THE SUBJECTIVE

Jaakko Saaristo

THE SUBJECTIVE

Copyright © 2020 Jaakko Saaristo

All rights reserved. No portion of this publication may be reproduced in any form without permission from the author, except for the purpose of quoting in a book review, or where permitted by copyright laws.

First softcover edition January 2020.

ISBN: 978-1-9163340-0-7 (Ebook)
ISBN: 978-1-9163340-1-4 (Softcover)
ISBN: 978-1-9163340-2-1 (Hardcover)

jaakkosaaristo.co.uk

To my heroes and the Unknown Philosopher

CONTENTS

Preface

Introduction ... 1

PART I. The Basis of Thought ... 20

    I-1. Existence and Subjectivity ... 22

    I-2. The Method of Linguistic Analysis ... 84

    I-3. The Mechanics of Meaning ... 108

    I-4. The Subjective, the Objective and Truth ... 136

    I-5. Philosophy, Religion and Ethics ... 156

    I-6. The Nature of Ethics and Aesthetics ... 183

    I-7. The Nature of Reason ... 218

    I-8. The Four Types of Reason ... 236

        I-8-1. Justification ... 241

        I-8-2. Logic ... 250

        I-8-3. Teleology ... 270

        I-8-4. Causality ... 280

PART II. Common Misconceptions ... 290

    II-1. Linguistic Confusion ... 291

    II-2. The Dual Nature of Philosophical Problems ... 302

        II-2-1. Meaning ... 307

        II-2-2. Reason and Cause ... 313

        II-2-3. Truth ... 318

        II-2-4. Agreement and Understanding ... 321

        II-2-5. Allowed and Imaginable ... 325

        II-2-6. Free Will ... 328

        II-2-7. Dreams ... 331

    II-3. The Subjective Nature of Morality ... 341
    II-4. The Metaphysical World ... 370
    II-5. Religious Language ... 401
    II-6. The Spiritual World ... 431
    II-7. The Social Nature of Religion ... 451
    II-8. Technological Argumentation ... 510
    II-9. Computationalist Science ... 544
PART III. Socio-political Analysis ... 591
    III-1. The Basis of Democracy ... 593
    III-2. Democratic Developments ... 613
    III-3. The Decline of Morality ... 645
    III-4. The Invisible Hand ... 665
    III-5. Information-Age Rhetorical Tactics ... 703
        III-5-1. Personalization ... 705
        III-5-2. Caricature ... 707
        III-5-3. Facts ... 709
        III-5-4. Mystification ... 711
        III-5-5. Ignorance ... 712
        III-5-6. Victimizing ... 714
        III-5-7. Umbrage ... 720
        III-5-8. Prudential ... 722
        III-5-9. Pathologizing ... 724
        III-5-10. Propaganda Inserts ... 728
        III-5-11. Experts ... 732
        III-5-12. Dictatorship vs Democracy ... 736
Acknowledgements ... 738
About the Author ... 739

"Don't do that to me! It's not this 'if you want' or 'if you agree' business I want to test. It's you and me I want to put on the line, and I think the argument will be tested best if we take the 'if' out."

—Socrates, *Protagoras*

PREFACE

I will describe the background and circumstances that led to this book.

After my master's thesis, I went to study Wittgenstein abroad, as recommended by every Wittgenstein expert I approached at my home university, where they in fact store some of Wittgenstein's estate, such as his walking stick, as it is also the home university of G. H. von Wright who was close to Wittgenstein and succeeded his tenure in Cambridge. They instructed me to gain better expertise on my matters of interest abroad. So, I went abroad, and abroad they pointed out to me that people like me have no future in academia. I think they were right; it turned out I've been mostly doing something else since then. Unofficially, I got the most contradictory feedback; that academia is in deep crisis and needs people like me who can criticize it outside its own functions. I think they were maybe right about that, too, because they don't seem to be doing so well; I think the institution is mostly battling for survival and many people today believe philosophy is dead and surpassed by modern ways that involve both science and technology. How wrong they are. Anyway, I forgave my personal disappointments but nevertheless felt that I have an increasing number of things to say that are just waiting to find the correct medium. To write a book was an obvious choice; this just unfortunately meant steering off the academic path, but the question for me was this: How much respect does a PhD in philosophy command these days? My main motive for leaving was that philosophy is the highest intellectual work, but academia today isn't an environment to support this kind of work. Philosophy requires *freedom* and *leisure*, and real philosophers, the ones in our past, were not productive researchers, but rather working at their time of productivity and often suffering long periods of unproductivity in between, and this was understood as a part of the business of philosophy. I also believe that philosophy, rather than being a professional discipline for some people, should be something *every intelligent person* and professional should cultivate in themselves, both as means of elevating themselves and nourishing their spirits and souls, and as a *test* of their level of understanding and civilization to avoid being absorbed into grandiose thoughts while reaching for the mastery of their chosen profession. In this respect I feel the same about both philosophy and art.

Around midway through my writing, I asked if my book had any chance of becoming a PhD thesis. I received flattering comments on my style of writing, but also that I am not allowed to write like this in a philosophical PhD thesis but only *after* having produced one. I understood that it was somehow unexpected or shocking that I have read the originals and not secondary Wittgenstein... the truth is I haven't learned a thing from secondary literature, and philosophy is not an exercise where I would write thoughts about what somebody might have meant. I have my own interpretations of Wittgenstein, as anybody should, and these opinions translate to politics; trying to defend them will create a political struggle within an institution that is doing all it can to create customs that convey a sense of objectivity. Academia has taken a path where lines of study in philosophical topics ritualize into *academic discussions* (this is a derogatory term outside academia) and lose their original motivation, and therefore philosophy hasn't produced much of value in decades. It is an unspoken but accepted truth that academics write to each other, not unlike art circles where artists put on exhibitions mostly visited by fellow artists as an exchange of favours. This unproductivity has not passed without notice, so now in modern cost-effective times these artists are losing all their funding, which is a shame but also the right thing to do to encourage change where passion for the subject matter has been replaced by a desperate search for the fortification of one's position. Philosophy is not science, and all the secondary literature, written for academics to understand Wittgenstein, has already proven a wasted effort, because Wittgenstein is mostly forgotten today. If the literature was valuable, people would read it and love Wittgenstein more. But they don't read it, and I don't blame them, as I never read it either to learn something; just read this and that as a part of the ritual of showing academic competence. This is what I was taught to do but I didn't learn anything from it, which makes sense as these are rituals that derive their function from maintaining an institution, as any ritual will. And now I am told that PhD

PREFACE

theses are also such exercises ... and this is not true; they should produce new research or whatever the product is considered to be in philosophy. I will not write *another* ritual study that nobody will read just to justify the existence of an institution that is not doing its job. Even when some academic writers do find interesting or apt perspectives to the work of real philosophers, they leave their work unfinished and communicate the perspective. To formulate this more clearly, they say: "As a philosopher-scientist, I don't care if what I am saying is true or not, but this is how this stuff *could be argued* to be"—a hypothetical explanation of someone's thoughts that are considered so valuable they require explanation. If Wittgenstein's work will find rejuvenation after this era of ignorance, it will be done using the originals. I consider Wittgenstein the greatest philosopher, but have never recommended his work to anybody because he is too difficult. If you think this is an arrogant thing to say, just remember that Wittgenstein considered Kierkegaard *too difficult*: arguably the greatest philosopher of the 20th century considered the man *he* found the greatest philosopher of the previous century too difficult to read; the best in his class couldn't figure out the works of the best in his class a century before. If this is the case, how do you think you can build an academic discipline on something so recondite? It is no wonder philosophy has been unsuccessful wherever it has tried to be a systematic team effort, and the systematic approach carries with the discomfort of a long-standing but so far unsuccessful investigation where the new joiners are forced to inherit the mistaken presuppositions of their predecessors to avoid humiliating them with a successful new idea. The original effort transforms into a bureaucracy where the main everyday effort is in politics and in not exposing oneself by stepping over boundaries; keeping the boat running and keeping yourself and your close partners on the boat. I trust all readers are acquainted with an example of this type of organization.

I'm not sure if this book is academic or non-academic philosophy as I'm not satisfied living in a world where these words mean something. I tried to write to "normal" readers as much as possible, but these days philosophy is an expert topic and these matters are very rarely seriously discussed outside the communications of people who are somehow personally drawn to them. I believe we should rather live in a world where these considerations are a matter of honour to all capable and intellectual people instead of intelligence reducing to memorizing a few smart quotes to use at social occasions and the professional discipline not producing anything new that's worthy of such quotes. I remember myself having been interested in exactly these questions as long as I can remember, and just happened to find myself having reached enough clarity to write about them. Due to these controversies I'm not good at saying what kind of people would like to read this book; I think it might intrigue those who have a personal wish to struggle for philosophical clarity and are willing to dedicate due effort to it without this activity having any immediate rewards in terms of, say, money or social respect. My only hope is that I won't severely disappoint precisely those readers.

THE AUTHOR
LONDON, JANUARY 2020

INTRODUCTION

This book contrasts with modern philosophy, as it would have contrasted with the mainstream of the philosophy of, say, 100 or 200 years ago. I consider it *existentialism*, by which I mean something laid down by Kierkegaard, and it involves a complete and intellectually grounded rejection of the effort to describe the world as a *conceptual system* (such as a philosophical or scientific system). Kierkegaard saw his works, such as the *Concluding Unscientific Postscript*, as being about how to *become* religious, and he saw that the most difficult things are to be communicated most indirectly. He saw that the point of his book was to lead the reader towards something that cannot be taught directly. I would liken this communicative goal to what a priest would like to achieve with his symbolical sermon. This approach was adopted also by Socrates and later Wittgenstein, both of whom didn't publish at all. The early Wittgenstein had similar mystical goals in mind in *Tractatus*; he saw, among other things, that any relevant things are such that they cannot be expressed in words, and that the reader must throw away the ladder after reading him, because meaning is actually outside the world. These goals are something quite opposite to what most people are trying to achieve with communication, be it spoken or written. But these authors have their similarities in emphasizing the everyday aspect of philosophy as an activity in which one *exists in thought*, and being logical, rational, opinionated, critical and judgemental as personalities to the extreme of abandoning social norms, often to their own disadvantage. I'd like to say they were 'keeping it real' in philosophy where others would lose their way. I think in philosophy we combine intellectual logic with actual personal life, and produce value by becoming capable of clear logic, after which we can provide critical value by pointing out critical weaknesses (critical, as in potentially causing crisis) in, say, the functions of our civil systems and institutions. In a democracy, who do you think will do this if not philosophers? The institution of philosophy must also be its own critic. We are not trying to tell people how to think and what is the correct system one should adopt. One is free, and doomed, to think in any way

INTRODUCTION

one wants; we will only be interested in pointing out the problems that thinking in a certain way produces and trying to assist in solving them. My own thought is peculiar in a way, and I see many admirable people thinking differently from the way I think. There is this huge illusion that a person's quality is produced by his brain, which can be somehow observed and analysed to be normal or abnormal, or right or wrong; in reality, all people are unique individuals and they think in various unique ways, and there are differences in our values and moral constitution. Other contrasting differences in this existentialist method are the dismissal of the hypothetical scientific method in questions that are essentially critical, and *the acknowledgment of subjective morality as an inherent feature in all thought*: the act of looking at things from a particular perspective is an ethical deed, and clarity is achieved only by making a clear distinction in both language and action between what is accessible to everybody and what is accessible to the private subject only.

The central themes of this book are, first,

> *a clarification of **the subjective** and **the objective** as grammatically defined by their criterion, and their roles in constituting linguistic meaning,*

and second,

> *a revitalization of **subjectivity** essentially as the home of both truth and morality.*

I have drawn my thought mainly from Wittgenstein and Kierkegaard, the great critics of their respective times and, in my view, kindred spirits: the Wittgensteinian method of linguistic analytics combines with Kierkegaard's subjective-objective distinction and promotion of subjectivity. Science is an effort towards full objectivity and spirituality an effort towards full subjectivity, and the correct place for philosophy is outside both, providing a critical perspective to both directions. This much should be self-evident, considering the full history of philosophy. Yet this is not the practice in philosophy. The book aims to explain linguistic meaning using notions and methodologies inspired by the said authors, and to apply this to a great multitude of real-life problem areas within society and modern science. It aims to unveil certain persistent controversies as Wittgensteinian linguistic misunderstandings, but also aims to explain this method and to bind it to the realm of subjectivity extensively explored by Kierkegaard but methodologically left untouched by Wittgenstein. The book also touches political issues as they directly exist in the subjective realm. The book seeks to cover quite a lot of philosophical ground—everything—and doesn't fit into any contemporary model of academic work where one is to restrict one's scrutiny to a certain topic and to provide a historical dissection of what others have previously said about that topic as a frame of reference and evaluation. I could well do that, but it would be another kind of work for another kind of purpose; in my understanding good philosophical work is something in which the author reflects *his thought* on relevant topics. In this work I am writing about my own findings that, in my thought, relate to all traditional topics of philosophy and that I wish to be understandable and original, but not in the scientific or academic sense; rather in the sense that philosophy shares with art and craft: some will relate, understand and recognize value, and some will not, as the capability to understand such things is a subjective skill that relates to talent and experience in the related art, which few have but most don't. To be able to judge whether my subjective findings are enlightening or just complete gibberish should require some familiarity on these topics from your part. I see that our entire world is on the wrong path; what philosophy can do is to point a finger to the exact problem points that exist in virtually every field and following the same pattern, and I have chosen dismissal of the subjective in favour of the objective as the main motif. There are only a few academic references. Preliminary reading of Wittgenstein will probably help in efforts to overcome the philosophical foundations, as the later Wittgensteinian linguistic approach, which is a monumental piece of Western philosophy, is in this book not reiterated but briefly explained and heavily built upon. The parts of the book concerning meaning and sensibility will likely be unintelligible to those who hold the common worldview that words denote objects—for a Wittgensteinian they don't, and as a reader you'll

INTRODUCTION

need to set yourself into these shoes the best you can. Then again, being a Wittgenstein expert won't guarantee any success, as he is a controversial author and you might well disagree with my interpretation of him; I suspect that marrying a woman opposite to your own personality and field is easier than marrying somebody from your own field but with whom you disagree. I try my best to explain the foundations of linguistic analysis in non-Wittgensteinian terms; Wittgenstein left a bunch of concepts so baffling that they have given birth to "new" interpretations. I try my best not to "be Wittgensteinian" by building upon his specialized terminology; rather I try to explain things from varying viewpoints because Wittgenstein's concept of language-games is just his approach of describing something that is *an actual thing* and that we can describe using any literary devices. I read *Philosophical Investigations* several times before it gave me anything other than disgust and a headache, and I did this because of his fame and my anger at my inability to make sense of him (I will also admit I am a rather poor reader). He was the first author I ever read who I could see was striving to explain a point with clear language and examples, but I, so proud of my smarts, was too stupid to understand it. Following this personal experience, I understand well those who give up on him. But as this book deals with distinct real-life philosophical problems both in individual life and in society (instead of trying to build a system) it might contain parts that are an interesting read even to the many who face challenges in reading Wittgenstein.

Now, the word 'philosophy' is a mixed bag, and I will explain my understanding of the correct philosophical method. There are two things: *language* and the *subject* (human) that uses it as a natural trait. Whereas classically in philosophy the philosopher might for example ask: "What is goodness?" and start his scrutiny from the object of the question—in this case 'goodness'—, in the philosophy of both Wittgenstein and Kierkegaard this question most essentially also involves the question of the *subject* performing the actual question or uttering the word 'goodness' as a part of the activities of his life. To try to search for 'goodness' through grasping its idea or essence would be the Platonic way, which is the path our Western science has taken as a general guideline. In the Wittgensteinian approach the problem regarding a concept includes not only the object of the question but rather how the word is used and what can be learned about the human in relation to his use of language, and in this sense, I often consider it 'second order' philosophy; it is an approach that takes a look at approaches; takes a look at *how* you are trying to do what you are trying to do. The problem involves not only *what* is said, but also *how* it is said and *that* it is said. This approach involves a perspective on language that emphasizes its connection to human thought and understanding in a totally different sense than in a clinical scientific model, which in a contemporary setting mostly disregards the subjective individuality of humans when they first learn a language in a certain environment and as a result to a certain extent existentially *become* extensions of those cultural linguistic traditions. Methodologically, the inherent second perspective calls for a separation of the two perspectives—that of the subject uttering and that of the philosopher analysing—since the analysing philosopher is not necessarily the subject making the utterances his scrutiny targets but rather is more of an observing anthropologist. After the great Kierkegaard, I will generally use the term '*the subject*' to refer to the human in a *unique* sense, which, used this way, will rule out any possibilities to imply or assume anything about him that is not, human as we are, evident through our shared natural language, and which will include everything related to whatever we can, through natural language, understand every human to be affiliated with in his life, such as his ethical choices, his responsibilities, his emotions and his spiritual life. Instead of 'the subject' I considered using '*He*', but that would carry a mystifying sense that I am trying to avoid. 'The subject' does not refer to a test subject in an experiment; it refers to both *subjectivity*, as explained later in this book, and the *grammatical subject*. It is a psycho-socially observable fact that humans are spiritually connected, not to other humans, but to other subjects, and this connection, through shared human psycho-social trends, is also unique, which is related to the subject's own unique nature: essentially the human relation to another is coloured by how he sees him, or as we might say, what he represents to him. What we speak of as God, spirits or suchlike, are subjects yet not humans, and in this role integral in our spiritual life.

INTRODUCTION

And by this *I am not saying anything about the existence of any spirit or making any form of religious or spiritual commitment* but simply mean to include the hidden psychological and spiritual human life in its full depth and complexity in philosophical scrutiny, which itself is an external viewpoint to the subject's behaviour. I find spiritual and religious life particularly interesting, but as a philosopher I will only look at them from the analytical perspective of what religious life and language are. The philosopher is not a theologian, but in order to write about humans he needs to honour and address spirituality, an inherent human disposition, or he had better not write anything at all. Personally, I don't consider such a writer a philosopher if he, firstly, doesn't address *full* humanity including human subjectivity (but instead rules out some *human* features as pointless or uninteresting), and secondly, doesn't mean his text to be ethical; something to guide towards a *correct way* to relate to facts. Due to modern academia ruling out the subjective and ethical perspective in favour of scientific objectivity, I generally consider academic philosophy as a set of academic exercises related to philosophers who are already dead; either analysing the work of those philosophers, or taking the concepts developed by those philosophers and extending them beyond their original context. Being ethical (or moral) is behaviour where something is chosen for a subjective reason and shown to others by the example of one's action; not by trying to prove one's perspective via scientific facts or by reference to other texts bearing the academic seal of approval. Something is supposed to be right and true because it is the strongest argued, and argument is something that takes a courageous individual who believes in his thought, is ready to present it and to have it challenged to see if it is indeed true or not. Many people are drawn to philosophy, but to be a philosopher is a considerably more difficult task than, say, to be a scientist, since it requires self-scrutiny of one's own thought, and to be any good at it, it requires absolute intellectual honesty and the related ethical self-criticism, which causes personal suffering of the most severe kind, dismantling one's most fundamental beliefs acquired in childhood. And, unlike with a scientist, a philosopher publishing something half-baked will publish simply junk, since the thought being half-baked means that the philosopher himself is half-baked and not yet ready, and because he is in this state something he discovers the next day might lead him to renounce everything he ever said before. As a rule of thumb, those who don't clearly know what to do can't lead by example, and those who do seem to know and to take the initiative, can only be admired and only partially understood by others.

Regarding language, it is as Wittgenstein would write: philosophy may not interfere with the actual use of language—such as by trying to formulate rules of how to use it correctly—but must leave everything as it is.[1] This means that the philosopher simply performs analysis; he might succeed or not succeed in his analysis, depending on how good he is at it. The analysing philosopher can never take the path of trying to correct language in terms of portraying the existent language as inadequate, such as by requiring the introduction of new terminology, but his analysis may imply that the already existent language is being incorrectly used on some occasion.[2] Only this can make the philosopher valuable: he needs to be able to display what others fail to see because it is inherent in the language we use. Also, a philosopher doesn't preach, moralize or politicize, but through his persona simply provides a perspective to human facts everybody can verify and understand, and whether this perspective is good or not—exactly like whether a piece of art is any good or not—is not determined by the author but is left for others to determine. For example, regarding religion, whenever I would write 'God', I would actively mean "whatever the subject might mean when uttering 'God'", having myself witnessed and thus being

---

[1] The same ideal is interestingly expressed in the Buddhist concept of *sunyata* ('emptiness' or 'void'), which, in its simplicity, means detachment and freedom from *dharmas* that in turn are phenomenological constituents of human experience. It seems to me that Buddhist dharma finds its Western equivalent in *conceptual framework*, which for us constitutes how we experience things—our linguistic viewpoint on matters at hand. To be empty, as an ideal, means not to assume; not to be bound by any framework; not to be bewitched by language. This neutrality, I believe, is an absolute requirement for any successful analyst.

[2] The willingness to control speech is a phenomenon has sadly (again) gained popularity in contemporary West under a trend called "political correctness", and could be briefly described as a tendency to condemn public speakers and to try and control what they are allowed to say by calling it e.g. *wrong*, *unscientific* or *hate speech*. This kind of a dark world of rule by moral institution is, of course, pretty far from the spirit of democracy or science, and, rather, what science originally effectively saved us from.

INTRODUCTION

able to imagine such linguistic events. I hold no opinion about these matters apart from my personal perspective of seeing this as somehow philosophically relevant, and the validity of this follows from the fact that uttering the word in practice is a philosophically interesting feature of human life. The whole question of if God exists seems completely pointless to me; I think people who are haunted by this question have some other (subjective) issues but are instead addressing the question as if it was an objective question to debate. The real question open for investigation is a linguistic one: What does it mean to speak about God? It seems natural for certain forms of human behaviour to attribute subjective qualities to objects of interaction in a particular manner—one that is completely different from our interaction with objects that we use, for example as tools. Examples of such activities targeting non-humans are nurturing pets and dolls, shadow-boxing against a sack, talking to oneself, playing chess against computer software, prayer and confession (personally, I remember once confessing to our pet cat as a child). As such, one's subjective relation aligns with one's inclination to use the grammatical subject. Now, the subject himself, by definition, cannot be scientifically studied, as the objective methodology of science will only see the objective realm and whatever is not unique but uniformly repeating over individuals. Scientific information produced by behavioural and social sciences and theology (wherever theology studies the divine, it effectively studies the subject's relation to what the subject treats as a divinity) produces objective information about humans, but not the unique subject, as the science can only express what can be shared in the language and methodology of the scientific discipline at hand. The fundamental trap most Western philosophy walks straight into is not understanding the logical difference between the subjective and the objective and thus to try and talk or write about the subjective—the unique and hidden—in objective terms that are shared and public. If someone tries to express something that by its nature (the meaning of its associated word) only he himself can see, but using a language that implies objective criteria, he will either not be understood at all or will be misunderstood. This activity of expressing the subjective is the fundamental target in artistic expression, and the responsible artist is aware of the impossibility of expressing his subjective existence (the way the world appears just to him, being who he is). The main effort of his artistic work is to bridge his subjectivity to a medium and audience that represents an objective (shared) reality and history. Also, for this reason the established forms of artistic expression are different from the forms of language we use when discussing things. Art is always meant to be taken as art, and furthermore, if what the artist expresses through his art could be expressed also with words with the same effect, the artist wouldn't feel the need to express himself through art.

Another paradigm I adhere to and want to be clear about is the requirement for *natural language* in philosophy. Academic philosophy has effectively hogged and academized every possible natural language concept that is philosophically interesting and created special definitions connected with trails of debate and will feel justified in snubbing anyone using those concepts with an expectation of enlightenment regarding those definitions and debates. This process has nothing to do with philosophy, philosophical interest, the principle of charity, or collaboration on the level of society, but is the result of violent elitism within academia and the intelligentsia, doing to language what the white man did to the lands he conquered, proclaiming in the name of his deity that the land belonged to him, and giving the natives permission to step on his lands only under the name and blessing of his deity. Whether or not crusades yield favourable political effects is a question I am unable to answer (in the old days this was determined through which side of the battle Gods chose to favour), but it is certain that they don't serve the scholarly function that philosophy as an organ of society has been established to serve. Therefore let it be said that anyone who understands the word 'conscious' as used in e.g. "Henry was conscious of Martin's attempted provocation but chose not to respond" or what the word 'consciousness' means as used in e.g. "Peter slowly regained consciousness", "A suspicion of planned treachery entered his consciousness" or "We must bring these facts into common consciousness", is *justified* in using the word 'consciousness', provided that—and this is a requirement for any argument—he is ready to further explain his meaning if necessary using natural language through e.g. examples, metaphors or any other natural means of explanation people generally use when talking about things. An academized definition of a concept should be considered specialized expert terminology—on the basis that the meaning of the word is verified *against* that definition—and therefore meaning something different from the original meaning of how the word is originally used in language. I try to write simply and to avoid philosophical jargon and scientific text as much as possible; I feel that if I have grasped something, I can also express it in various ways, and simple language is the best choice. Populist natural scientists act as obscurant religious interpreters of the modern age and they use their professional authority to preach politics, but they do it not as social commentary but by attaching their professional authority to the picture. Sadly, in the current academic crisis modern academic *philosophers* have either joined a freshly emergent neo-naturalist bandwagon or accepted a politically insignificant role within academia with no higher wish than to be able to practise their beloved profession for their own personal sake, having found no means to attack modern computerized natural science. As such, it is my opinion that academic philosophy serves little function in society and should be revisited, revitalized or reinvented, in a manner similar to the way in IT technological debt is something that accumulates over old codebases and should be methodologically cleaned out via refactoring and a revisit of the meanings and purposes of individual system pieces. This would bring philosophy back from where it has no place but has become entangled—back on the streets, back to common people and to any free spirit with a heart and mind, back where it is beautiful due to its ethical nature. Perhaps, as of writing this book, this development has already taken place and philosophy has lost all its funding.

I find myself unable to determine in how much depth I should explain different topics and will try to apply a method of minimal explanation in favour of simply accurate terminology. The points I present are ones that *I* have found relevant, both in terms of history of philosophy and in terms of modern needs, and I will try my best to be honest and not venture to cover any more ground than what is directly available to me: that information is available to the distinguished reader from other sources. By this, I hope to distance myself from the dishonest philosopher, who describes his best understanding or most plausible theory about the nature of things, and in fear of his own doubt covers this by stating "This is how it must be" instead of an honest "This is how I hope it is". The expectation of intellectual honesty between the author and his readers is the same as the trust between an employee and his employer or a party member and his party; the philosopher is an expert suggesting a perspective, and in this work it is as easy as in any other work to appear better than you actually are by painting your suggestion with more confidence than you actually have in your sayings yourself, thus creating a psychological effect on your readers. This honesty is a subjective quality, and in any area of life, the more we give importance to the objective, measurable end-product and disregard the producer as a person, the more likely the product will be somehow flawed in subjective terms. Let it be reminded that these subjective qualities of work (sincerity, authenticity, accuracy, relevance...) do matter to us gravely despite we don't pay attention to them too much these days, as we don't have tools to measure them.

I use the word 'phenomenon' as freely as 'cause' and 'effect' are used in natural language. The word can refer to anything and doesn't have any logical boundaries, but I use it in cases where I am unable to find any established terminology for whatever I need to refer to. Thus, I wish to distinguish my use of the word 'phenomenon' from e.g. Kant or Leibniz, who had self-defined meanings for the word (and thus were writing about something totally different from whatever the world so far had meant by such a word). By 'faith' I mean the quality signified by acceptance and unquestioning but that is also accompanied by the disposition that the target of the belief is *ethically right*, signified by ethical duty: "It *must* be like this".[3] This is distinct from the use of 'believe' in other senses, such as "I believe 1+2=3", which is void of any ethical component, or "I believe we are all going to die tomorrow", which doesn't signify faith but is an expression of the lack of it, as one will

---

3   The idea that 'must' is a give-away word, betraying the *a priori* character of thought, is from Lars Hertzberg in 'The importance of being thoughtful' in D. Moyal-Sharrock (ed.), *Perspicuous Presentations: Essays on Wittgenstein's Philosophy of Psychology*, Palgrave Macmillan, 2007.

INTRODUCTION

hardly find it *right* for all to die tomorrow. Faith, in this sense, is the same type as often described as "religious faith", but a religion need not be involved—an example of this would be a father's belief that his daughter is beautiful, which could be said to transcend physical beauty, as the father will also feel that in his role it is his duty to tell his daughter she is beautiful. I use the concept of *idealism* in terms of referring to an *ideal*, and not relating to philosophical traditions.

I might provide references at times but due to the rainbow of existing Wittgenstein and Kierkegaard interpretations there's simply no point in trying to argue for the correct interpretation—I am convinced of mine and if someone wants to know more about their work, I recommend going out and reading the originals. Then again, I am not in the business of exegesis; all I care is that I have learned from these authors—there has been a process of revelation, insight and humiliation, followed by admiration and gratitude—and I like to be very clear about whose ideas I am presenting, to myself just as much as to my readers. The risk is that I might have learned wrong lessons from these authors, in which case I am sure these mistakes will be reflected in my own thought and work, and this risk I am very willing to take. I expect experts to find me guilty of misinterpretation, having themselves published books containing contradicting interpretations that constitute the basis of their professional positions within academia—positions they have originally also sought via means of conducting alternative and new interpretations in the name of science. They will feel that they have well earned their academic positions and have a responsibility to defend their position. Because of this political setting I will not utter a single word to try and argue back. Also, readers may find that the things I write about have already been said before. This argument is a misguided application of the rules of science to philosophy, which is not science. First, the things I'm saying haven't been said before, because, unlike hypothetical scientific results, *I* am unique, and, I believe (this can be contested), have lived only this one time. Second, whether or not something I write about has been said before, makes no difference, as declaring those things is something that supports and completes *my* philosophical thought. If it was any other way, I could just write about a restricted topic and dismiss everything else, and my readers would have no clue what kind of a person I am, which is exactly what they need to judge in order for them to tell if my writings are worth reading or not. The only type of authors who will benefit from this are the ones who will not care if their readers know them or not. Furthermore, with said argument, "This has been said before", one could dismiss most philosophy after the ancient Greeks. The ideas I present here are *my own ideas*, unless otherwise referenced, and whether I am successful or an utter failure in my work, this is the right way of doing philosophy, and the way they do it in academia these days is the wrong way. Readers will find me unsystematic and obscure; they would prefer to see one subject exhausted from the perspective of comparing different hypothetical perspectives to the subject matter, as things are presented in philosophical textbooks. They will feel my carefully chosen examples fail to elucidate by being far-fetched or even deliberately outrageous or provocative. To this accusation I reply that I am simply trying to be evocative, but I hope that I am never guilty of being provocative, which implies an effort to provoke a *reaction* by saying things that one doesn't mean or even fully understand. Some readers will feel it was the custom of earlier times to write obscurely, that modern philosophy is systematic and organized as a science, and that my way of writing is an easy escape from the modern requirements of scientific rigour. Anyway, no matter what I did, I expect that the text would not satisfy most academic readers, or, to be honest, readers of any kind. Moreover, as we live an era in which anything considered worth publishing needs to be built on top of our extant scientific discourse, I am quite positive that my interest in dealing with spiritual and existential matters, and my willingness to disregard and disrespect the authority of the scientific institution, will have me academically categorized in the same bracket as the mad. But mostly I believe I will be dismissed because we live in a time in which we don't really have an institution for philosophy, and the pervasive scientism takes care of guiding people's attention to scientific news instead of the subjective. Luckily for myself I don't care because I don't need to share their bread and table. I am writing about things that the reader will not understand if he doesn't himself have the will to (yet even having the will won't guarantee understanding) and presenting the work in the form of a systematic study would be totally unnecessary and off track. If somebody found me more credible if I did that, and not simply credible because of what he can interpret of my character through my text as I now very particularly choose to write it, he obviously wouldn't be looking to find something in what *I* am writing about as a philosopher and a human being, but rather to find support for his already established beliefs. Such a reader should read no further and spare himself from trouble and possible offence by dismissing this book in favour of other books, and should those books by any chance be found in the library section containing philosophy, he should choose authoritative books the reading of which is expected to grant his beliefs social support, and not observably unsystematic and obscure books like mine. Furthermore, being able to technically apply a formal system of logic through its comprehension has absolutely nothing to do with where the roots of logic (and *'logos'*) and every common use of the term 'logic' are and have been before a school of thinkers of a particular kind gave it a branch of formalist meanings: *being* logical in terms of not contradicting one's beliefs in one's existence. Thus, the point of the book is to display my own subjective philosophical thought—not by presenting individual opinions on questions, but rather by applying these opinions to all the relevant topics, so that experts (if there are any, please step forward) can judge whether I am making sense and being *consistent*. To be inconsistent would mean that my work is ultimately incomplete; that I have thought about matters from one side and a bit from the other side, too, but due to ignoring and escaping the difficult problems on the other side, there is a tension left inside that is bound to crack and demolish the whole perspective. To point me out as inconsistent, or otherwise in error, is not a technical procedure, and one can only do that in the realm of philosophy, where one would take the trouble of addressing the meaning of what I am saying instead of its external formal expression. *This is philosophy, not science, and my results are not scientifically debatable.* Furthermore, I find science a poor proof for matters of reason. My observations, I hope, are such that anyone can agree with, but my results are related to my subjective perspective, which can be valuable only in ethical implications and is something one should never try and objectively justify but only appreciate or leave without appreciation. Having extensively discussed different artists and works of art with different people—including highly intelligent academic people—it has become clear to me how even those aesthetic qualities, that to me seem to signify values of the very basic and elementary kind, can be completely and blindly disregarded by people that I otherwise might respect and value in social life. People of intelligence can show extreme variations in their moral constitutions. In this kind of work, where one writes extensively about many topics from the same existential *human* perspective, it is not enough to be strong at one or many things: it is most essentially required *not to have any weaknesses*, as in all combat and warfare where one is only as strong as one's weakest point—this weak point being any topic the philosopher is unwilling to address in a satisfying manner. You can think of logical inconsistency this way: the philosopher is trying to create a picture out of a puzzle where the pieces fit together, and he starts his work from what some authors have written that he agrees with. This way he can finish half of the picture by putting together some pieces he is able to join. But after that he will try to come up with the other half and he notices that starting from what other authors have written that he agrees with, the size, shape and the theme of the pieces is different. So, he continues using those pieces, arrives at the middle, and notices that the two halves are built with completely different sizes, shapes and themes, and that even the idea of unifying them into a complete work is utterly hopeless and to a large degree ridiculous because he is essentially trying to build one picture out of two distinct puzzle sets; two different branches of language he has originally learned and taken for granted, but not paid attention and seriousness to the inconsistency between them to the extent of rebuilding the other half, which is a painfully necessary act unavoidably required. He feels appalled; he feels like a failure and a fraud, and wishes for nothing apart from mommy's arms and the peace of a mental asylum. But in our modern system his work is rewarded: he has done his duty—created something. Work was done; something was produced with the expected size and shape; time and money were spent on a good purpose. Compare this to software development; this is like a multi-sourcing development hub

INTRODUCTION

where software modules come in from vendors that come and present plans of a module in a brief description to get the go-ahead and funding from the project management. Only in this hub there is no architect to initially specify what kind of modules are needed in the first place, to specify the modules or to check the modules against the original specification. Thus, all they can do is to check plans and finished deliverables by their formal qualities (such as word count, number of references, font, grammar...), but not remotely from the perspective of whether they are useful or doing what they are supposed to do, or if the management are getting their money's worth.

Wittgenstein and Kierkegaard are my only philosophical teachers, and they, without challenge, stand out as bright beacons in the history of what we call philosophy—men who were anything but grey officials but as the main ingredient in their genius first and foremost radical freedom fighters and ethical human beings with love and passion to give up everything for the sake of their mission purported to ultimately serve mankind. The purpose of this book is to convey an ethical message; one that cannot be said with words. Trying to utter it would destroy it, and this destruction would not occur in a great flash but timelessly, like in a psychological thriller where two opposite realities can seamlessly alternate—the very act of trying merely constitutes the *proof* of its failure. It is so because, firstly, finding a person uttering nonsense is a very valid reason for, instead of trying to understand him, showing him he is not making sense, and secondly, in order to train a beginner to play badminton, it is senseless to bring him on the court and to tell him to drop if he doesn't know what the word 'drop' means, and furthermore senseless to keep telling him to drop if one can see him executing the stroke incorrectly—in a way that will not make him a good badminton player. That's what bad teachers do. But also, it is not correct to present what I write as a theory, because theories in this sense don't have means of validation or invalidation. The only sense in which you could call it theory would be to consider it a hypothetical opinion; somebody could consider it a hypothetical possibility for himself to adopt my position ... but this is not how opinions go; opinions involve ethics and faith, and one cannot, by choice, make oneself believe—rather, the truth is *revealed*, not chosen. So, it is not a theory at all and moreover strictly not a theory in a scientific sense; for me these things are not assumptions or hypotheses but something I believe, and the reason to believe them is not a rational choice for anybody but perhaps it is for somebody with similar motivations as I have. If you're just looking to make it through life and fit in, why do you care whether some word is subjective or objective? You can just deny the whole sense of the dichotomy and justify this by saying that everything subjective is undefinable. You can say the subjective doesn't interest you and ignore the fact that all discovery is by nature inspirational; it involves a highly subjective individual breaking the rules, discovering something new and then inspiring those around him. Only if what I am saying was a scientific theory would we have objective grounds for debate and you could approach me with your better knowledge, but this is not the case. And only if you were motivated as I am, to go in search of ultimate understanding and not just a justified position, would you have a motive to expose your subjective self in a dialogue where you can also be outright wrong and not just justifiable from various angles. I am very capable of presenting theories and my knowledge is based on many very useful scientific theories, but regarding philosophy I see the approach of theory as fundamentally misguided and think that the vast majority of people simply do not understand why it is so, which I very much link to our understanding of the basis of our own knowledge, which in itself is something specifically to be developed via the means of philosophy. Consider Peter seeing the dog on the yard and saying: "My dog is out in the yard", which Sarah immediately translates as "Peter presented a theory that his dog is out in the yard". Is this valid; is it valid to say that Peter presented a theory? No. It is valid to say that *Sarah* is presenting a theory that Peter's dog is out on the yard (as she is unsure whether this is the case, Peter is not), and her evidence is Peter's testimonial.

I wanted so much to write this book in a different way. I even considered writing it in two parts: the first part without nonsense and the second part only nonsense.[4] And, by doing that I might win some read-

---

[4] Wittgenstein says in his preface of *Tractatus* that the book consists of two parts: the one that he wrote and the other that he left out. I sympathize. The way I think

INTRODUCTION

ers who would be impressed by my *character*. But I cannot lead them anywhere! A display of achievement is worthless: for the viewer it is either entertainment or it will lead him on the ultimately wrong track of mimicking somebody else instead of discovering himself. Writing a book that way would be so easy. But what would be even easier would be to write a speculative book, a book about how things *must be*; to boldly, for the sake of mankind, say "I don't have the slightest idea" without admitting it to myself but by asking the forgiveness of others. That is the easiest thing to do: the only thing one needs to do is to know how to write, and that can be learned by repetitive practice, if one has the talent. It's like a singer who has trained her voice but has no idea what to sing about or who to sing to. The audience would see the whole room radiate when she produces her act, but fail to pay attention to *how* she uses her voice, who she chooses to perform with and what songs she chooses to sing: that in reality she is asking somebody else to decide all those questions for her, and she is doing the best she can to produce how a vocalist in her role *is expected to* behave; that in reality she is *fooling* everybody, by selling them an image that touches their dreams, but hiding how it is built in reality. To produce that, all that is needed is some luck to have the talent, mindlessly following an experienced teacher, and the disconnection from one's own emotions to force one's face into an expression without emotion, like a beauty queen. No, as a philosopher I can't be the leader or the actress. What am I, then? I suppose I am the terrifying memory, if anything. You might want to read something in which the author is taking you somewhere, or where the author compels you with his prowess; this is what you might think is good philosophy. Trust me, it is not. Philosophy exists to make you realize things; bad philosophy is something that has the external image of being profound but that disguises its moral emptiness behind its intelligence. It invites you to mimic and repeat it and implies you're a no-good moron unless you agree with it. It is charming and seductive; it invites and coerces from an intelligent higher status, like a beautiful woman who invites you to sit next to her but makes it clear that unless

---

about my own text is that the things that I write are the things I 1) find relevant and 2) believe to be true strongly enough to write them down. A person believing in science will find no glory in writing about his beliefs. He has yet to assess his conceptions of truth and knowledge.

you do what she expects you to do she will dump you with a snap of her fingers. You might even be unworthy to read such a work in the first place. There's thought that actively tries to reduce its readers to a like-minded group; ask a stupid question and you'll be told you don't have the merit to question it. Anyway, my failure might lie in attempting to write about ethics against the example of my idols who either saw the study of ethics as something that had no value, or something only expressible via action and linguistically expressible only through humour. Because of this my text will appear arrogant and pretentious. Moral argument is easily attacked by trying to show that the actions of the speaker contradict his values. This is the attack I anticipate on myself, because it is the attack with the most power against somebody who speaks for morality; to work to show his immorality. This attack will be made by those who wish to deny moral argument in general. But this is my choice between being a philosopher and human; as an analytic philosopher I feel compelled to make ethical statements about groups or types of people that immediately place me under judgement for expressing such things, and I used to hate myself for such attitudes; for wishing to wield the right to judge men. But I have grown to accept weakness in myself. It is a most reassuring thought that transcending this human nature and constant fear is an act not done by any man.

PART I. THE BASIS OF THOUGHT

In this part of the book I aim to bring together the various domains of thought that any person's thought process will comprise and that include both rational capabilities and morality. The target of scrutiny is *linguistic meaning*, which is the key philosophical subject matter that acts as the medium between our external world, our thought and our communication with other people. If you are not acquainted with Wittgensteinian philosophy, you are likely coming from a background where you don't place much importance on grammar when asking about the nature of things, and regarding philosophical questions you might be asking "What *is* this?" instead of "What does this mean?" You'll likely feel that the way a thing is expressed grammatically is of little importance, as it is rather the "point" or "idea" that matters more. Also, you might not have been getting very concrete answers to your questions, and you might think that the sort of answers philosophy altogether provides are of the vague type of "It could be like this, or it could be another way also, depending on how you want to look at it". If this is the case, I'd like to urge you not to settle with a resolution that essentially doesn't provide you with any real answers but only hypothetical ones; the questions a person asks in philosophy are subjective and personal, and they should be approached subjectively and personally and not academically and hypothetically. Then again, I am not the one to argue that the things that I am explaining here are the correct way for *you* to look at things. I am saying that in order to get different answers you should read different philosophy, as the things I am writing about here are my own personal findings that don't bear the insignia of the related institution to help you distinguish them from dangerous quackery. If you are on a quest for getting real answers to the questions that disturb you, you should not read my words as a final explanation of anything but just the thoughts of somebody who has been on a similar quest for a long time and has found clarity at least to the level of wanting to share them after having passed rigorous personal critique. Regarding any such subject matter you should be careful and ask any related questions about the character of the person who is offering such thoughts as wisdom.

PART I. THE BASIS OF THOUGHT

I-1. EXISTENCE AND SUBJECTIVITY

I consider myself existentialist, and I will explain here what I mean by the word. I use the word 'existentialism' in reference to an anti-theoretic philosophical method that Kierkegaard started, and I can see existentialism as having certain features that distinguish it from, say, mainstream philosophy. Existentialism can most concisely be described as an effort to combine *logic*, the intellectual rational effort, with the *moral* aspect of one's personal life. It is an effort to live and exist without contradiction. This is not simple to describe in a concrete manner, but I will try to give some highlights. An existentialist is interested in the subjective, but not *the subjective experience*, which is the realm of phenomenology. I want to stress that the subjective experience is a completely fruitless topic, and existentialism and real philosophy should be completely distinguished from the doings of writers who discuss it. The existentialist is interested in both morality and logic, which comes down to the basic questions of right, wrong, true and false, the follow-up question of what the correct action is, and the question of the correct way of conducting one's life. The subjective experience, by contrast, is a domain for all the various types of escapists, not for serious thinkers. As a philosopher, everything always looks like something or feels like something. So what? It is a misconception to think that others could share that experience, and moreover, following Wittgenstein's beetle analogy, people's private experience of something (the beetle) might be changing all the time without you even knowing it. Personally, I find it arrogant, and a definitive feature of contemporary cultural narcissism, to consider one's personal experience important when dealing with matters that touch everybody. I also find it both irrational (as opposed to rational) and feminine, as the female sex is more famous for basing decisions on subjective feelings instead of reasonable argument. No, if you want to dwell in feeling or act based on feeling, which I highly recommend to everybody, you should keep your pen in the drawer, since the willingness to announce one's love and passion should be considered a sign of lack of reason just as love is known to be blind, divine madness, a chariot of both noble and wild

I-1. EXISTENCE AND SUBJECTIVITY

horses pulling in different directions, only to be guided by the charioteer—intellect and reason with the motivation towards truth. You should live like that but not write like that; best is to hang the pen in a decorated box on the wall, with the inscription: "To be used when the head is cool, and reason is in charge". In philosophy, which is an intellectual and rational discipline, the whole subjective experience needs to be clinically and dispassionately reduced out. But this does not mean that the word 'subjective' is useless—on the contrary I find it particularly important in distinguishing the border of what is private and what is shared; it is so important that it is the central theme of this book. If you want to learn, say, music, there are two things that you *shouldn't* do: 1) lose yourself into the *experience* of music, because this experience *is not* music, as music is what is meant by the word and others can't share your experience; and 2) look at the appearance of making music; trying to look like somebody who is playing an instrument instead of playing an instrument.[5] It is not the subjective experience that interests the existentialist, nor the objects he sees and their names, but the totality in which he, as an individual subject, sees objects and calls them by names, that again are received and shared by other individual subjects; and in the middle of this problem-setting, shared by every single individual, lie the philosophical questions, such as what things are and what they are not, and what is right and correct and what is wrong and incorrect. If this problem-setting should sound banal to a modern scientific-minded person, I would like to point out that there are not many people who have much real understanding of this problem area in terms of being able to give definite answers, and the scientist is simply externalizing the problem and setting himself above it, and quite typically just a short conversation will bring out the philosophical problems in the underlying world-view that the individual will just work to hide due to his personal uncertainty. This is the real philosophical problem area and it is shared by all individuals, and success in this area of life can yield personal clarity and opportunity for growing to an authentic individual, as opposed to someone whose fun-

---

5 I remember a quote attributed to Michael Jackson that if you want to learn dancing, you should remove all mirrors from your training room. This makes sense as dance schools typically have mirrored walls to make it easier to observe how the dancer appears.

damental thoughts are derived from external authorities and essentially originate from other authentic authors. It is possible to be a highly successful individual in society without any understanding of the existential realm of life, which would translate to a career of work that is either disguised to be authentic or made in hopes of it being authentic without the introspective clarity or courage to realize that in fact it is not. These subjective problems of individual life are often carefully studied in fiction and drama, but rarely written about in a serious academic sense, which is the task of the existentialist philosopher.

Why would anybody live in an unauthentic way? We know that some people do this more than others, but why? Why would someone become something that he despises? We would likely say: they don't mean to. And we would be right. But this is not an answer to the question of what makes them do it. We are understanding them empathetically and calling their behaviour human, but we are not giving a reason ... which implies that the actual cause is not rational but irrational. And it is irrational because it is emotional and reduces to the emotion that we know is behind most irrational behaviour: *fear*. The correct answer is that life is terrible; it is not just sometimes terrible, but every day is full of absolute terror. What are we afraid of? Each other, mostly, in modern society. We are mostly afraid in reference to things such as our reputation and the judgement of other people. We are afraid of appearing ridiculous. We are hardwired in our bodies and minds to be afraid of uncertain things, and the thoughts of others and their opinions of us are the fundamental uncertain thing to us, as these thoughts and opinions are something that people hide every day—as they are required to hide them—because saying them out aloud wouldn't be proper in modern society. This is a fear that only exists in a society in which we need to be constantly careful about how we appear and what we do or say, because every potential action comes with a potential *faux pas* and social disaster. This is the real explanation why many people steer away from the authentic subjective path and start to focus their lives on the security brought by correct impressions and the mastery of social codes. And this development can easily start at a young age and carry through to our adult life: every child works to fulfil their parents' expectations, and we first learn to please our parents if this is what they expect from us. But isn't this fear that we feel just a pointless fear? Far from it. Before school age, most of us are protected in the security of our homes, but school brings us the first taste of the reality of life where our kind, trusting actions are met with ridicule and open hostility. We learn that some of our fellow humans, even at a young age, are vicious predators who don't just attack us but use their skills of social domination to probe and sense our fears. They concentrate not just their personal attacks but the coordinated attacks of their circle of lackeys to gain at least small social victories of humiliating us, but in the worst case physical or material victories where we end up hurt or our possessions stolen. We also often painfully learn that some people cannot be trusted but will opportunistically betray our trust, and due to this reality trusting new people becomes an act associated with fear; we need to ponder the motives behind their words and actions before placing our trust in them. And as if it wasn't enough that some people are scary, whereas in a primitive society we would be busy fighting the dangers of our surrounding nature, in a modern society our enemies are our social competitors; we are from a young age placed in competition with our peers, and in this competition there are many chances to fail and to put ourselves in disadvantage. Thus, even by surrounding ourselves with trustworthy people we are hardly ever protected from the chance of making mistakes in, say, career or human relations. But there is yet another source of fear, which is the fear of failing the expectations of others and our own expectations. Here our free society grants us some personal choice; we can choose what we hold valuable to a degree, yet whatever that ends up being is always the reflection of an existing social norm; just in the case of choice this is chosen by ourselves rather than imposed on us. Say, if your parents make you choose doctor studies, your career success will be judged against the norms of a doctor career, but if you yourself choose to go for actor studies instead, you still have every reason to be afraid of becoming a lousy actor. Due to these realities in our existence I'll say that if somebody is in the experience of living where there is no danger present, this situation is somehow perverse; we have examples of e.g. very wealthy people who become socially isolated due to their riches and this is a consequence of them not having to struggle to gain skills that reflect social norms. Most people would likely say they'd like to have more money or to be rich, but in fact there is no skill or related social norm to being rich, apart from that wealth can be successful entrepreneurship. Those who become rich without earning it with their own skills tend to be poor at holding on to the money.

It seems to me that the existentialist approach is laid upon two basic assumptions. The first assumption is that humans are *primarily moral* creatures in their existence, which is to say that, given that they have the freedom of choice, they make their choices and choose their leaders based on their moral sentiments of good and bad, or right and wrong. This is best elucidated by not analysing their brains but just listening to what they say (the language that they use) when they describe people or ideas they follow and subscribe to (accompanied by the powerful words 'good' and 'right'), as opposed to those they reject. The existential way of learning about people is talking with them. Whereas sciences steer away from any subjective matters, the existentialist is always bound to the subjective moral aspect of life. The second assumption is that people seem to differ in a way that could be analysed to have common features for everybody; that there might be universal human tendencies regarding how humans grow up to be the people they are. This is to say that the existentialist is looking for similarities in humans. And here it is so important to realize that to *show* that something is the same for everybody is a completely different thing from *assuming* something is so for everybody—it is a whole different business to point out that e.g. children develop similarly in a certain aspect than to assume that the subjective experiences and feelings of people are the same. From the existentialist viewpoint human life is a mystery because it is incredibly difficult to find any patterns or trends in observable human appearance or traits that would comply with our moral thought of right and wrong: people who seem to be right or good are consistently found to be the very opposite, and vice versa. People who portray moral virtues can be the least moral people we could think of. So, the existentialist is drawn to the question: what is it *within the human* that makes something or someone good or bad; that makes

I-1. EXISTENCE AND SUBJECTIVITY

one either be good or bad, or to perceive another person to be either of these? I believe this problem has proven to be so difficult that any attempts to solve it in any objective way have failed, and this can be seen in our concept of *equality*: we Westerners wish to believe that the only allowable starting point is that all humans are the same and nobody is better than anyone else, and any other way of thought would be wrong. Modern society in particular is experiencing a peculiar wish to increase the rights of any minorities, and this is always accompanied with egalitarian rhetoric and ideology where the very fact that these groups are minorities is regarded as the justification for the effort of bringing them up to the level of the majority in terms of rights (not responsibilities). In my understanding this movement reflects our modern loss of shared moral frameworks: because we are distanced from our original moral codes, we are drawn to emphasize that everybody is the same, sometimes even to a disproportionate extent. At the same time, we don't believe that people are the same, and we also don't treat them the same, which is unavoidable due to said first assumption; the fact that we humans are moral creatures and make our choices based on our moral sentiments. As moral beings it is the very starting point that some people, or actions, are good and some are bad, and speaking about the lack of this prerequisite means speaking about immorality that equates to being unrestricted and unbounded in behaviour; being somebody capable of any kinds of actions regardless of right or wrong or good or bad—in other words, psychopaths and monsters. We have just lost our understanding of who is good or bad, or right or wrong, and therefore we are suckered with egalitarian rhetoric that says "Shouldn't everybody get the same?", the answer to which of course is 'no', but we are being forced to accept this rhetoric as we are ourselves in a state where we are unable to answer questions of morality and justice. We are confused: we treat people based on our moral conceptions, but we are unaware of these conceptions and ignorant of what they should be; apart from, of course, the egalitarian starting point, which, however, is not possible to implement on the individual level to start with. Now, regarding existentialism, due to the subjective, individualistic quality of morality, and the absolute refusal to externalize himself from existence by acting as a professional whose work is not judged by its moral extent but just by professional codes of the institution that funds it, the existentialist is not a psychologist or psychiatrist, who are formal expert professions and base their language on scientific information with objective standards. Existentialism is an attitude; an approach to life and a way of doing things, and as such isn't ascribed to philosophers only. The language of the existentialist is rooted in the natural language shared by his subjects; the existentialist writes about humans but also about what it is to be human, implying the possibility to empathetically (and not only rationally) understand the existentialist. The existentialist exists, which means that his actions would have a moral extension. And this is strictly opposed to a professional who receives payment whether he is good at his job or not, is at his office at 9 am whether he is humanly in a state capable of productive or creative work or not and violates his institutional and professional code every moment he is a human instead of a professional. The relation of an existentialist and scientist seems to me to be the same as between a politician and a professional politician. Also, as the existentialist exists, he also aims to *change himself* and become better, and secondly, he aims to share this wisdom; the existentialist is *searching for truth* in order to help himself and others. I find it difficult to consider other ways of doing real philosophy, as it is such a truism in the conceptions of the general public that the philosopher should be one to live as he preaches, one who isn't just empty words, and so on—Western philosophers have expanded the meaning of the word 'philosophy' to mean a whole lot of academic exercises and *tatemae*.[6] But I also like to distinguish existentialism from all religion and spirituality that provides a body of symbolic concepts about the subjective. An existentialist might use metaphors, allegories and descriptive language to clarify his point, but his goal is to make his audience *understand* his point and not simply to trust, agree and follow him without understanding.

The definitive feature I would attribute to an existentialist is the conception of subjective truth. An existentialist truth-relation is one in which 1) *truth and reality are always derived from the existentialist's*

---

6   The Japanese have a dyadic concept distinguishing the true personal feelings (*honne*) from the publicly acted façade (*tatemae*).

I-1. EXISTENCE AND SUBJECTIVITY

internal system of beliefs, and 2) *the relation to external reality is a constant process where new and surprising observations are assimilated into the existing system via wonderment*. The internal and subjective dominates, but the relation to the external is something that updates instead of remaining constant. To clarify this, consider the two opposing typical modes of truth.

1) The sheep: one who takes assertion by external authorities as the primary constituent of truth and rationalizes his subjective beliefs to match these assertions. This kind of person will not challenge assertions coming from the authority even if it contradicts his beliefs or moral sentiments. He is essentially afraid of conflict with others, as his view might appear weak and stupid in the eyes of others.

2) The stubborn dad: one who remains persistent in his subjective reality and refuses to update it according to new observations. Instead he rationalizes surprising evidence in the light of his persistent subjective beliefs (prejudices), even when his beliefs can be seen to contradict the evidence. He too is afraid of changing his beliefs, as changing his own mind and beliefs will make him contradict himself and thus appear weak and stupid in the eyes of others.

Both contrary positions should lead to some degree of loss of reality, because to hold a subjective system but also to respond to one's environment are both fundamental human requirements, whether one agrees with them or is aware of them. Also, they will no doubt enrich the subjective experience with feelings of guilt and shame, whenever the person needs to conflict either with his own sentiments or with others. I believe the only way out of this cycle is the mode of subjective truth. Particularly in the modern-day public discourse, common conceptions about truth are dangerously biased towards "the sheep": truth is passionately (and submissively) defended as a scientific, external, evidence-based construct. The concept of *proof* is equally biased towards the meaning of "being supported by strongest evidence" instead of its central other, subjective meaning: "being supported by the most credible testimonial". In real life, however, people's relation to truth has not changed, and rather actually it is the social, subjective conception of truth as testimonial and loyalty that dominates people's family and private lives, and evidence-based proof is *tatemae*, as it carries the sign of being scientific and more civilized. It should be noted that there is nothing more rational in believing evidence as opposed to believing a person's word or testimonial; evidence can be used to deceive just as much as words can deceive, and everybody knows that an ordinary person will have great difficulty achieving courtroom justice against e.g. a corporation with a lot of resources to use to produce various pieces of court evidence. I find it very rational to predict that a single individual will lose a generic court case against a powerful corporation, or at least that he will not achieve public victory in court, as in the worst case for the corporation the case will be settled outside of court, to avoid conviction and public loss of face for the corporation. Then again, politically motivated rhetoric commonly deceives using, particularly, picture and video evidence; leaders of nations have been pictured sitting higher than their rivals, cuddling babies on their laps and so on; we all know how a planned appearance can be manipulated as evidence. Truth, however, is pronounced correctly only in the case where the individual, or a group, is adjusting an observation, or something that has been said, against his/its own belief system. Therefore, it is also correct to say that truth is both volatile and passionate; it doesn't remain constant. Truth represents the desirable *political* outcome and ceases to be true after this outcome has been reached. This applies to both science and religion; in science, a scientific truth is the scientific consensus, which means the dominant theory that is by design meant to be surpassed by a better one. Once a theory becomes consensus and the passion to defend it settles down, it by design immediately becomes, or should become, the target of criticism, and the motivation for new scientists to come up with a better theory. In Christianity, where God as truth is passionately defended, the separation of God and man is crystal clear: man can never be God but can only exist in a relation where this truth can be revealed to him. Here truth could be said to be mostly the individual's association with his moral sentiments that derive from his belief system: the individual will pronounce true any outcomes that he accepts to be morally right in accordance with his beliefs, and the word 'true' will not differ from the word 'right' or 'correct'. Then again, whenever the true, desirable outcome is reached in some matter, the

I-1. EXISTENCE AND SUBJECTIVITY

passion to defend such an outcome settles, and human passion is like love in that it can be blind. It is possible to passionately defend some outcome as right because the principles that imply it are believed to be true, and after having reached the outcome, come to the rational conclusion that the beliefs that led to the outcome weren't true at all. Scientific truth is no better than the subjective one in its capability to err; the human quality simply is such, to see just a little bit into the future at a time. And thus, enter the existentialist wisdom: what makes a difference is the individual's relation to truth: whether the individual accepts his limitation or tries to protect himself from humiliation by being the sheep or the stubborn dad. I find the best parallel to this in competitive sport: a good sportsman is one who competes in his own class, where he is constantly trying to update his performance and beat his earlier results, while accepting his obvious limitation by choosing to compete in a class where he can get beaten by a competitor. Bad sportsmen don't get better, because they are protecting themselves from humiliation: for example, they say things like 'look how bad I am!', hoping to elicit the response 'That's ok, nobody's perfect'. Or else they subjectively make believe they are good enough already and deliberately compete in the class where they can mostly win. But every good sportsman says you need to mostly lose in order to win.

Three existentialist philosophers deserve attention: Socrates, Kierkegaard and Wittgenstein. And these are only the philosophers—there are many people who have found the importance of the subjective and the impossibility to communicate it in words and chosen to cherish that in their lives. Asian philosophy has throughout the ages cherished the unique subject in its spiritual ideal and its conception of philosophy, but Asian philosophical *work*—relying heavily on subjective aesthetics and requiring a living connection of tradition between master and apprentice—has suffered from the same problem as the institution of the church in the West: trying to turn *spiritual* existential ideals into religious doctrines produces *political* doctrines instead. First, the followers may well follow those doctrines for different subjective reasons than their masters, and second, the masters themselves might simply be repeating the original work as political doctrines without being subjectively related to them. A (Western) lover of wisdom cannot take on followers exactly because of this problem but must exist with his fellows in dialogue. By letting someone follow him the philosopher would not teach the follower wisdom but teach him that *his* truth is the correct one—which is always exactly the wrong lesson. The three philosophers mentioned were fully aware of these difficulties and reflected it in their method and work: Kierkegaard wrote it and Wittgenstein, in personal conversations, expressed pessimism about whether he had done anybody any good even if they had spent many years together. Another striking common feature about these philosophers is their fundamental *intellectual honesty* which, of course, is not an intrinsic disposition but a quality that can only be achieved through painfully existentially striving for emancipation from self-deceit. Intellectual honesty is different from answering honestly when questioned; it requires active research into one's subjective contradiction. These philosophers took pains to reach their subjective status. I think Wittgenstein was first and foremost an existentialist although he never used the word; nor would he ever write from the perspective of the subjective using terms that he knew to require an objective criterion of meaning. Instead he always strove to use examples and thought-experiments applying meaningful concepts in terms of shared language-games. The main thing that drove his interest was something he wouldn't try and talk about due to his awareness of its impossibility. He baffled the philosophical world by at the same time *being* ethical, in terms of primarily leading a responsible lifestyle following his ethical requirement and extending his ethical requirements to people around him, and in his philosophy nullifying the whole philosophical or scientific study of ethics. He wrote about God mainly only in his personal notes. He considered Kierkegaard a saint and "by far the most profound" philosopher of the 19th century. Wittgenstein and Kierkegaard were simply clever enough to recognize both the personal nature of ethics and the trap of trying to write about it and to thus treat it as something different than a purely subjective thing. And because they were aware of this and the fruit of their personal ethical struggle in the value of their philosophical thought, they could both clearly recognize their own greatness and their rightful place in the history of philosophy. Interestingly they both

I-1. EXISTENCE AND SUBJECTIVITY

led a thematically and ethically similar philosophical life in attacking a Platonic tradition—Kierkegaard attacked Hegel as Wittgenstein attacked the Platonic idealism or mental representations as the basis of meaning. In addition to, obviously, Kierkegaard, I also find later Wittgenstein very much akin to Socrates in interlocutory method aimed to mainly discard contradictions of thought, and an ethical lifestyle. Just obviously irony, embraced by Socrates and Kierkegaard and in the sense of aiming to provoke a humorous reaction, was something quite alien to Wittgenstein (although baffled readers who'd like to find ways to dismiss him have also suggested to read him as satire).

Yet *existentialism* has been most popularly attributed to people in a *totally* different kind of business from Kierkegaard or Wittgenstein, such as Sartre, Heidegger, Nietzsche, Camus and so on. The difference is in the separation of existence from ethics: placing unrestricted emphasis on the uniqueness of the subject and having the ethical reflections merely on the level of personal emancipation from social norms (which is a challenge and a requirement for the capability of being good). That they dismiss the whole problem of communicability to others with a wave of the hand is reflected in the bulk of their work being littered by ontological gibberish. To Sartre or Heidegger, ontology—as a written art—was not a mistake altogether, but rather limited because all these wonderful things that they can experience are not expressed in it. Such a limitation is, of course, the limitation of *sensibility*, but these writers weren't too concerned about such a matter; they enjoyed talking straight-faced intellectual gibberish while their listeners were gasping as they were not intelligent enough to figure them out or to distinguish their gibberish from the writings of the great masters, whose writings look equally cryptic to the untrained eye. What a masquerade! From a subjective point of view, if one happens to be blessed with a considerable intellect, the easiest thing to do (possibly easier than living happily without using it at all) is to use it to create something one fancies and to then leave its judgement to the astonished readers with lesser intellects; surround yourself with a like-minded intellectual elite to get peer support in the face of opposition to your thought, which is inherently controversial as it is an unanalytical amalgamation of political opinion and rational analysis that is in its nature acknowledged to be halfbaked and incomplete, and meant only to compete against the similar efforts of your elitist friends. Such work is a mere display of skill and an act of narcissism; not an ethical deed. Ethical people take responsibility over others instead of trying to astonish them, and clarity in philosophy comes from a will to be clear to everybody. Such work is the popularization of philosophy via its intellectualism, and in the past it was the philosopher that was the popular intellectual, whereas today that seat is firmly occupied by popular scientists—partly, I believe, because of the popularity of philosophy eating away its quality. Both Wittgenstein and Kierkegaard have been accused of obscurantism, but their communication is not the issue; it's just that a lot of people do not understand their point despite their efforts that were often extended to repeating the same thing over and over. This is an expected result, clearly expressed in their predictions about their popularity and reception. From an ethical point of view, one can never appeal to everyone, but the subjective ethical struggle is in doing one's actions for the right reasons, not e.g. for (possibly unrecognized) reasons of immediate social respect. Making this point clear has far-ranging effects in terms of appeal. No arguments exist that point to objective facts to show how, say, Wittgenstein's work is any different from Heidegger's in value, and this intrinsic subjectivity indeed is the questionable wisdom behind the commonplace cynical attitude towards philosophy in general: "In the end, they all speak of the same thing". Yet from an ethical point of view all actions are not equally valuable; and from a Christian point of view, inherent in all Kierkegaard's work, people won't all be treated the same in the afterlife (this expression gaining a concrete meaning when evaluating the historical influence of someone, for example Kierkegaard himself). Also, from the standpoint of art, it is a very different business to use artistic expression to convey an ethical message rather than to borrow techniques and styles developed by artists (in their efforts to produce art) to produce something that externally looks awesome in terms of being e.g. intelligent, profound, technically masterful and difficult to capture. And indeed, what distinguishes the extreme of an insightful creator from the other extreme of a skilful narcissistic manipulator is the subjectivity: a stolen work can objectively be

I-1. EXISTENCE AND SUBJECTIVITY

identical to a created work, but the manipulator, as a subject, abuses and claims in his own name things essentially discovered and created by other subjects. The only proper standard for the ethical value of a piece of work of this kind is determined by the motives of its author in his society (reflected by the work), and it is not possible to assess these motives through any formal method or by consensus through public argument, but the capability for such evaluation simply takes an ethical individual. This is made obvious by the choice of method in the first place, since *if* the message were not subjective, the ethical author would be right to—as the scientist does—just point out in clear language what is evident but for some reason not publicly known (such as that on such-and-such a remote island lives such-and-such unrecorded animal species). Evaluating the subjective remains a subjective task and the subjective and the objective realms remain perfectly and cleanly separated.

Existence was prevalent throughout Wittgenstein's work as "what cannot be said" or "the background against which everything I might say gets its meaning", with a similar description by Kierkegaard as "something that cannot be thought of"[7] yet something combining with thought, since the ethical thinking subject *exists*. In the meaning of "what cannot be said" it is important to note that for the expression to be meaningful at all, there needs to exist something that one is disposed to utter but leaves unsaid due to the lack of (shared) meaning of what would be uttered. If the distinguished reader has not had such an experience, he might imagine something very personal he always wanted to say but never had the courage to say—and then imagine himself once in a lifetime having the courage to say it, but realizing that if he does so, nobody will understand or appreciate his words, and that this is a true and inevitable fact instead of just a fear to protect him from personal disappointment. Of course such a metaphor is quite meaningless apart from describing the nature of the experienced difficulty on the level of emotion, but I could characterize the form of 'existence' as the unique totality of his beliefs and dispositions as something that underlies his thinking and gives everything he might utter or do an

---

7   Concluding Unscientific Postscript, Part Two, sec. II, ch. III, §1

PART I. THE BASIS OF THOUGHT

ethical aspect: why did he do/say it in *that way?* I sometimes tend to visualize this uniqueness as a complex object conforming to the form of the subject as a thinker and an agent that is fundamentally static but slowly changes through existential change. It is an interesting idea to compare *this* to the neural basis of thought, as this sort of change is exactly what can be witnessed to be happening in the human brain; the so-called neuroplasticity of the brain. To me the existential approach seems highly compliant with what we know as a scientific fact about the human brain. One just needs to be clear that *the brain doesn't produce thought*, yet can be observed to physically behave in correspondence with reported mental events ... perhaps in a similar relation as exists between the sea—consisting of water particles in motion, and waves—consisting of the movement of the water body in response to stimuli such as temperatures, air pressure, winds, subterranean events, magnetism, planetary gravity fields and e.g. mechanical stimuli. Neither sea nor water produces waves but rather they constitute the platform of the phenomenon—one that is described by, and studied under, completely different laws and relations. Then again, to say that existence is changing doesn't reveal much about the subject's subjective relation to one's existence, but it is key in the existential approach to acknowledge that the human subjectivity has a *concrete basis*, which means subjectivity isn't random or incomprehensible but just unique. It is very possible to understand another person, but don't think that whatever you're doing at that moment could be successfully carried over to understanding another person. For all individuals there exists a basis that is unique but concrete and constitutes our character and the basis of our actions as individuals, and throughout history there is great wisdom related to understanding characters and being able to know how a certain type of person would behave in a certain type of situation. I find the word 'ethos', meaning something like "ethical character", very similar to how I see existence—it might be used interchangeably. Then again, *the human body* has the same characteristics of at the same time strictly following a determination that is actively researched via e.g. physiology, genetics and medicine, and being completely unique with such certainty that our methods to determine a person's unique identity are based on the body, such as fingerprints and, lately, DNA

I-1. EXISTENCE AND SUBJECTIVITY

sampling. Modern cognitive science and neuroscience are methodically reducing this human individuality to study of the brain, but this is clearly a pointless and obsessive overconfidence in our capability to predict the behaviour of a living system based on observational data from some constituents of this system. It is so clearly obsessive that I find it much more interesting to psychoanalyse this obsession than to believe any of the vast promises of this field of study. But at this point let's just take note that, irrespective of one's methodological preferences, uniqueness and subjectivity are in no contradiction with empirical science; but cherishing the subjectivity means to very strictly deny all the commonplace strong assumptions held by many scientists—assumptions that are not scientific but held as latent beliefs to guide the direction of scientific work. You could say that to refer to subjectivity means to strictly keep in mind the subjective, human, individual factor within a context where it is easily overlooked, but to really understand subjectivity means to explore where this individual uniqueness comes from; how it is constituted. It is a professional philosophical concept and has strictly no meaning outside philosophical discussions; it is an abstract marker to distinguish realms that constitute meaning. Now, although existence is a subjective quality and cannot be meaningfully described (in the absence of a criterion), it is easy to understand that it is a different thing to *see* something and as a result utter a related word in an effort to describe what you see, than just to be able to use a word in communication—which can be achieved through mimicry. Anybody can become a guitarist by following what other guitarists do, but nobody can become a good, inspirational guitarist that way.

The word 'existential' is often used in reference to the subjective change—the subject *becoming* something—as existence implies a concrete basis of subjectivity that changes. As Kierkegaard would write, the existing subject is in a constant state of becoming. To call a question existential means that its answer has implications for one's character. If one is at the crossroads one can see it e.g. as a practical question of choosing direction, but it can also be an existential question, meaning how taking that particular direction will change you in comparison with some other alternative, and here we can see what can feel disturbing to logically inclined thinkers: whether the choice can be called existential is a subjective question related to the individual and also the particular situation. Crossroads are not always existential; there are people to whom crossroads are seldom existential and there are people to whom crossroads are always existential. Also, it is an existentially interesting idea to get to a crossroads and not to make a decision at all but to proceed without choice—an idea depicted in the beginning of the Kurosawa film *Yojimbo* by the hero who at crossroads chooses his path by throwing a stick in the air and walking in the direction it points to. This is interesting because it highlights the role of making choices from the perspective of life and existence; no matter what choice we make, after we have made the choice we will still continue to exist as the people we were before the choice, but making choices is still burdensome to people who are afraid of the existential perspective; afraid of acting against their acquired identity. The boldest person is somebody who doesn't care what material choice he makes: his life is built so strongly on his confidence in his own capability that he can take on any consequence, so he trains himself by distancing himself also from his choice. Also, the concepts of *meditation* and *trance* as methods to attain spiritual enlightenment can be seen as existential practices: because existence has a concrete basis and a state of existential becoming is contrary to distanced theoretical rigidity, it is possible to train existence itself like a muscle. This behaviour where the mind is trained alongside the body is common to all religions but it vanished from the practices of standard forms of Western Christianity along with the process of secularization (which has led Westerners to seek these forms of enlightenment from outside of organized religion with collective morality, unavoidably leading to cultural segregation via alienation). To take an existential approach to something means an anti-theoretic approach in which one is ready for subjective interaction and ready to both learn and to change oneself through learning. This sort of approach implies fundamental honesty and humility, and it may be noted that this sort of approach was much more commonplace in earlier societies where people lived closer to nature. It seems to me that the way a human normally exists *in nature*, observing one's environment and immediately reacting to one's observations, has been

I-1. EXISTENCE AND SUBJECTIVITY

disrupted by organized society, with its complex social codes and the vast amount of abstract knowledge that needs to be internalized in order to successfully exist as an urban citizen. Civil society forces upon us identities (say, male, female, child, adolescent, person of age, father, teacher, doctor, neighbour) that *help us justify* our actions, which is a required civil norm, but the identities can contradict our moral sentiments, which will cause an existential dilemma and crisis. We might be, say, fathers and employees, but regarding successful life that's not all there is to it, or is it? The theoretical-conceptual way of assimilating new information has, to a large extent, surpassed the natural, existential way; in nature, humans don't weigh incoming information, or, on the other hand, abuse their habitat via e.g. littering but habitually take care of it, and they don't feel superior to or distant from their habitat but exist in a natural sense of fear towards ultimate higher powers of nature. And I'm not at all romanticizing primitive life or wishing for cultural degradation, but establishing the point that an existential approach to life is not something supernatural or utopian, but on the contrary something that existed before our modern society, which gives the word an interesting connotation, as what is existential is a reference to what already exists and needs not be created. As such, 'existential' is in the same realm as 'scientific', as both are the logical opposite of 'idealist'; both the existential and the scientific are interested in *what already exists*, which is juxtaposed with ideas and idealism that in their essence deal with what we wish or dream should exist. Science is interested in what already exists in nature, but the existentialist differs from the scientist, as he is invigorated by the *hidden potential that already is existent in the human*, and concepts such as "existential truth", "existential question" or "existential discovery" relate to the human discovery of this hidden human potential. Does this sound mysterious? Not at all! It's easy to see that this sort of "wasted potential" exists, because our society, as a side effect to all produced benefits, distracts us from the archaic human existence. Actually, many people get distracted by the *expectations* posed by modern society that present life as a sort of ready-made furrow in which the human simply acts according to an expectation and makes only minor decisions in their life, such as choosing a house once they move away from their parents, choosing their major study, choosing a company to work for and choosing their spouse. And to look at it honestly, it is very common to not even make these minor decisions yourself but instead resort extensively to the predestined expectation of your parents or to choose a dominant spouse who, from the moment of establishing a relationship onwards, makes these choices for you. This path provides exactly the comfort a lazy and cowardly individual wishes for, instead of existentially growing up and taking real responsibility over their life, and hopefully over other people, too; to satisfy any hopes of respectful acceptance or even remembrance at the end of your life, instead of being written off as a nobody. Existentially, the human beings we are, the terror of life that compels us is that we all dream and can't stop dreaming, and these dreams depict our wishes. In our dreams we see what we wish to become and to achieve, and to become like our dreams and wishes is a faint ideal that only a few people can achieve, but existentially it should be considered an absolute requirement. If we compare our modern life in contemporary society to an archaic life in the wild, did the people of the past have these issues? No; they were, so to say, forced to *fight for their existence or be wiped out of existence*. And it is misleading to say that they were forced to, because nobody is forcing; to fight for your life and your existence is normal in life. On the contrary, what is not normal is a society where one is distracted from, or restricted from, *living existentially*. We can safely say that our human minds and bodies were not designed to do chartered accountancy from 8 a.m. to 6 p.m., and by this we mean that to live this way is an unnatural achievement, and that it would actually be more natural and in many ways easier for us to use our minds and bodies in a different way, where we more directly express our natural needs and instincts, free from the *restrictions* of the *controlled* (not free) modern life. These restrictions require powerful *psychological inhibitions* to maintain and are an impossible feat for somebody without the capacity for such inhibitions. If you try and force this kind of work on, say, a healthy, vigorous individual with a normal sense of control over his environment and a healthy social need, he will not fit in; he will express extreme discomfort, rebel, and in the absence of a capability to flee he could

I-1. EXISTENCE AND SUBJECTIVITY

even fight for his life in a fight-or-flight situation.[8] When speaking of 'existence', we mean our *human existence as given by our natural needs and instincts*, in juxtaposition with whatever our society is expecting from us in terms of behaviour. And the hidden potential of existence is whatever would be natural for us, but we are, likely subconsciously and without any awareness, psychologically inhibiting ourselves by following the expectations our upbringing and society have imposed on us since birth. To speak of existence means to speak of life from this *natural, healthy* and *individualist* standpoint; from the perspective of what would be beneficial for us *if we got to choose freely* instead of being adapted into an inhibited, organizational role where we never made a free choice but were following something imposed on us by group expectation. To look at it from the perspective of justice; if the group imposes rules on an individual, the group is also expected to *take care* of the individual. But this is not the case in the Western world! From the standpoint of society, we get rules to obey and to follow, but we don't get the love and care we would expect from a society that governs our individual choices. Instead, we get *freedom*. And this freedom is good for nothing unless we use it to benefit our free democratic society where one *is free to choose*. To live existentially is a requirement for someone living in a free society, and if we, free Westerners, don't think and decide individually, our society will obviously collapse into an authoritative tyranny, which is the case everywhere where people don't have individual freedoms as the 'care' of society and government extend to all the areas where we are accustomed to having free choice. In the West we are free and individualist because we want to be free and individualist and we believe that it is natural for us to live this way, and that our modern society is a development from a society in closer harmony with nature —a society where one was not "forced to" make *individual* necessary arrangements to survive, but where living this way would be the only natural way and to consider anything else would be laughable or mad, and mean either death or the shame of slavery through lost freedom.

---

[8] This is one moral story in the wonderful movie *One Flew Over the Cuckoo's Nest*, which essentially shows that a healthy, active individual will in fact be destroyed by an environment that is controlled enough.

PART I. THE BASIS OF THOUGHT

A viable way to learn more about Kierkegaardian subjectivity and existence would be to perform this experiment: Imagine an object that is *you*, and let's name this object *O*. To be able to perform this, you need to satisfy the prerequisite of being able to look at yourself (some people are said to be unable to look at themselves in the mirror). Having succeeded in looking at yourself, looking at *O*, the following question brings about the *subjective problematic of sentence x*, as the question of what is, so to say, humanly possible: *What would it take to become somebody who is able to mean x?* (We are assuming x is a meaningful thing to say and not nonsense.) Can *O* say x and mean it? How would *O* need to change in order to be able to mean x? What would *O* need to *become*? This difference (Δ) in existence, ΔOx, is something somebody else has but you are missing, and to somebody else's existence (*P*), ΔPx might be all different. You are not *him*, and what you are missing is, by definition, different from what he is missing. Sounds vague and quite stupid, right? But that is the best you will get from a theoretical perspective; to become properly acquainted with yourself and others takes a long period of familiarity and experience. But you will achieve nothing in this matter unless you accept the fundamental human starting point of uniqueness. If you naively assume people are fundamentally the same inside, you are quite wrong; there are social and psychological frameworks in the light of which human behaviour is to be interpreted, and to succeed in this means to be able to gain skills to better predict how a certain type of human would think or act. But you can't 'read' other subjects or successfully categorize them. You can tell yourself you know people are all the same, but for this to be possible you need to completely ignore your own failure; you need to ignore where people deviate from your expectation. This is the story of Javert in *Les Misérables*: a police officer wielding authority and mastering procedure but incapable of mercy, having built a career ignoring the deeper moral aspects of the laws he is to maintain, believing instead that high morality cannot coexist with those who he puts into prison and categorically deems criminal in nature. When he himself is met with mercy, which he knows to be moral yet has so far ignored, his world crumbles. Subjectivity essentially means humanity; something typical to a human, and humans are not just psychological and

I-1. EXISTENCE AND SUBJECTIVITY

social animals. Humans are traditional cultural animals and in their behaviour are known to employ the cultural knowledge of hundreds or thousands of years. In earlier times humans were differentiated from, say, dogs and savages, by exactly this quality—having a deepness to them; possessing a soul. To know a human, you'd need to know, as it were, where he is coming from. Here the most useful thing you'll find out is the traditions he employs in his behaviour; traditions related to his society but also traditions employed in his family. This might touch on culture to some extent, but you can never fully know even your own culture, let alone the culture of another. When we discuss human subjectivity, we discuss a world of infinite extent and complexity, but one that is not as visible when we start our exploration as nature is for natural scientists. This infinity of subjectivity is the source of its uniqueness. As humans, people will be predictable to some degree at best, but they will never cease to surprise you, and if you think you have them figured out you are seriously fooling yourself. Also, you shouldn't be disappointed to find that there are many individuals who, due to this ultimate unknowability, never succeed in trusting other individuals; for them to trust they'd need to be able to predict: they are looking to trust their own prediction, not another person. To achieve that much subjective capability of reliance on others—*trust*—is already a subjective achievement to be proud of. Trust is the factor that both creates a community and binds it together and is often a prerequisite for joining a community and is required to be formally established. For example, the males of a hunter society would not be allowed to join hunts or to marry without having enacted the relevant male rites. Trust between both separate individuals and communities is formed via the means of such symbolic acts, which in our culture start from a handshake.

Kierkegaard would write about a subjectively existing thinker, in contrast with a thinker that doesn't exist. Wittgenstein would mention writers who continue writing while having stopped thinking. Both describe a thinker who is not just thinking but thinking in a certain way. If you're somebody who believes knowledge and success come in the form of rigorous, unquestionable facts, this approach is not for you. Also, it is highly dangerous to try and make subjective qualities into rules, because they cannot be described. If you describe a subjective way of doing something, a person will try his best and do it in a certain way ... but what is the criterion for him to know if he is doing it correctly? The written form of text, or any form of word, cannot convey this subjective understanding; the correct way would be the way of a teacher and student (or master and apprentice), where the teacher passes on his subjective understanding, evaluating and correcting the student in a subjective relationship that takes a long time, and in which the student needs to exist in a trusting relation with the teacher—first accepting the teacher's ways via his authority and later, hopefully, growing to understand them, and to eventually perhaps surpass his master. Learning by yourself is also possible, and either successful or unsuccessful ... but this is no worse risk than being under the supervision of a bad teacher, which will guarantee bad success, or trusting a teacher whose merit is unknown, which only puts you at risk of learning wrong lessons. But even if you study by yourself, taking an existential perspective puts you into the position of a *learner*, as you need to be in a state of becoming, and someone who feels ready will not become anything. Persistently tell yourself: "I am a learner; I am a beginner; I am not ready, not even close, but just at the beginning." With this sort of humble approach, you'll be able to fight the urge that we, as social creatures, have to show confidence or skill and prove our worth to others for admiration and status, or the willingness to see results as a direct outcome of invested time and good motivation. These are vices of impatient students that, in a learning model of teacher and student, the good teacher is to weed out and punish using his superior expertise. In a good learning relationship, the teacher has ultimate authority via his expertise and his word is not questioned by the student. The general formula for success in just about any subjective skill is something like the following:

1) Try something.
   - Use what you know to be good from others before you came along.
   - Don't repeat a path you took earlier but make corrections. Big failure → big changes, small failure → smaller changes.
   - Be courageous and adventurous.
2) Ask yourself: was the outcome a success or failure?

I-1. EXISTENCE AND SUBJECTIVITY

- Be honest about failure and cherish it.
- Distance yourself from the emotion of success or failure. Be analytical like an ice-hockey commentator in the comfort of his workspace.

3) Analyse.

- Was it a partial success/failure? How big a part was success/failure?
- What was the ingredient that made it successful? Keep that part and use it next time.
- What was the mistake that made it fail? Discard that part and never repeat it.

The formula applies both to learning something to become permanently better at it, and to any live interactive situations where skills are applied. The formula seems simple enough, but just to make it clear; there are a lot of people studying any subjective skill that progress fast, and a lot of people that don't make much progress at all. Looking at the methodology of learning can easily bring out a very valid perspective to what constitutes the difference in result. The key intellectual dispositions for success in any field are being honest, neutral and analytical, resisting the mental temptations of fear, shame or overconfidence. Also, it is necessary to be able to analyse and to distinguish success from failure, for which one needs not only honesty but a sound and objective criterion of success. There are many distinguishable patterns of learning in a wrong way, but we can easily see that many people don't use a criterion: they try and fail, then, instead of accepting the failure via its objective standard, try to see something positive in their attempt and reject the negative emotion related to failure. Failure is *supposed to feel bad*, and repeated failure is supposed to make us feel *angry*; these emotions have a purpose to them, and they are not to be avoided, and they are very different emotions than feeling guilty or ashamed. You're actually supposed to feel "I am just a failure" in order to get to the question of "What are you going to do about it?" and "If you don't think it is *you* who needs to do something, do you think somebody else will come to guide your hand to success?" These are the fundamental subjective questions determining a transition from an external moti-

PART I. THE BASIS OF THOUGHT

vation towards a self-induced motivation.

In philosophy, the answer—the correct way—doesn't come in the form of the most correctly written rule or statement; wherever philosophy has anything like this in mind, it is simply looking for that unicorn horn that is to be brought to the king who himself will take no trouble to find it. You could extend this metaphor by pointing out that even if you did find the ultimate answer or enlightenment, as the result of a process of searching, you yourself would not get it, as it is the legal property of your king. You are just a lackey, sent on this mission by your king, who has no clue whether the object of your search exists or not, and doesn't need to care if it exists or not, as you, his workforce, are cheap, if not free, whereas he is rich, and your time, not his, is wasted. But secondly, because existence is *invisible*, particularly to the subject himself (to others it is more visible), the best contact point for the subject to his own existence is *symbolical expression*. We must speak indirectly of invisible things, and symbolical expression is likely the easiest, most comprehensible way, yet it should be noted that there are also many other classifiable indirect ways, such as ellipsis (omission), speaking in the third person (as girls do when they play with dolls) or speaking in opposites, as typically in forms of humour. Generally, to speak indirectly means to deliberately address the *subjectivity* of the listener. According to a generally supported idea of meaning, meaning—at least in many cases—comes from "the context" of discussion ... but it is rather obvious that it is not the context but the shared subjectivity of the listeners that can be used to communicate. 'Context', as a reference to the conversational situation or a continuing thread of discussion, fails to do credit to human subjectivity, which is infinitely complex, and within a conversation there are multiple subjects instead of just one, meaning that the opportunities for the indirect speaker range from addressing the subjectivity of a single individual to that of several individuals. This essentially means that a careful choice of words can address something meaningful to a single listener or a whole group of listeners. An example is Master Yoda's "So sure, are you?" This comment does not address any contextual information of the discussion, but just addresses Luke, who is expressing certainty instead of

I-1. EXISTENCE AND SUBJECTIVITY

having an open mind to his master's teaching. Then again, 'context' is very vague for an abstraction, whereas 'subjectivity' is very particular, because it addresses a particular subject or a particular group of subjects that are both easily available for scientific study. To know what knowledge is available for "contextual" indirect communication, one just needs to know what the target audience (subject) knows ... and not only is this particular and scientific, but rather it would be something taught as an elementary principle in communication classes or, say, general guidelines for either written communication or an oral presentation. Therefore, subjectivity is the link from linguistic meaning, which is often thought to concern objects of thought, to psychology and sociology, which are known to concern not objects but how we relate to them—subjectivity is just a good choice of word in linguistic discourse as it is a reference to the *grammatical* subject. In my opinion, this Kierkegaardian word is a sort of missing link or component in later efforts of linguistic philosophy; if you don't properly accept that subjectivity is unique and infinitely complex, I expect you will try to enforce objective knowability where there is none, and likewise, if you don't accept the rigidness of grammatical logic, I expect you will attribute uncertainty to where an alternative actually is not imaginable. According to Wittgenstein in *Tractatus*, what we cannot speak of we must pass on in silence, and this is true if we consider words to be representations, which Wittgenstein believed at the time of *Tractatus* but then denounced. It seems to me correct to say that *symbolism is the view outwards from the subjective*; a view from subjective meaning towards the shared, objective language, where meanings are established by their use. So, for example (from the movie *Kagemusha*): the emperor could decide that "a mountain doesn't move", by which it is meant that not moving (standing your ground), like the mountain,[9] is the correct tactical choice. Here the mountain is the symbol, or *metaphor*, of not moving, but what does this mean? I can read a description of metaphor, that it is "a situation compared to the real thing", and that metaphors are figurative tools used to give effect. These are good descriptions, because in the example the emperor is using the metaphor of a mountain *in a situation*, but the fundamental and philosophically rel-

---

[9] The mountain, as a military tactic, is a reference to *The Art of War*.

evant question is the borderline between when people are speaking in concrete established meanings and when they are speaking figuratively or metaphorically, because *an imagined thing* is not the same, and not "almost the same", but in many ways the absolute logical opposite of *a real thing*. Here it is key to differentiate between the person's *subjective meaning* that the person is trying to communicate *using objective meanings of words as figurative elements*. I know a lot of people don't like the idea of a hidden subjective world, but they should then explain why anybody would try to use metaphors in communication, instead of simply speaking in clear established meanings, as it is an easily verifiable fact that people passionately engage in this sort of activity. If a person doesn't approve of the subjective, then he should intellectually explain the pointlessness of *all* such activity, and not just some subset of this activity, where people are e.g. passionately speaking of religious experiences that don't seem to refer to actual real-world phenomena. If somebody, like Richard Dawkins, wishes to call this "hallucination", he should notice he is using a *medical* word used by experts who need to try and help people who may have the problem of *not being able to distinguish* between a subjective, wishful, metaphorical world and the real world, which is a mental condition with possibly very severe consequences. He should take note that it is a medical fact that normal people *do* distinguish between their dream and the real world, and that there are quite a lot of people with very vivid imagination in whom this imagination is considered a skill and a talent instead of them being uncontrollably and dangerously driven by it. Extending the use of medical terms outside their scope, to categorize and to demean people exhibiting a very fundamental human behaviour, does not make one a medical expert, and people like Dawkins should address the question intellectually instead of making a mockery of it. So, the situational meaning in a metaphorical or symbolical expression is essentially subjective meaning, and the person using such expression is *existing subjectively*, using his imagination and using established objective meanings as his ingredient, and the symbolism is a perspective from his subjectivity outwards into the shared world. He is being subjective, creative and personal instead of being an objective and impersonal carrier of something somebody else has established.

I-1. EXISTENCE AND SUBJECTIVITY

His primary interest is not if he is being understood or not; he does not explain and is not looking to please. When meeting such a person you should first notice that you don't understand him, and you should understand that this does not mean he is not being rational or doesn't have a plan—on the contrary, a very highly subjectively developed person is likely to be immediately unintelligible, like a piece of art. Secondly, you need to decide your response to him. There are two correct ways of treating such people: promote him, if what he creates is good for all (genius), or oppose, limit or restrict him, if not (crazy). The correct way to evaluate people is by the consequences of their actions and creations, not their intelligibility or accessibility. In any case you should resist the modern ritualized institution of knowledge that doesn't have any clear conception of what an intelligent or good man is supposed to be like, but is just a system and a model of behaviour that has already lost most of its credibility and doesn't know how to renew itself— a model where the members are mostly just playing their part, trying to maintain a proper appearance and ignoring issues, leaving free space for all sorts of rhetorical con men to abuse the authority of the system, as it is essentially a system of correct knowledge and the masses are led to believe the utter falsity that publicly and confidently acting these rituals of knowledge is the same as being right. The falsity of public personae is in that through publicity people only see what they *do*. Actually, the key thing in order to judge a person is to know the things he *does not do*. This is akin to diet; in order to have optimal weight it doesn't actually matter much what you eat. What matters is the ratio of energy released in your digestion against the energy consumed by your body through your activity; roughly put: that the nutrition your body receives is in proportion to the energy your body needs to recover from what you have given and done in action. And for just normal people who don't exist in too much physical activity on a daily basis, coupled with the fact that the foods most available to consumers are foods that contain absurd amounts of fast energy, the key factor in achieving balance is not what you eat but what you *don't* eat. Oftentimes you'll see an obviously overweight person who publicly eats just salads, but not only that, she makes a big number out of eating only salads. The truth is, eating only salads it is not physically possible to gain weight, as fresh plants contain such an amount of fibre and water, in proportion to energy released during digestion, that they will fill your stomach before you are able to consume an amount that would release its energy fast enough for that to happen.

Because to exist is to be becoming, the Kierkegaardian existence signifies an ideal type of subjective state that is difficult to capture. It is therefore tempting to dismiss the whole concept as obsolete and to be replaced by something more modern ... but actually it is exactly the subjectivity that our whole modern psychology is unable to explain in its obsession with studying the mind via the brain and the body. When is the subject changing and becoming and not remaining stationary? In Kierkegaard's time, psychology and related psychological concepts didn't exist, but he considered the difference between a subjective thinker and an objective thinker, and juxtaposed subjective thought with objective thought in many ways. For example, objective thought may be complex, but it is *direct* and suitable for memorizing.[10] Kierkegaard used the concept of *double reflection* to signify the importance of both the object that is being thought of and its relation to the subject who is existing in thought. This could be understood via expressions like "I must not think that way", in which we can see the subject that is reflecting on himself as well as on the object of thought. And because of this, it is obvious that such thought cannot either be memorized or captured in full in written language, as the thought contains an active subjective component; it requires a subject to think it in order to have context. Kierkegaard expresses this necessity as a divine requirement: the subjects must stay separate and cannot meld together into objectivity. Wherever subjectivity is of interest, the language of expression is *art*, and wherever objectivity is of interest, a goodbye is said to subjectivity. So, it seems existence implies an ideal of thought that is subjective and double-reflective. In a contemporary setting, we might contrast types of thought by setting *creativity* and *original* thought against *patterned* thought by e.g. calling it "thinking out of the box", and subjective thought indeed is creative, but creativity is not really thought. Rather, creativity is a metaphor from creation, and as with

---

10 Concluding Unscientific Postscript, Part Two, sec. II, ch. II, §2

I-1. EXISTENCE AND SUBJECTIVITY

thought, one can mould clay or paint in a manner that is following a readily available pattern instead of originating it in a creative manner. Maybe creativity is the ability to employ one's subjective imagination in one's work instead of mimicking what one has seen others doing before—and these surely are two clearly distinct subjective activities; the difficulty is in distinguishing how the subject is doing whatever he is doing, as the subjectivity of another can't be seen, and typically a person is unaware of his own subjectivity and others see it better. It is rather obvious that others see the subject better because they have a direct view of him; the subject himself can only have the double-reflective view. The subject might be completely unaware of *how* he is doing what he is doing, due to lacking the double-reflective view. A copy-cat might be first accused of copying by somebody else, deny it, think about it further, and then become aware of what he is doing and accept the accusation later. Typically, the copy-cat will defend against such an accusation by saying that he is just doing what everybody else is doing. But dreaminess by itself is not what we call creativity; creativity is a subjective skill in which the child-like dreamy component unites with rational thought and human interaction. Creativity being dreamy rationality, the Kierkegaardian subjectivity is still a necessary word as it means something different, because creativity is a quality that doesn't imply ethics or any subjective change. I can easily imagine somebody being highly skilled and creative in their work, but not existing as an individual; using their creativity to weave an interesting story about themselves that is essentially a lie to please and fool others into believing in a personality that is actually artificial. Thus, creativity is a skill, but it doesn't imply any ethical-political existence. Being *associated* with creativity, originality and ethics, the type of subjectivity meant here can be *contrasted* with at least two distinguishable modes of action. Firstly, *mimicking* is behaviour in which—usually—one has been impressed by and admires the actions of another, and therefore works to become like him in one's actions. It is also the most basic animal social constituent that happens unconsciously and automatically when a social hierarchy has been established between the individuals: the subordinate repeats the action of a superior. It can also be called 'following'. Secondly, the predominant mode of human social behaviour is acting according to *social roles* that carry expectations and approval of a type of social interaction, and which is formalized in the concept of a profession. One can adopt a role, develop and become good in it, and this almost exclusively constitutes the general conception of being good. However, subjectivity obviously contrasts with this role as the personal contrasts with the social, similarly to the way art is said to be "above society" or "larger than life", which relates to the subjective realm involved in artistic creation. What we can also see is that as social roles relate to the form of society as what is deemed important for the society, the existence of roles and professions implies the possibility to criticize these roles, as society overall is subject to criticism. So, although society employs roles that take skill and professionalism—being good at something—to fulfil well, it has been a part of the spirit of democracy from its early days to subject these social functions to criticism from the perspective of the question of what is a good society, and in the spirit of democracy, these questions have lain outside the social frameworks themselves: in the realm of subjectivity, together with all the moral questions one needs to also employ in successfully fulfilling these roles. So, subjectivity is clearly distinct from social roles, and the whole concept of democracy implies a socially active but fully independent subject and not an army of mindless voters or MPs, and subjectivity is simply a realm that has recently not been studied under this name, or at least not as a separate science that would combine ethics, psychology and sociology. Works of art—studies of the subjective—are considered purely entertainment, and this misunderstanding is simply due to the lack of an effective model to explain what art is.

The existential, personal philosophical method is the opposite of the hypothetical, impersonal method. The existentialist way of finding the best answer is becoming as good as possible in an ethical sense. The existential method for philosophy is like the method for an artist: one can't make art without existing. I read that the writer D.H. Lawrence, a highly existential character, once bitterly raged to his friend: "All scientists are liars!" The clear subjective meaning of 'liar' here is reflected in that *all* scientists, not just some, are liars, since it is exactly the scientist who is sworn to objectivity. Also, Socrates' refusal—in his apology—to

I-1. EXISTENCE AND SUBJECTIVITY

take back what he believes in and to show penitence, would be a refusal to lie in a subjective sense. He knew perfectly well that he *could* do this, since he was being forced to it against his own will. Yet because at this point his quest for subjective truth (showing people that underneath their objective honesty they live a subjective lie) had already been deemed criminal by the city-state of Athens he loved first and foremost, this would have meant exile and the end of meaningful life for him. He lived and taught in utmost devotion to his nation and gods (those two being inseparable in discourse at that time), and denouncing his faith, because people were demanding this, would have been committing a lie towards that which he subjectively served. He chose to die for his nation as a martyr. In existential terms, *truth* is a type of *action*, revealed by expressions such as "that is not the *whole* truth" or "I have *found* the truth". The whole business of self-deceit is possible by avoiding a type of action, which is directly related to *confession*. Confiding, in turn, is something that people normally do with close friends or relatives, but for which there has been the institution of Penance in the Roman Catholic Church, similar institutions observed by monks in many parts of the world, and lately the secular institution of therapy. It is a matter of human social nature that, *existentially*, matters can come into existence only when one commits the action of pronouncing them, and only after a matter has come to existence this way is it possible to consciously silence the matter. There is an absolute difference between a truth one knows but keeps silent about, and truth one is unaware of—the first one being a truth that exists for the individual, and the second being a truth only somebody else can attribute to the individual. Equally, there is a difference between a man who knows the truth and chooses to say certain things on certain occasions, and a man who, by similar choices, strives to hide his lack of knowledge. And, essentially, here the word "truth" can refer to any matter under scrutiny: what is distinctive is the behaviour of these two men. The first man is certain because he believes in the truth in question, since he has become aware of it, and therefore also knows *why he* believes it and is ready to present that. This doesn't seem very complicated presented in this way, and this is the very basis of how we come to learn things in life. But the second man is fundamentally uncertain and thinks: "May-

PART I. THE BASIS OF THOUGHT

be that really is the truth, it certainly seems so; some others seem to be thinking that way, too... then again, I might be totally mistaken: what a shame that would be!" The second man has never pronounced such a thing and is missing the existential relation to such a truth. And it can be said with absolute certainty that no matter how much evidence he could gather about the matter, such a *process* will never make it true for him; the whole method of trying to gather evidence about it is learned from other areas of life where it can be very successful, such as studying nature, but in the case of subjective truth it is a pointless effort that one desperately grabs hold on to in the absence of the particular skill required for the job. The truth is *revealed* in a subjective process that requires living existence and a *trusting* subjective relation, and no amount of evidence can create this; the subject creates it, possibly via having exhausted all his questions and doubts, after which he can accept and trust the conclusion. And this is a very important thing to understand: *the truth does not follow from facts*. It is the subject that accepts the truth, and here the question is whether the subject is a rational person or not: whether he will have the rational discipline to change his beliefs based on reason and logic, or whether he will e.g. not believe any amount of reasoning, believe irrational reasoning, believe compelling rhetoric, or just change his mind seemingly (from the perspective of rational argument) on a whim. Few people possess the mental discipline to demand subjective logical soundness in the face of comfortable lies, amusing rhetoric or a threat of unfavourable consequences that they know to follow from a public announcement of disaccord with authority. The vast majority rather seek to please: to try and seek out the favourable expectation of social authority and attest it as truth if necessary; to use weaker forms of expression where they subjectively tend to disagree, or, when the disagreement is obvious, not to say anything at all unless forced to express their opinion.[11] Should anybody claim truth to follow from fact, what they essentially mean is that the combination of factual argument, rhetoric and, if necessary, coercion, is in almost all cases a successful tactic to mould agreement, and that the cases where this will not succeed are so few as not to pose

---

11 Here Jesus' prediction that Peter would deny him: Jesus predicted his persecution, which would catch on to all his disciples, which would require public denial in order to escape.

I-1. EXISTENCE AND SUBJECTIVITY

significant trouble in their resistance. It is a warped view favoured by tyrants, drunk with power, and a view that can easily be suggested by somebody in direct service of such authority; with a motive to walk over the individual. If somebody suggests that truth generally follows from proof of some kind, he is correct on the level of surface, because in the collaborative process of judgement this convincing with proof, and the possible acceptance of proof, is what can be seen to take place. Yet only in the case of formal systems—a very remote case from everyday life—is the truth of proof captured within the formal system, and this is done by generally restricting the formalism to allow only a finite set or combination of possible values. The way this is done is quite simple: consider that I ask you: "How certain are you that you saw this man yesterday on your way to work?" You'll reply something like "I might have seen him, but not sure. Possibly." Considering you're honest, this answer could be called the subjective truth—the opposite of which could be called a lie, semi-truth, diversion or such. I'll continue: "OK, well, if you have only two possible answers: yes or no … what is your answer?" You'll reply: "OK, then *no*." And what I do next is just give a name to this limited set of answers, such a 'truth-value' or a 'truth function' … and I have created a specific language with the word 'truth' appearing in it … but that has nothing at all to do with the subjective truth in your first reply. Under absolutely no circumstances can it even be called an "aspect", a "projection" or an "estimate" of the subjective truth, because the manner with which you limit the reply from "possibly" to "no" is a *moral choice*: you need to consider the consequences of what happens when you skew your answer. Here a possible relevant moral framework is e.g. "You shall not give false testimony against your neighbour", which implies you should rather choose *not to implicate* under uncertainty … but as it is a subjective choice, you are free to choose, and the choice is dependent on the unique *you*.

Essentially, whenever we use the word 'truth' we refer to something that *could* be seen but *is not* being seen—it could be seen via the means of this subjective action. By using the word 'truth' we imply that there is a possibility to see such a truth; by saying "The truth is…" we imply that we can see the truth and some other person can't, but we can also use the word by saying "This issue seems murky ... I wonder what the truth about the matter is", by which we admit we are being uninformed. Truth is never, so to say, a final and absolute state; in all simplicity, truth is the step from an uninformed state to a better understanding. Now, because subjective truth is an action, the subjective process of truthfulness is something that may be exercised, just like any other skill for action. After Kierkegaard, this has been called the "leap of faith". It is a personal, wilful action that essentially requires a component of trust. Proof can only constitute a social factor to motivate the expression of belief contra suspicion. Therefore, even vast amounts of fabricated evidence and an oppressive social environment that tries to force an individual to attest something that the individual doesn't trust to be right, cannot be successful. Even if the coerced subject submits and attests, he will still internally hold a conflicting view that he believes to be true and justify to himself that the falsity he attested is something he had to do. *One can't force belief, as somebody who forces is somebody who will not provoke trust*—but rather provokes fear. In a modern setting, as subjectivity is not paid any attention, this question of coming to believe is not raised and there is a sort of understanding that external proof creates credibility or plausibility, so it is assumed that a person is persuaded if he is in the correct state of mind. This is of course an utterly false assumption and missing the most fundamental key component—the *subjective* component. No amount of evidence can or *should* cause a person to be persuaded if he has valid grounds for doubt, and it is when the person, internally, has no grounds for doubt anymore, that this process should be initiated. *I* should convince *you*—not the other way around. And the subjectivity of existence and the fact that it takes *courage* to think correctly is why *self-expression*, a seemingly vain and pointless business by itself, is an equally important exercise towards subjective truth as training one's physique is towards one's capability to perform physical acts—in the same way that sport can seem pointless without a proper perspective of its roots as basic training for human existence involving hunting and warfare. Self-expression subjects one's personal creations to public scrutiny, which is something that cowards avoid. Only by lots of active exercise, having to take courage and being met with trial and error and the results of one's own actions, can one develop existentially to a higher social responsibility and thus the respect that contributes to one's happiness. It might be mentioned that most of what nowadays is called 'art' are really just works of self-expression; not serious work but just exercising one's freedom—not unlike the difference between dancing and having the courage to go to the middle of the dance floor to aimlessly wave one's limbs in public (possibly even in rhythm), which of course is a requirement for actual dancing. Similarly, in existential philosophy, a very tempting thing to do would be to write about subjective qualities, such as love, happiness or fear, but I find this the job for psychology as a science, and for art as a study of the subjective. What is to be considered philosophy is only the analysis of the rightful place of these disciplines and the sensibility of what is being produced by these individual fields. The job of the philosopher is to notice what an artist means by artistic expression and what a scientist means by his scientific results, and to resolve any confusions and incorrect implications caused by the fact that all these different forms use the same methodology of human communication: *language*. Language is systematic communication as a shared practice and has many other forms in addition to obvious written language, such as gestures, signals, signs, code words, and most importantly, *symbols*, that have throughout the ages also carried cultural knowledge in the form of metaphors and allegories. Spoken and written language is a development and an extension of these human communicative functions and has developed in complexity in step with the complexity of the form of the society in which it is applied. In a similar way as the system of justice has to develop together with society, the scholarly function of philosophy is an effort to impose intelligent criticism on society, and just as empathetic *insight* (seeing inside) is key to understanding other subjects, so *intellectualism* means the capability to entertain a thought, on the level of language, without committing to it in existence—without believing what one is saying—and is the key virtue of a philosopher. This mental function differs from the way that thought and intention are typically interrelated in people. *Intellectual honesty* is an attribute that Wittgenstein vigorously fought to achieve personally, and he vividly berated the lack of it in his colleagues. I understand intellectual honesty firstly as a personal existential requirement when doing philosophy; honesty about the things that in one's subjective existence remain hidden from others—later Wittgenstein used *confession* as philosophical methodology. But more broadly, I see honesty as the general relation of one's work to one's existence, and as such, an honest philosopher won't theorize over what he can't see, and this makes theory a tool unfit for philosophy. This can be likened to not giving testimony over what one doesn't know—biblically, not to give false testimony against one's neighbour—and it is most often simply not even considered that expressing belief is an action. By contrast with theorizing, philosophy is a methodology to come to understand what one knows and doesn't know, or in other words, the limits of one's knowledge, which is an essentially honest quality, as people quite naturally tend to hide rather than expose their lack of knowledge. This honesty is the opposite of empiricism, which works to posit a theory about how the things that one doesn't know, seem to be, and tries to test it with evidence. The intellectual needs this honesty the most, because he is the most capable of thinking things that he doesn't in fact mean but are just his ideas about how things could be. Therefore, the honest existentialist, who has the capability of double reflection, doesn't *assume* what seems to be; he notices *that* things *seem*, and works backwards by trying to understand *why* it is that they seem that way. *That* is real philosophy. Theories are tools for the situation where one can validate/invalidate one's theory with *objective* observation, which means that others can also share the validating observation and the criterion for the validity of the observation.

There are certain sad features that characterize modern Western conceptions about humans and their social behaviour that could be described as a biased concentration on the individual and a disregard of the social. It seems we have adopted a rather left-wing concept of universal freedom, which leaves the individual alone in his mind only as an individual agent and makes it sensible to concentrate any study of the human mind within the individual only. I will list some noticeable features here.

1) The standard conception of the human as a psychological, physical

I-1. EXISTENCE AND SUBJECTIVITY

and social *totality* has been lost, and these aspects of humanity are now studied in isolation from each other. We have lost both the psycho-social and the psycho-physical.

2) Individuals have been reduced to individualistic fact-processing machines whose brains are seen to process facts produced by science. The traditional concept of *dialectic*, as old as the history of Western thought, is forgotten in favour of this alternative model. The dialectical model of thought involves a social dimension, namely that knowledge is not final or separated from beliefs and is meant to be socially tested and verified.

3) The loss of the social perspective has caused the subjective themes of social harmony: morality, justice, religion and spirituality to disappear from interest. These are the themes of importance regarding the efforts of the individual to become a socially harmonious and productive member of society. Any remotely spiritual themes are described from their individualistic perspective of producing some effect on the individual, such as that instead of saying that the sauna is a place to relax, it is said that the sauna experience is relaxing. Moral themes simply don't exist as questions, problems or dilemmas—what exists is moral blame.

The individualistic perspective yields unsympathetic behaviour that is rather sickly and irrational in nature, such as, in a situation of disagreement and quarrel, a quick reaction to classify the other as mentally ill instead of trying to understand him. If we believe people are individual agents whose thoughts and behaviour are produced by their brain, it is only natural to think that incomprehensible behaviour is the product of a faulty brain. So, disputes in principle, that in practice are also territorial disputes between individuals sharing the same social space, can be resolved by agreement to disagree: "I go this way and you go that way", which is not a *resolution* in a social sense but just an alternative to it, just as a divorce settlement is not a resolution to marital conflict but an arrangement to avoid one. Humans have a social need for sympathy, so any leftover sympathy is directed to children and animals and takes place outside these disputes. In addition, Because the problem of morality has disappeared, authenticity of work is increasingly subject to doubt. Published texts, videos or even seemingly authentic news articles are constantly under suspicion of being unauthentic and having been produced with a hidden agenda.

Perhaps the clearest illustration to highlight the separation between the individual and society is the concept of *identity*, as Westerners are experiencing a colourful mass identity crisis. Identity essentially means how an individual is identified, and the role of society here starts at the birth of the individual, where the doctor identifies the sex of the individual and he/she is given a social security number, passport, etc., which in turn are used by officials to identify them as a citizen of a country, which determines their rights and responsibilities as per the laws of their home country or other countries, such as education, opening a bank account, military responsibilities and so forth. The concept of identity has sprouted uses in two distinct realms of meaning: 1) the social meanings of identity as practical (technical) means of identification, and 2) the personalized concept of identity, meaning essentially one's experience of what social groups one belongs to. There is a highly emphasized individualistic aspect to the latter meaning: various social groups promote individuality and freedom of choice by any means necessary and with no imaginable borders, and portray social identity, such as passport or marriage status, simply as technical registration information without any real function behind it. This is in fact the absolute extreme to which it is possible to diminish the dominant social identity in a society that degrades to a left-wing fantasy of metaphysical freedom of the individual and a wish for social anarchy. This can be seen just in that the noun 'identity' derives from identification, which is an act made not by the individual but everybody else except him: identity is, primarily and originally, anything but a personal feeling of what group of choice brings you comfort. It is the group that you belong to; the group that you are a member of; *the group that grants you all your rights.*

These conceptual and identity issues don't result from wrong thought, but their prevalence reflects the incapability to address real social issues

I-1. EXISTENCE AND SUBJECTIVITY

in the absence of proper tools of thought. The contemporary perspective sees it as *natural* that people are helpless individualistic subjects in a production machinery of national or corporate competitiveness that they themselves can't influence. What philosophy should do, in order to make any difference, is to show them why this can't be the case. But I see modern philosophy as a failure because nothing is produced on the level of thought that would in practice help these social issues everybody is aware of. Academic philosophy has distanced itself from the living reality: the *existence*. The modern successful philosopher is not best described as an enlightened sage or a passionate advocate of correct thought, but a professional writer with a comfortable armchair, many academic friends and many prospects for next year's university post. And instead of accepting the ridicule of this position and being part of diminishing the general popularity of philosophy altogether I would advise one to think about the correct way of conducting philosophy also outside the minimum requirements posed by academic studies. Accepting a vacancy as a teacher, doctor, policeman, architect, salesclerk, construction worker, cleaning lady, masseur, flight attendant or bank teller is different from accepting a funded position in which there is no practice and one doesn't produce anything that people would read. It is a different existence being useful; giving a different meaning to one's life. Maybe good philosophers ought to have schools and circles completely on their own.

In the contemporary world scientists constantly argue against religion through a false dilemma or some other fallacy as if having religious faith was incompatible with science, while themselves obviously believing in the prevailing scientific hypotheses in a metaphysical sense. This is farcical. Human existence is based on beliefs and thinking that one has no beliefs equals believing without any awareness of one's beliefs, which in practice results in complete subjective irrationality. Ask a scientist of this kind why a rock thrown in the air would fall and he might reply with a reference to Newtonian mechanics. Ask him if he *believes* in Newtonian mechanics and if he's honest, he'll answer positively and add that he's willing to change this view in the emergence of a theory with better explanatory power (if he is dishonest, he will

PART I. THE BASIS OF THOUGHT

evade the subjective question in some interesting way). We don't need any theoretical model of thought, in addition to the one that our beliefs form the basis of our thought, in order to conclude that denying believing in the theory will contradict the scientist's position of originally presenting the theory as an explanation for an observed phenomenon. Also, we might press him to answer whether the theory of Newtonian mechanics is *true* and show that a positive answer is sensible even by classical philosophical standards only if he believes in the theory, and a negative answer will result in a tied game between science and religion by his own standards. Before having to ultimately admit that his support for the theory in question is based on *faith*, the scientist might still try and halt us with the addition that the theory is something he *knows*—meaning he has lots of experience and support from others applying the theory. Since theories essentially are replaceable *tools* of explanation, this odd argument would be like claiming that having used a blue snow shovel for all his life would result in snow clearing requiring a blue shovel. But this kind of absurdity very typically results from the popular modern paradigm that information resembles some kinds of units that are in the mind—one that Wittgenstein ravaged in *The Blue Book* almost a century ago and has been forgotten only because he is dead and intellectually dismissed, not because he has even once been rebutted or somehow challenged intellectually.[12] The scientist holding such a paradigm would say that it *must* be the case like the theory suggests, because that is the only way he can comprehend it: the only way he is able to theoretically set the phenomena captured by the theory in compliance with all the other related information he possesses. And this is what ultimately displays his faith in the theory,

---

12   In any field there are people who make a career out of causing controversy over dead giants; by mocking the dead who can't defend themselves anymore; by poking them with a stick. This is an ultimate insult to one's legacy and built to a symbolical extreme in Mozart's opera *Don Giovanni*, where Don cravenly orders his servant to mock the statue of the man he himself killed. If the criticism is not made against the work of the person but in some moral or personal sense against the person himself (symbolically, against his statue), then the valid critic needs to be a peer who outranks him, and in the case of giants whose moral legend is elevated after death, there often are no men alive that are comparable in terms of influence (the man to mock the statue would himself need to be a statue). This doesn't mean you can't challenge him by saying the man was wrong, in a part of a body of work that contradicts him.

I-1. EXISTENCE AND SUBJECTIVITY

since it is the only available option for him (now); likewise, with anyone with genuine religious faith. Likewise, to a true believer he would say that it is something he believes now but that he is willing to change this belief if new information appears. A true scientist—one who fully understands the hypothetical nature of science and the necessity for him to believe, and a true believer—one who truly follows, neither contradict each other nor differ in an existential sense, being honest about their faith. However, the idealist (Platonic) manifestations of these characters clash. The idealist believer might consider that every scientist believes in something created by man instead of viewing them as believing in the creations of the same creator that they just verify with a different method. The idealist scientist might dismiss every believer as simply weak minded and incapable of systematic thought, because his idealist relation to a communal criterion has so far blinded him from seeing his own faith. I believe a quick test to bring out this anti-scientific scientism on the subjective level is the question: "You promise that science explains. Do you believe science will one day explain everything?" A person affirming this question essentially affirms a contradiction: a hypothesis equals truth, the real equals the imaginary, and the objective equals the subjective. Likewise, if you say to a Christian: "You promise that Jesus saves. Do you believe Jesus will one day save everybody?" he will answer you: "He has already saved all Christians", and he will not contradict. Like the promises of scientists, the non-contradicting Christian salvation via following Jesus should be juxtaposed against the promises delivered in business talk; take e.g. technology prophets like Steve Jobs who, in his thoughtfully delivered speeches, portrayed an Abrahamic leader, offering salvation via his company's products. In our Abrahamic world this is a powerful rhetoric, and you'll find such a speech making a lot of sense when you ignore the subjective contradiction and make the presupposition that he *really* is selling salvation and that the applause he gets is based on the truth of this salvation. Of course, the underlying resolution is not salvation of any individual but monetary profit of the delivering organization. Sales talk is the art of borrowing spiritual rhetoric for sales purposes; the art of creating an appealing appearance; the art of lying in a manner where the words are not lies from the objective

PART I. THE BASIS OF THOUGHT

perspective.

Regarding *faith*, one could describe it as a state of unquestioning, and the key thing about questioning is to notice that it is an inter-subjective facility: to question information means to question the source of the information, who is always a subject. And from the subjective point of view, believing *somebody* is not a one-off action but a constant process: when somebody is convincing, you believe what he says, but this in practice means that you believe *so far*. If you believe somebody, and afterwards the person starts to behave suspiciously, you can brush off a few suspicious acts as personal quirks, but after that you'll notice yourself questioning *everything he has said so far*, which means you are suspecting his *character*. This means that we subjectively place our trust in a person's subjective character and not the individual things he says. The external sign of faith is *compliance* in behaviour, and this behaviour is essentially disconnected from any subjective state of belief. We tend to describe somebody who complies with everything as naive, which implies lacking judgement. Somebody who might not comply, but is inclined to, we call good-natured, and this implies that there is judgement being made but no resistance. Then again, some people are stubborn; they don't believe or comply, and stubbornness is considered a positive trait against injustice but a negative trait against justice. But faith is beyond both belief and compliance; faith is something in the context of which we can say: "Please have faith", by which we mean to ask not to be suspected, and this is something we could e.g. ask when we know that something looks suspicious on the surface but has a *good explanation* to it that is not yet evident. But why would a person refuse to question something he believes? I would like to point out that this is not just what some people do; this way of existing is rather the standard way for everybody, and it relates to psychological processes that are said to protect a person's *identity*: some things are such that a person will in practice refuse to question, and those are the ones that constitute his identity. Now, people have all kinds of identities, of which we can say that strong identities are those that are not likely to change, and weak identities are those where the person is constantly looking to change himself and to reassess his person according to his experienced social expectations. This is to say that the fact that a person stalwartly believes something as a part of his identity doesn't mean that his identity won't change, but it needs to be pointed out that defending one's identity is not *a reason* to hold onto one's beliefs but rather just an objective explanation for observed behaviour in a person. The person might change his beliefs if he had a reason to, and rather, when we see a person defending his beliefs, we must make the charitable assumption that he is defending them *for a reason*. But what would such a reason be? Of course, anything he believes to be right, his *moral* beliefs. Obviously, he defends his beliefs because he believes they are *morally*, not objectively, right. Thus, we can conclude that

> *faith is a state where the person refuses to suspect the foundation of his belief, because he considers it morally right.*

Against this definition, and remembering that people are *primarily moral* actors, we can understand how people tend to speak about truth with conviction; they believe that whatever constitutes this truth *should not be questioned*, and that they would be bad people if they did so. This rather simple formulation defies the unfair modern tendency to put subjective faith in contrast with science using the standards of science: to have faith in something that contradicts evidence is, of course, a vice in any work in which truth is derived from evidence, but it is so strictly within that scope. Within a *moral* framework, to defend the justice of an individual against the injustice of the many is always correct, and secondly, the just outcome of a trial can be in support of a single critical piece of evidence against whole masses of evidence that are not critical. This could be reformulated to say that evidence only points out what is *evident*, which is not always the case with truth; on the contrary, people can be very crafty in working to hide the truth in such a way that what seems evident is merely a crafted distraction that is essentially a fabrication and the opposite of truth.[13] The formulation brings about several things. First, we can see that, regarding faith,

---

13 Somebody who believes that evidence implies truth is a fool, because he is easy to fool. He will not venture beyond what is *evident*. *Truth* will always escape him, as truth is something to be uncovered, implying that it is hidden. The scientist is much stupider than the average man; just put some evidence in front of his face and he will methodically believe it.

whether we are speaking about spiritual subjects doesn't matter—we can equally say "to believe in the right god" as we can say "to believe in the right things", if the faith implies correct action. Second, we can see that what fundamentally constitutes an *opinion* (or a *position*) is not the argument or rationale (or evidence) that is presented in its support, but a single opinion can be supported by many arguments, and, likewise, a single rational observation can lead to many alternative positions as a conclusion. Opinions are guided by moral beliefs (one's ethical nature); a person believing in a certain moral way will refuse to take evidence in support of an action that contradicts his moral beliefs, and it is rather his moral thought and his understanding of just action that determines how he will interpret given evidence. And here lies the perimeter of subjective ethics that must be left untouched when trying to say anything definite about the human quality: it is never possible to determine the *justice* of actions objectively—the only thing that can be said is that people who take objective evidence to somehow objectively conclude correct action are blind to the subjectivity of their own ethical character. Also, when saying that a person is "brought to believe" in the subjective sense of complying with another subject, I am referring to a very particular phenomenon. Compliance with a formal authority without personal relation is what we do in the military and in business life, and when we follow the captain's orders, we don't need to know his name. This is reflected by the fact that in the military we don't use first names, and might not even use last names but nicknames, to further enforce the domination of the hierarchy over the subjective. But the *subject-relation of compliance* is a very particular phenomenon that relates to love and respect, and this sort of relation takes very particular circumstances to come to existence: typically, the subject needs to be at his weakest and in a state of willingness to accept help. Such a relation can perhaps be formed between a man and a woman, or it can be formed in military partnership, and is characterised by unquestioning compliance and loyalty by setting the needs of this partnership relation to the highest priority. The classical movie depiction of forming a love relation is where the man is somehow brought to need help or assistance from the woman, and the woman accepts and takes care of the man. One aspect that is perhaps worth noticing is that homosexual relations were common in antiquity (compulsory in Sparta), particularly in the military where brothers in arms needed to trust each other with their lives. The change in culture, I believe, was brought by the citizenship of women, which introduced the formal roles of man and woman in society and limited what was acceptable for a free man to do—after this, homosexuality became unspeakable, and monogamous relationships where courting is to lead to matrimony were enforced. In Christianity, the subject-relation is said to be made with God (or Jesus), and is considered the foundation of being genuinely religious, as opposed to somebody who is just complying with tradition and rituals. One good way to describe Christianity is to regard it as anthropomorphising ethics, where one's relation with God, who is considered *love* and *truth*, is a symbol of this personal subject-relation (love relation) with what one considers right.

I was asked if I believe people always have the right to know the truth, and I must answer negatively. If truth was a *right*, this would mean that there is nothing to be revealed by truth, as one can just claim truth as one's right. Then again, if we think of truth as "the truth", "the ultimate revelation", that would effectively mean that truth equals God, which e.g. St. Augustine would say, or, as Jesus said, *he* is the truth. In this case if people had the right to truth, this would mean that people have a right to God or Jesus. It is only society and its institutions that grant rights to its members. And this is exactly how religion is misused: by believing that an institution, ritual or, say, an experience of revelation, will grant an individual the right to God; that the individual is corrected and therefore above criticism or requirement to justify his actions, being simply restored to holiness or truth. We might also note that this is not so very different from how the academic platform or ivory tower works these days: many academics believe, or at least act according to the assumption, that the rituals of the academic institution grant them the right to truth. This behaviour sets a horrible example that is passed on to students and educated people: instead of trying to stand out as critical thinkers or scientific bookworms they commonly superficially mimic these elitists' behaviours and arrogantly act as if they were the messengers of truth simply by quoting some a few modern political pseudoscientific myths. Meanwhile they remain scientific illiterates, having perhaps never read a study or even the abstract of a study, let alone having gained an overview of the relevant scientific literature or discussion, which would be the academic ideal. I'm quite limited in my scientific knowledge, but at least I know that anybody claiming to know something at the same time shall expose himself to criticism, and traditionally we would exempt only God from this critique, as all of us humans are known to err. Then again, it wouldn't occur to me to defend the truth of my claims with scientific literature, except only in the case of this being the context of the discussion. I tend to try and quote science to people whom I believe would be convinced by science ... which is never the case with said scientific illiterates; their troublesome attitude will lead them to try and quote science to you as best they can, but they will never listen even to scientific argument or admit their lack of knowledge within such discussion. Instead they will hide behind some comfortable authority or just make a run for it when difficulties arise in the discussion. Books will bring you no shelter; the basis of one's knowledge and confidence must come from somewhere else than knowledge of literature. The same applies in both religion and science.

Existence and subjectivity are something more fundamental than knowledge, and a fast way of seeing that this is necessarily so is to understand that there are different ways of knowing something. Firstly, there can be knowledge that is false, which is the case when there is shared information that turns out to be false. We can understand that every piece of knowledge we have could theoretically turn out to be false, and this does not invalidate the grammar of knowledge; it is still sensible to talk about knowledge and to affirm it. Knowledge implies belief, and in the case of false knowledge we *believed* something was true, but this belief turned out to be unfounded. Secondly, there is a sense of talking about knowledge that implies a subjective factor: How well do you know it? This use of knowledge has somewhat diminished in use in the modern day, but it is quite essential regarding the nature of knowledge. When we talk about any subjective phenomenon, such as an art or a skill, there is a level of knowledge starting from "I have

I-1. EXISTENCE AND SUBJECTIVITY

seen it" and "I know its name" to something that often in professional life is measured with years of experience with the subject. Let's recall that the openly fundamentally religious Socrates passionately emphasized that he *does not know*, and that his mission in life involved helping Athens by civilizing his fellow men wherever they *think* they know, but really don't. Here Socrates obviously is talking about knowledge in said sense where it is possible to know something on a surface level and to be master in this knowledge, and he is rhetorically emphasizing that he is a beginner, not a master. In fact, it is actually rather obviously the case that Socrates was himself a master in none of the arts whose experts he admired on the Agora of Athens, and his "I know nothing" means just a profound acknowledgement of this fact and an expression of respect and admiration towards anybody who truly is the master of his art. Aristotle would say that knowledge is superior to belief in that he is in a *healthy* state in relation to truth.[14] This means that when somebody knows something, he might still be believing something that is false either partially or completely, as the experience of life is fundamentally uncertain, but at least this man is essentially healthy compared to the man who holds his false beliefs private. This "private knowledge" is characteristic of a multitude of mental illnesses (e.g. schizophrenia, narcissism, paranoia...) that are essentially states in which the individual drifts away from the sphere of shared knowledge into believing his own untested beliefs. A key aspect of belief (and hence also knowledge) is that it is not possible (for one subject) to both assert and deny the same thing truly at the same time,[15] and this is the real nature of contradiction: a person is contradicting *his own thought*. If we think of a person who tries to escape the subjective contradiction by saying that he is both right and wrong at the same time, he is not able either to speak or say anything intelligible and is no different from a vegetable.[16]

Now, *knowledge* is a queer thing if you try and look at it as a faculty, because of the subjective nature of faculties: like a hand of cards vis-

---

14 Aristotle, Metaphysics Γ.4
15 ibid.
16 ibid.

ible only to the player, one's knowledge is in one's own possession (if anyone's) and the result is people using the concept in very different subjective ways. But just like it is in our social nature to extend our material possessions, we are very prone to collect answers. Consider someone learning life as a series of Trivial Pursuit (TP) questions: he is first confronted with a question; then tested on whether he knows the answer or not, and after that he hears the right answer. The key to the game's success is in that, firstly, such a learning model is traditionally applied in schools, and secondly, this is basically how most Western people exist: from the perspective of their existence, life presents them with challenges in which they are tested. They want to succeed in their efforts and are afraid of disappointment, and some people are more apt to admit they were wrong and to justify this with a negative self-image: "for a failure such as me it is only natural to be wrong". Some people do the opposite and never admit that the other was right and justify this in a similar way to an athlete that blames his equipment: "since I'm the best, it is only natural to end up with a support team that's worse than me". The healthy man between these extremes finds himself humiliated, and then updates his knowledge to do better in the future. And this he does because he feels he *should have* known that; that's how he sees himself, as someone who knows such things, and he has worked hard to gain such status, and this status constitutes his experienced responsibility. This phenomenon is integral in Christian social behaviour, where status as "simply men" is highly honoured and is something that is earned and not appointed or inherited. As examples of such healthy lines of thinking one may say "I want to eat some chocolate", followed by "Why did I eat so much chocolate?"; "That man is only interested in himself", followed after closer acquaintance of the man by the admission "I was all wrong about him!"; and "The opponent is clearly better than me, so there is no point trying to win". These simple examples can be seen to involve subconscious emotions that in practice extend to more complex thinking patterns when people manage to avoid testing them and instead enforce them. And quite often when the truth is revealed in such an experience of humiliation, the lesson people learn is a totally wrong one, relating to some *object* present in the situation instead of their own subjectivity. This scapegoat-objectification indeed

I-1. EXISTENCE AND SUBJECTIVITY

is the source of fetishism.

Now, consider the TP existent to keep on learning this way; what he ends up with is a collection of answers, and as this collection grows, so also does his sense of experience. After a while he will know he has lots of experience and knowledge, but that those lessons haven't helped improve his capability to overcome such disappointments—instead the same process keeps on repeating: first he *thinks he knows* something, but then he is faced with the humiliating truth. So, he knows he is in possession of a collection of answers, but this has not changed the fact that his interest is guided towards new things. He cannot help facing these things with the same pattern of first thinking that he knows and then finding out that he was wrong. And this is because in TP you are expected to give an answer regardless of whether you are certain or not, and more specifically, sometimes it is necessary to simply take a guess. Sometimes you know you have no clue; sometimes you have a strong feeling about the right answer and find out that you were right, and sometimes this strong feeling still is followed by finding out that you were wrong after all. Consider if our hypothetical man wanted to change this pattern; now, because he *does not know* if he is right or wrong (since, due to the nature of the game, he cannot see what is printed on the answer card before being told the answer), the first thing he needs to do is to give up something he has learned about how the game is played: he needs to give up pleasing the sadistic questioner by thinking that he *does* know the right answer, and instead acknowledge that he doesn't *know* anything at all. He needs to acknowledge that he is uncertain, because even in the case of a question where he might be completely sure of the *right* answer, he still cannot be sure if that answer is printed on the answer card. After all, that is the criterion for correctness in this game, and even if the game might sometimes be unfair, it is this game he has chosen to play. Therefore, he needs to fundamentally stop playing TP; stop existing as if in pursuit of trivial knowledge for a reward: in order to gain *any* certainty at all *for himself*, he must gain his *honesty* by acknowledging that the rules of this answer-knowing game forbid him to have any, since he is ultimately dependent on the relentless answer card. And this path to humility must feel ultimately humiliating; it is not just one question he was humiliated for not knowing the answer for, but *every* question.

And what is left after one accepts the fundamental uncertainty? Can a man live without knowing? Won't this somehow reduce the man's intellect? Ah, but unlike certainty, knowledge is not a subjective faculty as it implies not just belief but also truth. In the case of TP, we can say without a possibility of error that no answer will qualify for knowledge, since the criterion of the correctness of the answer is compliance with what is printed on the answer card; the answer cards can even hold false information. One might say that proneness to declare one's answer as knowledge may comply with another use of the verb 'know', namely one in which one might be expected to show one's knowledge, such as when a teacher asks the class: "Who knows such-and-such? Hands up!" But this is not the case in TP. In TP, the question here is rather a matter of eliminating the pretence of knowledge, and what is left after that is a group of expressions such as "I am certain",[17] I hope" or "I believe". Technically, the question here concerns acknowledging that the verb 'know' has multiple uses, and personally refusing to use the verb in a discourse in which it doesn't make sense since one cannot meet its validating criterion. Subjectively, the question is about taking more *responsibility* for one's words, and this requires (and morally follows from) understanding of the correct nature of words; that words by themselves are not equivocal but only their uses may be ambiguous. Now, a direct connection can be seen between TP existence and learning in general; such a learning method is deliberately used widely in schools, since it immediately forces the answerer (and any listeners) to reflect their own knowledge against the question by trying to answer. It is just that in school the criterion for knowledge in the case of an answer is not an answer card or the teacher's book, but rather the school is connected to a system of objective information. But most unfortunately, the model contemporarily conveyed by cognitive psychology and our school system completely dismisses the whole problem of belief against knowledge, and the word 'belief' rather enjoys a negative con-

---

17 To say "I am X per cent certain" is meaningless because certainty is subjective and percentages are a language to objectively quantify.

notation meaning something like a prejudice against knowledge that is considered scientific and infallible. Our children are basically taught that science produces information, and via perception their brain processes it into knowledge in their memory, and whether that knowledge turns out to be false is a matter of whether the process functions correctly—a model that would make perfect sense if discussing robotics: an automaton is functioning incorrectly if it fails to correctly internally represent its input. As if knowledge was a question of whether you can apprehend information or not! All information has a source and can be criticized! A person thinking like this will be completely unaware of his own beliefs and the ethical perspective of thought, and quite obviously blind to validate his information sources himself, since even a secondary source displaying the authorizing stamp of science renders the content unquestionable. There is no question that children should be taught to think for themselves and not only to be efficient in searching for authoritative information, which can be most quickly done by reducing source criticism to verifying the authority of the source. On the level of society, this sort of system will produce sick and mindless assimilators of propaganda instead of creative and spiritually grounded human beings. To exemplify this, there was a recent news article in Finland that said "the health effects of rye bread are *already* quite well known" ... as if science had made so much progress that we had already learned that rye bread is healthy. Rye bread is a traditional food in Finland and its health effects have been known for rather a long time; it's just that this article uses the word 'know' in the sense that applies *only* to scientific information. Given this approach, it is correct to say that our society has grown considerably dumber, as traditional wisdom has been forgotten and we externalize what we need to know. The amount of information has increased, but knowledge, as in being the opposite of mere opinion or belief, has reduced in amount. And this is reflected by people being less healthy, which means that people don't know what health is and how to live healthily. And this truth can be seen in the fact that all discussion about the health effects of foods is coloured by *contradictory* information and news. Just recently *Time* magazine published a cover page story declaring *butter* healthy, which was based on multiple recent studies. But butter has long been the epitome of un-

PART I. THE BASIS OF THOUGHT

healthy foods, and a visitor to our planet might be puzzled to find that *Homo sapiens* has discovered space travel but not yet discovered what is good to eat. When we induce knowledge from scientific information, we tend to overlook the fact that such information can be contradictory, as the outcomes of studies can suggest different actions—consider if we had, say, 1000 studies about rye bread, of which 450 suggest it may have some negative health effects and 550 suggest it may have some positive effects ... does this mean that we know the health effects of rye bread quite well already since it has been long studied? Rather it means we are increasingly undecided about the food and uncertain of the correct action; indeed, recently the American Food and Drug Administration banned certain blue cheeses for the official reason that they contain bacteria, whereas in Finland we use patented bacteria in sour milk products because of their known positive effects on the digestive system. This implies that in the scientific sense *we* don't really *know* anything about the matter, because the mark of knowledge would be uniform action. Instead, following the scientification of dietary information, food habits are still based on tradition as always, but the contradictory information is confusing, and consumers are given dietary recommendations that are increasingly dangerous, and, as a result, are more and more torn between senseless health fads.

We tend to talk about knowledge today in a warped sense; one that does not allow that knowledge 1) is also belief, and 2) is inherited from a historical body of knowledge in which its credibility (how sensible it is to believe it) is partly historical. In a subjective sense, the fact that your father believed something should make the same thing more lucrative for you also to believe, because your father is more experienced than you and therefore holds expertise. Our modern society places an immense trust in people called 'experts' because expertise is seen as something very valuable, but does not understand the very basics of expertise which is that experience in a particular field is usually measured in years, and this expert knowledge extends from the level of individual expertise to institutional expertise, and again, in a higher scope, to historical truth, where the truth of something derives from the fact that it is most remembered and least forgotten over generations. Most

I-1. EXISTENCE AND SUBJECTIVITY

of the stuff we learn in school we accept as truth with the logic that if it was false it would already have been corrected during the years it has been accepted as true. If we know that information about something can be found via Google or Wikipedia, we rush to claim knowledge, to defend our honour and status as somebody knowledgeable. But do we also believe it to be true? We could call this feeling "a strong hunch", but there surely isn't anything that would justify calling this knowledge instead of a personal wish.[18] Attesting knowledge upon a wish is not belief, and this is not distinguished by e.g. how strong the related emotion is, but by the fact that it is not supported by a *belief system*. When we ask whether e.g. Wikipedia is a belief system, the answer is negative: there is no *reason* for anybody to believe what is written there, as it would serve no *moral* purpose. A belief system, in practice, translates to religion, which, in turn, is distinguished by its morality. Then again, consider a man who first is certain about some matter, but after being fed an increasing amount of contradictory information, grows less and less certain and, as a result, starts to behave in a less and less uniform manner regarding the matter. Does he now know the matter better or worse? He has more information, but he lacks any certainty, so I find it more apt to say he knows less as he has grown weaker in holding his own opinion and thus attesting knowledge. Due to this, he will be wise not to make his own decision about the matter but to follow advice instead. This lack of reason is exactly what distinguishes people with intellectual disabilities from rational human beings; lack of his *own* reasoning—ask the disabled for his reasons and he will repeat to you what his carer has said.[19] So, too, behaves the man who is not certain; he will trust himself to the knowledge of a superior. This contradicts a common prejudice of the information age; that a man who is somehow lacking in intellect would be more wrong or false. Because information is valued so highly, there is an expectation that someone who holds information is righter, and someone who doesn't know is expected to be

---

18   *The French Connection* is an enjoyable movie where the protagonist police detective works based on hunches and causes tragedy by letting personal professional ambition overcome professional ethics. The movie teaches that a hunch is not knowledge by putting it into ethical setting, and in this setting, the willingness to put others to risk based on personal hunch boils down to immoral self-importance.

19   Applies equally to people who just act like morons.

wrong. This is, of course, true, according to the completely unfounded assumption that the information held also translates to expertise, which is seldom the case when information is just digested by reading, and never the case when the information is not even assimilated but just catalogued and accessible to one. The majority of those who are unsure do anything to hide their lack of knowledge, and they don't appear wrong but, to the trained eye, unopinionated and predictable. In general, the masses in the information age are superficial: they do a lot of work to appear unique, interesting and opinionated, but they don't hold onto their opinions. This is reflected by the fact that they change their opinions quickly and hide them when they sense those opinions won't bring them social support, and also because they tend to be highly sensitive about their opinions, and when confronted, very quickly turn from defending their opinion into attacking their opposition, which is always the sign of a weak base. This doesn't mean that these opinions would be somehow wrong, but it reflects the fact that they are assimilated without independently rationally checking them, and the main constituent in assimilating opinions is group identification and peer pressure. This mass superficiality equals loss of identity, and it is also reflected in the prevalent belief that truth is something ultimately impossible: one needs to constantly lie a bit in order to belong.

Take the system of knowledge as a game of knowing the right answer (TP), in which the word 'know' is used to signify one's subjective certainty and willingness to refer to an authority with knowledge. Take as an example the sentence "I know that the Earth revolves around the Sun", which is quite commonly used to refer to the enlightenment of modern science, contrasting with previous knowledge that the Sun revolves around the Earth.[20] That the Sun revolves around the Earth

---

20 Furthermore, it is interesting to note how commonly Galileo and Kepler, and this example of the Earth revolving around the Sun, are used within the context of advocating science. Galileo has essentially become a symbol of the victory of science over religion, and this has a historical basis, since these discoveries took place in a time that was followed by the European scientific revolution. This revolution was not just a change in thought but essentially a change in the European balance of power, uniting countries over the institution of the university. To advocate science meant to advocate a victorious movement over unjust oppressive authority, and this is the constituting fact in the victory of science over tradition in Europe. Had

I-1. EXISTENCE AND SUBJECTIVITY

can be quite easily verified by simple observation, but a person who would claim to know the contrary would refer to a heliocentric scientific theory rather than his own eyes. He would simply refuse a geocentric truth, because the heliocentric theory reflects the scientific consensus, but without noting that both claims: 1) the Earth (along with the rest of our solar system) revolves around the Sun and 2) the Sun (along with the rest of the universe) revolves around the Earth, are true in the light of General Relativity. The conception of the Earth revolving around the Sun applies a conception of revolving that is based on mass and gravity: if one were to draw a picture of the revolving motion, one would draw the body with the higher mass as the centre and the one with the smaller mass as the satellite, and this relation between the two is dictated solely by the significant difference in mass—the same picture could be equally drawn with the smaller body presented as the central piece. If the Sun and the Earth were close to equal size and exist in mutually revolving motion we wouldn't call one a satellite. Now, is it a *false conception* what the people of old used to think, that the Earth is in the centre? It is false only in the sense that the later concept of gravitation (Kepler's laws), that our ancestors didn't have, is more applicable in explaining the observed movement of celestial bodies in terms of making predictions about where the bodies will be located next: it is better to base the concept of movement on mass rather than the location of one's own viewpoint in the astronomical picture. But it is not false in the sense that it would not be true that there is a revolving motion between the two celestial bodies, and that one can observe the Sun revolving around the Earth. Only to the modern advocate of science must it be true that the Earth revolves around the Sun because all the scientists say so, which to him means it must not be like his ancestors used to believe. As an analogy, an ancient Japanese clansman might at one point believe in the greatness of The Mountain as the protector, but after being conquered by another clan, will say that The Mountain

---

the religious systems of the time not been so blindly departed from what can be disputed by evidence, science and the university would never have had the chance to cause a crisis of such extent through discoveries based on evidence. So, the victory of science was made possible by the weakness of the system it replaced; a system that was seen to produce injustice as it presents as facts things that can be shown to be false. And this victory brought an era of people who believe in science, and who will reign until they in turn have departed far enough from reality.

showed its weakness as a protector when its mines were flooded by the waters of The Great Sea Serpent, the true power. What the scientist is doing is simply believing in a new *system* of thought and its truth as *adherence* to a body of authority, one accepted as more *powerful* (*applicable*, in the context of science) than the alternative, which is human religious existence, only it uses a misleading word 'knowledge' to denote subjective certainty instead of the correct word: 'certainty'. The word is misleading because it is meant as a final, definitive and unquestionable answer, whereas what is actually denoted is a reference to a scientific *theory* created by a system that by definition never produces anything definitive but just applicable hypotheses, and this example of geocentric vs. heliocentric truth should well enlighten the concept of theory as a perspective, as one can easily see how the revolving movement is related to one's perspective. But such "knowledge" ultimately means simply knowing whom to trust: the board of scientists. Sociologically this doesn't differ from a religious system governed through holy men and scriptures, and another similarity is that the individuals that are the most vocal in electing science as an almighty power are the same class of fundamentalists that in religions are inclined to portray (an image of) following the scriptures and teachings to the letter. This behaviour in itself reveals that such people are the least subjectively committed to and aware of the principles they adhere to, and instead the most committed to the authorities within those institutions; they strive to prove themselves by making their adherence *seen*, like a dog trained to follow his master closely by his side instead of having a degree of leeway in his leash. Great scientists have always been great individualistic minds that have deeply subjectively comprehended their scientific principles, instead of advocates who preach their principles as ritualistic sermons, and in scientific breakthroughs typically standard methodologies are replaced with ingenuity.

Theory and information both have a light quality compared to wisdom or opinion. It could be said that there is something subjectively terrible about wisdom, because whenever we contrast wisdom with information, knowledge or, say, intelligence, we emphasize the *long-term* results of a choice or method, which is the time that needs to pass before

I-1. EXISTENCE AND SUBJECTIVITY

one gets to see its *negative* outcomes instead of simply positive hopes. Wisdom has a face that is compassionate but weathered and constantly troubled, because wisdom needs to deal with the consequences and take heed of bad choices, such as those depicted in the tragedy of Oedipus Rex. Wisdom is something that *takes responsibility* even when met with the worst of things, whereas an intelligent man might just reason to ignore responsibility. Subjectively, responsibility is a truth that needs to be accepted, and dealing psychologically with bad but inevitable things has a universally uniform development in stages, depicted in traumatic injury recovery self-help pamphlets: denial, anger, bargaining, depression and finally acceptance. In the case of the most uncomfortable truths, it is human to first try and deny and fight it; only it happens that in the case of traumatic injury the truth is bound to the victim's life forever, so ignoring it is impossible. But in the case of such truths that *are* possible to deny or ignore, this denial should be considered the expected behaviour. I will present some examples.

1) Mafia wives would be kept aside from the "family business" to protect their moral emotions and enable them to ignore the moral aspects of their husbands' job. They would be able to live the role of a wife if staying ignorant did not become overwhelmingly difficult.

2) Propaganda works because the lie depicted in propaganda is easier to accept than the truth that one's own government is actively colluding to mislead one. It is a comfortable lie against an immensely uncomfortable truth.

3) Legend is where a person becomes so agreeable that agreeing with his legend becomes the norm and the details of his life, which might contradict his legend, become an uncomfortable truth.

Similarly, an opinion that contradicts the norm has the subjective quality of terror, because presenting opinions means inviting conflicts of opinion, and conflicts are terrible for everybody—in Western democracies showing courage in open conflict is promoted, whereas in Asia open conflicts are commonly feared and avoided, and instead the skill of discreet conflict resolution highly promoted. Information doesn't have these qualities, and indeed the nerd-like character with thick spectacles, who babbles useless information at the moment of danger and decision, can be seen as the comical contrast to the bold hero character in films predating the rise to power of the information culture of the information age—nerds became heroes at the same time as information geek became a viable profession when companies started hiring such characters. It is no secret that our relation to knowledge in favour of wisdom is an unhealthy relation: knowledge is a highly desirable quality, which is shown by our high inclination to, wherever there is a chance, *portray* knowledge, however unrelated to any matter at hand that knowledge may be. But at the same time this concentration on knowledge leaves us vulnerable to the exposure of our lack of any deeper understanding of the subject matter, which is harmful to our social image and produces the phenomenon of us concentrating our efforts to portray knowledge on *trivia*, since trivia is free from any expectations of knowledge imposed on us and thus it is safe to be wrong about trivia. Moreover, this social phenomenon of having to portray oneself as an expert is why the increase in information in society divides people into social subcultures that share an interest and can span globally over the Internet. And this has a possibly counterintuitive effect, as one might expect division into expert groups to produce specialization and deeper understanding over the relevant interests. For example, one might expect a person identifying with "techie" subculture to be an expert on technology so that this phenomenon would have the general effect of producing subculture groups that possess wisdom in their relevant subjects. But this is not the case, since the phenomenon is of *social fragmentation*; such subculture groups typically possess shallow understanding and, instead of passionately studying their subject matter, tend to alter their interests and themes of identification closely following the latest trends within the subculture, changing their themes of interest before they have a chance to develop real commitment to them. As such, the phenomenon is not akin to specialization or professionalization, but to subculture identification and portrayal of status, which is a psycho-social mechanism to protect the individual in the plurality and change of the social expectations of a larger society. This can be easily observed by comparing the street image of the people in a large city against smaller cities. These phenomena reflect the fact that the recent explosion in the amount

I-1. EXISTENCE AND SUBJECTIVITY

of information produces more social pressure for society to digest it, and this distances us from the natural group harmony related to both knowledge and wisdom, leaving people in a socially conflicted state and dependent on the authority with the new information. After all, the children of the information age—young or old in physical age—in their efforts to portray knowledge to each other are just like schoolchildren in a traditional classroom, where the teacher asks: "Who knows *this*?", and children clamour to show they have the right answer.

In the wake of the rise in information there is a misconception that we have gained more understanding, but the opposite is true: we have not become wiser, older and better, but, as a subjective basic defence, regressed to the level of children along the Freudian concept of regression. We are fighting over a status or appearing knowledgeable and at the same time making ourselves vulnerable to completely uncritically believe all information that comes from a source that we trust without asking if it is trustworthy or not. From a psychological perspective, this is a *healthy* reaction that works to keep us *sane* and to protect us from a complete mental breakdown in the face of our total inability to comprehend what we are being presented with. In fact, this relationship of trust resembles the helpless reliance of a child to an authority: trust that is not blind and irrational beyond any doubts, but just undeveloped, naive and vulnerable; reliance that is not a choice but a necessity. The constant psychologically regressive state necessary for basic survival in itself is a very serious impairment of basic emotional life; from an existential perspective it is an isolated stasis. It will in itself produce feelings of guilt and shame, but the regression essentially puts an individual in constant risk of being subjected to abuse by authority, be that governmental or institutional authority, authority of expertise or just social authority commanded by rhetorically skilled or famous people, and such people will smell an opportunity wherever they sense people to be in a gullible state and not normally alert. The regressive state is isolated essentially because it is isolated from social responsibility; the cause of elderly people degenerating to a level of children is related solely to their lack of social responsibility after they leave the work life, and this doesn't happen to people who don't consider their work to be their formal profession and their responsibility to do work to be bound to the employer. Old people don't mentally degenerate as per human nature but as per human society that allows them to become pensioners. Being subjected to abuse produces even more emotions of guilt and shame that remain as an emotional burden and need therapeutic solutions, traditionally provided by the lately diminished Western institutions of family and the religious community. As a result, the demand for basic mental health services has risen to the extent that many people draw the conclusion that the phenomenon cannot have a real cause but that people have become lazy and started to abuse the system. Now, on a *social* level, belief systems tend to form *cults*, which is a phenomenon where people turn to follow an influential character without the ability to criticize him. In a cult the followers accept what the leader says without criticism, which is the social equivalent of religious faith as a state of not questioning. This phenomenon is common anywhere where the social roles of actors involve different levels of understanding over the commonly shared issues: when your superior says something that you cannot comprehend, you may be forced by social rules to follow without understanding due to your inability to question. The follower might feel puzzled but is forced to follow, and this superiority granted by better knowledge is the natural human hierarchical element. As an example, a senior white-collar worker once told me he took the role of leading a team of experts and interns, succeeding his predecessor, and found out the team had certain practices everybody was committed to follow "like holy rituals" but that didn't make a lot of sense to him. He was able to contact his predecessor and to ask what the purpose of those practices was and to ask if changing them could be taking into consideration. The answer he got was: "Oh those ones; well, they just happened to be necessary at that particular time but with no further reason behind them", and that changing them was not only possible but a recommended action. As another example, consider an isolated tribe meeting an invading party of modern men in an automobile, something they've never seen before and are unable to comprehend: the natural tribal reaction is absolute submission due to the unquestionable yet incomprehensible technical superiority of the device. And this doesn't mean the tribesmen would from that

I-1. EXISTENCE AND SUBJECTIVITY

point onwards unquestioningly follow what the wielder of the automobile would do, but it just means that the technological wonder is striking them with both interest and fear, and as the initial diplomatic step they are submitting in front of something dreadful, thus signalling their subordination, which is a method of avoiding conflict in the social behaviour of many herd animals. Submission is a skill for survival. Similarly, in any human group subordination in the face of superior knowledge is a natural way of avoiding conflict with the leader, and typically in a cult the leader is a powerful character that also actively works to coerce the hierarchy of subordination under him. The way a cult differs from religion is that religious faith is a voluntary act, and the choice to follow without question is a *rational* choice, meaning the religious person can present reasons to justify his choice, and is able to make the choice again. Argumentation for the irrationality of religion constantly ignores the personal subjective aspect of reason: the person is acting rationally if what he is doing is the best choice from *his* perspective and standards, which are subjective to him, and the only correct method of showing such a choice to be irrational would be to show the person contradicting *his own* beliefs, not some objective standards of correctness. And to further push this result: the act of accepting a subjective reason is the honest and enlightened alternative to trying to satisfy objective standards of rationality for subjective reasons invisible to oneself, such as, in the case of a scientist, wanting to be a scientist just like one's own father was and never really considering other alternatives. Such adherence to surrounding norms is the irrational choice that the subject is only able to justify with reasons that might be acceptable due to their social outcomes within a particular discipline but that he might not even personally believe in: say, a scientist might be a vocal supporter of accuracy and scepticism, but only apply these to his field of interest and be described by his wife to be completely inaccurate and unquestioning.

PART I. THE BASIS OF THOUGHT

I-2. The Method of Linguistic Analysis

Wittgenstein rewrote meaning in a way that is so far unchallenged. There is no point in iterating his work of genius, but I might begin by mentioning that the process of reading his work totally changed my whole thinking and made my experience of the problematic nature of at least the majority of philosophical questions vanish altogether, and I swear I fail to find, as some might expect, that the experience somehow made my intellect deteriorate or made me some kind of fundamentalist or cultist. On the contrary: I felt that his work answered exactly to the problems I had found myself in a dead-end with for years in my lone and primarily nocturnal efforts to understand the meaning of all this yet filling my notebooks only with big maybes. The idea of "meaning as use" that has been summarized and attributed to him is something like the most profound thought ever uttered, and the profoundness of Wittgenstein is of the kind that gives us a powerful philosophical tool to make sense in human communication. To repeat, I will not try and analyse or explain Wittgenstein here—there is a lot of secondary literature which does just that—beyond noting that the expression implies *an observational philosophical method for assessing meaning*. It means that meanings of words, in general, are not at all to be assessed by searching for their correct definitions or trying to capture their essences in what is found to be common with all uses of a particular word, but instead a philosopher is to educate himself by observing how words are used in their actual contexts in order to comprehend the varieties of uses for words. Naturally, the philosopher is not simply an anthropologist with the intention to only record how words are used, but the invaluable legacy of later Wittgenstein is his results. First, the conception of language that was aimed to completely destroy the work of philosophers trying to renew or perfect language in a quest for a theory of meaning or a formal super-language to, as it were, replace natural language as the Holy Grail to redeem us from conceptual misunderstanding. And second, that only such a humble method would bring the philosopher into an understanding of a particular word and thus the capability to spot when words are being used in a confused man-

I-2. THE METHOD OF LINGUISTIC ANALYSIS

ner.[21] Wittgenstein would actually instead write that *for a large class of cases* our use of 'meaning' complies with a definition that the meaning of a word is its use in the language, which implies cases that escape this definition. For these cases we use 'meaning' in such a manner that calling the meaning just simply the practice is not adequate. For example, take allegory,[22] where the meaning need not describe states of affairs but contains a subjective imaginative element and expects the receiver to share something subjective on the level of imagination. Yet in this case too we would speak of the meaning of the allegory: what its presenter meant by it. An example that Wittgenstein mentioned is the use of proper names: we would use "John, come here!" and "Francine, come here!" in an absolutely similar manner, but they cannot be taken to mean the same thing, in which case it wouldn't make a difference which expression one chose to use. So, clearly "meaning as use" doesn't provide us with a sort of mechanical method to derive meaning from, e.g. listing all the practical uses of an expression. The word 'meaning' is tricky because the expressions "to mean such-and-such" or "to mean what one says" are related to the subjective existence of the subject making an utterance, but the meaning of an utterance, as Wittgenstein would show us, is related to the shared practice: how the word is used.

Words have so many established uses, and in order to understand what is being said, we might need to distinguish between them, and many of our very basic forms of expression have many established meanings that have sprouted from the subjective experience of different subjects. These people have first acquired the words by interacting in a particular social environment; then they have used the words in order to communicate as a part of social interaction, and then these words are in turn received by people trying to understand what *they* mean by those words, using their full knowledge and understanding of the people that utter the words in their process of interpretation. As an exam-

---

[21] Hopes of destroying the quest for a super-language didn't die, but just switched direction from the logical structure of language into new directions, such as formal languages and computing. Very soon Chomsky started saying that thought consists of strings.

[22] Wittgenstein once suggested that philosophy should be written entirely in poetic composition.

ple of the actual complexity of this, take the common figure of speech "such-and-such needs such-and-such". We might ask: "By saying: 'This wall needs repainting', did you mean that you would prefer it in some other colour?" and get the reply: "No, I meant that I find the old paint beautiful but unfortunately stained". Here "to mean X" translates to "to have X in mind"; to imagine X, and the scope of X will translate to a person's imagination, in practice to mean anything at all. The evolution of language is complex and doesn't have any logical boundaries, as linguistic expressions themselves have, and this unrestricted nature is the basis for the need for a philosophical approach that simply analyses language instead of trying to categorize what seem like the common properties or features of objects that concepts refer to. That is simply a confusion that disregards the actual complexity of linguistic evolution and has its roots in the *logic* of concepts—as Wittgenstein would put it, the grammar tends to mislead us. To clarify: language does not reduce to people's subjectivity and whatever they have in their unique minds, nor does it reduce to human psychology and the tendencies that various types of personalities might have in their thought and expression, and nor does it reduce to the people's culture and all the various roles, authority relations and such that are involved in it, either. But these factors, I believe, can all be quite effortlessly demonstrated to affect and interplay in what gives birth to established uses of language (Wittgenstein's language-games), which are the point of contact for our analysis, and this is because what philosophy is trying to do is to correct the misunderstandings that arise in communication—the use of language.

The problem with analytic philosophy has been that Wittgenstein's later work was left unfinished. Young Wittgenstein, in pursuit of the highest intellectual challenges, had jumped into the world of logic, a path already laid down for him by an array of philosophers, most closely Russell, who might have in a way considered Wittgenstein as his intellectual heir. But Wittgenstein was altogether appalled by the dogmatism of analytic philosophy, and while finding a way around it in the *mysticism* of *Tractatus* that literally left the world speechless, he found only later that the problem of language runs deeper than how

I-2. THE METHOD OF LINGUISTIC ANALYSIS

it seems from the clinical formal perspective of analytic philosophy. From this perspective, language looks like a device that could have a correct syntactic form as a shared model for everybody, which indeed is an intriguing idea because, firstly, we are taught grammatical rules starting from our first year in school, and secondly, we have a long history of philosophy that sees that thought is dialectical, reason is argument and '*logos*' is 'speech' or 'word'. It is an inviting thought that the idea of language, the *ideal* language, is already in our minds—because this is where school leaves us, having first put the idea of clean and correct language into our minds—and that the work in philosophy is to find out what the correct language looks like and how it produces meaning. This method is in full compliance with our Platonic and Christian tradition, where the true idea of God is to be found via personal contemplation as the result of long hours of sitting cloistered in a monastery. Later Wittgenstein realized that this whole conception of language as a syntactic device was a philosophical error in the sense of a hopeless attempt and was able to produce great amounts of text that, due to his fame, was relatively well received during his lifetime given its unsystematic and non-definitive style and experimental approach. In this process, he himself was existentially on his way to clear the methodical eggshells of analytic philosophy altogether and wasn't at all happy about the lack of clarity in his later work. His time ran out, and it became easy for academics to dismiss his work as obscure. In addition, many analytic-minded philosophers were left to believe that perhaps there could be some novel approach to linguistics that Wittgenstein had missed and were left to think that maybe there is a theory of meaning after all; maybe e.g. computers could compute it. And I believe this is a point where the modern scientific philosophical approach kicked in: we have started thinking that maybe Person A can solve the mystery of the syntactic structure of language, and, possibly later, Person B can produce the related semantic theory. And I am sad to point out that this development has been a lobotomy and the incapacitation of analytic philosophy, similar to using "divide and conquer" to split a unified group into two halves that each by themselves are unable to produce anything. There are *many* problems that *can* be worked on individually by splitting them into separate subtasks,

PART I. THE BASIS OF THOUGHT

but to do this to analytic philosophy is just to *assume* the analytical syntactic-semantic nature of language. And this is sad, because it is so easy and inviting to produce work that is valuable from this scientific perspective, but that sort of work will not address the actual issue of language in its relation to thought and argument, because it doesn't address *language*. It addresses *a feature* of language, such as its syntactic form or its 'cognitive' features, which is simply a reference to the relation between language and thought, but I don't see either of these issues requiring any philosophical work except in the sense of clarification of concepts, as they are studied separately in the fields of linguistics and psychology. Rather I see grave and dramatic errors being made in both fields that have taken the step to try and gain information about the phenomenon of understanding via the metaphor of a computer, and no philosophers pointing out these obvious errors in a manner that is influential enough to get any results that would reflect on our society.

I promote linguistic analysis as the absolute tool to assess meaning and thus to tackle philosophical problems in order to solve them altogether via the clarification of relevant concepts. People who are not particularly strong in logic often dismiss linguistic arguments, because on the surface they look like correcting grammar or spelling; stressing details where one would like to say details are irrelevant. People feel that what is important in communication is the *point* that is being communicated and not the particular form of expression. This sounds like a strong argument, because it is clear enough that when we have a point in mind, we can choose various alternative forms of expressing it, with one form perhaps more accurate or appropriate than another, but all essentially a clear effort to communicate something that is assumed to be somehow universally reachable, if one so desires. People who come to this conclusion see only a part of what language is; they see that it is a flexible tool to communicate something that, maybe after some efforts and hardship, will reach an understanding in the listener. Often people feel content with this understanding, and accept that in addition there is a "philosophical" extension to questions of meaning, where things are not clear any more, but that venturing

I-2. THE METHOD OF LINGUISTIC ANALYSIS

into that area is a waste of time, since philosophy until now has been unable to say anything definite about those matters in terms of being able to clearly communicate it and, for example, educate children at school about these important matters. Now, although meaning cannot be reduced to a formal rule and a theory, linguistic analysis is a very *real* tool to solve very *real* cases of linguistic confusion, but the difficulty is in that these cases of confusion are *subjective*; it is not language but an individual that gets confused and thus is inclined to misuse language or misinterpret what is being said by another. And what happens next is that any use of language, be it clear or confused, by itself forms linguistic traditions—discourses or schools of thought—in which certain expressions are simply repeated and taken at face value, and these branches of discourse can be said to have a life of their own. Then again, to conduct such linguistic analysis means to be interested in *particular actual* problems, as opposed to an effort trying to build a *system* of thought that would somehow explain what anybody can already see. The philosopher should be somebody who takes on actual problems; a hands-on repairman that is not called in to perform a structural analysis of a building but rather to look at the things that will cause problems now or in future if not addressed early enough. A good analysis of such a problem is not one in which the problem point is pointed out and one is told how to deal with it to make it go away... this sort of cowboy repairman is good at making his own work very important by establishing a relation in which he is regularly called on site, and here poor quality of work is actually a benefit to the repairman. A good repairman is one that will analyse why such damage has arisen in the first place and recommend ways to change one's behaviour and habits so that the irritating damage won't recur. The shape of such a philosophical work is necessarily a patchwork (like this book); one sees things here and there that deserve attention, and they can be interrelated in ways that don't have any clear structure. This doesn't mean that there isn't clarity in analysing them, it just reflects their origin as problems of actual life, and actual life, unlike imaginary life, is always complicated and multi-faceted. But outside of academic, professional discussion, you can't tell a person these days that he has committed a logical error. He is too sensitive to this sort of criticism. Logic does not exist in, say, political rhetoric. Logical analysis is the ultimate tool, and to say that your thought is logically (*a priori*) erroneous is experienced as an attack, to which people will respond in a hostile manner. Then again, people don't really strive to develop their thought; they don't understand that thought is to be developed. They believe their thought is as good as any others, and that they can technologically overcome any shortcomings in their knowledge, that the mind is just a tool for processing and retrieving (remembering) information from an external (online) source. They believe information is power, and information is something that comes wholly from outside of your own thought, so, they essentially believe they are dependent on this external power. This contrasts with reality, in which intelligence and thought are power, and a person's power is in how he can use his mind.

As such, the practice of linguistic analysis is also a subjective *skill* and one cannot, for example, give instructions on how to correctly analyse confused language or to tell if an analysis has been correctly performed. The basic point of interest in this analysis is the *etymology* of words, which means recording when meanings of words change, but which doesn't endeavour to draw any conclusions or corrections from misuse of language. Because philosophical linguistic analysis deals with the *logic* of concepts, the results bear logical rigidness instead of, say, criticisms or notes that are subjective opinions. Language, when used, has clear and absolute logical commitments regarding the words and expressions that the speaker chooses, but that one simply won't see without an analytical look at this logic of expressions—and this is the very starting point of analytic philosophy; it's just that it so happened that analytic philosophers were back then, and still are, looking for the source of these logical rules from the wrong place; from the *syntactic* composition of sentences. The practice is something that follows from a Wittgensteinian approach to language instead of a metaphysical one; the analytic linguist knows how to look for the use of words in their home and to pay attention to the context that forms the logical boundaries of their sense. Armed with this method, he can say definitive things about the phenomena at hand. Wittgenstein used the word 'nonsense' to rule out confused use of language.

I-2. THE METHOD OF LINGUISTIC ANALYSIS

The word has been so mysterious that authors have been trying to suggest Wittgenstein meant different things by the German 'sinnlos' and 'unsinnig', but I doubt that he meant anything else except a refusal of certain sentences. But what is mysterious about this refusal (as always when something strikes us as very weird in philosophy) is its *ethical* nature: we *must* not accept such language, even if we want to. And why is that? Because, from the standpoint of linguistic analysis, we humans have a weakness: we tend to say "Ah, I know exactly what you mean" using our *empathy;* to politically *agree without understanding*, and this is what Wittgenstein was so passionate and relentless to resist. And what is nonsense? —Breaking the logical boundaries of concepts. A good example is from Wittgenstein: "Has the number 3 a colour?" to which both a positive or a negative answer is impossible, since the question itself breaks the logical boundaries of numbers and colours. A common approach to language would be something like "Could the word *xx* mean *this*? Could it not?" and then striving towards a social agreement about the matter. But the philosopher's answer is similar to how one could ask "Could the Moon be made out of cheese?" and the expert astronomer could answer "No, the Moon is not made out of cheese"... only the philosopher will base his answer on a detailed study of the subject matter and the use of tools and methods not available to the layman: the method of linguistic analysis.[23] Logic (in this meaning) doesn't refer to rules of inference that since the times of Aristotle have been "captured" in formal systems, but rather the transcendent nature of logic derives from the logical boundaries of the concepts we use—it could be said that 'logic' in this sense doesn't refer to the rules of inference or the line of study that studies them, but whatever it is in our thought and language that makes the study of such rules sensible in the first place. The most common use of 'number' is associated with mathematics, in which numbers are described in various ways. In this use colours can't be seen as properties of numbers, but this doesn't mean that other sorts of uses could not exist, and with a bit of imagination we might well imagine such uses—for example a particular coding (mapping) between numbers and colours that might be useful in some

---

23 Like any method that brings authority, linguistic analysis can also be abused. This would mean giving an incorrect analysis.

specific kind of use. But even in this sort of case the common verb 'has' would be used differently from the way presumably implied by the question "Has the number 3 a colour?": the question seems to treat the number '3' as a physical object which might be verified to possess a particular colour with a similar method we use when generally identifying objects with colours, but given the case of a coding the verb 'has' would obviously refer to a particular assigned association. We would effectively mean: "Is it the case that number 3 has been associated with a colour (already)?" The distinction between different meanings of the concepts is based on the practical *method* we use to verify them, as will be explained later. We *experience* the logical conceptual boundaries as something akin to transcendent categories—they are experienced with such unquestionable strictness that if numbers were to have colours, nothing would make sense any longer, and if everything actual in the world would suddenly disappear, those boundaries would still exist: the logical equals the imaginable. Yet their transcendent nature, outside our subjective belief in their existence, is purely grammatical, and will vanish when we unlearn this conception of language. We can experience their boundaries through having adopted the concepts in an existential sense: believing in them and believing that it is right to use them in the sense we have learned. This is a part of how we acquire new information and how it changes our beliefs and our existential nature. Logic is transcendent because it is rooted in our existence through the grammar of the concepts we have acquired, and the meaning of those concepts is in turn bound to the practical method of their verification—and these practices differ in an unquestionable way. For example, physical objects with colours we verify in a very different way from numbers: with objects we use our senses, yet numbers are only related to their grammatical symbols. If someone were to tell us: "Bring me number 5", we wouldn't know what to do because we wouldn't be able to look for one or to get hold of one—we wouldn't be able to perform what we have learned to associate with the practical process of bringing someone something. The imperative wouldn't make sense to me, not having learned such a language.

As a demonstration of how the boundaries of concepts are *logical (a*

I-2. THE METHOD OF LINGUISTIC ANALYSIS

priori) and not empirical, take again the word 'number', which can be seen to have multiple meanings (uses), and consider the following two uses.

1) "What is the number X that fits the series: 1... 2... X?"

2) "Each of you are handed a folded piece of paper, holding a number marked on it with a coloured crayon. Please look at your number and tell me its colour."

The first thing to ask is whether the sentences are sensible at all, and I myself would opine that if somebody saw fit to object to such English sentences, he would have to object to quite a lot of natural language altogether. Now, for each case, let's ask the question: "Are numbers necessarily colourless?" Applying the meaning in case 1, somebody might see the answer as positive, but in fact the question itself is senseless, since colours are not at all attributable to such an abstract meaning of 'number'. Applying the meaning in case 2, the question is sensible, and the answer is negative; on the contrary the test subject would likely be able to report the associated colour; the colour of the crayon used to draw the number. Now, consider somebody disrespecting the logical requirement presented in the first case that made the question senseless; namely, that numbers cannot be attributed to have colours. He would say that numbers are colourless, and Socrates would take note that the man thinks that he knows that numbers are colourless. Socrates would then request for affirmations whether numbers can be written on pieces of paper and if this can be done with coloured crayons. Having received them, he would then ask: if he wrote a numbers on a piece of paper with a coloured crayon, handed them to a class of students and asked them to report the colour of the number on their piece of paper, would the students understand the question and report their given numbers? And after getting the affirmation he would conclude with the contradiction: "How can they do this, if numbers cannot have colours? You seemed so certain that numbers cannot have colours, but you don't seem to understand numbers at all!" And the ultimate strength of the Socratic method is in that no matter what sort of escape his opponent would try at this point, such as claiming that the colour on a coloured number on a piece of paper is not a property of the number itself is, firstly, that the opponent himself had earlier declared that numbers are necessarily colourless, and secondly, the question at hand is not about whether he believes numbers to have colours or not, but whether the rest of the students are justified to believe that numbers can have colours. He cannot escape into refining his answer and to say that drawn numbers are not numbers, since the test subjects are being asked to report the colours of numbers and are reporting them; it is quite a weak argument to say that the whole class of students are wrong about the colour of numbers and he alone is right, or that the class are being misled to believe that numbers can have colours. It is simply a fact that the word 'number' has two distinct uses applied in the examples, and that it is *his job* to be aware of these distinct uses; not the job of others to restrict their language to fit his understanding. Thus, what Socrates brings out is a *logical inconsistency* in his opponent's thought, that he is looking at a particular use of a word and drawing overly powerful conclusions from it in that he thinks the same meaning can be applied wherever the word is used, and that such thought will lead into a logical contradiction when jointly applied with another meaning of the same word.

So, the said Wittgensteinian perspective to meaning is a scrutiny of the role of meaning in interpersonal communication as constituting both the correct interpretation of linguistic expressions and their credibility in distinguishing sense from senselessness. But meaning can also be analysed from the existential perspective by making note of some features of meaning, such as the following.

1) The subjective sense of lying equals saying things that one doesn't mean.

2) Psychological depression correlates with an experience of lack of meaning and senselessness.

3) The act of experiencing, acknowledging and accepting something as meaningful, but not asking why it is so, equals *faith in destiny*. The meaning is attributed to a factor named destiny.

4) Meaning carries a strong social power: unless you stress what you

I-2. THE METHOD OF LINGUISTIC ANALYSIS

mean, you will in practice be ignored, and those who speak meaningfully are taken seriously.

Moreover, an experience of one's *life having a purpose*[24] is a state I suggest associating with the ambiguous word 'happiness'; and I believe I am far from the first to suggest this, but the question of what "meaningful life" means is something that needs to be answered for such a naming to have any value. To answer this, we can rely on the power of language and use a metaphor of tools. A hammer is a tool to be used for a particular purpose. Broadly put, the purpose of having or using a hammer is to be able to hammer nails, and let's look at the agent: it is me who has the purpose for a hammer to be used, and the use of the hammer without exception lies outside the hammer itself, broadly described as building or constructing something. The other thing we can learn here is that the hammer example is apt because the hammer is a tool, and the quality that identifies tools is *usefulness*—the quality of Socratic beauty. Thus, it seems correct to infer this relation: *if A is useful to B, then B is meaningful to A*; meaningfulness is the inverse of usefulness.[25] Now, take the tool analogy to human life; one needs to notice that for it to make *sense* to talk about purpose, there needs to be a context outside of the subject himself in which his actions, life or existence has a purpose, and which constitutes the frame of reference against which his purpose will be interpreted. And from this perspective the question of the meaning of life boils down to the question of what the social frame of reference is that one identifies with; to what groups the individual extends purpose and responsibility in his thought; what groups the individual takes into consideration in his actions. "Does my life have a purpose?" is inverted: "Are there some groups you are useful to, and do you consider them a part of your life?" To the subject, this is an existential question, and as such,

---

24   In this sense, one can use any of the following: 'purpose', 'sense', 'meaning' or 'function'.

25   The clearest way to see this is our Christian religious relation where we are being useful to God, and this way of living is considered meaningful. But I think this is clear to see as the core of all human relations: one is being useful to another and experiences gratitude as meaningful. This is a human requirement of a relationship, otherwise we are talking about temporary or random human interaction. Sometimes the same relation exists mutually both ways. The real difficulty of looking at this is that it is so prevalent in our lives we can't see it.

PART I. THE BASIS OF THOUGHT

a purpose cannot be assigned to a person from outside himself but in order to experience any purpose the person needs to first understand and accept his role in a particular purpose—to identify with it. Let's say two men are returning home from work; one man goes to the bar for a drink, but the other man goes to the shop to buy groceries for his family. From the perspective of purpose only the second man is acting with a purpose, because his action gets its purpose from his role in his family. The action of the first man has *no purpose* (or "serves no purpose"), and it is confused to say that his purpose is to drink, because drinking will not bring use to him in any frame of reference outside himself—there simply is no sense to say that the purpose of brushing one's teeth with a toothbrush is to clean the toothbrush; yes, the toothbrush might be said to get cleaned in the process but what is key to the concept of purpose is how the word is used in language. Tools are, by their nature and without exception, *applied*, and their application lies outside the tool itself. And this observation about purpose doesn't imply that it is wrong to act without a particular purpose. From the perspective of society, this psycho-social relation of *identifying with a social function*, experiencing purpose via one's function within a social framework, is the basis of all human professionalization. Now, we know that *happiness* is around the world probably the most desirable subjective quality people would wish to acquire for themselves, and even people that focus their lives on more material ambitions tend to justify this via the happiness of others, such as their children. If you think the West is focused on happiness, look at Asia: all they say is "Happy! Happy! Happy!"; the image of happiness is the desirable image. Consider the suggestion that happiness equals purposefulness ... to test it *empirically*, we would like to observe people all over the world wanting to be purposeful and admiring purposefulness. A good way to validate that this is the case is to look at the fashion and entertainment industry, which purports to produce images of what seems desirable to most people in order to make a profit. I will present a few observable examples.

- Hollywood movies aimed at large audiences solely portray hero characters that look purposeful. The quality of a movie hero, in contrast to how real-world people exist, is to act as if he knew every mo-

I-2. THE METHOD OF LINGUISTIC ANALYSIS

ment exactly what he was doing: walking among people without hesitation, speaking only in pithy punch-lines that are so good they seem practised, and so on.

• The look on the Western fashion model's face can most aptly be described as purposeful, and the appearance of subjective purpose is called confidence. Serious and intense looks with a hardened face and tense lips signify people absorbed in responsible, thoughtful work; it is the stereotypic expression of a person with responsibility and power, such as a military leader. The female fashion model resembles an emancipated and equal woman with responsibility and power, which represents the ideal of what a Western woman can be if she wants. I just read that the latest look that women try to achieve in photos is the "surprised look" with mouth open … the popularity is explained by the fact that it is the face of a badminton doubles service receiver; that's what humans look like when they are fully concentrated on the purpose of being ready. Before the 'surprised' fad there was the 'duckface' fad where your lips are extra puckered, which is what e.g. a painter might look like when absorbed in his work … a look of a person considering options or making choices.

• The models for the most popular Western classical fashion outfits, such as high heels, shoulder-padded jackets with buttons, vests and neck ties (cravat), tend to have a military origin. The Finnish Defence Forces used to run a TV advertisement for employee recruitment with a literal message reading (translated): "Do work that serves a purpose." A soldier is the epitome of purposefulness; someone who has given up all individuality for the (military) service of a higher cause. But the military origin also reflects the practicality of the designs, having been created to be maximally functional when used in battle.[26]

• In Asia and increasingly in the West as well, a women's fashion trend known as 'kawaii' competes with the Western "high-heeled and independent" purposeful look. This trend tries to portray women as children and to portray all kind of things as cute, fluffy and harmless toys.[27] This reflects that, especially in a world where people don't have

---

26 This reflects the practical dominance of the conception of beauty as usefulness, held by Socrates.
27 The Japanese, with their unique control society, have a sort of kawaiization

much individual freedom for existential choices, *the life of children is purposeful* in contrast with the life of an adult, which can be experienced as being forced to follow a predetermined course of life and choices set by society, instead of choosing the course of life one would come to by existential and ethical choice.

- Dance is a display of primarily physical qualities from the practical perspective of matchmaking. The dancer shows his/her body, which predicts matrimonial satisfaction: men display particularly the strength of working legs, where women mostly work to provoke the primal interests of males and can typically portray birth-giving capabilities by a wide stance, hands on the hip or skirt moves. Lately, European dances have involved displaying aristocratic social class, which of course signals wealth and thus matrimonial satisfaction.

I believe these observations support my case. Another thing to notice is that the concept of happiness as purposefulness extends very well to cover our feelings about domestic animals: a happy animal is one that is kept in a way in which its life serves an active purpose, and this purpose is the interaction we humans use these animals for, such as company, guarding the house, riding, etc. Dogs really love fetching the ball, don't they? Why wouldn't they; it is a clear task assigned and they can show off their skills that are better fit for it than the skills humans have. The happiness of animals, of course, is a vague thing to measure, but my point is that the concept is better extendable to animals than some other concepts for the same purpose, such as happiness as an emotion or satisfaction, since the pleasure behaviour of animals, apart from perhaps only cats and dogs, differs so much from our own pleasure behaviour. This difference in behaviour might be the reason why domestic animals, such as chickens, pigs and cows, are mass-produced

---

movement to fight the helplessness of the individual against the power of society by making especially scary and important things look cute and helpless. I find this an alienation subculture; quite similar in function—albeit different in look—to the Northern European subculture in which it is cool to express disregard of society in favor of various fantasy themes and a general thematic of death to symbolize the death of the individual against external forces. The prevalence of kawaii in Japan reflects this thematic, having reached mainstream status; the social culture having a complete stranglehold over the individual, which is a Japanese reality. Talk about the wrong things in Japan and you will one day find that your neighbors have all decided to exclude you.

I-2. THE METHOD OF LINGUISTIC ANALYSIS

without too much guilt, as we don't relate to their suffering unless they are made to bleed: we are both made to bleed, and our blood looks the same, but animal faces don't show human signs of agony. If it were cats and dogs that were killed, our animal rights advocates would demand that the killer be slaughtered; not because they are animals that are suffering, but because they relate to the suffering. When an African tribesman kills an antelope, he thanks it for the life it gives and typically eats its heart or drinks its blood as animal sacrifice. The life of the animal had served a purpose, and now it will serve the purpose of feeding the hunter, for which he will show humble thankfulness. Our mass-produced animals might not look as if they are suffering, but first of all, their life doesn't really look purposeful, in the sense that secret agent James Bond's life is purposeful, and secondly, if we think of them from the perspective that they are being fattened and ultimately their purpose is to give their life *in our service*, we don't really show much thankfulness for this service ... and this should make us feel guilty, since the problem lies with *us* who are not compensating a service received, not with *them*, whose suffering we are unable to determine. In older societies animals were sacrificed with due rituals, and later at least a grace was said in reference to the God that created these animals.

The Kantian distinction between analytic (e.g. "shoes are clothes") and synthetic (e.g. "shoes are on the table") judgments can be explained in terms of this refined notion of logic that escapes the metaphysical idea where words refer to objects and thus the idea that, in contrast with analytic judgments, verifying synthetic judgments would require "looking at the world". Verifying an analytic judgment also requires looking at the world in the sense of coming to learn the related language: in order to understand what "shoes are clothes" means, one needs to learn the meaning of the words via learning what shoes are and what clothes are: briefly described, clothes are something one puts on one's body, and shoes are something one wears on one's feet. Here it is essential to notice that I provided just a description and not a definition, and anything one wears on one's feet, such as socks or toe-rings, are not shoes. To understand the word "shoe" one needs to know a human *culture* where pieces of clothing are designed and constructed to be worn as shoes; originally produced by individuals for their own use, and later on by shoemakers. Having understood this, one needs to understand that other things are also produced to be worn on the body, and producing shoes is just one part of this culture of producing clothing. In this culture, pieces of clothing are produced to be worn on the body, and this constitutes, among other things, shoes, to be worn as the outer layer of one's feet. Now, looking at the analytic statement "shoes are clothes", the thing that relates 'shoes' with 'clothes' is the culture of producing clothing, and not e.g. that such pieces could be worn on the body: as a counterexample, plastic bags can also be worn on the body yet they are not considered clothes, except that we have the possibility to borrow the pre-existing concept of clothes metaphorically and to make it understandable by stating that one is wearing plastic bags *as* clothes or shoes. We could say that shoes are clothes because we live in a culture in which such a thing as clothes and shoes are *designed* to be worn. This *purpose* for a particular use doesn't itself create the logical relation between these types of objects, but it creates the need to talk about them, as the purpose needs to be actively communicated: children need to be taught how to use objects and customers need to be taught how they could use the objects that are on display. It is this *need to communicate about objects that are designed for a particular purpose* that, for *homo faber*, makes it *convenient* to refer to them via their *classes*. Consider a shopkeeper showing a completely strange new object to a customer; for example, a strange musical instrument:

– *What is it?*
– *It is a South-Framsian strumbug.*
– *And what is that?*
– *It's an instrument.*
– *How do you play it?*
– *You hit it with a stick.*
– *So, it's a kind of drum?*
– *Not exactly, it doesn't have a drumhead. You hit the wood which makes the contents rattle.*
– *So, it is a percussion instrument. What do you call those instruments?*
– *I don't really know; suppose there is no class for them.*

I-2. THE METHOD OF LINGUISTIC ANALYSIS

– *So, it is a South-Framsian strumbug!*
– *Indeed.*

Only if we needed to refer to such objects in language a lot would we need to grammatically establish a class for such objects, and the idea of having classes of objects is the same idea as organizing different types of objects into, say, separate shelves in separate sections in separate rooms, in order to locate them more easily. We can also verify that 1) if the instrument was not designed to be used as an instrument, or 2) if there was no intention to pass on these instruments to other people, there would be no need for such a classification of objects. So, it is this human quality that constitutes the logical relation between the concepts in Kantian *analytic* judgments or statements. A truism like "shoes are clothes" is a statement, yes, but not very useful except exactly in the said purpose of *teaching* somebody the logical relation between the words 'shoes' and 'clothes'; it is a reference to this logical relation. Kant correctly established this as a property of the logical relation between the grammatical subject and predicate (and not the sentence) but was clearly wrong in thinking that the logical relation and the *a priori* nature of an analytic judgment is a property of the 'judgment'—the cognitive thought process about such matters—and originates in the mind. It rather obviously is a property of the living culture in which such concepts exist, among its practices of dealing with objects in particular ways. Kant can be effectively refuted by attacking the relation between an assumed mental representation and its assumed real-world counterpart by showing that the grammatical structure of a sentence doesn't establish such a reference: we cannot know but just assume that when somebody says "shoes are clothes" he is actually referring to the logical relation between the concept of shoes and the concept of clothes, as we had *assumed* in this particular example. And *if* he is referring to such a relation, that relation is culturally established and does not follow from the grammar of the words; if one would like to take it as a given, one is simply not looking at its cultural basis but generalizing the grammar he has learned into metaphysical properties of the mind. The challenge of showing this is in that we are operating within just one language and culture, in this case the English language and a culture in which there are shoes and

PART I. THE BASIS OF THOUGHT

clothes. To show my case is very simple; let's devise a judgment in the language of an imaginary culture: "all botoes are wapooh", and ask the question: is this an analytic or synthetic judgment? Kant says this is an operation on the mental representations of the referred objects, so now, come on, Kant, show me the power of judgment; explain to me how I derive the analytic/synthetic nature of the judgment from the mental representation of 'botoes' and 'wapooh'. I know that one should be forming a judgment here of the subject 'botoes' and the predicate 'are wapooh' that contains the copula 'are'; how do I know if 'wapooh' is contained in 'botoes' or if it lies outside the concept? The truth is that we can't know this as we don't have the cultural reference, but the question now is: how will we find out whether it is an analytic or synthetic judgment? We will need to know what the words mean. And I'll begin this phase of coming to understand the meanings by painting a picture of the variance in what they *might* mean for somebody who doesn't yet *know* them. For the sake of simplicity and instead of writing a long description of whatever people in their culture are doing when using the related word, I will here *assume* that the culture is like ours, having concepts that we also use but just with different words. Now, we can derive many logical options from the grammar of the sentence, but let's just limit it to a few obvious examples of a different type. In these examples, whenever I say, "A *means* B", I mean "the word A *is used* similarly to how *we* use the word B".

1) 'botoes' means 'men' and 'wapooh' means 'humans' → "all men are humans" → analytic truth

2) 'botoes' means a physical object and 'wapooh' means a physical quality, such as colour → "all knives are blue" → synthetic judgment, can be true or false

3) 'botoes' means 'humans' and 'wapooh' means 'men' → "all humans are men" → analytic falsity

4) 'botoes' means an abstraction, such as 'statements', and 'wapooh' means a colour → "all statements are blue" → logical senselessness

Depending on the meaning of the words, the logical nature of the sentence might be any of these cases. Fair enough, I think Kant would

I-2. THE METHOD OF LINGUISTIC ANALYSIS

agree that the nature of the judgment is, not just partly but completely, a matter of the meaning of the words (what the words refer to), and that not having lived in the culture he wouldn't know those meanings. Everything in the mind just, as it were, magically works like it is supposed to, when one happens to exist in the culture, but doesn't work when one doesn't exist in the culture, and this quite boldly constitutes a sound basis to call oneself a man of 'reason' and the representative of another culture irrational, or, say, savage. But would Kant now say that he didn't have enough input for the test; he didn't have a proper mental representation of 'botoes' or 'wapooh', which voids the validity of the test? So, what sort of data does one need for the proper mental representations? An observation? A textual description? A symbolic picture on a card? Suppose now that 'wapooh' refers to an unknown species of fish and 'botoes' refers to fish of that species that have been farmed in fresh water (similarly to the farmed Kamloops trout). Let's give Kant a good look at these animals; for this test one pen is set to contain only botoes and the other pen wapooh: please take as long as you like to inspect them and tell me if all botoes are wapooh and if all wapooh are botoes; surely there is enough *sensory data* to form a mental representation of these animals; these "objects of experience"? Surely a man with enough powers of reason should be able to use his rational machinery to deduce from the mental representations of these animals whether there is such a logical relation between these classes or not? The answer, of course, is that it is logically impossible to deduce from observation, as the fact of whether the fish have been farmed in fresh water or not is not deducible from observation but is a property of what these fish *are called in a culture* where such fish are farmed; it is essentially a property of the farming, not the fish. Kant would think that the *a priori* nature of analytic judgments is a subjective property of the mind, which is a sensible thought, given that it clearly is not a property of the objects themselves to be in a logical relation to each other. However, while it is not a property of the mind, it is a subjective property nevertheless; it is a cultural subjective property—something we could either describe as being carried in the minds of everybody living in the culture, or as a feature of the related natural language. That all shoes are clothes is *undefined*, because there exists no definition for

PART I. THE BASIS OF THOUGHT

the natural language concepts of shoes and clothes, yet the concepts of shoes and clothes nevertheless *are used* in accordance with such a logical relation, which *is explained* by the fact that shoes are to be worn on the feet and clothes on the body, and shoes are in a similar relation to clothes as feet are to the body. And one does not come to this explanation via either logical grammatical deduction from the concepts or observation about the real-world objects the concepts are said to represent (if one can be thought to exist in the first place), but observation and analysis of what the concepts *mean*. The relation between a class and an item of the class is like the relation of a brand and a product of that brand; just that the association between the class and the item is not enforced, unless objectively standardized, such as currently with e.g. 'champagne' or 'feta cheese' as EU standards.

What is often not understood at all, because it is too common and obvious to attract attention, is that one's capability to *identify objects* ("*That* is a daffodil, I know!") is restricted to the concepts one has acquired via education, and this education can be transmitted via various teaching methods, but also simply via books, which by nature are more accessible to the more conceptually intelligent. In aa modern context, one might think along the lines that if someone sees a daffodil, of course he will identify it as a daffodil but just not necessarily know its name, and he'd believe these properties of daffodils are all visible and accessible via looking at the daffodil and possibly to be discovered via scientifically researching it. But this couldn't be further from the truth; a truth that could easily be scientifically tested via the correct test setup, but that is unnecessary if one simply understands the mind correctly: a person who is uneducated about daffodils is not uneducated about the *name* 'daffodil' but the *concept* of daffodil, which involves all the knowledge about how *we*, as a people, typically interact with daffodils, and that one might e.g. read about on Wikipedia. This information is not contained within daffodils but is, in all its totality, cultural information contained within our living culture and passed on via the process of education. In addition to this conceptual element of the mind, with which we identify objects and assimilate our cultural education into our rational thought, the mind needs to be recognized

I-2. THE METHOD OF LINGUISTIC ANALYSIS

to have associative capabilities that assemble these concepts with our personal experiences and emotions in a way that is uniquely subjective and holistic in terms of our whole body as a system. As an example of this holism, thought consumes energy, and a hungry and tired individual tends to reason differently from a well fed, vigorous one. Due to changes in chemical balance, a hungry or tired brain loses activity in the frontal cortex, which will decimate focus and working memory, and these will cause rational failures that can aggravate and demotivate the individual but can in turn increase imaginative creativity.[28] At the very end, before bodily collapse, starving individuals degrade rationally towards dreamy hallucinations and an inability to rationally distinguish actual reality from hope- or fear-evoked mirage—an individual losing his will stops caring about reality and gives in to fantasy (in psychosis, the same phenomenon seems to take place, which implies that there is a similarity in the chemical constitution of the brain in these states). Logically the principle applied is *ex falso quodlibet*: when logic fails in a contradiction, the person will come to a 'creative' solution that effectively is pleasing to their imagination. In the brain the way this obviously works is that logic and rationality are to be considered higher brain functions that gradually switch off along with resource deprivation, such as lack of rest or nourishment, which obviously are reflected in the chemical constitution of the brain. Then again, rationally and logically particularly simplistic people or personalities that manage to be inspirational and hold a high status, can often compensate the irrationality by being empathetic, creative and moral.[29] But following the

---

28 Keith Jarrett described the conditions of his Köln Concert solo performance as abominable: he had been sleeping poorly for many nights, was exhausted from travelling, wearing a brace on his sore back and had decided to cancel the whole show hours before the start, which was at almost midnight. The resulting recording is the all-time best-selling piano album in existence.

29 A high rational disposition is a requirement for higher independence and self-control, and those without primary rational dispositions will always need to rely on other people, because being primarily motivated by one's emotions and drawing inspiration from a "positive feeling" has a dire weakness: the inability to cope with negative feelings. This inability will cause a person to 1) become overwhelmed by emotions of guilt, shame, fear, anger or hatred, and, because of his lack of rational ability to recognize his condition and to restrict himself, going out of control and a danger to himself or to other people, or 2) being forced to restrict himself via self-deceit, which is to avoid negative feelings on a conceptual level and to turn a blind eye to whatever things provoke these negative feelings. The

restrictions of thought imposed by the brain or mind as a sort of system that alternates between controlled rationality and uncontrollable imagination, one may dreamily imagine limits to the concepts one has acquired, and this is where psychology and literary analysis meet in the concept of an *archetype*: something that exists in literature as it is essentially cultural information, but at the same time something one is disposed to subconsciously imagine in one's dreams—in the West, human stereotypes such as priests, nuns, police, firemen, blondes, brunettes etc. *One cannot imagine what one hasn't acquired a concept of*; the logical equals the imaginable, and the boundaries of logic play with the boundaries of the meanings of the concepts being used. I remember a nightmare when I was very small, and it involved a troll monster staring at me in the dark ... but it seems I had just been reading grandma's troll book with pictures; it was that particular kind of troll. I've had repeating dream themes of natural phenomena such as floating in space, flying, being underwater, a painting-like dream of a great hurricane ... if you take a look at people's recordings of dreams (where you write down your dream thematic immediately after waking up), I suspect that they will be easy to understand conceptually because every concept used in the description will be familiar to you. This is because you share the language of the dreamer; he is dreaming within the concepts that both of you share. When we ask, "Is it *logically* possible?" (contra "Is it practically possible?") we essentially mean: "Is it imaginable?" Thus, I could imagine or dream about being on Saturn, which can be translated from the idea that Man has apparently visited the Moon—if I ever dreamed about visiting Saturn, the related activities would probably be like visiting the Moon. Visiting Saturn is something we, as humanity, certainly could *try*. But I couldn't dream about a logical contradiction, such as a car with a sore throat (ruling out a cartoonish anthropomorphized car, which is essentially not a car). Then again, I know I *could* dream about, for example, a living human baby floating in space. Why could I imagine such a thing but not a car with a sore throat? Because the *concepts* of space (as vacuum) and baby *don't logically contradict*: we could place a living baby in space, only the baby

---

second option is latently just as dangerous as the first option, rather like a buffer or a spring that accumulates negative emotions until it's ready to burst and fire.

I-2. THE METHOD OF LINGUISTIC ANALYSIS

would *in practice* die. This practical impossibility is what our dreams are free to omit when evoking images, while being strictly restricted to the concepts we have acquired, such as, here, the concepts of baby and space, which are both physical entities in respect to our conceptual world-picture. In the world-picture of, say, the year 1000, such a dream would be impossible due to the nonexistence of the concept of space as vacuum capable of being inhabited by human objects—something we have acquired via first launching objects into space, before which there existed a very reasonable doubt that such a thing was possible. Our concept of space as vacuum is the result of scientific advances and their popularization, and before these advances our concepts relating to the sky and the heavens logically ruled out such a thing as placing human objects outside Earth (and before naming planets we didn't call it Earth). Isn't it sensible to say that modern science has created things our ancestors couldn't even dream about? You should now understand why, but if you have understood it correctly, you should also realize what our modern scientistic discourse, which names things according to their status in objective *natural science*, bars you from dreaming about, which is the subjective reality that we have at the same time equally lost. This should be empirically testable by showing images or videos of things that are somehow obscure to groups of test subjects, making it impossible for them to distinguish what they see, and refusing to reveal it to them. It should follow that it is impossible for them to dream about them the next night, unless, of course, they clearly relate what they see to something that they already know (think they saw something unintended), and they dream about this thing instead.

PART I. THE BASIS OF THOUGHT

I-3. THE MECHANICS OF MEANING

An individual that has inherited our standard world-picture from school is brought to see the world such that there exists some sort of relation between the external—particularly *physical*—world and the mind; how we think about this world. There have been many philosophical attempts to describe this relation in various ways, such as how external reality is transferred into our minds via senses and observations, and I think a modern 21st-century person would most likely say something along the lines that our mind assimilates or, rather, processes, observations and data about events or suchlike. Here we might notice that in order for it to make sense for some sense-data to be transferred into our minds, we are following the metaphor of a computing machine, and such a machine, by nature, has input and output—as a computer is essentially a processor of data, it doesn't make sense to talk about a computer with just input. Thus, in such a picture, we would perhaps like to see the output of a human as *action*—at least for me it would make sense to say that a human takes input via observations that are translated/processed into actions/interaction; in the context of robots or autonomous agents we would talk of sensors and actuators, and so on. But in such a model we are assuming that senses and actions are logically comparable, like the way in a Turing machine both input and output consist of a tape, or many tapes, containing data *in the same grammar*. We quite naturally speak within a discourse in which we see something, think about it *and* interact with it, as if thinking about an object was conceptually the same as interacting with it. This follows from grammar; as Wittgenstein would say, the grammar is misleading us: in subject-predicate-object we just alter the predicate. Simply due to this grammatical relation we tend to think along the lines that thought and interaction are the same, but here we should be like Socrates and point out that a good definition for a mad person is somebody who supposes that he knows what he in fact doesn't know; one who can't tell the difference between imagination/idea and reality. Transfer this difference to such a sense-data machine, and we will notice that sensory input and actions as output don't meet the same

I-3. THE MECHANICS OF MEANING

logical boundaries, as, firstly, senses are private and thus unreliable, and even in the favourable case where the reliability of the motives of the individual are not under question, sensory reports can be disputed. Imagine the soldier on guard sounding the alarm and having the following conversation with the captain who arrives on the scene:

- *Captain, sir, I saw something in the bushes, so I sounded the alarm.*
- *What did you see?*
- *I'm not sure, possibly the enemy.*
- *How many men?*
- *Difficult to tell. I thought I saw something.*
- *You are sure you saw the enemy?*
- *I am sure I saw something.*

Similarly, whereas robotic actuators can be quite reliable, sensors tend to be semi-reliable at best, which is naturally overlooked by researchers as just a technical inaccuracy the future will fix, but in reality normal people's senses as such are not accurate but act in accordance with both the person's judgment and the judgment of his group, when needed; actually it is not so rare for somebody to need to check with his comrade: "Do you see the same as me?" The case of robotic sensors is worse: simple cameras or, say, combinations of light-detecting photodiodes and an illuminating light-emitting or (infrared laser) diode, commonly used in computer mice, tend to accumulate dirt that can break the sensor ... but even if this wasn't the case, the software that processes the measured sensor data into a meaningful representation of human sense, such as facial recognition software, typically is also inaccurate and can be made to work only with a much more limited set of input data compared to the performance of human vision when applied in a practical setting; and this is irrespective of the researcher's or the software sales rep's promises that they will be better in the future update. Contrasting with the private (subjective) nature of sensations, actions, at the other end of the sense-data machine, are public (objective). Eyes are not cameras; the visual sensation we have is not a translation process of objective data into a sensory experience, because experience, by definition, is subjective. No matter what you try you can't produce a subjective quality from this objective source; it is not a practical problem but a logical distinction; success is not imaginable. We cannot overcome this boundary between the subjective and the objective by any means except by overlooking it, but the logical power of grammar is so strong that the sense-data machinist will have many objections to this result; he will be inclined to say that there *must* be a *real* relation. This he will say until he accepts the primary nature of language in the constitution of his thought via the concepts he has acquired. And there should be nothing to be afraid of in this result; in fact it will bring a Western mind into harmony with the rest of the world where world-pictures are not built on the Platonic tradition of abstract ideas and a scientifically boosted search into their true nature—a search that nevertheless engages in constant dispute about this "true nature." Outside this tradition, more care is invested in the problematic of what is the correct way of expressing things such that what is said is in harmony with the social setting in which it is expressed. Along the Socratic line I might say that our world-picture taught in schools contains an innate contradiction which is a solid base for madness one can only hope to redeem oneself from, should one wish to strive for conceptual clarity, which will never be in the curriculum. What you learn from school is not a full understanding but just the basics to enable you to get along with the ways of the world; striving for non-contradiction is a task meant for those who wish to take on this particular challenge. The everyday lives of ordinary people are rife with conceptual contradiction, and they are happy with it, which is how it has always been and how it always will be. This is to say that philosophy will always remain an expert work for those who have the free time for it, and normal people will more or less painfully settle in their lives to everyday conceptual contradiction and the moral contradictions this implies. They must either live in a state of distorted reality and a state of terrifying madness whenever they, as people often say, "spend too much time with their own thoughts", or morally accept these contradictions as a fundamental human incapability under a religious system that promotes it. Our whole system of thought, that natural phenomena are the result of natural laws, is an illusion, as early Wittgenstein infamously noted,[30] yet it will be inescapably

---

30   Tractatus 6.371

I-3. THE MECHANICS OF MEANING

mystical to claim illusion without explicating how this is possible. I believe the simplest way to see how it must be so is to understand that natural phenomena have existed before the explication of any natural laws, and Western science has essentially continued the Aristotelian project of classifying what already exists (and has been created). How could natural phenomenon P be the result of natural laws L, if P existed before L?—if this indeed was a causal relation, the absence of L should result in the absence of P. Natural laws have been derived from observing natural phenomena, and the question is: would it have been possible to derive different sorts of laws from observing the same phenomena? To try and answer this in the negative will invalidate the scientific method and posit fatalism.

Meaning is a complex thing, yet as it is a human basis for both thought and language, it tends to be overlooked and taken for granted. Let's say that Mark tells me: "There's a chair by the pool." Being interested in the meaning of 'chair' used here, I will ask for a criterion: "How did you get to know that it is a chair that is by the pool?" and this is not a single question. Mark saw there was a chair by the pool, but that doesn't make what Mark saw a chair. What Mark has already established before that is how to denote certain types of objects with the word 'chair', and what happened in this event is that Mark looked at the pool and associated what he saw there as being a chair. And these two distinct things both have related possibilities of error: Mark might take a look at the pool area and, firstly, see something that he doesn't clearly recognize, and take a guess that maybe it is a chair, yet find out that it is, say, a trash can (maybe there was low light and he couldn't see at all clearly, and he was making assumptions based on the placement of the object as it was located where he would normally expect to find a chair). As the second option, he might recognize what he sees as a chair, yet still be wrong about it, as the object he saw is something that from his angle clearly looks like a chair, but is something not to be justly called a chair, such as a work of art that is actually a papier-mâché replica of a chair that cannot be used for sitting. It might also be that Mark sees something that he can clearly recognize to be something he cannot associate with anything he knows. So, what Mark saw can be questioned based on his subjective observation, and the possibility of error via the senses, and the question of whether Mark *knows* there is a chair by the pool, are the standard philosophical starting points. But what Mark saw can also be questioned based on the concept of chair he has acquired earlier: it might be that Mark doesn't understand chairs the way I do or the way everybody else does; it might be that if Mark attested a chair by the pool, we mean something different by 'chair'. There exists a question here of whether it is *sensible* to question that,[31] and this is something not answerable in an objective sense: it requires that one consider whether Mark is a rational and sensible person instead of somebody who likes to provoke people's interest as a means to get attention, if he is a novice or veteran in the language that he is speaking, or if he is somebody who would have a personalized, subjective conception of chairs (many artists and intelligent people are known to maintain and actively develop personalized conceptions in contrast with people normally doing their best to understand what others mean by words). In any case, because the English language is a shared communicative element and not just a secret language between me and Mark, the question of what the word that Mark is using means rather boils down to the question of what *one* might mean when calling something a chair; what is the shared communicative element Mark is using? This meaning is something he has, firstly, at some point acquired, and secondly, is now associating with his observation—both activities having a possibility of error that is easily exemplified.

Let's proceed. Words can't fruitfully be said to denote objects, but this doesn't mean there is no sense in saying words are denoting something, and surely it is clear that words subjectively denote something very particular to us, since sometimes we say "But that means something completely different!" But it also means that what words denote is not very clear, since we can often say "I'm not sure if these words mean the same thing," or can say "these two words are equivalent". The definite and most profound constituting factor between logic and language is that

---

31   On Certainty #2

I-3. THE MECHANICS OF MEANING

linguistic **meaning** *is a convention that exists in a shared* **praxis** *and is logically constituted by* **criterion**.

Praxis is an activity or a custom of some kind. I think the meaning is equivalent to how Wittgenstein used the concept of *language-game*, yet he caused some confusion by not being very precise about these games; for LW language-games are either real-world or imaginary, argumentative examples of linguistic practices ... and this is exactly due to the presupposition that each concept *de facto* is, and will be, bound to an underlying practice of using it, in a particular way, following particular *rules* of usage. When we assume that language use is bound to practice, it doesn't matter whether our examples are real or imaginary; rather the possibility to imagine a use associated with a word translates to having understood the relation correctly. Instead of 'praxis' I could re-use the word 'game' ... 'language-game' ... but I tend to dislike the word because, although I appreciate the reference to chess moves, using language isn't really the same as playing games in my opinion. It is not a care-free activity but rather an activity where spoken things can and do have consequences, which contrasts with children's games. Besides, playing chess is a considerably different thing from using language because it involves careful logical thought and consideration, which contrasts rather with the typical flow-like ease of using language when one is adept with the concepts. So, I wholeheartedly subscribe to the underlying idea, just suggest changing the word to reflect less eccentric thought. Praxis indeed involves rules of how the concept may be used. LW related the concept of language-game to the concept of *criterion*; some substantial evidence, a measuring-rod, with which to come to know if something is the case or not. Looking at the criterion related to the use of a word is something through which its meaning can be arrived at. I will take a closer look at criterion a bit later, but here I would just like to describe criterion as roughly equivalent to courtroom evidence; evidence doesn't constitute what actually has taken place, but is considered a necessary means to come to a conclusion about what has taken place, in a system that is motivated to reach justice instead of conclusions being drawn simply from allegations. This rough conception of 'evidence' actually doesn't get us much further in assessing what a given sentence actually means, but it is imperative that there should be some actual way of knowing what a word means, because, similar to legal proceedings in a court of law, communication is something that takes place *between individuals*, and individuals have rights and needs that, if not respected, will inevitably result in all the quarrels, anger, blame, hurt feelings, need for apologies and compensation, need for forgiveness and such, that persistently attach to misunderstanding in human life. If we accept the plurality of meaning (which is unavoidable), without tools to assess meaning we will slide into: "no meanings at all", "meaning is what the speaker meant by it", or "meaning is what its interpreter receives".

Now, philosophy for a long time tried to formulate *truth theories*, and even today the most popular truth theories are correspondence theories where the motivation for the theory is the ability to determine if a given sentence is the case or not; whether what is expressed is in correspondence with the state of affairs. This was the idea in Wittgenstein's *Tractatus*, but later LW said pretty much the opposite in terms of meaning. In a correspondence theory the motivation is to determine whether the statement is *true,* and thus to distinguish *facts* from falsities. This means that a proponent of a correspondence theory sees truth as a correspondence between something said and something considered as *reality*, and he assumes some method (criterion) of comparing a given statement with this reality. This, as I see it, would be a very elementary and natural continuation of how we learn to use the words 'true', 'false' and 'real'; we would understand that some things that are said are true, some are false, and that what is real is in contrast with what is imaginary or falsely believed or assumed, and what can or cannot be in correspondence with another person's statement. What we would like to gain from philosophy in this problem-setting is some clarity or confidence over whether in particular cases something said is true, false, or, say, half true, partly false and so on. But contrasting this motivation, what Wittgenstein means by criterion is that it is aimed to know if what is said *makes sense*, and furthermore *what sense it makes*, and this sense is completely irrespective of whether the statement is true or even whether it refers to reality or just imagina-

I-3. THE MECHANICS OF MEANING

tion. Thus it is applicable to *any expressions at all*, whether they aim to be factual expressions or not ... as it is a rather dire limitation of any correspondence theory, which motivates to tell truth from falsity, that actually quite a lot of language use is not aimed to convey any facts at all, or that the truth or falsity of this kind of language in many cases can be seen to be conceivable yet not attributable to the factual nature of the statement. Such as:

- You need to capitalize Butterworth as it is a proper name. (Reference to a grammatical rule)
- You need to keep the left lane here. (Giving driving directions)
- What a great idea! (Value judgment)
- Money makes the world go 'round. (Metaphor, proverb)
- I just love getting beaten up! (Value judgment, irony)

Factual expressions like "There's a dog barking on the street" are actually a very limited subset of expressions of natural language, and the idea that *truth* is only applicable to this sort of ignores the fact that people experience many kinds of expressions as true or false and right or wrong, and attribute the behaviours related to truth or correctness to these kinds of expressions on many, if not most, occasions. This is to say that considering whether statements, expressions or utterances tell the truth is a completely incorrect starting point for philosophy, as if philosophers could assess truth and others couldn't, and as if you would need philosophy in order to be right and not wrong. No; first, philosophers are to assess meaning, second, truth or falsity belong to everybody, and third, the meaning of a sentence is irrespective of truth. Look at Jesus Christ; he has billions of followers after 2000 years, so he must have been at least a tiny bit right about something despite being remembered only from sentences like "Blessed are the meek", the truth of which cannot be assessed in reference to any observable state of affairs.

So, meaning is something non-private, already existent in language and bound to some existent praxis, and for any given word in each sentence there can be multiple possible meanings that the word might

be used to signify. Take the following examples:
- "There is a pussycat on the table"
- "This guy is a real pussycat"

What is meant by 'pussycat' in these sentences? Let's distinguish that in the first sentence 'pussycat' refers to an animal, and in the second one it refers to a quality. How do we know? Because of the logical commitments implied by the sentences: something on the table must be a physical entity of some kind, and out of the known meanings for 'pussycat' only the one referring to an animal (an informal word for a cat) will qualify. In theory there might be other meanings for 'pussycat' that also signify physical entities, but I believe in practice there are none, so, we can be confident in our answer that 'pussycat' here means just a normal cat. In the second sentence 'pussycat' is used in reference to a person, which rules out the possibility that it could mean a real cat, since no people are cats.[32] Instead there is an applicable meaning for 'pussycat' that is an amiable or compliant quality and that is used of a person; so, in the absence of other logically applicable alternatives, we can be confident that 'pussycat' here refers to this quality. What happened here is that we have used the logical commitments of the words in the sentence of application in order to *rule out the logically contradicting alternatives*. Logic was applied, but not in the sense of deduction or induction in order to know if a statement is true or false; what was found is that, because no people are cats, the word 'pussycat' cannot mean a person in the given sentence; a possible meaning was eliminated. Now, as there are multiple possible meanings and elimination reduces these to a subset of these possibilities, can we use this process to reliably come to a definite single applicable meaning? No, but we can use the method to eliminate what Wittgenstein called *nonsense*, and anyone who has not paid much attention to these logical commitments might be surprised at the amount of sheer error that is committed, even in academic research settings. Very particularly, armed with this conception of language and meaning, we can spot quite many cases in which a word with plural meanings is being used in a manner as

---

32 These types of sentences like "No people are cats" or "All doctors are humans" would constitute the Kantian analytic statements, and typically would be used as premises in deductions in propositional or predicate logic.

I-3. THE MECHANICS OF MEANING

if the meaning was the same. This is *metaphysical* use; confusion or, to use another word, *bewitchment* of language; use of a word as if it constituted a reality, instead of understanding its more complex nature. One who is bound by this metaphysical conception of language takes a word and in a big "A-ha!" sees something beyond; a hidden reality woven into the structure of reality that this word refers to, and what he from then onwards uses as a base and starting point to build his model of reality. Not only is metaphysical thought an error but it is a dangerous error as it tends to carry around it a fascinated sense of mystery instead of the rigorous criticism one should be applying whenever one feels that the concepts are not clear. It is a fascinating feeling, I'm sure, to see a given word as a blueprint or model of the world, with unrestricted and limitless possibilities of application. No matter how much LW toiled to eliminate this thought in his time, today's scientific world is likely to be just as full of this linguistic error with hyped concepts, particularly in the area of computational research where computational models are wildly and unrestrictedly applied. Criterion and meaning relate, not only to the truth of a statement, but equally to any qualities we might consider a statement to have, such as aptness, accuracy, cleverness, funniness or whatever. Equally a statement can be analysed in terms of its sense or truth, but also in terms of any other qualities. Statements don't necessarily refer to actual states of affairs, but they can be imaginative or deliberately counter-factual or, say, humorous, and in every use case there is a possibility to use concepts correctly or to use them incorrectly. Truth, then, becomes a secondary interest and meaning the primary interest of linguistic analysis. This doesn't mean truth is not significant; on the contrary, it is more significant because its assessment lies outside the limited expertise of philosophy. It means that truth is not a quality of statements but moreover the subjective quality of the speaker, and thus not the target of interest for philosophy but of interest for life in general; the philosopher has just to clarify what was being said, and the question of how to react to this is left to others after this clarification. The philosopher can, of course, in addition to clarifying the meaning, also clarify whether what was said is factually (objectively) true, and also clarify connotations, references or other points of interested related to what was said. Perhaps a

PART I. THE BASIS OF THOUGHT

philosopher is to language and communicators as the art critic is to art and its audience. That truth is not a quality of statement completely reflects our psycho-social nature because we tend to trust people or sources that we deem superior or credible and distrust those deemed inferior or incredible, quite regardless of the factual content of what we receive from these sources. Being wrong reduces our trust and, in the larger sense, the credibility of the source ... and here "wrong" can mean either factually wrong or morally wrong. Being factually right is good when fact is at issue and being morally right is good when morality is at issue.

The amount of imaginable practices obviously is not limited in any way and essentially reflects any imaginable activities. If we think of what "1+2=3" means, we can imagine a society at one time in history where, say, there was a practice of calculating things using knots on a string, and after some time such an activity disappeared from use, being replaced by a practice of drawing simple calculus on a piece of paper-like tree bark. Here we have two different praxes that constitute the meaning of the simple numbers and addition operation, but is the meaning different or the same in these two cases? In a certain way both are true, because the activities are different, but both can be physically performed by anybody who can learn to use the symbolism on the medium,[33] and this is the important factor that places the activities in the

[33] The problem of what is going on when a person is applying mathematical rules, *rule-following*, was of interest to Wittgenstein and caused some controversy in interpretation. I have no further comment than to concur that a person cannot be said to follow a mathematical rule because the mind doesn't consist of mathematical rules or their interpretations, but rather we know from psychology that the human mind is highly apt to associate practices with symbols. The concept of *algorithm* seems apt here; algorithms are typically associated with programming but in a general sense they mean the association of a process or a list of activities with a symbol, which seems to be a highly universal mental faculty. An example would be how factory-workers need to pick up their time card from a holder on the wall, punch in the card and then place it back into the holder... this can be quickly taught to a new worker on one go and easily associated with a symbol. To be clear, there is a prevalent idea that the mind is somehow a computer that consists of algorithms... this is just classical metaphysical nonsense. The mind is something that can learn a process and associate it with a symbol, that's all, and clearly the causality goes the other way around: computers are used to implement algorithms because algorithms are a basic human facility and therefore it is handy to use a computer to repeat an algorithm because this model corresponds with

I-3. THE MECHANICS OF MEANING

same *class* in terms of meaning. Now, what would such a class mean? Let's first establish that as meaning is bound to praxis, this praxis is not something arbitrary or private, but something bound to society, and this *social* nature of praxis and meaning is key to identifying that *the fundamental constituent of meaning is the possibility to communicate it* from one person to another, as was also pinpointed by Wittgenstein's famous "no private language" result. It seems to me that what forms the basis of the sensibility to identify and establish distinct classes of meaning is *access to the criterion*; for example, sensory observation and introspection are accessed in completely different ways. The class of sensory observation forms a class because and only because humans *can be expected to* have senses, and likewise the class of introspection because humans *are expected to* be able to introspect: it is *sensible* to establish such classes as the constituting standards of human communication. This is no different from how, in network engineering, it is sensible to define a network communication protocol on the *capabilities* of the *expected* communicating agents: such agents can be added to the network later by having them implement the protocol,[34] which presumes the capability to implement the protocol, which was a key factor in defining the protocol. This possibility of repeating the practice that constitutes the meaning is a requirement for *understanding* the meaning of a concept, and the requirement for its communicability. And hence, I will establish criterion the following way:

> a **criterion** *of a word or expression is a* **practical method** *of learning about its meaning and coming to understand*

---

our mental capabilities.

34 The Internet operates mainly on the protocol TCP/IP, in which the IP protocol expects the agent to be able to chunk the data into packets that carry routing information that is handled by IP routers. The TCP protocol expects the agent to be able to form a reliable communication channel with a target TCP agent with a "handshake" operation, in which the data, chunked into IP packets, is transferred between the sending and receiving agents following a predefined scheme. In short, the scheme defines a process to send datagrams at a quickly increasing rate until the speed is so fast that acknowledgement responses fail to return quickly enough, and then to resend failed datagrams, lower the sending rate and to slowly increase the rate again until the same happens again. This way the protocol works to optimize the rate of sending datagrams based on the actual transfer capacity of the channel, in which the actual route is determined by the IP routers in a manner invisible to the TCP layer.

it.

To ask, "How do you know?", in reference to a word, means to ask for the sense of the word, which translates to looking at the praxis that constitutes it. In this way, it is rather equivalent to asking: "What do you mean?", which can be answered by referring to, or explaining, the praxis one sees the word associating with; for example:

– *You're it!*
– *What do you mean?*
– *I touch you and say, "You're it". Now you must touch me and say it!*
– *Ok I see, let me catch you first! Ha! You're it!*

You can think of words as being related to a collection of praxes where the word is used, but in which the various criteria can set slightly different logical rules to how the word can be used. The criteria are of different types and accessed in different ways. If we take two distinct criteria for the meaning of the same word or expression, it is *undefined* whether they relate to the same praxis or different praxes, as a word or expression can have multiple meanings. It can be that the uses are identical, but they can be different, either subtly or very concretely, and the only way to find this out is empirical observation to how the words are actually used. Furthermore, this difference in uses, the grammatical deception, is the primary source of philosophical confusion. This seems to me to be Wittgenstein's case about pain: in the distinct cases where the criterion of pain is a private sensation and where the criterion is external behaviour, it is undefined whether they refer to the same meaning of the word 'pain'. Here LW noted that we would never say "I know I am in pain", because knowledge is not something we attribute to private sensations, and to extend this by trying to claim that "Only I know I am in pain" is both false and nonsense because others often know it too, via the external behaviour of pain. This is to say that if you think only you know you are in pain, maybe you are not hurting enough yet. The word 'pain', in the sense of both a subjective criterion and an objective criterion, refers to the same praxis in the sense that the word is used to communicate harm or injury; the related practice where one is in pain and is given compassion or treatment would be

I-3. THE MECHANICS OF MEANING

the same, no matter whether the pained subject reports it or the observer notices it. Thus, although it is formally undefined whether the distinct criteria refer to the same meaning, in the case of pain they do ... with the clarification that what is meant here is the act of communicating one's pain to a fellow person, and one should note that people typically strive to refrain from showing pain behaviour to those that they consider somehow dangerous. Several things should be noted. The first is that because the criterion is separated, you don't have access to another person's subjective pain experience, so you can only be sure that he is hurting based on his external behaviour. Secondly, because nobody else has access to your pain experience, others will only know that you are hurting if you express the pain through behaviour. Thirdly, for the same reason, if you see another person expressing pain behaviour, you have no criterion for knowing if he hurts a lot or just a little, or if he is inhibiting his pain response or exaggerating it. Let's ask now: considering the subjective and objective criterion of pain, is the related praxis of the word 'pain' the same or different? The answer is that they must be *both the same and different*. They must be the same because we learn words in social interaction where one exists both in the role of a subject and an object of observation, and these words constitute a language, which can only exist if it is shared. But they must also be different, because we learn to associate the word 'pain' both to our subjective experience of pain *and* to the external pain behaviour, and *we will use the words according to a different logic* with respect to the criterion. With respect to the objective criterion of pain, we consider anybody who looks as if they are hurting also to be hurting, and this is the basis of how some children learn to fool their parents, and in later lives other people, by feigning pains. With respect to the subjective criterion of pain, we consider ourselves hurting whenever we have an experience of pain, and this can apply even when nothing is physically wrong with us. When we look at our *experience* of pain, when the criterion is completely subjective, this experience is actually identical to *believing* that we are hurting. I'm sure many would like to disagree and to separate the subjective experience from subjective belief, but I would have to ask them for some evidence to support this. The truth is that such evidence cannot be imagined because both phenomena exist strictly in the subjective realm. From this impossibility to distinguish belief and experience it follows that a person who, for one reason or another, believes he is hurting or being hurt by somebody, also experiences this pain, and vice versa: if he is being physically hurt, but, for one reason or another believes he is not being hurt, will also not experience the pain. To further look at the experience of pain, I would like to point out that it is clearly wrong to say that the *experience* lives in the brain and is created by the nerve signal; according to the grammar of 'experience', if we are hurt or, say, tickled, in the arm, we will say that we experience the pain/tickling in the arm. There is (often) a nerve signal involved from the pain/tickling area to the brain, but this nerve signal is to let us react consciously to the pain, as opposed to just a simple local response of pulling away from the pain, which is a common reaction for even simple organisms. This signal helps us to think about what happened and to react to it on a conceptual level of thought. But this is greatly confused and mystified by expressions like "conscious*ness*" or "conscious experience"; 'conscious' just means something that occurs within our rational capability as opposed to behaviours that don't, such as bowel movements, or that do so partially, such as breathing. Then again, to experience anything at all, and then not use it as information for our rational capability to help commandeer our bodies and lives, is quite pointless. And this translates to the teleological meaning of the nerve signal: it is clearly there for the sole purpose of our rational capability to process; otherwise we could do away with a body that just pulls away from pain but doesn't recognize it on the level of thought. Take another example of a case where the distinct criteria of a word *do not* refer to the same meaning; consider the word 'peace' as a private sensation vs. as a white flag that represents peace or truce. Let persons A and B be in battle, and A waves towards B the white flag of truce and shouts 'Peace!' Should B conclude that they now *are in peace*, that a state of peace exists? No. B should take note that to wave the white flag and to shout 'Peace!' in this case are meant *as a signal*, and this practice of saying 'peace' here is irrespective of whether either A or B, in their private sensations, *sense* peace in the current situation as an observation. He should understand that using a signal of peace doesn't mean peace as a state of affairs between par-

I-3. THE MECHANICS OF MEANING

ties; on the contrary, the signal can be used as a deceptive tool with the intent to make B lower their guard to make them easier to attack. And the key factor here to distinguish the meanings is the praxis: these two senses of peace indicate different practical situations of use.

To highlight the meaning of 'expected' regarding the ability to repeat the practice, consider code words (signs, gestures…) that are intentional units of meaning that are meant to exclude comprehensibility from others. This incomprehensibility is based on others being unable to reproduce the practice of understanding them, whether it concerns a simple private oral agreement held in the memory of just two people or, say, defined in a private document of a secret society. As an example, imagine coming to hear an unknown expert concept 'gizmorph' and learning that it means the output of a scientific device that, by pressing a button, performs some complex calculations and outputs a gizmorph as a result. The word 'gizmorph' is communicable because there exists a possibility to repeat the practice of producing a gizmorph by pressing the button, but the meaning of the word will not be understood at all by somebody unfamiliar with such devices. It can be understood in the sense of being an output from a device by somebody knowing of the existence of such devices, but it can be understood as a result of a particular calculation only by the scientist who is able to repeat the calculations performed by the device. And here we can establish the sensible classes for the criterion of 'gizmorph' as 1) something being output by a gizmorph device, as humans can be expected to use devices, and as 2) something which is the result of a particular calculation, as some humans can be expected to perform such calculations. Working with gizmorphs would be something that, for example, a web editor would do for work: the web editor writes content for the World Wide Web and is expected to know what the word "WWW" means, but is not expected to understand how WWW or any of its constituting technical elements work. As an example of how the lack of shared practice implies lack of communicability and meaning, take the private language word 'dazzledum', said by its author Mr Haywire to denote the emotion *he* feels while stepping out of the shower. The word 'dazzledum' is not communicable because, due to the nature of emotions as something else than shared practices, nobody will be able to experience the emotions of Mr Haywire, and thus it also makes no sense for Mr Haywire to try and communicate using such a word. If Mr Haywire instead tried to argue that 'dazzledum' denotes the emotion *one* gets while stepping out of the shower, one should point to Mr Haywire that what he means is his own emotion and that he knows that nobody can *be expected to* feel what *he* feels (although one *can*, by use of empathy, know how he feels). And this is not to say that emotions in general are not communicable with words but that the words generally used for emotions function as established standards of communication and have had much more to them in their history than somebody just claiming them, and their communicability is based on a practical process of people identifying similar conditions in their own subjective state as what is being described by others. Let it be remarked that there are actually quite a lot of people who expect others to understand them and to know how they feel and to respond to their feelings instead of their communication, which is likely due to their being brought up in an overly empathetic environment. It may also be noted that this objection to private meaning doesn't lead to solipsism, and to saying that observable objects are no different from emotions, as in saying that nobody can see what Mr Haywire sees. It is the *meaning* of the word Mr Haywire described to denote an *emotion*, a subjectively identified state. The question is completely different considering the case where Mr Haywire would argue that the word 'ablacack' denotes a particular observable external object, than the case where he argues that the word denotes *his sensation* of observing that object. Only the case of the word denoting a private sensation one must rebut on the grounds of inability to reproduce the practice of its meaning; anybody can be expected to reproduce the practice of observation, but not to reach the same sensation.

I will here try to distinguish *classes* of meaning, based on different sorts of criteria in terms of how they are accessible to an individual. This list is not meant to be comprehensive or accurate but a rough characterization of types of things based on their grammar.

I-3. THE MECHANICS OF MEANING

1) Individual *external objects* or, say, people or living creatures, can be directly denoted by association; sensory observation.

2) An individual or an institution can have the power to constitute meaning via *authority*. These are any influential individuals such as a governor, a rock star, a poet or a prophet, and their authority implies their public opinion. This kind of meaning is a reference to what a known person has said. The concept of oracle formalizes this.

3) *Definitions* are written descriptions of phenomena that *are to be taken* as the meaning to establish a concept. For example, grammar rules are of this kind.

4) Existing written *text*, such as an archeologically recovered writing, can describe something, and that something can be referred to in the sense of the written text.

5) *Types of objects*, such as 'chair', 'bag' or 'houseplant' generally have no definitions but denote objects with some distinguishable characteristics that relate to their *practical usage* instead of their external appearance, and all that there is to bind the word to anything distinguishable is established practices of human life. Types of objects can be exemplified by individual objects, but such examples don't constitute the meaning of a type. An object is a chair in this sense if you use it for sitting; an object is a door if you use it for opening or closing something, and so on. This can be called metaphorical use.

6) *Private sensations* and *emotions* are inaccessible to others. What is accessible is the related external behaviour.

7) *Abstractions*, abstract objects, by definition, function grammatically as objects but cannot be observed. Many if not most abstractions are derived from verbs that denote action, and have emerged around events that relate to those actions, such as 'love', 'wish', 'assembly' or 'agreement', but also for example 'pain', which is an abstraction of hurting that Wittgenstein studied in length. One can notice that in the general case abstractions have no related practice, yet abstractions can give names to institutions (e.g. 'government' or 'corporation') or something else concrete relating to a shared practice.

PART I. THE BASIS OF THOUGHT

8) Tradition is the living entity of individuals to pass on primarily skill. The role of tradition in passing on knowledge has been greatly reduced by the increase of the role of written text, but tradition dominates as the source of opinion and thus the criterion for what is being said.

9) Anecdotes[35] and *hearsay* refer to something said by somebody, but the information is not meant to be public.

Now, out of these examples classes 1-5 have something in common that classes 6-9 lack: the possibility to *share the criterion* between individual subjects. Written text or the spoken word is (when performing in this constituting function) collectively received, external objects can be collectively observed by means of natural science, and individuals within a society can be asked what they might have meant. But emotions, abstractions and hearsay are examples of grammatical objects that, unless specifically bound to a particular shared practice, have their meaning constituted in a manner that is not collectively accessible, and as such, they are susceptible to Wittgenstein's Beetle argument; the only thing that is accessible to all is their *grammatical form*, which is how they can be seen to be used in language, but because there is no related practice one cannot observe this practice to come and understand together what they mean. The case of tradition is the most interesting one regarding criterion, because what is passed on in tradition is not only knowledge but *skill*, and here we can see that the concept of criterion is only borrowed by linguistic analysis from a much larger tradition of knowledge: the question "How do you know?" regarding our knowledge in the context of grammatical sentences is essentially the same question as "How do you do it?" regarding matters of skill, where the master is asked to show and *prove* his knowledge; to show the *basis* of the instructions he is giving, his expertise and seniority. An expert can take offence at the question "How do you know?" and reply with: "How dare you question my authority?" This reply, of course, doesn't signify very strong expertise, but we all know humans to be weak, and also it is a common human phenomenon to try and portray expertise, which can be seen in that we don't just repeat the

---

35 Originally the word 'anecdote' meant gossip, literally 'unpublished', which explains why in the contemporary setting the word has come mean table talk.

words of experts but also mimic the style in which they speak, and in the modern day it is common to try and "speak like a scientist", to inaccurately refer to scientific sources instead of admitting that one's view is based on tradition or anecdote. I believe this social role of expertise and knowledge relates very strongly to the common antipathy towards philosophers; we can see Socrates as a professional public questioner of people's expertise.[36]

In modern everyday public discourse, and also deeply rooted even in the basic concepts of scientific professionals, 'fact' equals scientific fact. But then again, say, a religious Christian can present the Bible as 'fact'. Now, instead of stating that the other party is *wrong*, we can simply bring out the criterion by means of analysis. But wherever this analysis of the meaning of words, or the latent *commitments* in what is being expressed, is omitted, that is when things start going wrong. For example, it is commonplace for a scientist to present fact in contrast with *opinion*, and this is clearly wrong and an indication of confusion. The word deserves a full clarification, as it has deviated from its original meaning, *"done"* (*factum*, "deed, achievement", from *facere*, "to do"), and I have heard some interesting formulations of what the word is supposed to mean. Today, the word seems to simply signify *objectivity*, and this we know now not to mean an absolute truth but a shared criterion, and this is why two people, who don't agree on the criterion, can't agree on factuality. Say, a Christian might say to another Christian about some Bible verse: "This we know as a fact", as both share and accept the standard. In contrast, the words 'opinion' or 'politics' work to especially distinguish what is being said from these agreed standards, and they can be used to denote either another person's view or one's own statements to acknowledge deviation from agreed standards, which is an essential requirement in both scientific writing and (real) professional journalism. The scientific inclination to speak of "simply facts" is a form of elitism; the position for one's statements is justified by one's institution in disregard of its potential weaknesses: science is often wrong, and, looking at science from both the theoretical and his-

---

36   In the *Apology*, Socrates' accusers call him a 'gadfly', and Socrates ironically accepts this, calling himself a gadfly given to the state by God.

torical perspective, can in fact be known for sure to be wrong, as the results consist of hypotheses that are to be corrected in the future. With respect to the reliability of scientific statements, the question is not so much *whether* they will be corrected in the future, but rather *how soon or late* they will be corrected. It might be illuminating to notice here that 'objective' essentially means 'shared'[37] and not e.g. 'final', 'absolute' or 'necessary', and "objectively true" means accepted as truth based on *shared* criteria instead of e.g. private criteria.

Metaphors are very interesting grammatical devices because of their prevalence, their close relation to *metaphysics*, and the enthusiasm with which contemporary empirical science uses them. Think of the word 'ball'. The origin of the word is to describe a round object, which reflects the shape of the object, but in addition balls have many practical characteristics that make the use of the word sensible, such as that they can be moved by rolling upon a surface and adhesive matter compressed in the shape of a ball keeps it shape, making the ball a good shape for portioning rice, compressing snow into snowballs and so on. In addition, because of this same quality of being able to keep its shape in the face of gravity and erosion when in a rolling motion, the ball form can be observed in nature in e.g. underwater air bubbles, celestial bodies, pearls inside seashells, and in rocks and sand particles under the freely moving and grinding motion caused by sea currents. Now, none of these qualities *defines* a ball, but on the contrary, the word 'ball' is always used metaphorically relative to these identifiable qualities and *our related practices* regarding balls. In fact, one can directly turn nouns to verbs via either their external features (most idiomatic to American English), such as "I was *sandwiched* between two opposing players", "As soon as I came in, the men started *eyeballing* me" or "Don't *Bogart* that joint, my friend", or their use, such as "I *scooped* a couple of

---

37 'Subjective' and 'objective' originate from Kant; to him pure objectivity means "das Ding an sich", which is something independent from the senses or the mind (and highly controversial). One should notice that for Kant these objective things are not just blueprints of external objects but include inherently psycho-social things such as objective values, ends, necessities and principles. Setting Kant's objectivity to my own thought, I would say Kant means exactly sharedness, as to him also this category is the logical opposite of 'subjective', which is equivalent to how I see subjectivity in terms of knowledge.

I-3. THE MECHANICS OF MEANING

dimes from my pocket" or "He started *clubbing* the door with his shoe" or "His idea was quickly *trashed*". But returning to balls; the idea of the physical forces behind natural balls, both in the sense of compression towards a converging single point by a surrounding heavier substance in the case of underwater air bubbles, and the sense of a rotational movement around a single central axis point, is captured in the mathematical definition of a sphere, and the mathematical ball is defined with the help of the concept of mathematical sphere. But essentially, both words 'ball' and 'sphere' existed in language before their mathematical definitions because the related physical phenomena have been observed in nature, and we had practical uses for balls before such efforts at formal definitions. One could say balls were created both before our related words to communicate about them and before our related definitions to further describe their qualities from the perspective of making better use of these qualities—that is if the metaphoric use of the word 'create' wouldn't meet such harsh resistance in the name of scientific principles. And this idea of the same common word having many metaphorical uses relative to its surrounding practices and its observable features is Wittgenstein's concept of *family resemblance*, which itself is a metaphor of the feature of a family that everybody is united under the same last name and heritage but still obtaining both unique qualities and qualities shared by only a subset of the family. The idea of family resemblance is very useful in fighting against the persistent desire to categorize and unify phenomena for the sake of one's own simpler understanding, which blinds one to the observable dissimilarities and the overarching uniqueness and variance in the real-life phenomenon that one is in practice investigating.[38] A very strong and simple point against the sensibility of metaphysics altogether is the linguistic fact that any object can be successfully used to create a metaphor; all that is needed is for others to be able to see or use the referred objects to know what they look like or how to use them. So if one feels inclined to think metaphysically, seeing reality as a reflection of some

---

[38] One might also note that the family is one of the more successful metaphors in creating harmonious tolerance towards difference, used consistently in Christian symbolism, often in e.g. in-house corporate values, and basically all around the world to signify acceptance. To be considered family is a social status meaning protection and freedom from any hostility or otherwise normal suspicion.

sort of transcendent reality or Platonic world of ideas, the divine and compelling nature of such is very easily challenged by simply observing language and that Man can freely and effectively invent words if they relate to something concrete, such as an existing practice or type of object, but more importantly, that one can create metaphorical uses of a word very easily and they will gain popularity if they are insightful and apt. This demotes the metaphysical world of objects "more real than physical" into the status of an invention. This feature of natural language is the basis of its unrestricted evolution, and understanding this unrestricted nature implies understanding that there are no grammatical rules for the philosopher to search for. *Any* forms of linguistic expression, along with gestures, signs and so on, can be used to convey meaning and to successfully communicate, but then again, any of these forms can be used in a failed effort of communication, where the intent of the communicating agent is not correctly conveyed with the expressions used. Then again, linguistic grammars are tools to standardize the rules of forming sentences and thus enhance communication, but these grammars are always created to reflect a linguistic practice that already exists but is just in need of systematic rules. The syntactic rules of grammar are separate from the idea that a philosopher could rule out some ways of using language as false, but—similar to the way a language teacher can correct one's syntactic formulation of sentences and also guide one to the use of the correct idiomatic expressions in given language—the philosopher who has grasped what constitutes meaning for sentences can correct where language is used in a confused manner regarding their meaning; where utterances sound grammatically correct but lack meaning.

I was recently told by an academic that Saul Kripke has *shown* that there exist necessary *a posteriori* truths, and he seemed to see some importance in the fact that Kripke is currently celebrated within academia for having discovered important philosophical theories—a feat Wittgenstein did not achieve. I was able to read that Kripke—in the same celebrated work—has also shown that there exist "contingent" *a priori* truths, meaning that they are not necessarily true or false. Among the examples Kripke gives of 1) a necessary *a posteriori* truth

I-3. THE MECHANICS OF MEANING

is Frege's Puzzle, namely that the ancients thought that Phosphorus (the Morning Star) and Hesperus (the Evening Star) were two distinct stars, whereas it has turned out that they are both the same star Venus. His examples of 2) a contingent *a priori* truth include that the (until 1960) standard metre stick, which defines the meaning of 'metre', is one metre long. Here the length of the stick is *a priori* because, referring to his self-proclaimed concept "rigid designator"[39], 'metre' is defined by the stick itself, but it is also contingent, because the actual length of the stick could turn out to be something else than one metre. I will analyse the two examples here. Let me first comment that this mystical nature of language which, by examples, allows one to show that the traditionally accepted philosophical conceptions (such as that *a priori* implies necessity as it means something that precedes; something "taken as a given" akin to a function parameter to our understanding or knowledge) are *not true*, is exactly the sort of linguistic puzzle one will be able to create by forgetting what Wittgenstein has already shown and that in its time temporarily put an end to searching for truth from the logical form of sentences. If you understand what concepts actually are, you will understand that this result is equivalent to "discovering" that it is not true that 1+2=3. Wittgenstein meant to demolish the metaphysical conception of language and the conception that words refer to objects, but his work has simply proven too difficult to understand: in order to understand what is going wrong here, one must be ready to think of language in a different way altogether. Kripke is applying an Augustinian conception of language, and advances to show that this leads into a contradiction in certain cases of language use. Fair enough, this is a point that philosophy had reached 100 years ago, but his conclusion, that our traditional conception of '*a priori*' is mistaken, is simply taking a step in the wrong direction. As a parallel, consider a man wearing his brand new MetaReality™ spectacles and then, during his daily walk, meeting a creature he knows to be impossible because it has feet but it is walking in thin air, hovering above him. Then, after examining the creature from different angles and without taking his glasses off, he determines with certainty that what he needs

---

39   Kripke's "rigid designator" is something that 1. designates, 2. rigidly, the latter of which means that the designation exists in "all possible worlds".

PART I. THE BASIS OF THOUGHT

is a second pair of glasses, and urges his friends to boycott MetaReality Ltd. Now, from Wittgenstein we have already learned that words cannot be separated from the context where they are uttered and from the people who utter them. And now, applying the conception of meaning from Wittgenstein to Kripke's example of Phosphorus/Hesperus (1), *forgetting the model of language where the words* ('Phosphorus' and 'Hesperus') *refer to something* (such as a planet or an observable spot of light), one can see that when the ancients *uttered* 'Phosphorus' they *did not mean* Venus the planet as we understand it, but they meant something that could possibly be described as something observable in the sky and appearing in the morning, and probably something that held many more *a priori* features that were true because of the things they believed about stars (they were not at all something describable by our physical theories, and in their time to even suggest that stars were spheres of gas would be completely ridiculous). So, the ancient conception of a star didn't even denote a planet. *They* (the ancients) did not find *a posteriori* that Phosphorus is Hesperus; rather, *because* for them Phosphorus and Hesperus were distinct stars *a priori*, they did not venture to look for any relation between these stars. After all, in the absence of science, what use would that have been? Stars made (and still make, if one cares to look for it) people feel very grateful by providing light in the night and providing a means for finding routes on land and sea, and thus, why should one question the stories about how such individual stars came into existence? All this planet business is modern astronomy, having its value in a modern world. Let me simplify and transfer the puzzle to a non-epic setting. Tell me, *is* Dr Jekyll Mr Hyde? If you say yes, what do you mean and why do you call him Mr Hyde if he in fact in your opinion *is* the same person as Dr Jekyll? Ah, so by calling him Mr Hyde you were referring to his *characteristics* or his *personality*, not to his *identity*... but you'd perhaps like to call this *a posteriori*, something to be discovered only via observation and not included in the concept of Mr Hyde? Well, how do you know that Mr Hyde exists in the first place? Ah, I see, the 1886 novel by Stevenson. And how would you describe to another person, in a short summary, who Mr Hyde is? Let me guess: you'd describe him as the alter ego of Dr Jekyll. So much for the '*a posteriori*'; your knowledge of Mr

I-3. THE MECHANICS OF MEANING

Hyde's identity is without doubt *a priori* and derived from the concept of Mr Hyde as a fictional character, the criterion being the novel. When you say 'Mr Hyde', you mean Mr Hyde of the novel, and if you look at it closely, you'll notice that you would not be able to answer the question of who Mr Hyde is unless you *already knew* (*a priori*—"from the earlier") Mr Hyde exactly as portrayed in the novel. Between the two instances of time, the moment of *you* understanding the novel, that Mr Hyde is Dr Jekyll's alter ego (t_1), and *you* being able to answer my question of who Mr Hyde is (t_2), there are, so to say, no time frames (before or after); they are the same thing, from a different viewpoint; $t_1 = t_2$. What is necessary to understand here is that, firstly, *you* cannot separate yourself from the concept as the whole idea of *a priori* is respective to your understanding of a concept, and secondly, 'Mr Hyde' is a reference to a work of fiction that acts as the criterion to the meaning, and we can sensibly talk about Mr Hyde only with the premise that we both share this criterion. It is not a question that one would need to resolve with observation, looking for Mr Hyde from, say, under the bed. Now apply this to the concept of a star in an ancient setting and replace 'you' with 'they'—*they could not* talk about a star unless they were already in possession of the concept used to communicated it, and its meaning is bound to its *criterion* that in this case is traditional knowledge and not the school books and such that constitute our understanding of Venus. And let me emphasize that it is not a 'minor detail' that the criterion is different; along with it comes a whole world of difference in praxis where the ancients would use the stars for navigation, prediction and many things that we simply have nothing in common with in our understanding of planets and are unaware of and unable to reproduce without fundamental study of stars in the sense that our ancestors would refer to them. So, we can conclude this matter by understanding that the claim that Phosphorus and Hesperus denote the same star is not *a posteriori* truth but a misconception about the meaning of 'Phosphorus' and 'Hesperus', created entirely by a known misconception about language. But this result doesn't apply just to this case but has a much deeper extent; it is in general the case that

> *the **a priori** is derived from the praxis.*

PART I. THE BASIS OF THOUGHT

This should already be obvious, given that *a priori* is generally understood as the knowledge from the domain of concepts; we are clarifying that the actual source of the necessity (what makes it "already given") is *the necessary existence of the praxis* in order for the concept to exist, and the concept carries with it everything that is relevant to the praxis. I'll give just a quick example: consider the word 'vaccination'; what is *a priori* is that something is administered into an immune system, but what is not *a priori* is that this is done with a needle or that the target subject is a human. This is because the word is an umbrella term for *various practices with the same aim*, and it is strictly whatever is common to all these practices that is considered *a priori*. These common features could well be described as "the spirit" of the concept or "the idea" behind it, but this kind of description is just for convenience and one shouldn't be distracted by its vagueness, as one is well able to actually accurately determine what is *a priori* in a concept by analysing the meaning of the word via the related practices. Now, Kripke's second argument (2) about the definitive one metre stick being one metre long being an *a priori* truth not necessarily true or false; one can see exactly the same linguistic mistake taking place where one takes sentences without asking the meaning of the concept of 'metre' applied in the sentence. When saying that the stick is one metre long by definition, nothing more is meant than is said: from this meaning of 'metre' it *a priori* follows that the stick is one metre long, and anybody taking this concept and applying it in other contexts can *a priori* see things in units of metres, by which the length of that particular stick is meant. Now, when saying that it is *contingent* that the stick is one metre long, meaning that it is not necessarily true that it is one metre long, something very different is meant by 'metre', and it is argued that the stick could in fact turn out to be longer or shorter. This sentence is obviously senseless, because, holding to the meaning of 'metre', defined by the length of the stick, the length of the stick is one metre, and only a very confused person would consider measuring the measuring-rod itself using the length of the measuring-rod as a basis for scale (however, I can imagine a comedy based on this exercise). If this is not what Kripke had in mind, then he had in mind some other meaning of 'metre', and this problem turns out to be a simple contradiction in

I-3. THE MECHANICS OF MEANING

terms. After all, 'metre' has multiple meanings related to objective yet distinct criteria, such as "That table looks to me about 1 metre wide" or "I have measured this table to be 1 metre wide", which can be brought out by the question "What do you mean by metre?" It's just that there is this temptation to forget this and to treat the occurrences of the same word in a metaphysical sense. The instant the meaning of 'metre' was changed to the same one used when saying the rod is 1 metre by definition, the measurement would not make sense anymore; rather, the 1 metre stick would be used as the basis for assessing the accuracy of the chosen method of measurement. This is a standard equivocation fallacy.

PART I. THE BASIS OF THOUGHT

I-4. The Subjective, the Objective and Truth

We should now understand natural language as an unrestricted human communicative tool where meaning is bound to some praxis referred to by the criterion that also constitutes the *a priori* aspect of our understanding. I now turn to the inherent logic of words and expressions.

> *Something is to be called* **objective** *if its* **criterion** *is* **public**.

This means that the criterion exists for *everyone*, not just a group. Examples are the possibility for sensory observation, a particular public scientific theory or any other form of verification, such as a wise man, oracle or a holy writing. To call something objective implies a shared criterion which determines the sense of the utterance and limits its sensibility. I believe "water is H_2O" is true, but that's not the only thing I would call water, it is equally objectively e.g. "the binding force of all organisms" and a "purifier". Although all events of expressing objective facts involve a subjective factor implying the question of whether it *should* be expressed in the way it is being expressed (or whether it should be expressed at all), the objective factor is the part that *implies a criterion* that is shared. Because the criterion determines the sense of the description, there is no logical contradiction between "X is a liquid" and "X is H_2O" whereas there would be one between "X is a liquid" and "X is a gas": to find out whether something is liquid or gas is bound to the sense of the words as states of matter, and this use of those words (along with related physical theory) treats them as mutually exclusive, hence the contradiction. Nothing is objective in a transcendent sense: uttering 'objective' merely implies the subject's faith in the correctness of, and the commitment to, a shared criterion, and in contrast with 'subjective', the distinctive factor is that the criterion is shared. This methodologically scientific requirement is something a philosopher needs to distance himself from in order to be able to point it out when analysing the language that is being used. Objectivity doesn't imply a scientific theory except in the sense that many if not most of our basic concepts are today bound to a scientific explanation due to its attractive qualities. *Calling scientific knowledge 'objective' means subscribing to the scientific* (system of) *criterion.* Often in common discourse we require an objective basis for truth and this reflects our need for an authority to set the standard for a shared basis of language, but objectivity has nothing in particular to do with *truth* except within language regarding objective matters: it is true that water is H_2O and this truth is in reference to the objective scientific theory. Science is *the* public criterion of the modern day and the authority and "wise man" we tend to turn to when in doubt, but it is a mistake to take 'scientific' for 'certain', and moreover a mistake to search exclusively for a scientific answer whenever one is merely in need of counsel and subjective certainty.

Let's then look at the opposite of the objective.

> *Something is to be called **subjective** if its **criterion** is **private**.*

On a social level, the subjective creates the ethical-political realm. The word is not related to knowledge and solipsism; the standard relation between the subject's mind and things is *belief,* and the subject doesn't need to be (and in the average case isn't) conscious of the criterion. The word 'subjective' is used negatively in the context of public discourse to imply unreliability, but the word here bears no negative connotation and is crucial in understanding the qualitative and unique nature of the subject's beliefs, and psychologically has its birthplace in the dichotomy between the self and the others (or the internal vs. the external).[40] Things in the subjective realm are related to a subjective way of looking at things. Our subjective thinking forms our traits of character that in turn form the basis of our social behaviour and affect our social response; it is not essentially the things we say or do but the *way* we say or do them that intrinsically communicates with others. These personal traits can be met with admiration and sympathy but also with hostility, sarcasm, distrust, fear or repugnance, and words such as 'consideration', 'norm', 'code' or 'etiquette' refer to social practices requiring

---

40   Also, the word 'philosophical' is used negatively in the context of public discourse.

willingness to yield our personal preference for the shared good. We have an intrinsic tendency and motivation towards checking and configuring our appearance in relation to the social, and starting from our first years we learn to correct our behaviour in accordance with external reasons, such as our parents' will, and suggestively believing them to be true, telling ourselves in shame: "I shouldn't have done that" or "How very stupid of me". Guilt and shame are good examples of fundamental and extremely powerful psychological forces in determining our lives that avoid any conversation and therefore the subject's consciousness. A person struck with guilt or shame will tend to comply with what the emotion suggests as a punishment or reparation, similarly to how he might admit to hurting or slighting someone and accepting that justice demands amends to be paid … yet subconscious guilt and shame are such that there is no criterion or measurement for the amount of this reparation. In normal life, hurt can be amended by concrete means and this can result in restored honour and healed relations, but subconscious guilt and shame apply the same psychological mechanic but without a concrete action to resolve or relieve the psychological tension. Thinking of guilt and shame, one should notice how the subjective realm is, as it were, *personal*, and therefore much more difficult to see or take a look at or to talk about than the objective realm, just as it is easier to take on work assignments as a member of a group than to take them on alone without any help. As a result, we have a strong tendency to treat the world and our beliefs as objective, and even the thought of admitting one of our beliefs as subjective would subject it to a social consideration and the humiliating doubt that we have been wrong about it so far. The objective is what we learn to see first, since its meaning is conveyed to us from others and thus in a shared manner, and the subjective poses us the major existential challenge, as is also implied in the expression "coming to terms with oneself". The subjective realm was what Wittgenstein saw as impossible to talk about, and this is caused exactly by the lack of a shared criterion. Consider me watching an enthusiastic dog in the bus. Subjectively, to me the unrestricted enthusiasm of the dog represents lack of skill, self-control and responsibility. The man sitting next to me is also watching, and for the sake of argument let me assume that to him the dog represents undying loyalty and an unrelenting attitude of entrepreneurship. How these sort of aesthetical values reflect existential change is explained later on. In this brief moment our gazes meet and I am urged to comment. Now, I choose my words carefully and say: "Keep trying and you shall be rewarded," and the man responds with complete agreement: "Truly". Superficially it seems that we understand one another, but if I now would explain to the man what I meant by my comment, our political agreement would turn into disagreement, since I don't believe that a worldly reward is worth pursuing, as the man obviously would; rather, I was relating to the dog simply sympathetically. And this is possible and *de facto* standard, because for what I just said there exists no shared criterion, no matter how tempting it would be to believe that you are being understood. And it is not a *nice* idea at all that your words are not being understood, which is why Wittgenstein would see that it takes effort to resist such temptation. We crave agreement: it is safe, comforting and appealing, and its opposite, conflict, is generally disturbing and also often socially disapproved of.

The simple subjective/objective dichotomy is a very efficient linguistic tool. As an example, take the word 'headache' and ask what it means; the answer is found by asking what one means by it. Headache as an emotion is a subjective concept, since one accesses one's emotions privately, but headache as an attribution based on external behaviour is an objective concept, and so is headache e.g. as a neural phenomenon. Any analysis of a word or expression must first start from asking the sense in which the word or expression is used. But there is a class of meaning that exists exactly in the border area between the subjective and objective and involves an *expert* criterion. As criterion means a practical method, there exist practices that require special subjective skill. For example, law text is the objective criterion for laws but requires subjective expertise to comprehend. And Wittgensteinian *language use* is in the same class: it is objective due to the impossibility of private languages, but then again, the prerequisite of linguistic analysis is a subjective expert skill. Furthermore, it is exactly this partly subjective, partly objective nature that creates *institutions* around expertise, and institutions are necessary wherever there is a subjective practical skill that is deemed socially important. The word 'institution' can mean any of the organized social functions related to a particular skill that is passed on in tradition via learning, and in the simplest form an institution around a skill is a culture where a master passes on his knowledge to his apprentice; or the word can mean the formality of this function, which historically has taken the form of guilds. The question of whether the institution is formal or not is rather a practicality, as the tradition of maintaining and passing on skill is what is essential to an institution. For example, *government* is essentially an expert institution that is founded by the rulers for the reason that a society needs common rules, but there is no need for a government to be formal apart from the need for the people to accept the rules of their governance—in parliamentary democracy we trust the governance to expert MPs after accepting the form of their office: their rights and responsibilities. An expert is expected to understand the related expert language, to be capable of subjective interpretations regarding matters that are involved, and to be responsible over the social matters regarding his field of expertise.

As an example of the subjective/objective distinction, take a common belief: "It is the man who puts the food on the table for his family". Although it is not a scientific statement, the person uttering it would probably see it as a fact, responding, if questioned, something like "That's just how it is" or "You don't understand", which essentially is *reference to tradition*. An outsider from the tradition the person learned that way of thinking from—such as a family tradition or more generally something shared in everyday conversations in the world of men—won't share the criterion, but this doesn't bar him from the capability to understand that what is being said is objective due to reference to tradition. Another example is the commonly reported experience of learning ethical lessons as objective facts—so-called "hard facts of life"—solely through personal experience but with a stubborn insistence on their objectivity, e.g. "I used to believe that people are all honest, but then I found a fool and his money are soon parted." Here the person doesn't see the subjectivity of his belief, but what is important to note is that as someone outside the criterion (tradition,

I-4. THE SUBJECTIVE, THE OBJECTIVE AND TRUTH

personal experience) one could be inclined to call the belief subjective in a derogatory manner and to conclude that the utterance is *false*. But this would be wrong, exactly because one doesn't share the criterion and the *sense* of the utterance: one would not be speaking of the same thing. The utterance *is* true for the person making it, given that he is being *truthful* and not lying. Since he would see the utterance as *true* and not just e.g. being an agreed rule of conduct, it is either of the two cases: either 1) the subject himself doesn't see the subjectivity of what he is saying, or 2) he does see it. Simplified, he might mean that what he says is true because it's what his mother taught him and sons must take heed of their mothers' advice, *or* that what he is saying is true because it's what his mother taught him and *he* wants to be a good son. The difference between cases 1 and 2 will lead to totally different actions, and thus it is the person's *awareness* of the subjectivity of the utterance that affects his actions in an ethical sense but has no impact on the truth of the utterance. This equals the Socratic paradox of virtue being knowledge: the subject who holds some particular belief and is aware of the subjectivity of this belief[41] will behave differently from the subject who believes the same but hasn't become aware of his lack of knowledge and thus believes everyone must believe the same as he does. In practice the unconscious believer will be prone to blame others for not believing as he does. It would obviously be senseless to claim that truth implies objectivity which implies independence of socially shared beliefs, since taking this path, first of all, we couldn't point out any things that are necessarily true, and secondly, we wouldn't be doing justice to all the people swearing on their lives that they're speaking the truth (in using the word in their everyday life) and thus rendering oaths and vows meaningless, which certainly cannot be the case due to their universal cultural commonness. The concept of truth is rather related to the process of apprehending new information against our existing beliefs, and the use of the concept is closely bound to the related subjective experience: e.g. "What is the truth in this matter?" implies searching for the *correct way* the implied information is to be understood. This subjective nature can directly be seen in the original

---

41 He believes it but at the same time is aware that he doesn't know it, and on the contrary, knows that he cannot prove it.

PART I. THE BASIS OF THOUGHT

Greek word for truth ('*aletheia*': "the unforgotten/unconcealed") and is reflected in the classical effort of the philosopher: searching for truth. Thus, how Wittgenstein saw it[42]: the truth of (certain empirical) propositions belongs to the frame of reference (meaning), and the truth of one's statements is the *test* of one's understanding of those statements. Philosophically—meaning from the standpoint of external linguistic analysis—truth must always be analysed in terms of the subject believing something to be true and never in transcendent terms as "truth as such", and the whole philosophical business of e.g. trying to capture truth with a theory is a result of confusion arising out of how truth functions grammatically. Before evaluating whether what someone says is true or not, one must first understand, and, if necessary, find out, what he means by it; as an example, it is most violent and senseless slander practised by certain contemporary scientific authorities to attack religions on the basis of evaluating the truth of religious people's testimonies of God against a meaning of "God" that has nothing to do with what those people mean by the word. Non-philosophically, one is right to utter 'truth' or to declare something as true when one is certain and willing to put one's honour upon what is being said: the word functions as signifying devotion, whether or not characterized in religious terms, such as willingness to say what is being said in front of God. The correspondence between religious and non-religious terminology of devotion while serving a social function is illustrated by both Finnish oath of office and military oath having interchangeable terminology: one can take the oath in the form of "I ... promise and swear in front of God all-knowing and all-mighty..." or in the form of "I ... promise and affirm by my honour and conscience..." Moreover, the word 'truth' not only signifies devotion to others in a utilitarian sense, but the experience of subjective truth is fundamental to the subject's devotional life and his experience of a meaningful life. It is not a random coincidence that psychological depression correlates with an experience of lack of meaning or purpose and a lack of knowledge of what is the truth, as it also correlates with philosophical angst that can lead to searching for truth; it's just that not very many people possess mental skills to personally search for meaning and would rather have it imposed on them

---
42   On Certainty

I-4. THE SUBJECTIVE, THE OBJECTIVE AND TRUTH

by somebody else. The problem for the modern depressed Westerner is that he lives in an individualist egalitarian society where he is protected by laws and norms against another person determining his purpose and using him for a purpose, and he believes he needs to find this purpose alone without anybody imposing it on him. Christianity used to provide people with this purpose; now what the depressed man has is a therapist to listen to his problems and to wait for his self-realization and self-identification with a larger whole. Christianity used to be a far more efficient therapist, too, because the Christian rhetoric of God overseeing people and their families is something that provides consistency over the previous generation, one's childhood, present and the future, and the next generation. And this consistency is exactly what one would psychiatrically require in order to overcome one's Oedipus complex: one's guilty feelings that carry over from the previous generation and one's childhood. I believe that out of all the people that have been permanently drugged and stripped of their chances to naturally heal by our shameful modern psychiatric machine, those that survive will carry severe traumas to the next generation, which will become highly socially unstable. I believe the results are already showing, as modern parents have lost their capability of authority over their children; and now we wait for the power to pass on to the generation that has grown up without a home-grown model of authority into a society of historically maximal authority.

The word 'truth' serves a social function and is most clearly related to the *subject's faith that he is being correct* by the standards he sees relevant and not the correctness of a statement. A *standard rational* way of communication is where a subject implies the truth of his statement with perhaps a degree of certainty, which can be tested by asking how strongly the subject believes his statement to be true. This is standard, and speculative, hypothetical forms of communication are to be considered higher forms, as they require the abstract intellectual skill of disassociating oneself from believing one's statement, which is not shared by all. Also, manipulative communication, where one is intentionally portraying faith in a statement or outcome one knows to be false, is in the same category of a higher intellectual skill, as it requires the same detachment from the truth of one's statement. This detachment is something that someone with a very low intelligence is unable to achieve, as he is best characterized exactly as being bound to the truth of his statement and what he sees, which makes him predictable and readable by others; he cannot imagine an alternative to what he sees, or if he can, he cannot put it into a meaningful statement.[43,44] As this way of communicating describes the way of a standard *rational* person, to signify complete confidence means to imply *knowledge*, which implies the person has reasons of *objective criteria* to back up his statements, and he believes both that these reasons are true and that his statement validly follows from these reasons. A normal rational person understands that the conjurations of his own mind are different from reality, and to him truth and knowledge relate to objective standards within a community whose values he adheres to. This is true about normal children in a family, and it is true about all people in normal and healthy communities in adulthood. Religious statements completely qualify with this type, as the objective criteria are the various people, practices, writings and traditions that are actively and openly shared within the community of the religion, and I say this in hopes to put an end to the recurring problematic of whether religious statements are rational or not. In contrast, people with mental illness involving hallucinations[45] typically acquire these symptoms at the

---

43   A 'beautiful idiot', a man incapable of suspicion, malice or deception, is portrayed at least in Dostoyevsky's *The Idiot* and the later movie *Forrest Gump*. This is a theoretically possible idealization of a mentally retarded man who receives a good and supportive upbringing and can develop a strong identity to protect his personality despite his lack of mental competence. This kind of man is loyal and helpful, yet harmless to, and unharmed by, others, and this personality naturally draws people to him once they clear their own suspicions and inadequacies out of the way of friendship.

44   This also seems to me to be why the early (pre Star Wars) sci-fi portrayal of robots was always psychotic and malicious, as robots relate to intelligence, which relates to the capability of deception and malice, and on the other hand, to both "no faith" and "no soul".

45   Manic and/or psychotic states can involve hallucinations. Personality disorders like schizophrenia, borderline personality, bipolarity and narcissistic personality, are states with idiomatic recurring mental state patterns that typically involve mania or psychosis, which can be summarily described as degrees of loss of contact with waking reality in favour of dream-like imagination. In a hallucination the imaginative imagery, normally present in dreaming, is present in the waking perception; the dream takes over, not just on the level of thought, but on the level

I-4. THE SUBJECTIVE, THE OBJECTIVE AND TRUTH

same time of steering away from the communities that constitute their values, be that their family if they are younger, or their work or friends when adult; the hallucinations relate to being detached and isolated from community, and occur together with emotions of being alone, bad and not being worthy, together with suicidal thoughts. In contrast with rational people whose beliefs are constituted in the shared, communal objectivity, irrational people harbour beliefs that are constituted only in their imagination, and they can't tell the difference as they don't do a reality check to see if their beliefs are real or not. It seems to me that manic states, and various mentally unstable states, involve a rather abnormal escape that I would like to call self-deceit.

As the correct conception of truth is a subjective one, so is the correct conception of lying. The first thing is to note that 'liar' is a very strong term *in a social sense* yet reports of people being presented with extreme accusations by their guilty conscience are commonplace. The commonplace use of the term 'lying' relates it to objective (verifiable) states of affairs, and in an objective sense, to lie is to consciously report states of affairs that are, in an objective sense, false, meaning that there logically (not necessarily practically) exists an objective criterion for their falsity. But to commit an act of this kind of lying doesn't make one a liar, and to steal doesn't make one a thief; the liar and the thief are made by their existential nature: their existential change to become a person who tends to resort to these acts. Also, a single act of this kind can rarely count for loss of trust and can be excused. In a subjective sense a liar is one that lies habitually; one that has become one that might lie in certain subjective conditions, and the liar can actually train to be adept in lying in a manner where no objective content of the statements can be shown to disagree with reality. To correctly determine what is lying one needs to forget the objective content of what is said and to look singularly at the role of the lies as a justification: the liar creates a justification by presenting some statements that can be more or less accurate, but a lie takes place only if some *social responsibility is being omitted*. To lie is to misrepresent or omit *relevant* information, and this relevance is only determined by the subjective frame-

of perception.

work of justice applied, and the related expectation of justification. We describe lying as deceiving or misleading, not because of the objective content of statements, but because the expectation of giving information in the social framework in question is not respected. However, just as in the case of truth, the problem of lying doesn't reduce to just social responsibility but the objective content of the statements along with the logical commitments of the concepts comes into play, yet indirectly and via the subject's existence: the liar can be spotted by logically contradicting justifications. In short, the liar gives a justification that can be seen to originate from a certain kind of thinking... but because the liar essentially has no rational principle behind the lying, next time he will use a justification that seems to originate from different kind of thought. If you assume somebody is lying, it won't help to pursue him about some particular statement or situation of lying, because a single event can be excused in various justifiable ways. The liar needs to be pursued about the *contradiction* in different things he has said and shown that these statements cannot be justifiably originating from the same person. This should be considered the secure, infallible way to corner a liar, should one wish to confront one, and is also the method the police and courts of law use: they interrogate people for statements and find various evidence, and show that either the evidence presented, or something the accused has said before, contradicts with his presented statement. In the US when somebody is arrested he is read his "Miranda rights"; this clarifies for the suspect the nature of the process, where his sayings and doing will be compared to one another for contradiction. This is not a guaranteed method; the success is related to the pieces of evidence that can be used to find contradiction... but it complies with our common knowledge that liars always get caught in the end. This is because the process of determining a liar involves comparing the liar's justification with the liar's reasoning and spotting that the various justifications in different situations don't seem to originate from a single identifiable individual who can be expected to be unique, but who uses sound reasoning. Because we respect people's uniqueness we will accept different kinds of reasoning from our own, but not if the reasoning seems to change with every justification. Also, due to an *accusation of lying* targeting essentially *the person*, not the actual objective content of what they have said, it is a very powerful accusation. It implies that this person is of a lying nature, and not just that this person would have committed an act of stating states of affairs that just happen not to be true. An accusation of lying cannot be responded to by the accused; it implies that trust is gone and communication is over.

To side-track a bit on this particular topic, imagine a self-deceptive individual remaining in said existential deadlock where he needs to uphold a lie, such as a bad marriage, or a mistaken career choice; eternally making himself believe it was not his fault instead of confronting the personal responsibility of his choices, dreaming of another life he could have had, had he made that one choice differently—the choice he actively wants to forget. To keep constantly escaping the guilt is hell in itself, but one day he will notice he is getting old and his life is over in the sense of being able to repeal his choice. What happens now? He will want to forget, not only his bad choice, but his whole life after that; his whole life has become a sham. This is what will happen, and this phenomenon is studied as forms of dementia, such as Alzheimer's disease, which results irreversibly in the collapse of memory and mental activity and leads to death. The physical collapse of memory is the perfect justification for the need to forget his shame: responsibility for the whole life of the patient is shifted away from him to relatives. It is not rocket science to say that shame and a wish to forget are related, and so are forgetting and memory loss. Shame is directly and singularly related to memory loss: ashamed → don't want to confront → don't want to remember → repression of the shameful memory, represented on neural level as a reassembly of active neural connections. But unfortunately, our cognitive psychology is a miserable failure in dealing with psychiatric issues and is looking at Alzheimer's purely as a brain defect and speculating about its causes and is thus inclined to see Alzheimer's as causing shame and not the other way around. The psychiatrist will declare the patient a lost cause and instead tend to the relatives who need to tend to the patient; while they're at it, they might as well tend to the back pains of the pallbearer. "Oh, this case. Broken brain. For a price, I'll take a picture of his brain for you with my special equipment. No? Next!"—as if the relatives didn't know there is something wrong before they entered the office; why would they need photographic evidence of that? But to be accurate, this failure is one of society and not psychiatry, as it is related to the lack of *spiritual institutions* in the constitution of society, to help people alleviate repressed shame. Such spiritual 'services' are available, but they have been secularized out of the daily functions of society. Alzheimer's as a cause of death has skyrocketed since 1980s and is currently considered an epidemic in Western countries. Currently in the US, it is the sixth leading cause of death and a third of seniors die with it; two-thirds of them women, which makes sense as women are traditionally more willing to make adjustment in life choices; more willing to, say, marry for money. Comparing the high numbers in Western countries with the low numbers in developing countries is surely interesting; they speculate, say, sanitation,[46] high intelligence[47] (you see, people in developing countries are stupid), sleeping pills[48] or computer games as the cause. Yes, a big difference is expected between these worlds, and it's not sanitation but the lack of spiritual communities in the constitution of society to overcome isolative shame. But of course, this is just an analytic result from my part; I lack any empirical study to back it up, and modern science only values empirical studies, not the use of reason, which it considers fallible. In such studies, dementia has been recently repeatedly linked to depres-

---

[46] University of Cambridge, 'Better hygiene in wealthy nations may increase Alzheimer's risk, study suggests', Science Daily, 4.9.2013, http://www.sciencedaily.com/releases/2013/09/130904105347.htm [26.12.2019]. Original source: M. Fox, L. A. Knapp, P. W. Andrews and C. L. Fincher, 'Hygiene and the world distribution of Alzheimer's disease', EMPH vol. 2013, issue 1, pp. 173-186.

[47] N. Rogers, 'Alzheimer's origins tied to rise of human intelligence', *Nature*, 21.5.2015, http://www.nature.com/news/alzheimer-s-origins-tied-to-rise-of-human-intelligence-1.17589 [26.12.2019].

[48] H. Briggs, 'Anxiety and sleeping pills "linked to dementia"', BBC News, 10.9.2014, http://www.bbc.com/news/health-29127726 [26.12.2019].

sion[49,50] and cynicism,[51,52,53] which is close to what I am saying here, as these mental states are the representation of an existential deadlock. This hidden area of the human subject—the things the subject will actively repress and ignore—is something our science completely ignores in its effort to be humane. Our science heavily favours the empirical at the expense of faith: faith that there is more to a human than he will show—there is something he will work to hide. He is not an empirical object but a subject; by nature, unknowable unless he is willing. In the case of people with nonverbal autism, our science will look at their brain in an effort to find a cause for their being mute, and disregard the fact that many of them are mute by choice, simply to avoid shameful misunderstandings where they lack social competence; a very humane choice. The novel/movie *One Flew over the Cuckoo's Nest* well portrays a person with autism presenting himself as deaf and mute, as well as a whole ward of mental patients all committed by their own choice and in escape of the shame of their social conflicts. Such, too, is our motive to commit people to a mental institution in real life; people are free to live by themselves until they start to cause consistent social conflict, and are committed (known as 'sectioned' in the UK) mainly by the action of their family. When a person accepts such commitment, he accepts it as 'help' because it is in everybody's best interests; because he feels it is justified as he is ashamed of the trouble he is causing others: "Yes, there's something wrong with me, please help me." I am pointing this out to bring about the question: Why are we obsessively looking into the *brain* of those we consider mentally defective, since the rea-

---

49 V. M. Dotson, M. A. Beydoun and A. B. Zonderman, 'Recurrent depressive symptoms and the incidence of dementia and mild cognitive impairment', *Neurology* vol. 75, no. 1, 2010, pp. 27-34, http://doi.org/10.1212/WNL.0b013e3181e62124.

50 J. S. Saczynski, A. Beiser, S. Seshadri, S. Auerbach, P. A. Wolf and R. Au, 'Depressive symptoms and risk of dementia', *Neurology* vol. 75, no. 1, 2010, pp. 35-41, http://doi.org/10.1212/WNL.0b013e3181e62138.

51 E. Neuvonen, M. Rusanen, A. Solomon, T. Ngandu, T. Laatikainen, H. Soininen, M. Kivipelto and A. Tolppanen, 'Late-life cynical distrust, risk of incident dementia, and mortality in a population-based cohort', *Neurology* vol. 82, no. 24, 2014, pp. 2205-2212, http://doi.org/10.1212/WNL.0000000000000528.

52 N. L. Marchant, R. J. Howard, 'Cognitive Debt and Alzheimer's Disease', *Journal of Alzheimer's Disease*, vol. 44, no. 3, 2015, pp. 755-770.

53 K. Bokenberger, N. L. Pedersen, M. Gatz and A. K. Dahl, 'The type A behavior pattern and cardiovascular disease as predictors of dementia', *Health Psychology*, vol. 33, no. 12, 2014, pp. 1593-1601.

son why we consider them to be so is not their brain but their social capabilities and social constitution as members of society? The brain doesn't *originate* anything; despite being complex like the climate system, the brain is a system that acts in response to external stimuli and its chemical balance, not e.g. some latent programmer source code that mysteriously awaits revealing. Alzheimer's patients are usually placed by relatives in retirement homes, and I don't understand why we study the brain because we *know* we can't fix the brain despite looking at it as if it was the cause and originator of the issues we are facing. Why don't we look to socially rehabilitate and integrate those with mental impairments instead of using them as guinea pigs for the brain study of our own pleasure? Why do *we* expunge our parents away from society, the context of all meaning, into homes for the depressive, or let them wallow in self-destructive cynicism, and then act as if it was *their* brain that is defective? Our society is what is defective. In a traditional society, each member of the society is considered and newcomers taken in, but in our modernized society, the needs of work life and individualism preclude this, and there shouldn't be anything surprising in that this causes psychiatric issues.

The conception of meaning presented here, along with the dichotomy between the subjective and the objective, calls for an explanation for what *association* is; how are we able to associate words to things? The answer is simple: association is a human psycho-social function that just is distinct from the meaning of a sentence. As an example, take proper names and the sentences "Where is John?" and "Where is Francine?", which have the same meaning but just point to different people. And this doesn't mean that John means Francine, but just that John and Francine are both used in these sentences in a similar manner, as proper names. As another example, take pronouns[54] and the sentence "Take *that* piece and join it together with *that* piece", accompanied by suggestive gestures. Here the pronoun 'that' is used similarly in the sentence two times, yet the gestures will appoint the instances to something different. Now, the main difficulty about the word 'meaning' can be seen in that it may be that the person uttering the previous

---

54 The word 'pronoun' means "in place of a noun": a noun substitute.

I-4. THE SUBJECTIVE, THE OBJECTIVE AND TRUTH

example will continue: "No, I didn't mean *that* one, I meant *that* one!", which is to say that the association is not *evident*, and that in addition to that our sentences are said to have meanings; also *a person* is said to mean something by an utterance. And here, based on our established concept of criterion, we can see that the verb 'mean' is used in another meaning, namely one that cannot be clarified by pointing to how language is commonly used in such situations, but by somehow pointing or referring to something. And that it is *necessarily so* is actually very simple to understand, because we share the same language and the same word with others, but our subjectivity is unique to ourselves only. The subjective meaning of 'meaning' where there is no criterion but the word relates to *showing* or *proving*, forms a discourse in itself, and the concept might be used in this manner: "You said that you are worthy of our club membership. Now show us that you mean it!" or "Run, Shadowfax! Show us the meaning of haste!" Consider the following examples.

1)

– *About what I said that you are an idiot... I didn't mean it.*
– *What did you mean, then?*
– *I was angry and I didn't like what you said. But I had no right to call you an idiot.*

2)

– *We have a baboon for a prime minister and I am not ashamed to say it!*
– *What do you mean? That he is of the genus Papio?*
– *Yes, that is exactly what I mean.*

The examples aim to show that whether a statement is objectively true or false is no criterion for the subjective question of whether it should be said or not, and the philosophical effort regarding meaning is only related to understanding what is meant by statements; understanding what people mean by what they are saying without distorting the message, and thus acquiring the ability to e.g. explain the conceptual difficulty to different parties where there is no mutual understanding, or proposing objective criteria for common standards of discussion. In

PART I. THE BASIS OF THOUGHT

the examples we can see that in natural language the subjective and objective meanings are intertwined, and that objective meaning can be used in subjective communication with no inherent contradiction even if the statement would be false in an objective sense. To describe somebody or something with words that are not true in an objective sense is very commonplace,[55] and can be ethically valuable, which is something that lies outside the scope of philosophical problems. The key part for a philosopher is to recognize that even the concept of meaning is a linguistic tool that serves a particular purpose, and to give up his idea to come up with a theory of meaning—as 'meaning' itself obviously has various senses. Regarding this matter, the job for the philosopher is done when he is free from trying to look at meaning as a natural phenomenon following some universal laws of nature. It is a social phenomenon with distinguishable characteristics as such.

As my final point on this matter, now look at the intersection of the subjective and the objective, as they are not transcendent metaphysical categories but rather reflect different areas of life: the individual life and the shared, social, political and civil life. How can it be that objective things exist; what constitutes an objective criterion? An objective criterion is a shared standard, but people don't need to be aware of the criterion in order to use a word the meaning of which it constitutes. Just to state that something *is* a standard, while at the same time there is no process of standardization, doesn't explain where this kind of standard originates, as distinguishing a standard here is an *observation*, not a *definition*, and something doesn't really become a standard by itself, does it? The process of a word coming to existence is that there are some people who start using it according to a certain praxis, and then this praxis is learned by others, along with the associated word. After that the word needs no definition; the *existence of the praxis* carries it over to new people. This is very simple to

---

[55] To state something that is not true is a common basis of humour with the capability of enforcing trust. Like a gesture of pretending to smack somebody but then not doing it, successfully telling a joke is a means to show that one is capable of deceiving the other, but with no intention to harm him. Jokes most often incorporate linguistic deception: one is led to expect something based on grammar, but this expectation is then shown to be deceptive.

I-4. THE SUBJECTIVE, THE OBJECTIVE AND TRUTH

demonstrate by creating a new word and associated practice, and then teaching somebody the practice and the word, and testing, within the context of the praxis, to see that he has learned the word correctly. An example is builders' game,[56] which involves two roles, the builder and the assistant, and the praxis involves the assistant bringing a construction element to the builder when the builder shouts out its name. Let's continue with this game and imagine that the element was just newly created in a factory, and the only people who know about it are the factory employees. They will name it BG. If somebody now wanted to learn what BG means, what are his options? Basically, only asking the employees, each of which might have their own subjectively coloured description of how the game works. In my simplistic scribbling of a classification of meaning by criteria,[57] a person's criterion for 'BG' could be classified under tradition, anecdote or hearsay, and is strictly subjective in nature. This means there is no reason to assume that when you different individuals, they would teach you how to play BG in the same way. Now, let's say the factory recognizes BG as important and it becomes standard practice to minimize misunderstandings... this is a process that can be done in many ways, the obvious ones being writing a definition or a manual to describe the game, and/or appointing an authority, like a BG master or coach, to maintain and develop it. At this point we have the first *objective* criteria to learn its meaning. The switch from a subjective criterion to an objective one significantly changes how the employees will talk about BG, as the new definition or authority for playing BG correctly becomes the *norm*,[58] given that it is *accepted*. So, it is important to note that in order for a norm to be accepted it needs to be *agreeable*, and countering this ideal, it is possible to forcibly dictate the terms of discussion that are not agreeable, and this sort of activity happens every now and then where an authority (in the example, the factory management) enforces standards without considering if they are agreeable or not. This sort of standardization will likely cause more trouble than such a process is purported to dis-

---

56 Philosophical Investigations §2
57 p. 81
58 The meaning of 'norm' is comparable to 'criterion' from the practical perspective. Criterion is the standard for meaning and knowledge whereas norm means a standard in assessing correct practice.

PART I. THE BASIS OF THOUGHT

solve, because the employees will likely feel highly uncomfortable talking about the BG they already subjectively know under the new shared criterion that doesn't comply with it. So, the objective standardization is something that involves authority and both ethical problemata and a possibility of abuse. But if the norm is accepted it sets aside both ethical and political aspirations *between individual employees* about how the game is correctly played. However, these aspirations can still exist respective to the norm; two individuals sharing a norm can't challenge each other, yet individuals can challenge the norm. This is why even the successful introduction of an objective standard won't, so to say, wipe out all subjective problems of justice and correct action, but will just change the problem-setting as the accepted norm justifies individuals following it. Let's proceed with our example and take note that after the introduction of an objective criterion there exist both subjective and objective criteria to know what BG means, but are these references to the same praxis or not? Before the objective criterion there actually was no way of knowing if 'BG' was referring to the same practice when different individuals were asked what it meant, and this is because there was no norm to use as the standard of correct practice. We can now see that the norm dictates a way of playing BG, but let's say there is a group of employees that finds the dictated way ineffective and among themselves agree to play BG in a slightly different way, say, to use agreed mnemonics to refer to the building elements. Let's assume they won't agree a different name for the game but just call it BG; if you ask them, they will explain BG as a game played in their own subjective way, using the mnemonics instead of full element names. It would be correct to say that the norm defines the correct action, and when we speak of BG, this is our only way of knowing what 'BG' means, as individuals can play BG in their individualistic ways. When looking at the praxis of some people seemingly playing something, we *refer to the norm* to check whether what is being played *is BG*. So, as a conclusion, in order to know what 'BG' means there are many types of criteria to use as reference, each of which refer to some praxis that may or may not be the same, as people are both highly obedient and highly individualistic at the same time. To know if these practices are the same requires one to compare them, but instead of comparing all

I-4. THE SUBJECTIVE, THE OBJECTIVE AND TRUTH

of them to one another what one would like to do is to compare them against an agreed standard, the norm. Trying to figure out the meaning of a word would quickly become an uncontrollable chaos unless one could trust that the norm carries *a social agreement* with it, which makes referring to norms *safe* compared to thought or behaviour that, as we say, acts on its own and deviates from the norm. To deviate from norms is to leave the safety and protection of the society that is committed to these norms, and this relation I would picture as similar to all our relations to other people; we need the safety of agreement by others or we risk hostility and rejection. In this manner we also *risk* our mental health... and here it is important to note that people who are individualistic are different from people who are mentally ill. Individualistic, creative people often think in terms of subjective concepts that sometimes differ radically from norms, but they are also aware of the norms; so to say, they know and trust the norms well enough to have the courage to take independence from them, similarly to how a baby and a child are fully reliant on their parents to take the individual steps into adulthood. Individualists don't forget or deny the norms, they take conscious freedoms from them, being in possession of both their own subjective conceptions and the norms, and taking rational and ethical transferences into the conceptions of their preference... whereas the mentally ill simply are in the possession of their own subjective conception due to an acquired, often traumatic, distrust in the norms. These conceptions can be deemed wrong, as in the absence of their argumentation to defend their subjectivist conception, the only valid measurement is the norm. This complies with how we generally perceive crazy people: they seem to *think wrong*.

PART I. THE BASIS OF THOUGHT

I-5. Philosophy, Religion and Ethics

Philosophy has no subject matter; thus, it is not a science, but the motive of philosophy is ethical, in a similar way as with art. On a subjective level, natural motivation towards philosophy is something arising out of personal angst and may be followed by the recognizing of philosophical self-scrutiny as a means to rational self-advancement through changing one's relation to the concepts one understands. Because the inner change requires willingness, philosophy by nature is rather meaningless to people who do not understand the connection between one's own satisfaction with the outcome of one's actions and philosophy as a means to change oneself through gaining, not more knowledge, but more understanding in relation to concepts already familiar to one. Thus, it is also pointless to teach philosophy to someone unwilling to see this connection. From the perspective of language, the only purpose of philosophy is to *abolish contradiction*, and contradiction can be seen as both confused and senseless use of language, where the contradiction is in breaking the logical boundaries of grammar, but also a contradiction between one's thought and action, where the subject can be seen to utter things that contradict his existence. This latter form of contradiction can be exemplified by the sentence "I never write anything in English", which is grammatically correct but contradicting only when implied that someone would actually *mean* those words, and it is a result of the assumption inherent in natural language that the speaker himself understands and believes what he says, and not just that he produces expressions that are formally given a meaning from outside his existence. Thus, philosophy aims to free us from the trap of having good intentions but ending up believing contradicting things by trying to understand and please all parties. Another way to present this purpose is to say it is to become less crazy. In science, people who believe what the scientists say without scrutiny of the extension of the meaning of the expressions used in a scientific field, and instead somehow expect that the scientists would do it themselves, will easily apprehend contradicting thought. Of course scientists of today will not clarify their concepts; in their discourse the concepts that their

I-5. PHILOSOPHY, RELIGION AND ETHICS

field of expertise produces are used as currency for credibility, and only the great scientific minds of old were in addition philosophically enlightened to understand the limits of their own knowledge by having the time alongside their work to also read philosophy. Because scientific terminology is also scientific currency for credibility, philosophy—the effort to clarify—is mostly disregarded given modern philosophical arguments targeting language. Clarification would be an asset for all, but not necessarily an asset for the individual scientist. As an example of confused language that works for the benefit of creating additional study, the question of if one could programmatically produce an artificial speaker: it is somehow seen as an interesting question of if we would 'project' to a "speaking computer" (a machine seen to output grammatical sentences) the subjective emotions we are said to project to humans—of course not, we only use the word 'speaking' in reference to subjects, and we don't 'project' emotions onto humans but absolutely on the contrary, humans are used in psychology as the method and criterion of defining emotions; the context of humans constitutes the sense of the word 'emotion'. When I say that Betty is tired, I am not *projecting* any emotion, and psychological projection is a completely different thing (a defence mechanism). But AI has since its birth lived off the hype by which new study is made to look necessary or potentially beneficial, leveraging exactly the confusion of language. One could perhaps go as far as saying that the more rampant (crazy) the scientific language, the more work there is for scientists to spend resources in chasing the various apparitions the linguistic confusion conjures up.

Both the subjective and the objective realm are directly connected to ethics via the question of whether it is right to see things that way—the objective can be questioned through questioning the norm. Both philosophy and art can help the subject to change his thinking in order to become good yet apply different methodology. Good in the sense of personally maximizing effort leading to an experience of success instead of disappointment, and, equally importantly, the sense of receiving approval and respect from others, both of which functionally contribute to what is called happiness. The realms of goodness are both the personal and the social, and they obviously must be. The personal, subjective aspect of what is good contributes to its universality, and the social aspect to its cultural nature. As 'good' is a psycho-social aspect, the basis of the universal nature of what is good is *empathy*, and this is an analytical result based on how the word 'good' is used. There exists a standard philosophical confusion to relate 'good' to the object experienced as good but let me characterize the word a bit here. First, from the early steps of our life, 'good' is used as the standard signal for encouragement, which relates it to a certain emotional basis of rewarding appreciation. Secondly, since people generally perceive very varying things to be good, the word clearly relates to a purely subjective appreciation, which is to say that to call something good carries no objective information. And for somebody to share your subjective emotion—to understand your subjective appreciation—they need to be empathetic, but you yourself must also have a motive to share your appreciation and to be understood in order to express it in the first place. This is why when unempathetic people call something good we may experience it as false; we experience the lack of empathetic understanding of the subjective appreciation and thus the contradiction with the standard meaning of 'good'. And it is common for society that this original, encouraging meaning of 'good' becomes distorted because of the interest it creates; if something is really good, successfully reaching the empathetic appreciation of many people (touching people's hearts), it creates mass interest and there suddenly appear masses of people who don't have the empathetic interest but who have a social desire to comment about the phenomenon at hand without understanding it. This happens to any subjectively powerful work: first it creates some interest, but after the level of interest reaches the mainstream, there appear both critics and also people with a desire to exploit the cultural value by expressing (empathetic) understanding over the subjective issue without possessing it. From the grammatical perspective, the word 'good' *references a norm*, similarly to how we refer to the norm to check whether something we see is something we know... but involves subjective questions about the norm in question and the performance in reference to the norm. Let's imagine we see somebody performing some so far unidentified action. There are several important questions involved.

I-5. PHILOSOPHY, RELIGION AND ETHICS

1) What is he trying to do? Is it X? Is it Y? This question is about the objective norm that the person must be trying to achieve in his action. Actions are not random spurts of energy, but we can safely assume that the person is trying to act according to *some* objective norm, yet without any knowledge about the person in question we can't yet know which one it is.

2) What is his performance in reference to the norm? If we have established the norm in question, we can evaluate whether the person is over- or underachieving in his performance, or, as we say, simply meeting the standard, which implies there is no real motivation but just the requirement of passing standards imposed by others.

3) Is he trying to do the right thing? Is this the correct norm he should be acting in reference to? I find myself very often forgiving people their shortcomings, given that they are trying to do the right thing, and to guide a person to correct action I find it best not to judge the actual performance at all but only his choice of norm. Also, many people pathologically set their standards either too high or too low; facing too high a challenge where they are doomed to fail and somehow self-deceptively rationalize the failure or facing no challenge, so they fail to learn anything new. The correct path for them would be to apply a norm according to their own subjective skill and not according to an idealized standard that somebody else seems able to meet with minimal effort.

Ethics is not at all science or a system of doctrines but a word related to a particular human psycho-social phenomenon called morality, and the subjectivity of ethics is always clear and accented when dealing with moral questions such as "What is right in such-and-such a situation?" where asking the question would make no sense at all given that some written law or code, or an agreed conduct, in itself constituted morals. It is connected to, but not to be confused with, politics, which deals with the form of the society (such as group, family or nation), which again dictates the *form* of what is good. A thought or a deed cannot justifiably be called ethical based on its outcome, but solely based on the subject having undertaken an existential change in order to become someone inclined to make it. In this case it can be said that the subject would do the deed for ethical reasons. The word 'ethical' is predominantly associated with types of deeds that suggest (symbolize) an existential change, such as e.g. giving money to charity or helping the poor. But once a type of deed is labelled ethical and becomes a social norm it is possible, and often the case, that people might choose to do such deeds for external reasons such as social respect, without actually having undertaken the existential change that originally made some people inclined to make a social intervention that originated the norm. As an example, buying free-range eggs might be called ethical due to the emergence of that type of egg production having its roots in the ethical thinking of some people and there having emerged a social norm promoting it. But one can buy free-range eggs without having ever given a moment's thought to egg production, in which case the deed is not actually ethical because it wasn't done for ethical reasons; these being the reasons for the subject carrying out the actual deed. After the habit of buying free-range eggs becomes culturally valuable, a corporation could appear and buy those eggs in bulk to gain popularity as an "ethical corporation" while just making a profit for the stockholders without any ethics involved. Take as an example the scene in *The Godfather Part II*, in which Don Fanucci, the dreadful Mafioso known by all to be brutally extorting his own countrymen for money, makes a public charity donation, abusing the PR function of the established charity system. This perspective of ethics conforms to Kierkegaard's perspective on Christianity: being a Christian does not equal participating in the life of the official Christian social institution, such as going to church, but the right God-relation is achieved only in private within a subject. This also explains why a replica is not a work of art itself, as the maker of the replica doesn't share the motivations of the maker of the original work. Ethical progress takes the form of *inner change*, which changes the subject's relation to the concepts he understands (changes his understanding) and in practice changes the way he uses those concepts. The inner change required for ethical progress requires that the subject is, for one reason or another, *willing* to make the change, which makes it rather difficult as it challenges psychological self-maintaining forces such as the need for social acceptance: one needs to accept that there is a reason to change oneself, which is likely

I-5. PHILOSOPHY, RELIGION AND ETHICS

to produce an experience of shame and guilt, and which takes *subjective courage* to overcome. Thus the result that completely contradicts the idea that public altruism is ethical: to be able to be good, implying eventual approval and respect from society, also takes one to be a courageous individual and to base one's actions not on the expected social response but on one's own subjective ethical reasons, which implies a psychological process of turning away from society and what other people would expect. In short; to give others what they need (or to oneself what one needs) requires one not to listen to what they want, and taking this position gives the subject a personal, private responsibility of knowing what they need. It is precisely the ultimate subjective nature of ethics that makes the pursuit of existential change in order to become good a very lonely task.

To further analyse ethics and ethical change *as citizens of a democratic nation*, we must briefly look at the meaning of 'freedom'. There is no "freedom in itself"; people are not free by nature, but we are *primarily* members of a society and only secondarily free to express ourselves. This primary nature of society is rather easy to see if one understands the function of a stable society as providing safety from external nature, criminals and such, but it is also empirically visible if one observes unstable societies where government often alternates between democracy and a centralized dictator-like rule by a strong individual. The democratic state, where people have more freedoms, can exist in a peaceful time, but in dire times the freedoms create behaviour and activities that are not beneficial to the survival of the nation, and therefore these freedoms need to be revoked. The standard error of left-wing thought is that a freedom simply exists in itself and is not meant or designed to be used for anything, and when this idea is radicalized, it leads to the aggressive defence of freedoms and promotion of further freedoms while the purpose of such freedoms is simply ignored. Democratic freedoms instead have a similar relation to academic freedom at the university: they are meant to provide variety, experimentation and a birthplace for surprising new developments and results, while serving the scientific interest of research. All freedoms are to be used responsibly; why allow freedom if this can't be expected to happen?

PART I. THE BASIS OF THOUGHT

Only a bad parent or teacher would do this. A freedom provided by a nation is meant to provide said variety *in service of one's nation*, and in the case of a widespread abuse of this freedom to divert from this purpose, this freedom will be revoked to protect the nation from falling into anarchy. Anarchy, in turn, can be described as a state of self-defeating regression similar to the daily activities of an insane person that completely lack the personal planning or advancement that a person is normally expected and encouraged to have in relation to their life. Now, regarding the topic of existential change, there are two kinds of existential change: one that takes personal responsibility for social phenomena and proposes to change things through action and showing an example to others, and its opposite: one that uses social phenomena as a rational justification (excuse) to escape personal responsibility and action. I would like to call the former *ethical* and the latter *self-deceptive*. Both types of change are characterized by a sense of renunciation due to being compelled, and in the sense of the ethical, it is correctly characterized by *a sense of duty and responsibility to reflect the freedom one's society has granted one*. The changing subject changes because he believes he is forced to; that any other alternative will just postpone what is essentially unavoidable, and the existential change is always *believed* by the subject to be necessary for the right. Ethical and self-deceptive existence both are *active qualities*, but they are first acquired via the process of existential change, involving renunciation of angst, which is not a light process but fundamentally painful and horrible, involving a powerful and death-like experience of *epiphany*, which involves subjectively understanding the *reason* and *necessity* for personal change of ways. Psychologically, it is the culmination of a crisis, and this crisis can take a long time to develop, accompanied by an increasing feeling of angst and depression; a sense of lack of meaning, created by the acknowledged lack of capability to solve the problem in one's life with any of the existing methods one possesses. And as these existences are active qualities, once the subject has shifted into such an existence, existing in such a mode involves a process of active remembrance: the subject will feel tempted to fall back to a standard aesthetical existence, but needs to actively remember his personal subjective reason for the existential change. So, the change is not like a switch to another personality, but more like having internalized a reason to behave differently than how one would normally be disposed to be behaving, and once this reason has been internalized the subject needs to get comfortable in existing in this new existential mode requiring active remembrance, which will become easier with experience. Accepting the active and continuous quality of remembrance, first of all, imposes a sense of *humility*; it is as if one was permanently deprived of the comfort of following one's subjective inclination, compared with the completely unrestricted pleasure-seeking of the aesthete along with its associated arrogance through feelings of omnipotence. Secondly, the fundamental subjective tactic to maintain one's elevated existence is *passion*. To correctly analyse passion, one must first take a look at *love* from the perspective of it targeting *subjectively undesirable* things. I will present some observations to support this.

- Falling in love is classically preceded by a feeling of annoyance towards the loved one. From the male perspective this is related to desire and a wish for ownership: it is an annoying feeling to see something highly precious that you don't yourself possess. The female perspective (on which I can unfortunately only speculate) seems similar to me; an exciting man is experienced as annoying due to a defensive reaction to protect from disappointment. Classically the true lovers hate each other before falling in love; the desire unearths a subjective weakness and helplessness that is experienced as annoyance.

- It is sometimes said that one *must love* something one can't change; for example, one must love one's job, or "You've got to love Mondays" (implying that you would be more likely to say you hate Mondays). This is to say that love gives one the subjective capability to cope with what is undesirable but necessary. This is also reflected in that the characteristic features of our loved one, such as physical quirks, tend to become most lovable; the difficulties in accepting the other are successfully overcome with love.

- The recommendations for maintaining a romantic relationship often include doing surprising things, such as presenting gifts or doing impulsive activities together. This indicates that while the monogamous family unit is a standard dictated by society, the ingredient of love is not about prioritizing conformity as a family unit, it has the power to disrupt the comfortable routine of the unit.

- The quality of being *lovable* is a sense of helplessness, which provokes our empathetic capability (the Japanese fashion culture of cuteness, "kawaii", dominates the girls' and women's market throughout Asia). Helplessness is a highly undesirable trait and we ourselves wouldn't want to be helpless, so, seeing this undesirable quality provokes loving emotions. Similarly, here in the West, it is said that women fall in love with 'bad boys'—ones with a visible weakness of bad habits—where they can find a purposeful role in getting rid of the bad habits and healing the bad boy.

The words 'passion' and 'love' are in many uses interchangeable, but 'passion' reflects an active quality, a passionate way of existing, whereas love is often considered as something also persistent and unchanging and is related to partnership and commitment. Passion is something to be experienced *in defence* against something else, and for a subjective cause believed to be right. In the case of a passionate athlete who has changed his existence by taking responsibility for developing his own body, health and fitness and by setting an example in this for others, his passion represents the difference between two subjective worlds: the world of a person with those qualities he favours against the world of a person who lacks them. The passion of lovers is akin to a defence against losing their loved one: a desire to fulfil the needs of the other to protect oneself from abandonment; and the passion of an ethical activist is a struggle between a world where there is only a need for others to follow his example, against a world where nobody seems to be doing anything. So, all in all, passion is not just a strong feeling or desire to do something, but it is essentially a subjective ethical struggle where one feels the *duty* to act and choosing not to act would mean surrendering to defeat. And this passionate defence of what one believes to be right, as opposed to aesthetical pleasure-seeking, is a requirement for ethical existence.

Self-deceptive existence, however, by its nature creates *cynicism*, a subjective state of self-protection, because of its constant need for a rational basis to excuse one from responsible action. Cynicism is said to concentrate on the negative side of life: for example, everybody knows that some people are lazy, deceitful or corrupt, but for the cynic it is the people who are lazy, deceitful or corrupt, and by persisting in this perspective, and actively enforcing it, the cynic is excused of his own similar behaviour. One might describe this as self-imposed absolution without confession. For the cynic, there is no point in trying because the negative outcome is already perceived as existing and persisting regardless of any effort to change things. The deceitful nature of this can be seen in that the cynic doesn't provide suggestions of any alternative course of action, but simply states his cynical view in subjective defence against having to himself act responsibly, and also in that the cynic often has other excuses available for situations where the social situation would render his standard excuse unusable. But because of the necessity to actively enforce his *perspective*, and not to see fault in his own lack of action, the cynic can easily come to hinder the progress of the efforts of other people. A theoretically oriented cynic has abstract excuses such as "There's no point in looking for work because the employment situation is so bad" or "There's no point in studying for my exam because this subject is not really important", but a less theoretical cynic needs actual people or groups of people to blame for his own shortcomings, such as "I can't get anywhere in life because of this lousy marriage" or "I can't get work because foreigners are flooding in to take the jobs". But it is important to note that the cynic doesn't actually *believe* his negative perspective but just superficially acts according to it, as cynicism is a state of disbelief, not belief. Take as an example the cynic who says there's no point in looking for work because of the poor employment situation; he can be seen to be superficial because he is not preparing for a life without income or somehow contributing towards helping the employment situation, for example by increasing political awareness of the dire lack of jobs. Rather it is something he has succumbed to say without thinking or believing it; something he doesn't take any pride in saying. Cynicism is somewhat similar to but different from *detachment* in that they are both self-protective mechanisms; the difference is that self-deception is an active denial of responsibility that is caused by guilt or shame, whereas detachment doesn't involve denial but suppression of emotions to cope with accepted submission. In case of a relevant undesirable event, the self-deceiving subject denies that it happened or denies his involvement with it, but the detached subject knows it happened and that he is involved; he just chooses not to care about it. Adults can be capable of rational manipulation of emotions, sort of steering their emotional life and selecting the moments when they choose to feel, but detachment is a highly dangerous state during psychological development and develops into personality disorders, such as narcissism or co-dependency, where the subject learns to unconsciously and thus uncontrollably manipulate one's emotions. Children are susceptible to traumatic detachment reactions because of their rational helplessness in the face of strong undesirable events. That both narcissism and detachment are considered very visible 21st-century social issues is well explained by their relation in psychological development. Looking at a narcissist, he is an individual who distances and detaches socially due to the unethical popularity and admiration he gets from others and which acts as the empowering source of his very particular behaviour. The popularity typically builds upon some single traditional quality of admiration, such as beauty (the classical story of Narcissus), intelligence, physical strength or some particular individual ability such as skill at singing. This source of narcissism is unethical because it is not a trait that is acquired for a social purpose, such as skill at bricklaying that is useful in building houses for the good of society, artistic skill which involves cultural understanding to convey ethical perspectives, or spiritual skill applied in an effort to create social harmony. The ability functions as a social asset for the narcissist, and he abuses it for his sole individual purpose, as opposed to using his abilities to a common purpose. Narcissists typically appear extremely charming in a social setting due to their efforts to build their social persona upon their individual social asset. But in reality they are socially isolated due to their missing empathetic skill and are completely oblivious to the emotional life of others, relating to others from the perspective of either personally gaining from them (admiration and status) or protecting themselves from experienced danger via methods of control. Then again, the word 'narcissist' is thrown around a lot, but the easy and basic check to know

I-5. PHILOSOPHY, RELIGION AND ETHICS

whether somebody is narcissistic—as in being in a mentally unstable state fit to qualify as a personality disorder, as opposed to being narcissistic as in just very full of himself at the moment—is to ask how realistic he is; how much his vision of his own competence matches the goals he has set for himself or the role that he sees himself fit to undertake. In the case of a narcissistic disorder, the self-image is typically persistently an *idealized* (imagined, unrealistic) grand saviour. There is typically no stable goal associated with the narcissist's life achievement, but, firstly, the goals the narcissist presents as his motivation are often not related to the his own life achievement but manipulatively directed towards involvement in another person's life choices, and secondly, the goalposts tend to change whenever the narcissist is forced, in a secret and hidden moment of shame, to realize his own inability to meet the previous goal. The pathological narcissist elevates himself by depressing others because it is his way of living but doesn't really possess any passion or motivation to excel in whatever field he happens to be promoting himself, as his primary motivation is just to look superior in the eyes of others.

There is no logical basis for the ethical but logic is applied to the perspective of a subject—as one might say e.g. "With that logic, what you say is true and reasonable, but with *this* logic it is not". These translate to alternative ways of reasoning. Ethics takes place within society, and the domain of ethics is the subject's relation to the society that granted him the freedom to choose what kind of person to become, instead of assigning him his duty as a totalitarian state or family would do. But on the level of the subject it is the case that—as Kierkegaard would write—the subject turns to ethical duty in order to save himself, and essentially, should this ever occur, the subject himself makes a subjective choice to do that. The willingness to change oneself is initiated by a subjective choice that results from understanding the connection between how the subject lives and his own despair. Without ethics and social responsibility man's actions are predominantly driven by immediate urges (including carnal urges), but because of the social aspect of what is good, satisfying those urges doesn't lead towards the satisfaction the subject ultimately wants: social respect. This is because there is nothing difficult in satisfying urges; nothing that would require any effort towards the good of society and nothing to respect as something that sets an example to other members of society. In fact, the contrary applies: unrestrictedly following one's urges, while disregarding the social aspect that yields the reward for one's actions, leads to *perversions*. The original term 'pervert' has meant, not just as we contemporarily connect it to sexual perversions, a person strayed from *truth*, and in this meaning includes also e.g. drug abuse or any activities that have a publicly condemned "escapist" nature. The pervert not only disregards socially approved ways of reaching personal satisfaction and subjectively boldly ventures into new possibilities, but he essentially abandons the possibility of receiving social approval and respect and needs to pursue his activities in private or within a small close community, or totally in secret. Also normally approved activities, such as playing games or using alcohol, can become forms of perverse escapism when separated from their social forms: an alcoholic is recognized from, not how much he drinks, but how socially approved his drinking is—meaning that the substance use doesn't hurt the social feedback of his actions.[59] The pervert will gain momentary relief by enjoying the objects of his desires, but as with addictions in general, in the absence of social approval they will not provide him with the stable satisfaction we get from social life. Typically, if not interrupted, the perversion evolves to a more and more deviant form in the pervert's search for satisfaction through means that won't produce it. Thus, the argument called "gate theory", which holds in any escapist activities involving social isolation (but not related to any particular form of substance

---

59   In a similar way, there is no known cause or reliable measurement of mental illness; to be mentally ill is just a label for observed pathological behaviour with certain characteristics that in addition cause harm to others. This is to say that if a person doesn't commit himself, it is impossible to be mentally ill without causing some trouble to others that is big enough to trigger the need for an intervention that includes the diagnosis to determine the name of the mental illness. And this is in contrast with physical illness that often can, eventually, be distinguished from its physical characteristics. Many of the unidentified states of illness are such that they involve both mentally and physically distinguishable symptoms, such as that the patient seems to be unreasonably opinionated about the cause of his physical symptoms. Doctors will have a hard time distinguishing such a sickness as it doesn't match the fingerprint of any known physical sickness... and this is because the patient himself conjured it simply by believing some particular thing to cause it.

I-5. PHILOSOPHY, RELIGION AND ETHICS

or other pleasure). The argument is that since isolation is a gradual process it is not the substance of the drug that makes it a gate to more problems, but the cause is the process of isolation from a stable society that is associated with the use of the drug. Then again, the relation between truth and *fetishism* is in that a strong emotional (i.e. traumatic) experience causes the denial of the responsibilities underlying the event (e.g. a feeling of guilt from believing one has caused an unwanted event as a child) and the cause of the event is transferred to an object, an abstract object or another subject. Hence the supernatural nature of fetishism: an object that *causes* events as if it was a subject instead. The same desire to escape personal responsibility underlies e.g. the phenomenon of pointing at scapegoats to blame for strongly undesirable events, and the common case in which someone gets irritated for some reason or another, then breaks his activity and directs his frustrated anger towards an external object, such as noise, heat or the personal qualities of another person: "Must you make that noise all the time; it breaks my concentration!" When a person is known to have such a habit, the people around him can often easily predict when the person will start "lashing out" and connect this to the situations when his weaknesses are exposed.

I will comment on homosexuality, which is as taboo a subject as ever, although the phenomenon has entered the mainstream and there is social pressure to "make it normal" by promoting baseless beliefs about its physical constitution to justify it and attacking naysayers. Homosexuality is obviously a fetishism as studies about the childhood parental experiences of homosexuals report common deviant features, which would not only explain the identification with the opposite sex but also the abundant fetishist features in gay culture.[60] As a subjectively initiated effort to deny personal responsibility, fetishism is always correctly

---

60 According to many studies, experienced disinterest, remoteness or violence from the father, and/or experienced disappointment in the sex of the child from the mother is a likely finding in the childhood experiences of homosexual individuals, which will lead to identification with the opposite sex. The idea that homosexuality is genetic or innate is yet another contemporary topic confused in basic scientific terminology, as identity is both a psychological concept that refers to the person's experience of his/her social group, and also a social concept referring to the way the group identifies an individual.

viewed as self-deceit and not, as sometimes represented by outspoken gays or sexual fetishists, a normal rejection of social norms and expectations. That sort of defence is intended to protect against the common social antipathy that classifies and discriminates against such people as groups, and the word 'normal' used in the defence is essentially used in the social meaning, indicating that the groups don't deserve any special attention from society. Regarding contemporary discussion about homosexuality, the ambivalent meaning of the word 'normal'[61] has had the effect of distorting discussion to accept the weakest forms of any assertions about the status of homosexuality, whereas in history there was no need for this, since there was no data about the phenomenon and society could easily accept it as a mental disorder. To put it ironically: when asking the truth, a fundamental issue that bothers the mind is: "What *is* the truth?" but when it comes to talking about homosexuality, the fundamental issue rather is to commonly agree upon all the things it is *not* (or if it must be something, then let's call it "splunge") which means the search for a common agreement on dropping the whole issue as too difficult to confront. This is, of course, the mark of violent denialism, and if there was no social prejudice against sexual fetishism or homosexuality, there would be no reason to try and stubbornly portray as "normal" what essentially is deviant (which is the source of the whole prejudice)—and saying this has nothing to do with how society should deal with such phenomena or to imply any ethical countering doctrine that would try and tell a person how they should conduct their life. In the psychology of denialism, in your attempts to come to agreement with a denialist you can only hope to get as far as being told that what you said was factually correct; but these facts don't really matter as it is the point/heart/something of the issue that matters more, and so it was inappropriate for you to say it and you should now apologize. And if you ever raise a hornet's nest by talking about it again, you will be treated similarly, or rather worse, as you should already have learned the lesson from this incident. Denialism is the wish to silence a painful truth, and just an observation of the behaviour of denialism is a clear indicator that what is being denied is no

---

61 E.g. 'normal' as in "healthy natural process", 'normal' as in 'commonplace' or 'normal' as in something that doesn't require attention.

I-5. PHILOSOPHY, RELIGION AND ETHICS

less than the truth, as falsities are easy to counter factually but denialism is a desperate attempt to force away a painful internal conflict. Psychiatrically speaking, homosexuality is an identity disorder, which essentially means identifying with something that is beyond your possibilities; having a *false identity*, similar to the way an identity-problematic person could present himself as a rock star or, say, Napoleon, by acting their manners and trying to look like them. That gay rights are on a crash course with particularly religious institutions has to do with the fact that these are institutions that work to maintain *morality*; not simply *social order* on the level of society as rules enforced by laws (elements of which can be seen in the sacred texts of all major religions), but morality as correctly understood as a subjective quality in terms of truthfulness, which means not presenting yourself as somebody you actually, in truth, are not. The Bible itself cannot maintain subjective morality as its codes are effectively political doctrines, but the living *tradition* in the form of the Christian institution—the collective of subjects working within this institution—forms the organ that works to maintain this subjective quality, as is the case with all that is subjective. Never in a democratic world has it been the job of the government to care for the morality of its members but simply to provide rights and responsibilities that apply equally to moral or immoral people, and this shift took place during the Enlightenment. Europe changed from a place where the government was also a moral arbiter to a place where the government operates on objective principles and leaves the problem of maintaining morals to the hands of Christian institutions and the democratic public, which maintains its morality from a reformed Christian tradition. And by saying this, of course, I am not (yet) saying anything about morality but just framing its role in society as something by its nature to be correctly left out of the discourse of equality (morality is a subjective quality whereas equality refers to an objective standard), and if our social discourse focuses on equality only, morality will be dismissed and lost altogether and we can be expected to enforce an immoral society. It is quite possible to enforce equality in an immoral way; an example is the contemporary treatment of transgender individuals that are seen to have the right to change their sex, and, as a result, are somewhat encouraged to change

PART I. THE BASIS OF THOUGHT

their sex. This, as I see it, takes place at the expense of medical ethics, as expressed in the Hippocratic Oath.[62] People who have a tendency to hurt themselves (by e.g. having their bodies cut or by not eating) should be correctly seen as the weakest group—the group that needs the most protection from society. But the current trend is a decline in such moral principles, which liberates high-earning surgeons to make a profit from their bodies, not vastly unlike the organ trade. Statistically, the risk of transgender suicide attempts is elevated by both undergoing surgery and revealing one's transgender identity to others instead of concealing it,[63] and this highlights the nature of transgender identity as a *false* identity that is actually better concealed than revealed, as with any shameful action. I can draw a parallel with the story of Florence Foster Jenkins (1868-1944), the worst opera singer of all time who, with the help of her wealthy inheritance, socialite antics and dutiful supporters, was able to maintain a deluded identity of a distinguished opera singer despite being notably poor in her singing abilities. Her delusion was real to the extent that her friends convinced her to book a concert at Carnegie Hall, which, unsurprisingly to anybody who knew her true singing abilities, became a sold-out fiasco and a public laughingstock in the newspapers. She died of a heart attack shortly after the concert. As the moral of her story it seems to me correct to say that her opera singer identity was a false identity that she should have struggled to leave behind instead of enforcing, and that her socialite friends were not real friends but partners in crime to create this destructive identity that was set to kill her, not to make her happy. 'Morality', in general, is a highly unpopular word these days, associated exactly with religious traditions that are experienced as unjust; speaking of morality gets one associated with unjust enforcers of moral systems, but the sad irony is that speaking of an immoral society will just create helpless nausea. Morality, as a concept, has been to a large extent forgotten and there seems to be no intellectual framework

---

62 "I will remember that there is art to medicine as well as science, and that warmth, sympathy, and understanding may outweigh the surgeon's knife or the chemist's drug."

63 A. P. Haas and P. L. Rodgers, 'Suicide Attempts among Transgender and Gender Non-Conforming Adults–Findings of the National Transgender Discrimination Survey', The Williams Institute, American Foundation for Suicide Prevention, Jan 2014.

I-5. PHILOSOPHY, RELIGION AND ETHICS

to e.g. stop people from blaming others for the same faults that they are guilty of, and such people are easy to provoke into mass hatred. Economic values and capitalism replace morality, and in their wake push any ethical standards from their path. As a quick example, the Finnish disposable packaging manufacturer Huhtamäki has received publicity for its efforts to fight the workers' union at one of its factories in California. The company publicly supports ethical standards, expresses commitment to support the organization of the employees and strongly denies any allegations of hampering such organization, but at the same time it pays high fees to law firms and consultancies that specialize in tactics that are targeted against workers' unions.[64] It seems that the trick here is that the company can deny involvement in such activities as they are discreetly performed by an external consultancy.

The ethical choice to change oneself is made out of personal reasons and not as a consequence of logical necessity. One can present logical reasons for doing things in a certain way, but it can be that they are not logical to the person addressed because of the ethical difference. Take as an example: "Why did you take such a long way around? If a person wants to get from point A to point B, it would only seem logical he would take the straightest route", and the response: "To me it was only logical to take the most scenic route, since being new in town I need to learn the surrounding areas." Because of this, discussing the ethical is pointless outside subjective terms, and trying to enforce morals over others works to no ethical avail beyond perhaps getting others to follow what one says without understanding the reason why. Rather, as every good teacher, parent and youth worker knows, the ethical only transmits from one person to another through example, and speaking about the ethical, failing to set an example in compliance with what is said, serves at best a comical purpose. Later Wittgenstein would say that there *is* no ethics, by which he meant there is no such thing for objective science to study. He meant it in the way he would say "There is no problem", which is both a substantial claim about it not being subject matter for philosophical study, but also as a moral claim, to

---

64 H. Jokinen, 'Huhtamäki maksoi liki 400 000 euroa ammattiliiton häirinnästä', Central Organization of Finnish Trade Unions – SAK, 4.5.2015.

point out this is not a topic philosophers should be morally concerned about. The word 'ethical' exists due to our subjective capability to distinguish between our own motives, but not as a tool to debate them over the motives of others. Someone might ask another person: "Why won't you eat meat?" and receive the reply: "Because of ethical reasons", which would make his choice understandable to the person asking. But it would never make sense to say: "You are not being ethical", since one cannot see the subjective reasons behind someone else's actions, unless one can know the other person well enough to point that he is somehow contradicting his own ideals. The subject is trying to be good according to the standards he believes everyone would be right to follow, and the ethical is different from the political in that ethical deeds don't target the good of just society but good in general as the subject sees it. The related experience carries an objective quality: the ethical deed is not something the subject might choose to do at will, but rather follows logically from what the subject believes, and from the subjective perspective the ethical struggle is related to the fear of *remembering* what one believes during the event of making a decision because of the consequences of the action that one is aware to logically follow from those beliefs (people reason very differently when under threat). The ethical struggle is this: "I know *this* is the right principle, but *if* I follow it in this particular situation, what would happen? Can I follow it? Am I brave enough?" The problem-setting for *an ethical person*, one who has internalized a reason to behave in a particular way instead of some other way, is not whether he gains some advantage out of the deed, but the problem of whether he himself—as one defined through his actions—*is* good or bad, and rather the struggle for the ethical person is how to have the strength to live that way. Also because of the logical subjective nature of the ethical, one who—out of fear under threat—submits to reasoning differently from how *he* normally would, will suffer from a guilty conscience. Perhaps because of this Socrates would say that the ethical choice, "to do the right thing", is the *safest* way of living, except that most would likely agree that his demise didn't really testify to safety in the traditional sense. But it is always the difficult choice, and the ethical subject is placed between two forces: his own sense of duty to be good through his actions, and his own limits in, through his deeds, advancing the change on the level of society that his sense of duty targets. Everyone has an ethical conscience because everybody is brought up according to expectations of correct behaviour, but the subject can protect himself from seeing the subjective nature of ethics through self-deceit, and live in a constant loop of despair: having a guilty conscience, performing some deed in order to see himself as good because of the reflection of the deed in the eyes of others, and then again after a while waking up again to the guilty conscience that one is bound to suffer by not *living* ethically. By following norms of "ethical deeds", such as giving money to charity or performing voluntary service, the subject essentially buys himself the possibility to defend his ethical nature in the eyes of others, as does the wife who sacrifices herself by pleasing her scornful husband without question. This way the ethical doesn't create a subjective burden of responsibility, but the compliance with the norm justifies the action in the eyes of the majority and thus saves the subject from the painful process of thinking further about the limits of what such deeds will achieve and what his value is in the light of existing as someone performing actions that work to no avail. And this is not at all to say that a person cannot be ethical at all, but to point out that the ethical is transmitted through example, and if someone wants to be ethical it is not sufficient to think "If only everybody would do this, things would be better". This argument can be seen as an attempt to justify one's own peculiarity by expecting everyone to do what one wants. Because the domain of the ethical involves actions to make the world better, advancing an unrealistic utopia can surely be seen not to achieve such, and simply taking a look at this might help one see the subjective nature of ethics, since after all utopia is not the real world but something created in one's mind only. It's not enough to say "By donating this money I am setting an example for everyone to follow", but one must also take seriously the question of whether others in practice will follow that example or not.[65] And if one understands this, one will also understand that voicing that principle serves no ethical purpose; only the action does.

---

65 This is the second perspective in the Kierkegaardian 'double reflection', a subjective ethical process that creates *truth*.

PART I. THE BASIS OF THOUGHT

The intrinsic subjective requirement of objectivity against subjectivity for one's beliefs has throughout history proceeded hand-in-hand with religion and religious experience. It might just look like a peculiar coincidence or even like a deliberate act of deception that the persons holding social status as the mediums through which the gods work most often happen to report divine testimony in support for their political agenda, and not so often against it. Moreover, both on a personal scale and a political scale, the subjective willingness for change, showing itself in spiritual turmoil, *is calling for* an objective justification. This makes it fruitful grounds for religious dreams or visions, or counsel from religious officials or moments of enlightenment reading religious scriptures, as the commonly accepted divine testimony will provide the required objective basis. However, this objective basis has in the contemporary West to a great extent been replaced by results of science and the religious scriptures replaced by semi-philosophical[66] texts authored by famous scientists, and currently we are experiencing the direct impact of this tremendous change. Science, when accepted as a basis of subjective beliefs, is no different from religion in its psychological function, and a scientific argument, when used as a justification for one's subjective belief or political argument, is no more valid and holds no more objective power than a religious argument: they gain their credibility simply through authority by referring to an objective criterion holding status in society. The contemporary Westerner is tricked by wordplay regarding the objectivity of science and that the scientific system is very complex and hard to for an ordinary person to comprehend (which, unsurprisingly, is also a quality of all existing collections of religious scriptures). The system of science is objective in the sense of being based on empirical knowledge and applying methodology of self-correction, but any ethical-political argument—such as "such-and-such is the right action" or "such-and-such is the right way of looking at things"—still takes place in the space of subjective *beliefs* in the context in question.

---

66 Semi-philosophical writing is a way of toying with classical philosophical problem areas but without actual philosophical argumentation or problem-setting.

I-5. PHILOSOPHY, RELIGION AND ETHICS

The intersection of the subject's unique tendency to use language, and the established and shared meanings of the concepts he must ultimately use, equals *the mystical*. The subject can always choose to use concepts outside their standard meaning (to produce nonsense), such as metaphorically or by choosing the concepts in a particular manner to communicate something special within the particular context in which the utterance is made. Looking at the mystical gives the subject a mystical experience, which is the basis of all artistic expression. The sensations of infinity and lack of constraint, and the presence of something indescribable by words, all related to mystical experience, are in reference to the subject's freedom to use a concept, limited only by the subject's creativity and skill in indirect communication. If it makes any sense to describe the mystical experience as an altered state of consciousness, it is altered due to the subject's awareness of his own freedom in giving meaning to utterances, as opposed to an experience of being imprisoned by what the words already mean to other people. This emancipated experience allows the subject to experience more closely his own emotional connection to linguistic expressions but is characterized by a sensation of the presence of divinity instead of a sensation of looking at oneself as something external. As God tells one what is right and wrong through allowance and denial, the experience of the presence of God equals the categorical absence of other people in determining what one is allowed to meaningfully utter. Wittgenstein never meant the concept of nonsense as some sort of crime to be avoided; on the contrary, he saw it as an essential feature of life. But in a similar way that *faith* is a *sin* (a corrupting human weakness) from the standpoint of *science*, nonsense is a sin from the standpoint of logical analysis: you cannot live without it, but cherishing it you will walk down a steep path into darkness. I see a perfect parallel in the relation between *sex* and *lust* and describing it with words is pointless because we all know that even among the smartest people some people don't see any difference between these two, and some people do. Some people call the first one good and the second one bad, and out of those people some people accept the first and some people refuse both. Some

PART I. THE BASIS OF THOUGHT

people call the first one pretentious and the second one honest, and out of those people some people accept both with "Anything goes"; and some people are incapable of the first one. In any case, as the mystical can be distinguished as the subjective freedom to think in opposition of the established meanings of concepts, *mysticism* or *occultism*[67] can be established as the *objective* study of the *subjective* meanings of concepts. A good example is the fully established occultism behind Nazi ideology that approached the subjective human concepts of God, soul and religion via the objective human concepts of race, external features, economic status and so on. Those who were seen as exemplary by external standards, such as being rich, powerful or pure of appearance, or in any way useful from practical point of view, were taken to be descendants of freely and inspirationally evoked spiritual ancestors and favourable to the predetermined ancestral mission of the German people, whereas those who were seen as deficient by objective standards, such as being a certain colour, poor or having physical ailments, were taken to be deficient in subjective spiritual sense; disfavoured by the Gods as bad material for the mission and to be genetically discarded. But take as a practical example mind-reading and the study of telepathy: there would be nothing supernatural at all about telepathy if humans were known to have the capability of telepathy as a sense, similar to seeing. Instead, humans are known to be highly empathetic, and many individuals can be seen to have developed the skill of recognizing micro-behaviour and assimilating this skill to their empathetic skill of being able to say what the other wants to hear, and this art has throughout history been professed by artists called fortune-tellers. These artists have often been nomadic in nature because their art is a risky business since it postulates a skill that essentially is an illusion.[68] We could perhaps say that mind-reading is the occult extension of the skill of

67 The study of the paranormal, arcane, esoteric or supernatural
68 One of the first chess-playing machines in the world, the Turk, was a very detailed construct that hid a small framed human inside, and this says something about the illusive nature of machine intelligence. But furthermore, as a general starting point for evaluating the *credibility* of any presented *miracle*, one should ask the question why circus acts are nomadic and not stationary; why is it that they move around showing people magic, and not the opposite way that people from all around travel to see their magic? This distinction between the *perspective* in science and miracles is addressed in Wittgenstein's (rather notorious) *Lecture on Ethics*.

using "reads" or "tells" that a professional gambler needs... these reads and tells are essentially hints about the psychological state of the person sitting opposite you, and, depending on how good the subject's poker face is, can be used to gain hypothetical information essentially on how *satisfied* they are, either with the fortune that was just read, or the card hand they were just dealt. Another example of similar hypothetical psychological information is the concept of the "sales lead" commonly used in any professional sales; a lead is a good guess for a potential buyer. There are common metaphors of e.g. reading the mind of the other and seeing the thoughts of the other, and advanced skill in this kind of reading implies psychological and sociological knowledge of human behaviour; knowledge that involves associating behaviours, expressions or gestures to the psychological states that underlie people's strategic decision-making in a particular context. The strategic contexts of gambling at cards or real estate sales are clearly established, but also one should note that a session with a classical fortune-teller is always restricted to a particular context that is articulated beforehand, for example finding a life companion or making a strategic investment. A classical partner-finding session will not say who the right partner is, but will produce suggestions about the *appearance* of the right partner (the hair colour), which translates to attempting to give confidence about what kind of partner the client should be *looking for*... naturally, as the fortune-teller has no idea who the people in your life actually are. The context needs to be restricted beforehand, and this rhetorically looks like the fortune-teller needs to know what you are trying to achieve, but actually what happens here is that the restriction of context is essentially the restriction of the context of discussion, which is why you are asked to restrict it yourself before starting the session. It means that *you* need to know what you are looking for before entering the session, and the consultant is just using the restriction of context to make *you* focus on that context only, which simply has the effect that the behavioural "tells" you display are tells of *your* satisfaction or dislike of the outcomes *in this particular topic*. It means *you* are not allowed to be thinking about anything else during the session, while the fortune-teller basically shuffles through various options veiled in his routine rhetorical act on this topic. You need to be in a *suggestible state*, *commanded* by the rhetorical act, and if successful, one of the options *suggested* by the fortune-teller will snap, resulting in a big "Yes, this is the answer I was looking for!" You have now received "advice" (and a bill) from the fortune-teller, which, to be accurate, is not advice, but simply an act where one of the options you already knew was somehow made subconsciously desirable to you while you were in a suggestible state. And this has nothing to do with whether the option is right or wrong, as the source of its acceptance by you is your own desire, not reason; rather you entered the session exactly to escape your reason, which you found gave you no peace over the matter. This is no different from how some people like to escape life dilemmas by hitting the bottle, and the result should be expected to be of similar reliability. The metaphoric nature of mind-reading can be seen by asking for the criterion of reading, which is completely different from reading text, since text is objective but thoughts, feelings or emotions are subjective, but the sense of mind-reading is evident and supported by the fact that there exists a tradition of mind-readers that profess an art to make a living. It is just reading in a different sense—a sense that is easy to subjectively imagine. And this linguistic confusion regarding reading is what gives an occult nature to anything that views mind-reading in the sense of reading or tries to study mind-reading with the methods one would use to study reading.

There is no such thing as ontology or metaphysics. From an objective perspective such is a logical mistake, and from a subjective perspective, devoting one's intellect to attribute qualities to objects is a way to guarantee one's object-relative life as a subject. To believe there is any sort of final solution to be found with such an approach is simple confusion, since the finality of an ontological system would require it to be satisfactory, which is not an objective quality. Such philosophy will miss the whole point of satisfaction, which is a subjective state and related to the relation between one's effort and experience of success. An object-related intellectual—since he is object-related—misses the connection between what he is trying to find and why *he* (as a subject) is trying to find it. A satisfactory result for the subject is one that serves his purposes, and in the case of a philosophical system this would imply its communicability for everyone, because he is not trying to find *a* philosophical system for himself but *the* philosophical system for everyone. Yet if it is going to be a system for everyone he surely hopes that everyone with a desire for philosophical enlightenment would read it and understand it, which might have implications for the form he chooses to express his thoughts in. But secondly, if he sincerely hopes that people would read it he should ask himself the question: Why *should* they read it? He would surely not be ridiculous enough to imply that his system is "the one and only system" he has discovered. Instead he would most likely refer to some objective qualities of the system, such as clarity, simplicity or explanatory power. Yet it can be seen that these are not qualities that people generally expect from philosophy unless interpreted from a very specific context. One might say of such a system: "When I asked for the meaning of (e.g.) 'truth'—I meant something different by 'truth'. I have lived my life, learned the word 'truth' and used it all my life but found that there is something I don't understand about it. Now you are asking me to study and learn something I have never heard of—but I swear I never had such things in mind when I asked my question in the first place!" This is to say that a philosophical system is a red herring, since it tries to answer a question with an alternative meaning of the word—creating a novel objective criterion, being the system itself. Another potential answer the object-related intellectual might give is that the question is not up to him to decide; an approach made possible by academic philosophy that borrows from the quality of science that factual information produced doesn't need to be useful at the time when it's produced. This is wrong, however, since philosophical systems are not factual information but suggestions for a subjective way to relate to factual information. They have no empirical grounds as scientific information does but only a subjective guarantee that it would be worthwhile to apprehend the system, and the question of whether one should apprehend it is an ethical one, related to whether apprehending the system will make one better or not. If a philosophical system won't receive a favourable response from the actual readers to whom it is presented, there is no reason to think it would get such a response from future generations. And this is unlike scientific results, which may well find later application.

Furthermore, following from the fact that ethics is not a system of doctrines and that there is no ontology, the following two definitive conclusions can be made.

1) There is no such thing as philosophy as a science, since philosophy doesn't study objective reality and cannot use empirical methods.

2) There are no philosophical systems to be found.

Instead any philosophical result in the form of "The state of affairs is such-and-such"[69] may potentially be valuable only in its *ethical* quality, in the sense that apprehending such thought implies becoming a better human. Implying the *truth* of any philosophical statement is equivalent to believing it and that apprehending it and thus seeing it as a truth would be helpful for *any* subject. This, however, places the emphasis in philosophical work on totally different kinds of activities than engineering philosophical systems that require from their audience something more than a willingness to understand *more* via understanding the philosopher, the *human*.

---

69 Such as the statement "There is no ontology", c.f. *Tractatus* 4.1 and 4.5

I-6. The Nature of Ethics and Aesthetics

I would like to express my awareness that my writing about ethics or aesthetics is hypocritical, since these subjects lie in the subjective realm, and so the basis for the claims I am making is not, relatable by an audience. I will never write about my personal aesthetical appreciations, since they are subjective to me, and I treat them as such and keep quiet about them. But many statements I make in this book are generic, relating to human nature as it were, and I consider them subjective in the sense that they strictly are not theories and I wouldn't want anybody to take them as a basis for further *study*. However, if somebody were to learn something from such philosophy, by all means one they should relate to what I have written, consider it and evaluate it, and along with this evaluation, evaluate *me* as a subject. The hypocrisy lies in my requirement to write about such things in a universal sense, by stating things that are the result of my subjective perspective, as a result of my self-important feeling of having acquired some subjective wisdom to generalize about humans and human nature. If I was completely honest, such things should not be expressed as generalizations at all, since they have no objective criteria. If I was a very wise person, I should rather just make friends with people and try to spot opportunities where I might have the potential to help them grow to overcome their existential trouble, *and then not talk about the troubles objectively* but subjectively. This is something I have never been very good at, and any good teacher will be better than me in it; I am somewhat cursed to always remain an abstract theoretic who tends to exist in thought. By generalizing my subjective observations, I am making an *expert authority* of myself; making myself into somebody who can announce objectivity without objective criteria for his claims. In early societies this role was that of the holy man, who, by this formal role in society, himself *is* an objective criterion. And I suspect that my credibility is not at all elevated by the confession that such behaviour comes with a related feeling of being unashamed: I am fully aware of my incapability to ground my subjective arguments objectively or rationally, yet I shamelessly generalize because I *believe* what I say to be the case, and many of my related beliefs are such that I would be unable to denounce them *or* to change them in response to an argument, since no rational or objectively factual argument can touch the subjective realm, and I believe that, in the dialectic via which I have come to my conclusions, I have already taken into account enough subjective argumentation in order to reach certainty. This certainty is a subjective quality and can't be defended; it can only be challenged by somebody else, which I invite. Surely such a statement is an absolute faux pas in any academic discussion where, by the very ideals of the institution, only objective and rational grounds create institutional equality. Thus, let my writings about human nature be accompanied by this apology for the dishonesty of pretending to be an expert in something in which there is no presentable subject matter, and no related special skill as a means to prove my expertise. If I am to be a problem-solver, which I seem to see myself as, I should be clear that the solutions I offer are *my* subjective solutions, even though I can't seem to help presenting them as universals, which equates to promoting myself to the status of an authority, which I believe I am not. The way to correct myself would be to write as Kierkegaard did; to completely cherish the subjectivity and to make my writing directly incomprehensible, and to make the *exercise* of deciphering it the actual goal for the reader.

The universal basis of ethical concern and thus all ethics is *empathy*, and because our empathy naturally targets all subjects we are able to communicate with, the coherent form of ethical thought is universal among those subjects. I believe this is the explanation for why the word is so often mistakenly understood to have an exclusively positive meaning; something like 'caring'... whereas empathy is not just a positive skill but also the basis of e.g. mob mentality (repeating mob anger) or children repeating parental guilt or shame. Empathy can be characterized as a universal human capability to subjectively feel the emotions of others and is related to an experience of understanding. The relation of the word 'understand' in cases of empathetic and rational understanding (understanding meaning) is in that empathetically we understand that what we interpret the target of our empathy to be feeling, we also could feel ourselves in a similar situation, which contributes to

I-6. THE NATURE OF ETHICS AND AESTHETICS

an experience of sameness and also a conception characterized by "I could be in your shoes" (although in a physical or social meaning this would be impossible). The empathetic comment would be: "Although I can't be you or share exactly what you feel, I understand how you feel." This *personal* nature of empathy, firstly, makes it possible for us to feel empathetic also towards e.g. dogs or dolls, and secondly, means our capability of empathy is directly affected by our personal capability of dealing with our *own* emotions: roughly, denial of personal emotions results in denial of empathetic emotions and thus impaired social existence. The essentially *social* nature of empathy contributes to the social aspect of what is good: since the empathetic subject is capable of sharing emotions, in his effort towards being good he is also drawn to maximize the experience of success of other people in the social group he identifies with. Having this effect on others provokes a response of approval and respect, contributing functionally to the subject's happiness. An empathetic motive by itself by no means equates to being good or doing what is right but is distinctive to any actions regarded as good. As an example, the good actions of an idealist war hero (for a war that is considered justified by the people) are based on an ability to maximally nullify empathetic feelings towards the enemy in an extreme empathetic effort to do good to his own people. He would not be able to intentionally perform those actions without empathy towards his own people regardless of his personal well-being, and a way of keeping a clear conscience while silencing his empathy towards the enemy. Rather, uncontrolled use of empathy is equal to suggestibility, and a person like this is prone to repeat the rational suggestion made by another when it is delivered with an emotional request for approval. This is all the more likely if the request for approval comes with some kind of threat, such as disapproval or confrontation, or in the worst-case violence, abandonment or some sort of material harm. The sort of people who respond to this are easy prey for manipulators of all kinds that can smell this suggestive behaviour from miles away and take similar pleasure in being in the position of control over another person as, say, a truck-driver feels when being in control of a large vehicle or a classical composer feels being in control of a world of musical expressions and an orchestra. Every person is capable of empathy; it is an intrinsic pack animal disposition shared by at least dogs and monkeys. Yet, the subject's existence dictates his conscious relation to it; whether he will cherish it, abandon it or remain internally undecided. In order to be ethical, to take responsibility, one needs to be empathetic, since ethics is action intended to show example, and not action intended to invite attention to self. In order to feel responsible over others one must feel the need to help others; that others are in need and dependent on one. Every child is born to empathy, wanting to be good relative to what our mother expects of us: we are linked to our mother without a conceptual language and without question, with trust and hope. We never lose this capability—as they say "there's good in everyone"—yet the subject can lose his trust in empathy and his hope in its usefulness in reaching success in his life and choose to reject it. Such a decision is made after a prolonged experience of actions based on empathetic feelings leading to emotional disappointment and suffering and involves an experience of relief and satisfaction out of the denial of empathetic feelings and the destruction of the aesthetic symbols related to those feelings. This should be called an existential change since it is connected to what the subject finds necessary, albeit that because of the social nature of what is good and appreciated it can be said for certain it won't contribute to the subject's happiness but quite the opposite.

Only through empathy can one share another subject's emotions, which is a requirement for the ability to evaluate his choices: to approve or reject them—otherwise a display of appreciation or disdain isn't genuine but based on something else, such as personal wants or official position. These emotions in our relation to other subjects lay the basis for our willingness for existential change: we either follow someone's example or advance to avoid having to follow someone else's, and hence the subjective necessity for role models and heroes, but also for examples of the opposite (anti-heroes). Now, the subject that has undergone an existential change would often describe the experience in terms of having *found* a solution, or that he has found the right way of thinking. The experience is such that the subject is becoming aware of some objective rule or quality that already applies for everyone. So, the ethical shows itself as objective *for the subject*, and this is the impor-

I-6. THE NATURE OF ETHICS AND AESTHETICS

tant factor of the meaning of 'ethical'. If the subject now writes this out in the form of a doctrine or a rule, whether it can legitimately be called an *ethical* doctrine for anyone else is solely a matter of whether those other subjects have undergone a similar existential change that yields the doctrine as a discovery, or if they are willing to do so. The doctrine might be very useful in the sense that a lot of people find it agreeable, which is a *political* function (in the sense of general society-level change, not in the sense of the political system), but political doctrines are always followed by the masses for non-ethical reasons, which are many and varied and include peer pressure or a sense of justice of general adherence to existing rules and laws. Thus it is a fallacy to think that ideals or actions themselves (by their results) are ethical because ethical thinking involves an experience of universal necessity, but they are ethical only in reference to having emerged as the result of certain individuals having performed ethical thinking and undergone a subjective existential change as a response to their environment. To call an action, an ideal, or, say, a product, *ethical*, implies a precondition in the society where such a change is desirable for certain individuals. If free-range eggs are called ethical, this is only because our society induces a sense of injustice among some people which has given rise to demand for the product, and free-range eggs have been associated with ethical thinking to better highlight them in distinction to other eggs. Should society decide such that free-ranging should be the norm in egg production, there would be no need to call free-range eggs ethical, and because of this it would be false to call a doctrine promoting free-range egg production ethical (instead of political), despite its sense of universality. The conclusion is that *every effort to pronounce an ethical doctrine will result in the birth of a political doctrine instead*, and the scope of the ethical is restricted to the subject only. This explains why an effort to "find" an ethical system in form of universal laws—initiated by our sense of the universality of ethical necessity—has not in 2400 years of Western philosophy resulted in the emergence of a system that would to any extent satisfy our philosophical search for what is right in the form of producing the right answers in particular situations. The word most closely related to ethics, 'right', is very similar to the word 'truth' in its subjective nature; from a linguistic perspective, neither word denotes *any* particular *type* of thing, but a subjective relation to something that, from the perspective of existence, could be described to be in a semi-existent state such as concealed, forgotten or emerging, but one that is already in an existent state in the perspective of the subject inclined to use the word. To be able to call something right there already needs to exist a subjective alternative of wrong, and in situations where there is only one choice for action such words are never used. In such a subjective state, it is the *act* of admitting the truth that brings it into existence, and this is something that can be very difficult for people with a self-deceptive inclination in relation to some matter: they can avoid the act of facing and admitting the truth despite expressing no clear objection to any fact. And people often need the help of others to overcome this difficulty: it is the main constituent in what is called *confession* and the motivation behind *therapy*, but it is also a very basic human social requirement. Every day people need to talk to others in order to see and understand themselves; to bring themselves into a situation in which they are *socially provoked* to self-reflect and to reveal truths at the same time to the other person and to themselves; to bring themselves into a situation where the shame of not admitting the truth overcomes their shame of admitting it. People who actively or methodically self-reflect or search for truth outside such social interaction are rare, and for many, if not most, showing oneself constitutes the major subjective challenge as a primitive subconscious fear. The social function of both 'right' and 'truth' is to bring change into people's understanding, and thus it can be said that 'right' and 'true' are used to *teach* somebody something or to communicate in an effort to share a perspective, as they imply a subjective conviction of seeing that such a thing is true or right—interestingly, both words are used in English for signifying agreement in subjective perspective: "Paul can be a real bore sometimes.—Right/true". The subject is inclined to say "Yes, you are right" or "I was wrong" after something happens in his subjective existence, and what this is cannot be described due to the subjective nature of this process; different people have different internal dialectics. But both signifying agreement in opinion and saying sorry are very significant social acts, having strong effects in the social fabric.

I-6. THE NATURE OF ETHICS AND AESTHETICS

The subjective nature of ethics also gives birth to a phenomenon called *ritualization*, which is both a subjective and a social process. That the ethical—what is right—cannot be expressed in doctrines, doesn't diminish our wish, firstly, to pass on to others what we feel is right, and secondly, to follow the individuals that impress us and that we find exemplary. Consider a man who spends many days in introspection, sitting by himself, distancing him from others by looking down (or up) and isolating his hands from impulse for action by crossing his fingers. His efforts bring results, and one day he experiences an epiphany; a revelation that instructs him what to change in his own life in order to be relieved of his problems. He is unaware of any psychological basis of what happened; all he knows is what he did, how he was sitting, how he held his hands, and also what the content of his revelation was. So, these factors form a causal model where a particular kind of action possibly leads to revelation and spiritual healing. Others see the change in his character and are impressed and interested; they'll want to learn what he did to reach such a radical change. So, what he can tell them is that he was sitting with his head bowed and fingers crossed, and that he didn't *do* anything supernatural (even if what happened to him might be called supernatural), which means that if one man can do it, another man can, too, which means it is possible for *any* man. So, he guides everybody to follow his example. And this is where the ritualization kicks in: the student will be asked to repeat the external form of the behaviour: to sit with his fingers crossed and to utter words that follow the example of the man with the epiphany. The only standard against which the correctness of this action can be evaluated is the external behaviour; to do so means to be on the right path. In a ritualized institutional form, action—doing the right thing—is not the result of *subjective thought* (more accurately put: rationality is not the standard against which the correctness of action is interpreted), but *that* the action is committed is interpreted as its standard. Whereas rationality is human social behaviour where action is socially justified by giving reasons that originate from underlying subjective thought, ritualized action is something in which no rational requirements are presented for the underlying thought. And this is a form of social action that has the quality of giving complete freedom to the subjective motivations of individuals participating in the related rituals, as long as they appear in the *role* of a person who performs such actions adhering to their ritualistic form. The example I'd like to give here is modern science: it is something that in its earlier form used to be close to both religion and philosophy in rhetoric; there were deeper subjective questions to be found out whenever science was to venture to find out something. All our fascination related to science, our image of science as something mysterious and wondrous, is related to those times and our success in related discoveries, mostly in the area of physics. But times have changed; now science is trying to achieve "full objectivity" ... and it is exactly this that gives research plans maximum subjective freedom; there are no rational requirements anymore; the plans can be as conceptually contradictory or pointless as they like. Science has succumbed into a ritual role, where the only thing that matters to succeed as a student or researcher is to repeat the various rituals of correctness, and the role of those studies is also not creative but instrumental and subjected to external use: corporations and politics fund them and use them as a rhetorical basis to communicate their wishes to citizens; politics and corporate power are communicated through the mouth of scientists, the new ritual clergy.

A subject's relation to the concepts he understands is *unique*, and words and methods of expression bear a personal emotional connection, related to the subject's unique personal history and past emotional experiences. A scientific correspondence can be seen in the theory of neuroplasticity of the brain in which changes in the neural connections in the brain are seen as a function of the experiences of the animal in question: every person surely has a unique history of experiences. And this is not at all to say that the mind has some "neural correlates" to be found in the brain... such an idea is assuming that perceptions or memories are data, which they clearly aren't; data is essentially messages of communication from one person to another and is created and received by a subject. What I am suggesting is that as we could interpret consciousness as the full brain state, we should expect to see existence as a brain neural constitution; to think the same way ("along the same lines") means to employ the same neural patterns, and to

I-6. THE NATURE OF ETHICS AND AESTHETICS

start thinking in a new way means that this pattern is somehow structurally altered in a way that is novel to this brain yet has no significant similarity to other brains. In any case I don't find the brain at all philosophically relevant, as that would be the same as trying to teach sport and concentrating focus on the macro- and micro-level functionality of individual muscles, which is not at all relevant; the only thing that's relevant is how to use and train those muscles in the sport. Because the subject is unique in this way it cannot be fruitfully targeted with a philosophical approach that gains its relevance from attributing the universality of the subject's relation to the concepts he understands, such as phenomenology. A *philosophical problem* arises from a conflict between the subject's relation to a concept (the way he understands its meaning) and his satisfaction with the outcome of his actions in using the concept in his environment. It is as Wittgenstein noted—philosophical investigations are conceptual investigations… and I might add that as they are conceptual investigations they are also purely *rational* investigations. Misusing concepts, meaning *unwittingly* using concepts in a way that is different from the way the people addressed use them, *de facto* will result in not being understood or some sort of a conflict, which in practice affects one's satisfaction with the outcome of one's use of the concept. On the other hand, deliberately using concepts in a different way from the way the people who are addressed use them might serve an ethical purpose through implying that it is the right way of using them. An existential change not only changes the way the subject acts but furthermore changes the way the subject *thinks*. In the subject's experience this has the paradoxical-seeming result that philosophical problems can vanish and new ones can emerge, and it happens to be the case that philosophical problems generally are problems that the subject won't solve theoretically but can *overcome* through changing his subjective relation to the concepts he understands. Thus philosophy is essentially a process of therapy regarding the way the subject thinks: as opposed to a classical view of philosophy as an investigation of what *is*, the philosopher essentially asks because *he* is not satisfied with the outcomes of what *he does* as a result of how *he thinks*. Then of course, having reached some enlightenment, the philosopher can try and assist others on the same path—in the same

PART I. THE BASIS OF THOUGHT

way as Wittgenstein saw his work as erecting signposts at junctions leading into linguistic traps.

To avoid accusations of being a cultist Wittgensteinian, I think it is good to point out that as much as I admire him, I believe the main cause of him disliking ethics as a philosophical topic was that he simply didn't understand it, and that he was, so to say, a slightly unusual character in this sense. It seems to me his approach to philosophical work, and the people he respected as professional philosophers, was that he was striving to create a professional atmosphere of relentless philosophical work that would minimize wasteful moments of empty socializing. Workaholic? —no, just one of those greats in their field who has realized that the key to success is absolute commitment and immersion into one's professional role. But he could never be a leader of people (or a successful teacher) because he didn't understand human weakness; he denied it in a way that is rather traumatic. Considering him as an intellectual authority among his peers, it is one thing to expect full commitment from your work crew but quite another thing to take their moments of weakness as a personal insult. He knew *precisely* the categorical subjectivity of ethics and the futility of trying to teach ethics, but that's where his analysis ended: he saw that ethics has no place in science or the sort of philosophy that strives for conceptual clarity. As a philosopher, he could pinpoint the rightful place for ethics, but refused to touch the subject because it was too personal for him; his private notes reveal he had profound secrets about himself that he didn't want to face. These secrets were related to his tendency to lie and caused him a lot of guilty feelings. He confessed white lies to his colleagues that they found insignificant. He showed a way to analyse the use of 'good' to mean approval in most cases of its use, but that the use of the word is infinitely *complex*.[70] What is "complex" about goodness?—I would call that part of life simplex: empathy, approval, acceptance and forgiveness; but I know this is simple only for the people with a capability to it. He saw that 'good' is used—along the lines of his standard chess analogy—in a "terribly complex game" along with pieces like 'ought to do', 'conscience', 'shame', 'guilt', 'bad', etc. Now, this chess analogy is a

---

70   Conversations with O. K. Bouwsma

I-6. THE NATURE OF ETHICS AND AESTHETICS

metaphor for *language*, but given the question of what might be going on in the mind or soul of a human when he is inclined to use such game pieces, this sort of an answer, of course, says absolutely nothing. What strikes me, however, is Wittgenstein calling the use of ethical concepts "terribly complex" and also his examples of the use of 'good' drawn mainly from contexts such as encouragement in moral training for children and religion. From Wittgenstein's life we know that he tried working as an elementary school, primary school and secondary school teacher, and we know that although he was a passionate teacher he had no skills whatsoever in dealing with children apart from those favoured by his selected learning topics and methods (whom he favoured to the extent of trying to adopt one). He was described as a nervous and tyrant-like teacher who had little concern over what might be expected from a student. He switched schools and expressed his disdain towards his students in letters. When his antics of excessive and sexually egalitarian corporal punishment started bringing him serious trouble from the rest of the school staff, he repeatedly lied about the corporal punishments and had to end his career by resigning and lying to the court in the subsequent trial. The judge suspected that he was mentally ill, and this seemed to be the shared general understanding of the villagers and school staff, who were concerned about the welfare of the children. Years later, he returned in an effort to apologize to the students he had hurt, which shows that he regretted his own actions and wanted to make amends no matter how shameful, clumsy and ridiculous that action might make him appear. These reports very clearly indicate that Wittgenstein respected and was interested in teaching, but he—to the detriment of both himself and to others—could not relate to the children's emotional world to understand what kinds of games they play. A roomful of children can psychologically overwhelm an inexperienced teacher, so he must silence them by means of authority and punishment if he knows that he can't win them over in social intercourse. The nervousness of a teacher is a sign that he doesn't feel he is in control of the social situation; that he feels anything might happen and he doesn't know how to respond although he knows he is responsible for what happens in the class. I believe Wittgenstein was fundamentally missing the skill of empathy in social interaction and therefore, as an ambitious teacher, he was doomed to fail. It is impossible to diagnose someone who is no longer living, but LW would definitely not be the first high-performing person with autism (Asperger syndrome?) in the hall of geniuses. Autistic people are not incapable of empathy like sociopaths, who tend to completely avoid empathetic levelling with others and isolate themselves into constant grandiosity, but the tendency of a high-performing person with autism is to replace empathetic social interaction with an abnormal intellectual feat, and this passion for using intellect instead of empathy can easily lead to paranoia, as intellect elevates suspicions and not using empathy incapacitates the ability to read other people's intentions. Empathy is like a sensitive pain the autistic person shuns emotionally and reactively, yet they might intellectually understand its necessity and restrict its use to private moments (I have observed this in someone with autism who I know well). This would explain perfectly why LW didn't *like* ethics—a discourse based on our capability of empathy—and at the same time he held Kierkegaard (a highly ethical and socially intelligent author) in extremely high value yet paradoxically said that K. was too difficult for him or that he could sometimes only read a few lines at a time. Ethics puzzled him; he could see to reject the errors that other thinkers were making in writing about the subject and he didn't neglect the subject by any means, but he himself, in his role of a strictly professional philosopher, found the topic desperately unintelligible—and therefore to reject the whole matter showed perfect intellectual honesty. He saw that in each of the different religions the leaders of the religion presented their religion as 'good', but when different religions contradict each other, a big mess ensues that he could make no sense of. Wittgenstein would never actually live a harmonious social life in a social group either, but because of his lifestyle, also supported by his wealthy background (which greatly bothered him), he managed to avoid the necessity to do so. Wittgenstein would present moral upbringing as the sort of authoritative process he might himself have been brought up to. However, in order to develop morally to acquire a higher social responsibility, a child actually needs *humility*, which can only be achieved through being confronted with the consequences of one's own actions. Otherwise one's moral judgment over others is simply hypocrisy, up

I-6. THE NATURE OF ETHICS AND AESTHETICS

to the point of the fundamental empathetic revelation: "Who am I to judge others? *How* do *I* determine whether their sins are greater than mine?"

Following Kierkegaard, existential change involves a personal process of renunciation to escape angst. It seems to me that angst is nothing more complicated than a personal *sense* of dissatisfaction with the outcomes of one's actions; a feeling, once one has acquired experience over the outcomes of one's actions, that something is not right. This evolves through crises that result from changes in our *social role*: the thinking that we have adopted, and that has served us in an earlier social role, fails to serve us in a new role. Such roles change typically when moving from childhood family to school and from school to work life and moving from original family to a family of one's own with parental responsibilities, and again, moving from parental responsibilities into seniority. Most visible in more traditional societies and Asia than in the highly professionalized Western society, there is a certain level of responsibility and respect related to a person's age, and that forms an ideal of how a person of a certain age, existing in society in a certain role, should behave. A good child is to obey his parents, a good parent is to take care of his children and good worker to take care of his company's business, and a good senior citizen is to command an even larger responsibility. This creates a natural path towards more responsibility in life, and in Kierkegaard's philosophy this forms the ethical path from aesthetical (pleasure-driven) to ethical (duty-driven) and from ethical to religious existence. It also complies with the observation that the few ethical idealists tend to be adolescents and young adults, and the even fewer very religious wise tend to be of older age. One can see that aesthetical existence reflects the life of a child without responsibility: he is expected to seek simple pleasure and to be taken care of by others, and his decision-making process is dominated by unrestricted immediate liking or disliking. Now, take the aesthetically living subject and put him in a new role in society in which he is to take responsibility over certain matters or other people; or the subject might seek such a role himself by the competitive drive that works to raise his social status. His pleasure-seeking ways will no longer work in view of his new responsibilities, and gradually he will become more and more aware of this, which will be reflected as increasing angst. And it is a matter of the subject's subjective honesty whether this angst will initiate a change to an ethical mode of existence, or if the subject will escape the angst by self-deception. It is a matter of honesty because only the change to ethical existence will give him the social feedback of acceptance and respect from fulfilling the ideal expectations of society, which will satisfy the subjective need for such respect all humans share. The self-deceptive existence in practice impairs psychological development that would match the social development of the individual related to his role in society. Religious existence implies the most responsibility over others, and this is, first of all, reflected by people in religious existence requiring the largest amount of time spent in active remembrance of one's subjective reason to exist religiously, meaning time spent in prayer or religious contemplation. Religious existence is where the subject turns to observe, not only his own capability to act and to show example, but also how this example would be perceived by others. Ethically, one might preach: "You should all do *this*; look, I am doing it!" and disregard the fact that the vast majority of people either ignore you or express interest and conformity out of sympathy yet fail to perceive the subjective reason to take up such an existence. But becoming aware of this ultimate disinterest of others means acknowledging the failure of the world the ethical existent is trying to subjectively create, and so he is passionately trying to disregard it by believing that a change will come. That is why ethical existence leaves the subject desperate, and often leads them to reach towards an idealist utopia. Religious existence is where one sees the need for action but starts paying attention to how to appeal to other people. And this is where the subjective and symbolical language comes into the picture as a much better way to make an impression on people. The skilled preachers of the past would mesmerize and win over their audiences, but also be warm and approachable people. To reach out to people one needs to touch their hearts, and touching people's hearts is not just a matter of cleverly choosing one's words as a speaker but coming to exist as a person with this sort of quality. And from the standpoint of ethics and ethical existence, religions should be seen as a reach towards a higher

I-6. THE NATURE OF ETHICS AND AESTHETICS

form of ethical existence. When people subjectively evaluate whether to listen to the subjective advice of somebody, they will first ask if the preacher himself "practises what he preaches", and they will also ask if the preacher gets some direct benefit from his message, for example whether he is paid to deliver the message. Earthly possessions are the major discriminator; if one wants to preach equality, one needs to do so without earthly reward in order to have any credibility. A paid promoter of subjective equality is a contradiction; such a person can promote equality only as a political device—equality in the sense of some particular political agenda that will be said to advance equality. In this case we speak of equality in certain particular terms, but not equality in the sense of the subjective ideal.

Aesthetics is the subjective emotional response to symbolical qualities expressed in a sensed medium that represent what is valuable to the subject. I also like to call aesthetics the *footprint* of subjective change. As an example a martial artist, in order to be effective and successful in his work, needs to undergo an ethical change to maximize his self-control over his mind and body, and this calls for an ability to clear his mind from distracting thoughts that otherwise are part of normal human experience. This has the effect of bringing simplicity and clarity to the martial artists' ethical effort in becoming good in his profession, and simplicity and clarity become themes of *faith* that help the martial artist overcome his distractedness. The outcome of this process within the martial artist is that he will *want* to be someone characterized by clarity and simplicity, he will be naturally *interested* and see *beauty* wherever he sees reflections of those qualities, and he will *look up* to (openly respect or secretly envy) other people in whom he recognizes such qualities. Another way to put this is that features of external beauty directly reflect the values one subscribes to: what one finds valuable and what one has apprehended in order to become the person one is. Aesthetics is what develops inside the subject when undergoing an ethical change and reflects what is ethically valuable within the context of life where he wants to succeed, and because aesthetics is based on themes of faith, aesthetical values are characterized by a sensation of *sacredness*. But it is not only ethical change but also its opposite, abandoning one's experience of empathy through a sensation of necessity, that develops a corresponding aesthetics. This is what happened with Hitler but is actually very commonplace. Common amoral aesthetic themes are themes of unrestricted profanity, which represents glorifying what once was considered forbidden for the subject: fulfilment of sexual desires. But there also exists a more sinister aesthetical realm that involves obtaining pleasure out of others' misfortune, such as by stealing sweets from a child: working to justify that what once happened to you was not your own fault but could happen to anybody; doing evil in return for the evil you once had to endure and that proved to be life-changing—"loving vengeance". For example, there are many kinds of films that portray violence, and among those films the violence normally takes place in reference to an ethical framework: either the hero is being subjected to unjust violence, or the hero is using violence in a fight for a moral cause. But in addition, in a strictly postmodern setting (deliberately detaching art from its meaning), there are films that portray senseless violence, and I can only understand the aesthetic of this as relating to an experience of having oneself been subjected to unjust violence. The word 'art', as it is correctly used (it is contemporarily used mostly in a meaningless postmodern sense), is to be related only to *ethical* change, and it is precisely this ethical nature of art that makes it both interesting and impossible to define. Art can only be produced by an ethical individual, and it is a means of communicating ethics.

One can see art as *symbolical* communication of *subjective* things, and in its symbolical nature art is akin only to *religious* expression, as a priest in his sermon might apply the symbolical language of the Bible to a practical setting where it touches the everyday moral life of the congregation. Yet there are also forms of symbolical expression that touch the subjective aesthetics of people but that should not be called art, and these constitute the forms of cultural *entertainment*. Consider, for an example, a symbolical work that elaborates the wish to commit infidelity (I am thinking of a particular popular song by a Finnish popular artist). These can be seen to be commonly shared feelings related to partnership that anybody can relate to. Everyone

I-6. THE NATURE OF ETHICS AND AESTHETICS

knows how difficult it can sometimes be to live in a relationship and so they relate to such work, feeling that the artist *understands* them by sharing this sentiment—understands in the sense of how a dog can be said to understand you by showing loyalty that is experienced as an emotional bond. But at the same time there is equally strong consensus that committing an act of infidelity is morally wrong, and this moral nature is what distinguishes art from the commonplace activity of romanticizing things that are, in fact, agreed to be morally wrong. To be justly considered art, the artist should, through his work, also make a moral statement about the matter at hand, but of course, this is not something he can do by simply trying hard enough, because morality is bound to the ethical existence of the artist. This is to say that in order for a work at hand to be justly considered art, it should be *made by an artist*, which, as a word, in itself carries a presupposition of a particular type of ethical subjective existence. Then again, the given example is just one description of what could be *interpreted* to signify the *ethical nature* of the creator of the work. Classically this has been bound to observable features such the technical command of the artistic instrument and a distinguishable personal style. However, these observable features in a work themselves don't justify calling the work a work of art but can only be taken to signify the creator's ethical nature, which constitutes his role in society in a broader sense. The original role of an entertainer in a more primitive society has, however, been akin to a jester or beggar (beggars also provoke our empathetic sentiments); it is only in organized societies that have developed art forms as *cultural institutions* where jesters and beggars can create a real profession out of entertainment, and this activity is based on the abuse of those cultural institutions, presenting their activities as equals according to the norms and standards of those institutions. Governmental or municipal funding of art is justified based on the presupposition that the money is spent on *art*, that beautiful and precious thing that everybody is acquainted with but unable to define, and it is the impossibility of having objective criteria for art that just creates the abuse of such a system. This is why I generally believe it is a really bad idea to fund art in any manner that is reliant on any form of objective criteria, as governments or municipalities are obliged to do due to their democratic nature.

Rather, the question of "What is art?" should not be answered through any attempts at objective definition of art, but should remain a subjective and culturally *active* question, a process where produced works are evaluated and some of them taken as artistically significant, others (most of what is produced) not. As a subjective parallel, consider if we wanted everybody to, in a Christian sense, go to heaven... so, should we set a government office and taxpayers' money to make people good? No, that would just corrupt the sense of the word 'good'; people would work to comply with the set objective criteria and be called good, while everybody would know perfectly well that these people are not actually good but just the boldest abusers of a rigged system.

A successful artistic work succeeds in transmitting an ethical message by means of an aesthetic, grounded in a form or forms of media, such as painting with oil on canvas or musical instruments, and the aesthetical interest will result in an effort to communicate the subjective through the medium. As the artist will see beauty in wherever he sees reflections of those values, he will also feel *disgust* wherever he sees them being profaned; for example if something is presented as a work of art but he can recognize it as a creation by someone who does not share the aesthetical values, which implies that the work has been made for other motives than the aesthetical interest implying the ethical values. Due to this connection between ethics and aesthetics, artistic *taste* can be an effective means for recognizing people's ethical nature. In artistic expression, there is a path in which someone first creates something to find his skills through feedback, and then develops the skills in such a manner that he grows confident that what he is producing is well received. During and after that process, he can become self-aware of his earlier efforts to produce what is pleasing to the receivers, and using his acquired skills, start to change what he used to do, and do it differently instead; and this is where the personal, unique style is developed. What we see from such an artist is work that can be seen to be skilful enough to be easily made to please, but instead is something we can't understand, although the display of skill proves that the artist himself must know better than us. So, such art is a portrayal of ethical change; the portrayal of the subject turning away from his orientation to try and please others, as we all need to do when we are to take any responsibility in life: we need to acquire skills to be useful, but in order to do *good* we need to apply those skills according to our own choices. For the ethical-aesthetical subject who understands a form of art there is a right way of doing, just as there is a right way of living and dealing with other human beings, and witnessing a violation of those values will result in ethical concern and a willingness to actively intervene with the violation. Now, as the purpose of art is to convey an ethical message, the success of an artistic work is related to the ethical nature of the artist, and this can be said to be seen in the subjective choices the artist makes in his work. As Bob Dylan said about his major inspiration Woody Guthrie, he found Woody's music such that one could listen to it and *learn how to live*. I see this as a good basis for the purpose of all art; the artist is to *teach* his audience something, and a great work of art is something of a constant reminder and lesson about what is held in high value in society, or within a class or trade—such as the example of themes of simplicity emerging as valuable for a martial artist seeking clarity of mind. But in a modern society where art is a profession of its own, a work of art that at first glance can seem to embody great ideas, skill and innovation, can instead be mimicry, stolen ideas or just attention-seeking via shock effects. The subjective question is whether to *trust* that the artist's motives in the sense of self-criticism are genuine: if the artist has the morals not to sell stolen goods. The prerequisite of art is a display of skill, and this gives the artist an *expert* position, which from the viewer perspective implies trust that, like all trust, can be abused: something portrayed as art can be opportunism and abuse of the contemporary institution of art. What one asks when admiring the work of an expert artist is: "He could have easily done such-and-such, but instead he chose not to do it, and do *that* instead. Why did he choose to do *that*? It doesn't make any sense!" And these questions are asked in a *subjective* sense, trying to ask what sort of the *subject* the artist is; what is it that he knows that we don't know; what can we learn from him? It seems to me that in all art the valuable content is everything that is original, unpredictable, genuine, inspirational and sensitive. These all are qualities attributed to *children* as they highlight our subjectivity and uniqueness in relation to others, and remind us of

PART I. THE BASIS OF THOUGHT

our childhood: art can touch our hearts and heal our wounds wherever it can *remind* us of who we were when we were still innocent. The question of "What can I learn from the artist?" doesn't need a concrete answer because the answer can come from one's subconscious via remembering who one used to be, before having to face the hardship of adulthood and any existential choices. For example in Western popular music I find the method of recognizing value so simple that I often find it surprising how few people seem to actually the understand artistic value in it, given that popular music has so many consumers: what is valuable is the original subjective choice, which is contrary to the obvious choice of copying what somebody else has made. Recognizing what is original and not obvious just requires understanding of the musical tradition; it takes an understanding of music, the related instruments and technology, and the musical tradition. For this quality there can exist no objective measure, as any objective measure could immediately be associated with a non-ethical motive, and there have always been and there always will be good and bad teachers. The difficulty of ethically evaluating people is a recurring beautiful theme in the films of Kurosawa; for example in Sanjuro, the motives of the enigmatic, harsh and bad-mouthed *ronin* (a *samurai* without a master) hero of the film are constantly evaluated by the resistance fighters he is said to protect; the question is: is he a great hero or a back-stabbing scoundrel? A *ronin* is somebody who is, by definition, disrespecting the samurai ethical code (*Bushido*) by having outlived his master without committing *seppuku*, which will create an ethical problem of trust as he is a traitor from the perspective of his role of serving his *daimyo*. In one particular scene, when the *ronin* suddenly announces laconically that he will sell his services to the opposite side, the resistance fighters are left to ask the question: is he planning to abandon them for cheap money, or is he planning to become an undercover agent in the ranks of the enemy? The opinions are divided: half of them are convinced that the *ronin* has betrayed them, but the other half evaluate his character further, and the main and winning argument is that even though the *ronin* was seen to be impolite towards women in his speech, he did help a fleeing old lady who refused to climb a fence in the same way as men did, by making a ladder out of his own body, low-

I-6. THE NATURE OF ETHICS AND AESTHETICS

ering himself on all fours to enable her to get over. His supporters felt that the *ronin*, although seemingly crude in nature, was not angered by the stubborn impracticality of the lady but was humbled by her purity of soul. And this alone was seen as proof that he is a *samurai* true to his class, despite disrespecting his code—a code with questionable ethics. The smart people in the group took the effort to evaluate the ethical character of the man and chose to trust him after reaching agreement on how to interpret his actions.

Both philosophy and art have *angst* as a common *motive*, but the philosopher and the artist are fundamentally different in that the artist essentially *expresses* his angst through his artistic (public) persona that develops into a *fictive* character. An artist might claim genuineness essentially for the sake of distinguishing himself from fabricated art, but this can be only partly true; he might have invented his character himself, and might identify with it, but it is still his character, not himself, and this distinction of person would often be materialized with the help of an artist's name. The artistic character, that creates the art, is a requirement for the artist, and contradicts sharply with what we mean if we call a person genuine—this is something that entails what we would call being comfortable and in balance and peace with oneself. The quality of being genuine is actually the logical opposite of acting or performing; people who are non-genuine are all the time acting to try and satisfy a social purpose. That the artist is essentially an expressionist correlates with the artist's role in society and the expectation society would have over the artist: we all experience angst, and the work the artist produces, when successful, can help us in advancing with the processing of our own angst. We experience angst because we subconsciously sense that we are seeing the world in the wrong way, as if we were living in the wrong world. A successful artist succeeds in appealing to our aesthetics—the footprint of our already ongoing ethical change—and thus gives support and enforces our faith in our experienced purpose of our ethical change. And he does this through his artistic persona and his artistic medium. It is said that in order to be an artist one needs to have "a wound", which refers to his angst having a traumatic emotional source, which functions as a catalyst. The world of personal experience for an artist is filled by the symbolical repetition of the personal traumatic experience of injustice in everything that he sees, which results in an experience of angst. The case is the same with philosophers; they too tend to come from similar backgrounds, and there is a history behind a man who loves truth more than people. Russell described[71] himself as a man with "cosmic loneliness", with which I can also identify someone I know personally very well. Also, in philosophy the easy temptation is to reach for appeal by putting into words what others already know. The challenge is in being unique but also fresh and contemporary. The same seems to apply to art. But the job of a philosopher is profoundly different from the job of an artist. Whenever the artist experiences angst, he can channel it through his artistic persona as an intentionally dramatic act of communication to others. Simply put: "Why is it that things are like this? — Oh, the pain of it all; woe is this tormented soul, please someone take a look this way!" While the artist externalizes his personal angst into his artistic persona he at the same time escapes the possibility of his angst initiating an ethical change in himself, since the pathetic question "Oh why?" directed at himself from the depths of his conscience is instead rewarded by an external audience. This may result in the artist desperately, obsessively and in vain seeking for consolidation to his personal conflict through his art. The philosopher does not have this option, nor can he have an external persona for communication, but he must, *as himself*, engage himself in the existential search for the answer to the question he finds himself asking. In this process he must cast aside all masks and veils, the comfortable identities that keep us socially mimicking the behaviours of others, which leads us to contradict our own rational and ethical mind in our behaviour. Only after he has come up with some results is he allowed to try and communicate it. That classical philosophical questions (e.g. "What is the meaning of life?") *will* not be answered by searching for an answer to a grammatically wrong question (a question that someone seeing things right would and *could* not ask) is something that produces the suspicion towards philosophy that so many people have. In this modern information age philosophy is totally confused, which is no wonder since the world has changed dramat-

---

71   History of Western Philosophy, Introduction

I-6. THE NATURE OF ETHICS AND AESTHETICS

ically through rapid development of technology. Academic philosophy has been incompetent in addressing the confused questions emerging along with the technology using philosophical (personal) methods, but nearly all of the produced work that even tries to be 'real' philosophy (and not e.g. more or less interpretive biographies of philosophers of the past) has slipped to the dark path of trying to answer the questions with the scientific method: trying to answer the subjective questions with the objective framework. Due to this, despite whatever those philosophers might think or want, philosophy is not respected today by the common man even in a mythological sense but is rather seen as something antiquated and ultimately pointless. The real *philosophical* question of "What?" essentially means "What does it look like?" which, in turn, means "How am I looking at it?" which, in turn, entails "Is this the right way to look at it?" The modern world simply turns a blind eye to these questions; the modern student is uneducated about the fact that these are real questions. He believes he can potentially find out about everything from a single source. The stupidest part is that he believes scientists will ultimately answer these questions.

There are no scientific studies of subjective phenomena, apart from, say, studying how people tend to behave in situations, which can't be called understanding of the related phenomenon due to the subjective being transmitted via *empathetic* means. In fact, there are many such attempts but they fail through either providing no understanding or being unscientific. Objective study of the subjective creates occultism. It is rather subjective *art* that can be seen as the correct way to *study the subjective*, and this explains the global cultural pervasiveness and importance of art due to its importance. It also is the reason why I like to use examples from the world of art when discussing the subjective.[72] The purpose of art is to *portray* the subjective, and it has this purpose because, due to the nature of language, there exists no sensible way to talk about the subjective; subjective understanding needs to be passed in a way that one can emotionally relate to via our intrinsic faculty of

---

[72] This habit can be portrayed as trying to defend real arguments and solve real problems using fantasy examples. To that I would like to respond that not all people can tell fantasy entertainment from art–a subjective study.

empathy. As an example, the purpose of a work of *drama* is to transmit understanding of a subjective phenomenon, such as hate, distrust, envy... or various such phenomena. The dramatist creates scenes with characters that, similar to the way *an example* works in language, bring about an ethically relevant subjective phenomenon. He also writes the dialogue, but more interestingly, *monologue*, which is a highly interesting theatrical form because it is usually written to portray the subjective "inner dialogue" the person is experiencing and that can be empathetically related to. Operatic lyrics are classically a pure mixture of spoken dialogue and experienced monologue; something like "What do you want from me? I feel so confused, why is this person talking to me?" and so on, and this form of using language emphasizes and *portrays the subjective* we call *dramatic*. Nobody speaks like that in personal life, but dramatic expression is extensively utilized in political rhetoric, where the person seeks public support for the things he expresses as his personal beliefs. In this sense, a dramatic or a political role is role like any other, except that in drama and politics, what is represented are personal beliefs. Inner dialogue is sometimes dramatically expressed with a voice that is heard yet the character is not seen to say. Next, an *actor* performs the given character in a staged manner that we also call dramatic.[73] An actor is a professional at portraying the subjective. He will use expressions and gestures with the proper practices of the dramatic form: stage actors learn to use e.g. accentuated facial expressions and primitive body and vocal gestures to overcome the low visibility and audibility of the theatre arena, opera singers learn to not only technically use their singing voice as a part of the orchestra[74] but also to transmit the dramatic content of the play, and the highest virtue of the modern film actor is to excel at portraying difficult subjective states with maximal realism, such as to portray authentic crying (although this has been to a large extent replaced by technical methods). Now, these professions and methods are the *instruments of drama* that the writer, the actors and the rest use to por-

73 In cinema, the dramatic tradition has recently been challenged by a movement emphasizing realism, which reflects the capability of film to transmit dramatic content with technical means such as camera close-ups.
74 The emblematic 'prima donna' is a technical term from the perspective of writing musical score. It means the first female voice in the operatic vocal ensemble that typically consists of male and female voices.

I-6. THE NATURE OF ETHICS AND AESTHETICS

tray the dramatic study of the chosen subjective phenomena, and this activity has a very clear scholarly function: to provide subjective understanding and wisdom of relevant human social phenomena. Art can help us better understand our own emotions and reactions and thus give us better rational control over our decisions in our lives in organized society, and similarly art can help us understand the reactions of other people in social situations that would otherwise seem unknown or novel and thus threatening to us. This invaluable function of art and the related fame and respect gives the historical works of art their astonishing monetary value and can be observed in tourists flocking en masse to photograph the great cultural works of other countries while not necessarily even being aware of the historical or artistic meaning. Now, from this very evident but often neglected perspective the contemporary postmodernist/structuralist conception of art, which on the level of definition is absolute Wittgensteinian nonsense of the most severe kind, is brutally violent as it functions to exterminate art in this scholarly function; denial of faith and extermination of religion being the standard atheist motive and postmodernists and structuralists being outspoken atheists: Derrida, Lacan, Lévi-Strauss, Foucault and so on. Many of these atheist writers would cherish the atheist Nietzschean theme of God being dead, which in itself symbolizes this exterminating function. These are people to whom the writings of the worst case of documented God-hating paedophile sexual offender, one whom both the king and his own family wanted to incarcerate and erase from history books, the Marquis de Sade, are to be considered the highest philosophical existential works, because they allegedly reveal the dark side of contemporary elitism. This is simply a revolutionary political move and a below-the-belt argument to associate contemporary leaders with paedophiles based on upper class status—with the same argument one can present murder as good and a murderer as a hero: it brings out the dark side of human nature and the political fact that murderers exist; and following this line, serial killers are the greatest heroes, as their deeds portray the most scientific value. One might perhaps elaborate the popularity of de Sade by noting that he is the most condemnable creature in what he chooses to express, which makes him a particularly valuable character in the struggle to overcome the king's private court of justice in his time, and as such, a symbolic hero in the future revolutions that these writers participated in, in arts and humanities. As art and religion both share the method of symbolical expression, it is quite impossible for me to imagine an atheist artist, because an artist should be one to understand a symbolical language, as he is using symbolical language himself. However, an atheist by definition refutes all religious symbolism, which implies a complete lack of willingness to understand. Taking a look at historical evidence of the religious thoughts of, say, Western classical composers, reveals an absence of atheist artists. And then again it is quite impossible for me to imagine an art scholar who is not an artist, except in the same way as I can imagine and witness paid telephone numbers with a recorded message telling you how to correctly place your bets on the upcoming football match in order to maximize your winnings, these recordings very obviously being made by exceedingly generous people who are very far from being rich themselves. Why should one believe anything on the subject of art that comes from a person who has never even tried to understand art but rather works to swindle his way out of trouble by denying or redefining the concept? A common conception for modern people trying to interpret something presented to them under the name of art, is to try and interpret *the work* in itself, detached from any preconception of an artistic motive, instead of interpreting the work from the perspective of what *the artist* might have tried to express with the qualities seen in the work. If one were to simply accept one premise of what art is supposed to be, the idea that art is supposed to *help* and to create a positive change in the world via a scholarly function, such interpretation is like interpreting the works of an expert surgeon as works of art; the surgeon killed the patient with elaborate incisions and cuts and leaves the room with a grand bow while the observing audience applauds, admiring simply the technical prowess of the work. And today especially the field of movies is free to roam for technically skilled directors who are able to create elaborate symbolical works with the purpose of making the audience feel revolted, and with similar addictive success as narcissistic domestic emotional abuse can create. The abused woman feels that if the man is able to make her feel bad, his ability to touch

I-6. THE NATURE OF ETHICS AND AESTHETICS

her on the level of emotion is proof of his importance in what she doesn't understand about herself. Such emotional abuse can use many calculated methods such as baiting: showing understanding and care until the other is perceived to be in a vulnerable state, and then blasting with emotional attack—the method of "cheap spooks" in virtually every modern thriller is legacy from exploitative B-movies that used to be shunned. To see that it is abuse, one can notice that the woman will leave the relationship only after she feels he can't hurt her anymore; she will stay as long as he is able to hurt. So will the audiences addicted to exploitative 'art'; something disguised as art as portrayed under its name, but that is only meant to hurt for control and power.

Regarding the postmodern conception of art in the 21st century, it can be foreseen that a widely accepted nonsense conception of art produces efforts at self-expression that are not ethical and thus artistic even though they are conceived under the concept of art. This has produced certain observable common themes in what is conceived of as art, of which I will here list a few.

- *Decadent* cultural forms are the degraded remnants of ethical norms that are no longer followed because of their experienced ethical value but to fulfil the norm and thus gain popularity and acceptance, and thus distance from their original forms into forms best described as perverted. In short, the loss of common ethical base values results in mass superficiality. The prevalent decadence of the 21st-century West can be observed in the role of filling the subjective emotional void of societal detachment and isolation one brief moment at a time as a behaviour of impulsive, marketing-reactive and ritualistic appraisal of *the symbols* of traditional values, most visibly the values regarding *personal wellness*, including prosperity, comfort, cleanliness, health, power, skill and intelligence. A short list of examples includes the following: hipsterism[75]; promoting an active sex

---

75 I'd call hipsterism an effort to claim the social status related to cultural values, but one that is free from any effort to try and gain any skill in these cultural areas. Typically, the hipster will direct his interest to exotic and extravagant items to portray selective taste and to guard himself from being directly associated with the item, that is essentially a cultural item because of its cultural value that requires skill. The hipster is a collector of cultural items but without the ownership

life but with a focus on receiving personal pleasure; working out to look good rather than get healthy; men joining women in wearing make-up and shaving intimate areas; young adult groups identifying with a subculture of luxury, accompanied with words like 'amazing' or 'extravagant' for women, and 'player' or 'V.I.P' for men; promoting exquisite foods under the pretext of health; mainstream popularization of money games; portraying musical ability by musical subcultures instead of musical interest or skill; portraying intelligence and high education by dictionary-assisted online punditry; constant holiday travelling to portray an exotic and experienced online existence, and the subculture use of recreational drugs the pretext of gaining experiences. These themes will appeal to people in large numbers and are common in entertainment as well as marketing. In decadent social behaviour, the underlying ideology, or the "subject matter" of the interest, doesn't really play such a strong role in determining the behaviour, despite the testimonials of the decadent. Rather, the decadent will use the eroding cultural items to build his own social identity and forsake them the moment they cease to feed him social benefit.

- *Portrayal of cynicism*, cynicism being the emotional disassociation from social phenomena. This is most visible in the portrayal of *senseless violence*, where violence is not seen in the form of traditional social phenomena but most often occurring in a setting of fantasy or a setting where violence takes place but there exists no means to expect or to avoid it and no means to relate the violence to the functioning of society. This sort of portrayal of violence won't help anybody learn anything about the violent nature of humans. It is rather ironic that the general worry about the educational effects of violent entertainment is targeted towards violent computer games where the player controls a hero who *is* existing in an ethical setting, with the violence generally is seen as understandable action, such as Doom, where the character needs to fight his way out of a planet of monsters, or Grand Theft Auto, where the character is a social outcast making a living with crime. This is educational regarding the nature of crime, since many people don't understand that crime and related violence are often born out of poverty. These computer games contribute to the

---
of collecting.

I-6. THE NATURE OF ETHICS AND AESTHETICS

tradition of fiction that portrays violence in an ethical setting, unlike the trend of entertainment where crime or immoral actions are portrayed as inevitable, with the implied mental strategy of dissociating oneself from it.

- *Regression*, which is a psychological defence mechanism (named, by but not necessarily discovered, by Freud) to cope with undesirable events, in which the subject's personality reverts to an earlier state of mental development. Such aesthetic themes are highly popular and commercial in Asia where the role of the individual has been diminished for a longer time than in the West, where the lack of options for individuals rather reflects the relatively recent rise of global capitalism. The most common themes are women trying to look like children and the romantic idolization of toys, pets or fluffy animals. In the West the development of infantile romanticism is making inroads into the consumer market, providing decadent Westerners with aesthetic pleasures guaranteed to be disconnected from any ethical duty or concern for one's society. One highly prevalent modern form of regression is people's preoccupation with pet dogs; dogs resemble children in being immediate, careless and empathetic. They provide an easy source of primal social interaction, and in modern terms are used for this purpose in an addictive manner, apparently due to alienation. I have seen many examples where people's relation to dogs resembles drug addiction in all relevant aspects; quite obviously the underlying neuro-chemical basis is the same.

- *Fantasy*, which is related to the theme of regression and provides a perfect setting for entertaining escapism. Western fantasy entertainment has extended its themes predominantly from Tolkien's book *The Lord of the Rings*, a highly successful novel published at a time when being infantile wasn't yet popular, which can be seen to be, and is confirmed by its author to be, a Christian *allegory* that very obviously borrows its powerful moral lesson directly from the story of Jesus in the Bible: Frodo alone succeeding to overcome the evil oppressor by unifying mutually warring tribes by means of sympathy, grace and self-sacrifice. The entertainment industry will no doubt take any available popular theme and exploit it as long as there is demand in the market, and these popular themes cannot by themselves emerge out of entertainment. Entertainment never innovates, only exploits.

- *Exploitation*, in general, is a common phenomenon in art where the significance of some already existing cultural work or institution is somehow used to gain interest. Such acts involve quickly copying and repeating popular art institutions or ridiculing unpopular institutions. Also, *obscenity* is a popular theme whenever moral institutions collapse. Exploitation movies have historically never been very successful commercially because of their nature as feeding off an existing institution; say, wherever there's an institution against nudity or violence, such as a censorship body responsible for granting ratings for movies, there will be an exploitative entrepreneur offering entertainment nudity or violence, working to slowly bend the margins of what is considered improper or violent to his personal benefit. But the digital nature of the modern entertainment business has brought a new scale to the repetition of themes, as the technology behind 3D graphics creates a lot of interest and is reused time after another in a slightly enhanced form in a very large and dominant class of related entertainment, provided by the digital effects companies in movie productions and the 3D engines used in video games. This rewrites the history of exploitation, as the two major entertainment industries base their income on such an activity.

- *Circus acts* and displays of individual skill without any related ethical theme. Individual skills, which often take years of training to acquire, are experienced as entertaining for a moment because they show something one didn't expect to be possible. Due to this effect nomadic circus productions have historically been providing career opportunities for people with special individual skills, and basically have extended their clown thematic from Italian *commedia dell'arte*, which literally means comedy created by craftsmen (having 'art' equal 'art' as in 'artisan'). Craft—the manner or way of doing something—indeed is the original meaning of the word 'art', and this can be seen to be equivalent to exactly the *subjective quality* of doing something; the skill and way something is done. The social function of art is to extend this tradition of subjective skill to society, just as art in the sense of craft originally did; skill in creating e.g. tools that are beautiful in the sense of art with the Socratic conception of beauty as usefulness, which has become more difficult to grasp in an era of mass-production.

- *Objectionable business under the guise of art.* Because in modern times art is primarily considered a right and not a thing or quality, this is a very alarming situation because it provides cover for ideas and activity that otherwise would be forbidden due to their objectionable nature. We can say that art is flirting with the sick and the illegal and thus providing leeway for this kind of activities; picture evidence from objectionable activities can be presented as art in court. I could give examples like selling elaborate torture devices as art pieces, or arranging occult rituals involving human trafficking or human sacrifice arranged as art performances. The police will have other things to do than to monitor what goes on in the art business, so looking at these things should be the responsibility of art appreciation. If certain things are allowed in art, they are closer to becoming reality; for somebody who wants to produce this kind of business, doing it under the guise of art is an option.

At the same time, stories showing *compassion* towards lower classes have disappeared altogether; no more *To Kill a Mockingbird*, *The Grapes of Wrath*, *Les Misérables*, no 'Hey Joe', no 'Ballad of Hollis Brown' ... no more works that once were shocking in their portrayal of compassion for murderers or criminals. Not because such work wouldn't have power anymore but because such emotions are difficult to portray and nobody ever paid much money for such works; great works of art predominantly involve a significant personal investment by the author for the required artistic freedoms. The superficiality of decadence and the calculation of exploitation work together with the opposite in mind: to maximize winnings in a production timeline and budget that is calculated to fit consumption expectations. The production of other kinds of work is not supported by the industry, which provides the latest technology and standards. The works of our time altogether reflect a lack of compassion towards crimes of passion or even towards people accused of crimes. Compassion is a rare skill; people that have been treated coldly and without compassion will find it rewarding to express themselves in a similar fashion.

Finally, the 21st-century 'art' forms can be described as having an *absence of both tragedy and comedy*, which can be interpreted as the *silent suppression of social critique*. Tragedy is a vessel for communicating injustice by getting the audience to empathize with the tragic character, and comedy is a vessel for communicating justice via having the audience empathize with the justice of retribution: somebody getting his comeuppance. Isn't it a simple expression of justice to laugh when, say, somebody falls over because his shoelaces have been tied together? He is bound to fall due to his own negligence, and to make him fall is to teach him a positive lesson. But if, by contrast he falls, having tried to walk because his legs are in chains due to enslavement, we won't laugh but feel his tragedy: he can't *even walk* because he is so enslaved. It's easy to observe that modern art doesn't contain these elements as means of social critique. Modern art can portray tragedies of things that are completely distant to us, such as Asian acid attack victims, or, say, gay rights (the last two works I have seen that try to use the method of tragedy), the latter of which is the most ridiculous goal because at the same time the art tries to argue the highly dubious yet popular claim that gays *are born* gay. So, the creator of such art is himself saying that he is completely distanced from ever being able to understand the tragedy of homosexuality (or the acid attack victims, as they are culturally completely distanced), yet he is asking us to empathize... but there is nothing tragic about this if we are assuming that the pain can't be felt; that the target character is assumed to be qualitatively different from us. Such ludicrous topics seem to have been chosen deliberately to avoid the real social issues in one's own culture; they escape the real targets of tragedy or comedy into areas where they are not art anymore because they do not function as social critique. Criticizing another culture or criticizing a social group for the implied mistreatment of a minority group, is not social critique but just fuelling the flames of hatred through blame; trying to show that a group of people are not human but barbarians. Real tragedy and comedy both imply a *higher justice*; they imply that there exists a *perspective of beauty to bad things* taking place, which is the ancient knowledge and higher wisdom that seeing tragic injustice will always be heart-felt by all, and that just punishment will always be heart-felt by all. *Critique* or *social commentary* is a more evolved form of communication than blaming; it is something that assumes shared good and common goals with one's opponent. In the great days of tragedy and comedy, Mozart wrote the most beautiful and remembered operatic pieces for the moments where the characters are saying the most evil things,[76] to bring out the *humanity* in the things we most easily want to forget and dismiss as inhuman or barbaric. And of course, it is this humanity that we humans share. But how is social critique suppressed? The answer is: silently and efficiently, by those who fund art aiming to maximize their predicted winnings by refusing to fund critical work. Disregarding subject matter and just looking neutrally at critical work; critical work is *risky*, and the risks involve both angering audiences and angering business partners due to related politics. The logic of the art business can be exemplified by professional poker; those who win in the long run are all players who follow precise, predestined patterns, and it is their ability to follow the pattern in the face of temptations to act upon instinct that gives them statistical advantage in the long run. It is indeed possible to win big with luck and high risk, but to take into that industry and to do it repeatedly—to be a player—one needs stability and planning, and from this perspective, to win by statistics means to win by *minimizing risk*. It is because the business is in the hands of long-term commercial players that there is no social critique and hence no art.

The safest way to assume what will happen next is to assume that history will repeat itself. The reaction against mundane art depicted using realist methods—today, photos and videos of the everyday using image/video editing—has been done before as the Symbolist movement against Naturalism and Realism. Symbolism is the tool to describe the

---

76   For example, the 'Queen of the Night' Aria from *The Magic Flute* ("Der Hölle Rache kocht in meinem Herzen"), and the 'Trio of the Masks' from *Don Giovanni* ("Protegga, il giusto cielo"), are *oaths of vengeance*. Who writes oaths of vengeance today? Evil antagonists are always portrayed as disproportionately inhuman and missing any personality. Both protagonists and antagonists used to be portrayed as humans and therefore as more realistic.

subjective, but this view is ridiculed in today's point of view, as the mundane is what is directly accessible by modern technology. People feel that they have invested their share of money in acquiring this new technology, so art better now be more accessible to them using it. At some point people will wake up enough to understand that art *is* romantic symbolism, and that postmodernism is just a denial of this value base to accommodate commercialism: being "weird for the sake of weird" to attract fast attention to make a quick buck. After this there will be a revitalization of attempts to portray the subjective via the symbolical, but in order for this to be successful, one needs to fall back to a shared *moral* and *spiritual* value base. Who cares about the subjective struggle of the artist if he can't relate to the struggle, being alienated from his values? Such a work is not art; art is made in an attempt to unify, and art will play the integral role of being able to rebuild this shared value base. There are possible paths of shared values, one of which is religion, but others are, e.g., naturalism, animism or shared racial and national identities, i.e. national romanticism. The prediction of what will happen depends on global political development, the integral question being the question about the political motive: Who are to be unified? If you consider being an artist and you'd like to speak to, say, Christians and Muslims, the question you need to ask is: What is it that these people share in terms of belief? Having found that, just express it in symbol and you have a chance to be a famous artist who has created something genuine, as opposed to creating something that has commercial value in being impossible to ignore. Another way is to make romantic art: express the unification by portraying a theme that causes both parties mutual strong emotions. Being a real artist shouldn't be too difficult if you understand and accept what art is and then work to discover the values of the parties you wish to bring together. And when you make real art, you don't need to mystify it by being deliberately unclear about what you are trying to express. Good art has the ability to speak clearly, and this clarity is in understanding what you are trying to achieve. I'd also like to clarify that by having the impertinence to give instructions on how to make art I am not promoting myself as an art critic. Art has this mystery around it due to its cultural value, and there is a preconception that in order to be able to

I-6. THE NATURE OF ETHICS AND AESTHETICS

say anything at all about the subject matter, one needs to be somehow formally qualified. This mystery, supposedly conquered by academic wisdom, is equal to the mystery around philosophy. But these formally qualified circles seem to understand nothing about their subject matter and are walking contradictions: they respect formal credit, because as members of an institution this formal credit is what they have to respect as it is the standard of their credibility, but at the same time they contradict each other's thought and are comfortable with this. So, at the same time they accept that they are right in their own account and position, and that they are wrong from the position of the standard that promotes them. Would you trust a man who says he is both right and wrong; who says you should listen to him but also that you shouldn't listen to him? He *can't* be right, because by trying to teach what he believes in, he would be corrected by the rest of the institution—the institution whose rules he has accepted via bearing its standard—for teaching wrong things. This sort of institution surely is not a place to learn any skill about one's subject matter; schools of art should at the same time be schools of subjective art thought, just as the word "school" would imply one being of a particular artistic school.

PART I. THE BASIS OF THOUGHT

I-7. The Nature of Reason

I would like to approach the problem of reason from the perspective of the modern scientific effort to explain scientific domains as a hierarchy of causally interacting levels. In this we tend to adopt a physicalist perspective where mental functions would be on the highest level, reducing to lower-level functions of an organism that in turn somehow follow the laws of physics. This sort of dream contains an idea of an infinite chain of causes inherent in such a causal hierarchy that was already present in Aristotle's thought, thus setting such a course for future investigation. This was considered by Wittgenstein[77] to be a misconception arising from confusing cause with reason, and indeed one can find *causation* to be an epistemological faculty with no logical limits of application. This is because the sense of the words 'cause' and 'effect' is not grammatically bound to any particular discourse and there is no *a priori* error in applying the words to any pair of concepts in some meaningful context, such as asserting that intestinal stimuli cause dreams[78] or that the phase of the Moon affects menstruation, and such statements of natural language can all be given a meaningful context. In general, we are in a very confused state about reason, and science in particular is in a dreadful rut regarding causation so that even the fundamentals of, say, genetics, are completely under suspicion because we don't really know what causes what. Genes were supposed to cause bodily and mental features, but now it seems the environment is also causing genetic changes, and we know for sure our mental state very strongly causes changes in our environment. Now, it seems to me that Wittgenstein didn't notice that the metaphor of an *infinite* chain in fact suits *reason* and not cause. Consider this example: "The bicycle is stiff to pedal because it is rusty. And it is rusty because it has been subjected to water. And this is because it was not brought inside for the winter. And it was not brought inside because you forgot it. And you forgot it because you forget things." This fluent example is not actually a chain of causes but a *reasoning* in a *dialectic form: you could* insert "Why?" between each sentence, and what is

---
77   The Blue Book
78   This was the dominant pre-Freudian scientific interpretation of dreams.

produced is something that contains many assertions and that binds the phenomenon of a rusty bicycle together with how it is normally stored and that somebody has a tendency to forget his duties. Taking a closer look; the *first* use of 'because'—why the bicycle is stiff to pedal—is *causal* and answered in terms of an investigation of the underlying cause. But the second, third, fourth and fifth uses are all *teleological*: what is implied is that it is purposeful not to subject bicycles to water, to remember to bring bicycles inside for the winter, and generally not to be forgetful. These implications of purpose all concern human practices that are subjective reasons and norms to behave in a particular way. Now, let's try to transform the example into a "chain of causes" with more than one investigative cause: "The bicycle is stiff because there seems to be rust in the chain. And there is rust in the chain because there has been water on it." Now, this investigative causal connection is of a very different type than the earlier examples that concerned norms; actually the second sentence could be better read as: "*That* there is rust in the chain *implies* that there has been water on it", which means that there is no logical other alternative, since we know that rust, as a physical phenomenon, requires water to form. Consider if the second sentence was instead anything else, such as: "There is rust in the chain because there is *a cover* on the chain"; we would rebut it with "That doesn't make any sense". So, the deductive reasoning here—from the general physical knowledge regarding metal, water and rust to the particular case of a rusty bicycle chain—looks like it is a requirement for the *sensibility* of the causal attribution. And this is a highly interesting notion about the sense of causal claims: an illogical causal claim is not false but senseless, and it is the implied causal attribution that creates this restriction—we could also replace the causal attribution and, instead of 'because', say: "...*and* there has also been a cover on the chain", which would make the sentence sensible. But look further: the deduction is not the only option here to make the causal attribution sensible; another option would be to say, "There is rust in the chain because somebody left it outside". This seems equally sensible as saying that "There is rust in the chain because it has been subjected to water, which, in turn, is because somebody left it outside". Weird... but let's imagine another sentence: "I missed the flight (A) because I overslept (B), which is because I didn't put the alarm on (C)". But wait, how is this possible? In both cases it looks like "A because B", "B because C, "A because C" and "A because B because C" are all equally sensible. Let's now switch context and separate C in the example: "I didn't put the alarm on" and add a cause (D): "...because Tommy always wakes up at 8". This "C because D" is sensible as is. Can we now say, "A because B because C because D"? Not so sensible anymore. But can we say just "A because D"? No; completely unintelligible. The "C because D" is a part of a separate causal attribution, because it is a part of a separate context of language use. To summarize this brief analysis here, let's take note that causality is an act of communication where the attributed cause is not arbitrary but an explaining factor within the context (or perspective) of communication, and relative to whatever the speaker is trying to explain. The sensibility (logic) of this causation is within this communicational context, and if one tries to take two separate contexts, where the seemingly same phenomenon or act is explained, they can't be sensibly merged. I know that as a scientist you don't like this answer, but this should be enough proof to show that an idea of an underlying metaphysics of these causes, such as a "chain of causes", is doomed, as the so-called logical nature of these phenomena depends on the communicative context where they are explained. This, in turn, reflects directly to science, such as physics, where the theories always reflect a particular *scope* that the scientist is trying to explain with the theory. A much better metaphor than to consider science as hierarchy of interacting layers is to imagine it as a set of different kinds of observational scopes ('theory' originally means "a perspective", having 'thea', meaning "a view" as in e.g. 'theatre') or other measuring devices, pointing into a murky space. Scopes are of different kinds and technologies and are erected at different vantage points, and their perspectives largely overlap. These scopes then act as tools of explaining phenomena: just as we say, "According to this view/position..." we say, "According to this theory...". This should also shed light on what it means to say that some theory is *true*... it means to subscribe to that perspective—no different, regarding *truth*, from subscribing to any political view. If you say something like "the world is *really* physics" or emphasize that such theories are true, what you mean is that you vouch for that perspective over some other perspective, but truth be told not many people are aware of any reasons *why* they do that but simply take things that are said to be true to actually be true. It is rather interesting to consider what your point of comparison is: do you mean that other scientific theories than physics are less true (if you are saying this, what is your criterion?), or do you mean to promote the scientific methodology altogether? If you promote the methodology, why promote the empirical methodology that is prone to error, over, say, mathematics? I understand very well Plato or, say, Pythagoras, promoting mathematics as transcendental as is, without any scientific institution to promote natural science, but the promotion of physics is difficult to understand except on the grounds of its popularity. The widely noted increase in the popularity of physics has been speculated to reflect the popularity of natural science overall. I can easily relate this to *modern technology* as, firstly, physics and astrology are gaining popularity in these, say, philosophical areas, via things like Higgs' boson, the "God particle" and the cosmological mysteries that people seem to relate to deep metaphysical questions as our technological abilities in scoping the depths of space or other planets increase. A second reason for the rise in popularity of these subjects is that mathematics, the historical "God subject", is not gaining any interest, which is explained by the fact that the study of mathematics doesn't apply any technology. What is experienced as interesting, mysterious, deep and ultimate, is whatever is being probed at with these new technological innovations, and that we have built machines to escape Earth.

The problem inherent in causation within science is that since causation is an epistemological faculty, *valid causes are subjectively and culturally determined.* What science manages to do is to give supporting or countering evidence by showing that a statistical correlation might or might not exist between phenomena. In the case of statistical study "finding" new information, what is always predetermined is the sensibility of the statistical variables, and in a contemporary setting (in dramatic contrast with the past) this just happens to be determined by science in terms of the sensibility of such qualities being attributed to the scientific system. Thus, for example, 'consciousness' is a valid causal agent if and only if there happens to exist a related scientific theory. For example, common social variables are those that are easy to classify due to the existing logical nature of related language, such as age (quantified in numbers), sex (genetically binary) or nationality and religion (distinct due to legislation). It is only the logical nature bound to the objective meaning of these concepts that makes them appear well applicable in terms of causation; if they were not so, we would just consider them less convincing. Thus, whenever a scientist advances to show a causal relation, he does so by either having chosen beforehand 1) the actual cause and effect to be studied, or 2) the statistical variables in a manner of causal applicability, and then advances to find supportive statistical evidence. It is not difficult to see how this liberty in the choice of cause and effect is in contradiction with any hopes of creating a coherent hierarchical (mechanist, reductionist...) system: in such a hierarchy one should be able to flawlessly show how higher-level phenomena reduce to phenomena of a lower level, and this is not in practice possible regarding *any* two such levels of naturalist research. On the contrary, such a model is the theoretical *ideal* that has set the direction of naturalist research since its infancy, with a similar component model in mind as a building architect has in mind when designing a new building and determining the building blocks from which it is to be composed. The value of such an ideal is in its ability to guide the process of building the system *in a controlled manner* (as opposed to a chaotic manner) regarding the people who work within the system and the fields of life that the field of science ultimately serve, and not in any assumed ability to finish the work or to guarantee that the work of the man who works on finishing the surfaces can (even in theory) be done by the brick-layer. Any such hopes are clearly caused by a misunderstanding of the role of science. Also, scientific attribution as the standard of the interpretation of causality has resulted in a constant *cum hoc* fallacy in drawing conclusions from statistical results, because the media have found out that the people involved are in practice unable to determine the sense of such claims themselves, since their sense is determined by the scientific institution. This is why we see so many commercial interpretations of statistics-based scientific results in newspapers; for example: "Musical preferences affect the tendency

I-7. THE NATURE OF REASON

towards drug use." Our world lacks authoritative philosophers to teach them the right way, as our trusted keepers of sacred truth sit relatively silently and with grim faces in the bandwagon of this scientific standard of interpretation instead of honouring the rationality inherent in natural language.

Scientific or philosophical thought that aims for neutrality, objectivity and truth via *criticism* is not *blaming*, although it is very easy to portray negative comments in this way. The common Western rhetoric of approval is the model of Abrahamic leadership, and it should be noted that the possibility of criticism reflects a politically stable situation: one is able to carefully evaluate options when one is in a relatively comfortable position of free choice. The opposite of this situation is one in which one is forced to react quickly to events that are out of one's control, and this kind of mentality is called reactive. Criticism is a particular tradition that presumes a model of action where the justification for the action is a matter of a collaborative decision-making process that either precedes the action or that is willing to steer current ongoing action in a new direction. In our reasoning and argument, the standard behaviour is where a person states what he believes in or shares an action he has committed or is planning to commit, and the rational grounds he has for it. Here he is primarily searching for social support, and when met with contradicting beliefs instead of support, he may respond in various ways. This may work something like the following example.

– *Today I bought a car. It's a good car because of such-and-such. Boy, am I happy with my new good car! (hiding a mountain of insecurity, asking for social support for one's choice)*

– *Oh, you bought that model. It's an OK car but has a bit of a suspension problem. (as if such details mattered in terms of cars, but only on the level of conversation where knowledge is social authority)*

– *Oh yes, I knew about the problem (lying to a social authority to maintain respect) but I chose it because it has such good acceleration. Boy, does it feel good to press that pedal!*

This is followed by the new car owner accommodating the new information into his rational justification for his choice. To say that people are primarily looking for social support means that everybody is willing to receive social support but some people are more willing to receive opposition than others. Receiving criticism, which means reasons that don't support one's actions, choices or preferences but the opposite, is considerably more difficult than receiving support, and receiving criticism is considerably easier within a strictly private conversation with no danger of one's folly becoming public. Then again, the concept of "criticism" here reflects the Western (Indo-European) culture of dialectic, where people express their opinions in public debate, and which implies the inherent equality of the speakers. In Asia, generally, but also in Western hierarchical military and corporate cultures, the rationale of a higher-ranking individual dominates over the rationale of the group, and there is no culture of dialectic: contradicting somebody's rationale means a conflict, and contradicting the rationale of a higher-ranking individual (without an explicit invitation) means social suicide. Also, generally, resolving conflicts between individuals, without resorting to public confrontation, is a highly respected skill. When a higher-ranking individual speaks, he speaks from behind the role of a higher-ranking individual: a contradicting opinion is not culturally appropriate and debating the rationale would only be appropriate in one of close to equal rank. A higher-ranking individual who asks the opinion of individuals of a lower rank shows weakness and jeopardizes his respect. The Western world is currently in a movement towards hierarchical elitism, where public discourse takes place in a setting in which open debate is not expected: the party in power shows its power by not participating in such conversation. This is seen in the USA whenever supposedly democratically elected officials meet the public for questions; asking the wrong questions often results in a prompt removal by force. This is quite a sharp move away from the culture of dialectic as the foundation of Western politics. All in all, the historical basis of this cultural dichotomy between the East and the West is that, unlike with Asian group culture, the Indo-European dialectical culture has evolved from hunting tribes: when two hunting parties meet, the party who wants to discuss (with the dialectic method) raises an open hand in salute, and if the other party responds, envoys can meet with

I-7. THE NATURE OF REASON

hands shown and finally shake hands, which can initiate the dialogue (this makes a lot of sense, since hunters typically carry weapons, so approaching someone and shaking their hand literally shows them you have no weapons).

When we say that *Homo sapiens* is rational as a species, we don't so much mean that we tend to give social reasons (excuses) for our actions, but something different. We refer to *rationalism*, which is an *ideological movement* in Western thought. We mean that one *should* be *rational* (with a little help from God); in the Age of Reason we started to see rhetoric in which God favours men of reason. But to say that we should be rational is to admit that we actually—in a scientific sense—*are not*; we have the capability but we don't generally use it, and to be rationalist means to believe in the capabilities of reason: to always use reason and to trust reasonable conclusions over mere rhetoric. We need to remember that both idealism and religion are grounded in morality that opposes science, and that there is no ideal out there to find out how things actually are. Instead, ideologies purport to enforce a desired outcome—the way things should be—and contrasting this with science we must take note that idealism is primary over the scientific, and science is a very particular and peculiar system that purports to act as a reliable highest standard of objectivity. Equally, it is more common to find people who speak only in terms of their plans or wishes—how they would like things to be—than to find people who speak in realist terms, acknowledging their limitations in achieving those goals. A good scientist aims to bring change by his choice of research, but he humbly enforces rigorous scientific standards upon himself in his work. Therefore, idealism doesn't contradict being scientific but rather is included in it, and the relation between idealism and science is that the rigorous application of scientific principles in work, along with a peer-review process and being subjected to scientific scrutiny, allow work to qualify within scientific standards. I would illustrate this with the following two-dimensional setting.

PART I. THE BASIS OF THOUGHT

	Rigorous methodology	Not rigorous
Idealistic	valuable science	advocacy
Not idealistic	waste of funds	junk

I use this illustration simply to distinguish the relation between the subjective quality of idealism and the objective quality of adhering to scientific principles; since idealism is a subjective quality, one cannot measure it and therefore assess the worth of a study in a reliable manner. Now, to call something *rational* means that *it involves a process of justification by giving reasons*. Reasons are something that also serve a function in our thought, but, essentially and primarily, work to explain and to justify things in social interaction—hence their relation to *argument*. Some people like to speak of rationality in terms of modern notions like "optimality of behaviour", but whoever says that simply means something else and wants to attach the word 'rationality' to it, and is in the business of doing something else than philosophy, such as economics or artificial intelligence. He most likely just wishes to borrow the important notion to make his theories and sayings more appealing, but with no interest in discovering what the word actually means, which is our aim in philosophy. Now, the common misconception is to think that these reasons that people are seen giving somehow causally (metaphysically) constitute phenomena. After all, it makes sense to say that they *should* constitute phenomena, by which we mean that our discourse and understanding should be justified via a collaborative process of reasoning. By this we also admit that to begin with this is *not* the case, because we say that it should be the case. Scientifically, we know that humans are *primarily* (primitively) apes, a fact that we should frequently remind ourselves of, because academic discussion tends to promote reason with a wish to elevate man, which is similar to how in music we wish to elevate keys such that a person's voice appears brighter and younger when it rings higher. This discourse says: "We are all men of reason", and means let's have a rational discussion, using the rational capability that we all possess to some extent, instead of using the other communicational capabilities that we all also possess to some extent. What we have here is a history of *idealism* where we mean that something *should be* the case, but that is—in rhetoric—attributed to *be* the case, which essentially means that we announce *faith* in the *morality* of the matter at hand. We say that it is true because we *believe* it for an ethical reason; we *want* it to be that way, because it is considered *right* in making one a better person. All religious discourse in the world is like this. When somebody speaks like that, one should realize that what is *scientifically* the case is the *opposite*; the statements being made are not scientific statements; an attempt to analyse them as scientific statements is an error, and to make a public entertainment show from this self-induced controversy—misunderstanding something as its absolute logical opposite—means to be Richard Dawkins. Also, to clarify the relation between reason and knowledge, which is not very clear to many, as people are often seen to confuse reasons with the objects of discussion, is to think about it through the metaphor that talking reason is just talking about signposts and deciding which way to go. Essentially, reason serves this *social* function of justifying and convincing people via argument; it's similar to the way a group of people at a junction can spend some time discussing whether to go in the direction of St Thomas' Hospital or Parliament Square— what is at hand is decision-making about which way to go; nobody is required to know anything about St Thomas' Hospital or Parliament Square, yet such knowledge might be useful in justification. Often, in a process of trying to convince somebody, the strongest way is to point out how the *rationale* he gives contradicts the actions he takes, or to find a way to make him open to an alternative rationale; one that he hasn't taken into account. This is called talking reason to a person. If we indeed were rational creatures whose actions follow from reasons, this shouldn't be possible, but rather it is a human basic. We are very pleased with ourselves in that we feel we are justified with the reasons we give. But if you manage to show a flaw in one's reasoning in terms of what action should follow from it, you should take note that this is not nearly enough; he will commonly come up with more reasons, and these reasons can conflict with what he has already said earlier. The reasons we give are aligned with our moral thought and our conception of justice, and if you try and convince somebody against their moral thought, using reasons, the person will be confused but his moral thought and sense of justice will take precedence. He may insist that the reasons are secondary relative to the point he is making, or he may steer the discussion away from this contradiction. To look at reasons correctly from the subjective point of view, they should be seen as a set of rationales that we believe to be true. But any given set like this never excludes the possibility for us to be convinced by a different rationale, which constitutes a different perspective. The role of *logic* here, as conceived in philosophy, is related to the question of whether the concepts that are being used are similarly understood by all parties, or whether there is the possibility for error purely on the level of grammar. But the art of convincing somebody is not a rational process. Rather, the problematic involves essentially the question of how to make somebody believe that your perspective is the right one—that it would be right for him to accept what you say and to follow your example—and in this process the rationale you are giving is secondary, and the primary thing that will reach a person and change behaviour is reaching the person's sense of justice. This idea is the basis of all *rhetoric*: if you want to get people on your side, you should appeal to their sense of justice; to touch on what people experience as wrong, and to offer them a solution via giving you their support. Philosophy, in general, involves the methodology of evaluating matters from different perspectives, and evaluating the credibility of arguments, which translate to these different ways of reasoning about different matters.

Homo sapiens really is rational as a species, but by this we need to mean something very different from reason as an ideal that people should adhere to, and particularly, to contrast *Homo sapiens* with other species in search of points where we differ. I recently watched a documentary[79] that aims to explain the difference in learning between humans and great apes. The conclusion about the key difference was

---

79   The documentary is called *Ape Genius* (PBS Nova: season 35 episode 12) and there is an associated interview with Rebecca Saxe, 'The Ape That Teaches', at Nova Online, http://www.pbs.org/wgbh/nova/body/ape-teaches.html [26.12.2019]. I found the cognitivist framework misleading rather than enlightening and the underlying concept of culture to be erroneous, but these are irrelevant to the conclusions.

I-7. THE NATURE OF REASON

something the scientists called a "triadic attention" or simply "magic triangle": an inclination to learn via a pattern where two individuals, e.g. a mother and a toddler, focus on a particular object, thus forming a trinity of these two individuals and the object. This seems to be something that human toddlers pick up instantly but apes miss a natural inclination for. I find this observation highly enlightening due to the relation to *Homo sapiens* as a *rational* animal—and here we require a correct understanding of rationality where the dispositions of the mind are not isolated but seen from the Wittgensteinian perspective as directly related to *language* and *communication* in a social setting. This particular conclusion the researchers highlighted is no less than the famous Philosophical Investigations §1 with a historical reference to St Augustine, highlighting the very basis of human thought where the elders name an object and the learner is to learn the word by first pointing to it by finger, and that takes place in every family with a toddler uttering his first words, here concluded to be a distinctively *human* activity missing from the skills of great apes. Today's cognitive researchers are equally fascinated by this quality (calling it a *magic triangle*) as was later Wittgenstein, seeing it as the basis of his philosophy along with the Great Minds of the Past. It is fascinating because it is the philosophical endpoint one reaches via the method of asking how one's own introspective mental dispositions and conceptual structures actually are constituted, and most importantly, because it is not an abstract theoretical construct but genuinely *scientific* in that it seamlessly integrates and won't contradict with the results we get from branches of science such as psychology, sociology, neurology, and here zoology. This quality is *not* shared by cognitive science, which is essentially outdated philosophical Cartesian theory. When we assemble the constituting facts—1) that the process of *education* essentially involves two individuals and an object, and 2) that thought is something that operates together with language—we will understand that thought by nature involves two inseparable realms: language as social interaction and language as the conceptual constituents of private thought. Chomsky and his ilk take part 2 as a given from his predecessors but completely ignore part 1, the primary interest regarding where our language, so to say, comes from. An interesting point to look at is desert island outcast survival stories, a theme so popular that it has been featured in a number of reality TV shows because it makes us wonder what it is that gives us skills to excel in a hostile novel environment (our traditional notion of *intelligence*). These stories historically portray *educated men* as successful survivors: the fictitious character Robinson Crusoe was well home-educated, and the likely real-life inspiration of the book—castaway Alexander Selkirk—was home-educated as the son of a shoemaker and tanner: skills particularly useful for survival. For a fresher example I'll refer to a likeable character study in this tradition, the movie *The Edge*, in which the capability of such survival is well summarized: most castaways die of *shame*, whereas the educated, intelligent man is saved by his ability to rely on reason, overcoming the emotional irrationality that takes hold of those who base their lives only on the norms and standards of organized society.[80] Now, the power of education is this: in the Augustinian triadic activity (the mother points at an object and names it, while the child watches and repeats) the subject learns the names of objects—the *concepts*. Say Selkirk had been taught the concepts of leather, tanning, types of needles, sewing, etc. When we think rationally, despite the experience of being free or unrestricted or limitless, we are subconsciously applying the concepts we have learned. When Selkirk looks at a feral goat (he used feral goats for his survival), he is unafraid because he has seen animals tanned, and he thus has the ability to *see them as* sources of natural resources such as meat and leather, and this is something an untrained mind is simply restricted from doing. Essentially, his success comes from him being a rational actor with a conceptual, educated basis to his action. The power of reason over primal emotion is easily observable in tournament badminton, which is a game employing both capabilities. Humans tend to succumb to varieties of emotional irrationality when their game is going poorly and their rational ideas of how to win have been exhausted; some get angry followed by shame; some regress and start behaving as if the game was just a friendly knockabout; some

---

80 The hero of this movie is a millionaire bookworm who is socially inept and withdrawn in daily life but who instantly emerges as a fearless leader after a plane crash in hostile wilderness. The power of intelligence over fear is depicted in the movie as an Indian motif: "Why is the rabbit unafraid? Because he is smarter than the panther."

I-7. THE NATURE OF REASON

apathetically displace themselves and become mental spectators. In all cases their performance collapses significantly; they make elementary mistakes and fail to follow their opponent—which makes sense as they essentially are not doing that but are lost and just trying to cope with the shame of their incompetence. The only successful mental tactic is to stick to one's reason and education; try all the things you know to work, and if you run out of ideas, you should "consult the book": have some simple basic game strategies at your disposal that you can use as backup when all else fails. Submitting to the state of having run out of ideas will lead to complete failure of performance as the result of loss of reason. The same priority of reason applies to showing emotion; some players like to play emotionally, which can be done to intimidate the opponent and might seem a viable strategy, but the downside of this is that if the opponent is reasonable enough not to get intimidated, the emotionality turns into primal anger and frustration, and soon works against its user causing lack of control and primitive reactions. In the higher-level game, players consistently show no emotion; so that they are not limited by their own emotions and also so they don't give hints to their opponent that could be useful in predicting their actions. In battle you need unpredictability and the element of surprise on every level, and if you, for example, show a sign of frustration at a specific stage, an experienced opponent may use that to predict a frustrated move, or if you appear overly confident, your opponent can expect you to try to play power-game and try to use your strongest weapon. Each emotion revealed will make your move easier to counter. When rational animals fight each other, the skill of victory and survival is built on the use of a variety of primal skills shared by many animals, such as physical power, cunning, blind rage, deception, communication, etc., but reason tends to give the higher capabilities of tactic and strategy that, in a sustained concerted effort, will overcome mere reliance on said primal skills. At some stage of evolution, reason has obviously been key to the success of *Homo sapiens* over other species, and battling both forces of nature *and* other tribes of men, *Homo sapiens* extended this victorious capability into a society firmly built upon reason and communication—the keys to the survival of a tribe.

PART I. THE BASIS OF THOUGHT

As a brief summary of the nature of rationality; reason is a human disposition with a conceptual, communicative basis, and something that we are both biologically inclined to, but most essentially, that is heavily culturally projected to seal our victory over other species and forces of nature we have evolved to dominate. But because the concepts involved in all use of reason are both communally acquired and passed on, there exists the dichotomy that has in philosophical attempts been called internalism and externalism, or, quite similarly, ontology and epistemology, as if they were some sort of distinct separable approaches each worth of their specific line of study. A more reasonable approach is just to recognize the dual role of reason in the separate discourses of *causation* and *justification*, just as we recognize our role both as an individual and as a member of society. Cause and effect relate to our interest to interact with the world, having related fields such as mathematics, mechanics, engineering, physics, architecture, electronics and robotics, whereas justification is related to the subjective and civil side of life, in fields such as politics, rhetoric, psychology, sociology, art, literature and theology. The *meaning* used in causal discourse in the modern day is objective, due to the existing lines of study that have produced the basic conceptual frameworks that such discourse is built upon. This means that there is no room for subjective interpretation in the concepts, which is why they are suitable for use in individual thought; there is no space for deviance from others to produce error when the results are later combined. A mathematician or an engineer, for example, can work alone and produce results that are directly verifiable and applicable by others. But subjective concepts always involve subjective interpretation. If you produce a work of, say, theological study, by yourself, your whole work will be subject to interpretation—as the subject is *unique*, meaning infinitely different, the degree of subjectivity translates to the likelihood of deviance in the generic case. Therefore, these kind of studies tend to slowly form schools of thought, consisting of like-minded individuals who are convinced of the correctness of the approach, which implies that the subjective justification (argument, message) involved in the work has been successful. While the role of objective science has increased in Western rhetoric, the role of reason as a justifier has equally diminished, and this can perhaps be best seen by contrasting Western social behaviour with behaviour among Asians, who typically do nothing without an articulated reason that justifies action; they'd be very afraid to act without such a reason, "just for the fun of it", as we might say. The movement in rational rhetoric from the subjective towards the objective in practice means an increase in individual liberties. For example, some years ago all Finnish men were conscripted unless pardoned; then the system changed so that one had the liberty to select unarmed service instead but was required to provide a reason. Currently, providing a reason is not required; there is a freedom to act without a reason in this matter. Here we can also see the second thing that justification involves, which is authority: the justification is provided by a lower social rank to a higher one, and a higher-ranking individual has more freedom and less requirement to present reasons for his actions. In a similar way as with loyalty, justification is something with which a lower-ranking individual will gain the favour of the authority: he will present his reasoning for an approval or a correction by the authority, in order to avoid conflict, and a lot of the explaining behaviour that people take on can be correctly interpreted as a request for (silent) acceptance. In the academic setting, originally started as philosophical dialogue, all meetings, lectures, conferences, proceedings, journals and so on consist of public presentations of results to peers, and the reason for this model is to simultaneously educate and receive criticism, the second of which—the test of public scrutiny—is accepted as providing the justification for the acceptance of presented results as facts. This publicity and scrutiny of the source of one's information is the very foundation of any validity of applying the word 'fact' to the results of science, which also constitutes the norm of what is meant by 'fact' in the West. Armed with this knowledge, one should be very careful regarding modern journalism or public discourse that presents information without any public source as *facts*; we tend to trust this word because our scientific model has been relatively reliable in this. But anything without a reliable public source is opinion, not fact; scientifically, it could become fact after scrutiny of this source. Today the average Westerner lacks subjectivity, and thus he does not grasp the idea of democratic opinion, provided by freedom of opinion. This is unfortunate, since Europe is made up of democratic governments. In the absence of facts, insecure and vulnerable, what he trusts is authority.

To compare a subject-relative spiritual explanation with an object-relative causal explanation by means of the concepts 'true' or 'false' is not philosophically fruitful, as the explanatory method is bound to responsibility and thus the form of society. Such treatment will unavoidably lead into an internal ethical conflict. Take an example of comparing explanations of rainfall by a Westerner and an African tribesman. The tribesman would not be responsible for an object-relative causal explanation of rainfall in his society, and to imply that his inability to do this would be the result of him seeing the world *wrong*, as e.g. a Western scientist might do, would be disrespectful. It would provoke hostility since it implies his society and what he believes in (his god) is wrong. It would also be an act of blasphemy within the Westerner's own monotheistic system since it implies the tribesman is logically able to worship another god (which the Westerner cannot imagine if he himself is monotheistic). The tribesman would similarly think that the Westerner sees things wrong, or, if convinced of the opposite, would be bound to see the Westerner as a deity, which cannot be true from the Westerner's monotheistic perspective either. When the subject says his world-picture is *right*, he is effectively announcing his *faith* in the correctness of the picture he possesses and his adherence to the values it implies, no matter what reasons he is able to produce to justify it, although those reasons have their value in their potential to convince others. However, the commonplace belief that these *reasons make it right*, just as a passing cloud creates a shadow on the ground (cause and effect), is exactly the result of misunderstanding the roles of cause and reason, and in the subject-relative realm of reasons only humans or spiritual subjects make things right, each in their specific domains they are believed to have control over. This preconception is the force behind the philosophical school of *rationalism* and is equivalent to a principle that there exists nothing higher than reason. It's similar to the way atheism is equivalent to a principle that there exists nothing higher than Man; and the word 'higher' here refers to a method of convincing via *argument*: the rationalist will hold fast to a principle of refusing an irrational argument (such as that we should go out today because it is such a beautiful day), and the atheist will refuse argument that attributes a deity. Given the example of the Westerner's intrusion in the tribesman's territory, the Westerner would believe in God and his system of values contradicting the tribesman's values, which at the event of conflict in values would justify his holding onto his own values. However, *to say* to the tribesman that his values are wrong, implying that he worships the wrong deity, would be an act of making himself divine; an act of pride and not humility, since for the Westerner it is God only who sees in all men's hearts and God only who judges men. The conquering Westerners have historically circumvented the requirement of religious humility by actively disbelieving the humanity of the invaded and treating them as non-humans, outside of grace. Once a society recognizes the humanity of the neighbouring society, invading acts of war become *prima facie* ethically and religiously condemned (for which we generally have science to thank, as it is through science that we figure out that barbarians are actually people like us), and crusades have through ages been justified because they target savages, not men.

PART I. THE BASIS OF THOUGHT

I-8. The Four Types of Reason

As explained earlier, 'reason' is a very confused concept. In a general case, 'reason' is the word we use in the subjective realm of justification and 'cause' the word we use for objective explanation of phenomena in a scientific sense—in reference to 'causality'. However, there is also a sense of 'cause' that means reason, such as in a political "common cause" or "For what cause did you put this money on the table?" Actually the etymological origin of the word 'cause' is equivalent to 'reason', yet the word has since evolved to have a scientific cause-and-effect meaning that is distinct from any justification but related to objective evidence, and this has happened hand-in-hand with our Western conception of justice evolving to courts of law requiring objective evidence instead of simply rational justification for one's cause. An objective cause for an effect is something that *can be shown* to have this effect, such as by showing that cancelling the cause also cancels the effect. After this objective meaning of 'cause' has been accepted, what has happened is that we have also started using the word in the sense of *attributed* causal relation, where the cause need not be shown but can be accepted as a hypothesis. And here we have two completely distinct meanings of 'cause'; one in the sense of cause as a reason, and the other one of cause in a cause-and-effect relation. The realm of justification is our conception of *justice*, which is distinctly a psycho-social context that involves argumentation where we debate with reasons, and that inherently has nothing at all to do with causal relations but more so with *social norms* that are used to measure correct and incorrect action. Justice is the basis of social harmony and involves our conception of social responsibility. The causal model is something later artificially added to our *justice system*, where we have established a rule that whenever somebody accuses another, he will need to be able to show his accusation true with evidence. A society without this kind of system would exist in a constant state of hostile blood feud where a relative state of equilibrium is reached only via having equally strong opposing powers; justice would mean nothing apart from the justice of nature where a man needs to kill or be killed. Because justice is a distinctly

I-8. THE FOUR TYPES OF REASON

subjective and psycho-social phenomenon, it is also completely culture-dependent and references our norms, which act as our measurement of correct action. This means that there simply are no theoretical restrictions on what kind of concepts can become cultural norms and, in turn, what kind of actions can become the cultural expectation of correct action for justice. Justice is simply an expectation that follows cultural norms and that has the function of seeking harmony over tension within society; seeking a state where each party can be content and not hold grudges or hostility towards others. What is philosophically interesting is the confusion created by these different senses of the word 'cause', as very commonly the word 'reason' is misused in a the sense of cause and effect,[81] in utterances such as "The reason for all these mushrooms growing is that it has rained heavily recently". It would, however, be correct to say "All these mushrooms are growing for the reason of us getting a good mushroom harvest", which means that "it is reasonable for us" to get such a harvest, which means an implied justification using the fact that mushrooms are growing, similar to saying "this is a reasonable compensation", meaning acceptable or satisfactory. It means that the good mushroom harvest is a common goal, and this implies reasoning to reach or satisfy this goal. However, because the word 'reason' is so often misused, when somebody says "The reason for the rise of temperature in March is..." what he likely means is to give *a reason* to *pay attention* to temperature rise by showing what he believes to be its *cause*, essentially meaning "Here I am giving you one reason, which is the temperature rise..." In such discourse, the reason to do something is intertwined with cause by the speaker, the subject.

It is crucial to understand that the world is not a reductionist house of cards built from the bottom up, because humans have various ways of reasoning and we have no established basis for *perspective*: there simply is no reason to consider physics the metaphysical basis because humanity does not consist of physicists and we have no need to train people to consider things from a physical perspective and to be less literate in the other sciences. Rather it seems that we should have few-

---
81   e.g. The Blue Book, p.15

er physicists now, because the golden age of great advances in physics seems to be over and our world is struggling with other kinds of problems. To think about these kinds of questions in the first place—the question of "What is the best way of looking at things?"—we will have to start by trying to understand ourselves, the human; to understand how a human thinks and reasons. Only after understanding this could we go ahead and try and say something about what would be the right way of looking at the world. This is no different from, say, if we'd like to make a comfortable shirt or jacket, or effective body armour for a soldier; in order to succeed in this practical feat, you'd need to understand human anatomy rather well from a practical perspective. Now, I will attempt here to give an analysis of the various existing modes of reasoning, and to sensibly bind them to the subjective-objective dichotomy, which, to me, seems to be the birthplace of these modes and the explanation why we have exactly these sort of modes instead of alternative ones. The way I see it is that our modes of reasoning are as shown in the following chart.

Mode of inquiry Domain	SUBJECTIVE (aiming to accept)	OBJECTIVE (aiming to convince)
SUBJECTIVE (values, responsibilities)	justification	logic
OBJECTIVE (phenomena)	teleology	causality

A phenomenon is determined to be subjective or objective based on its criterion, and here the subjective domain differs from the objective in that it relates to subjective values. The mode of inquiry is determined as subjective or objective based on whether it is private and personal or public and shared. The subjective mode of inquiry is a person's reasoning, which aims to morally accept and settle instead of remaining in a state of conflict due to injustice. The objective mode of inquiry aims to convince via finding relations that are shared and thus indisputable, irrespective of subjective opinion. I think my presentation most notably differs from how reason has been characterized by others in that the mode of inquiry aiming to accept or to convince is *inherently social*, whereas thinkers would often like to see reason as something happening outside of our social space in a sort of abstract world of its own. Logic has often been seen as a formal system instead of a tool for convincing via argument, and causality is often seen as a metaphysical relation instead of a way of presenting objective phenomena in an attempt to convince somebody. In my presentation a human is utterly and completely social, because he is unable to even think in a manner that would not be inherently social. I believe this presentation is in harmony with our basic humanity in that we are often described as psycho-physical-social creatures, but even more importantly I believe that social interaction is our primary nature, which means that if we remove ourselves from *testing* our thoughts against the thoughts of other people we soon start to think strangely and will make mistakes, but furthermore if we isolate ourselves from social interaction we will soon die one way or another, such as via suicide, provoking an accident or because of a physical illness such as cancer.

A key thing to notice is that in the cases of justification and teleology where the mode of inquiry is subjective, this means that the form of knowledge is *faith* and that the outcome of such thought is something that is *believed to be right*. It is a category error to present that something is believed that is morally wrong, just as Aristotle would say that all deliberate actions aim towards a goal that is good. From this it follows that *something is not a justification nor a teleological explanation unless the outcome is believed to be right* and hence justified or made purposeful. Furthermore, whenever people would support outcomes that they know to be morally wrong, or whenever they are living and acting in a particular way yet don't possess a subjective justification for their action, they do this as a result of a process that is not valid rational reasoning. It is a rational violation to accept the existence of things that are not desirable, and our natural inclination would be to fight against their existence. In the case of a disastrous event it is crucial to keep believing in a positive outcome; this activity keeps us within our rational capabilities and letting it go will release us into chaotic irrationality. But looking at the exact opposite of this requirement to justify, there is a class of things that are accepted to exist only and precisely because their existence is perceived as right and their nonexistence wrong, and this class is called *the supernatural*. Now, there is a class of bad reasoning with the following features: 1) something is pointed out to be the status quo; 2) justification or purpose is drawn from the status quo, and 3) this whole thought process takes place in the context of moral justification instead of analysis. The third point implies psychological rationalization instead of reasoning; it is an artificial reasoning that tries to shoehorn a valid reason into an outcome that is decided beforehand based on essentially moral sentiments that try to satisfy a social expectation. This fallacy was pointed out by Hume's Guillotine, and is also related to what Moore described as naturalistic fallacy. It is also akin to *argumentum ad populum*. Essentially, in this kind of reasoning justification is drawn from something that is seen to exist, and as we already know that real justification is a subjective perspective to subjective matters, in this reasoning the 'status quo' is actually an objective state of affairs that is used to justify the subjective outcome. So, it is closer to a teleological argument but just disguised as a justification; "It had to happen" or "It has to be this way"; drawing justification from an objective state of affairs like a natural law. Essentially is not *reasoning* at all but something that can look like it, and this is because it is neither a justification nor a teleological argument, because there is no need or purpose to be served and the outcome is not believed to be *right*. It is an excuse. Subjective reasoning and the search for acceptance is *primary* to people, and they will predominantly behave in such a way that if they are unable to come up with a valid justification, they will settle for a justification that is invalid, and might remain in this state despite knowing that they don't have sound reasoning behind their behaviour. The outcome comes first: "It might be wrong and I'm not proud of it, but I know I can't help it, so I must accept it." In this case people generally look for authority figures to follow and to associate themselves with, because one is actually unable to carry out deliberate action at all when one's independent thought is not based on valid reasoning. At this point a person is in a helpless state and unable to act at all without external authority. Another point to note is that in the cases of objective mode of inquiry (logic and causality), any subjectivity is a vice, and successful inquiry requires a significant skill of subjective detachment and hypothetical thought; *the ability to think about or say something without believing it.* Because of the primary nature of subjective thought, a high level of skill at theoretical thought is not actually very common, yet people commonly try to pretend to have this skill because it is prestigious to display it. Also, people who tend to think and argue logically are commonly misunderstood by the subjectively thinking man in the street exactly because of the hypothetical nature of thought: "If what you say is true, then I am the Emperor of Rome! ... No, I didn't mean I am the Emperor of Rome! ... No, I have never been to Rome..." The same hypothetical thought is used when pondering about causality ("What might have caused this?") and people with high skills in this kind of thought are able to cycle through potential alternatives in their mind and to come to a probable hypothetical cause, instead of just jumping into the first cause that comes to mind via association.

Let's now look at each of these modes of reasoning a bit more closely.

I-8-1. Justification

Justification is the person's subjective reasoning regarding subjective matters. To put this another way; justification is the person's way of thinking about matters that are within our subjective freedom and characterized by personal value, choice and responsibility. Matters that are not within this domain, such as paying taxes or going to school, don't need a justification, but a person is simply expected to do these things as a duty and obligation as per law and custom. But for those matters where a person has a free choice, we often ask for the person's justification or rationale behind his choices, as this rationale can reveal if the person is behaving morally, and this affects other people's impressions of them. These subjective reasons are primary to people. And because they are primary, the social requirement for justification is much, much more important than a requirement to be logically coherent. I read a newspaper article about an elderly lady being startled by removal men that came to her home because they had the wrong address and saying to them: "I don't want to move anywhere today because I am very late for work." Here we can see how justification is generally used in social intercourse: in certain situations people are required to give a reason—to justify—and the way they handle this is that often they have no idea what to say but they will give a reason because they are required to do so (or rather they believe they are required to do so), and the reason they give might not in the slightest be *causally* related to what it *grammatically* seems to be used in justification of; it is simply used in a sentence where a living subject is using it as a reason and responding to some event. Reasons like this we Westerners would likely call non-genuine excuses, but in Asia, where the social dominates over the individual, this way of responding is the norm; the question "Why?", in the standard case, asks for a *socially accepted justification* of action, not an objective cause. We might distinguish these kinds of social reasons from reasons that are *independently* believed and take note that these kinds of independent reasons constitute *conviction* and *determination*, which are considered virtues in a rational *individualist* society. But in both East and West we can note that when a reason is publicly given, and the reason is agreeable to others (because they share its criterion; in other words, they can see why it is right in a practical context), this is equivalent to these reasons being *true* or *right*. It just so happens that the West is individualist, and an acceptable justification is expected to portray *moral thought*. And this is even more so today than in the past, because nowadays religion doesn't provide much of a justification for action, so the result is that people try to portray themselves as more moral than before (and more moral than they are) by performing symbolic acts of courtesy by e.g. showing compassion to animals or immigrants. If we look at justification from the perspective of the subject, if you compare "I want this" with "I want that", you don't yet have a reason to choose one over the other. If you'd like to promote yourself by saying "because I deserve it" or "because it is better", you still don't have a reason, as those things need a justification, too, to have any social effect. Why do you deserve it? Why is it bet-

I-8. THE FOUR TYPES OF REASON

ter? And this is how people grow up: we start by doing actions without a reason, simply following others, and at a certain age we start to be expected to show independent thought in our action in the form of responsibility over our own lives and the lives of others. So, action without justification precedes action with justification in everybody's subjectivity. Let's set this against some exemplary norm, such as wearing a formal suit for a formal occasion; we all learn that people wear suits on social occasions, but do we understand why? We learn first that whenever our parents would take us to such an occasion, they would dress us up properly and tell us to behave correctly, which is uncomfortable for children who generally like to squirm and make noises when one is supposed to sit silently and listen. They have not yet experienced life where there are concepts such as honour and respect that are used to strengthen bonds between people who share something in common, instead of them existing in mutual disinterest. They don't understand that it is an honour to be invited instead of being left uninvited, and this honour is to be respected with due courtesy. So, the social norm is something that sets the standard of our correct social behaviour, but we differ in how much our behaviour is just mimicking the norm in our action—just like we were taught, or forced to, as children—instead of understanding, and subscribing to, the moral thought that underlies the norm. And this difference we would describe with the word 'genuine' as opposed to 'non-genuine'. This is where our justifications differ, and this is why we commonly ask for justification; to determine the subjective part; if we have respect for *the person* as determined by his actions as an adult with social responsibility instead of a child that is mindlessly following external rules. Justification can be called the civil aspect of reason; we are dealing with the subjective way of looking at something that in itself can be subjectively seen as many things. If we witness a man throwing a rock against the wall, the two subjective related questions are: 1) What did the man do? He threw a rock at a wall, but what should we call this action? Vandalism? Expression of frustration? Signal to his girlfriend who lives in the building the wall belongs to? And 2): What should we make of this action? What does this action reveal about the nature of the man?

PART I. THE BASIS OF THOUGHT

Aristotle would say that all deliberate actions aim at some good that is separate from the action itself, but some aims are desired only for the achievement of making higher aims possible. Firstly, we can see already here that all aims are good as they are, simply because they are aims, which implies that that there is reasoning behind them, and the type of reason here is obviously a justification. We can derive from this that even bad actions or outcomes have good justifications, which, I believe, is a universally accepted idea. Let's say I want to make somebody suffer. The right way to think about this is that *I am unable to deliberately carry out a conscious act* (to make somebody suffer) *unless I indeed have a justification for it*. And to see that it really is so, look at how kangaroo courts universally work: the guilt of the defendant has been determined beforehand, and before announcing the incriminating verdict, we just first need to find a suitable justification; a suitable crime. Here we can see that the mark of justification, as opposed to logic, is the subjective nature of the decision; the people have already subjectively decided whom they hate, but in order to make *the action* look *reasonable*, the action needs to follow a justification. Just as a man can't carry out deliberate action without a justification, the court is unable to condemn the man without a justification—a crime. So, not only does a justification make an action possible, but also the reverse: an action is to be socially considered just, or reasonable, when a socially accepted justification exists, and unreasonable when one doesn't exist. Secondly, there is an idea here of a chain (or tree) of reasons. It is commonly thought that "everything has a reason", but this is exactly the confusion between reason and cause, as every effect can be seen to have a cause, but in fact the actual chain of reasons is finite. What would, then, act as a *subjective original reason*; that is, the reason within the thought of one subject where the chain of reasons ends? For Aristotle the highest aim would be *eudaimonia*, which he derived with a certain logic from how he saw things must (should) be, and thus the concept is in itself politicized (answering to the question of what is good for the *polis*) and only semi-analytical. I would look at it objectively, outside my subjective commitments, and suggest that the subjective original reason is simply any social justification, and the question of what is the highest aim translates to: What is the most sensible/convincing

I-8. THE FOUR TYPES OF REASON

subjective original reason? This question is equivalent to: What is the most agreeable social norm? —What is the most agreeable standard against which to assess correct action? These are actual, scientific, answerable questions. To summarize the separation of the individual and the social good:

> *the individual, in a good case, has justifications to his action, that, in an even better case, correspond with social norms, but that in the best case correspond with the most agreeable norms.*

To try and conclude the best norm analytically does not make any sense; it is a subjective question determined by the basic question of politics, the question of what is good for the city, which is a living organism existing in a particular state of domestic and foreign politics. Also, it can be a scientific, empirical question of what is found most agreeable, and can be approached by methodology of e.g. opinion polls. From the perspective of the subject, the question of justification means that he can exist in two kinds of states: either he will say something like "This is what I *believe* to be *right*" and appear stalwart and determined, or he will have to admit he doesn't know why. In order to be truthful, he can't do it alone in his own mind, but ultimately the origin of all his subjective knowledge is simply a justification to others. If you are a scientifically inclined thinker, you will likely hate this result. But if you are not, you might be very interested in the question of what might be the ultimate justifier; the problem of *what is the most agreeable thing that can be believed.* And via this problematic we come to see that in religious explanations of the world and religious rhetoric, the question of "Why?" is always asked within the subjective and never in the causal realm; the religious thought consistently and persistently asks for an explanation in the form of a reason, with the logic being something like "It *must* be like *this*, because things *must* have a reason". This is because religion and religious thought are rigorously in the service of the subject: it is the subject who needs a reason in order to do anything meaningfully, and vice versa; in order for any subjective action to be meaningful it must be guided by reason, as the only logical alternative is to be guided not by reason but just by emotions and impulses.

PART I. THE BASIS OF THOUGHT

To highlight the importance of subjective meaning I could sum up by saying that no matter how complete your world-picture, as a system of causes and effects, is, if *you* don't have subjective meaning you're *as good as dead*, and, firstly, you would not be the first intelligent, popular, famous, etc., person to commit suicide, and secondly, you would not be the first person to suddenly find subjective meaning to your life and choose to resign *all your past life*, including your precious and refined world-picture. A reason is right, or true, when it is agreeable by other subjects, and this quality of being *agreed upon*, a common cause, is the basis of objectivity and a prerequisite for group cohesion.

Looking at the other side of subjective reasons, when we *blame* people, our thinking seems to incorporate causal objectivity on a subject, and when we say "It's all your fault!" we mean that the appointed person is the *cause* of something that has happened. A simple thought experiment can show us that for any objective effect one is actually in a position to blame anybody by just changing our conception of subjective responsibility—for example we can blame the mother who gave birth to him or his friends who didn't stop him from doing what he did. In both situations, where one is looking for a cause-and-effect explanation or a rational justification, reasoning can be faulty, related to exactly this confusion about which one is meant. Often people who have suffered a shocking experience will behave erratically in terms of trying to rationally explain the experience. I am reading a self-help pamphlet by the Red Cross for people that have experienced an emotional shock, and it gives examples of events such as the death or suicide attempt of a person close to one, suffering injury or being subjected to violence, or witnessing or being involved in a shocking or threatening situation. The typical reactions, among various stress symptoms, include finding it difficult to *understand* or to *accept* what has happened, and a need to understand why, such as by discovering the cause of the event or finding out who is guilty. The symptomatic experience is described as a conflict: at the same time, one feels 1) relief from having oneself survived or evaded the danger, and 2) guilt from having been luckier than others. That shocking experiences have such typical symptoms shows that our *need to justify* goes hand-in-hand with our subjective,

I-8. THE FOUR TYPES OF REASON

personal safety and comfort: we ask "Why?" in the subjective sense only regarding events that we experience personally meaningful, and the rest we can pass over with "Who knows?" The need for justification and support is the standard and primary human rational mode of enquiry, and this means the justification for one's *actions*. And we also naturally extend this thought to animals, most importantly where we justify eating them via honouring their life, which is a normal part of hunting and eating animals in all primitive cultures. We need to understand, in our subjectivity, why it is correct to eat the animals, and it is quite understandable that eating farmed animals is difficult to justify because they never had an honourable chance to defend themselves, nor do we, in a strict sense, have a *need* to produce and slaughter them, which would be our natural way to justify, say, killing and taking over the neighbouring tribe or conquering a neighbouring country. Such aggressive killing of outsiders will only feel justified to us if there is an overwhelming need that cannot be avoided, for example that they are somehow endangering us with their hostility, and even in modern times this type of—usually fabricated—rhetoric is an absolute requirement to justify any territorial takeovers. This is why people have strong sentiments against meat production; because animals are not endangering us and also we are distanced from times where hunger was so close that killing an animal would be considered a holy ritual. For hungry people the need to kill animals is evident.

Finally, justification is the disposition of mind where *self-deceit* takes place. Unlike conscious lying, which is just a normal act with a purpose that can be subjectively justified, the nature of self-deceit is very philosophically profound and can be characterized as emotionally initiated subjective manipulation of one's own reasoning. The manic behaviour I have witnessed in people is behaviour in which the person steers away from unpleasant, guilty, shameful emotions into an area where he feels confident and empowered, and this movement is experienced *passionately*, similar to the way ethical or religious passion is characterized by a visibly powerful desire to transmute oneself from one existence to another. Like a person who decides not to be lazy today and to be active instead, the manic person is characterized by a *drive* that keeps him going, and he rides this drive with a 'must' mentality, as he knows that if he stops, he will soon fall back into defeating emotions again. Many of the particularly positive, energetic people we see are like this because they are actively escaping negative emotions into an active, empowered existence. Recognizing the results of one's own choices and actions—as the result of one's own thinking—as unexpected or unwanted yields painful, primitive emotions (sometimes "truth hurts"), which is a natural part of ethical progress as the initiating emotional force of existential change. The self-deceiving subject has succeeded in subjectively denying such a truth in a manner that resembles covering one's eyes to avoid witnessing a visual observation or the destruction of evidence during a trial; it is *active neglect* of some subjective truth. Like all lying, self-deceit is something the subject succumbs into and not something the subject likes or enjoys, but he chooses it, believing he can use it to overcome some other thing that he experiences as unpleasant. After this has been done once, one can get used to it, as one can get used to anything unpleasant, like changing a baby's nappies. Self-deceit takes the form of denying social responsibility over one's own actions as the cause of the unwanted results and instead blaming an external cause, and can be recognized from outside by the strong emotional reaction of denial and a cycle of *justification*; it is a painful truth the subject escapes from with an instinctive reaction of an animal responding to a danger of death (called "fight-or-flight"). The self-deceiving subject needs *constant justification*, a constant re-thinking and finding a justification, and simply watching this routine where a person is not being content but constantly coming up with justifying rationale, should reveal to a bystander that the only thing that can cause it is actually the absence of justice: the subject actually knows his behaviour violates his own moral thought, but he actively remains unconscious about it by believing the justifications that allow him to divert from responding to it. Should one pursue a self-deceiving person about the truth he is escaping, one will see him applying ways of escaping the topic, such as escaping the whole conversational situation, lying or hostility against the person who is questioning his action; the subject is barred from rationally handling the topic. Logically, it is a contradiction between one's existence and thought, and our normal rational disposition would invite us to recognize this and to correct our existence... only in this situation the self-deceiving person will behave irrationally. Because the self-deceiving subject essentially actively *escapes* social responsibility, in a manner similar to looking away—instead of believing that such a responsibility doesn't exist, which seems equivalent to how an agnostic differs from an atheist—he typically would see the line of responsibilities differently if some other person was in the actual situation instead of himself, and thus self-deceit is different from an existential change into one who thinks that in the context in question no person should be held responsible. Instead, he knows people *should* behave in a particular way, but pronouncing this becomes impossible because he has excused *himself* from behaving this way. He will feel uncomfortable about the topic and prefer distance from it, as the memory of the excuse causes guilt and shame. He loses his dignity. Dignity would be something that makes a person feel good about himself, to receive respect from others and to act honourably towards them. It seems to me that this dignity is a requirement for *reciprocal morality*; firstly, we need to be able to see our actions as justified, which has the requirement of dignity in order to look at what we are doing in the first place. But secondly, it is specifically morality in which our behaviour is based on *rational thought*; some sort of *principle* that we follow that acts as our guideline when we are met with our natural impulses that tempt us to primitive non-civil behaviours. In self-deceit, the person's capability to use his reason to *justify* is impaired; the person can no longer either justify his action or use his reason to control himself by setting his actions according to what he sees as justified. In the sense of the ethical and the civil, the act of self-deceit impairs a person's social responsibility and *sense of justice*. The subject cannot level with others and is impaired from empathy-driven existential change towards what is appreciated by society regarding the responsibility in question and will cease healthy spiritual development. In addition, the very fact that the self-deceiving subject escapes a truth—a *subjective* process of confronting the problem of the correct way of understanding certain information—implies that *he* has been confronted with such a truth. He cannot escape the truth itself, but can either undergo the possibly painful process of facing it, or live in self-deceit which holds him in a state of internal conflict and the need to every now and then actively escape the internal conflict and the memory of the excuse. The need to escape means that the subject *is not free*, and thus he can't be responsible. The denial of personal responsibility in self-deceit is generally possible through blaming an external cause for the results of one's own actions, and this typically involves blaming either other people, or alternatively any kinds of objective 'agents', the most common of which might well be society, luck, time and money. Another common form is to justify with norms, with arguments like "This is how things have always been" or "I'm just doing what any man/woman/father/mother/... would do in this situation", but it is obvious that norms don't determine the particular individual situation the subject is involved in and what would be the moral expectation of his actions, given the knowledge that is in his subjective awareness. In court, a judgement involves exactly the subjective element of a person's actions: whether he was conscious of the relevant environment and the consequences of his actions, which determine whether he could have subjectively chosen to act otherwise. This is also the stage of a subject's personal morals, in contrast with norms that are essentially social models and roles of respectable behaviour.

I-8-2. Logic

Following the four types of reason shown in the chart above, logic, or argument, is where one is trying to convince somebody over matters of subjective value, and does in an objective manner, using the shared meanings of the concepts as the rigorous basis. A good way to look at logic is to see it as the implementation of the *rationalist* principle that some things (the *a priori*) can be unquestionably known simply from a given expression or argument; it is just that there are differing ideas about how this knowledge is possible, and my (Wittgensteinian) way of looking at it is that this is not some innate knowledge but inherent in the concepts used and assimilated to our thought while we are learning to use these concepts. The rationalist principle is essentially juxtaposed with the empiricist idea that doesn't necessarily deny the

I-8. THE FOUR TYPES OF REASON

rationalist principle but essentially promotes the senses (*a posteriori*) as the true source of all knowledge. Now, we can probably agree that the rationalist principle is true *to a certain degree* and that we just wouldn't be sure how much we can rely on the *a priori*. Meaningful research in logic is essentially an attempt to discover reliable rules and principles that determine this scope and extent of the rationalist principle, but this research has also taken a wrong path where philosophers have extended the rationalist principle beyond its analytical origin. Originally, logic is research that has an analytical purpose: to figure out what language and argument actually are, and just as importantly what they are not. But misguided research on virtually any field would take its founding principles literally and start enforcing them by saying that the world needs to comply with their principle, or the world is being disobedient. For example, a bad psychiatrist will try to enforce his hypothesis on his patient instead of using it as a tool of essentially learning about the patient in order to be able to better help him, and in the case of logic and language analysis the wrong path is an attitude where philosopher-kings try to create rules of language as rules of conduct, to be used to point out whose comments and opinions can be dismissed due to being incorrect in form. Therefore, the question of *a priori* contra *a posteriori* is of utmost importance in any rationalist enquiry: What can we infer from argument and what can we not infer? How do we distinguish between 1) what the person meant, 2) what the person tried to mean but expressed incorrectly, and 3) what we can expect the person to have meant? From the perspective of *justice* there are two parties in communication, the one that is speaking and the one that is hearing, and what we are dealing with is an understanding and *agreement* of the parties about the communication: what is expected of the speaker to be understood and what is expected from the listener to understand the speaker. The whole business of the study of *meaning* is about how to solve this problem of communicability in a general case, but the best solution is to become an expert in meaning by becoming an expert in the use of language, similar to how one could become an expert in law in order to become a judge whose job is to know the law and the norms and to be able to, case by case, determine a situation of conflict (misunderstanding) *in service of justice*, which means ob-

PART I. THE BASIS OF THOUGHT

jectively in the best interest of the whole society and both individuals. And actually logic has developed hand-in-hand with our system of justice; it is exactly the need to *present one's case in court*, enforced by our established system of justice, that creates the requirement in society to present oneself via the method of *argument*, and in such a way that the responsibility to back one's argument is on the party that has *demands* and not the other way round. It is commonly said that the "burden of proof is on the party with the initial argument". But this doesn't reveal much, given the case where two opposing parties are in, as it were, the real business of arguing, which involves hostile exchanges of reasons and accusations, deliberate taunts and insults and possibly backing one's honour by physical means. This is a general human quality I am sure everybody has witnessed to some degree at least, and where there actually exists an underlying *social conflict* giving rise to the whole situation which essentially is a primitive *territorial dispute* in its psycho-social nature; a fight in defence of one's social space and boundaries.

To avoid such chaotic reasoning a system has been established to protect the honour of the parties, in which the party with accusations needs to publicly back them in court or to publicly lose the case and lose honour, enforcing the honour of the defending party. The origin of this system of justice is an interesting question: Why do we believe that people have a right to defend themselves in the first place? In a feudal society you wouldn't have this problem of having to bother to justify your accusations against an inferior; you'd just deal with him in the way you thought best. A truly ideal situation—for the one in the higher class. Until the end of absolute rule in Europe the king would hold his private court where one might expect little chance of victory against an accusation of treason. In any case, *this* system of *public* justice, by contrast with a system of centralized arbitrary justice, is where the idea of a burden of proof comes from, and this just happens to be the case for us in the West. Public argument is not encouraged at all but frowned upon throughout Asia, where the Western idea of human rights is also fundamentally alien and the structure of society is hierarchical, albeit with this hierarchy expressed in varying different ways. In such coun-

I-8. THE FOUR TYPES OF REASON

tries democratic society and human rights are simply mimicked on a superficial level as a political charade in order to please Western nations. I mean to say that our whole system of logic, as rules of argument, is something inherently Western and not universal; the world would generally prioritize subjective reasoning (justification, teleology) over public argumentative reasoning, and would believe that the grammatical form of an argument doesn't really mean anything at all or give any grounds of superiority over another in a dispute. The whole of Asia basically lives within a culture where *somebody* (not abstract reason) is telling you what you must do, and the favourite form of entertainment is ghost stories, as ghosts are the subject-like shadows of subjective reason. The way argumentative power works (for Westerners) is that the *validity* of the argument is a key factor in determining the essential *credibility* of the arguer. Giving valid, credible arguments is a quality attributed to somebody with *leadership qualities*; somebody we can trust in his ability to think and decide over people in general due to his capability of objectivity by sticking to reason instead of getting emotionally carried away and thus subjectively biased to favour one party over another. It is in our Western idea of *social harmony* that the leader is able to stand neutral with a cool head, and I emphasize that this is an *Abrahamic* quality fundamentally alien to people from outside the sphere of our religions. Look at our prophets: Moses was both an orphan and escaped the cruelty of the Pharaoh, Jesus Christ was born without a father and a was victim of the cruelty of the Roman Emperor; Muhammad's father died before he was born and he was orphaned at the age of six, after which his people faced persecution by the wealthy religious elite he was threatening. This same character (without family, fighting oppression) happens to also be the archetypical hero character of virtually every Western movie ever written. The orphan feature of the legend essentially signifies both the capability, and the disposition, to fight existing oppression, as only somebody without a family is capable of forging their own destiny and pledging it to create social harmony instead of having to take the path that most mortals are bound to take, which is to follow their parents' footsteps or guidance in profession and to give them grandchildren. This is why today we trust the scientific system so much; we don't think science is *right*, everybody allows that science is sometimes, even often, wrong. But we believe science is *credible*. We essentially trust its neutrality and thus its capability to enforce social harmony and to solve conflict. Similarly, when we assess whether an argument is *valid*, we assess that it is credible and not inherently faulty; we don't assess that the person putting forward the argument is right; a valid argument can well have a false or disagreeable conclusion. We assess whether the argument presented is what we would expect from an ideal man of wisdom and reason and is in harmony with his beliefs that also are correct, and we are historically inclined to follow this kind of leader. Thus, logic essentially targets the subjective domain; the subject; the person—it just happens to do it in an objective manner.

If we look at what the study of logic has been up to so far, we can see that in traditional formal logic we have logical connectives, such as 'and', 'or', or negation, quantifiers like 'for all' or 'there exists', and rules of inference such as 'modus ponens' or 'reductio ad absurdum'. We might notice the commonness of the connectives in natural language and also the practical connection of the rules of inference to our practical thinking. In order to understand this, we need to take a look at how we first learn words like 'and', 'or' and the negation, and what role they play in our practical life. Being the humans we are, very commonly we organize things or build something together; we tell other people e.g. what has happened or what we have seen as a part of our social interaction; we often deny or ask and get a negative reply; we present alternatives and so on. And this occurs perfectly in harmony with how we come to understand things—how we make our choices, how we struggle for clarity of understanding or how we need to follow some people and reject others. Just take a look at a person who says 'and... and... and...' when wanting to continue a sentence within a conversation, while not yet being able to articulate what he is about to say: he wants to continue his sentence and will do so when he has found the words, so he starts by using the *connective* of joining another sentence and *signifying to listeners* that he is about to continue; hence the 'and'. The basis of the traditional logical connectives is rooted in our natural language, which has evolved to serve the natural functions of our lives.

I-8. THE FOUR TYPES OF REASON

Only after those words were already in use did people like Aristotle begin to systematically pay attention to and to conceptually research what can be experienced as something structural emerging from these forms of language, which would be something similar to developing the grammar of a spoken language by giving it an official form, yet not done in the role of a government official but an independent researcher. Research in logic has advanced in a very similar way to mathematical research: logicians have discovered (created) new kinds of logical grammars. The result of logical research is a shared set of *rules* that has been developed and processed for the purposes of argumentative use of language, to determine whether a conclusion is valid or not. As with mathematics we can say that the rules of logic are not metaphysical and don't necessarily apply, but the necessity in which they apply is logical and bound to the meaning of the concepts in the first place, and in order to change the meaning one would need to redefine the concepts—something that has happened in mathematics several times. The experience of the absoluteness of logic is a result of apprehending and assuming these rules. The *discovery* of the rules of logic, starting from Aristotle's syllogisms, is research of the common features of language *that is already in use*, and the fact that it is already in use is the actual basis of why those rules turn out to be true. Since then logic has been formalized, and features of such formal systems (such as the quantifiers of second order logic) introduced into mathematical discourse, and logic can be thought of as a recipe book for correct thought to be referred to when irrationality is to be suspected in people. A parallel to mathematics, again: we can easily dispute that *1+2=3*; it doesn't have to be. But it does have to be that if we take the numbers and connectives to mean what they mean; in the simplest form, if we take the numbers *1,2,3* to denominate the amount of fingers, then you will indeed *find out* that adding two fingers to one finger will actually compute to three fingers, and you will find this with absolute rigidity, as the praxis of computation can be repeated by anybody, which lays the objective base of the concepts. And this is because we *are* humans with ten fingers, without exception; what we have here is, so to say, a God-given reality. So, it is not the mathematical relations, or mathematical reality, that is transcendent and God-given; what is actually transcendent is our *genome*—the unchanging human quality—that we have created this logical language to refer to. Returning to logic; what is then the unchanging foundation of, say, propositional logic? Clearly the words: 'is', 'if', 'then', 'and', 'or' and 'not'. Now, these are not static in the same sense as our genome, because we can, in theory, imagine a full language in which such words are not used. But these words seem to be quite universally used in various languages around the world. So, let's wrap this thought up and simply conclude that the rigid basis of propositional logic is the existence of those connectives *in the natural language*, and in order to dispute the validity of the rules of propositional logic one needs to dispute the meaning of those connectives, which means to step outside the language in which they are used. This is, of course, easy to prove; just found a commune of your own in which those connectives are banned and invite people to partake in the life of this commune... and you will see that the transcendent nature of those connectives will gradually disappear. To dispute them does not take a thought experiment but a real experiment with *actual* language that is in use. This test would actually prove that the logical rigidity of the *a priori* in rationalism is not innate or transcendent knowledge but learned... only it might turn out difficult to prove due to how central these connectives are to our communication. The sort of *discovery* related to logical or mathematical research is not discovery in the same sense as in "Columbus discovered America", because the sense of 'existence' when speaking of the existence of continents is different from when one speaks of the existence of logical or mathematical concepts, which derives from the fact that we verify their existence in a different manner. The occurrence of the same word 'exist' in two meanings is explained by the fact that the practical similarity of the experience has given rise to the logical/mathematical existential quantifier ('there exists') in the corresponding language. It might be noted that we often use 'existence' in a non-sensory meaning, such as in "Do you think that true love exists?", "The existence of free will separates humans from animals", or "Somewhere out there a better world exists for all of us", not to mention spiritual existence. Also, it is correct to say in a non-sensory sense that a mathematician is able to *see* mathematical qualities: the mathematical discovery occurs in the space created by the already

I-8. THE FOUR TYPES OF REASON

existent and subjectively apprehended language. What is important, however, is that the process of logical discovery is essentially a process of the *creation* of logical tools that are *useful* as the basis of other linguistic systems with inherent logical (indisputable) qualities, such as mathematics and argumentation. Because we want to be able to build houses that last and an egalitarian system of justice, we want to have a basis for such systems that is indisputable and universal, and it is this need and only this need that has (in the West) given birth to the need for logical discovery. We want foundations that are unbreakable.

There is a common cognitivist misconception that logic is related to *thought*, because we often use the word 'logic' in reference to thought, but related errors can be cleared up by establishing that logic is related to *spoken word* and *argument*, and can only be said to be related to thought via attribution. Logic is an objective framework that is based on shared language, and there is no way to 'think logically' by yourself, unless what you actually mean is the application or repetition of these same argumentative 'moves' within your inner dialectic that you would normally use in spoken dialectic. To the cognitivist I would like to say that to test this is not to try and imagine it in your mind but to look at the meaning of the concepts, which is something shared, actual and objective instead of a phantasm of one's imagination. When we call something logical, we mean that from something that *has been said* follows something else, which gives us the inclination to formalize what is being said into having a structure via the connective words that are being used. And this is done not to point out that the thought processes that the subject has are wrong, but with the purpose of clarifying language; whether what is being said is in accordance with the logic of the concepts that are being used and our understanding of the related connectives. People are free to use their minds any way they like; the only place where we have to start making corrections is communication. *Logical errors* are due to difficulties in maintaining thought that is in harmony with our society *in terms of social justice*, which in our Western society promotes many things, such as equality of individuals, rationality in terms of cause and effect and justification in the scope of *social norms*. Logical errors are all cases of "jumping to conclusions",

PART I. THE BASIS OF THOUGHT

and it should be clearly observed that jumping to conclusions is perfectly normal and acceptable if you are, as it were, within the comfort of your own home. In their own homes people are free to—and do—rage, kick the walls and blame all that is wrong in their lives on their neighbours' stupidity. However, stepping out from one's home, presenting *public* accusations brings the problem of escalating a social conflict, and this will definitely happen unless the rationale of one's argument is valid in said terms and, most importantly, social norms. This conflict might be escalated even if the argument was clearly valid but having a clear and valid argument is the best option if one is to get social support from surrounding neutral observers and thus to induce willingness to agreement from one's opponent. Take the following as an example (I'm not saying this sort of argument would be very common).

– *A(ccuser): You took my socks from the drier!*
– *D(efendant): I did not! Why do you say that? I don't want your smelly socks!*
– *A: I saw you in the laundry room today! I know it was you, it's not the first time.*
– *D: Have you ever thought there are other people in this building, too? Maybe it was somebody else?*
– *A: Don't deny it! Something always goes wrong when you're around.*
– *O(bserver): Excuse me, but from D being in the laundry room and the socks missing, it does not follow that D took them (non sequitur). Maybe there is another alternative?*
– *A: Well, I guess I might have misplaced them. But I'm still quite sure D took them.*
– *D: Well of course you're sure! You're always so sure, aren't you? Last time you were sure...*
– *O: Come on, now, whatever happened last time is unrelated to what we have at hand, yes? (hasty generalization)*
– *A: Last time? Last time it was my underpants that were missing... and you took them, too, didn't you?*
– *D: What?? You son of a... I would not touch your stinking...*
– *O: Now, settle down! Maybe last time something else happened? It*

I-8. THE FOUR TYPES OF REASON

does not follow from your clothes being missing that D took them (non sequitur). Do you have any other evidence except your suspicion?
- *D: Well... No...*
- *O: Well, do you agree that it is possible that D didn't take them?*
- *A: Yes...*
- *O: Well, D, did you take them?*
- *D: No!*
- *O: Well, would you help A to find out what happened to them?*
- *D: Of course!*

The need for logic comes wherever there is a need for social justice and harmony, and this implies a situation where the opponents are in relatively equal power relation so that both parties are willing to take part in argument instead of relying on raw power instead. To engage in an argument means to accept that one is expected to justify one's actions, which implies that one is unable to ignore the issue and must defend oneself, or, rather, that defending oneself is a favourable option compared to other consequences. This equality, of course, in Western society, is ultimately enforced by our system of justice, which tries to guarantee everybody an equal opportunity to make this defence. If there was no system of justice, the need for public argument would reduce to its primitive origin where it is simply a system of communication between opposing parties that can be used in an attempt to negotiate instead of avoiding or attacking one another. But if we do accept the premise of being equal enough to try and reach agreement, we will find out that being logical, instead of jumping to conclusions, is actually very, very difficult! We humans are passionate, emotional and aggressive creatures and known to attack each other on a whim! As an example, the word 'if' in natural language implies potential action or event, for example "If I catch you looking at other men, you'll know all about it!" But one can also use 'if' by simply pointing out a logical relation, such as: "If one merely thinks about rape, that doesn't make one a rapist" (as a side-note, rape fantasies are common)—however, presenting such a logical relation can have its 'if' associated to the 'if' as in potential action, which can unfortunately be interpreted as rapist sympathies, or that the person himself is planning rape. This is an example of grammatical misleading in Wittgensteinian terms where one form of 'if' is associating with another and causes confusion, and I deliberately chose rape as an example of a theme that typically arouses strong sentiments that routinely evade rational conversation. Another way to present this is to say that in thought, full neutrality is difficult, and one is easily bound to be associated with a social group. In the rapist example, the difficulty is in saying something neutral about rapists without being associated with them, and in practice it is the work of professionals to neutrally study such groups or to work to help them. The logical form to present this associative jumping to conclusions is *affirming the consequent*: "If he is a rapist, he has also been thinking about rape." The more controversial the topic, the more we are inclined to make these hasty associations that lead into simply wrong conclusions.

Yet it is much more interesting to look more deeply at the phenomenon of *irrationality* than to simply state, with the criterion of logic, that an irrational person is not being rational, as if there was simply something *technically* wrong in the thought process, and we could behave like teachers and just correct the error, and then the subject would think correctly. As mentioned, the alternative to using logic is avoiding, ignoring or fighting; it is not necessary to step into the argumentative arena where the rules favour the logical. People differ in their inclination towards rationality: some people are likely to jump to conclusions while others less likely to do so, but there are people who tend to be both often vocal and often wrong. Often there is something wrong, but it is not a technical issue; rather it is an *existential contradiction* that causes irrationality. I find this idea intuitive, since it is quite easy to observe that whenever people are being irrational, rather than this taking the form of a single instance of technical error it is instead a behaviour that they show after they are met with something subjectively undesirable: a conflict. And by this I mean a case where the person is otherwise calm and reasonable, but suddenly becomes irrational; it is common that in various anomalous states of mind people are highly irrational. During the state of irrationality, the subject may come to multiple irrational conclusions ... and in the end is typically willing to soothe this state by accepting something he knows to be untrue. This is like a state of denial where everything is no, no, no; followed by a state of acceptance where whatever presented is yes, yes, yes. One can explain this undesirable event psychologically, but it is also a matter of conceptual-level thought and can be explained with the aid of propositional logic and the logical principle of explosion,[82] as, most essentially, the self-deceiving subject is living a *contradiction* between thought and existence, and this existence involves a constant escape of this contradiction. Consider someone hiding a truth from himself; for example, consider an obese man and the horrible truth "I have an unhealthy lifestyle". He is aware of his obesity but doesn't want to say so and face its cause, so, he starts to eat smaller meals in public and goes to gym sometimes, remembering to mention this to everybody. He now has two presentable facts to support the claim "I don't have an unhealthy lifestyle", which is what he *wants* to believe about himself and which makes him feel positive and good about himself. Now, consider somebody suddenly confronting him with something that supports the claim about his unhealthy lifestyle, which he *knows* to be true; such as his wife asking him what happened to all the cupcakes that were in the fridge. This question is in support of the claim that his lifestyle is indeed unhealthy, but he also has his support for the claim "I don't have an unhealthy lifestyle". This is a contradiction, so, *ex falso quodlibet*: the use of logic has been ruled out from among the possible ways in which he can respond, and he will respond with anything illogical that he can use to escape the contradiction ("We must have rats in the kitchen"). And the key here is that the escape is *triggered* by the subjective conceptual contradiction; if he wasn't maintaining the logically contradicting view about himself, he wouldn't need to answer illogically but could admit to his deeds. Since Festinger (1957) the phenomenon that initiates the trigger has been called "cognitive dissonance", maintaining that we have a natural, physical inclination towards consistency of beliefs, which is disrupted by a contradiction in thought and which results in discomfort. I find this to be in accordance with said existential conflict that causes a brief, but soon settling, state of irrationality. It seems to me that this kind of irrational

---

82 The principle of explosion, or *ex falso quodlibet*, is expressed in formal logic as $(p \wedge \neg p) \rightarrow q$. It can be read as "From p and *not-p* it follows that q".

PART I. THE BASIS OF THOUGHT

thinking is very common, and evident irrationality is rather a sign of subjective contradiction: it is common sense that if you try to push something you know to be true to somebody who you know is in *denial* (he strongly believes a contradictory statement), you can expect that he will claim *anything* in response, and he will do so in all seriousness. The basis of the psychological phenomenon of denial (and likewise acceptance) is *involvement*, which actually is a social phenomenon. One can think about denial via the common reaction people have in a socially surprising situation: "I'm sorry, am I troubling you at all?—Oh, no, no, no!" or "Would you like a chocolate?—No, no, thank you"... in these cases the denial is a direct reaction of courtesy to an unexpected social contact with a stranger, and essentially the subject wants to signify he is harmless and considering himself uninvolved with any social issue at hand, not taking sides with anybody or having any intentions. The answer is not made to the letter of the question but is a diplomatic response as the first step of diplomacy, which is to signify peaceful intentions, as no trust has yet been established between the individuals (or parties). Similarly, denial is the psychological initial response when one is met with any criticism or undesirable news, such as news of a drastic illness; there is a course of psychological stages that starts from denial and leads into acceptance. This is our way of coping with *surprise*; things that contradict our expectation; evidence that contradicts our existing belief. There are situations in which people or groups adhere to contradicting ideals, and such cases can be expected to have completely wild and arbitrary results, not because they are bad people or incapable thinkers, but because of the contradiction and the human disposition captured in the principle of explosion: *the human rational capability will push out the contradiction by creating an arbitrary third assumption*. Some contemporary examples include: "One should not tolerate intolerant people" or "All white people are racist"... the key in these paradoxes is that the statement is not just a grammatical exercise, but in order to *say* that statement one needs to *exist*, which anchors the statement to the real world: somebody is actually saying the statement, and that the statement says something about real people. To say something like this obviously means one is *living* a paradox, not just randomly spouting a paradox as the result of an uncontrollable

I-8. THE FOUR TYPES OF REASON

release of gas from the mouth. *Ex falso quodlibet* says that people arguing from such premises will conclude *quodlibet*, and also that all conclusions derived from these contradicting premises rest on the same contradicting foundation and will collapse when the contradiction is finally abolished. The Latin word 'quodlibet' literally means "what will *please* you", so, *EFQ* can be read as: "From a contradiction, what will follow is something that will *please* you", which is where one can see the connection of acceptance in the case of pleasurable news and denial in the case of undesirable news. *EFQ* means that if you think in such a manner that your thought incorporates a contradiction, then you will rationally conclude from this contradiction whatever will please you, and this explains the irrationality of thought both in the case when a person is learning surprising news and denies it, and the case where the person remains in self-deceptive denial and is sometimes met with this constantly existing contradiction. Note that the irrational conclusion of a conflicted person is not something random but something that he wants to believe; likely something that will apparently make the conflict go away. The right way to think about the existence of this classical logical rule is that *over hundreds or thousands of years* thoughtful observers have discovered that people who think in a contradictory manner also *tend to* think in a manner that serves their own pleasures, not their own best interests or the common good; it is an ancient psychological truth. Let me demonstrate the explosion of the contradiction; consider if both A is true and A is not true ($\neg A$ is true), then also "A or P" and $\neg A$ are true... but if either A or P is true, and we know A is not true, then P must be true. To give a practical example: you're driving for work and your planned journey runs via Route 52. You check the latest travel information and find out that the route is blocked. Now you know both that you must take Route 52 and that you can't take Route 52. Now you are forced to take some other route, so your behaviour surely won't be random but instead you'll take the most inviting option. So, the 'quodlibet' is much more revealing than just to think that one would choose a random P whenever *EFQ* is applied; the wisdom of *EFQ* is that the contradiction *causes some P* to be pushed into the conclusion, and *any P is equally logically valid solely and exactly because of the contradiction*. We can reverse it: if you have an irrational arbitrary *P* as your conclusion, check your premises; if you find a contradiction, that is all the explanation you need, as the human mind will do this whenever it meets a contradiction. From the perspective of rationality, whenever we can observe somebody having taken action in this manner, we can call it 'intuitive', 'creative', 'ad hoc' or 'desperate'; for example we may say with a hint of irony: "Peter was forced to get creative", meaning Peter had to do something, even though he was out of reasonable options. In this sense, logical rules are not only syntactical tools but empirical truths about human nature, and the related systems exist to pass on the wisdom related to rational thought as a human phenomenon. It is highly ironical that at a time when we have the most computer-literate people—people who operate machines that consist of essentially logic gates and that contain a processor that is controlled with an operation set containing logical operations such as *and*, *or* and *not*—we have no people to deal with logical errors in argument, and in fact that the whole concept of *logical error* is non-existent in discourse. To be more accurate, it is because our society is so far away from *subjectivity* that we have so little interest in the logic of concepts; we are only looking at *evidence* but not at all at the logic of what is being said. It is as if whatever is said could have been said by anybody at any time and with no connection to who said it and in what context and with what likely meaning. To be furthest away from subjectivity means to be most objective, which means to be most shallow and taking what is being said as true on the immediate surface level only with no interest at all in the subjectivity of the person speaking. This is true even to the extent that we never notice or even think about logical error; the error between what is being said and who is saying it. For example, I recently read a newspaper column where the columnist expressed the hope that politicians would act against climate change because Finnish people are consuming at alarming rates and also because the Earth is warming at an alarming rate. We can see that both of these arguments—separately—make a scientific and testable sense, but bundled together they make no sense at all as it is rather impossible (or to be accurate, *occult*) to think that some particular cause was causing both high consumption *and* warming Earth temperature. It seems to me that such an argument is *impersonal* and thus not to be

I-8. THE FOUR TYPES OF REASON

taken seriously; it is simply the mindless, machine-like repetition of what somebody else has said, where one has forgotten that one actually needs to both think and exist both in order to mean what one says and to be logical, and if one would, instead of just speaking, try and actually *think* these two things together, the logical contradiction would emerge in one's existence. It seems to me that our whole age has taken the achievements crafted with the concept of logic but forgotten the whole history of logic as a study of correct thought, and there exists no organ to say what is correct thought *or* correct language. What will happen to those who forget reason? The implications of the answer to the question are sinister.

In a similar way as with logic, there is a lot of controversy over the nature of *mathematics*—not because there is something mystical or metaphysical about mathematics but because our society and natural science are so heavily based on mathematics and the history of mathematics is so long and there is so much human work behind it that it is not easy to understand what it actually is. In order to avoid the commonplace philosophical confusion created by a metaphysical approach towards mathematics, it essentially needs to be understood as a language; a logical grammar. This is most easily done by taking a look at the roots of mathematics in history in times when it was developed independently at different parts of the world essentially as notational system used for practical matters, such as commerce, architecture and tracking the seasons and time. After these practical uses for such a language had been established the need arose for a separate line of study further developing the grammar itself for greater precision and applicability, to allow new practical fields of application and to overcome problems in the overlap of the fields of application. The copious details and practice of this study are relevant to mention here only inasmuch as the study has progressed through a series of abstractions and extensions. The metaphysical perspective towards mathematics that a mathematician would typically hold is useful in allowing him a concrete perspective towards mathematics and exposes him to the often-cited aesthetic beauty of mathematics and the experience of discovery related to the thought process involved in mathematical study.

PART I. THE BASIS OF THOUGHT

It results from the existential change of the mathematician towards his standard of excellence in his profession, similar to the way a professional musician or a sound engineer might see sounds or tones as colours, a sculptor might see a block of stone as a ready-made sculpture, or a music professional will immediately recognize levels of structure within a complex piece of work. But outside such perspective it can be seen that the baffling question: "How can it *be* that *1+1=2*?" is valid because of the grammatical structure and properties of the mathematical language, for exactly the same reasons as we would say it is correct to say "Peter sleep*s*" instead of "Peter sleep" with such certainty that if this rule didn't hold we would need to revise the whole grammar and nothing could be trusted to make sense any more. The laws of mathematics we have been taught at school are the result of a long process of adjusting and refining the mathematical grammar such that it can be broadly and reliably applied, and as such mathematics provides a reliable basis in its special role in our society as the governing language providing the framework for the rest of science and many other fields of life. This is only to point out that the factual truth of a mathematical statement is no different from the factual truth of statements of other kinds in that a method exists for its validation and verification: one involving applying the mathematical language in mathematical proof. Of course, in practice this proof is never performed but we accept its truth as we trust the mathematicians (researchers) that, as a profession, have created our mathematical language. Proof is taught in schools to the extent that students are receptive, but it is essentially the tool for mathematical research unrelated to the application of mathematics, no differently than how the profession of a potter is distinct from the use of pottery in a household. Then again, the baffling question presented above was totally senseless in a world in which mathematics was not yet axiomatized; where the meaning of natural numbers was bound to their repeatability in an objective medium, such as a series of hand signs, knots on a rope, or simple markings or carvings. There is nothing baffling about the fact that a person can see three birds and place three rocks on a plank, or that a person can make a small carving on a rock every time the Sun rises, or that a person can teach another that a particular symbolic marking (of, say, three strokes) means he needs to

I-8. THE FOUR TYPES OF REASON

repeat a certain process and upon each repetition raise one finger on his left hand, until he has as many fingers up as there are markings in the symbol, and that after enough practice, validated by an inspecting teacher, he doesn't need to hold his fingers up as he can be acknowledged to have understood the process. Only after the usefulness of such activities was recognized in terms of making predictions did the men acquainted with these tasks begin to develop the qualities of the representational systems further. The baffling nature of mathematics arose only after the *already existing* mathematical language had been separated from such practical meanings and natural numbers redefined in different, solely theoretic, terms. What baffles us is that the whole mathematical grammar is carefully unified in modern terms, and this bafflement is similar to how the Egyptian pyramids baffle us because the amount of *human labour* required is gigantic, but the difference is that the details (axioms and proofs) of the human labour behind the mathematical grammar are hidden from the viewpoint of their application. It might seem to us that one plus one *simply* equals two, but the centuries of collaborative mathematical research underlying the *meaning* of those modern mathematical concepts is hidden beneath our simple lessons of their practical application. What we all learn in school is a precise formal language that is readily applicable to a vast multitude of practical situations, but we don't learn the meaning of the related concepts—just certain practical ways of how to apply them. Actually even elementary arithmetical operations have various meanings depending on the axiomatization of reference, and the interesting part is that these operations existed—in a different meaning—before the current standard axiomatization (Peano axioms); the axiomatization process, by many contributors, took what was already existent and suggested creating a foundation for it, which effectively contributes a new meaning to the mathematical concepts. The case for mathematics is equivalent to the case for any words of natural language: we learn to use a computer mouse and assign the name 'mouse' to it before we have any conception about the details of the construction and history of computer mice or the related evolution of the concept of computer mouse. Also, as in natural language, in mathematics the meanings evolve, just via a different process.

PART I. THE BASIS OF THOUGHT

The view presented above directly contradicts the traditional conception of logic in Western philosophy, in which *logical systems*, simply built with care upon commonly used words, are seen as equivalent to logic,[83] which is a fundamental misconception similar to taking an institution to equal the ethical ideology it has been created to convey. Logic needs to be understood as forming the boundaries of the meaningful use of concepts, and the purpose of this is to clarify communication in the interests of social justice, which is a very cumbersome task as our society is very complex and our primal tendency to attack one another is strong. There are other ways to reach social harmony, but I am doubtful whether there could be other ways to reach *egalitarian* social justice. Then again, if our egalitarian society collapses, as is to some degree happening due to the increasingly disproportional distribution of wealth and power, the need for logic also collapses as the upper classes simply won't need to argue with the rabble. And this social system is where the indisputable *a priori* nature of logic is rooted. Simply put, anything logical in nature should be considered indisputable, but any subjective position presenting itself as logical alternatives should not, as logic always boils down to a subject trying to convince. As an example, let's say I am at an intersection of three roads, A, B and C. What is *a priori* here is the number of roads: three. But the fundamental disputable fact here is the question whether I accept the premises; whether I am a traveller at all, to say I won't take any of these alternatives doesn't make me any "less logical". I might dispute the premise itself and claim instead that there must be more roads. In fact, the idea of people placing their trust in logic to resolve dilemmas in their life is comical, or even tragic, to me, since human reason is highly fallible in an existential sense, and instead there are alternative existential facts that are infallible. But there is a thing that can be called "being logical", which means being able to spot and avoid a contradiction in argument, which translates to a skill where one can apply this model to one's own thought and, hopefully, ultimately not contradict oneself in the concepts one uses oneself. This quality is essentially equal to the Socratic ideal. Let's say somebody presents a claim: "All science is innovation."

---

[83] Similarly, 'mathematics' is commonly taken to mean the application of mathematical language.

I-8. THE FOUR TYPES OF REASON

It does *not* make one logical to be able to formulate this logically, such as "For all s; $s = i$" or to be able to add further premises and use deductive reasoning to reach the given goal; in fact it is very sad that this mostly useless formal logic is taught in academic philosophy studies. It is mostly useless because being able to formulate one's logical reasoning is not considered an ideal anymore; then again, it is no standard for being skilled, intelligent or moral. What logic really is, and what is expected from a logical person, is to understand what 'science' and 'innovation' *mean*, and to be able to come up with counter-examples where something aptly called science would not meet with something aptly called innovation, and to make clarifications about and restrictions to the scope of the concepts in the sense of the claim; not to bar or deny a claim but to clarify its sense. The philosopher is critical, not because of willingness to contradict or to show fault, but because the more people rely on terminology that is inaccurate and misleading—ambivalent—the more destructive this fault becomes. But ultimately, this understanding about the relationship between logic and meaning should change the way the logical person himself speaks, since a person understanding this should understand what Wittgenstein meant by saying that anything that can be said at all can be said clearly. If someone knows what meaning is and the different senses of a word, he is ready to use the word without causing confusion or without possibility for philosophical criticism. In addition to being resistant to confusion, he is also resistant to *conceptual attacks* where language is deliberately redefined or alternative meanings used as a part of manipulation, psychological attack, propaganda or information warfare; we have several examples of deliberate conceptual redefinition to suit a political agenda, such as communist, fascist or feminist propaganda or e.g. Derrida's deconstructionism. Because of their simplicity I have always deeply admired the lyrical forms of both Wittgenstein and Kierkegaard, which are very different but both fundamentally beyond the possibility for criticism; simple text to read but difficult to grasp, like our most beautiful classical themes.[84,85] Writing philosophy doesn't re-

---

[84] A quote from Chopin reads: "Simplicity is the highest goal, achievable when you have overcome all difficulties. After one has played a vast quantity of notes and more notes, it is simplicity that emerges as the crowning reward of art."
[85] Similarly, the better I have learned the dominant language, English, and with full

quire coverage of some particular topic, as one would need to do for an academic subject. It doesn't even require complete understandability or accuracy. What is required is that *your thought is not contradictory*... and this is a much more difficult task, which can't be achieved by paying attention to what you are writing.

I-8-3. Teleology

"Why does the butterfly have wings? —In order to fly!" In this example the question "Why?" is asked in wonderment without any commitment to a particular sense of answering,[86] but the answer is given *as a reason*. We are looking at objective phenomena from the perspective of subjective purpose. A valid sense for this sort of an answer is not in that the butterfly once had an option to choose not to have wings, but that the *creator* of the butterfly had an option to create a wingless butterfly but for some reason chose to create one with wings. We can also say within the same discourse that the butterfly has wings for the *purpose* of flying, in the same way as we use 'purpose' in "The purpose of wearing a hat in the winter is to keep one's ears from freezing", which implies that we also have a choice of not wearing a hat, against which wearing a hat in the winter can be seen purposeful. The 'mysterious' sensation of determination related to teleology is related to the two choices of discourse to explain phenomena—the subjective and the objective—that overlap in the experience if one doesn't make the distinction. But importantly, the causal, objective explanation will never prove satisfactory regarding natural phenomena. As Wittgenstein repeated, after Frege,[87] the *meaning* of a word is what *gives life* to the word. Con-

---

respect to the archaic beauty of the language of an old civilization, the more I have come to appreciate the laconic linguistic culture of my native tongue in which it is a beauty to express concisely, using as few words as possible, making extensive use of the highly flexible constructive grammar instead of tonal variance. Finnish is a particularly suitable language for poetry and learning Finnish in school seems to produce relatively high skills in reading and writing, where, as it were, grammar reigns and social skills won't help you.

86   One could equally well answer within a causal discourse "Because natural selection has favoured this" or "Because it is of the order Lepidoptera".
87   The Blue Book

I-8. THE FOUR TYPES OF REASON

sider someone learning about butterflies from a book: "A butterfly is an insect of the order Lepidoptera with such-and-such characteristics and behaviour" and so on. Does he now understand what 'butterfly' means? He understands it through the criterion of the book he learned it from and its references, such as the biological taxonomy, and the question of whether it is correct to say that he understands the meaning of 'butterfly' is a matter of which standard of meaning we are referring to when asking the question.[88] It seems to me that a good criterion for determining whether he completely understands the meaning of the word 'butterfly' is whether he would be surprised by butterflies, since only things about butterflies that are new (to him) could appear to him sudden and surprise him. Consider our book-taught lepidopterist travelling to the Amazon to empirically study butterflies for the first time, finding himself standing in the middle of a thousand butterfly species. Could we imagine this moment not striking him with surprise and wonder? The empirical situation would allow him to use his own *reason* about butterflies, with remarks such as: "Why does this species have white dots in its black wings? It seems to predominantly prefer to sit on dark tree branches: are the dots there to hide the butterfly from predators?" and so on. We subjectively understand relations between phenomena through all forms of reasoning, and despite the fact that our understanding is hidden, the surprise is proof that we have learned something new about the phenomenon a certain word is related to. And this process of discovery is not limited in any way; the commonplace conception that "science has already explained almost everything" is a misconception related precisely to the two-fold role of science as providing both 1) the objective basis of our common notions and 2) authority over the process that produces new information. Thus, science can be depicted as a window of standardized meaning in the timeline of world history resembling the following cyclic process.

1) The current world status creates demand and funding for research.

2) Research provides new information that also functions as a basis of creating new concepts and renewing the standard criteria of the

---

[88] These commonly get confused and it is commonplace to say e.g. "You don't understand what such-and-such means" when finding out one's conversational partner does not share one's meaning and criterion.

meaning of existing concepts.

3) New information is popularized and apprehended by society and in textbooks read in schools by the new generation.

4) Apprehended new information plays a role in a change in the world status. → Go to step 1.

We can now distinguish this third sense of "Why? Because...", as a *teleological* concept, where the person is looking at an objective, shared phenomenon from the perspective of the framework of reasons. The word comes from *telos* and *logos*, literally meaning a goal-reason or a goal-explanation. The outcome is a meaning where something is seen as *occurring for a purpose*, and this purpose seems to be nothing more complicated than *a need*. The butterfly doesn't just use wings to fly, but flying is a prerequisite for its life and reproduction; it needs to fly. The baby cries... Why? We could answer either in the sense of causality: "Because he is hungry" or in the teleological sense: "Because he needs food"... and we can see that, similar to the subjective reason, the teleological explanation involves the perspective of what *should happen*; that is, the baby should be fed. Hence the need, which is a strictly subjective concept; the *teleological argument* is an argument based on the justice of *satisfying a need*. The teleological explanation, sort of, gives us an answer in the form of relief from tension, because the answer satisfies our sense of justice, in that it sets things into a perspective of how they should be. It just happens to differ from justification in that it involves an objective phenomenon instead of a private one. And hence teleological reason is applicable only within a moral framework about things that are not independent subjects that are expected to have independent, subjective reasons and related rights, such as animals and babies, but that we can agree to have respective needs, such as here the need to stay alive and the need to be fed. Babies or butterflies are mostly objects to us, and by this I mean that we would mostly think about them from the perspective of how to interact with them, and not from the perspective of them as independent actors or persons with rights. When we say of something that it 'needs' something, we are actually touching on the area that would normally belong to the person's rights as an independent subject, and if we say e.g. "Peter has a red jacket

I-8. THE FOUR TYPES OF REASON

today because he needs to attract attention from the ladies", we are not actually letting Peter defend himself against our judgement but objectifying him, implying that he has a need for attention, which might be true but nevertheless is not a very nice thing to say because it does not respect Peter's rights and personality as an individual. So, to take the teleological, subjective opinion about an objective phenomenon, the phenomenon indeed is regarded as an object.

Metaphysical commitment to any of the types of reason will produce the expected metaphysical confusions. As an example, consider the heart and arteries in the human body. The standard way is to interpret the heart as a mechanism that pumps blood into the arteries, and I have been told that it is sensible to research anatomy mechanistically because so many features of the human body seem to function analogously to machines. But this is simply an observation following from one's methodology, and there is nothing to restrict a teleological perspective to the same phenomenon; humans are *required to live* (or to, say, reproduce), and the heart performs a role in enabling this by providing the body cells with a blood circulation that is necessary for their life. And this perspective is very applicable when observing *phenotype*, because an organism's environment can be seen to set requirements, and the phenotype can be said to develop *in order to* fulfil a practical purpose enabling it to survive in its environment that is restricted in a very particular way: a monkey has long fingers, instead of short ones like humans have, in order to grasp tree branches better, and so on. The mechanistic causal perspective dominates science altogether because searching for causes reveals practical information that helps us humans to manipulate our environment to our advantage. To say that the heart pumps blood into the arteries enables us to design methods to interact with this process in a sensible manner, mostly from the important standpoint of curing people. Then again, the teleological, purposeful discourse is central in religious thought, but no more than it is central in any thought that emphasizes the subjective: as an example, once after a badminton training session I remember muttering to my coach something like "I should work on my game so I stop making such elementary errors..." but he came right back at me with "No, why

PART I. THE BASIS OF THOUGHT

should you? Humans often need to repeat the same mistake for years and years." I remember this lesson as a deep truth: why say "I *should* do such-and-such" as if asking for forgiveness from your coach, when you obviously are not going to do it now and the whole question is simply a subjective matter of when you are ready to make the difference within yourself—my coach had the wisdom to see purpose in failure: it is failure that can teach us subjectively, and the moment of failure is a subjective opportunity to see where we fail. Another example would be: "I should quit smoking", which can be answered with: "No, obviously you need to smoke more (since you don't yet see clearly enough why you should quit)." But now, let me say that there exists a *fundamental flaw in the mechanistic approach in science* altogether, which is this: that the mechanism, in the sense of 'mechanistic', is essentially a metaphor, having roots somewhere in Descartes' observations of early mechanisms and an idea that the body is a mechanism where the source of all movement is caused by animal spirits somehow operating in the pineal gland as a "force of the soul". He thought that the pineal gland *must be* "the seat of the soul" because everything else in the brain is doubled yet the pineal gland is a singular organ, which makes sense because our soul is surely a singular entity, and was thought to be the home of all our primary subjective qualities that separate us from animals: thought, common sense and so on. Descartes was looking for a singular place to satisfy the idea of the home of the soul, as this would be a sensible thing to do considering how the body can be seen to operate in accordance with our subjective experience of wilfully and consciously moving our body. Today we mostly agree that this place is the brain, and that we don't know how the brain does it, but it can be safely assumed it does it anyway and it will simply be a matter of time until this is finally discovered and all gaps closed. But where is the *operator* of the mechanism—the *soul*—in today's science? *All mechanisms have an operator*, and this point is equally forgotten in the study of AI; we can see this in the confused results of its practitioners, who base their explanations on occultism and fiction, trying to figure out why it is true that at the same time machines can and cannot operate on their own. If you're convinced the heart is a mechanism that pumps blood into the arteries, then please answer the question: who operates the

I-8. THE FOUR TYPES OF REASON

heart? A modern scientist would just consider this a silly question, but he is unaware of his metaphor and its history; Descartes didn't consider it a silly question at all, and after him others came, took him as a sage and then quite misunderstood or misinterpreted his theories. The *sense* of 'mechanism' in 'mechanistic' implies an operator. This devastating linguistic problem of bad use of metaphor—using an ill-fitting metaphor—exists no less in the whole idea of computationalism: if the brain is a computer, who programs it and starts it? Let me compare this to the phenomenon of crop circles, because I have noticed that many people share stories about these crop circles; people I consider will believe anything and become easy victims of hoaxes. Distinctive circular figures appear overnight in a farmer's wheat field without any evident originator. Following the mechanist or the computationalist, it doesn't really matter if we know or don't know who created them, as long as we know that such things exist, so, let's call the circles "space shuttle prints" because this borrow from fiction would be the most obvious and immediate point of reference (crop circles are sort of designed to match an idea of a landing spaceship, and the idea likely arose from early UFO TV shows with their flying saucers). We know that space shuttles exist, we just don't know who would land such a space shuttle on a farmer's crop, but because we are only borrowing the parts of the space shuttle analogy that we need, and not all of it, it doesn't matter at this stage since it sets the course for new discovery and adventure. Then of course *if* we were pushed to answer the question of who we believe might have landed the space shuttle (and there doesn't seem to be any way to escape the question), as we are already committed to a particular metaphor we would be left with no option but to resort to attribution of the arcane: we suspect that the prints were made by space aliens (or Chomsky's cosmic ray shower), but this should be accompanied by for once seriously downplaying one's conviction and stressing the fallibility of science to avoid being branded the witch doctors we are. The arcane is the bastard son of science; the commitment to a particular methodology while remaining blind to the linguistic commitments one has already made, and thus being haunted by them, as we learn the meanings of many words at a young age and they dwell in our subconscious. Your reason is in the concepts you use;

PART I. THE BASIS OF THOUGHT

you reason according to those concepts. If you happen to, through experience and exposure, learn a concept that you took for real but that is actually an ill-fitting metaphor, you are completely trapped until you somehow break out of it... that is, if you even want to.

The standard contemporary natural scientific way is to think in terms of *blueprints*, and this no doubt has been inspired by computers and the metaphor of program code. In computers and program code, it is the programmers that do all the hard work to produce the user experience. This is a reality that doesn't seem to exist in the minds of many thinkers, because they just see the end-result of programming and have no clue whatsoever about how it is produced. This state of *bafflement* about how things arise is then directly transmitted to wondering about natural phenomena, as they have been shown things that look impossible. This is easy to relate to Plato's ideas and Cave allegory, where what one sees is merely a reflection of a greater plan that is hidden but can be painstakingly revealed to one; in fact, computers are exactly something that hide a *great plan* behind them; an infinite amount of work by mysterious professionals! Genetics, initially having the gene as simply a unit of heredity without any material or idealist basis, has for some time been a thought where DNA is seen a *code* for building humans. But Chomsky brought this idea into linguistics, Dawkins brought the idea of reproducible 'memes' into sociology and cognitive psychology, etc., and the blueprint approach has gained explosive popularity since the 1950s when Wittgenstein died. Now, take Plato's Cave and ask the question: Who created the Sun and the objects that had their reflections projected on the cave wall? The answer is: obviously a divine creator. Ask e.g. Chomsky or Dawkins the analogous questions: Who wrote these genes/memes that work as blueprints for psychological/social phenomena? Or: Who created the syntactic device that gives account to expressions of natural language? They will give the same, rather brutal, answer: "I don't care, and the people who do are weak minded." They are, essentially, taking the Platonist approach that natural phenomena are *defined* (blueprinted; having a related divine, transcendent *idea* behind them), but their methodology is Aristotelian: trying to *describe* phenomena that in themselves are taken as naturally occurring and thus as given. Instead of following Plato or Aristotle, both of whom in their own ways attributed the cause and origin of natural phenomena to a divine creator, they patch the missing Platonist divine architect with Aristotelian methodology, and the missing Aristotelian creator with the Platonist attribution of blueprint. I believe this sort of sleight of hand in thought is possible only from somebody who has internalized the scientific method as a personal religion. It seems to me that such a scientist doesn't care about the missing parts of his partially applied metaphor because he doesn't have to, which means that he hasn't yet been caught by a worldly authority with a branding iron hot enough to burn his thick skin deep enough to create discomfort, and he has also renounced his fears of any such punishment in the afterlife. It takes a very particular person, I believe, to achieve this kind of thought; something possible for a professional and not the man on the street, who in general is very sceptical of his own perspective and conclusions.

As with phenotypic qualities, subjective phenomena can also very sensibly be perceived teleologically. Consider *pain* or *fear*, which are nowadays considered solely undesirable and negative phenomena. Both can be said to exist and take place for a reason—in order to keep one from injuring or killing oneself—and thus to be evolutionarily highly functional qualities. Pain is not bad in itself, but it is easy to see that pain that is meaningful is good, and pain that is meaningless is bad, and this applies to both physical and mental pain. The same goes for fear; fear that is meaningful—a reasonable fear—is good, and we would say that our capability of fear exists for a reason. It seems to me that in the modern scientistic worldview these qualities are considered negative because we have committed singly to a causal discourse where one must view pain and cause as something caused by something or somebody and ignore any teleological considerations. This is because humans are perceived simply as mechanisms in which *external stimuli* cause internal reactions, and not that humans cause their bodies to move or to, for example, become obese as a result of neglect. But this bias in perception is not confined to these features but extends to e.g. all of psychiatry, which, as a field, has reduced to a statistical procedure of classifying people under a medical taxonomy and a similar statistical procedure of prescribing controversial medicine in order to 1) maximize the chances of the patient maintaining a capability to work and to 2) minimize the risk of malfeasance charges by holding fast to overly standardized (ritualized) practices instead of performing actual medical work, which has always also been a highly subjective and experimenting practical art. These days if one wants to be a real doctor one also needs to be a defiant rebel,[89] and this situation has left the door wide open to lobbying by pharma companies who try to fill the gap left because the doctor, who is simply a cog in the wheel of ritualized medicine, is not actually subjectively making enough choices to be able to feel responsible for the choices he makes when prescribing medicine. To make it clear: if a doctor happens to recommend a new vaccine to the patient—whether this is for the sake of any of the personal bonuses promised by the medicine corporation or not is unimportant—the decision to take the vaccine is completely on the patient and not to any extent on the doctor. That is, many doctors would feel this way, whereas many would not— "I did not take any of the money but saw many others doing it". Along with psychiatry shifting from a socio-psychological approach to a solely psychological perspective with drugs as the primary method to alter the socially isolated patient's brain functions, there has been a move by countries to legalize the drug cannabis—with the supporting argumentation concentrating on the individualistic benefits of the drug as a relaxing painkiller instead of its long known psycho-social function of triggering schizophrenia and boosting alienation. Contesting this modern neo-Cartesian development of people as isolated individuals with their brains as fact-processing machines, in favour of the classical concept of human thought as a dialectical process inherently involving reason, beliefs, errors of thought and so on, particular emotions related to psychiatric conditions can very sensibly be seen as occurring within the subject in order to provoke some change in his way of life. The teleological perspective is basically seeing purpose for a need, so, events in a subject's life can be seen as occurring for a purpose of a need to change something. For example *depression* can, similarly to how pain protects the subject from moving and fur-

---

89 Something similar could be going on in philosophy, too...

I-8. THE FOUR TYPES OF REASON

ther injuring an injured part of the body, be seen as a condition to provoke change in one's existence that one has lost faith in; as a motivation to start changing one's beliefs and move along new routes. *Suicidal thoughts* can be interpreted, instead of dangerous emotions statistically relating to suicide, as placing the subject in an existential position of choice between two alternatives: holding on to one's current way of existence which, as serving no purpose any more, is about to lead to death, or accepting that one has been wrong so far and to be willing to learn a new existence. One can note that *changing one's existence* and thus healing is exactly the effect the psychiatrist would actually like to see in his patient; it is just that the tools of modern soul doctors are clumsy and ineffective, and our ritual institution works to make sure no doctor would prescribe external existential remedies lest he be promptly cast out as a quack. Another such observation is that people who tend to block (or deny) their emotions seem to think that they have no *reason* for such feelings; for example, "I don't see a reason to hate, so I don't hate". Emotions don't require justifications; *actions* do, so this sort of thought is obviously carried over from upbringing where the expression of emotions is dominated by the parent; it is the mother who doesn't see a reason for the act of expressing so-called 'negative' emotions, because she doesn't know what to do with a crying child or is afraid of being accused of being a bad mother due to having a crying child. Certain emotions are typically considered 'negative', whereas all of them are clearly positively functional in, say, a hunter-gatherer society. Our modern psychiatric methods are bound to a statistical wish for a favourable outcome instead of a *sensible* framework of interpreting the patient's emotional experiences as a logical outcome of how the patient lives or, say, what distress he has had to experience. Instead of accepting that humans are, as it were, designed to suffer under particular situations, the psychiatrist is resorting to a statistical guess, which is a methodology designed for phenomena that are by nature unknown. Surely there is nothing unknown about the fact that people suffer mental conditions and get mentally ill; that this is a known fact is the basis of the whole Aristotelian taxonomy of mental illnesses, and the whole sense of classifying them is based on the fact that there are similarities in people's mental composition, development and the responses to events in their environment. Then again, hand-in-hand with this development, the demand for varieties of belief-based treatments and greedy quackeries is booming, because people report that they are genuinely helped simply from being humanely understood; that *somebody* is actually taking care of them. This is something they can't get from psychiatry or drugs, so they turn to unlicensed treatments, and this reaction is easy to understand as modern psychiatry is not set up to understand patients but takes as a hard, methodological fact that they cannot be understood. Rather than curing patients it seems to me that psychiatry is playing an active part in the cause of such problems, as it is the *denial* of emotions that causes psychiatric conditions in the first place; if what you can expect from a psychiatric visit is classification and drugs, these simply enforce the idea that there is something morally *wrong* about having mental problems, and will contribute to their denial. Man is to express his humanity in all regards and inhibiting the hunting and fighting human will result in a human who has issues with fear and anger.

I-8-4. Causality

Causation is to be understood as a linguistic argumentative tool, which implies that recognizing and communicating causal connections between observed objects and events is a fundamental and essentially social trait. It should be also noted that it is an exclusively *human* trait. Consider the monkey mother cracking nuts with a stone, and the baby monkey observing. The baby monkey can learn to mimic the mother's action. But a human is differentiated from these monkeys exactly by his rationality and the triadic attention: the human mother points to the nut and points to the stone and refers to them by their names for the baby: "Mom is breaking nuts with a stone." The baby observes the nuts and the stone, hears the associated words, and something wonderful and inherently human happens. Here is the first causal attribution: the mom teaches (convinces) the baby using a causal attribution. To see causality as a language is quite contrary to the commonplace so-called scientific world-picture that regards theories of natural science as true

I-8. THE FOUR TYPES OF REASON

or false. But as a philosophical position, this reflects a fundamental misunderstanding about the role of science in our understanding and the concept of truth.[90] The following is a simplification of how the scientific discourse advances.

1) Man finds that placing a certain plant on cuts stops bleeding.

2) Man concludes that the plant causes bleeding to stop.

3) Man investigates in more detail and finds that the plant contains a certain substance, and furthermore, that the application of the extracted substance on a cut will have the effect of clotting the blood, which results in stopped bleeding.

4) There's a change of discourse: no longer does the plant cause bleeding to stop, but the substance causes the blood to clot.

There is no logical contradiction between the discourses here, but the new concept of the substance in question might be a more useful causal agent, since extracting the substance could be more practical, for example, as extracts can often be bottled and preserved more efficiently. Both scientific statements remain true and don't contradict each other, as they are verified in a different manner: to see whether a plant is of the desired species is a very different process from seeing if a given sample of extract is of the desired substance, and similarly to see if the blood in a wound is clotted can be a different process from seeing if a wound has stopped bleeding.

The hypothetical-deductive method of science—unlike religion—by definition regards *no* scientific theory as a truth as such but a mere assumption (hypothesis) that in turn is used to determine whether something is true in the light of this assumption. For example, according to modern chemistry, water is H_2O, but this statement is not true or false, but a hypothesis. Then, given a sample of liquid, one can apply the methods of chemistry to find out whether the chemical structure of the sample is H_2O, and thus verify if it is true or false to say that the sample contains water. From the standpoint of science, a theory can be *applicable* and useful and can be methodologically accepted as a

---

90   Wittgenstein points this out in *Tractatus* 6.371

hypothesis, but none of this concerns truth. To think that a very applicable theory *can*, for the sake of simplicity, be accepted as a truth because of its applicability, is an intellectual crime and an act of making a deity out of an instrument, which, however, is quite commonplace among people who love their work and is an integral constituent in the subject's devotion to his work. Just think about the dishonesty of saying: "Let's all just together decide *this* is the truth." If scientists were honest men, they would hold truth as the highest virtue and principle, which means they would insist and actively broadcast that the results of science are *not truth*; they would use their better knowledge to release us from such dangerous misunderstandings, while holding true to the virtues of their field and doing their best to come up with useful scientific discoveries. An expert skeet shooter might give personal subjective names to his rifles (and e.g. talk to them) and we would forgive him this peculiarity when understanding its connection to his expertise; it makes him feel more comfortable with his instrument. But as truth is the single most important target of philosophical scrutiny, to misunderstand the role of science in producing truth is the most dramatic category error conceivable; the skeet shooter who doesn't understand how his weapon works and therefore consistently keeps missing his targets. The philosopher must understand that scientific theories must be regarded as theories or he will be unable to perform his work; after all, it is the job not of the physicist but the philosopher to understand the relations between the concepts belonging to *different* fields of science, and the physicist is forgiven in his work for his commitment to the fundamental concepts of his own field. And since no theory (such as theories of physics) can be regarded as true, a philosopher can also notice the error in the kind of thinking that phenomena in the realm of an apparently lower-level theory (such as theories of physics) *cause* phenomena in the realm of an apparently higher-level theory—it is prevalent to argue from physics or genetics to e.g. biological theories or theories of social sciences. The theories give an appearance of a hierarchy of theories because they have been designed that way throughout history: since *Homo faber* uses tools he also designs mechanistic theories, and naturally he has been wishing for the unification of the theories of natural science so that ultimately everything would fall perfectly

I-8. THE FOUR TYPES OF REASON

under his command, analogous to how individual machine-like components could somehow be moulded from their edges to fit together to form one big super-machine that can be used for anything. A physicist might see causal connections between certain phenomena of physics and certain phenomena of other domains of life, and also a mathematician or a computer scientist might see causal connections between mathematical relations or computer algorithms and other phenomena in life, which gives them the personal pleasure of possessing a capability to generally apply in practice what they have learned through the results of science. But these causal connections only *exist* for the subject if he has learned the theoretical framework in question and *believes* in it—believes in the *truth* revealed by it. It is perfectly possible to learn a theoretical framework without holding such metaphysical beliefs, although holding one might be beneficial for the ability to apply the framework, because when the subject believes something and it exists for him, he can also *see* it—in a non-sensorial sense. It seems that advanced professionals in any field have this kind of a subjective relation to their profession. Also, very interestingly, they often have a personal subjective story that drives them towards that sort of relation towards their profession. But at the same time believing an objective framework as truth creates a guaranteed self-deceit that can only be cured by moving backwards and accepting firstly that, by definition, hypotheses are not truth, and, secondly, that the truth of mathematical relations derived from research through mathematical proof doesn't carry over to anything else outside the field of mathematics. Yes, according to elementary mathematics, *1+2=3*, but from the statements "There is one coin on the table" and "I add two more coins on the table" doesn't follow the statement "There are three coins on the table", and these statements are meaningless without a context in which they are applied, and no person is liable to sum coins unless such a context exists.

Let's look at the sensibility of causation. When we talk about causality, we don't talk about just seeing effects and their causes, but essentially the language of associating an effect with a cause, and here one should notice that the sensibility of the expressions is bounded by the fact that

PART I. THE BASIS OF THOUGHT

both cause and effect need to be objective, shared phenomena. Let's first establish this by looking at the following statements.

1) The ventilation system was blocked by accumulated dust.

2) John wants to go home because he feels ill.

3) I was issued with a restraining order because I am madly in love.

All of these are understandable statements and share the same grammatical form of cause and effect, but the statements all differ from one another in sense. The first one attributes an objective effect (being blocked) to an objective cause (dust) and should be called causality; we could say that the dust simply caused the ventilation to block up, and then verify and agree on this scientifically without any subjective controversy. The second one attributes a subjective effect (want) to a subjective cause (feeling) and should be called a justification. This statement would most likely be used in a context where we are excusing John to go home and asking somebody for a permission, like e.g. John's mother saying this to his father while they are out in the city, or John's gym teacher saying this to his maths teacher who is responsible for his next lesson. The third one attributes an objective effect (having been issued with) to a subjective cause (love) and should be called teleology; restraining order having needed to be issued for the purpose of restraining. Now, the difference between statement 1 and statements 2 and 3 is the subjective cause, and the subjective is related to both values and responsibilities. This is why these statements are used in a different purpose and context and should be referred to by their correct names. So, this is the high-level boundary of the sensibility of causation but doesn't yet say anything about the logical rules in particular cases in which the concept of causation is applied. Despite causality dealing with objective phenomena only, it is still *a language* and not any hard, real, metaphysical phenomenon, as it were, chiselled into the very bedrock of a singular reality. When we speak about causes, we essentially try to convince somebody to adopt our view, and actually the reason why we associate *information* so strongly with causality is because the purpose of what we like to call information is to convince. We tend to think of information, say, Wikipedia, or a recipe book, as a metaphysical entity, forgetting that it is actually *communication* produced by

I-8. THE FOUR TYPES OF REASON

somebody *for a purpose*, and we might liberally think that the purpose is just "to help" or to "share knowledge", but the more likely subjective motivation for sharing information is an effort to try and convince others to adopt our position on it. Now, the human quality is such that almost anybody you talk to would like you to adopt their position, but you would, and likely should, not trust anybody's position as worthwhile for adopting. The most trustworthy authority would likely be a teacher or a professor; teachers and professors are professionals whose purpose is *to educate* instead of, say, manipulate, which implies a social responsibility that is not just a word but something put to the test by commitment and devotion to this purpose, to the extent of devoting their lives to the purpose. So, statement 1, despite being attribution of an objective effect to an objective cause, can naturally be disputed by saying that it is not the case that the ventilation system was blocked by dust. The objective nature of causality just means that the cause and effect are shared and one is, in theory, able to access the ventilation system and to verify that this is the case, and here we will actually reach another boundary of sensibility when this access is not available any more. Consider the statement: "Our bank services were shut down today due to a technical error in a subsystem." Here "technical error" is something that can be objective or subjective, depending on whether the error is shared; whether it is possible to inspect it. And if there is no way to inspect it, we are dealing with an objective phenomenon being looked at from a subjective perspective, which should be called a teleological argument, which indeed it is, as there is an implied need and a motivation to create acceptance: the systems needed to be offline due to an error, and actually the error doesn't matter (statements like this are usually political statements politely hiding the real cause) as much as the institution's subjective responsibility and values. One should be careful to notice when something is being presented as objective causality when actually we are dealing with subjective causes, as the teleological argument hides the actual reasoning under a sense of predestined natural law that just happens and has its reason like everything in nature.

But let's look at the other commitments in actual causal discourse. Saying "the cue ball causes the nine-ball to move", or any such utterance, makes sense (in practice) only in the context of pool, and to understand the utterance correctly one must already know quite a lot about the practice of how pool is played. And because causality is an objective mode of inquiry set to convince others, to talk about pool balls in terms of causation only makes sense in the context of teaching somebody the game, or a context where people, say, argue about the correct rules, trying to convince each other that their particular viewpoint is correct. To play pool, and even to play pool well, one does not need to think about pool causally; rather a good player would be experienced in particular pool situations as patterns, experienced in hitting the cue ball correctly and experienced in using his body correctly when executing the shooting action. But if we look at pool causally, important things we realize are at least that pool is a game of two people in which balls, freely moving on a flat table, are struck with a cue stick. This preliminary already implies a particular sense of causation that is applied in people's practical activities: "How does this game work; how is it played? The player shoots..." Against this preliminary one can meaningfully ask: "Is it so that the player causes the cue ball to move? The balls are not in motion by themselves?" So, in this use, a human is seen to cause events, which is a sensible cause, since asking if the human was also caused by something else to do this would make no sense in the case of pool, since he is a player, and the rules of pool dictate that players may strike freely on their turns—yet there are many other contexts within which it might be sensible to ask if a human is caused to do something, such as "Your lateness caused me to miss my bus". The causation is sensible strictly within that context: within the context of pool it makes sense to explain what is happening on the pool table with such a causal expression; to explain that the events on the table on one player's turn originate from the player striking the cue ball. Now, in the expression "the cue ball causes the nine-ball to move" we are again bound to a very specific context, namely the analysis of what happens to the nine-ball on the player's turn. The question of whether something else causes the cue ball to move is irrelevant because of this: we are looking at the situation strictly from the context of how the nine-ball gets its initial momentum within one particular turn. If we wanted to talk about the

I-8. THE FOUR TYPES OF REASON

events on the pool table from a broader perspective, we would never be inclined to say that "the balls cause each other to move"—this would be just nonsense; the sense of causation is not a random mess but a particular relation—but it might make sense to use an expression like "the cue ball collides with one ball and causes it to move, then that ball collides with another and causes it to move, and so on" in order to explain something about how a player should be thinking when preparing a pool shot. It would make sense to say, "the player shoots the cue ball and then the balls bounce freely from each other and the walls whenever they happen to hit either" but saying this wouldn't say much about what pool *is*; how pool is played. I think an overall fair explanation of causation is that our use of the word 'cause' is something that exists in us as a disposition after having learned to use the word in the sense of causation, and after this we incline to use it to point to elements of attention when explaining phenomena.

One feature to distinguish reasons from causation is that, although we would often say that many reasons affected our decision-making, we usually find that a single reason suffices, whereas in the case of causation there is a latent preconception that a single cause is never enough to fully explain anything. As an example: "Mother, why can't I go out? —Because it's too cold.—Right." An adult might have many objections to the reason in the given example: he might like cold days, he might have warm clothing, he might have a reason why he absolutely needs to go, etc. The importance of his individual reasons depends on his level of personal responsibility in justifying his actions, which is socially determined. I also believe this confusion of reason against cause explains in science and philosophy what Wittgenstein called a "craving for generality" or a "contemptuous attitude towards the particular case"[91]: reasons are related to authority, and an authority often uses a sole reason whereas complex explanations lack authority and convey the impression that the problem at hand is not completely understood ... a single reason, instead of many analytical explanations, sounds more authoritative. Causal explanations differ from reasons, not in the sense that they metaphysically describe the world "in itself",

---
91   The Blue and Brown Books pp. 17-19

but in the sense that they nevertheless do *describe the world*, and when these causal descriptions are used in decision-making, it is possible for us to collectively agree that they also describe the world correctly. If you compare two ways of making decisions: 1) where an authority announces his decision and doesn't give a reason, and 2) where an authority announces his decision and gives a causal explanation as a reason, the second one can be disputed on the basis of whether the causal explanation is correct, which has the effect that this approach *in rhetoric* is more convincing, as it better appeals to our *sense of justice*, which, in turn, is the primary way of changing our behaviour by turning us into followers and supporters instead of subordinates.

Also, reasons differ from causes in that a satisfactory understanding of a certain phenomenon may require fitting together many different causal factors but taking other people's subjective reasons as objective causes will interfere with the process and may turn out to be emotionally difficult to achieve. The existentialist *emancipation* involves reaching awareness of social responsibilities in reference to the subjective experience, and thus reaching subjective freedom through correcting related misunderstandings. For example, consider someone who has grown up believing that his father is sometimes angry and violent because he has been such a naughty child, not doing what he's supposed to. Consider in addition that one drunken night his father committed suicide. Now, this connection from naughtiness to the father's violent behaviour is essentially a reason told to the child that is functionally related to justifying the parents' (either just the father's or both the parents') decision-making, but since children adopt their parents' reasons, he believes it to be true and thus sees his naughtiness as *causing* his father's moods and therefore his death. From an external viewpoint one can see things in perspective, determine what the socially determined responsibilities are for parents and children and conclude if a child's naughtiness is a *good reason* for violent behaviour, but the child, having *existed* in the situation, has had no option for this, and will only have a possibility for emancipation in later life. This belief formed through an act of violence will subsequently emotionally impair his reasoning regarding social responsibilities and without emancipation

I-8. THE FOUR TYPES OF REASON

can result in many forms of problems for him. A few examples of such are punishing himself because he believes he has done something punishable, punishing others when seeing others commit a similar 'naughty' deed, applying the same belief as a reason with his own children, or applying with his children the logical opposite of that belief[92] in a desperate effort to escape it. One more example of confusion regarding reason and cause is the commonplace method by which people, in an effort to solve some subjective problem, try to artificially support the burden of responsibility in their decision-making by listing "possible reasons"—by listing subjective qualities, as in: "Should I stay with her or leave her? She's good looking; she's smart; she's a good cook…" Such methods can never ground decision-making due to their subjectivity, because listing and compiling evidence is a part of forming judgment over the actions of somebody from objective causal factors, the purpose of which is to determine the environment of decision-making.

---

92 It seems to me that a common—and not only Finnish—model for parenting currently is that a child cannot be naughty and therefore punishable, and that the child is always right. I see parents generally expressing shame for their children's problematic attention-seeking behaviour. And I believe this is caused by guilt and shame in the parents.

PART II. COMMON MISCONCEPTIONS

In this part of the book I take a look at both classical and modern-day problems I have found topical and that I believe are a result of our unclear thought. The problem at hand is our blindness to the subjective and that we have developed many concepts into meanings that have lost their original sense, and in many cases, any sense. Solving the issues requires taking a look at them.

II-1. Linguistic Confusion

It seems to me that many of the common philosophical mistakes are a result of confusing the subjective and the objective by not realizing the importance of asking for the criterion. By 'philosophical mistake' I mean something that can happen to the man on the street and even to a 'proper' philosopher. Actually, quite a few mistakes arise because we do not ask "How do you know?" The confusion we experience as a result of not asking this question, and taking something at face value, is a feeling of mystery and wonderment ... it feels like it is a question that boggles the mind, is beyond our understanding and is overwhelmingly deep. To me the interesting part is that we experience this as a sensation of greatness, yet what causes it is a limitation and an error of thought; it is like looking at something huge because one is small, pushed against the very limits of one's reason and understanding. I will give examples of such misunderstandings here.

• *Confusing love with marriage*: love is a subjective disposition whereas marriage is an objective and law-regulated institution. As a purely fictive example, suppose a jealous man was to refuse his wife's testimony and to ask her to prove her love. Here he would be mistaken to look for such a proof, since testimony is the only form of proof for a subjective disposition, and there exists no institution to validate her testimony. No matter what actions or deeds the man were to require, none would prove satisfactory, since he is essentially lacking the subjective trust. To trust another is a subjective choice for a man with the subjective capability for it.

• *Confusing subjective opinion with measurable fact*: I read a claim that ideological questions are solvable with factual argument, and the example given was the question "Is same-sex marriage good or bad?" This was treated as a question of facts, namely e.g. the question of whether the children of same-sex parents are better or worse off than children of traditional parents. This claim has a latent presupposition that everything is measurable; namely, that whether children are better or worse off is measurable. Now, for it to be measurable, we would need a measure—a criterion. For the sake of argument, let's imagine that we *do* have such a criterion, such as that "worse off" children have more mental problems or worse test scores—any criterion will do here and we can abstract it away by imagining an oracle device that prints out "good/bad". Let's ask now whether the criterion is applicable; are you willing to say that your child is worse off than another child because his test scores are bad, or he has mental problems? I suggest the answer to be negative, but the interesting question is *why* it is negative, and here we would have to say that it is not children's *fault* that they measure poorly, but that it might be their parents' fault, or it might not be anyone's fault and that God made them special children with special skills. To be accurate, *any* parent would *ferociously insist* this, at least in the West where we believe God created all children equal and unique, and that no children are wicked, and that it is the parents' responsibility to stand up for their child and to put them first. The result of this is that the criterion (the oracle device) will be deemed immoral, because it will slight an innocent child. So, even if such a device existed, it could not be used for moral reasons, and this ethical perspective and latent inequality is simply unnoticed in the original argument. And on a broader scale, the same problem of subjective choice of criterion applies whenever subjective qualities are to be measured with objective means.

- *Confusing religion with religious institution*: one's religion is a subjective disposition, whereas the religious institution, for example, the Church, is an objective institution. Even the holy man of a village is an objective institution, because he is equally shared by the villagers and will be succeeded by another holy man when term comes to an end. The same relation exists between the Christian God and the Bible; if, according to the Bible, one is to devote one's life to God, who is defined as a spirit (a subject), then one surely is wrong to follow an objective medium defined as God's word (the Bible). It is a commonplace atheist fallacy to accuse religions of atrocities done in the name of religion,[93] and at the same time, ironically, to promote

---

[93] I wonder if the atheist blames Christianity for the invasion of Afghanistan and Iraq, as the invasion was launched in the name of God. This would effectively acquit the real perpetrators who wield military power in the name of religion. E. MacAskill, 'George Bush: "God told me to end the tyranny in Iraq"', The Guardian, 7.10.2005, http://www.theguardian.com/world/2005/oct/07/iraq.usa

II-1. LINGUISTIC CONFUSION

science—seeing no problem in the discovery of e.g. nuclear weapons. This behaviour is no different from holding a language responsible for the actions of its speakers or a race for cultural idiosyncrasies.

• *Confusing faith with ideology*: the standard idealist mistake is to think in terms of ideals and to suppose that everybody does the same. A typical idealist would list and analyse the ideals he believes in in an objective manner, then list the wrong things he sees his political opponents believing in, and his argument would begin with "If only everybody..." Now, yes, there are similarities in how all humans think, but ideologies don't qualify this. The idealist sees a person doing the wrong thing and supposes this is because the person believes in wrong things or ideals, and this false supposition justifies his judgemental attitude. But the idealist simply doesn't understand moral psychology: all people have justifiable motives, but the moral difference lies in the subjective manner of their justification in the amount of self-scrutiny the subject is willing to impose on himself; whether his actions indeed reflect his motives or not. Therefore, idealist argument fails. Take the atheist Marx; he blamed capitalism for his observation that workers saw (and still see) work as a utilitarian means to gain a reward instead of seeing it as valuable, which he believed was the correct view. He took it that such workers believed in capitalism, but I take it that the people believed in something that Marx himself didn't believe in and thus didn't see. His method of advancing to correct people's faith via an idealist theory was bound to fail ... the theory can only become an instrument of evil as the justification of malice.

• *Confusing subjective reality with physical reality*: this mistake gives birth to what we call metaphysics. Our subjective reality is built upon language and the concepts we have apprehended. Those are they eye-glasses through which we perceive the world. Take my friend, a computer expert, who has come to believe that "everything is ones and zeroes" (there are several of these guys working in any IT company), which, of course, applies to the data processing of a standard computer. Quite commonly I hear him wondering about how, say, the *rendering*[94] of *reality* takes place, or how emotions emerge out of a

[26.12.2019].
94 Rendering means producing the two-dimensional picture to be displayed on a

human body, which he essentially sees as a mechanical system. Here, the idea of rendering is a standard of three-dimensional computer graphics, but the "rendering of reality" is a metaphysical concept born out of disregarding the logical difference between the objective criterion for rendering and the subjective criterion for the reality he is speaking of. Similarly, the metaphysical nature of the concept "emergent emotions" requires an underlying mechanist (Cartesian) presupposition regarding minds and bodies and is born out of disregard towards the subjective criterion for emotions in contrast with the objective criterion for emergence. One more example is psychoanalytic theory that treats the subjectivity of the mind as an apparatus and is thus littered with pseudoscientific gibberish. Freud's empirical work, the main work of a true scientist, showed superb insight in recognizing common mental phenomena, and his theories give some direction about the relations between these phenomena that could have been used in establishing strictly empirical cases of particular types of development history having particular types of effects in the subject's psyche. He could have remained vague and true to his science, as empirical psychology is always vague; describing cases that have similarities but are highly unique. Instead he constantly went unnecessarily far in his ascriptions, describing the mind as an apparatus, which is simply an extra commitment that produces no value but instead confusion, which needed to be cleared by others after him.

- *Confusing biological sex with sexual social identity.* The concept of biological sex is bound to the methodology of determining men from women, which is typically done by the doctor at birth, and is the same method people in general use to make this distinction. This will be called 'identity', as it is the criterion for identifying one's sex. But then the same word 'identity', or the word 'gender', is used in feminist theory to indicate the (subjective) experience of one's sex—the experience of one's *sexual group*—the cause of which is attributed to society, which is a correct relation, as it is denoted by the same word 'identity' in psychology or sociology. The confusion mixes ethical problematic regarding minorities in sexual identity with the scientific questions regarding differences between sexes.

---

screen out of the simulated computer model.

II-1. LINGUISTIC CONFUSION

- *Confusing mental illness with physical illness.* The word 'illness' in mental illness is misleading, as mental illnesses are persistent mental conditions caused almost exclusively by psycho-social factors (subconscious social fears, traumatic events and shortcomings in parenting), whereas physical illnesses are caused by physical causes such as bacteria, viruses, genes or old age. The group of illnesses where a mental condition is caused by a physical condition in the brain is a borderline case. However, it is now common to see research studies where the physical nature of a mental illness is latently assumed. These are often accompanied by some sort of movement to ideologically support the idea that the condition really is physical in nature, as illnesses bring about strong emotions in friends and relatives, and they can network with people of similar experience to establish a contrary opinion to what the doctors suggest.

Let's look at a common theme in a discussion about the subjective/objective distinction: *colours*. This is an apt topic, not because the same problem of not having information about the subjective experience of another person (the problem of solipsism) wouldn't apply to all questions about subjective experience, but because our vision is known to vary measurably regarding colour, with some people, such as myself, being less receptive to colour variance than others, and in varying ways—we are able to measure colour blindness by certain tests where the colours shown to the test subjects are created with objective means. Colours are experienced in light and surfaces, and the physical criteria of colours as electromagnetic radiation with varying frequencies and intensities, and as a surface material reflecting light in a particular way, are measurable and highly applicable objective criteria and thus wonderful theories. Then again, there is no other reason to use these physical criteria of colours except the applicability (the explanatory power) of the theory, and no *a priori* reason why not to use an alternative colour theory, such as, say, a scientific library of standard light and material sources, like the 1 metre stick still recently used as the criterion for 1 metre. I am often told interesting facts about colour by computer boffins, such as that are at least 4 billion colours, but the human eye is unable to receive them all. Such abuse of language is not helped by all sorts of scientific studies producing suggestive and

PART II. COMMON MISCONCEPTIONS

hypothetical 'results'; for example, that a woman has been found who "can see 99 million colours" due to some genetic anomaly that affects the eye. Such preconceptions suggest that the speaker is using a metaphor from the display properties of computers, and also using a metaphor of the human eye as a sensor with a varying degree of sensitivity (resolution), which also would imply that one might build a better sensor than the human eye for colours. The colour display properties of computers involve *colour depth*, which is an important concept in the topic of computer graphics: colour depth is e.g. 1) a physical capability of the display monitor, 2) a physical property of the video card that sends the video signal to the display, 3) a property of the screen resolution of the operating system graphical user interface, and 4) a property of each image file that affects the data size of the file. As such, the computer science and mathematics used in these colour properties is no rocket science and has been available for over half a century, but the restraining factors have been the cost to produce display monitors with a capability to physically implement high colour depths in a way that offers enough precision, and also the practical data storage capabilities, as image files with high colour depth contain more information to encode. It is only due to these practical factors that there has been a development from early computers using monitors and display modes with limited colour sets towards modern high-resolution and deep colour displays, and thus the standards of how many colours a computer is said to be able to display have increased with time. And this was just to demonstrate one objective standard of colour that a person might mean when using names of colours; namely, a colour in the sense of a particular colour encoding in a computer palette, but also to demonstrate the fragility of a metaphysical conception of colours as just something bound to an existing objective criterion such as a computer palette. When the subject is using the name of some colour, he can be expected to be using it in some sense, although he might be unaware of the sense; and this is equivalent to saying that when somebody says something he can be expected to mean something despite the fact that he might be speaking nonsense. And whenever one requires clarity, one can always ask for clarification about the sense of the concept, and in this case one might ask: "What do you mean by

II-1. LINGUISTIC CONFUSION

'green'?", where he might point to an object he perceives to be green, or an object he knows to be green, such as by answering "Green as a forest". Asking further "How do you know that that object/ a forest is green?" is a tempting but non-sensible question, since it is not sensible to apply the concept of knowledge to subjective experience. We might ask: "Is the forest necessarily green?" to point out that forests may turn yellow in autumn and white in winter, but the answer to this won't answer the question of what the subject *meant* by 'green'; he didn't mean green as in a distinction between green and yellow/white, but he used a forest as an *objective* sample of something agreed to be green, as something shared in the language between the person asking and the person answering. The subject wouldn't be sensibly said to *know* that a forest is green; rather he takes it as evident, and does well to do so, since walking in a green forest gives one an experience of a particular predominant colour, and calling this colour green predates even all our physical theories of colour that have been produced to comply with the existing language of colours. There are many fascinating features in how we use the colour concepts, such as looking at a wooden surface that is painted black, partially hit by sunlight, which has the result that the experience of the light reflected from the lit area is considerably different than the light reflected from the unlit area, but still this doesn't disturb our experience of the surface as carrying a single colour. It seems to me this wonderment is due to nothing more than the fact that we use the same colour words for both light and physical surfaces. I might wonder "Why does a black surface hit by yellow light remain black in my experience?" but consider replacing the word 'yellow' with another word, such as 'cromulent' ("...black surface hit by *cromulent* light..."), implying that the words for colours in the sense of light would be different than the ones in the sense of surfaces. This has the result that the question doesn't look confusing any more, as black and yellow don't look like they belong to the same category any longer; the mysterious nature of colour vanishes, and this reveals that the mysterious nature of colours is related to our metaphysical conception of them and the related fact that the same colour words are used in various senses—in this case namely in the senses of light and surface.

PART II. COMMON MISCONCEPTIONS

Another highly puzzling language, due to the completely subjective nature of the criteria of its expressions, is *music*. For a long time, I was disturbed by the question of why minor keys carry sadness, because there doesn't seem to be a child born who would argue that they experience minor keys as happy and major keys as sad. This seemed to me to prove that the sad nature of the minor key must lie in the distinguishable tonal structure of the chords, and there are also many musical rules that are taught in the language of musical theory that seem to be making sense, such as the role of the musical scale degrees tonic and dominant: the dominant *creates* tension that *requires* tonic as resolution ... in a similar way as with to stress or muscle tension. This rule makes sense, because one can hear this chord progression being used all over the tradition of Western music: to learn the tonic and the dominant is to learn how Western music has been made. And the process of being subjected to a musical tradition starts at a very young age; my first memory of sad music was sung to me by my mother at bed-time, and it seems to me that the sad nature of the song's predominant minor key was first *associated* via the sad *lyrics* of the song. Children of a particular age are normally highly empathetic and especially prone to empathize with subjects which they experience as peers at least to some extent, which is not adults but, say, pets, toys and fantasy characters, and are able to empathetically relate to both tragedy and comedy as in children's play: girls more drawn to showing care towards tragic characters and boys towards comedy in e.g. the light-hearted side of a play character getting hurt.[95] It seems to me that this emotional basis is transmitted by the lyrical or other thematic and dramatic context of a song and then associated with the distinguishable musical characteristics, such as key, tempo or dynamics, and one can indeed distinguish also largo (slowly) and piano (quietly) as additional common characteristics of sad music, which obviously relates to our cultural form of feeling sad and depressed, which is something we tend to do alone or only in a closed company, at a moment that is separate from all activity. And this is to say that the association between sadness and minor key, after all, seems not to be intrinsic but culturally conditioned; it's

---

[95] The empathy of tragedy targets the injustice that the tragic character is subjected to, whereas the empathy of comedy involves the justice of retribution—both sensations are obviously not experienced by an unempathetic person.

II-1. LINGUISTIC CONFUSION

just that this cultural conditioning is just so all-pervasive and goes way back to one's childhood that the connection is difficult to see. And what we see here is the temptation of the common fallacy of appealing to nature as a constituting source of phenomena that are social in their constitution; there also exist human qualities that can be plausibly attributed to species (biology) or heredity (genetics), but the attribution of *nature* as the constituting origin will always produce results that contradict science, as science, in all its totality, is a process that rather works to analyse nature into more and more refined distinguishable constituents: *social* phenomena are a constituent of human *nature*.[96] Now, *music* was described by Kierkegaard as the art form that is "furthest removed from language" and also "the hardest of all media to repeat", and the sense of this can be seen in the fact that musical *expression* bears no objective criteria for meaning, but in addition, any subjective meanings given to musical expressions are independently, actively and artistically developed by the musical artists instead of, as is the case with most subjective concepts such as 'pain' or 'love', established to serve some practical social function. It could also be said that music is directly related to our sense of hearing whereas language is related to our thought, and for example the valued skill of musical improvisation is characterized by a sense of flow experience[97] free from abstract thought in the same way as, say, a sports performance. This quality is not considered a virtue in terms of spoken language; quite the contrary, it is considered admirable to speak with consideration and determination. In Western classical music there exists a long tradition of technical musical notation with the function to make collective performance of music possible as the passing of the musical intention of the artist to performers, and in addition there are eras and schools of musical thought in which ways to compose music are taught to the students in the form of theoretical rules. But the syntactic mu-

---

96 Perhaps it would be just as correct to say that a phenomenon is *natural* as it is to say that a phenomenon is *scientific*; and equally incorrect to take this as an attribution: to say that any phenomenon is caused by nature or that is caused by science.

97 A dance floor classic has the lyrics repeating "Let the music take control" ... the moment when abstract thought changes into thought about physical performance into rhythm—changing from an existence of planning to an existence of following—carries the sensation of giving up control.

PART II. COMMON MISCONCEPTIONS

sical vocabulary has also functioned as an inspiration for the artistic creative process, being a target of study for creating fresh-sounding music.[98] And this feature of freedom of expression on all levels is the definitive feature of Western classical musical, in contrast with musical traditions that normally align with a social function such as worship, harvesting or encouraging martial feelings. It seems to me to be related to the Christian moral conception of justice, where the relation with God and equality in front of God is seen as completely individual, in contrast with the view of religious worship as a form of worshipping an earthly authority. The great innovators in Western classical music have all created their work as passionate Christian artistic expression and would say that their work has been their best effort to produce what sounds beautiful to God. Yet still, despite this lack of rules and a requirement of free expression to express worship, we tend to, at least in musical terminology, speak of expressing *something* in the *language* of music. And this lack of established meaning, and especially, our Western tradition of *expecting* music to be an individualistic art form as an expression of Christian worship, seems to me to be the definitive feature of music as a language and why Kierkegaard appropriately described music as the hardest medium to repeat. Also, this difficulty of repeating explains why in the Western musical scene *singers* are the target of highest admiration: the singing voice is the most difficult classical instrument as the art of singing cannot be at all mimicked by somebody who doesn't possess the particular musical ear that is mostly developed at a very young age. It also seems to me that this difficulty of vocal repetition of a higher pitched voice, but also the rarity of child singers before voice change, is the underlying cause in the tradition of Western music of trying to raise the pitch of male singers (historically peaking in creating eunuchs), and, following singers, for manufacturers to raise the pitch of instruments in an effort to achieve a brighter (higher, more divine) sound than their competitors, which is an effort more recently settled by pitch-based standardization of musical keys. As seen in the case of gold, the rarity and the difficulty of obtaining something has constituted its value wherever the human has been a

---

[98] The examples that I have in mind are the pop & jazz tradition and *dada/Avant Garde*.

II-1. LINGUISTIC CONFUSION

collector of commodities.

PART II. COMMON MISCONCEPTIONS

II-2. The Dual Nature of Philosophical Problems

It seems to me that the classical philosophical problems involve words with a *dual* meaning, and it is exactly this feature of these words that gives them what classically has been called a philosophically problematic nature. Once this difference is clear, there is actually nothing problematic in the words any more, which of course doesn't free the subject from the ever-present problem of how to choose to use words in different situations of one's life—a problem that exists for all words and concepts the subject knows and which equates to the problem of *what to say*. That problem is not philosophical but is a very difficult one anyway; I often don't know what to say. The dual nature of the words related to classical philosophical problems arises out of the difference between a subject and an object, since it is either that the words are learnt by everybody in childhood as an object-relation and in adult life the subject has an ethical responsibility to change it to a subject-relation, or vice versa. Our role in society changes when we move from childhood to adulthood, which changes our ethical responsibility, yet we remain in a relation to the same words since they are fundamental in fulfilling the requirements of our everyday life. This *existential relation*—learning a word in one role but ending up in having to cope in another role with what we have learned so far—explains why it is so that the same words end up confusingly having *two* meanings, instead of a new word emerging for the second meaning of a word. You could say, things are easy until you need to exist... life's problematic is not theoretical but existential in nature. When people turn to philosophy, they have conceptual problems ("What does such-and-such mean?") and they want answers. What happens nowadays is that their short attention span leads to frustration and a brusque announcement that philosophy is pointless as it doesn't bring practical benefit. But the fundamental task on one's path to escape utter confusion is to understand the difference of objective and subjective things. This needs to be understood, because we feel that some problems can be answered *definitively* but there are problems that the philosophers don't seem to

II-2. THE DUAL NATURE OF PHILOSOPHICAL PROBLEMS

answer but to give only indefinite answers, which feels like a cowardly begging of the question. But this is just an impression that follows from the expectation that everything has a definite answer, and from not yet understanding that the subjective realm is inhabited by problems that have only a subjective answer, which translates either to an opinion or to a conviction. When asked my opinion, I might give it, but as an expert, I should clarify that my opinion is only as good as another's; it's something that works for me, but since you are asking, you are looking for something that works for you... and there is no objective basis of how to determine if my opinion is one to follow—only a subjective one. If I try my best and describe my opinion in an understandable way, there is no guarantee to protect against misunderstanding, as there is *no standard*, no criterion that we share. If you are buying a boat, you will expect the boat-maker to be a professional who is aware of the risks and hazards that boats are commonly subjected to, and you will expect these to be taken into consideration in the hands of a reliable expert. So, if we are to do any good in philosophy, we need to focus on making sure that what we are stating is true and reliable. If I should give you my subjective opinion as philosophical truth, you might tell me you see my point and that you understand, but when that happens, we haven't really tested if it's true, have we? Don't trust me so easily; there are a lot of people out there ready to use all their skills in sales and marketing to rip you off, and when the product you bought fails you, they'll imply you were stupid to expect too much from them. They were only doing their job as best they could; after all they also need to make a living. Ask for common standards instead, like a brand or hallmark; in philosophy, ask for the criterion as the sign of compliance to an agreed standard. As Wittgenstein would say, those (subjective) things *cannot be said*: "As a philosopher, I can't say yes or no, I can only clarify."[99] A philosopher who will give his opinion as an answer to a subjective problem is not acting as an expert philosopher but as a peer, and such an answer can lead to an abuse of this expert position. But in the case of objective things, the philosopher can point out that the criterion is actually shared: *this* is what is meant; given that that is

---

99 Wittgenstein's position on the role of philosophy was unchanged from *Tractatus* 4.113-4.115. What changed was his thought on the constitution of language.

PART II. COMMON MISCONCEPTIONS

what the subject indeed meant. This clarification of what is objective and what is subjective will point out your actual options: where you should seek knowledge and where you should have a conviction or refer to subjective advice of another. Then again, subjective conviction—certainty—is something that we can't talk about apart from it being a recognizable phenomenon that some people are subjectively more convinced than others, and that people respond to this socially. But we can relate this to ethics and a subjective realization that, in turn, can act as a subjective reason: one can be subjectively strong where one believes the way one sees things is the right way of seeing them, and the nature of this rightness is in accordance with some values one has personally come to believe. If the son of a shoemaker realizes that the best he can do in his life is to continue his family profession, he will act very differently from the son of a shoemaker who has been taught to make shoes but wishes to be a merchant instead. From a philosophical perspective the interesting bit is just to notice that this difference has nothing to do with shoes or making shoes but is the difference in existence between two individuals. Now, you might feel unhappy with this answer and find it elusive, and feel that there instead must be some objective common ground in human behaviour, such as logic or rationality; some means of predicting what a man should do... and here I'd like you to analyse what you are trying to do into two parts: Do you wish to 1) predict with certainty what a person is *about to* do, or 2) know for certain what one—anyone—*should* do? The first case contradicts free will and the second case contradicts human rights. The problem must lie instead in your expectations from philosophy and reason, but you shouldn't get frustrated; it is an intellectual coward's choice to accept something without profoundly understanding it, and the modern conception that intellectual challenges should be quick to learn is badly warped and based on the idea that all learning is just apprehending information.

When analysing language, the sense of a word used can be unclear without a context and even with a context provided. But the sense of a word can often be analytically determined, which is done by ruling out existing uses of the word based on logical commitments within the

II-2. THE DUAL NATURE OF PHILOSOPHICAL PROBLEMS

context of the expression. And in this case one might say "By saying the word that way, he *must* mean it in such-and-such a sense", because these meanings of a word are logically bounded. This sort of analysis can be aptly called bringing into light the hidden presuppositions of the speaker, and in fact it is very common to catch people logically contradicting themselves due to exactly the misleading nature of language that Wittgenstein pointed out. This contradiction is, of course, what Wittgenstein meant when he referred to 'nonsense'; leaving the academics writing piles of discussion trying to understand what he was getting at. As an example, take the word '*love*',[100] used in statements like "I love him" and "I know he loves me". The criterion in the first one is subjective emotion, but in the second one the criterion for knowledge must be different and related to the observed behaviour of the target of one's love[101] (if anything). The first one is related to a family of problems regarding the personal experience of loving feelings and filling the daily romantic struggles of many people, such as "How do I know if it's love?" or "Could this be true love?" or "Could this last forever?" The latter one is, however, related to different problems; namely, problems of trust and fidelity, such as "Does he really love me?" or "Would he do *that* if he really loved you?" or "Do we understand love in the same way?" In the case of love, I believe, it is a confusion of these two meanings of 'love', the personal one and the interpersonal one, that causes persistent jealousy in people who themselves are persistently inclined to thoughts of infidelity. The logical option, and the option that people with high empathetic skills would take, is to determine the trustworthiness of the other by empathetically analysing the rationale behind their actions. But because of the confusing word 'love', one is prone to misinterpret things. One way of doing this is to interpret one's own emotions regarding the basis of the relationship to *mean* love, and thus, when there is disturbance in one's own emotions, to expect something wrong in this shared transcendent object called 'love'. This might lead one to often accuse the other of causing the disturbance experienced, in spite of its self-originating basis. Such a person would be prone to think he is able to make another person love him, with effort,

---
100   Like the word 'pain' Wittgenstein analysed in *On Certainty*
101   And, as Wittgenstein pointed out, it is senseless to apply the concept of knowledge to subjective experience

similarly to how one can make oneself get out of bed instead of staying put, which is something that just takes more effort on some mornings than on others. The other form of misinterpretation is the opposite of this, which to interpret the external behaviour of the other to mean love also in oneself, and to say "I love you" when one can see one's own behaviour matching the behaviour originally initiated by the other, while one might be completely lacking the sort of emotions classically described by people in love. Both of these types of pathological behaviour are common in people with limited empathetic skills to correctly interpret the actions of the other, and therefore are restricted from existentially learning that when they themselves use the word 'love', their partner can use the same word in a different way but not be untrue in doing this. Their conception of love remains on the initial conceptual, abstract level where it begins when they first learn the word, love denoting an abstract object. The extremes of this type of partnership are 1) the pathological narcissist, to whom love equals his own one-sided emotions of desire and need for nurture, and 2) the pathological co-dependent, to whom love equals being the object of desire and nurture by the other. In both these extremes the lack of empathy produces behaviour of manipulative control over the other; the narcissistic manipulation works to make the partner dependent on oneself to protect the satisfaction of personal desires against the threat of abandonment, and the co-dependent manipulation works to satisfy the desires of the other via self-sacrifice, in order to make the partner dependent over them to protect them from the threat of abandonment. Since these pathological types lack empathy, they don't possess reciprocal motives involving thinking about the well-being and development of their partner, but instead they aim to secure their own position in the relationship with the means they know best. And this is because they believe their partner is being equally one-sided; because they believe that love means showing such unempathetic behaviour. Psychologically both types are deceptive practices one picks up in the course of one's development to disassociate (detach) oneself from shame and guilt; the narcissist manipulates others to escape his dominating feeling of guilt, and the co-dependent is playing victim to get sympathy from others in order to escape the same guilt. Whether we talk of guilt or shame is a cultural question; in the Christian West we are motivated by guilt, and in the East by shame. In any case this detachment is something that can be addressed via the criterion instead of the expression of the word 'love': How do I know I love him? How do I know he loves me?

Language is a constantly changing system and the process of moving between changing meanings of certain words is an existential requirement, caused by the fact that in addition to trying to understand the world we also need to exist: to first be born and after that to change roles in society. From this absolute necessity it follows to the philosopher that healing the confusion of language should be seen as a constant struggle related to life itself, instead of searching for theories or other forms of remedies to completely solve such issues. Thus, philosophy is work of healing ailments rather than producing theories. The following is an analysis of the dual (subjective/objective) nature of certain classically problematic philosophical words.

II-2-1. Meaning

We start off our life with the Augustinian, object-relative relation to the meaning of words presented in the beginning of *Philosophical Investigations*. We learn to deal with objects by learning their names: "What is this? This is a *cat*. Who is this? This is *John*. What does this word mean? It means *that* object." So, we learn to search for a corresponding object whenever we are asked for a meaning. This later develops into a capability to identify the meaning of a word with *abstract* objects, and in the case of learning an abstract concept we essentially retain the object-relative approach, yet (possibly) relate the object to some private mental representation and adopt a means of producing a description of it. Asking different people for descriptions of the meaning of abstractions gives an idea of the variance in how people subjectively relate to the concepts.[102] People often have particular memories they relate to the meaning and that they subjectively use when rea-

---

[102] This also shows that there is a big difference between people in the level of detail they can provide by description.

soning with the concept. Studying those mental representations is not philosophically fruitful since a subject's relation to the concepts he understands is unique, and the term 'representation' merely highlights a characteristic of the subjective experience that often is connected with the visual experience and makes "We create pictures of facts for ourselves" and "A picture is a model of reality"[103] seem like valid grounds for philosophical investigation. Yet the subject might relate an abstract object, for example 'kindness', to *any* kind of a picture, say, the picture of Jesus Christ with his open palms extended, the roots of this picture being somehow connected with the subject's past (unique) experiences. Somebody else might, and I suggest definitely *would*, produce a different mental image to the first person. Now, these two subjects might communicate perfectly well about kindness and be in complete understanding yet, if asked, produce a totally different description of the connected mental image. This insight was captured by Wittgenstein in the Beetle metaphor, and it has the effect of rendering phenomenology an effort sure to fail in assuming uniformity over something essentially unique. The way to express this in the right terms is to note that *concepts*, firstly, *are the basis of our reasoning*, and secondly, *evoke our mental imagery in a unique manner*. Taking the uniqueness seriously is difficult, because our concept of meaning holds onto the established basis we acquire at a younger age which relates it to objects. We experience them as objective and static and their meaning is related to this sort of image and questioning that image can give one a sensation of the loss of any meaning.

The Augustinian relation will suffice for us until we are required to start interacting and co-operating with other subjects instead of just objects, which introduces a totally different *world* of expression. As children we could find the answer to what something means from just looking for a corresponding concrete or abstract object, but in social interaction, an Augustinian approach poses serious difficulties in understanding what another person means, because of the uniqueness of the mental representation. One can see this effectively hindering one's effectiveness in functioning in society through limiting one's un-

[103] *Tractatus* 2.1 and 2.12

II-2. THE DUAL NATURE OF PHILOSOPHICAL PROBLEMS

derstanding of how other people in society work. The phenomenon of objectification (also sexual objectification) can be understood as immaturely developed capability for subject-relation, in which the subject still *sees* and treats people as objects, which is the primordial human relation to the external world. And the idea of *subjective meaning* changes this, and we are now asked and required to react to phrases like the following.

- What do you mean?

- Everyone's wearing a red scarf. What does it mean? (People may imply something by choice of clothing)

- It will be wise for you to forget about what you just saw—if you take my meaning. (An implied threat)

- Too much alcohol means the next day is wasted. (Communicating a *subjective* causal connection)

- That the shaft of the stuck arrow is pointing to that particular direction means it must have been fired from that direction.

- Listen! Do you know what that sound means? It means we must get out of here!

These expressions are related to social phenomena and involve increasing our understanding of how society functions or how one is expected to act in a particular situation. When we learn such expressions, they form the basis of our subjective models or patterns of thought and behaviour and understanding them may involve reasoning related to the meanings of the related grammatical objects. For example, in order to understand the arrow example, one must understand what arrows are and how they are used, both as the projectiles they are and also in terms of the related language, such that they are fired, etc.—and this is not related to the grammatical object referring to any shared basis, for example a particular physical object, the idea or a class of physical objects or similar mental representations. We understand the words in a unique manner through the practice in which they are used in society. Wittgenstein would write that the word 'meaning' is similar to the word 'rule', and this can be seen in the said examples, as one can interpret the meaning of a question as the answer to the question "How

PART II. COMMON MISCONCEPTIONS

should I react?" or "What actions need to be taken?"

So, one can see linguistic *meaning*—as something that, as it were, gives life to sentences—as moving from words denoting external objects and abstractions towards these subjective cases where one *is expected* to be a *rational* and *responsible adult* and *to mean* something by one's actions and words. Now "What do you mean?" is equivalent to "What do you have in mind?" which highlights the absolute subjectivity of this sense of meaning. "What did your friend mean; does he have a problem with me? —No, he didn't mean anything by it!" implies that the actions of the friend ought not to be interpreted as communication but something private to himself only. Then again, children are not expected to mean anything by their actions and are considered innocent and completely susceptible to external influence. If you ask a child the question "What do you have in mind?" he will probably *invent* something, which is essentially a response to the question motivated by an intent to behave well and to provoke a response in turn, rather than a result of introspection, and this phenomenon equals what we call the freedom and creativity in children's minds. And this doesn't mean that children are somehow demonstrably different in quality from adults or that there is some particular age or moment of change in children when a sense of responsibility is born, but it reflects the *expectation*, imposed by society and reflected in language by the subjective sense of meaning. To act responsibly implies to rationally think over the consequences of one's actions, and this thought clearly is a process children don't perform, but a sense of responsibility is necessary when one is exposed to a situation that implies responsibility over others, and this is a completely sociological phenomenon. The capability of freedom from the *requirement* of rational thought—a capability of child-like experience—is considered a very high mental skill present in geniuses, and developing such a quality requires a fair amount of freedom from social responsibilities where the subject is not required to give reasons for his actions.

The subjective meaning of 'meaning' is very important existentially

II-2. THE DUAL NATURE OF PHILOSOPHICAL PROBLEMS

because it functions as the link between the subject and society. I will present two linguistic observations to bring this to light; firstly, the "meaning of life" is probably the most classically asked question by people drawn to philosophy, and can be seen to contain a subjective meaning of 'meaning' combined with an objective abstraction referred to as 'life', that could be described as something like "*what*ever all these events around me are". Secondly, a depressed person experiences and reports a loss of meaning or purpose; a loss of the purpose of living; and at the same time experiences detachment from society. But what makes a man ask for the "meaning of life"? It seems to me that the meaning of 'meaning', in the case of grammatical meaning and in the case of tools or social phenomena, is *an answer to the question: "How is it used?"* The best formulation of "the meaning of a word" that I can think of is that it instructs how to use the word, and likewise the best formulation of "the meaning of a sentence" is an answer to how the sentence is to be used; in what sort of situation it could be used. And this sense is very similar to 'purpose' or 'intent'; it carries a presupposition that a word is not born randomly out of nothing, but that some human beings have used it in communication with a particular purpose. Asking "What is the purpose of a hammer?" can be answered by explaining its potential use, such as "To hammer things, such as nails", but one can also ask about the meaning of a hammer in a different sense, namely "What is the meaning of the hammer in the refrigerator?" which is not asking for the purpose of hammers, but for the purpose of having a hammer in the fridge instead of where a hammer would normally be stored. And this implies that *somebody* might have *put* the hammer in the fridge with a purpose or intent in mind; a plan of what to use it for afterwards. That question wouldn't make sense in a context where the hammer would be lying on the ground on a building site, where it would obviously be the case that the hammer has just fallen on the ground and been left there without any particular purpose or intent. Of course, studying purposes or intentions is not philosophically interesting as they are subjective by nature, but the presupposition of one can be related to the meaning of 'meaning', and this presupposition establishes a sense of inter-subjectivity: we *use* the word 'meaning' only where we *expect* a subjective intention or purpose to exist, contrary to situations where we don't expect one and that we experience as unpredictable, unknown or chaotic instead. This inter-subjective presupposition of meaning is interesting, as it is a subjective disposition in itself and carries along an experience of meaning. There is great variance in how much people experience it; this is related to trust and empathy, and it is a measure of our interpersonal skills. And this inter-subjective meaning is bound to both *society* and *tradition*, as these are the frameworks within which actions are interpreted and evaluated. We might say that it is meaningful to take exams at university, because tests are constituted within the academic system and tradition. Let's say that Peter failed an exam at university; why did he fail? We could say, and Peter might agree, that he failed because he didn't study enough or give the exam the attention that it required, but taking a proper look at it, this perspective is confused because it blames Peter's subjective qualities (study, attention) for inadequacy in objective terms (success in the exam). These empirical metrics are constituted within the framework of school systems, yet, strictly speaking, Peter's success or failure in a particular exam, or in a whole set of exams, doesn't determine his capability to study or pay attention. However, the confusion of the perspective of subjective quality against objective standard can be avoided by taking an inter-subjective perspective, which is to say that Peter failed *in order to* learn better in the future, or in order to learn his own fault, and the inter-subjective nature of such a perspective can be seen in the reference to tradition, as both being better in the future and the concept of 'fault' presuppose the tradition of that particular study. This perspective considers that learning, which is the meaning of study, is not just a single event of test, but a process and tradition within which the learning takes place and that the test constitutes. So, Peter's failure is *meaningful* from the perspective of the academic process and tradition of learning where tests are passed or failed, and this sense of meaning *forgives* Peter's failure, because it would nullify the whole sensibility of tests if they weren't sometimes failed; it is purposeful from the perspective of creating such a system that students pass or fail, and failure is *meant* to act as incentive to study more. And it is a very particular type of system and tradition that grants such freedom. As another example—one of group intent without tradition—consider a multi-national company sending Linda to Singapore in order for her to study to be their new executive officer. In this example the failure or success in her studies is not forgiven by the academic system and tradition, but responding to it will be solely in the consideration of her company, and due to this difference, life within private corporations is very different from the academic life of academic freedom. Corporate life is a relatively mild form of group duty, and the forms of group membership and allegiance vary greatly; in the West, corporatism has completely replaced feudalism, in which bonds between individuals were based on sworn fealty instead of legal contracts with mutual obligations and legally controlled extension. But all in all, the purpose of Linda, in her studies, is not to learn to become a capable citizen with an advanced education, as in Peter's case, but to learn the skill required to be the executive officer of the company that sent her to study with this intent. And these are the relevant frameworks of inter-subjective meaning available to Linda and Peter (frameworks relevant to this example); the frameworks within which to evaluate their skill and usefulness, to evaluate whether they have done poorly or well. Experiencing inter-subjective meaning is something that takes place within such groups and traditions and is a result of *identifying* with such a group or tradition. And this experience of meaning is the basis of all our action: desiring to act, feeling that it is purposeful to act, is the result of our experienced membership in a group or tradition. And the opposite also applies: alienation from an experience of meaningful action, related to depression, correlates with alienation from these groups and traditions. In a subjective and existential sense, these groups and traditions are all we have.

II-2-2. Reason and Cause

It is of great importance to notice that, within one's subjective existence, the subjective 'reason' is the primary initial concept that we learn, and the objective 'cause', or cause and effect, the later learned, specialized one. When a child answers the question *why*, he has no possibility but to understand the question in a subjective justifying sense, meaning the question means something like "*Who* has done it?" or "Why did *you/he* do it?" In a child's world, events are caused by subjects such as the child himself or adults, and this is because the child has no responsibility over his own actions or property, and the social expectation for his answer would thus be subject-relative. The child is first taught the use of 'why/because' in sentences like "Why did you do that?" or "Because you were so nice to your sister you can have ice-cream." Because he has no responsibility he could not yet learn to understand what it means when adults would say to each other e.g. "Why do we keep getting these letters each week?", except in the sense that someone must be sending them, or "Why is the washing machine not working?", except in the sense that someone must have broken it. Our responsibility to provide causal answers increases with our responsibility over our life and property. As an example, since American Indians didn't own land a spiritual explanation for the cause of grass growing would suffice for them. They simply would not need to cut or otherwise manipulate grass. This would have come to interfere with the natural human tendency to explain everything that man has no power over in spiritual terms, which is similar to the child's explanation of everything not in his power as external yet subjective. Also, because children have no responsibility, their reasoning is often inverted: "Why not?" The fact that the subjective reason is the *primary* mode of inquiry, and the objective cause only secondary, can be seen via the following points.

1) Subjective reasons precede objective causes when learning language.

2) Objective causes are an etymological branch of subjective reason; the words used to mean the same thing.

3) A rhetoric of objective cause is dominant only in the West.

4) The subject changes via ethical change that involves subjective dialectic; subjective reasoning. He doesn't change via e.g. acquiring subjective experiences or material possessions or achievements.

Because the words 'reason' and 'cause' are intertwined both in our learning language, and also share an etymological origin, it is very understandable that the question "Why?" has a strong sense of metaphysical

II-2. THE DUAL NATURE OF PHILOSOPHICAL PROBLEMS

mystery to it. Why do we exist? Where did we come from? These sorts of confused questions litter the field of Western popular philosophy, yet the questions become answerable when broken down to the separate grammatical constituents with a different sense. "What reason do I have to do this or that?" and "What is the cause my action is serving?" ... both very good questions, as it is quite stupid to carry out an action when one cannot find a sensible reason for doing it. We all start our life at a point where we have no independent thought but only the reasons our parents gave us for the actions we simply followed in their care and authority. We must transition into adulthood and citizenship where our parents are gone and the reasons for our action are something that reflect our own skills and possibilities, and the needs and opportunities of the surrounding world. This is the existential challenge in which it is possible to do well or do poorly, and this is why these questions come into every person's life. They are not objective but subjective questions and they will not be answered in a once-and-for-all manner in the form of a theory, but in the same way as teachers need to bring up every new generation into the necessary skills required in adulthood. In causation, our childhood wonderment ("Why?"), resulting in a subjective explanation, confuses us in adult life, since the new target of our wonderment—connected with the same word—targets causal explanations. As children, we are expected to follow our parents' guidance unless we can produce reasons to act otherwise. Therefore, it is only natural to feel that reasons produce what causes our actions, and thus we have a justified inclination to refuse actions without reasons. But the error lies in thinking that everything *must* have a causal explanation—it is perfectly unproblematic to require from oneself a reason for one's own actions, and to pass on such thoughtful behaviour, e.g. when bringing up children. However, this use of 'must' simply implies a subjective determination to refuse action when a reason for it is not known, and it contradicts the grammar of causal explanation: for any phenomenon we can—in an unproblematic way—have any amount of causal explanations (or none), and those explanations that we are inclined to use are related to what we call perspectives. It seems as if our childhood connection to our parents being responsible over our lives remains connected with us asking "Why?" and thus our spiritual experience of security rests upon trust that an answer exists. This makes it understandable why the endlessly interested and solution-seeking scientific mind so commonly blithely ignores the fundamental impossibility to bind together qualitatively (methodologically) different fields of science, placing all its trust on the ultimate possibility of the scientific method to eventually overcome such 'technicalities'. Moreover, throughout the history of science a certain confused argument has persisted in scientific political discourse: "We are only one small step away from the *final* explanation." This is an illusion emerging out of subjective blindness to the difference between reasons and causal explanations.

Let's take a simple example: I drop a ball on the floor, and ask the question: Why does the ball fall down? Now, possibly the first causal explanation coming to mind—due to this experimental setup—is gravity, and with this answer one is assuming a physical context to the question. But the question might have meant why did I drop the ball in the first place: what was my reason/meaning for dropping the ball that also explains why I didn't hurl it down instead of dropping it, etc. ("why does the ball *fall* down?")—and let it be pointed out that whenever we are struck by wonderment and inclined to utter the question "Why?" in our lives, no such assumptions have been made already unless we commit to making such assumptions ourselves. So, why would one presume the physical framework of gravity then? First of all, because our so-called high-level discussion is predisposed towards both a scientific and a physical answer. But more broadly, our presumptions, in the general case (true individualist thinkers are rare), are directly absorbed from social expectations that involve both social roles but also personal-level social dynamics—in the extreme example it could be that your correct answer will lead to a big reward and a wrong answer will lead to severe punishment, which creates a setting in which you don't have much space except to make your best guess about what the correct, pleasing answer might be. This tends to be the case in relation to Asian schools in comparison with Western ones and would be a defining feature of the Japanese social culture in general. So, returning to the gravity example, you might be presuming the gravity framework

II-2. THE DUAL NATURE OF PHILOSOPHICAL PROBLEMS

because the context of the discussion is scientific and you want to be a good boy and play correctly according to the rules of this type of discussion. And you would be right to do so, given that I, the instructor, wanted to demonstrate gravity (however, in this case I wanted to demonstrate presumption). From the perspective of meaning, having assumed a physical context makes you answer the question through scientific physical theories, the norms—and these come to mind because those theories and the related language have been taught to us as the correct way of thinking in school. Precisely and only because they are norms, I am expected to refer to them when asked this question in the physical sense. But what many don't know is that I am proud to call myself the inventor of a physical theory of my own, according to which balls tend to fall downwards, down being the general direction of my feet in relation to my eyes (very early physical theories were probably very similar), and my theory would perfectly explain this phenomenon in the immediate context where the question is presented and would thus have potential for acceptance. However, if I did this I would be contradicted and ultimately overcome with the fact that my theory has less explanatory power than the existing physical theories, and thus my theory would be dismissed in a process of choosing a common linguistic framework for phenomena of this kind. I would be the last professor of my theory. Now, the process of developing scientific physical theories works through a similar process in which theories that work for different kinds of phenomena are presented, supported and dismissed, linked to each other, enhanced to more fine-grained ones and so on. It should be equally clear that *this process has no limit*—as it has no set target level of accuracy or scale but rather responds to upcoming events in a society that creates hypes and fashions—as the idea that between any two rational numbers a and b such that $a < b$, there exists a rational number a', such that $a < a' < b$. If science is, by definition, an advancing process, what makes somebody think it is approaching some final destination? He might, confused by the language, take the objective research question "Why?" in the subjective sense, and faithfully believe the results of science as *truth*. This gives the fundamentally false impression that the question "Why?" currently being asked by scientists is just the small bit that is missing from the truth. The truth, of course, is subjective to him and related to his ethical nature: the reasons why he himself is living as he is.

II-2-3. Truth

The problem of truth seems to me to be the most fundamental philosophical one. In *Concluding Unscientific Postscript* a point is raised that truth can be asked in a subjective mode ("Is it true what you say?", implying that the question is whether the subject is being truthful) and an objective mode ("Is it true that there is a pen on the table?"), and that the method to find out the truth in these cases is completely different. To check whether someone is lying or deceiving themselves implies a very different procedure from checking whether his utterance is factually true, and the difference in criteria equals different meanings. Also, the main claim ("truth equals subjectivity") put forward in the work is essentially an ethical claim: a suggestion that despite different ways of using the word, truth *should* ultimately be understood as subjective.

We learn how to lie at a very young age and our parental relationship at this age strongly determines our subjective relation to truthfulness. For a child truth equals telling the truth when asked something. We might ask a child "Are you keeping anything in your pockets?" or "Is there a car outside the house?", and the answer will be empirically formulated and the truth behind the answers is empirically verifiable. After this when we become more socially blended—at school and at work—truth is associated with existing linguistic frameworks that determine the criterion. So our concept of truth—in its role as our understanding of what we are supposed to do when asked if something is the case or not—changes from a subjective one to a class of objective ones related to the existing discourses, and their use is dictated by our responsibility to get involved in society. This causes the confusion regarding the word and our puzzlement when we learn that people obviously subjectively apply different conceptions of truth (related to their general

II-2. THE DUAL NATURE OF PHILOSOPHICAL PROBLEMS

sense of responsibility): some people are apt to say they are telling the truth when they believe their lie cannot be caught; some people like to do that when they believe what they are saying accords with what some other people would also say. Some people would say they are telling the truth when they believe there exists an objective way of verifying it; some people would never call anything truth and say that truth is a matter of perspective; some people would agree that anything is at least partially true (for the same reason). Some people are apt to say they are telling the truth when they believe in what they are saying, and among those people there are those who have taken the personal effort to check the basis of what they believe in, and then again those who haven't—it is perfectly possible to remain in a child-like subjective world, believing in fairy-tales, but then again, it is perfectly possible to end up not believing in anything. Then again, the notion of *objective truth* is a methodological matter for communal work and implies objective verificational methods for the subject matter. In natural science it is, for example, perfectly valid to study the chemical structure of substances in reference to the theories of chemistry that have been widely verified by chemists adhering to the scientific method. Those theories provide the objective criterion for one's results; one can deduce: in this reaction of these-and-these chemicals, such-and-such a result happens because of such-and-such theoretical chemical qualities. Should somebody claim something that contradicts those theories, one would be justified in saying: "No, that is false! The *truth* is..." In the light of this, one can see that the contemporarily exploded study of subjective qualities, such as the mind, intelligence, awareness, etc., through means of natural science, is a scientific error: such research refers to non-verifiable theories about the features or structure of those subjective qualities. The motivation to conduct such research, of course, is the age-old puzzlement about the mind that also inspires philosophers, but any theories about the nature of whatever those concepts mean are worthless if they are based on subjective verification and are thus adopted just because they sound appealing—and any scientific research in reference to such theories *makes no sense*. Such research programmes should categorically be further explicated to, as a *minimum requirement* for clarity, exclude any subjective terminology from their subject matter, since the subjective factor will result in subjectively applicable results and hypotheses adopted unconsciously, advancing the segregation and disintegration of science and producing nothing with any practical value. From an existential perspective, subjectively adopting an objective notion of truth (to take something objective as truth without reference to its constituting frame of reference) is a form of self-deceit, firstly in terms of being blinded about whether one is being truthful or deceptive, since one will justify the use of a word through having in mind some particular meaning for it (and the formulation of such is the mission of Platonic philosophy). This preconception will void the necessity to actively subjectively search for the meaning of concepts while using them in one's life and thus to become aware of their actual use. Secondly, this self-deceit results in a form of thinking that it is correct to strive to reach for the reality depicted by the subjectively assumed objectively true statements, which in effect results in ethical reasoning where ends justify means. As an example, consider a religious person taking the word 'God' used in a Platonic sense as a reference to a metaphysical idea, and noting the neighbouring family referring to something called 'Vishnu' in a similar divine meaning. Now, from this standpoint the word can either refer to the same idea or another one—after all he has many names for the same idea too, such as 'Lord'—and a quick look at how the neighbours use the word reveals to the subject that their customs related to its use differ from his. For example, they don't go to church, which would imply that they don't consider churches to be built in in honour of their 'Vishnu', which in turn is quite a strong indicator that by 'God' they are referring to something other than what the subject means by 'God'. Now, this poses a rather serious conflict with (the traditional interpretation of) the First Commandment, and from the objective fact that there *is* only one God it follows that it must be the case that the Vishnu worshippers simply don't understand it and have it wrong. And in order to bring balance in society, the rest is simply up to the choice of means how to best convince them—the cause is already justified, and whatever the means would be, their justification would be interpreted in the light of the cause.

II-2. THE DUAL NATURE OF PHILOSOPHICAL PROBLEMS

II-2-4. Agreement and Understanding

The behaviour of *sympathy* has the appealing appearance of understanding ("I understand you"), but in a strict sense it should be seen as a *willingness to agreement.* Sympathy could be described as the social use of empathy as a means to reach agreement; *syn-pathos* literally translates to together-feeling, "the feeling of being together" (the word has been mixed with the sense of pity, which is a very different sense). It is clearly regulated by social status: a person will only show willingness to agree with somebody he regards as an equal or higher; the socially dominant individual is agreed with in an instant without question, and the socially inferior individual is questioned even if his sayings seem to be correct and don't superficially differ from the norm. It should be noted that pity is the opposite; pity, if anything, is something we show to socially inferior individuals. Empathy itself is a highly important subjective skill in terms of one's ethical development, and a sympathetic willingness to agreement can be seen as an important social skill in itself. However, regarding meaning, empathy becomes a vice exactly where language begins to function as a political agreement among *all* people who speak it, instead of the two people in question, and where meaning is bound to an objectively shared criterion instead of an agreement between two subjective views. The uniqueness of our subjectivity is related to our social nature and what is called 'inter-subjectivity': we develop our subjective qualities in close social interaction and in a subject-relation to other subjects. This inter-subjective emotional basis we share inter-culturally and with many animals, but we are very much separated from animals by our subjective rationality: our learning, changing beliefs and reaching subjective certainty involve a subjective process that can best be called *dialectic*. Before accepting something, a rational person needs to present questions, and these questions are subjective in nature, meaning that nothing general can be said about such questions, and it is not a standard process or algorithm how people learn. From the perspective of philosophy, it is enough to say that a person can believe anything that a particular person says, but reject everything that another person says, and the details

PART II. COMMON MISCONCEPTIONS

of this process are left for psychology and sociology to investigate. Here it is enough to note that 1) political (social) agreement, where something another party presents is *accepted*, and 2) *understanding*, which involves a sense of familiarity and can be said to have varying degrees, are two completely separate phenomena—not so very different from how one can accept and sign a written contract the contents of which one is partly or completely unaware of. They serve a different social purpose: agreement (1) is used to communicate and coordinate intentions, whereas understanding (2) is used to pass knowledge. Agreement (1) tends to look like understanding (2) and knowledge, perhaps because both are socially communicated with affirmation. However, an effort to understand can look like disagreement, and because of this reaching for correct intellectual understanding requires social strength, whereas children and the weak minded are said to simply look for acceptance. However, understanding (2) something (X), I believe, can be best described as being equivalent to *seeing the same reason*[104] that the subject who communicated X saw regarding X. "Do you understand?" translates to "Do you see the same reason as I do?", and here the person answering has an easy option to deceptively nod his head in acceptance (1) without having any insight (2) whatsoever, unless he will be pursued by the person asking; and this, I believe, is where people, who are called intellectually honest, differ in action from the norm, by resisting the temptation to claim understanding unless there is also a subjective experience of insight. Sometimes agreement (1) and understanding (2) are intertwined in expressions like "I understand how you feel", and this mixture is often simply called just understanding… but of course nobody needs to see reason in anybody's feelings, as feelings rather are the logical opposite of reason as a motivator—acting based on feelings is called impulsiveness.

Why can't things be clear from the start; why is it that agreement tends to deceptively look like understanding? We need to take a look at human social interaction at the age where we learn language: at first we

---

104 This is elucidated by the English word 'insight', which also has equivalents in other Germanic languages, such as in German: '*Einsicht*'. To understand another is to subjectively (inside, as opposed to externally) see the same reason as another.

II-2. THE DUAL NATURE OF PHILOSOPHICAL PROBLEMS

are simply required to agree and to comply. "Put on your clothes"—"Yes"… there is no understanding required; the reason to put the clothes on is known by our parents, who are in charge of our lives. Only after our status changes from childhood to adulthood are we required to understand the reasons for our actions, and we could quite reliably state that the goal for good parenthood is to give children the means to independently maintain their lives, which involves passing on select behavioural patterns as legacy but also passing on the reasoning behind those patterns, because behaviour that is not understood will be given up by the child once he starts to lead an independent life. The social interaction where our parents pass on authoritative directions to us, and we are expected to comply, later changes to a situation where we need to pass on reasons as adults. Also, we can take note that a person who is generally stuck in a habit of bossing people around and, for example, using violence to enforce his authority, is actually existing as a child, as he is repeating the only relation he has learned so far: an existence where the parent gives directions and the child mindlessly carries them out. When those who he is bossing around don't comply with this, he doesn't have a model of reasoning to back this behaviour and can only resort to violence. Hence the often remarked-on senselessness of violence: violence is used where reasoning would normally be used in harmonious interaction.[105] So, once again, the confusion between agreement and understanding is in our *existence*: because we need to exist as the same person in the same interaction in two different roles.

Once it is clear that what is talked about as understanding between humans is actually mostly social agreement of communicating intentions disguised as understanding in a technical sense (and this ritual act is a Western dialectical development), what is talked about as understanding between humans and animals also becomes easier to understand. In the correct sense of understanding, of course animals can't understand human reasoning in terms of insight, but in terms of agreement, they most certainly can. Social animals excel in clarity

---
105 Not all violence is senseless; only resorting to violence instead of reason is–literally–senseless. This applies only to situations where reasoning would be a more effective way of advancing one's goals. Warfare is a very sensible subject that can be developed into an art of its own; the art of advancing one's goals via violence.

PART II. COMMON MISCONCEPTIONS

of communicating intentions: a dog shows his open mouth and teeth to another dog, signalling what he intends to do unless the other dog backs off from the food. The other dog pulls his ears back and opens his mouth to show that his teeth are together (any biting is not going to take place, either of the food or the other dog), then lowers his body and leans away, signalling the intention to retreat, asking if this is enough to avoid the confrontation.[106] The other dog accepts by closing his lips, and an agreement has been reached; the confrontation has been avoided by means of negotiation. Any efforts to study whether animals are 'intelligent' are simply employing a misconceived model of the mind, where intelligence is seen as some sort of mystical or metaphysical power of the mind of which some great champions of the mind possess a lot while lower beings possess less. Clarity is needed in that thought and language are essentially the same thing, and an animal's communicative (linguistic) skill determines whether we can agree with them. And yes, we do; people are known to sleep every night with highly dangerous predator animals. How could one do such a scary thing? Well, aren't we only afraid of what we don't understand? Isn't the xenophobe just culturally uninformed, failing to communicate and come to agreement, and therefore afraid? Another thing we can note, after clarifying the difference between agreement and understanding, is that our general difficulty in understanding other people is related to the fact that we disagree with them; we don't wish to comply with what they are suggesting via their statement. We feel that if we take the opponent's argument at its face value and nod our heads signifying understanding, we are agreeing to what their argument implies, and at this point we say "No, no, no! I simply can't understand you!" What we really mean is that we don't feel sympathy with what he is saying; we have no willingness to agree. The difficulty of understanding another person can, in the standard case, be overcome simply using the scientific principle of charity, by assuming the rationality of the opponent... this works because it forces us into looking to *understand* (to see the same reason) instead of looking to agree. The enlightened answer is "Yes, I understand perfectly what you are saying and understand your

---

[106] Also, humans have the social signal of raising hands, lowering the head and showing closed teeth when backing off from a confrontation.

reasons. However, I disagree with you and will not comply."

II-2-5. Allowed and Imaginable

It is no coincidence that the words 'can' and 'may' refer both to a subjective possibility or capability to do something and either logical (imaginable) or probable occurrence of an objective phenomenon. As children we are taught the subjective meaning of the word in uses like "You can go out for two hours" and "You may watch TV". Ask a child a question like "Could it rain tomorrow?" and he will probably answer 'yes' or 'no', as he probably would if he was asked if he would like it to rain or not. Again, in adulthood our responsibilities change so that we are required to function communally and thus have objective clarity over the concepts we use, but the words 'can' and 'may' generally remain existentially available to us and are used in expressing objective relations, e.g. "In tic-tac-toe one space may hold either one cross or one circle" or "Finding a parking space at rush hour can take time".

The major difficulties related to the dual use of 'can' or 'may' lie in the complete distinctness of the subjective and the objective in terms of criterion and are two-fold. Firstly, one can misinterpret a concept of the objective realm to be explainable in subjective terms either by oneself or by another; in other words, someone may think he has the right to interpret an objective concept in any way he wants. Secondly, one can misinterpret one's own subjective experience of possibility, or the expression of such by another, as an objective question requiring objective evidence as proof. Both cases will logically lead into a philosophical dead-end. Surely the subject doesn't by accident produce senseless utterances, but his inclination to do so is related to a subjective process that has produced such beliefs in which fear has overcome his intellectual honesty. The subject protects himself by means of self-deceit, forcing the integrity of his subjective belief system through manipulation instead of facing the horror and humiliation of changing it. Here are some examples of the first kind:

PART II. COMMON MISCONCEPTIONS

- "My smoking may be addictive, but people who say so don't understand what it means to me"— 'addiction' is not a subjective faculty but diagnosed in an objective manner.

- *"One can achieve anything if one just wishes hard enough"*— 'anything', used in passive voice and thus general sense, calls for objective criteria, but wishing is a subjective faculty. Saying "I can achieve any goal I set for myself by wishing hard enough" would be an unproblematic expression of conviction.

- *"We can have better capitalism by having corporations invest in caring"*.[107] This is an inverse example of abuse of public naivety by corporate propaganda. "Corporate caring" doesn't mean anything without definition, since caring is a subjective faculty; it effectively means a marketing concept that is purported to increase profits for companies established enough to plausibly pose as caretakers instead of suppliers or service providers. And "We can have better capitalism" means nothing more than "I can have more money", since capitalism simply means faith in capital and no change of system in respect of, say, laws, is implied. This reflects the inherently contradictory American rhetoric of leadership that portrays the moral ideal of strong individuals taking care of weaker individuals; in this case of capital investment the rhetoric hides the contrasting reality that quoted corporations are legally obliged to maximally benefit their stockholders before anybody else.

These examples can be seen to relate to naivety: the subject wishes to believe that these objective words can somehow be subjectively influenced, similarly to the way a child might block his ears to maintain the integrity of his subjective world instead of letting it be destroyed by what he knows—since he blocks his ears—to be evident. The subject doesn't want to grow up. The same phenomenon seems to be involved in the human wish for *fantasy*: the full diversity of natural human existential interest is directed to a story that is imaginary, arising out of a subjective failure to existentially realize it. The silent subjective world, albeit inhabited by words that bear objective meaning, gets a subjective context, which functions as an ultimate protection, and this

---

[107] Rhetoric applied in a speech by Bill Gates, *TIME* Magazine, 2008

II-2. THE DUAL NATURE OF PHILOSOPHICAL PROBLEMS

is the common feature in the addictive nature of e.g. TV, fiction and narcotics, the use of which develops unhealthy features only in a socially isolated environment that maintains a possibility for the subject to live in his subjective world without social feedback. It might be worth mentioning that the criminalization of narcotics has always been a matter of the *social* issues their use can be seen to produce among minorities that use them for escapist purposes, and the "gate theory" argument, if applied correctly, should also be seen to apply to e.g. TV or fiction, which, however, is never the case in practice.[108] Narcotics have traditionally been used, in addition to medical purposes, in secret both by high-performing individualists, and systematically in military contexts, to improve individual performance.

Here are some examples of the second kind of difficulty:

- *"One can never be certain because one is always liable to error"*—certainty is a subjective state but this sense of 'error' implies shared criteria. It is indeed possible to act without possibility for subjective error, by holding fast to one's ideals or principles.

- *"I wonder what my odds of success would be if I tried…"*—probability, although defined as a means of expressing a degree of belief, is used in an objective manner implying an objective means of calculating the probability, such as a statistical method. 'Trying', however, is a subjective faculty.

- *"God probably doesn't exist since we have no supporting evidence"*—this sense of 'evidence' implies direct, sensory objective evidence, but the subjective faculty of non-sensory experience is the criterion related to spiritual testimony, through which the word 'God' gets its meaning.

These examples can be seen to relate to insecurity: the subject desires objective and external confirmation for what ultimately lies solely in his personal domain. By believing in the objective nature of the phenomenon in question, he escapes the related personal responsibility.

---

[108] The upper-class perspective of the good of the lower social class is for them to remain in a state of controlled stasis rather than to exhibit unpredictable behaviour.

PART II. COMMON MISCONCEPTIONS

II-2-6. Free Will

The question of *free will* is one that has had a long importance in philosophy and is considered important regarding ethical questions. We will clarify that the concept is utterly meaningless as a metaphysical notion; as a notion of e.g. some sort of Cartesian human "controller component" or "decision centre" that one might use as a metaphor. However, it is meaningful when used in juxtaposition against a setting where one would be *forced to* comply, or where the behaviour of an individual would be seen to rationally follow from the behaviour of a group or, say, a ruler, as the hierarchical behaviour of military units could be characterized as "drone-like", and in military humour you say that you follow the orders because you *love it*, to emphasize that free will doesn't exist in the military hierarchy. In Western thought, a *rational* human being has the capability to decide, but essentially he has *the right* to decide, and he is *willing* to decide instead of being dictated rules by another—as if this had anything to do with *rationality* (another metaphysical notion) as in being a rational person; as if it was any more rational to behave in an individualistic way in an individualist culture than behaving in a conformist way in a conformist culture. The concept of free *will* has never meant just the *capability* to decide, but the proud willingness, strength, courage, potency and vigour to decide for oneself, yearning for self-governance instead of being governed by another: "I am not an animal! I am a human being!"[109] This fundamental individuality is bound to our concept of rationality: that *it is rational to aim to govern oneself* instead of being governed by another. This conception is fundamentally Christian and Stoic, as Westerners are equal in front of God—in Asia, generally, being individualist is highly irrational, as the concept of reason is generally not individualist but refers to the will of a higher entity, and thus the problem of free will doesn't exist. But that the notion of free will doesn't relate to anything

---

[109] The cry is the climax in the tragic movie *Elephant Man* by David Lynch, and highlights the democratic problem of the free will of disabled minorities: to what extent are we justified to *govern* individuals with the *will* for individuality, like everybody else in a democratic society, but that are devoid of the practical capability for it? The concept of "elephant man" (animal man) well summarizes this problematic.

II-2. THE DUAL NATURE OF PHILOSOPHICAL PROBLEMS

with a concrete human basis, such as a "free will organ" in the brain, is easy to see from the fact that people don't statistically make decisions that would reflect freedom in the sense of independence from social governance. If people indeed were "individuals by nature", as we Westerners would like to see ourselves, we would expect to see mass individuality instead of mass conformity in e.g. consumer choices or political decisions. On the contrary, in the US democratic system it is a known practical impossibility for a presidential candidate who is not backed by big money to get to the final rounds of the presidential race. This is because big money buys visibility in the media, which, in turn, translates to a statistical expectation towards certain voter behaviour. And this empirical fact is based on the well-known truth that people's opinions are influenced by what they see, and this, in turn, sprouts various methods of advertisement (newspaper front pages, big, medium or small ads, TV or radio commercials on various channels by popularity, leaflets, walking advertisements and so on) with *demonstrable expectations of efficacy*, that, in turn, translate to the price of these services as per their availability and demand. Therefore somebody with a lot of money can buy lots of visibility for his *opinion*, which statistically translates to conformity to support this opinion, and this is something that absolutely contradicts the idea that people would behave in an individualistic manner because it is *in their nature* to do so. Thus, individuality, instead of being a metaphysical or intrinsic human quality, turns out to be a Western (ethical) *ideal*, as we would say that a person will ideally make individualist choices instead of succumbing to external governance.

We can now determine the concept of free will as nothing more intrinsic than a democratic ideal in the Western sentiment; the ascribed ideal model of an emancipated citizen deciding independently instead of being governed. That free will is an ideal can be observed in that, in the West, there exists a normative sentiment that one *is supposed to* make individual choices, which is a paradox caused by the juxtaposition of two meanings of free choice: 1) the *subjective* capability of free choice, as opposed to letting oneself be governed instead of passionately fighting to have one's *own will* (subjective quality) realized, and

2) the *objective behaviour* that implies free choice, which is verified by its accordance to the norm and expectation of free choice, imposed by society. Turning this around, *if* free will was *not* an *ideal* realization of a human *capability*, similar to loving, caring, being considerate, modesty, etc... but instead an intrinsic quality that essentially distinguishes us from some other species, such as thought, social hierarchy and bonding, linguistic communication or such, there would be no need for the norm of individuality and no need to be *urged* to be individuals making free choices. Isn't it quite ludicrous that individuality can be marketed to a person by e.g. the fashion industry: "To prove that you are an individual capable of free choice, do as we say and buy our product"? And this is not the only thing that's ludicrous—this paradox of a notion has been, and is, studied metaphysically by academic minds instead of simply analysing it away, and they have produced a mystical bag of mutually contradictory metaphysical answers to whatever free will *is*, *if* it is, and covered it with a warning label. I suggest calculating the value of this whole bag as a lump sum, using the Socratic conception of value as what it is useful for, instead of the Marxian conception of how much workers' sweat and blood has been shed to produce it. For anybody who offers a metaphysical explanation that free will *consists of* such-and-such, creating the new concepts of such-and-such as the *constituents* of free will, I ask the question: Where is the practical application of such-and-such? And don't say that it gives future work to other academics who can carry on analysing it. It certainly does, but it shouldn't; they should have done away with the concept already instead of further complicating it. I would also emphasize that an analytic explanation such as mine, one that explains what free will *means*, doesn't contradict anything.

But the asylum can't be run by the inmates forever; as Western individualism is degrading under the pressure of conformity imposed by the global economy, we are witnessing an increasing gap between the masses of people behaving as conformist herds, and the models in advertisements portraying images of people with the capability of limitless individuality: images of *rich* people. Our wish for individuality, as freedom of choice and freedom of the soul, is degrading into the ideal of earthly freedom and the *practical* capability to be an individual instead of a slave of industry without individuality. And this direction is exactly towards the Eastern notion of individuality, where individuality implies freedom, which implies practical capabilities for freedom and thus higher social status, and the human worship of the most powerful individuals that, at the same time, are the freest. In Eastern thought, free will is not considered intrinsic at all, but rather we could say that the *will* of those who *are free* is the thing that is to be considered. All in all, the talk about free will is a particular Western discourse and rhetoric, but nothing to be taken more metaphysically or seriously than just understanding its importance in the Western Enlightenment when individual freedom under democratic governments and a liberal economy was sought. But if we void the Christian background of equality and rationality, and announce that we Westerners would now like to have lots of free will but without Christianity—without the idea that we have been *given* free will—the notion of free will has lost all its meaning and will be discarded in the coming reform as an empty relic. Freedoms need to be earned or they are lost, and this applies to free will, too.

II-2-7. Dreams

There has always been a great deal of interest in dreams in the sense that interpreting them may be able to yield some wisdom, and I believe this is related to the supposed relation between dreams and truth: dreams represent the totality of our subjectivity instead of just the part that we wish to see, to look at, or to admit to others. Therefore, in this role our dreams are mirrors to our subjectivity, and our reminders. In this modern effort to try and learn more about the human by studying their brain, the underlying motive in the first place clearly is that we know that there is more to the subject than what we consciously see and such events have been, in the questionably scientific tradition of psychoanalysis,[110] described under the notion 'subconscious'. Any

---

110 Originally the word 'subconscious' was coined by Pierre Janet, who inspired, among others, both Jung and Freud. Janet himself accused Freud of plagiarizing

scientific study of this suffers from the same problems as everything studied under the concept 'supernatural', which originates from the problem that these concepts are metaphors that are interpreted in a metaphysical manner. One might take note that both 'subconscious' and 'supernatural' are qualities that grammatically are extensions of 'conscious' and 'natural', similar to the way 'metaphysics' is an extension of 'physics', essentially meaning "whatever it is that is not strictly physics", and further note that 'esotericism' translates to "of the inner circle", and utilizes the same grammatical device, implying something hidden buried underneath... as it were, underneath the scope of a concept. A subconscious wish or fear simply is something a person wishes or fears, but doesn't show it and is not conscious about it,[111] which puts it into a different category from wishes and fears of the other, spoken kind... and it is this difficulty of reliably uncovering a subconscious mental quality that gives psychoanalysis its occult nature. Freud theorized *all* dreams to be fulfilments of subconscious wishes, but this unfortunately is a rather pseudoscientific claim that, I believe, has been influenced by the persistent scientific desire to attribute a single cause or factor behind phenomena. One needs to go to uncomfortable pseudoscientific lengths to explain all dreams as secret wishes, although it is easy to see that the desire for something is strongly related to dreams, and this fact was not discovered by Freud but is rather self-evident. Very obviously dreams are related to our subconscious subjective relation to things: we dream particularly about everything we find important, and also in reverse, we say that one should sleep on important decisions.[112] Rather than being wishes, I would rather relate dreams to the concept

his notions, and it was rumored that Freud had stolen his ideas by listening to his lectures.

111   People seldom are conscious of any of their own fears, but other people are aware of their fears, as fear is something that can be read from one's behaviour and face. I would say every fear is first subconscious, because we have a social requirement to show strength. Then some of these fears are easier to overcome, which is largely related to how socially acceptable they are.

112   By saying "we say" I mean that in sensible times people did that. In the modern world people don't have enough time for a healthy subjective life, and they are taught and conditioned to constantly make fast and hasty decisions and not to worry about their consequences. This is related to the only 21st-century business model: make personal profit any way you can as quickly as possible, and when the vein has run dry, quickly adapt and change. You can call this modern banditry and easily relate it to lack of control and authority in business.

II-2. THE DUAL NATURE OF PHILOSOPHICAL PROBLEMS

truth via the concepts of *revelation* and *epiphany*. As 'truth' originally means 'unconcealed' or 'unforgotten', so dreams relate to revelation, as what is being subjectively revealed is something that is either *concealed* or *forgotten*. The things that are concealed are the things that are not yet understood well enough to be seen clearly, and due to this, the dream state is often the state where one gets the most important ideas and finds the answers to many questions. During the daytime we are not susceptible to deep thought about what we see because most of the time we are either focusing on something in particular or under social obligations and expectations to respond to observations instead of thinking over them. That is why our sleep time is time when the things that we have seen, and especially the things that we saw and thought over during the day, go through deeper processing with the totality of our subjectivity. This is where questions are asked and contradictions are solved: as a simplification, let's say I am a shepherd who's always tended white sheep but one day I suddenly see a red sheep. In my subjective world sheep are white and I have some explanation as to why sheep are white. This subjective construction that I possess is an entire meaningful system that includes a lot of memories and contradicting beliefs, but also a lot of fears, such as the potential dangers of red sheep or the social humiliation of what others will think of me now that I've stumbled on the fact that red sheep exist. It isn't a simple task of adding a red sheep into the picture; rather it has to be acknowledged that I have been wrong about this so far and I will face many questions about why I had never seen a red sheep before and what made me think all sheep were white... which, if successful, could lead to many revealing insights. And during sleep is the primary time for this sort of processing. The second case of dreams—as the forgotten—can be seen in *haunting* dreams that follow people who try and personally escape something. Let's say a person commits a crime and gets away with it. Now he has to act socially as if it never happened and to forget it, which is in the highest contradiction with his subjectivity in which he will remember the minutest details about the crime. These memories are now in contradiction with all his behaviour and can only lose importance to him if he manages to forget them further, and therefore such a person will try and minimize the chances of being subjected to things that will remind him of those actions. The haunting functionality of the dream reflects the contradiction in his beliefs, and I believe this works in such a way that when such memories are stimulated, the related thoughts are triggered. Recurring dreams and nightmares are obviously related to memories of experienced events that are somehow undesirable in nature (having committed a crime usually is not a matter of pride) and can be reminders of traumatic events that are beyond the reach of one's conscious memory. Here we can see that dreams can often bring back memories that have been completely forgotten in our conscious life, possibly due to our wish and tendency to repress what is undesirable,[113] and this function of dreams has been a target of interest in psychoanalysis and studying hypnosis.

But now we come to the same explanation that we always can find to be the case with every phenomenon that is mystical in nature: there are two major senses to the word 'dream' (and two distinct words for it in Finnish, 'uni' and 'unelma'). The first one is dream in the sense of distinguishing sleep from a waking state, which emphasizes non-sensory perception: "*He* is dreaming", which we know because his eyelids and body are showing particular motions that we know to relate to a state of non-sensory perception, or "I *saw* it in a dream", which implies a past tense because you will have to know first that you were dreaming, using some objective criterion such as an event of waking up. The second one is dream in the sense of wish or premonition: "I *have* a dream..." or "I *am* dreaming of..." where one is able to tell that one currently is dreaming. The *criterion* in the first case is strictly objective, as we can see that one is not subjectively able to distinguish whether one is sleeping or not, but we can observe whether another person is sleeping or not. But the criterion in the second case is subjective and related to something we are inclined to experience in a sleeping state. Taking

---

[113] I once met a woman that I had known before she disappeared for many years. She had completely changed from a, so to say, normal person, into a pale, detached drug addled state. She didn't recognize me when I went to talk to her; she had forgotten about me. But what stayed in my mind was her reaction when I reminded her of her past life: it was a reaction of painful horror. I am sure she had her reasons to repress all those memories of who she used to be and what she used to do.

II-2. THE DUAL NATURE OF PHILOSOPHICAL PROBLEMS

a closer look at this subjective meaning of a dream, it is not something that is strictly bound to a sleeping state but just something that tends to happen more during sleep; we have the word 'day-dream' and say things like "Stop dreaming!" But more importantly, *psychosis* is described as a state where the person has lost contact with *reality*, and one can see that the opposite of reality here is not 'falsity' or 'surrealism' but dream or fantasy. In a psychosis, a person can't tell the difference between dream and a waking state, and modern psychology acknowledges that the state of psychosis develops via the stages of hypomania and mania, and typically during these stages the subject tends to sleep more and more irregularly and, in practice, to sleep less. This phenomenon, where dreams follow us to the waking state if we don't get enough sleep, also occurs on a shorter timescale as what we call drifting, and a sleep-deprived person can enter into a sleep state via the initial stage of drifting. As a general rule, people seem to physically require a certain amount of sleep, and there is a lot of individual variation in how much sleep is required, how people fall asleep and how they sleep. Speaking of dreaming in the subjective sense, we can notice that the subject actually more or less constantly inhabits a subjective world of desires and fears, and the objective criterion of whether the subject is 'awake' or not is whether he is in contact with the objective (shared, observable) reality instead of, in his behaviour, responding to his imagination. The standard medical check to see if there is basic response to observation is to ask how many fingers are being shown: this requires the subject to *observe* instead of answering nothing at all or answering according to his imagination. The old problem of whether we *know* we are dreaming or not, and the Cartesian claim that we can't know that and therefore can't fully trust our senses, is quite misleading, as it is also the case that being in a sleeping state implies that the person is not monitoring himself and thus is restricted from asking the whole question. Only in the objective sense, in the sense of an observation, it is sensible to speak of knowing that the person is asleep. Also, at least personally in my dreams (I lack data from others), I have the experience that the act of doubting the reality depicted by the dream, and instead recognizing my experience as a dream and recognizing that "I am dreaming", also has the rather immediate effect of ending the dream and waking up. This implies that the subjective states of being absorbed by the dream and believing the reality it depicts (the subjective meaning of dreaming), and being an external objective observer to the dream, are in a logical contrast and are not at least normally done at the same time. There is a concept of a "lucid dream" which relates to a degree of awareness about dreaming during dreaming, and this observation dates back even to Aristotle. It seems to me that there is an interplay between the subjective experience of a dream and the objective check that one would make in order to know whether one is imagining something or whether it is real, as both of these functions are being subjectively routinely performed by everybody during their waking hours. Often close to morning I have states of being half-awake where I observe the objects in my room having dream-like qualities and sometimes get a fright, until I perform a reality check and realize they were the interplay of dream and observation. What we call subjective experience and objective observation, respectively, reflect classically opposing realms of our subjectivity, imaginative creativity and logical rationality, and are related to respective subjective skills and weaknesses in which one quite easily see the necessity for both skills: creativity and rationality, and the fact that the lack of either skill relates to psychological impairment. Looking at the extreme ends of both existences, 1) a person in ritualistic rational existence is one who can think only rationally and is afraid to think independently: he will stick to an externally imposed rational discourse, of which there are two kinds: either of cause and effect that is accessible silently in one's thought (a person who is locked up in his mind with his theories), or of social justification, which means constantly rationalizing one's actions to others for social support (a person who is constantly explaining what others already know). Both of these types signify lack of imagination due to social cowardice; the fear of appearing stupid in the eyes of others by expressing independent thoughts that won't get social support. The other extreme is 2) a person who is restricted to a ritualized imaginative existence; one who constantly absorbs and develops imaginative theories about, say, government collusion with extra-terrestrial aliens or government mind-control of normal citizens. Talking to such a person reveals that there may be no clear boundary

II-2. THE DUAL NATURE OF PHILOSOPHICAL PROBLEMS

between the products of his imagination and his observations, and he feels a sense of delight in this, which signifies an ethical change: the person is being imaginative for a reason, for example because they experience rationality as cold and inhumane. Such individuals will likely be challenged by a nightmarish daily life, and they typically actively seek out and join cults where they get social support and where independent thought is controlled by authority and routine. But there is yet another dimension to reality being contrasted with dreams, which is that the word 'fantastic' refers to both being phantasm-like, and being *ideal*, as ideas and ideals are born in dreams. Idealism is the logical opposite of realism, as the dreamed ideal is the logical opposite of reality. This is an important aspect to note, because grammatically ideals are often used identically to reality: people have a strong tendency to present a wish as the state of affairs, and *lying* is often a kind of behaviour where something not real, but wished to be real, is presented as the state of affairs. So, in a certain psychological way, a wish is close to reality, as people can exist in wishful thoughts and a dream-reality instead of "facing the facts" of life, or people can cheat a bit and present themselves as being in possession of things that in fact they'd just like to be in possession of, and in general falling asleep is a small, quick and humane event that normally happens to everybody every day and as such doesn't get much attention. But it is important to see that the dream or ideal is the actual logical opposite of reality, and as such is, in effect, as far from reality as it is possible for anything to be. An extreme example of where this can lead is in wartime, where a sleeping sentry is the greatest criminal of all, compromising the security of his whole unit by a minor lapse of attention leading him to drift into sleep.

Whenever dreams are interpreted to be guided by natural laws, this sort of thought or activity is in the same category as horoscopes, fortune-telling, palm-reading and so on, as these enterprises all operate with the assumption that there is a causal relation between two phenomena: one objectively verified and one subjectively verified. It is also in the same category as science that attributes a causal relation between, say, neurons and dreams—I once witnessed a university lecture in "cognitive science" that started by considering whether we might be able to *record our dreams* from our neurons, using some device like a tape recorder. Here one has obviously taken the step from considering dreams as visual images into somehow seeing them as storing visual images, but simply forgotten that the particular difference between how we speak about the visual images conjured by dreams, in comparison with sensory visual images, is that essentially dreamy images are *not real* but a result of imagination. Rather the image is a metaphor from the sensory images we have seen with objective criteria, and dream images are the logical opposite of real images. Then again, the motivation to record dreams must derive from our age-old wish to interpret them—we know that dreams tend to conjure symbolic images and stereotypic images, such as priests, nuns, police and firemen that essentially are cultural stereotypes; sexual stereotypes, such as a blonde or brunette woman; symbolic locations such as an empty plain, a church or a hospital, and certain commonplace symbolic events such as being in a high place, floating in empty space, seeing a disaster unfold, going underwater, et cetera. This symbolic nature of dreams is behind the high interest in the interpretation of dreams, but the key thing to notice is that the *motive* to interpret dreams, or to have one's own dreams interpreted, is completely subjective; only in history were the dreams of a king important enough for there to be an official to carry them out to make them real, because the kingdom was following the king's whim. *When* people want to interpret their dreams, they are asking "What does this dream *mean*?" but definitely not in the sense of causation. They are *not* asking: "Give me an analysis of how neurons (or such) *produced* my dreams." They are asking "Why?" in the subjective sense of the word, such as: "Why should I go to school tomorrow?" They are asking for a *sign*: "What subjective actions does this observation signify (imply, stand for)?" But not all people are in this sort of suggestive state, and those who are, tend to be in that state at specific times. I was once told about something that happened at a funeral: "When the priest finished his memorial speech, there was a sudden breeze that tipped over all the plastic cups on the table." This event would normally go unnoticed but on that occasion it was experienced as *significant*. Now, the word 'significant' is in itself very telling of this phenomenon: a phenomenon is experienced as subjectively meaning-

II-2. THE DUAL NATURE OF PHILOSOPHICAL PROBLEMS

ful when it is experienced as significant, or *relevant*, which translates to 'relieving' and reflects the emotional experience of significance—the purpose of the memorial speech is to *relieve* suffering, is it not? The priest gives a speech that is (ideally) received as significant and succeeds in bringing some relief to the suffering. But this relief, implied by the concept of relevance, is obviously supernatural in nature *if* one would like to look at it from an essentialist perspective, which I strongly advise against for anybody who desires objectivity and wishes to avoid the mystical nature of language. Rather, in exactly the same way as with meaning, relevance is something that is quite correctly described as "beyond" the syntactic expression of language, and this place is the subjective realm where people are choosing their words and causing this relevance in their choice of words. One is correct to describe a word or expression as relevant when it has been subjectively chosen in a way that succeeds in achieving the subjective result that is experienced as relevance or significance, and from the perspective of society, relevance and significance are subjective opinions. Now we can conclude that the experience of the relevance and significance of events implies the subjective state in which the subject is himself asking for a subjective *reason* and *purpose*. And this is the connection between the subject's observations and the subjective meaning of a *dream* which is psychologically connected within the subject and related to questions like "Where do dreams come from?" which essentially is asked in the subjective sense of "*Who* put the dreams inside my mind?" that derives from our inherent causal disposition, which, in turn, serves the rather inescapable human social nature of wishing for the security of a social order of things instead of uncontrollable and unpredictable chaos. While we dream, we could be said to be looking for the right way of looking at what we have seen, and in this sense our nature brings us from being scientists to being rational human beings that, in our rationality, have no other standard for correctness than harmony and social good: to see things as right when they seem right from the perspective of being right for all—all other subjects—in contrast with them being right to ourselves only or being right by an arbitrary standard. Hence the interesting supernatural nature of dreams, which is our only motivation for wanting to interpret them instead of regarding them as insignificant, boring and random in nature. And hence the status of dreams as *visions*; as signs of premonition; pointers towards correct personal choices in pursuit of looking at a world that seems right and meaningful instead of arbitrary and chaotic.

II-3. The Subjective Nature of Morality

The difficulty in conducting philosophy of morality is existential in nature; because we ourselves exist as moral agents, even saying something constitutes a moral act. If one articulates anything about morality, one can be questioned based on that very act, and this is reflected in all common argumentative rhetoric. How we look at moral questions is a moral question; things might seem one way from an objective point of view, but at the same time from a subjective point of view it can be wrong to look at things that way. When discussing ethics on a level that is detached from the agent, first of all, one has no tools to rule out hypocrisy where the speaker doesn't himself represent the values he is promoting. But secondly, if the speaker happens to be pious regarding the values he is promoting, the morality of these values can still be brought into question, and then the subjective moral question is: Why should I follow *him* and not somebody else? Morality is not a theory but a subjective *skill*: there are a lot of people who enjoy teaching and dominating others, but one who doesn't possess respect (the source of credibility) in the form of recognized abilities will make a fool of himself trying to do so. He can be right on the level of theory but be wrong to say it because he doesn't possess the credibility for it. Who cares if a wise-ass is right or wrong? —he likely just parroted a granule of knowledge from somebody who is actually worth listening to. The beauty of competitive sport is in that formal credits or qualifications are meaningless, as skill is constantly measured in success on the field. This rules out the phenomenon that plagues all institutions that employ formal credit systems: in time they tend to become overrun by false honour. Credit needs to be based on measurable skill or merit and not, for example, on time spent in participation (or the number of publications someone has.)

Regarding the relation between thought and language, even thinking about an immoral person can be considered an immoral act, similar to the way that planning the execution of a crime is considered a crime in itself if such planning can be shown to have taken place. For the great majority these questions pose a fundamentally difficult task to address, as one cannot think or talk about morality beyond the morality one already exhibits in one's own existence, and therefore people's moral argumentation is seldom intellectually defensible. Actually, people in earlier times were much more correct in passing on moral understanding via sayings and proverbs instead of adhering to a rational tradition, trying to articulate moral understandings as scientific statements and failing to do so. It is a very strong act to say that some form of behaviour is *wrong*, and it takes a moral *authority* to say that, rather than a scientific neutral analyst. Because of this, the fact that moral argumentation has to a large extent disappeared altogether reflects the disintegration of shared base values provided by religion, and what is left as an argumentative tool is reference to scientific information. Instead of using a moral argument saying that the action is right or wrong, what the common rhetoric usually tries to do when dealing with moral issues is to refer to statistics, popularity, evolution, cost-effectiveness or, say, pseudo-philosophical frameworks such as cognitive capabilities, neural functions and so on. From a moral perspective, the current Western atmosphere of public discourse is a farce and cannot continue for very long; it is simply dishonest to present scientific argumentation where one is in essence trying to influence people via moral argument, and the prerequisite that allows such behaviour to become dominant is a world where nobody actually personally knows or is related to the people who present such arguments in order to criticize the subjective moral basis of their argument; to ask: "*Why* is *this guy* presenting this information?" Information from the news and media is consumed as a constant flow, and it is completely separated from the morality of the agents that produce it, thus rendering the information immune to moral reproach. An early 21st- century media company is very blatantly an automaton to produce information with the intent of gaining the interest of people, and any attempt to *morally* reproach a fallacious newspaper article will be met with formal regrets at best, and then only after great effort. This despite the fact that a reproach strong enough to elicit even this stilted formal response already implies significant moral outrage on the part of a number of influential individuals. I doubt that the editor in chief of a newspaper could be

II-3. THE SUBJECTIVE NATURE OF MORALITY

fired for other than financial reasons, and when newspapers make a move to consciously publish controversial information as fact, they employ tricks to escape responsibility. The world of public discourse is going through a 'Wild West' period due to globalization, when it comes to morality or the validity of the concept of argumentative fallacy. One can see that the *rational basis of morality* has now been challenged, which is understandable in the light of the history of rationalist philosophy in the West, which founded itself on a particular platform of shared values that has now eroded.

Consider the well-known Kantian ethical doctrine ("categorical imperative") which states that one should act only according to a maxim whereby you can, at the same time, will that [the maxim] should become a universal law, and that one should always see humanity as an end itself instead of a means to an end. This can be seen to be a normative principle: it says that in order to be moral one *should* follow *a maxim*, instead of, say, following one's heart or acting according to one's conscience, religion or advice. It is not a scientific descriptive statement that tries to capture and describe how humans seem to be thinking or acting, but an attempt to define morality as behaviour where one is following such a maxim. And to be accurate, one needs to actually follow a maxim that Kant doesn't himself articulate; he just formulates that *a maxim* of duty *must* exist in order for the action to be moral. This part I agree with; I believe it is a correct analytical statement that morality distinguishes from other activities in that a moral person is subjectively following a principle; he is acting in a principled manner. The categorical imperative is a simply a call for people to behave *morally* instead of behaving in some other manner. But Kant further explicates that the maxim must form the *actual* basis *in the name of which* the action is fulfilled, instead of just a possibility to show afterwards that the action happens to conform with some maxim. This part is most problematic, because *a name* is not subjective anymore but a part of shared language; when I say that somebody is following a *subjective* principle, this is a whole different thing than to be following something with a name. Kant assumes that a moral agent needs to be aware of his moral principles and able (and willing) to state them. What if it was obvious

PART II. COMMON MISCONCEPTIONS

to conclude from the actions of an agent that he was following a subjective moral code, but the agent utterly refused to call it such, instead insisting that his actions were based solely on subjective feelings? As an example, take an artist who profoundly believes all humanity should be treated equally, and this quality would be reflected thematically in all his work; yet when interviewed, he would strongly object to the idea that his work had any underlying moral principles? Or take the mysterious Harmonica character from the movie *Once Upon a Time in the West*, who basically doesn't say anything but just acts. Would Kant say that this kind of person is following a maxim but is just not aware of it? If yes, how can this be distinguished in terms of his own requirement, that the maxim must be the source in the name of which the action is made, and not that the action just happens to conform to a maxim (by outsider view)? Or would Kant simply say that the artist is not being moral, or that he is being just partially moral? I might emphasize that I find these provided examples to reflect a particularly high, if not the highest, morality. To be accurate, the fact that that the principle is not spoken out is precisely the proof that the principle is completely subjectively assimilated as a part of one's subjective character that one does need not need to articulate in justification to others. In contrast, someone who would need to articulate the principle would be somebody to whom the principle is partially external, like something taught by one's parents and repeated yet not subjectively assimilated. This kind of person, who repeats and tries to follow maxims formulated by others, is clearly not moral, as also for Kant morality is a subjective quality and not an external feature of action. Secondly, it is problematic that an action should treat humanity as an end in itself. First of all, we can see that this definition of morality doesn't conform to actual cases in which people have acted in history in a manner that we would, without controversy, be prone to describe as moral. For example, look at defending one's country in a war; what would be the principle according to which one would perform this action? For "my country"? And what is the action? Defending? Shooting? Killing? If I take it that my action is defending my country, and the name of the principle in which I perform the action is "defending my country", I could perhaps wish for the whole world to join my act of defence against an illegit-

II-3. THE SUBJECTIVE NATURE OF MORALITY

imate attack and be confident that I am wishing for a universal law. But how do I know that my action is not treating the humanity of the enemy as a means to an end of retaining independence? Defending something is a non-human abstract, so it seems to me that unconditional surrender should be the evident Kantian action. Socrates and Jesus Christ should be seen as immoral by this standard for causing their own deaths through treating their own humanity as a means for some other end. Maybe a Kantian should think here that Socrates, albeit a good guy otherwise, in the end made a mistake and forgot the moral maxims (Gods) he otherwise followed. The problem with this, however, is precisely that in his apology he was passionately holding onto exactly the same principles he had been advocating during his life and refusing to withdraw them even under the threat of certain death. Wittgenstein, too, seems immoral, volunteering to serve in the war. As a pure idealist, Kant argued[114] that governments are morally obligated to pursue peace, armies should be abolished by governments etc... that governments should act towards one another as moral people within a nation should morally act towards one another. When we speak about moral obligation we simply are doing something other than analysing who is being moral and who is not.

It seems to me that the said shortcomings of being unable to distinguish a moral agent disintegrate not only the Kantian ethical principle but also any normative ethical doctrine; if we have a list of qualities that we feel a moral person *should* possess, at the very least we should expect the list to describe a real-life person that we *actually* consider ideally moral. But it so happens that because one's ethical nature is ultimately a subjective quality and the society in which one needs to act as an ethical individual is unique, any attempt to give an objective account for morality will result in people trying to judge morality in terms that defy the nature of morality. This is rather a violent action that, if applied, will lead to condemning exactly the passionately moral agents and promoting those who aren't passionately moral, but just pretend to be so—not completely unlike what a particular super-state is currently doing in Middle East under the flag of democracy. The

---
114   Essay: Perpetual Peace

PART II. COMMON MISCONCEPTIONS

categorical imperative is interesting, though, because it is precisely a metaphysical rationalization of the Christian principle of "Do unto others as you would have them do unto you" (henceforth *do-unto*). To be accurate, *do-unto* is not original to Christianity but I called it Christian because Kant was of the Christian tradition; *do-unto* is a repeating pattern in nearly every religion and has been termed the "Golden Rule" or "law of reciprocity"; it is almost a definitive feature of religions in general, not just Christianity. In the categorical imperative, "universal law" can be seen to denote the system of justice that would "do unto you" according to a law, and just like the Christian "as *you would have* them do unto you", the Kantian imperative states that you yourself should suggest this law in a universal manner through your own example. Kant comes to this conclusion via the fact that people in general follow conditional reasons (hypothetical imperatives) that are reasonable as means to another end, but moral principles must be unconditional (categorical) in order to be universal. This method seems to me to follow Aristotle's programme of classification, and the distinction presented here strongly resembles the Aristotelian distinction between things good in themselves and things good for the sake of things good in themselves; as means towards some other end considered good in itself.[115] However, Aristotle doesn't conclude the categorical imperative as Kant does, and this makes sense, because there is no logical basis for the ethical but logic is applied to the thinking of a subject—which is to say that whatever the reasoning the subject presents, it is universal only in terms of the logic of the concepts he uses, but it doesn't mean universal in the sense that a man living on another side of the world would be bound to conclude the same, given that he applies the same rational methodology. It is universal within the group that shares the concepts. The general misconception about logic is to consider it somehow "simply universal" without taking a look at the sense of this universality, which binds it to the language and concepts being used and, having been apprehended, that carry along their culture and norms. Of course it doesn't follow from this that ethics has no logical basis and that Kant and Aristotle conclude different morals, but, just for the sake of example, contrasting two such noted thinkers

---

[115] Nicomachean Ethics, Book I

II-3. THE SUBJECTIVE NATURE OF MORALITY

with high ethical aspirations and rational capabilities, and considering that they still conclude differing morals despite the claims of the universality of morals, can bring to light an important aspect of ethics. It contradicts the assumed universality of reason that Kant assumes regarding ethics; the categorical imperative makes sense to Kant because he is a Christian, but Aristotle had never heard of such moral religious writings. To him it would simply make no sense to claim *do-unto* as *just*, as for him there exists no Jesus Christ having unjustly been crucified for his moral message of the equality of submissive tribes as a united power against the evil Roman Empire. To a rationalist this culture-relative approach to ethics predictably seems wrong simply because it undermines universalist ethical claims that are assumed somehow necessary and valuable, but to correctly see ethics as a subjective faculty removes the inherent self-contradiction created by metaphysical thought: to *think* one is being universal and rational when one is in fact being culture-relative. Or, if one thinks one is *justified* in considering one's 'way' of rationality the correct one and that the rest of the world *should* share one's moral views in order to be right, despite their inability to rationally come to the same conclusions, one should consider the ethical consequences of this sort of thought regarding all the various nationalistic movements in the world (as in many Nordic countries, Italy, Germany or Japan) where the people of that particular group and mind-set are considered descendants of an ancient higher totality such as spirit, family, race or people.[116] In morals, one leads by example: the one whose skill and better knowledge is recognized, sets an example for others to follow.

As further examples of unsuccessful moral theory take hedonism and utilitarianism—the principles of pleasure and usefulness. Both are ac-

---

[116] Heidegger begins *Being and Time* by saying that the idea that 'being' cannot be defined is an ancient prejudice, and that he is able to define it as it is (subjectively) available to him. This idea is the basis of all occultism: the sense of a concept is subjectively available and put under objective study. A similar idea is found in postmodernist 'analyses' of art that are essentially redefinitions of art instead of analyses of what *is meant* by the word. Any such results are philosophically uninteresting. There are people who take Heidegger for a philosopher and not just a clever opportunist in the service of German National Socialism. With them I can agree that *Being and Time* is very thought-provoking.

tually so easy to refute with examples that the support of either cannot reflect any intellectual honesty. This can be done by showing that the pleasure or usefulness of an action is a quality that can't at all be known at the stage of considering an action before committing it, and it is exactly this stage one is interested in when considering the value of a moral principle. Rather I would like to point out that both pleasure and usefulness (being of use to somebody) are primitive human values and reflect a stage of behaviour associated with quite a young age: pleasure-seeking is the centrepiece of aesthetical existence and being useful (being a "good boy/girl", doing good deeds) is among the first things taught to children both home and at school, and one might take into consideration that children don't yet have any responsibilities of the kind generally related to the word 'ethics'. Both pleasure and usefulness are generally used to argue simple cases with something immediately rewarding. Then again, determining the moral outcomes of an action *after* it has been committed—the work of courts of law—is a judicial question and a different question altogether because it implies different methodology. Here the first thing to notice, from the standpoint of ethics, is that the trials in the Athenian People's Court 2400 years ago consisted of public hearings in front of a jury where charges and denials were attested to be true by both the prosecution and defence, and this is the same model applied in courts today. The fundamental change in the judicial process in the West, since those days, is the acceptance of *natural equality* of individuals. This idea is of Stoic and early Christian origin and became dominant in the 18th century. It remains a Western concept in contrast with the Asian moral perspective that generally disregards individual rights in the face of the group that can contain individuals of different status and authority. It is very interesting to contrast the morality of Plato and Aristotle, or the Asian group morality, which both accept individual inequality in modern Western terms, with the modern egalitarian moral conception, and to see that the ideal of individual equality, along with the later declarations of universal human rights contemporarily implemented in Western judicial systems, is not a rational necessity or even a modern discovery but rather a recently implemented religious ideal with a rather old origin. There is absolutely no rationale behind saying

II-3. THE SUBJECTIVE NATURE OF MORALITY

"All individual people should get the same X" or "All individual people are equal regarding X", apart from tradition and the Stoic and early Christian origin that basically just stipulated individual equality. And the senselessness of asserting equality as-is, without even pointing out the frame of reference, is a popular contemporary moral rhetoric in the West regarding 1) the rights of minorities and 2) the morality of non-Western nations. The rights of minorities are being aggressively used as a means to abolish traditions in Western nations, whereas the concept of individual equality, without reference to local traditions and concepts of justice, is being used as war propaganda to support invasive action against oil-rich countries in the Middle East. But the whole Middle East knows that such morality is hypocritical, and it is hypocritical exactly because the rational basis of universal individual equality is assumed to exist and thus to be universally rationally conceivable, whereas in reality such a thing doesn't exist but is a Western cultural extension of Western moral writings and the Western achievements of the Enlightenment era. In order for us, the West, to hope for any credibility among the Eastern countries that we consider ourselves justified in moralizing to, first of all, in order to be intellectually honest, we should deliver our moral concepts openly through preaching Christian equality and not covertly under the flag of universal moral principles, and thus to place oneself on the same ground with one's target audience, applying religious moral principles alien to one another. And secondly, we should first and foremost first live ourselves as we preach, because what country would listen to rhetoric based on universal human rights from countries that are well known (yet not acknowledged) around the world to be shameless violators of their own principles in action? The morality of UDHR Article 1[117] is that if you don't treat others in the spirit of brotherhood, then you don't earn human rights yourself. And this applies to individuals and nations likewise. But the human rights rhetoric, as presented in the mostly corporate-owned and centralized Western media, is not moral but functions as modern-day propaganda, intended to draw attention away from the *real* human rights violations in the Western countries (as universal human rights are a Western

---

117 "All human beings are born free and equal in dignity and rights. They are endowed with reason and conscience and should act towards one another in a spirit of brotherhood."

PART II. COMMON MISCONCEPTIONS

concept) to the *attributed* human rights violations in the East. This is the rhetorical tactic of scapegoating innocents to escape one's own guilty moral sentiments, and it never has good results. Human rights are the modern-day justification for war, and the sense of this can be understood by the fact that they are a Western moral framework of a Christian origin that has replaced Christian morals in popularity. As more Western people are united by human rights than by Christian morals, it is more effective as a justification for war against political enemies. Then again, if some other framework was more effective than human rights in uniting people, they would choose that instead for their rhetoric of justifying warfare: in a battle, such as a legal battle, any means will be used, and the means are chosen based on their effectiveness, not their morality.

At the risk of appearing banal, I'll mention that a moral theory that succeeds in actually providing information due to the accompanied *empirical* study—the theory of moral stages by Kohlberg—complies well with the empathetic foundation of morals that I have articulated. Kohlberg suggested a set of universal levels in the development of morals that start from obedience-and-punishment and self-interest, and advance through social roles, conventions and laws to the higher-level morals of social contracts and universal ethical principles. When we grow up we gradually extend our social group of identification from our family to larger and larger social groups such as school, work, local town community and ultimately the nation and the world. The growth of our influence most essentially involves coming into contact with people from those groups and coming to understand and to consider their roles in society. We come to understand that these people are working in order to advance something that ultimately affects us too through society, but if there were no empathetic connection between us, there would be no basis to take into account interest groups with different needs from our own. Let's consider the effect of human empathy by considering its hypothetical absence: consider any social minorities, such as criminals, or the disabled: since they have caused so much trouble throughout history, *why* does society advance to reintegrate them rather than to dispose of them? If we silence our empa-

II-3. THE SUBJECTIVE NATURE OF MORALITY

thy, disposing of them should be a rational choice. It is because of our empathy (and not an assumed maxim of respect for humanity) that in earlier societies the disabled (sometimes) were not euthanized at birth but rather abandoned, as this would save the mother from having murder on her conscience. Why doesn't the mother choose between raising the child and disposing of it, but instead chooses to abandon it? There doesn't *exist* a rational ethical principle to be *found* from which it can be derived that such behaviour is right—one may only be *attributed*. Ethics rather works the other way around: an ethical principle is never universal, but it may succeed in providing the rational basis for the acceptance of behaviour that takes into account our empathy towards all members of society and doesn't leave us in conflict with our empathetic emotions. It can be seen that, in the development of civilizations, tolerance towards difference increases along with the evolution of the civilization. But more essentially, we can see the nature of morality as *mental skills* that require work and development by the individual subject. I believe the subjective attributes related to morality are the following:

1) Empathy is the skill to experience the emotions of another.

2) Trust is the skill to cooperate without being hindered by fear and without the need to try to predict and control the behaviour of others. Trust requires exposing oneself to other individuals in terms of security and letting go of our natural protective traits of fear and suspicion. Individuals who are incapable of trust are generally protective over personal matters and unwilling to expose personal information and form their close human relations by the more primitive patterns of domination and submission.

3) Acceptance (tolerance) does *not* mean non-reaction to an outcome by another that is experienced as negative. That can be achieved by controlling oneself and is not genuine acceptance. Acceptance means a deeper understanding about where the qualities of another originate, and the capability to *empathetically* and reciprocally level oneself with the other: to understand that both come with human features that can be experienced as negative by others. Individuals incapable of acceptance appear judgemental and easily aggravated by others, and can e.g. live under an outspoken personal moral system of codes that allows them to judge others, or be smart enough to hide these shortcomings in public life by not expressing the constantly experienced discomfort the proximity of others causes them.

4) Forgiveness is the skill to take responsibility over the actions of another and generally requires extending the sphere of one's responsibility to cover the actions of other people as well. This extension of responsibility can be best seen in the extreme example of Jesus Christ, who took the sins (shortcomings) of everybody on his own account, including the sin of punishing perpetrators with the inhumane cross. The concept of forgiveness can be defined in relation to the rights of an individual: consider that the basic human social requirement is to take responsibility over one's own actions; this is what others will expect of you. In the skill of forgiveness, the requirement of responsibility is extended beyond that, and this is something the subject must develop internally, as it is never required by others. In the case of forgiveness, the individual is always considered to have the moral *right not to* forgive (and to demand compensation for personal damage by e.g. legal means), but the forgiving individual chooses to give up that right at the act of forgiveness.

All said skills are such that the possession of a skill doesn't require using it but grants a capability of using it at will. It seems to me that a normal healthy person's moral thought derives from basic moral emotions that innately, if not disrupted, involve trust and empathy, e.g. "It was not his fault as he couldn't have helped it" or "He didn't mean to do harm". Empathy allows one to share the emotion and to think of oneself in the same role, and trust allows one to generalize one's own emotional basis to also apply to another: "I myself in that situation wouldn't have done such a thing intentionally, so *I trust* that he wouldn't do it either." These sentiments should be, in a normal setting, cultivated by normal family relations in a harmonious life of overlapping generations where one needs to accept and tolerate the other generation without necessarily relating to it in thought. This should be the basis of our morality, and via this it is also easy to understand why Christianity chooses to use the family structure (father, son and the holy spirit) as a moral

II-3. THE SUBJECTIVE NATURE OF MORALITY

model: the tolerance and harmony towards others is cultivated within every family's own family unit, and the Christian model is the extension of this family harmony to a larger context.

Having proposed moral mental skills, I can relate their absence to an attempted formulation of things that are called *evil*:

- Rationalization is used to overcome and silence the empathy that would otherwise naturally take place.
- No moral justification of action, but justification, if any, imposes *blame* on premises that e.g. 1) are not true, 2) don't apply to the person accusing, or 3) refer to values not shared by the group.
- They lack a relationship of trust. Trust replaced by means of abusive control, such as violence, humiliation and breaching of privacy.

Evil, within a subject, starts as a social phenomenon. First one is evil to gain attention, for example with bullies who only bully when others are present. Then, if it is not corrected, it develops into an *identification* where the subject justifies his immoral behaviour with his identity; any empathetic emotions are dismissed with determination: "I will do what I want here, because that is who I am." There is a common question of whether an individual is 'really' evil… this is a misleading question, but understandable in the sense that evil is also presented here as *lacking* skills. All children are born with trust, but since a person with evil traits doesn't trust, he has, at some point, stopped using this skill, which indicates that there actually *is* something more to this person than he is showing. But essentially, these characteristics should be seen as patterns of behaviour, and, as such, they are as unoriginal to the person applying them as any other pattern. Then again, any individual lacking trust is likely to use abusive means of control over others, by which I mean that such patterns need not be acquired by learning from another individual. The question whether somebody is *really* evil, or if they are evil only on the surface level, boils down to the question of how much this individual identifies with such behavioural patterns. If they don't, the question loses its meaning, reducing to the idea that nobody is really evil, which resists the truth that the word 'evil' has some existing situations of valid application. Another noteworthy thing is the

PART II. COMMON MISCONCEPTIONS

reference to *group*: the scope of evil is the group; evil is something that takes place within the reference group. Defence (or warfare) against outsiders lies outside of this scope. It is commonly said that war is evil; this it may be, but it is so strictly in the case of where the justification of warfare, from the warmongers to the people, falls into said category of lacking morality, as an *attacking* war does without exception. Attacking wars are started via 1) provocations and 2) propaganda, with which people are led to support the belligerent actions by supporting ideas that escape the internal morality of the group. Provocations are blamed on the opposing group that is dehumanized and demoralized by means of propaganda... at the moment, the West is painstakingly led to believe that Muslims are inhumane aggressors, through propaganda that leads us to forget our shared base values of Christianity and human rights. This evil as the *absence of morality* is what commonly causes evil behaviour to escalate in places that are left outside of effective law enforcement, such as ghettos, high-security prisons and the battlefield. Such behaviour should not be seen as standard primitive human behaviour; primitive humans are very moral, too, just less organized. The study of ethics hasn't made us any more moral, but it has resulted in the *systemic application* of moral thought in the form of written law and its specialized enforcement. Places of evil, void of morality, are places of neglect, void of attention and law enforcement. They are places where people, who normally exist under the guidance of an enforced moral system, are left without this guidance.

Any traditional moral question of the form "Is it right/wrong to do *this*?" can in practice be distinguished into either of the two questions: 1) the question regarding one's own action that is not yet committed or articulated, and 2) the question regarding the actions of another person. This distinction exists because of the *criterion of action*: when we ponder our own action, and also when we either consciously or subconsciously (conscience) reflect upon an action we ourselves have done, the criterion for action is subjective, but when we evaluate the committed action of another person or the actions another person can be seen to prepare to commit, the criterion is objective. The criterion itself, in both cases, can be brought to light by asking "What action?"

II-3. THE SUBJECTIVE NATURE OF MORALITY

In the first case we could call it something like a thought, a wish, an intention, a memory or suchlike, whereas in the second case we will have some evidence of the action available. The subjective question of right/wrong regarding any person other than oneself is not a moral question in the same sense. It is very common to want the best for your loved ones, as it is also common to try and persuade other people to carry out actions that can be expected to have consequences somehow useful to oneself (to use other people), but the question involved in such consideration should not be called *moral*, because one doesn't *exist* as the other unique person (doesn't share his existence) and thus, for example, one doesn't share his values. And one also won't be affected by the consequences of the actions committed by him. If I ask myself if e.g. John was right to steal to satisfy his hunger, the things I can say would reflect the laws and norms of society, or reflect my own morals… but it is not a moral question because John's action is not directed at *me*. The same restriction of morality applies on the level of comparing societies: it is, especially at this particular time, very common for one society to argue about right and wrong with another society using its own moral conceptions that act as the shared criteria within society,[118] but such problem-setting must not be considered moral, because neither the values of the other or the consequences of the implied actions are shared. Only question 2 is one that concerns justice and equality, because it should not be punishable to have criminal intentions; not because it is often said every person has bad thoughts sometimes and this commonness would justify them, but only because intentions are by nature subjective. It is only committing an action that makes the action associable to others, and the social questions of how to organize the system to resist the moral wrongdoings of individuals can be targeted to this phase. This is where we build the system of justice: reacting, not to actions that somebody believes to have been committed or that can be said to have been committed, but to actions that can be shown to have been committed. The question of justice involves not only the question of whether the planned or committed action it-self is right or wrong, but also the question of whether the method of

[118] I read in the papers every day about how morally bad the strategically chosen countries with which the US is in conflict are in terms of claimed but not shared Universal Human Rights.

PART II. COMMON MISCONCEPTIONS

coming to verify the action is *sensible*: accusing somebody of having certain intentions based on external observations of his behaviour violates the logic of intentions. And the sort of trials where the accusations are based on attribution of subjective qualities based on external observations are the showcase of injustice, such as verdicts of being a witch or of corrupting (subjective quality) the youth and disrespecting (subjective quality) gods. Such a verdict can intuitively be seen to "make no sense"; only it takes this careful observation to point out why it makes no sense. This is why a legal system must take the effort of creating *standards* of objective criteria that will *reflect expected* cases of moral conflict, and judge them using the concepts of *right* and *offence*, reflecting cases where the subject can be expected to have acted in a manner that would receive general acceptance or rejection in the subjective meaning (question 1) of action. Thus the evolution of laws, regulations and judicial standards within a system of justice is a process of interpreting the plausible subjective moral questions within society, evolving together with the form of society, towards the *consensus* of the subjective moral sentiments of its citizens; towards the form of most general acceptance. For example, the US Constitution Second Amendment grants US citizens a right to bear arms, which is an exceptional right from the perspective of the Western world. And the way to understand this correctly is to put it into the perspective of how the United States was born as a country: a massive flow of colonists and prospectors, most of them European misfits, claiming a newly found continent as the Biblical Promised Land for the Christian world from barbaric natives and exotic animals using superior weaponry. In such an environment it is very understandable for an individual to wish to carry a gun, because, apart from constant military use, guns were commonly used not only for hunting and defence against hostile inhabitants, but also as a self-defence measure within a society that was not yet organized and sometimes faced internal violence. There is no 'moral' entity, such as a universal rule or some transcendent human property, which would make it sensible to say that having a system that permits carrying guns, or having a system that doesn't, would be the right or wrong one. On the contrary, the concepts of right and wrong are used within the moral framework of such a system: within a society that bans guns

II-3. THE SUBJECTIVE NATURE OF MORALITY

it is considered wrong to carry one without a special permit, and within a society that allows them it is considered right to carry a gun if it suits your purpose for it, and extending moral concepts outside these cultural contexts puts one into a position that is not moral.[119] And now when the US has long since become a highly organized society, there's no way for another country to moralize about the United States constitution or laws; they can be condemned, ridiculed or threatened, or then again praised or admired, but not moralized about.

Having said all this, we can analyse the *do-unto* as comprising two parts: the part suggesting a subjective way of action, "Do unto others", and the part attributing objective standards of morality, "as you would have them do unto you". Kant saw it as a categorical imperative in the Kantian sense that it doesn't refer to any particular actions. Instead it is suggesting that the subjective criterion of right action should be that it is *exemplary*; serving as an example expected to be agreeable by others, since laws evolve in a process towards a consensus of moral sentiment. And here there's an emphasis on *expected* because acting as an example to others doesn't mean doing something arbitrary and expressing a sacred wish that others would see that as morally agreeable, nor does it mean action that could be externally seen as and fitted into a moral justification.[120] Rather it means doing what *one oneself* would expect the others to, in practice, find morally agreeable. And of course, subjectively behaving like this is a completely subjective disposition beyond any chance of being distinguished by any objective criteria, and therefore what *do-unto* suggests is a way of moral *existence* as a subject. But moreover, it can be seen that this sort of ideal moral existence is not possible by following a *rational* principle: take *do-unto* that Jesus preached, and apply it to the Biblical event of Jesus chasing the money-changers out of the temple and pushing their tables over. Given that Jesus, if anybody, as the highest and the first preacher of Christian principles, could be believed to have lived and *existed* according to the

---

119 To emphasize the distinction, one can verify that "You should fuck off" shouldn't be interpreted as a moral statement but "I should fuck off" should.
120 Taken out of the original subjective context, any action can be made to appear morally justified or morally condemnable by simply attributing a suitable subjective quality as the basis of the action.

principle of doing unto others as he would have them do unto him, and whom we instead believe to have been falsely accused and died as martyr—what is the interpretation of him cleansing the temple from the perspective of rational morals? And it can be pointed out that any historical controversy about Jesus doesn't really matter here; the example nevertheless works as a thought experiment via the legend of Jesus. Did Jesus overturn tables because he would have his own tables overturned by others? No. Instead, he would have his actions corrected and, symbolically, his false tables overthrown, in the event that he himself had ever succumbed to committing a subjective moral crime, a sin, as he believed the money-changers to be doing: defiling a holy place of worship by turning it into a place of business. So, the Christian morals of doing unto others is in practice itself referential to the fundamental subjective moral factor, sin, and this reference can be brought out most clearly by applying *do-unto* in any practical situation where one would be seen morally as simply taking some sort of action that involves defiance, such as, say, intercepting an attacker by force or even peacefully resisting tyranny by demonstrating on the streets.[121] In Kant's categorical imperative this subjective factor can also be clearly seen in "Act only according to a principle that *you can wish* to be extended...", as we all know people wish for very different sorts of things for themselves, and, accordingly, very different sorts of worlds of justice.[122] And this clarification reveals the categorical imperative to be, in Kant's own terminology, a *hypothetical imperative* instead, conforming to his definition of *rules of skill*, which he described exactly as subjective instructions of *how to* perform something in the most reasonable *way*. It can be seen that the so-called categorical imperative describes a *higher* moral standard, since it dictates a subjective mode of behaviour with the high responsibility of having responsibility over the whole of society instead of just pleasing oneself. But it is a *subjective* moral standard nevertheless and not "commanded by reason" except for a Christian who has assimilated the concept of sin, and thus sees punishment for one's as

---

121 The morality of laws is not very complex when one understands the subjectivity of ethics: laws have nothing to do with morality and occupy a different logical realm. One can find a law just or unjust and should act according to one's morality instead of being confused with terminology.

122 I remember in my childhood wishing to live in a castle made of candy. And I have nothing against anybody living in such a castle.

II-3. THE SUBJECTIVE NATURE OF MORALITY

sins *reasonable*; sees that it *makes sense* that committing sin is a moral crime—in the same way as it seems reasonable for a thief to steal some bread when an opportunity has presented itself and capture is unlikely. To follow one's conscience is a high moral principle, but there's nothing reasonable about it unless one subjectively sees a point to living without guilt; that is, avoiding sin. And as the Kantian conception of morality fails, unveiled as the abstraction of one's moral upbringing into universal rules, so, too, fails e.g. the Rawlsian abstraction of a universal social contract that builds upon this. It is undoubtedly wrong—wrong as an error but wrong also in the moral sense—to claim that anybody can see what anybody can't see. We can subjectively see (imagine) only what we have acquired a concept of, and these concepts constitute the scope of our rational logic. Whenever we make the jump into: "Any rational person can see this", this argument is akin to something I heard from a musician presenting his musical equipment: "Any self-respecting bass-player will want this amplifier." By saying this he means that he is in possession of something particularly valuable, which also constitutes *an ethical norm*, and that if a bass-player did not happen to want the amplifier, he *should* want it, because it is in some particular sense a legendary product—not the newest or necessarily the most expensive, but the one most respected by the relevant artistic community (the artistic guild) that maintains the subjective skill necessary to evaluate properties of musical equipment. To defend rationality like this means to promote rationality as a value in itself, which indeed is the business of philosophy in the Age of Reason. To say "Any rational person can see this" in this *ethical sense*, actually translates only to "Any person who calls himself rational *should* see this", meaning that rationality is an expert skill that the speaker happens to be in possession of. And the word 'should', used in this way, should be a red flag to anybody who is interested in how things *are* (factual claims), because to say that things should be, means to admit they are not. It is a form of rhetoric that means: "I'm sure you can see this, because I hereby promote you to be one of us: a rational person (despite knowing that all people are not rational)", and asks us to accept the invitation to the gentlemen's club and to say 'yes', whether we see it or not. This sort of rhetoric is a sense of irony and common in all communities that involve some sort of competition between individuals. It is not a factual claim about what somebody or anybody can actually see or not; it is a jump from rationality to the shared moral framework, using irony.

In history, the Western moral question has indeed been based on the subjective moral concept of sin, and to commit a criminal offence has rather been *proof* of the sinful nature of the condemned. This makes sense regarding the subjective existential nature of ethics: it is common wisdom that a bad person is bad in a more persistent way than just being a good man who accidentally commits a bad deed. Classifying people as good or bad people, where good people are treated as one's own kind and bad people are to be harshly treated and even killed without remorse, is a very primal and universal human quality that in past times would rather naturally divide humans into warring tribes that would treat each other similarly to the way monkey packs treat other packs of the same or different species. Also in Asia, where criminal punishments are generally much more severe, it is a group-think not to show remorse over bad people who have succumbed to criminal behaviour, and one that people don't pay much practical attention to, once the *bad nature* of the individual has been established by the system of authority. This is our primal heritage and a mode of thinking to which people tend to succumb most when in a social state of arousal, which relates the behaviour to warfare and hunting in our primal past; by nature, these activities were social events marked with arousal and rituals. So, it seems to me that the existential nature of ethics, that it is the common wisdom that one becomes a person susceptible to crime (however crime is understood) via subjective change more or less permanent in nature, interplays with our tendency to segregate others into groups of kin and others, which is the norm in tribal form of life outside an organized society. And this phenomenon produces the basis of our subjective moral feelings: the sort of people we identify with and the sort of people we tend to discriminate against.

Morality, as the word is used, should, instead of trying to describe correlation to a moral ideal, be used to describe behaviour that is in-

II-3. THE SUBJECTIVE NATURE OF MORALITY

tended to be moral as it follows a *subjective ethical change* and is an intentional and rational form of social behaviour, and guided by the subject's sense of justice. And by giving this sort of vague description I am not trying to *define* morality by articulating what it should be but trying my best to portray a living real-life phenomenon that can be observed in human behaviour. Let's say a person steals from the shop and is caught, and after feeling the guilt decides never to steal again, and, say, goes on tour to schools to tell children how shoplifting is wrong. Now, one might immediately say that such action is not an act of "real morality" because it is simply a counter-reaction to having been caught, and there are other things that can be argued to be wrong in the same sense as shop-lifting, such as theft in general. But, following Kohlberg's approach of classifying levels of moral behaviour, it only does justice to the use of the word 'moral' to recognize morality as a subjective and unique phenomenon but with the distinguishable ethical motive. The changed shop-lifter is moral *in this respect* because of the ethical change that has taken place inside him, which is not just an impression of goodwill but a very concrete change comparable to the flick of a switch in the constitution of his behaviour (and probably somehow physically reflected in the neural wirings of the brain). The philosophical study of ethics as a science has traditionally noticed this plurality of how we wish to talk about morality, and has been making an effort to try to find the metaphysical "one true morality" along with trying to find some unifying constitutional feature in the types of behaviour that we deem moral. This goal should today be nullified by Wittgenstein's concept of family resemblance. Instead, morality can be distinguished to be a *type of behaviour* where, instead of a direct effort towards personal gratification, the subject holds some *reason* to distinguish himself from such behaviour. The existence of a reason distinguishes moral behaviour from simply following a social role or a social norm, as it is not a moral deed to, say, protect the people by fulfilling one's job as a police officer, but it could be considered a mark of moral behaviour to do so outside such role. The existence of a reason also implies that the subject has undergone an ethical change, and someone that has not undergone such an ethical change one won't see the behaviour as reasonable. Now, this says absolutely nothing about

PART II. COMMON MISCONCEPTIONS

what sorts of *actions* or *things* are moral or immoral, which must be correct, since, say, stepping on the lawn is clearly deemed immoral when it is breaking social rules, but deemed moral when it is done in order to save somebody's life. Morality lies within the subjective; and the subjectivity in this case means that the morality of an action is not even relative to the reason the subject presents for his action, but it lies in the fact *that* he does it for the particular reason that he presents. Morality lies in the unity between the person's reason and action that is found socially commendable; it lies in the social *responsibility* a person can be seen to incorporate in his thought. And this now relates to what sort of a person we call a "moral person"; to call somebody moral carries the expectation that the person applies his reason in a socially responsible manner. And the concept of responsibility is now key here: in order to be considered a responsible person it is not enough to do some useful or good things, just as in order to be a responsible parent it is not enough for one to just feed and clothe the child and then present these deeds as evidence for being a good parent. The concept of responsibility implies *care* and protection from harm; it implies that one can trust another person to a responsible person's care without having to supervise them. And this human quality of the capability to look after another person cannot be reduced to any distinguishable characteristics, but people, complex creatures as they are, are mysterious and carry secrets, and—even worse for the sceptic—are volatile and impulsive, and due to these qualities even in the year 4000 one person will say it is possible to trust another person and another will say it is not. To deem an action moral or immoral can be done based on whether the action is socially motivated and reasonably grounded, but to deem some*body* moral or immoral is a matter of trust and appreciation, and bound to the sense of what activities one is expecting the other to express moral behaviour in: for example a moral father to a child can be an immoral husband, which simply implies that in terms of fatherhood he has grown to express responsible care, but in terms of being a husband he has not, but is existing in the pre-ethical mode of gratifying personal desires.

To better understand morality; there are commonplace types of morality that are worthy of description because, unlike language in itself, they are not passed on and learned as traditions, but rather there are cross-cultural similarities of thought. And as such, this perspective on morality is not culture-relativism but, on the contrary, tries to establish universal features in moral behaviour, but just by following an empirical instead of idealist method. I will list a few obvious moral frameworks here and what their key features seem to be.

- *Friendship*. Friends are morally expected to support each other in difficulties, and to be loyal to each other and not abandon each other in the face of difficulty. Socrates promoted a strategy of making friends that can be *useful* to one by performing friendly deeds, and this sort of behaviour can be seen as generally human, because a person who shows competence at what is deemed valuable by the group needs less effort to make friends than those who don't make themselves useful. This tendency could even be pre-human, since studies suggest that social rank doesn't play a significant role in primate allogrooming. Rather the grooming behaviour takes place in pairs who have a strong preference to groom each other, without the dominant individual receiving noticeably more active grooming. This suggests that, in a similar way as with humans, the equivalent of friendship in primates is about individual usefulness, respect, or something along those lines, instead of hierarchical authority.

- *Partnership* implies joint responsibility over something concrete, such as shared property, investment or family, or e.g. the hiding of shared secrets. Criminal organizations often work by imposing partnership on members by acquiring incriminating evidence against them.

- *Brotherhood* is a reference to the concept of *family* and implies an equal position as children of the same father, sharing of resources and shared fate, as the family unit is dependent on one another. The Christian brotherhood is symbolized by the Eucharist, where Christ is shared over supper table, a place where, in many if not most traditional cultures, it is customary to give thanks. Brotherhood is the constituting morality behind the concept of human rights, expressed in the first article of the Universal Declaration of Human Rights by

PART II. COMMON MISCONCEPTIONS

the United Nations, and obviously following Christian tradition. The brotherhood of arms is a standard military norm and related code that serves the members of the unit that in war are highly dependent on each other.

• *Group membership* in groups with *collective responsibility* (excluding groups with no such responsibility). Collective responsibility generally has the pattern whereby the group membership brings some privileges without a material contribution by the individual that counts as a payment for those privileges. Under this condition the group membership forms a reciprocal relationship between the group and the individual. The most commonly shared group membership of this sort is *nationality*, and others, in the West, include clubs, societies, groups of friends, and similar groupings. From the Western perspective the Chinese model of teamwork might be highly alien due to cultural differences, but one must understand the power of a moral framework in contrast with, say, contract services governed by money: an individual will give himself to the group out of his own will, when he is morally bound to it.

These moral frameworks are in different from certain other frameworks that are respected due to the related honour system. These include the following.

• *Law* and *norms* are the basic frameworks of decency. Laws are a necessary means to stabilize a society, and instability is related to difficulties in enforcing laws. Norms constitute the expected social behaviour of groups from individual-level house rules to larger-scale cultural rules, and that norms generally are not challenged by the majority of people goes hand-in-hand with the fact that public adherence to norms is the universal standard means to pursue social status.

• *Codes* are rules and principles related to groups or professions and constitute the sort of behaviour that is morally expected from the member of a group or the practitioner of a profession.

• *Agreements* are formulations of *promises* between parties, and in social life promises are used in coordinating cooperation and communicating intentions. Even though the capability to hold up to

II-3. THE SUBJECTIVE NATURE OF MORALITY

one's intentions is considered a virtue, failure in doing so is generally viewed with sympathy rather than condemnation. The concept of a formal agreement has only gained importance in the Western world, enforced by trade laws; humane promises have been replaced by law-regulated, and often inhumane, agreements. In other parts of the world, and also in the Western criminal underworld, and generally anywhere where the letter of the law has less weight as the legal system is less neutral without applied human rights (a Western concept), business life doesn't really operate with agreements but with the concepts of partnership and friendship instead. Generally, in Asian business no agreements are signed before a long-lasting partnership has first been established via diplomacy, and even deviating strongly from agreements is always understandable if the action is moral from the perspective of partnership. Also, as an agreement is essentially established between individuals, the inability to settle disagreements as individuals and having to go public court over them is immoral as it violates the powerful cultural norm of a moral public image.

Now, as the definite answer to the question of what *morality is* (as opposed to what some person should be doing, etc.) we will note that the prevalent moral idea of *reciprocity*, also present in almost all religions as the "Golden Rule" (*do-unto*), is completely reducible to the reciprocal nature of said *moral* frameworks of collective responsibility, as such mutually shared behaviour constitutes their functionality. On the other hand, subjective moral behaviour in terms of a reciprocal moral framework is everything that is seen to support and enforce a functional reciprocal relationship; it is shared trust between individuals to fulfil the shared expectation of behaving *responsibly* according to a moral framework, and moral laws, for example "Don't sin; don't entertain thoughts about your neighbour's wife; don't be nasty to another...", can be seen to enforce harmony via restricting behaviour that would be destructive to such reciprocal relationships. The difference between moral laws and the laws that today are applied by the legal institution is that moral laws target the mental phenomena that underlie one's behaviour and that are subjective in nature. The history of law has seen a movement from laws regulating subjective phenomena towards laws that target phenomena that can be shown without too much need for subjective interpretation; before this the interpretation of law had given an absolute power of judgment to the moral authority. In contrast with the legal systems of old, the higher success rate of modern legal systems to impose what is experienced as just by the people is achieved by the protection of the rights of the individual from misuse of authority, which in turn is achieved by the reduction of *subjective legal terminology*. To summarize:

> **morality** *is subjective loyalty (actions and sentiments) in accordance with a reciprocal framework of collective responsibility that functions as a norm.*

Because the loyalty and responsibility in morality are subjective qualities, the subjective question of whether a person is moral in some regard or not equals the question of whether the person is *acting responsibly* in that regard. This essentially involves the question of the subjective reasoning (dialectic); the question of why the person is doing what he is doing. It seems to me that this problematic involves two key factors: 1) whether the person is working to advance outcomes that imply responsibility, and 2) whether the person's actions imply responsible behaviour with respect to these outcomes in terms of his personal knowledge and awareness. Due to the subjectivity of morality, these questions can only be approached via the external features of the person's action, and because of this, firstly, the conception of morality is vulnerable to the disguise of the image of responsibility, which is the adherence to behaviour that aligns with the external features of moral norms. For example, a socially responsible person can be seen to take care of others at his own expense, which makes charity and public donations an effortless symbolic task for wealthy people to portray responsibility. An even easier way to do this is through the modern concept of ethical 'eco-shops' where you can portray your morality while doing your grocery shopping. The model of adherence to the public image of morality forms its own traditions. Jesus labelled as *hypocrites* the sort of people who work to portray the image of good deeds in this way. Secondly, it is pointless to try and argue for the morality of an action or the morality or immorality of a person. Because morality is subjective, calling somebody moral or immoral is simply an expression

II-3. THE SUBJECTIVE NATURE OF MORALITY

of subjective trust in the person's morality or the lack of it, and should be correctly expressed via subjective belief and trust instead of claiming it somehow follows from some actions or other objective evidence. Thirdly, whenever the responsible behaviour of a person needs to be questioned, the related problematic (questions 1 and 2) needs to be answered by a court of law instead of argument, where the individual is allowed dialogue to present his subjective reasons to individuals who judge his reasons against his actions and the expectations related to his position. And finally, there is no need for any general *moral rules* apart from the rules that enforce reciprocal behaviour within the collectively shared moral frameworks. This result completely contradicts Kant, who felt we should expand our collective citizen morality to other nations as well; since we and the outsiders do not share any moral frameworks, we should agree to settle in our neighbouring territories under our own moral frameworks, and this understanding of the universal human moral quality should act as the constituent of a harmonious coexistence where territory is not shared. To behave morally regarding, say, friendship—to be a good friend—one should act like a responsible friend, and this doesn't follow from some list of responsibilities for friendship, but from our subjective understanding of what friendship means... and the result is, obviously, that some people have a more responsible idea of friendship than others. To behave morally regarding a democratic society, one should act like a responsible citizen and look after society: exercise one's democratic rights in voting, express one's opinion and look after fellow citizens wherever there are issues of public concern—this is the only way for a democratic society to flourish and develop: in addition to the parliamentary form there needs to be a spirit that encourages the exercise of democratic rights. These rights are currently in decline, from which it follows that the democratic spirit is in decline, and democracy is in decline. This doesn't make us more in harmony with our neighbouring countries, however; on the contrary, like all humans, we also have an international tendency to blame our own shortcomings on the other party.

Justice is also a subjective concept and is often described with a reference to people's sense of morality. As morality is a reference to a norm,

PART II. COMMON MISCONCEPTIONS

it seems clear to me that a person's

> ***sense of justice*** *is subjective commitment to a norm where accordance with it (actions that are right) is approved and discordance with it (crime) is disapproved.*

It is a subjective commitment, because norms are many and conflicting, and it is the subject who, in *his* sense of justice, is committed to a *particular* norm, and draws his sense of justice from it. This is simply how people reason morally; they might have awareness of many and conflicting norms and an understanding that a person's actions are not all good or all bad, but they have their own, independent, personal sense of justice that they draw their concluding attitude from, which equals their personal commitment to a particular norm. This quality is exactly and precisely why trials are decided by a *jury*. Because a single juror will be subjective by definition, having multiple independently acting jurors reduces the risk of having the decision based on a single particular norm only, as these norms in reality are many and conflicting and can each be defended with correctly chosen rhetoric. Using a jury makes the decision better reflect the moral opinion of the majority, which is exactly correct, as the source of this morality is not some rule or law but the subjective sense of justice and moral norms that happen to hold value in society. Another important thing to notice is that because morality is a *loyalty*, morality and justice are linked to a person's knowledge and awareness, and we correctly believe that it is the event of becoming aware of something that creates the related subjective *moral obligation*. This obligation is the same as loyalty to a group: as it is a subjective quality, it can be tested and questioned. For example, if a member of a war party sees the enemy, he is expected to inform his group. If he fails to do this the result is punishable disloyalty and a valid suspicion that he has colluded with the enemy. In a trial we try to assess justice via the question of whether the person was acting in an obligated manner towards the norms, given his knowledge about the matters at hand. If a person knew but did nothing, he is guilty, therefore the most fundamental thing a criminal needs to deny is knowledge: I know nothing! I saw nothing! I am hearing it for the first time! I have never seen this man in my life! He can claim that he is innocent or good, means no harm to anybody, never did anything to hurt anybody... but these things are of no importance to the trial; the only thing that is being assessed is whether he knew and whether his subjective quality, given his knowledge and his actions, reflects disloyalty in terms of what is expected of him. When an event takes place, for the stability and security of their society the people will want the event resolved and actions taken, and this process equals finding out *who is responsible* and taking sound corrective actions. Many people could be considered responsible, but the process aims to identify those who are most responsible regarding their duties and to punish them accordingly... and this will generally satisfy people's sense of justice. Knowledge—information—is the target asset in financial crime, which is the fundamental type of crime our modern society is battling.

PART II. COMMON MISCONCEPTIONS

II-4. The Metaphysical World

Our object-related world-picture that starts from naming objects and naming abstract objects, develops into a big object-related theatre; a skeleton; a background of reality that in our understanding acts as a mould to form particular phenomena. By 'metaphysical' I solely mean this kind of thinking, similar to later Wittgenstein, and the word can be related to Platonism or essentialism. From the subjective perspective the model seems to be an ideology of *abstraction*; convinced faith in abstraction. It is a learned pattern of thought where an abstract concept is simply taken as a name tag for something somebody has seen, and it is very human to have acquired this model, because this is how everybody learns language in the first place: somebody uses a concept and you trust him and take for granted that it stands for something. Not only is this not a negative way of thinking; it is really difficult to think in any other way than this way, and particularly difficult to think in another way that isn't in some other fundamental respect wrong. Not just our parents, but our school system mostly rewards us for thinking like this: they call out a word and ask you what it is a name tag for, and reward you in front of all your classmates if you can put it into one brief sentence. The school system doesn't aim to produce people who excel in this sort of activity, but it is a necessary evil of the system; the school system is actually supposed to work in such a way that in between the formal requirements set for the pupils teachers work to educate the students to become real thinking people instead of the sort of machines that merely repeat the rituals of the system. But suppose we have a school system like that, all we need is to cut down funding and reduce the motivation of the teachers, and what we have left is a system in which students are simply rewarded for performing this sort of shallow ritual of "knowing what something is". Complement that with having a huge, free online dictionary to extract more detailed information from, and pupils will start thinking that all they need to know is the high-level name of a concept, and they can use the dictionary for the rest if they have to. This issue is similar to the question of whether pupils should be allowed to use calculators in

II-4. THE METAPHYSICAL WORLD

maths or whether they should be required to also actually perform the elementary calculations by hand... but it is a far more dangerous issue, because calculations are mechanical, objective procedures that can be performed by a machine, but *understanding* and critical thought are not. If the understanding is not taught, it will not be learned, and the person can live all his life without coming to understand much about the things he learned in school, but is left to an existence of repeatedly finding out in later life that "Oops, it wasn't like that after all", blundering through life bouncing off the edges of the system without a skill to direct and guide his own life. He will learn later that the information he absorbed in school, even when complemented with all the information available in the world, isn't equal to a subjective, independent understanding of a particular subject. He will learn that even if he reads a Wikipedia article, he will not understand much about the subjective part of the subject matter if he doesn't subjectively know the correct approach to come to an understanding by asking the right questions and being open to observation and critical thought. While the subjectively aligned thinker takes as a given that in any subjective matter there is always the "It isn't necessarily so" and is ready to put under question both his own understanding and the credibility of his source to a relevant degree, the metaphysical thinker takes a thing for granted with a feeling of entitlement, silences critical voices by slamming the desk with his fist and saying things like "If it walks like a duck and quacks like a duck, then I will assume it is a duck". In the duck example the evidence only shows that it seems to you to be a duck—the rest is your assumption—and this method might perform well in a context of observing animals where we are framed to a set of existing species and recognizable animal characteristics, but it might perform very poorly when you extend it to another context without this comfortable framing, like this: "If it walks like the enemy, wears green like the enemy and carries a gun like the enemy, I will assume it is the enemy"... no, it might be your own squad mate.

In Platonism, thought is to be used in search for *proof* that something abstract exists 'beyond' particular phenomena and associated words, and taking this into a primitive society, one can see how the model

PART II. COMMON MISCONCEPTIONS

relates to Man trying to understand natural phenomena through using his intellect to establish the origin of those natural phenomena: their *creator*. Being baffled after being born into a world full of mysterious life forms and seeing how birds give birth to eggs, beavers build dams, etc., he starts to wonder what gave birth to all these animals. For Plato *ideas* were related to phenomena that *already exist*, such as animals, plants and physical objects but also concepts of virtue such as love and courage, and from that he deduced that e.g. a smith (the creator of objects) must also have the idea of the desired object in his mind when he begins to fashion it. Very importantly, the phenomena Plato attributed to ideas were *observable* phenomena, not e.g. scientific theories that are known to be man-made, and both he and Aristotle were aware of the obvious problem of what sort of phenomena sensibly qualify as attributable, since the attribution was a method rather than a result and had no logical (grammatical) limits. Breaking the Platonic model into a form of argument in predicate calculus: "X creates p; p; therefore X", one can see how, as such, it is a clear fallacy of affirming the consequent. Also "(X creates p) OR (Y creates p); p; therefore (X OR Y)" is a fallacy, and this seems to also be the case with any sensible ways of trying to present Platonism in predicate calculus. The Platonic model is deeply rooted in the foundations of our scientific system and especially natural science, in which what lies beyond has been named "laws of nature". The contemporary scientification of philosophical questions in practical terms is a separation of philosophical questions from rationality, and this process should be interpreted to confirm that Platonism in itself *is not rational*, but the dominance of Platonism has never been a result of it being a reasonable choice or a choice or a result of any kind, but rather because it is a natural existential continuation of learning the names of objects when growing up. Indeed for Plato *ideas* were not simply grammatical abstractions but transcendent in the sense that they are eternal and *supreme*.[123] This quality of superiority clearly implies faith in an *authority* and reflects the human spiritual search for truth through the divine, and there exists a human quality that favours security through what one already has over subjective honesty. This makes it possible for one to continuously resort to the eternal possi-

---

[123] A linguist might ask: How can a *word* be more supreme than another?

II-4. THE METAPHYSICAL WORLD

bility of simply assuming a hypothesis and deciding that a lot of work needs to be done—for oneself or for someone else—in order to clear up any problems it poses. We don't choose to see things the way we do, but if we are able to maintain an observational approach instead of, due to our ethical commitment to an *ideology*, closing our eyes and saying "This is how it *must* be",[124] we might succeed in noticing whenever our results don't conform with the actual use of language and the beliefs and functionality of the living human society that underlies it. Then again, the Platonic perspective manages to gain credibility from the *authority* of the scientific system, and one might be deceived into thinking that questioning the metaphysical way of thinking equates to questioning the results of science. This is a simple misconception: science has never claimed that the more or less applicable theories it produces that effectively act behind our common understanding when interpreting the nature of different phenomena are somehow final or equal to reality—after all, that's why they are theories and not definitions, and who (if not an assumed architect of the world) could define reality? Of course, many if not most scientists *believe* this about their own field of study and some of them are more able than others to distinguish this personal faith to theories appearing subjectively plausible from the objective nature of science. Natural science validates theories with observations and in the shared process of unifying results some things are accepted as agreed conceptions—but none of this has anything to do with 'reality' or 'truth' although people might use 'truth' in relation to such theories as signifying their subjective belief.

Why is it so compelling to think along the lines that the "true nature" of the universe is physical, comprising e.g. atoms, quarks and quantum phenomena? The use of the word 'true' in this way (similarly to the original Greek meaning of truth: "the unconcealed") implies *a reality* that lies "beyond", as in myths the afterlife has always lain beyond, say, a river, or as a popular Finnish tango[125] begins: "Somewhere beyond the vast sea there is a land...", implying faith beyond the unknown

---
124 The *duty* of an ideology, or religion, is revealed by 'must'.
125 "Satumaa", Unto Mononen, 1955. Translates to "The Fairytale Land"; the name is also revealing.

or incomprehensible. The framework of 'truth' or 'reality' can be just about anything, such as:

- a memory, as in "Sorry, I misremembered; truth be told, I never attended that meeting";

- history, as in "Official records claim six million Jews were killed in WWII, but these numbers are highly suspect, the reality being likely considerably less"; or

- the future, as in "The truth is that Europe is living a modern era of trade and economy, and the British decision to exit the EU is not based on reality."

These examples should point out that rather than the frame of reference, the key part of the meaning of 'truth' or 'reality' lies in the use of the concept as a grammatical device to highlight something that is *unfoundedly believed*, and the beauty of the tango, and, no doubt, the source of its popularity, is in the outspoken acknowledgement of being a fool in unfounded love, which is classic tragedy. At the same time, in this use, the true nature of something is what the subject announces faith in *instead of* another referred reality... and this nature essentially refers to a *methodology*. This can be seen in the light of more practical non-theoretic examples that nevertheless remain completely understandable, such as "The truth about potatoes is that in reality they don't provide much in terms of nutrients", where the subject promotes a particular diet methodology instead of another one, or "Real men don't hit women", where the subject promotes a certain conduct; again, instead of another one. Take away the grammatical reference to an alternative methodology, and the concept becomes confusing, such as "This is a real bottle"... immediately we must ask what the 'real' refers to: are you implying, for example, that in this context I should suspect the existence of fake bottles, imaginary bottles or bottles that are somehow inferior to the bottle in question, and if so, in what way are they inferior? Thus, via these examples we should understand that the words 'true' or 'real' don't yet refer to anything unless they are used in a particular context, and that a person attributing the true nature to a physical nature is promoting the power of natural science over something else. Furthermore, as there can be no truth or reality apart

II-4. THE METAPHYSICAL WORLD

from being the alternative to another, false reality, this should give rise to the question: what is the alternative to the truth of natural science? This must be a historical alternative: the truth revealed by science is correct in its relation to the alternative which was truth revealed by something else. This brings us to the roots of science, as scientific truth is something that has replaced something else as the norm, and it also gives rise to the question of why it is that we blindly insist on using the words 'truth' or 'reality' in reference to scientific results, because the justification to call them truth is simply that it is a norm. We can clearly understand that natural science can't be the answer to *everything*, because you can't churn milk with natural science, and so on... but it becomes somewhat understandable that a natural science advocate might attribute reality to natural science and to simply forget to address his implied alternative. If somebody says: "The world consists of physical particles", this is correct, as he is simply implying a physical context to his use of 'the world'. But if somebody says: "The *reality* is physical" or "The *truth* about the world is that it is simply physical", then we must immediately know to ask: the reality as an alternative to what? This question would force him to make the claim sensible by bringing his further commitments under scrutiny; *why* does *he* choose a physical reality over another reality? What is good about *this* reality that you promote over another reality, and does your reality have any known flaws? I would personally ask these questions when considering buying any property, because the 'real' in 'real estate' or 'real property' originally meant immovable; property being defined as something that you are potentially stuck with and can't easily get rid of—actually it is non-contradictory to combine the logic of sales and reality: "If you *buy into* this reality, you are stuck with it." If somebody says e.g.: "The truth about the world is that it reduces down to series of physical events", we need to ask in return: "Do you mean sex reduces to a series of acts and positions?" and when he says he didn't mean that, we need to ask: what *did* you mean; *why* do *you* believe the reality is like that? Down this path we would come to see things in the subjective light; any explanation of the world, even a physical world, demands the subjective moral question of whether the explanation is *good* in the sense that one should adopt it, implying that adopting it would make one better. And

PART II. COMMON MISCONCEPTIONS

the crucial thing to understand is that there is no 'reality' outside of this subjective question (a metaphysical reality), but any concept of reality already implies this subjective choice of the promoted reality over another one. *The subjective is primary and the objective is secondary; our norms change but the human is guaranteed to remain.* The next generation is born with the same brain as the previous one, and this is a scientific truth and not a matter of faith, and something we modern people cannot question but that actually contradicts old norms such as the belief in royal blood; that the earthly status of royalties is passed on in the blood and that there must be a divine reason behind a royal being powerful and being permanently commemorated in imposing statues.

Some light can be shed by tracing 'physics' back to its origins where the word ('fysis') meant nature, and it can be seen that in this meaning "the nature (of the universe) is physical" is a tautology. But the original meaning of physics meant natural science: the empirical study of nature such as the soil, the weather, animals and plants. Atoms and such, the building blocks of the universe, are a later discovery, and much further away from observation as being for the most part founded on theory of the existence of something that *per se* is not verified by observation, but the theory is validated by the fact that it can produce predictions of the behaviour of actual observable phenomena which actually turn out to be correct. So, what did 'nature' mean for Aristotle? He meant a reality of moving bodies, all affecting one another, but behind which there had to be something that didn't itself move but instead was perfect in setting everything into perfect movement with perfect consideration (a deity). So, in this conception it is obvious that the 'true nature' of the universe was not physics, but on the contrary physics was the study of the *effects* of what was the true cause, and this came to exist as a tradition of systematic study of nature. This conception was something that laid a *basis* for the empirical method of natural science; something without which the whole activity of natural science would have been meaningless, since it contrasted with the view that the nature of the universe can be conceived through reaching for the ideas behind real-world phenomena using one's intellect (Plato).

II-4. THE METAPHYSICAL WORLD

It can be noted that natural science has throughout history existed in this oppositional role against religious idealism, saying: "Yes, we don't deny that God is behind everything (regarding that question we take no stance, since it is not our primary interest), but what you are teaching contradicts with the evidence we have found using the empirical method." So it is that the meaning of 'physics' *in the sense of natural science* is a process that, instead of getting mixed up in metaphysical or theological considerations, has chosen to ground itself strictly in observation and evidence, and its relation to the divine is fully neutral *assumption*. What has happened since the times of Aristotle is that natural science has proven very useful and powerful in terms of gaining better control over natural resources, which has made investing in natural science politically fruitful, and has given natural science a strong authoritative position and great visibility. Today the authority has outgrown the institution and the situation is totally out of control, and concepts traditionally rooted in human sciences are being reformulated in naturalist terms (under 'cognitive science'). The rapid emergence of the digital computer has enabled the use of the computationalist hypothesis to create a confused enough situation to waste resources in this false pursuit: academia simply feels that it is easier to justify technologically motivated research plans. It's commonplace today to read articles implying that the mind is a computer, and as we all know, computers are built out of physical components. This is why today it is compelling to see the nature of the universe as physical: it is the quasi-religion of the materialist world born out of a second industrial revolution launched by the innovation of the digital computer. In contemporary work life, humans, along with their minds, are seen as parts of a mathematically available mechanist whole, and their lives and behaviour interpreted in terms of tendencies and probabilities used in an effort to maximize efficiency, which bears every similarity with the way the original fascist factory owner would look at his workers from the standpoint of how their productivity as extensions of the machines (that constitute the major investment) could be maximized. And it seems to me the Marxist ideal has failed: today we are in an at least equally desperate situation regarding Marxist alienation (which follows from the workers not owning the production machines) as in

PART II. COMMON MISCONCEPTIONS

the early post-industrial era, and workers more than ever regard their work as a utilitarian means to reach a reward (money) rather than seeing it as valuable in itself.

Taking a look at the popularity of metaphysical thought, I believe that the value of transcendent idealism and rationalism expressed in both Plato and Kant can be understood in the light of attributing transcendence to *individual* thought, which means that the individual is capable of reaching the highest value in his mind only, in contrast with, say, an idea that an individual can be most worthy by placing himself in the service of another. 'Transcendent' generally can be translated to "the highest in value" or "supernatural in value" or "with a *given* value", with value beyond doubt; for example in Christianity, God happens to be transcendent and the highest in value, but this quality is not reducible to Christianity but on the contrary, the transcendence of God in Christianity *means* God has the highest value, and that *only* God is transcendent means that *only* the value of God is a given, and the value of everything else is susceptible to doubt and relative to particular conditions. Furthermore, in Platonic idealism we can see the transcendence of *abstraction*, which is essentially an act of placing abstract thought on the highest pedestal in terms of value, which further develops into the science of mathematics. And this makes sense in primitive terms, since the capability of abstract thought is the essential feature that distinguishes humans from other animals, and is a requirement for the sort of language animals don't learn to apply: a language that applies e.g. the subject-predicate-object sentence structure to *concepts* instead of something directly related to the immediate context, such as the expressions of emotions that have primitive responses, or gesture expressions of "I want you to bring the object you have associated with this picture". It is precisely abstract thought that gives humans the capability to transcend the nomadic existence of simply using tools by learning and passing on related traditions, into life in civil nation-states where working with objects involves also expressing them in language. So, such idealism can be interpreted as an act of giving the highest value to the activity of individually reaching for abstract and rational thought, which also happens to be the most human evolutionary asset, and I believe this sort of thought can be seen to produce high value in terms of cultural evolution and related evolutionary competition. But I believe the transcendence in Platonism or Kantianism should correctly be interpreted in a similar way to religious transcendence: in idealist terms reasonable thought itself is the purpose and endpoint of action, and to think abstractly and rationally in a worthy manner is an act *in service of* reason, essentially contrasting with an unreasonable mode of thought; one that is uncontrolled and whimsical, and easily succumbs to vices such as fear, anger or lust, or chasing dreams or apparitions produced by the subconscious. To value the legacy of Plato or Kant is to value the human *capability of reason* in spite of urges, dangers, chaos or anarchy; to value the human faculty of being able to reason but also to be reasonable with each other. And by this I mean to say that such thought should never be interpreted in the sense that some sort of "final answer" could be given by reason, which is an abstract quality—how could it give any answers? But it's possible to note how it shows our humanity when we turn towards the transcendent in search of personal, existential answers. Reason is a private capability similarly to e.g. trust or loyalty, but how could one expect to find some *answers* from reason, as we can see that one doesn't even *learn anything* using reason, but the role of reason in learning is in its relation with reasonable *argument*. Reason is a disposition, not an act, and it is related to the manner in which we learn, as well as the manner in which we argue. To further describe reason as a disposition, it means that a reasonable person is not one who behaves reasonably in every aspect, but reason is applied in behaviour and interaction, and whenever we call a person "a reasonable person" we mean they are likely to take a reasonable approach to presented matters. People who are highly reasonable in some particular aspect of life can be completely unreasonable in some other aspect, and it is rather painful to meet a person who places Kant and reason on a pedestal and possesses high skills of abstract thought, but at the same time argues only in a fallacious manner, displaying a complete lack of reason. A person with a capability to apply reason can be seen to be reasonable in a particular respect if he wants to be. But looking at the tradition of embracing reason, one must recognize its very particular nature, as people normally apply reason in order to solve some task at hand. On the contrary, for Plato and Kant the exercise of reasoning in itself is *service* to a higher power, which reflects that they considered reasoning to be the most valuable type of activity. And this explains why the role of reason in the activity of searching for answers cannot transcend the role of analysing one's options in the process of making *existential choices*, just as the role of analysis is invaluable whenever making decisions—if one wishes to embrace reason, one should embrace it as it is, a useful and valuable tool and skill for a mode of thought and behaviour, and not confuse it with God or one's mother. Wittgenstein thought it erroneous for the whole Western history of philosophy to run against the limits of language, and I can't produce a better description of this process than his, seeing how creating transcendent metaphysics out of our capability and *freedom* to independent thought produces such an evident contradiction of thought where a transcendent, given nature is attributed to something that demonstrably functions as a practical tool for thought and communication. An intellectual should make his existential choices with his best rational effort, but then take a look at the world today and think about what is the most useful thing to do with one's analytical skills; the information age is full of information, which has produced confusion, and just as reasonable analysis is the best way to deal with existential questions and confusion, the best way to deal with linguistic confusion is linguistic analysis. Or at least one could try to raise some public questions about our confused language instead of confining oneself inside the illusive safety of one's own mind. Also, there is no longer any need to compete with the Church over the nature of transcendence, because today the Church has no authority.

The naturalist worldview consists of entities in motion that are discovered by the naturalist method at various levels of precision and detail. For example, modern physics is divided into four domains that deal with phenomena whose entities are either slow or fast (close to the speed of light) and either small (smaller than atomic) or large in scale: classical mechanics, relativistic mechanics, quantum mechanics and quantum field theory.[126] These domains have isolated applica-

---

126 I don't know much anything about these fields but if you have been stupid enough

II-4. THE METAPHYSICAL WORLD

bility, which essentially means that *predictions* made by applying the theories *have proven* to match observations only within phenomena falling into their domain of scale, and become less and less reliable when approaching the limits of their application. This is evident regarding what the concepts of physics *mean*: they don't associate to anything material, in the way that e.g. a library catalogue points to material books, but, contrary to the function of a library, the meaning of physical existence is *attribution* verified with empirical evidence resulting from experiments. Thus it is expectable that the predictions are most reliable in a scale close to the scale of the phenomena used in the experiments that constitute the validation of the theories, and actually any reliable extension of scale is rather miraculous and truly a great achievement of scientific intuition regarding the formulation of the originating theory. But any true physicist can understand that the limit of scope in the domains of physics is a *proof* that they are not *true* in the sense of the goal of science: the concepts attributed by the theory imply a metaphysical model of the world that is proven false. A physicist just doesn't need to deal with this problem, since he is a physicist and not a metaphysicist. Physics should correctly be seen in the light of its history as a constantly refining set of theories that have been categorized to the said domains only at a fairly recent point in time. If natural phenomena today are commonly seen as sets of rules governing, say, atoms, quarks or quantum phenomena, one should correctly see these as a *refinement* of what previously used to be bodies generally having larger mass, since the related experiments were conducted with bodies of higher mass, for example the spheres Galileo used when he conducted his experiments at the Tower of Pisa. Another example of modern hypothetical 'high truths' (they are very passionately defended) is our popular cosmological conceptions of the universe such as black holes. The theoretical basis of this is Einstein's theory of General Relativity in 1915, which implies that certain areas of space can have such high mass that light cannot escape; and this has been complemented by Hawking radiation (1974), which, using a different theory—quantum mechanics—implies that such an area (event horizon) will emit radiation in a particular way. Since then, areas have

---

to read my book so far it proves I don't have to.

been located in the cosmos via different measuring techniques that are consistent with such radiation. One can evaluate the reliability of this model from the facts that the founding base of this cosmological model is less than 100 years old, and General Relativity is not the only theory, but the *simplest theory* consistent with experimental data, on top of which other theories and observations, that support the existence of black holes, have been built. But in addition, since we are dealing with matters that can't be experimentally replicated, we are resting on a highly speculative assumption that is true only because no better candidate has been suggested. It seems to me that the point of popularizing such speculative pseudoscience is only, as it were, philosophical interest; dealing with matters such as *creation* people want to hear the 'scientific answer' to... but there is a great contradiction between the fact that science is so immensely popular at the moment and the fact that the results of science are much less applicable than what the scientists before these times could produce. Hawking came to the conclusion himself that black holes don't actually exist, as he thought that quantum theory contradicts the whole notion of an event horizon.[127] Then he joined the AI-world-overtake doomsayers, a tradition of consistently false predictions started by Turing and proudly held by characters such as Ray Kurzweil whom the tech companies cherish as the best-selling traditional fortune-teller in AI. As of today, Hawking's final submitted paper has not been peer-reviewed. To give another example, popular cosmologist Esko Valtaoja, along with many similar people, would say: "The most profound question is why anything at all (the universe) exists, and this question has no answer", to which I would reply with a claim of my own: "The sweetest of all jams is the jam made out of squashnacle berries, and this jam cannot be eaten." Why does a person with enough intellect for a scientific education claim to know something, but in the same sentence also claims that nobody knows it? "It is only I who can lift this rock! [tries to lift it, fails] Nobody can lift this rock!" Isn't it more *credible* to say, "The best of all beings is God, and I know him but many do not"? When one says something like "The world doesn't *really* consist of solid bodies, but instead consists of at-

---

[127] Z. Merali, 'Stephen Hawking: "There are no black holes"', *Nature*, 24.1.2014 http://www.nature.com/news/stephen-hawking-there-are-no-black-holes-1.14583 [26.12.2019].

II-4. THE METAPHYSICAL WORLD

oms/quarks (or the like)", the word 'really' is a reference to the reality imposed on us by *modern* science as opposed to *old* science that has been discarded from use because of the higher explanatory power of the modern theories. Using such reality as a basis for metaphysical exploration is a complete waste of time by definition, since these theories of natural science by definition are our best existing hypotheses and mistaking hypothetical reality for truth is a very serious error, similar to mistaking a dream to a waking state. In subjective communication, it is a mode of thought that by itself creates disagreement and resistance by any party that doesn't share the metaphysical preconceptions, and such thoughts are simply communicated in a much more efficient manner without a fanatic commitment to them. Instead of saying "It is as I say because *the world* is like *this*", it is much more effective in terms of potential reception to say: "I believe this is how it is because in our such-and-such tradition *this* is what we believe"—and the tradition could be a scientific tradition or simply any cultural tradition; they behave the same in terms of social function. This sort of softness of approach doesn't hurt the reception of the message but quite the contrary, what happens is that the fanatical nature of the metaphysical perspective is experienced as frightening, and the acceptance of such a perspective is not made intellectually but via submission, like a distant tribe throwing themselves to the ground at the feet of their invaders, not because they are wearing fancy clothes or speaking the right words but because they are wielding superior weapons—in this case scientific theories unintelligible to the masses.

Metaphysical speculations presented by scientists should be understood in the light of their love for their work, as any romance requires a degree of blindness, and true love requires complete blindness to the faults of the other. But it seems to me that currently the phenomenon in question is a gradual process of subjective falling in love with an *object*, and this differs from the philosophy of Plato and Aristotle in the sense that the love is targeted towards the object instead of something considered beyond, or the creator of, the object. Science has evolved to a stage in which, to many scientists, scientific concepts are no longer seen as reflections of God's work, but as existent independent of such

PART II. COMMON MISCONCEPTIONS

creator, which can be said to give them an independent life. I will demonstrate a fictive gradual metaphysical relationship of a student towards an abstract object of arbitrary choice, *letters*.

1) The student learns that the words we have spoken so far have equivalents in the written word, and there the words consist of letters. She learns to read and write, starting letter by letter, advancing to a mature skill of reading and writing.

2) The student learns that *beyond* what she has learned so far, the structure of sentences is bound by structural rules called grammar. Grammar dictates a certain order of words and certain structural rules of forming words in her language. There is much joy related to finding the equivalents of the grammatical rules in the natural language she hears.

3) The student learns that *beyond* what she has learned so far about her own language, languages of other cultures contain different alphabets and completely different grammatical rules. One common feature about these languages, however, is the use of letters in forming words. This testifies that letters are an important feature of languages that otherwise sound and seem arbitrary.

4) The student has learned the *fundamental* importance of letters as the common ground beyond languages. For her it is not the case that letters are textual components, but on the contrary, text is an *embodiment* of letters that are transcendent and omnipresent in nature. In seeing a natural phenomenon, she is essentially seeing a configuration and permutation of letters, being the cultural and textual equivalent of the given name of the phenomenon.

What has happened here is the human spiritual process where one comes to understand the nature of a phenomenon as the force behind that phenomenon, which might be called the *spirit* of that phenomenon. But the spirit here is not treated as a subject but instead as an object, and this is bound to confuse, as we only usually regard subjects as a mystery. Only of subjects do we humbly ponder: "What could he have had in mind when making this choice?" when trying to understand the actions of the subject, which implies a working method of trying

II-4. THE METAPHYSICAL WORLD

to come to *understand* the phenomenon considered to have been created by a subject. And contrary to this, if we consider that an object is causing or creating natural phenomena (such as that the cue ball, as it were, *causes* the nine-ball to move, or gives or produces its momentum), we would not try to understand it but rather we would just observe it or take it as a given. This relation seems to me to be all wrong in modern natural science and also seems to me to have been perceived correctly in the earlier stage of science called natural philosophy. Scientists are unaware about attributing active spiritual qualities to the objective phenomena they attribute as the causes of the phenomena they study, because such spirituality simply is an inherent human disposition. I think this is the professional sin for a scientist in the same way as greed—falling in love with money—is the professional sin for a businessman, but such a sinful profession would require means of absolution via a third party, meaning somebody with particular wisdom about the nature of science itself instead of a particular science. This role has in the past been held by philosophers, but this is no longer the case. I relate this to the fact that academia follows the rules of corporate life in terms of careers and funding. Corporations are often reluctant to accept criticism in their internal processes, because change via acknowledging mistakes is a slow process requiring a long-term investment and commitment, whereas careers, positions and market opportunities tend to be short in cycle. For a corporate boss, rather than publicly discussing, say, bad terminology or bad processes, a more lucrative option is to fire somebody or to buy a ready-made solution to replace the old one. And the abyss into which academia is descending more and more deeply is the same abyss that many large corporations fall into before being dissected into smaller entities, bought off the market and sold to competitors. Unfortunately, this fate doesn't seem to be an option for science, so the crisis persists and will continue to do so.

The attribution of a metaphysical world is inherent in the methodology of natural science, and this would pose no problems if the results of natural science were correctly interpreted against such attributions, because one can say what one likes as long as one is being clear about one's commitments. There are considerable difficulties in achieving this clarity in the formulation of research plans, and furthermore in publicizing the result of scientific research in the media. However, the situation is totally different regarding *philosophical* metaphysical theories: they fail to provide us with any practical use. This is why Wittgenstein saw the work of the philosophers as dissolving the rampant metaphysical use of concepts and returning them to their everyday use. The philosopher is not to jump into the trolley of bad scientific language, just as a priest is not to give absolution by simply stating "It's not your fault, I would do the same!" After all the priest is in a highly valuable position as the trusted mediator between a man and his conscience, and absolution is sought with the predetermination that sin has already been committed. It is not enough for a philosopher to present a theory and assert that the theory—like scientific results—*can* be useful, but since these theories don't come with the applicability of science, he should also explain why such a theory *should* be used. As a response to this problem I have heard e.g. that philosophical theories bring more clarity to the issues at hand, but such an answer is based on a misconception of the meaning of 'clarity', which, in this sense, is a subjective quality: bring together many subjectively clear systems and one will not have a clear result but a soup of mutually meaningless systems and considerable disagreement.

In linguistics, a *phoneme* is described as the smallest unit that distinguishes *meaning* between words, which builds upon the assumption that meaning is related to the sounds that are produced when a word is pronounced. But this quite obviously can't be the case, since words with the same pronunciation or the same spelling carry different meanings. For example the Finnish language is particularly rich with constructive capabilities to produce identical words with different meanings; for example the word for *Finland* is 'Suomi' but 'suomi' is also the imperative mood of the verb that means lashing; or the word meaning *a vein* is 'suoni', but 'suoni' is also the word 'suo' (swamp), with the first person singular possessive suffix '-ni', meaning "my swamp". These examples indicate that the phonetic or grammatical form of words has absolutely no relation to their *meaning*, and words with identical pronuncia-

II-4. THE METAPHYSICAL WORLD

tion and spelling can mean completely unrelated things. It is better to say that the phoneme is the atomic unit of a spoken language and reflects the capability of producing sounds within a linguistic group, and not the meaning of expressions in any way. The status of linguistics between the passing of Wittgenstein and the publication of Chomsky's *Syntactic Structures* was that linguistics is a classificatory science, a sort of "verbal botany",[128] which is a much more fruitful approach in terms of coming to understand a new language, yet the related science happened to be infused with the idea that meaning, as something that linguistic expressions carry, is a product of the mystical object, the mind. This might be historical continuity from Kant feeling that this was the case. So, this problematic was challenged by structural linguistics that provided a sense of rigorous science to the matter, as thinking of words as esoteric character strings was very compatible with emerging computationalist ideas preceding physical computers. Science has a lot to do with exploring new methodologies, so it seemed as if computation could perhaps solve these problems, and indeed I was quite recently taught Chomskyan context-sensitive and context-free grammars on computer science theory courses; techniques that produce *formal languages* out of generative rules. Even today the notation for a context-free grammar is the computer scientific standard for describing the syntax for various formal languages when building information systems. This very linguistic development is likely the sole reason why we use keyboards with characters on them instead of, say, colour codes or pictures of fluffy animals. Computers are controlled with instructions that come as languages, originally (and still predominantly in Unix tradition) via character input terminals, similar to the way soldiers are controlled with military keywords, and this development has fundamentally been influenced by thought that generally relates the string representations of words with meaning. This is to say that structural linguistics and the power of the technological innovation of the digital computer have supported each other, which could help to explain why we have come to a false theory of meaning as syntax from the alternative of another false theory of meaning as a cognitive process. By

---

[128] J. Searle, 'Chomsky's Revolution in Linguistics', *The New York Review of Books*, June 29, 1972.

saying "meaning as syntax" I simply mean the idea that it makes sense to study the grammatical form of expressions in a language via assuming an underlying imaginary generative process—something that I fail to find any sense in to begin with, since, speaking of scientific rigour, real natural languages are produced, strictly and without exception, by people who are real and natural instead of imaginary. It has been noticed that syntax is not meaning, and optimists believe that we can overcome this problem by complementing the notion of syntax with another notion of *semantics* (or its study, *semiotics*), which is a sort of placeholder word for "whatever it is that constitutes meaning" that one can attach to the syntactic form of a linguistic expression (created by an imaginary generative process) to create a holy unity that explains everything. This is yet another metaphysical attribution: meaning is not cognitive process nor syntax; thus, it must be something else; let's call it semantics and throw some money at a guy with a beard to figure it out. There's money, there's research for all; so, what's the problem? —these problems don't solve themselves, so, roll up your sleeves and sing it out: "Hurrah, science!" This is the standard form of corrupt expert work, to guarantee your own job by working in a way that won't produce anything final while at the same time becoming the foremost expert in your particular field of work. Maybe many of these optimists feel this way because formal languages have so many undiscovered applications within the field of computation that they simply have no idea yet what remains to be discovered. There's no sense to relate the word *syntax* with the formal properties of *languages*; on the contrary, whatever Chomskyan context-free grammars generate is something that has nothing whatsoever to do with languages in the sense of natural language. They just happen to be called formal languages because they have been named as such, and this process is quite similar to drawing a picture of a cat: drawing a body, four legs, feet, head, ears, eyes, mouth... and after finishing, saying: "Look, it's a cat!" They are *models* of reality, and I'd say the best way to do away with the related confusion would be to rename them "models of language". Formal languages are languages as much as this picture of a cat is a cat; they are not 'partial' or 'incomplete' languages missing only semantics, but in a very strict sense they are not languages at all but models; something that has the alphabets and grammars of languages as its inspiration, and the tag 'language' attached to it. When somebody is speaking of *syntax*, he is most likely speaking of rules that govern the structure of meaningful expressions in a *formal* language but applying the word to natural language is simply senseless; a rather grave mistake due to linguistic confusion. Natural language has no such rules, and rather the formal grammatical rules are worked in the opposite way: not generating sentences from rules but by linguists identifying key features of languages and laying out rules to unify the language; how to *ideally* structure one's sentences. A key feature of natural languages contra formal ones is that we tend to understand them despite them being grammatically incorrect (e.g. "H3ll0, h0w arr yuu d0ing?"), and this process is rather similar to *dress codes*: to produce sentences of natural language that are grammatically correct is equivalent to dressing formally, as opposed to dressing casually, and the opposite of this behaviour is not producing senseless arbitrary strings or meaningless grunts, but producing expressions in *informal* language that one has learned at home and picked up from here and there: something an uneducated person might do by contrast with a person who has been educated in his mother tongue, and that essentially has *spoken language* as its very core basis. In fact, spoken language seems to me the core of our linguistic skill, due to the following reasons.

1) Prevalence of reading and writing, not speaking, are the ways to measure societal advance, as speaking is something that already exists in any culture but reading and writing don't exist in all cultures.

2) Spoken words generally precede read or written words in infants growing up.

3) One of the best ways to understand a sentence is to read it aloud.

4) My experience of thought often involves something similar to imagining or remembering spoken thought, and the language in my thought changes according to the language I need to use every day.

The primary nature of spoken language is what explains how a grammatically incorrect sentence is understandable. It seems to me that to some degree we directly associate the written form of a word with its meaning, and to some degree we speak out (aloud or in our thought) written sentences and associate the auditive result with the meaning, and these sorts of activities are repeated in a process that is sometimes a flowing, effortless experience, and sometimes slow and clumsy where the meanings don't just 'jump' into our mind but we need to perform various activities to come to the right meaning. This is to say that reading is not a simple, automatic process to bring strings of text into the understanding in our mind, but rather a complicated set of subjective skills that need to be learned, maintained and further developed. We apply these skills only partially consciously while reading, and we apply, in various ways and at different times, different energy and attention levels and so on.

It is a silly idea that syntax would somehow 'need' semantics as its pair; what for? You can have a lot of fun with just syntax, but what are you trying to do? You are playing with a picture of language but what do you think it would take for a picture to come alive? When we speak about the pair "word and its meaning", we are not describing a binary metaphysical entity; that's just what it looks like based on the grammar of this expression. This is quite similar to the way we could say "body and soul" to constitute a human, but we could also say that "body and its life" constitutes a human: Dr Frankenstein would take a body and, in his tragically twisted mind, only needed a bit of science to puff life into this body. Look carefully: when we pair "word and its meaning", we not describing two *constituents* of language but two *aspects*. We are not talking about two separable Lego blocks or puzzle pieces; we are talking about a 360º theatre stage with seats ranged on both sides of the aisle in front of it. We are looking at the *phenomenon* that we have named 'language' and have found two important perspectives from which to describe it and named them 'grammatical form' and 'meaning'. And these two aspects are strictly bound to our *scientific methodologies* at hand: grammatical form is to be analysed in terms of written language or its phonetics, and meaning has historically been understood in terms of cognition, which involves things such as the soul, mental images, will, desires and so on. What the grammatical form and meaning *constitute* is the *approaches* (paradigms)

II-4. THE METAPHYSICAL WORLD

we have available to the phenomenon of language. These aspects don't constitute or create language; if you want to ask what creates or has created language, you must look elsewhere, and regarding these matters just be satisfied by the perspectives you have been given on an already existing phenomenon by fellow scientists. Rather you should ask what has caused science to get to the point where scientists no longer feel as if they are describing phenomena that they acknowledge to exist simply because they can be observed to exist, but have started to obscure this very role of science with occultism that doesn't feel like observing, describing and identifying, but instead like crafting, and very importantly, portraying an *image* of being *capable* of crafting, and selling this service for a price. This art of shameless deception is in the nature of alchemy, the elixir of life and the philosophers' stone: promising the funding party that one is very close to being able to produce wonders. When philosophers or scientists say that they are very close to producing something marvellous, this is said simply to humour the big man, who is growing restless at their lack of productivity. And looking at it from this perspective it's easy to see why scientists give baseless promises: science had good results (in physics, and therefore, in warfare) and the big man noticed this and increased the funding for science. Scientists became well-funded, and so many of them grew fat and arrogant. The big man is not stupid, so he said that he might have been overly generous, and each day one scientist would face the sword until real results came rolling in. A great deal of philosophical work presented in history concentrates on trying to describe the subjective in objective terms—as Wittgenstein would put it: trying to "run against the limits of language". Mostly this activity is due to a false or limited metaphysical conception of language—one resulting from the fact that the crucial question of how language is learned and shared between individuals is not raised at all. Then again, this is only natural for anyone who has not paid enough attention to the issue since, first of all, the words we use are normally understood by others in the contexts we have learned them in and then advance to use them in, and secondly, *grammar*, in its traditional meaning, doesn't describe the boundaries of the meaningful application of words, but just dictates a framework for producing sentences with a particular alphabet. The grammatical rules don't give meaning to sentences, but rather they are an effort to reach better communicability through a shared structure of sentences, and these in the West have had emphasis on the structure: subject-predicate-object. Within these structural rules it is still easy to produce nonsense by breaking the logic of the concepts. When we learn words, they produce for us some sort of a sensation of their meaning, and we follow this sensation when we apply the words. But this sensation is a part of our unique subjectivity, and no assumptions can be made about its nature—from psychology we know for certain that people assimilate new information in very different ways. Very importantly, many words are learned with a strong emotional connection to their meaning, and this emotion may be carried over from the context in which we learn them: the learned meanings may be personally dear to us. From a grammatical perspective, changing our conceptions is a technical issue, but from our personal existential perspective it can be very drastic and painful. We *want* the words to mean exactly what we have learned them to mean, and we don't want to change this. In psychology, this is expressed by the fact that humans tend to work to enforce their subjective world-picture instead of dismantling it. In this perspective the philosopher is a very odd fellow.

The root of conceptual problems is in that natural language doesn't have (or require) any standardized definitions for concepts, and we therefore don't have any objective medium to verify whether we have understood a particular concept correctly. Rather, understanding a concept is related to our experience with it, but then again, long acquaintance with a word doesn't automatically result in us correctly understanding it (I remember somebody who had all her life believed that wasps were the same as bees), just as long acquaintance with another person doesn't guarantee familiarity about him as a subject, particularly if we don't show any curiosity about his subjective character or if he is unwilling to reveal his character. The search for a correct definition is a completely different business: from an objective perspective, definitions of words or expressions of natural language can be useful in the sense that dictionaries and encyclopaedias are useful, but from the subjective perspective it is rather like trying to find a very compelling

II-4. THE METAPHYSICAL WORLD

picture to match your taste in an effort to show it to the people around you so that they will change their behaviour to match your taste. This sort of thinking is so deeply rooted in Western philosophy and science that even laypeople often say, when met with a conceptual problem, "It depends on how you define the word", which basically means that the problem is to be ignored and the person saying this is trying to sound smart and enlightened. This has its roots in the attempts by science and philosophy so come up with a definition in the effort to describe the subject matter correctly. As a matter of fact I have included some definitions in this book myself, as an attempt to give a compelling picture of how I see the nature of some concepts... but these definitions are meant for experts who want to understand the mechanics of meaning, and not for normal people who just want to learn how to use or to understand a word correctly. Many words have multiple meanings, and certain words are especially difficult. The normal way to approach understanding would be to try and learn as many of them as possible, but what I am trying to do is to provide the tools for how to learn them all. The major thing required to overcome problems with meanings is to simply have a correct perspective on language: not expecting words to refer to things and not to look for definitions in the case of conceptual problems, but rather look for different real-life contexts and *traditions* in which words are actively used. This sounds simple, but to a person who believes that words refer to things it is unfortunately an extreme challenge *existentially*, as it can be seen to require a change in a core belief. Also, to such a person, observing the actual use of words seems a very uninteresting business. In my understanding, once the fundamental problem is cleared any confusions should be gone, too, and the actual analysis of the meanings of particular words is potentially left as an interesting subjective hobby, but not something that would require significant philosophical *struggle*. After that, the question of *why* we use particular words in particular ways, becomes highly interesting, as the illusion of philosophy as a simple objective analysis disappears and one is left to observe the subjective realm with more clarity.

I will illustrate the logical commitments of a concept by taking as an example the word *'layer'* and investigating what it means. I chose this particular word for no other reason than that it is an abstract concept. Now, it is essential to see that we *don't* need a dictionary to understand the meaning but we can learn the word through being acquainted with its use in language. The description of the meaning of 'layer', as stated by a particular description in a particular dictionary, refers to (describes) *one* meaning of the word. It doesn't define but describes, but the dictionary entry can well function as a shared criterion: when using the word, one can mean the word in the meaning of the dictionary entry. The dictionary description is written and reviewed by people who also possess a high practical understanding about how the word is used and it serves the role as a point of establishment for scientific communication, and the process of reviewing and revising dictionaries is a part of the systematic unity of scientific communication. Therefore if I used the word 'layer' and someone asked me to elaborate on what I meant by the word, I might point to the dictionary if this was asked within an academic context, but otherwise this reference to a secondary medium might imply that I don't actually know the meaning in terms of how the word is used. Now, often when discussing abstract concepts people will say "it's hard to define", but this implies that we *should* be searching for a *definition*, which is a presupposition from a standard of a certain type of approach to meaning. A definition is not necessary in order to *apprehend* a word, although it might be necessary for two or more subjects to *share* a *criterion* of meaning, which the definition itself would provide. But a definition will never serve to 'capture' the unique nature of the way in which the subject understands the meaning of a word[129] in terms of its use. However, it just might give this impression to multiple subjects, since it would accord with how the subjects would describe it—just as I might describe an elephant as a rather big mammal with big ears and a trunk, etc., but *any* description of such phenotypic qualities would fail to substitute the *practice* of observing elephants that would require someone to be qualified as an expert in elephants. The apprehension of a word is unique, subjective and hidden, and definitions won't replace experience, although they might otherwise be useful when working as a group. In relying on definitions

---

129 The idea that a definition can "capture the nature of" something is figurative use of language and in strict sense a contradiction in terms.

II-4. THE METAPHYSICAL WORLD

there lies a great danger of interpreting other people's affirmation of a definition (their stated subjective *belief* in it) to mean the same as subjectively understanding its meaning. To repeat this matter briefly, this kind of affirmation ("it is *exactly* as *you* say") is a natural psycho-social phenomenon, but from the standpoint of philosophy it is a trap: that two people are in full agreement with each other has absolutely nothing to do with whether they are in any understanding with each other. The agreement could be the result of a complete misunderstanding but could just have some hidden social cause. The political human nature in play here can be seen in the following story. A non-citizen wants to pass through the city gate but the gatekeeper won't let him, insisting that access is only granted to citizens. The man tells the gatekeeper: "But it is very important for me to enter, it is my sister's wedding today!" and is repeatedly denied access. Then the man slips a bundle of money to the gatekeeper and asks him: "Fellow Christian, don't you believe in holy matrimony?" and he receives the reply: "Come to think of it, matrimony truly is holy. You may enter." I chose here the religious discourse and money for the sake of illustration, but the same political phenomenon regarding ideals, common assets and the individual asset, is at work at all levels of society wherever people congregate, and academia (and in the past religious institutions), being the highest authority in providing meaning for common language, is no exception. An extreme example of agreement without understanding is rape, in which the woman is forced to submit under threat. And it is seen in the way the protagonist Luke was broken in the film *Cool Hand Luke* by repeated punishment and being asked: "Have you got your mind right, Luke?" This sort of agreement is similar to the relation between a man and an animal: we consider we are in 'agreement' if the animal behaves the way we want it to. Furthermore, our tendency to agree is very much akin to our tendency to affirm knowledge; to say: "I knew it!" It often strikes me as very odd how readily people say such things, and I believe this phenomenon is a psychological strategy to allow the objective to dominate the subjective without recognizing one's earlier subjective misconception. It can easily be noted that whenever somebody says "I knew it would turn out this way", one could very well imagine the person saying the same thing even if the actual objective outcomes were completely opposite.[130] One is simply affirming knowledge instead of subjectively comparing outcomes with one's expectations, which is probably what is called *suggestion* in psychology. Consider the following conversation:

- *I think we ought to go shopping.*
- *Yes, exactly!*
- *No, on second thought, we shouldn't. We should stay home.*
- *Yes, exactly!*

Here we might say the person agreeing is being suggestible, and that he is focusing on external clarity: the clarity of political agreement and cooperation. But if, as a serious thinker, you allow this sort of thought, you might as well throw in the towel as you can't tell even extreme logical opposites apart from one another where the level of skill needed is the ability to distinguish subtle shades and grades of difference. If you take agreement for understanding, as a philosopher, you are like a colour-blind painter. It also seems to me that people subjectively differ very fundamentally in respect of how willingly they affirm a political outcome, and that there is a psychological process of *rationally enforcing* the politically accepted outcome: *after* one has affirmed with "Yes", one comes up with the reasons why, and these reasons are set to agree with the political outcome. It seems to me that this is standard and healthy human psychology, and the intellectual process, where one is to subjectively rationally come to the conclusions one expresses agreement with, is rather in contradiction with it, and an extension of our long Western tradition of dialectic. To rationally agree with outcomes is how *children* reason: an adult gives the outcomes, and the child's imagination comes up with the reasons why this outcome took place. The accepted reasons are satisfactory until they come into contradiction with the subject's own rational thought, and how readily the subject will accept this subjective contradiction—life in self-deceit—is a matter of intellectual honesty.

---

130 In an episode of *Futurama*, Bender makes a sudden return, and everybody is rejoicing. Then:
Fry: "I knew he cared about us!"
Hermes: "You said you knew he *didn't* care about us!"
Fry (embarrassed): "Leave me alone!"

II-4. THE METAPHYSICAL WORLD

Now, returning to the topic of the meaning of 'layer' and approaching the meaning of the word with an observational method through its *actual uses*, I might start by describing layer as "something laid upon something else", and noting that this is not a definition (because we wouldn't in practice be satisfied with it because of its generality) but a description. I also might recognize the verb 'lay' and the grammatical '-er' suffix in accordance with this. Now, I know *a* particular use of the word in a sentence like "The wall needs two layers of paint". In this use the paint is laid upon a surface, which accords with my original description. But how do I know what the word 'layer' means here? This is illustrated by considering if I asked the person uttering the sentence about what he means by the word. He would reply e.g. that it's a layer because the paint *is laid* upon the wall. I might ask him how this is done, and he would show or describe the practical process. I might ask further if, firstly, paint could be applied upon other things too, and secondly, if something other than paint could be applied on the wall, and if this would produce a layer—and I might get a positive answer. But taking this further into imaginative examples such as whether paint could be applied on top of e.g. numbers or feelings, I would be greeted with odd looks because that wouldn't make sense—you only paint objects and with a substance that is in practice suitable for being applied as a layer. So I might enrich my description of *this particular use* of 'layer' with those restrictions, and furthermore, because of my criterion for this meaning (asking a painter) it is correct to further specify the description of this use of 'layer' with "something a painter might produce when painting a surface". The word 'layer' in this use is a *metaphor* referring to the praxis of applying a substance over a surface with some instrument. This is crucial, because the word 'layer' has other meanings with which this metaphor is not fully compliant, such as a layer of snow that has fallen and has not been laid by anybody. Although snow and paint in this sense can both be described as covering something or being laid upon something, the practical processes related to how we understand snow falling and how we work to manipulate it are completely different. For example, unlike paint, we don't (usually) apply snow in a determined way and therefore decide how the layer is formed—snow falls and covers on its own, through phenomena that

PART II. COMMON MISCONCEPTIONS

we work to understand in terms of meteorology and physics. Thus, a layer of snow is something we rather witness and observe than ever plan to apply and thus would associate with questions such as choice of material or the method of application. Consider e.g. a child having just learned the word 'layer' anew strictly in the meaning of painting in the form "a painter layers paint on a wall" and didn't know any other uses. Then someone said to him: "When I was walking past the church I saw ice layered on its windows." The child might well ask: "Who put the ice on the windows?" and an answer "Nobody put it there" would surely not satisfy his confusion and curiosity, since he'd be looking for the painter of the ice until he learns a new use of the word. The same would apply if the child was replaced with an adult that didn't know the language and how ice is formed, for example as an uneducated foreigner who has lived in a country in which there's never ice.

Now, the word 'layer' has many derived uses in different abstractions and e.g. in architectural patterns because of its natural comprehensibility through the practical uses in contexts of e.g. painting, building and observing formations in nature, that are historical and thus deeply grounded in the evolution of language. Take as an example the Internet Protocol Suite that underlies the Internet as the communications protocol set and their architecture that the interconnected hardware routers and application software use for communication. The suite defines a hierarchical stack of abstraction layers and related network protocols, each of which operates on a particular layer. The various application software used in the Internet each communicate using the highest-level protocol on the stack, and the different levels of the protocol architecture, supported by the operating system, translate the messages ultimately into small packets compliant with the low-level protocol, and only these are communicated between the underlying hardware routers. The messages are routed in various ways to the target computer identified by its network address, and once they reach there, the protocol stack builds them back up into messages understood by the application software. Now, there exists *no technical necessity* behind this layered architecture, apart from just the need to separate the different technical features of message transmission related to the nature of the Internet as a dynamic network, but the layered design has been chosen because of the easy conceptual comprehensibility of layers. Consider someone not already familiar with the word 'layer' learning the functionality of the Internet Protocol Suite and finding this in the protocol specification. What does he have to know about layers in order to correctly understand what he is reading? A specification is a special device in the controlled technical production process to establish, among other thing, concepts. Therefore, unlike in natural language that consists of groups of people sharing a linguistic practice, the meaning of 'layer' in the context of the Internet Protocol Suite is how it is used in the specification, and this doesn't have to have anything to do with layers in other contexts apart from ease of understanding through association with a concept in natural language. The specification could have each occurrence of the word (wherever used in its particular specified meaning) swapped with an arbitrary word of choice with no caused change in the meaning, causing only a change in how the word will be associated and therefore an effect in readability. Because the concept of a protocol layer is derived from other common uses of 'layer' (such as layers of snow, layers of paint etc.), it will probably ease the understanding of the concept (to "get the picture of it") to be familiar with some other uses because those uses provide one with a metaphor and an associated image of something being layered over something else.

Now, there lies a fundamental *danger*—causing conflicts, inequality, persecution, death and war at the very least—in the very natural phenomenon related to natural language of taking the analogy between particular uses of the same word to denote that the word to refers to the same object, idea or 'nature'—in this example, "the idea of the layer" or "the nature of layers/layerness". As Wittgenstein brought out, the way of conducting philosophy through searching for such common objects is a fundamental misconception that leads into complete darkness. He used the concept of *family resemblance* to illustrate the similarities between different uses of a word, and I suggested that "the spirit" or "the idea" of a concept is a reference to the common features of all the practices that the word is associated with. The logical error in metaphysical thought can be cleanly described with set theory: imagine these family similarities and dissimilarities as a set of partially overlapping meanings (uses, praxes). Metaphysical thought would like to take the idea of a word as the *union* of these meanings, whereas the correct way is to take *intersections*: there can be multiple intersections, and each of these intersections would translate to a separate idea. If you think about the layer example, there are various uses of 'layer' that reflect how something is laid upon something else, and whatever is common to these uses would translate to one idea of layer… but then there are uses in which the word functions like a technical design principle, and such uses would have something in common which would also translate to an idea. But this is just to make sense of *what we should expect* when somebody talks about the idea of a word or concept; I don't recommend such an approach to words at all but want to be charitable and understand when somebody is talking to me this way. If this 'idea' of a word is taken in said incorrect way, it will be impossible for him to understand an alternative conception without endangering his whole model of language, and although he might yield to accept alternative conceptions, he will not be open to understand them and will probably distance himself from them by deeming them inferior. The experience of a rational or logical necessity in this illusion is created solely by the apprehended false model of language: the word *must* mean what the subject believes it to mean, or else, subjectively, a whole system of meaning will collapse. This quasi-philosophical use of 'must' within science has been rightly condemned by many Wittgensteinian academic philosophers. There shall be no use of force in philosophy, and wherever people use force in order to convince people, they use it as the last resort in a sorry act of existential despair—trying to protect their own world-picture from a destruction that is evident, since an act of force is already found necessary.

II-5. Religious Language

Religious claims are probably the best example of why metaphysics is a self-destructive way of thought. As an example, consider the claim "God lives in heaven", which, I believe, has a concrete origin yet has a contemporarily symbolical meaning. This is similar to how the Church supported Aristotelian geocentricity before Galileo, which makes sense, because Christianity concentrates on the subjective self where the (both geometrical and spiritual) origin is inside the self—one's soul and connection to God—as opposed to it being in the Sun like e.g. the Egyptians (Ra) or the Japanese (Amaterasu) would believe. Now, one might think that balloons, blimps, aeroplanes and such would demolish Christianity by allowing humans to venture into the skies to find nothing; to conclude the falsity of the theory that God lives in heaven and then to move on. But how come Christians *still* believe in heaven? Obviously it means that even the original Christian meaning of 'heaven', whatever it was, was different from a sensory meaning. But from the metaphysical perspective, this creates a contradiction: it can't be at the same time true and false that God lives in heaven, so the metaphysicist will deny that God lives in heaven and be fundamentally baffled by his inability to convince any Christians with his arguments. He would personally like to feel that the problem has been solved in the name of reason—due to the contradiction being a logical contradiction—but what will he do when he meets people who reason differently? A common solution seems to be to go on indefinitely arguing against this perceived false reasoning, instead of approaching the issue with philosophical, reflective thought that targets the underlying concepts.

Although they inhabit different realms in life, the closest equivalent to religious claims are *mathematical* claims. And I don't think mathematical formulas, practices or, say, shapes, have anything to do with religion, but they are both realms of full *abstraction*. So often one hears the sceptical question about religion: "Why should I believe anything I don't see?", to which I proffer a rather obvious counterargument: "Why do you believe in numbers?", which generally leads to a squirming dismissal. Indeed, mathematics was a religious concept to the great minds of antiquity such as Pythagoras, Plato and Aristotle, not only in terms of beauty, but also in the sense that the abstract space of concepts equals reality and that in order to reach for this reality one needs to reach for it in one's mind and soul using one's intelligence; one's conceptual capability. Whatever was discovered using the conceptual capability of the mind was considered real, and whatever was reached using one's senses was of lesser importance, imperfect, changing and fallible. This is not the same as Christian theology but it shares the same approach where both connection with God and sin are considered personal and private matters only to be touched via the private, personal methodology of prayer, religious contemplation and confession. Religious concepts describe the subjective in an ethical sense; concepts such as 'humility', 'guilt', 'shame', 'pride', 'righteousness', 'truthfulness'… these are concepts for which we have no external criterion, yet they relate to distinguishable forms of human behaviour and related subjective emotions. They are concepts that describe what happens completely unseen within a subject, and therefore they are most distanced from external criteria, in a way that is analogous to the role of mathematics within science as the field of pure abstraction. Then again, the whole of Western science is the child of Christian theology, and the role of mathematics is a sort of a back-bone and basis upon which every field or rigorous science has been built, which would parallel our Western society being built upon the basis of Christian social order and core beliefs. The said quality of religious claims (such as "God in heaven") being unaffected by empirical observations applies equally to mathematical claims; neither types of claims are empirical claims but their truth or falsity is derived from outside of the senses and what we see is just the concepts. Both mathematics and religion involve a body of basic assumptions that makes discussion meaningful using the basic expressions within the realm of language. In mathematics these are called number systems and in religion they could be called core beliefs—in religion everything is always susceptible to interpretation but there more or less exists a body of claims that are not questioned but accepted as fundamentals that have been *proven*. In mathematics we have the mathematical proof, which is, more or less, a bag of differ-

II-5. RELIGIOUS LANGUAGE

ent methodologies, each logically proven not to contain error. These methodologies are used to proceed from certain mathematical expressions to other mathematical expressions and are called e.g. properties of number systems. The *proof* constitutes the foundations of the basic properties of our mathematical systems, such that, working with mathematical formulas, we can say for example, "With *this* you can do *this*" while making a transition from a particular mathematical expression to another, and by saying that you *can*, that it is possible, we mean that such a move is allowed within the system of numbers and expressions, by which we refer to the properties of the system that have been proven. But the methodology of proof is fundamentally different in the case of religion, as is the constitution of the set of core beliefs of any given religious system, which is susceptible to alteration with time and prone to disagreements over interpretation—something unrelated to the use of mathematical language. Proof in religion—any religion—essentially means a *test of faith*, and here it is implied that people are capable of expressing faith towards something that they in a general case *don't* have faith in. This rhetorical turn is identical to ideologies: things that are *ethically desirable* are said to exist (or that they must exist), and the whole rhetoric presupposes that in an empirical sense they *don't* exist... and this presupposition also makes it sensible to test faith. There are many kinds of tests with which faith can be tested: at least we can 1) test if the subject fully *understands* the matters of faith he is talking about or if he has understood them incorrectly—similar to school tests; we can 2) test if the subject knows what he is talking about but is *lying* about his faith in it; and we can 3) test if the faith is *strong* in the sense of personal commitment, or if the subject would give up his faith in the face of a temptation. Here we can see that understanding, honesty and strength are all subjective qualities that can't be derived from just looking at a person, nor can they be believed by simple testimony of personal experience, from, say, whether a person swears and attests that he has seen God, talked with him, and so on. Such reports don't affect the credibility of religious claims despite the numbers of people disposed to report them due to their powerful experiences in the realm of the deep and personal. Externally testing the seriousness and personal *commitment* of asserted claims is traditionally involved

PART II. COMMON MISCONCEPTIONS

in, for example, the various institutions of dowry and male initiation rites, and these are performed by the *institution* that exists to validate the commitment, such as the male warrior group sending the initiate to take a test of courage to prove his capability to take part in battle. Similarly, various tests of school students, and the related monetary investments, can be interpreted as a test of the commitment of parents to the interests of their children. In Kurosawa's movie *The Seven Samurai*, the villagers were hiring *ronin* to work for them, and the related test was that they were invited to a hut and there was a man hiding behind the door who would bash them over the head with a club—no real samurai would value his work prospects above his *Bushido* code of intelligent courage and follow an unknown person into a trap. So, all in all, *proof in the subjective sense is a test of one's commitment to the ideals of the related institution*, and these will be performed by the institution as an acceptance rite.

But in a particular sense it can be said that mathematical language is subject to interpretation: consider the ultimate example *1+1=2*. Now, the symbols used in this expression can each mean many things; that is, as many things as we have constructed systems to interpret them. And considering mathematical systems, it seems to *make sense* only with the interpretation of a particular arithmetical system—or probably a few different systems—but essentially, there exist countless practical human-built notational systems that employ the same symbols (1, 2, +, =) but in which the example doesn't make any sense. This is to say that whenever one applies the mathematical language—expresses that *1+1=2*—this expression in itself already holds a commitment to a particular system of interpretation, which the listener will have to be familiar with in order to understand what is being said. As with the Wittgensteinian idea of family resemblance, which applies to the whole of language, we can imagine the mathematical expression as, say, a set of cards that belongs to a particular deck of cards, and that altogether there are myriad variants of those decks of cards, each of these decks specifically constructed by some mathematician. And they are printed indefinitely and put into circulation, and each deck holds cards that look exactly the same as the cards in another deck, cards that look a lot like the other cards but just a bit different, and cards that are completely unique to the particular set. And essentially, it is meaningless to play with different sets as the players will simply be confused about the game that is being played. It is not as if there would be any danger of confusion in the study of mathematics about the language that is being used, but this is just to point out the role of mathematics *as a language*. Firstly, in order to use it there needs to be an understanding between parties about the language that is being used, and the mathematical symbols don't in themselves carry this quality; and secondly, as a language, mathematical expressions are meaningless unless applied in the context of human action, such as "I wonder how much money I need to invest in order to host all these wedding guests?", or a context where one is applying them e.g. to show something or to prove something.

Now, if someone wanted to compare the *credibility* of mathematical and religious claims, instead of promoting mathematical claims as infallible, he would instead do so by applying these languages to real-life problems. Let's take the aforementioned context of wedding planning: the wedding planner aims towards a successful wedding, and depending on his personality he might be inclined to calculate the number of guests against the estimated prices of necessary products and services, or he might, say, be inclined to just "go with his heart" without any exact numbers, justifying his *way* of doing it with the teachings of his religion. This might be a slightly ironical example, as both options can easily be seen to be fallible, and the passionate defendant of mathematics would probably like to say that mathematics is fundamentally not like that: if you take the expression *1+1=2*, the result will hold true no matter what the context is. And while saying this, he might not notice that his religious opponent would use the exact same words and would equally passionately promote his religious approach to *every context* and potential application imaginable. He might wish to say that it is *true* and an *unconditional truth* that *1+1=2*, which will equally be repeated by the religious person regarding questions of his faith—the unconditional nature of both religious and mathematical claims follows from their lack of empirical connection. Now, one could expect

PART II. COMMON MISCONCEPTIONS

some difference to be found in mathematical and religious claims in terms of what it means to *understand* them, and, as a question regarding meaning, we ask for the criterion: how do we know that a person actually knows and understands what he is subscribing to? Well, in the case of both mathematics and religion, this is achieved by *peer evaluation*.[131] In the case of mathematics, the higher the level of mathematics, the more skilled the peers required to evaluate the work of another. For example, the eccentric Russian mathematician Grigori Perelman was awarded (and rejected) prestigious prizes for being the first to solve something called the Poincaré conjecture. It took his peers two years to confirm his results; to be able to jointly conclude that what he produced is to be considered a proof of the conjecture, after which it is justly promoted to the status of theorem. And this essentially means that after this collaborative conclusion the theorem can be trusted and built on. Until that point it was something that seemed highly trustworthy but that was to be methodologically doubted. So, despite the willingness to describe the nature of mathematics as unquestionable and absolute, the process of coming to mathematical truth is hardly best described as a *clear* process that contrasts with the unclear religious truth, as it is produced via a complicated process by enlightened scholars. In the case of Christianity, the Christian variant of proof—testimony—means describing how one became a Christian, and thus subjecting the event to the scrutiny of the community and masters; allowing them to reflect on the event and the person's description of the event against related traditional wisdom. This would be something not expected from normal churchgoers but from those who wish to have a career in the church and to dedicate their lives to the study of God. In many religions, and also in forms of Christianity, to avoid variance in interpretation and thus to impose harmony and unity, this process is ritualized into e.g. ceremonies involving recital of ancient texts, that are interpreted to symbolize understanding of the ancient traditional wisdoms and moral truths that are seen as essential. To

---

131 If the distinguished reader is under the impression that one is able to somehow deduce and know for certain that somebody has grasped a mathematical rule, I would like to direct him to Wittgenstein's writings about *rule following*; for example *Philosophical Investigations* §54 and §201-202, and the *Blue Book* (Blackwell) p.13 example about squaring cardinal numbers.

II-5. RELIGIOUS LANGUAGE

compare with said mathematical proof, the respective collaborative process that yields religious proof has been the step that brings the respective community over the phase of doubt into a phase of belief; the step that casts away all doubt. And in the case of religions—say, Christianity, Islam and Buddhism—this is constituted by the legend of the prophet: the testimony of the collective that is passed on as tradition; in Christianity, the communion. The role of this can be seen by presenting the following question. Considering that *I don't know* if Jesus existed or if he ever did what I have been told he did; *if* Jesus never did exist, that would essentially mean that all these Christians, churches, holy events, psalms, hymns and such would exist *accidentally* or in some sort of error or a result of some evil mischief that all those people were unable to register.[132] It means they exist for *no real reason*. Now, which one is the more credible explanation: that all these millions of things exist for no reason, or that *you* just don't have the insight to see the reason? Where the need for a religion emanates from is *reason* not *cause*; it is primary for people to have a reason they believe in and only secondary to understand causes and effects and to have understanding of what it was that particularly caused this and that—what they need to deal with is their real life, their sentiments and their decisions, and for this purpose reason is a fundamental requirement. Atheists often argue that all religion is just the result of somebody's calculated evil mischief, such as the will to dominate, but they don't intellectually follow the claim in explaining how one would achieve the feat of getting everybody to believe in the religion and pass onto their children something that is essentially a lie. For example, the will to dominate is a fundamental human quality with likely positive and negative aspects to it; its presence by itself doesn't devalue religion. On the contrary, where religion has been eliminated e.g. in communist transitions, the same human quality has been present stronger than ever and the results have been more chaotic. So, the idea that religion is mischief seems to boil down to a vague suspicion that a person carries because

---

132 I stumbled upon a funny caricature of atheism: "Atheism—the belief that there was nothing and nothing happened to nothing and then nothing magically exploded for no reason, creating everything and then a bunch of everything magically rearranged itself for no reason whatsoever into self-replicating bits which then turned into dinosaurs. Makes perfect sense."

he fundamentally doesn't accept religion and must somehow try to intellectually justify his rejection. Then again, why wouldn't it be this way, because throughout human history religion has always existed but the right to follow any religion is a modern invention, and because religion has always existed, it is correct to say that *Homo sapiens* is a religious creature; it organizes its communal existence around religious concepts and behaviour that impose group harmony. If you want freedom from religion, just as you might like to have freedom from your parents, you have it already in this modern society, but you don't need to try to intellectually deny religion any more than you need to denounce your parents to gain freedom from them. Atheists often liken religions to closed cults or sects that are typically relatively short-lived and in which free thought is actively suppressed and doubters violently disowned, whereas all religions build rather heavily on promoting personal, communal, active and continuous interpretation of moral questions against the exemplary divine path laid down by the holy prophet—even Islam, which is perhaps more culturally inclined to restrictions by *modern* comparison, can easily be argued to promote this on the level of scripture. And the case is essentially the same for anybody in mathematics: anybody is welcome to learn higher mathematics and the path of a mathematician, but without the required wisdom *and* fellowship, one has no business to venture into e.g. questioning proofs of conjectures presented by fellow mathematicians, which is something that happens every now and then; for example something called the Jacobian conjecture has a history of multiple presented proofs, each of the proofs later refuted by a fellow mathematician by showing a related error. To be accurate, our whole concept of *study* is derived from Christian theology; to study anything at all used to mean to study the ways of God, or the gods, as far back as when this activity first started. And to look beyond Christianity, let's take an example from studying, say, the art of weapon-smithing, which would mean studying how to make weapons in such a way that they maximize your potential to gain victory in battle. The idea of being a victor or conqueror would be synonymous with being the gods' favourite, so, to strive to make weapons that bring victory means to serve the gods' favourite in battle, and to study this art would mean to study how to best

II-5. RELIGIOUS LANGUAGE

serve the gods' favourite in battle. Why would studying mean something different these days and why would religion somehow mean suppression of free thought? That is a regressed idea arising from a confused mind.

The similar status of religious and mathematical claims is, of course, strictly related to their criterion as they lack external reference: the concept of, say, *a number* doesn't refer to anything sensory, nor is it derived via abstraction from anything we normally experience. Yet, both the language or religion and the language of mathematics speak of e.g. existence, truth and proof, all of which are concepts that have a meaning *also* in an empirical sense; that is, a completely different meaning. Existence, in this non-empirical sense, means *attribution* (or ascription), and to be honest I find myself wanting to say that these are completely different processes in mathematics and religion, but am baffled. Consider the following in mathematics.

1) Take the concept of the square of a negative integer, which yields a positive (natural) number; say, to do x times backwards taking x steps back, $(-x)*(-x)=(-x)^2$, equals taking $y=x^2$ steps forward. Consider this a *logical idea* with a particular *sense* that we can grasp and that the example of taking steps forward or backward illustrates—there is a particular point to saying that the negation of negation is positive, and nothing that restricts us from thinking of negation in some wholly different way and thus having a different meaning.

2) Inverting the idea, we'll say that if we just took y steps, this can always be presented using *either* 1) the model of doing x times taking x steps, *or* 2) the model of doing x times "taking x steps backwards", backwards. And this is because of the forward/backward metaphor of negation: in the context of turning one's back it makes no difference regarding the outcome if we turn our backs twice or if we don't. We denote this with $x = \pm\sqrt{y}$.

3) Let's ask: what if we just took y steps *backwards*, what is this equivalent to, in said terms of square root? We will reply that it is *meaningless*, which is to say that $\sqrt{y}$ is undefined for $y<0$; it was in our idea of squaring that squares are positive.

PART II. COMMON MISCONCEPTIONS

4) Be that as it may, but as an example consider the action of *pounding* as a means of impacting force via striking. Pounding a nail with any object will impact some force on it, right? Now, is it *imaginable* to *pound* something and to impact *zero* or *negative* force?—Yes, but you would have to pound with something that is not an object—let's call it an immaterial object: imagine pounding a nail with all your force, using an object that somehow sucks the nail out with every hit relative to the power of the hit, because it is impacting negative force when we pound with it. A tool like this is an object that of course doesn't exist. Now let's ask likewise: what if we take the said *idea* of a square root and forget that we are counting steps or even the idea that we are using it to apply to anything real... now, can we *imagine* a negative square?—Likewise, yes, but that will have to be the square of something that doesn't exist; something that is not a number. Essentially, the word *idea* here—the idea of pounding and the idea of a square—means the *practice* that we associate with the concept; such as how we can imagine pounding as an action and disregard the object used.

5) Thus, of course, the motivation for a definition of a *complex number*, which consists of a real part and an 'imaginary' part i, such that $i^2=-1$, and with which one can perform calculations that involve negative squares. And this is because it is the practice and the result that matters, not whether the grammatical object we are using is a reference to anything that exists.

What happened here was an extension of the definition and sense of the applied concept; an abstraction of the concept of squaring to involve also numbers that are not 'real', namely complex numbers. And we can do it because we can *imagine* it, because of the *logic* of the concept of squaring that *appears* to us after we have become familiar with its *practice*, and likewise with the example of imaginary pounding. Now, turn from our example to the concept of *seeing*, used in a religious sense: it is an extension and a metaphor from the practice of seeing; let's just call it doing whatever sensory seeing is, only something that is performed without senses. What is left is the practice of seeing and a result of something happening which we can evaluate in terms of whether it's good or bad, but the object of seeing is missing.

II-5. RELIGIOUS LANGUAGE

Fair enough?—If you are baffled by how this works, you should read again the example of complex numbers, and understand that these are real, non-imaginary mathematical tools that yield real results, but just contain things that are imaginary and not real. But then there is this character, an evolutionary biologist by training, who will listen to what you've explained and tell you, in the name of Science[133]: "That just proves that you're hallucinating. Non-sensory seeing cannot be seeing at all, since there is no evidence of anything to be seen." The serious mathematician is already confused and searching for his Fields Medal for a reality check, but I have the sense of humour to point out that my parallel to mathematics here should show that if the quote was true, then it would also be true that complex numbers are dangerous and mathematicians are hallucinating lunatics, which, no doubt, could also be argued with the help of a psychiatric perspective on some individual mathematicians.[134] But I rather suggest that we should understand that fear, and the ascription of danger, is a healthy primitive reaction towards everything that one doesn't know or understand.

But what actually happens when we reinvent meaning based on practice, such as in the case of extending the concept of seeing to a non-sensory meaning? I suggest that this move is the basis of all *metaphoric* or *symbolic* use of language: the ability to see *practical similarity*; to grasp an idea through familiarity with its practice. I will explain the birth of symbolical language in steps of examples.

1) Consider the concept of a *helmet*. Let's try and describe the idea of a helmet: a pot-shaped object worn on the head to protect... and so on—I just want to exemplify that there is no 'true' definition or de-

[133] Richard Dawkins was widely reported to have said that fairy tales and Christmas can be harmful to children, but he later came out with a bold defence against his own thought. He said that he had been worried about fairy tales imposing supernaturalism on children, and that he is "now thinking that they probably don't" and that "[i]t could even be the reverse". He also said *he genuinely doesn't know* if stories damage children's critical thinking. I personally would suggest that the famous critic should not express his concerns in public if he doesn't know if they are legitimately grounded concerns or fantasies. (Weaver, M. 'You can call me a big bad wolf but not a bore, says Richard Dawkins', *The Guardian*, 5.6.2014).

[134] The movie *One Flew over the Cuckoo's Nest* contains a delightful scene where escaped closed ward mental patients are successfully presented as famous professors, based on their external appearance.

scription; just some perspectives or approaches to description—but with a Wittgensteinian mind, you should already know this. Now the question: do you understand what it means to use a helmet as a *bowl*? Or to use a bowl as a helmet? If you do, why? After all, bowls are not helmets at all. You can ask a 4-year-old girl, and you will find out that she will quite correctly *know how to use* a bowl as a helmet. Give her a punch bowl and ask her to show how it can be used as a helmet, and she will gladly show you what it means to use a bowl as a helmet. Now, do you know how to use a lighter as a bottle-opener? Fair enough, but do you know how to use books as shoes? (Tip: you might need scissors, rope or some adhesive.) We use this sort of language because of the practice associated with objects, and it is the wonder of children's creativity to be particularly smart with this sort of language.

2) Continuing in the same line of examples, do you know what I mean if I say that children are little monkeys? Please answer: "I might know what you mean", but please ask me to clarify, and I will say that I meant that they are playful and practical little monkeys, and not for example stupid little monkeys. This clarification is the answer to the question: In what features do you find children *resembling* monkeys? And if you find in your heart this certain lightness to use language in such figurative, non-concrete manner, you can agree with me, and we will have successfully communicated a feature of children via the metaphor of little monkey. The lightness is required because of the unpredictability of *subjectivity*: if you agree to understand me, you will also have to accept that you will never have criteria for showing that you actually *did* understand me, and as there is no criterion for correctness, there is also a risk of looking stupid via using expressions that cannot be shown to be true via objective standards. You will have to step into the uncertain waters of subjective communication between two human beings, and that's why *I* was *asking* you to understand me, if you will. I was not expecting you to attest what I said; nor did I expect what I said to be self-evident. Also, it should be noted that it is a (subjective) *choice* to see children as little monkeys; and, expressed, it is an *opinion*.

3) To emphasize the subjectivity, let me ask if you understand me if

II-5. RELIGIOUS LANGUAGE

I say that marriage is a prison? Or do you understand that children can be a burden? Or do you understand that the police are pigs? We can notice several things here. Firstly, the word 'understand' becomes more difficult, as these things are usually said by signifying subscription via understanding, and, for example, understanding a criminal can be misunderstood for acceptance or subscription—one can denounce this by emphasizing: "I understand what you mean but I don't agree." Secondly, even though the subjective element is of the same degree here, we would call such examples "more opinionated", because we can identify them to be less widely subjectively shared.

4) The previous examples were about the use of metaphor to express subjective opinion over words that commonly have objective criteria. Now, do you follow if I say that art is a flow? Or that a woman is a distraction? And let's move a bit from the form of subject-predicate-object... what if somebody said: "No woman, no cry"? In this move, we can see that the grammar of the used concepts loses all its meaning, and what is left is simply the communication of something subjective, using words that otherwise are often communicated in an objective sense. And again, we have two aspects to such communication: we can either understand or not understand, and we can either agree or disagree with what is being said—we can be completely in support, completely in rejection, or have sympathies or doubts. Now, how do we know *if* we understand what is being presented? The answer is: because we have no criteria, we *don't*. We could ask: "What does this expression represent to you?", and we might get an answer, but if we would wish to apply the concept of *truth* to the answer, it will be used in a different way now. It is no longer possible to show that it is true by some objective standards, but only to *attest* truth.

5) Finally, we come to examples like: "People are primarily good", or, as I was once very tenderly and passionately asked: "Is every person innocent?" This sort of language is not uncommon at all, but we should recognize that we are in utterly senseless waters in Wittgensteinian terms (the favourite waters of public orators); senseless because of the *complete subjectivity* of expression and complete possibilities for one person to agree completely or another to disagree

completely, with nobody ultimately possessing a criterion to tell who is right from who is wrong. And Wittgenstein would not mean senselessness in the sense of lack of importance or interest. His judgment was for no other reason than to dispel the illusion of sensibility that is *based on grammar*; that such subjective sentences would be sensible in the manner that objective sentences are because they share the grammatical form. He would say: "Very well, what you are saying might have a meaning, but it is your job to give it; thus, I am compelled, at this stage, to dismiss it as senseless." He wanted to stress the very essential truth that *it is an error to take grammar to convey sense*; an error that takes one into perilous, dark waters.

An artist is, in his profession and role, free to touch our feelings with expression that is essentially senseless, such as putting arbitrary words together, inventing new words, turning them backwards, mixing and blending words together, creating geometrical (or, say, geological) formations of words ... and so on. But the reason why it is generally the job for the speaker, and not the listener, to produce sense is that, from the perspective of the listener, such sentences might be of two kinds: 1) they might contain subjective commitments that the listener is unaware of, or 2) they might simply be erroneous, such as containing self-contradicting beliefs, logical errors, faulty observations, be poorly explained, be hasty generalizations... there are all sorts of ways to describe *how* one is *not* making sense, if one wishes to do that. But essentially, they *might also* be of the first case and to contain *subjective commitments*, an example of which is that one is expressing something that would be obvious if the listener shared some related subjective experience. For example a speaker might insist that "There is a *letter A* behind the building", which would sound like a category error and a completely insane claim, but could be clarified by pointing out that somebody had indeed erected a commercial sign of the shape of the letter A behind the building and it was being referenced by the speaker, only the listener had not seen it and it didn't occur to the speaker to clarify this deviance from an obvious linguistic norm. In this case a very reasonable way of coming to understand what is being said would be to simply ask for more clarification, and we might describe it e.g. that the claim sounded senseless but the speaker had a point and had a capability for sensible speech. Now, having first presented a case of subjective commitment that is clarifiable by observation, we come to the ultimate example of sensible subjective commitment, the one in which the *subjective commitment is the product of tradition*. Consider again the example of 'letter A' being reported to be found behind the building, with the exception that now it is not found behind the building:

– *The letter A is right here in front of us.*
– *I can't see it.*
– *I didn't mean a letter A that could be seen but one that can be sensed.*
– *I can't sense it.*
– *I didn't mean that you could sense it with your eyes or ears.*
– *How can you sense it, then?*
– *Ok... do you know how to latifah?*
– *No.*
– *Ok, how to start then... do you know how to ginx your phasma before going to latifah?*
– *No.*
– *...*

Here I introduced some gibberish to exemplify references to traditional wisdom in terms of subjective *skill*. Any crafts and arts behave this way in terms of language and have been maintained by guilds and institutions; examples could be smithing, bricklaying, mathematics, programming... but also arts such as fortune-telling, dowsing, "the force" in Star Wars and so on. Essentially, the listener doesn't possess the subjective skill required to evaluate what is being said, and I believe this is all that can be said about the language in such a situation: it will be up to the listener to choose to *trust* or not to. Typically, what is required in matters of craft is a portrayal and proof of skill and competence, and because of the required trust, this is also an opportunity for abuse of this trust. Fortune-tellers and e.g. Greek sophists were both 1) hired for money and 2) itinerant in lifestyle, which made them highly dubious professions, as any smart person will understand that such an itinerant character would easily be able to feign or fabricate the required proof

PART II. COMMON MISCONCEPTIONS

and thus gain the trust required for a relatively short-lived transaction of consultation for money. There is the very legitimate question of why such a person chooses not to settle; why does he take quick money for his services instead of the indirect yet higher wealth of good name and respect of society? Illusionists seek to change place because the nature of enchantment is momentary, and once it vanishes, the artist—like Mozart's Don Giovanni—will be chased furiously by disillusioned victims, who, on the other hand, will be sufficiently cooled in their anger at the time of the next visit not to pose too much danger. Thus, Greek philosophy grew as a stationary *guild of wisdom*—alongside organized religion—that actively condemned the said signs of con artistry. All in all, this example should point out that *the higher the proportion of subjectivity in what is being presented, the higher the related trust required and the greater the danger of abuse*. Objective standards, on the other hand, provide the security of authority, and high objectivity is completely analogous to the prevalence of guards in a city: it provides security as long as the guards are fulfilling their duty. But the atmosphere of full reliance on those guards will enable the misuse of their position in terms of organized crime, just as full institutional reliance on objective standards soon causes those standards to develop into something untrue that will be enforced upon the people whom the standards were originally devised to protect and serve (this, to a great extent, is the current status of the policies of the UN and EU). So, contrasting a tradition of full subjectivity to a tradition of full objectivity, the wisdom and truth are passed on from one subject to another, with the scholarly model or the model of master and apprentice: a responsible master, in possession of valuable wisdom (subjective knowledge), passes his wisdom on to the next generation, trying his best to oversee the truthful conservation of this wisdom. And this model is based on a relationship of trust between the individual subjects participating in the tradition.

So, as I wanted to point out with this approach, the obvious example of *religion*, as traditional subjective wisdom, doesn't in this respect differ from any of our institutions of skill. I'll take my personal favourite, *programming*, as a point of reference to parallel certain institutional similarities between these arts. Religions involve the moral art of how to live correctly, and programming is the art of commanding machines, and—once again forgetting the metaphysical perspective of looking at words from the perspective of the objects they denote, and instead looking at *how language is used in an active community*—the similarity of the institutions can be surprising. Any religious person or a programmer will admit the following *ideals* about his institution.

• The institution can be described as both conserving and developing a fascinating, sacred and arcane *skill* (art), in which one is dealing with deep truths and an open, unforeseen end.

• It involves highly valuable knowledge in the form of absolute and unquestionable truths. Written expressions of the art are often called script or code. Code does not describe observable real-world phenomena but is of the nature of instructions and deals with abstract objects. The instructions relate to the *subjective skill* the institution maintains and develops; they answer to the question: *how* to do it (how to live; how to make the machine perform tasks).

• Participation in the related practices is generally found both intellectually and spiritually rewarding. But the foundational truths are to be discovered by pioneers and to be passed on to later generations by scholars. Truths require proof, which involves practices that are beyond simple participation in institutional practices.

• The most important discoveries become holy principles and paradigms to be acknowledged as best practices. They are assimilated by at least the great majority of the community, and they can have a far-reaching influence but can also be replaced in popularity or made completely obsolete by new discoveries.

• The greatest pioneers are considered geniuses or visionaries, and characterized by child-like creativity, technical command and hands-on field involvement.

• Participation and membership are voluntary, and respect and rank are based on proven skill.

• Any and all of these ideals can be compromised in a rotten commu-

PART II. COMMON MISCONCEPTIONS

nity, and it is not difficult to find examples where this has happened. The central dissimilarity is that religions are *moral* and involve the skill of how to live and how to behave, whereas programming—as with the majority of institutions overall—deals with the skill of using objects to some valuable purpose. But with the base argument of the importance of the institutions of subjective skill, we will firmly snub any attempt to disqualify symbolical languages based on the fact that they don't refer to anything sensory. Rather we will feel justly fascinated unearthing *evidence* of essentially the same human practices from, say, 5000 years ago in cuneiform script or Egyptian hieroglyphs, and we will be fascinated because we won't think that these people must have been out of their minds producing such language, but instead feel genuine wonderment over what they might possibly have meant by it. Generally, whenever somebody is asking for evidence, he is asking for intellectual support over a presented claim—unfortunately there is a misinformed yet popular pseudo-naturalist neo-Cartesian tendency to treat the word as if it meant an external observation, like some sensory particle that is fed into our mechanistic system via receptors for further processing.

We have now established the nature of religious linguistic expressions as non-sensory and abstract, traditional and institutional—as with e.g. mathematics or programming—and that such expressions convey wisdom in the form of the subjective skill of living. I believe that anybody who understands this much about these expressions will admit that they make sense, in terms of understanding the *motive* for expressing such, whether or not one is interested in further understanding such matters. Understanding the nature of religion as a traditional *vessel of subjective skill*, carrying the skill between individuals *from one individual to another*, one can also understand the general form of its practice and institution all around the world, which implies a scholarly role of an elder passing on his wisdom to pupils. I am particularly trying to explain this to my stubborn atheist friend who is confused and stuck with the method of hypothetical thought and has been brought to believe that knowledge is *information* and therefore belief or faith is

II-5. RELIGIOUS LANGUAGE

unnecessary. The tradition of skill involved in religion needs to be understood in juxtaposition against *symbolizing, signifying* or *representing* the skill for a mass of people: religion utilizes symbolic expression, but it itself *is* not a *token* or *symbol* of something. It is a *living* tradition that you can't invent and bring into existence by imagining it in your mind, which is exactly the function of symbols and signs: means of expressing something. An example: when Judas betrays Jesus to the soldiers with a kiss, the kiss is obviously symbolic; the symbolic meaning is open to interpretation (I believe it is the symbol of superficial love, but my opinion doesn't matter here). However, what is not open to interpretation is that it *is* a symbol of something. And that the symbol exists in tradition and culture makes it available for reference and reuse, as Coppola did in *Godfather part II*. There is *something* existential and human that is being conveyed with the symbolic expression of religion, if you miss the meaning of these expressions in an existing language, then it is more appropriate to say you are illiterate regarding that language instead than to say the language means nothing. I mean if you don't understand what expressions in an existing language mean *if* whatever religion conveys *could* be passed on without tradition, it wouldn't be subjective, it wouldn't be a skill, and you wouldn't need to change or involve yourself in order to understand it; and if no things existed that require subjective change, no things should be called subjective opinions, and *you* wouldn't be a unique subject. And this is not a proof of the necessity of religion from its existence, but the proof of the necessity of the existence of various subjective traditions, given that it is sensible to speak of such a thing as subjectivity in the first place. A typical hostile atheist might also say "So what?"; that my analysis of religion is a truism, that all I did was mouth of an empty explanation about how a particular word is used about a set of practices that happen to exist, and that doing this says essentially nothing about religion in the sense of whether it should or should not exist in the first place. First of all, this is to nullify the value of any analysis altogether, not just the analysis of religion, but secondly, my analysis says quite a lot not only about what religion is, but also about what is not a religion. For example, *atheism* is often presented as a religion, and from a particular perspective it can look like a religion, but from the perspective of subjective skill it most evidently is not: there is no skill involved in being atheist, and no skill being passed on in how to be correctly atheist. Furthermore, atheists can often be heard arguing that being religious is easy because one doesn't need to do anything to prove God, but just to say one believes in God... and this argument can now be thrown back at the atheists: it is rather the attitude of *not believing* that is *particularly easy* to announce, because there is no related community and no consequences for doing so. And a quick glance at the newspaper headlines on any day presents gives some good examples of things that are *announced as true* instead of untrue, and conveyed in statements by people who say things that they *believe to be true* instead of things that they don't believe to be true or believe to be untrue. On the subjective level the atheist error is of the nature that the simple act of cynical disbelief—an act with no social consequences in a secular society—is misunderstood as an objective justification, such as a rational or scientific proof. These objective frameworks can only justify but never prove, yet the atheist insists that he is convinced and has no doubt, whereas things have only been argued yet not proven beyond reasonable doubt. And here lies the idealistic nature of atheism; it is akin to an activist attack aimed at the institution of religion where the only thing one needs to do is to step out in public and repeat a slogan. Because of this idealistic nature of atheism, the same applies when comparing religion with any ideologies: the support of an ideology is not something in which one would be expected to have *learned* some subjective traditional wisdom, but instead, to be atheist, feminist, communist, humanist, etc., one needs to simply announce an attitude as something one feels is the correct attitude towards political matters. Looking at religion as an institutional vessel of abstract wisdom makes it very difficult to distinguish it from *cults* rather than ideologies. But one more thing worth noticing while assessing the status of religion as something conveyed by tradition is that it brings light to the fallacious juxtaposition of scientific knowledge against religion. The comparison is made sensible when one considers *traditional wisdom* (instead of *religion*) as the counterpart of *science*: *that* is what science has replaced. Science has replaced traditional wisdom because it is supposedly more reliable... but looking at today's science, it's hard

II-5. RELIGIOUS LANGUAGE

not to ask: Is it really?

We have now established the status of religious claims but said nothing about their meaning or how to approach the question of their meaning. The whole of religious language is symbolic, metaphoric and allegoric in nature, which completely voids any effort to use observational means. Now, first, let's establish that there exists symbolic communication that doesn't imply a religious context; I could use the previous programming example, but let's instead just say that "a doctoral dissertation is an armour, but a tenure is a horse". Now, what we can see is that there is a way to describe such a symbolic reference, but no way to establish its correctness; a horse has many typical connotations by reference to practice: you can ride a horse, but also, a horse is fast in comparison to moving by foot, it eats a lot (we say "eating like a horse" meaning eating a lot)... The key here is that in order to use such a symbolic expression, the speaker subject is already implying something that is expected to be shared with the listener subject: in this case, there is something about the nature of a dissertation and a tenure that is desired to be shared. It is not, like objective information, neutral as in being unrelated to its speaker, but carries along the subjective intent of its speaker. Thus, the sense of such an expression is that it carries a wish *not* to be understood by *everybody*, but only by select people, namely the people with *the subjective quality* to understand it: in order to understand it, one needs to *be* of a particular subjective quality. And this is to say that the expression is *discriminating* its addressees by nature. This indeed is a quality of symbolic expression and all religious expression: I commonly hear a comment against Christianity that Christians promote themselves above others—which is quite an apt description, as Christians speak of heaven and hell as places literally above and under the ground. 'Discrimination' can be a negative word, so let's first disassociate it from the sense of discrimination based on unchangeable things such as gender, ethnicity or heritage: when religious people discriminate in expression, they at the same time welcome in action. So, clearly such religious discrimination is not disapproval of people themselves, but *moral* discrimination that targets their ways of life. Generally, when Christians speak of heaven

PART II. COMMON MISCONCEPTIONS

and hell, they are not condemning people to hell, as what would be the point of such expression? What they are doing is telling people they are condemned *unless* they convert and change their ways, and they do this by using symbolic language that implies that it will only be understood after having converted into a subjective existence shared with the speaker. The language plays a crucial role: I don't see why a Buddhist couldn't understand the Christian concepts of heaven and hell, and particular concepts are essentially shared across many religions. The question is whether someone understands what he is speaking of when he talks about some people going to heaven and some people going to hell, which could be roughly described as the question of whether one understands that the personal choice of how one lives determines the highest outcomes in terms of happiness: the basis of morality, expressed in a symbolical way.

After the moral discourse of heaven and hell, the second integral component of a religion is the discourse of continuity between generations: something that binds our past generations to the current and future generations. On the level of institution, this is reflected by the ritual institutions related to birth, marriage and burial. On the level of discourse, the component that precedes the current generation is served by *legend*, and the component that succeeds the current is served by the concept of *afterlife*. I find it aptly summarized that the fatal necessity of the existence of God translates to the necessity of the existence of an intergenerational conceptual frame of reference for the survival of a conceptual social animal. Now, we know that *truth* is a very *profound* thing... when we say 'profound' we don't mean complexity or difficulty of the subject matter or the matter of expertise involved in order to deal with such matters; we don't call a skilled chess player or a mathematician profound. When saying 'profound' we are dealing with *historical* depth, and a profound man or a sage would be one with historical wisdom. We are dealing with depth that surpasses generations; the similarities and differences between us and our ancestors. It is a fundamentally fascinating feature how the preceding and succeeding realms come together in the concept of *truth*, namely, in the sense of truth as *unforgotten*—the afterlife of the future meets the legend of the past. Such a conception of truth could be called 'religious truth', but the concept doesn't differ from 'truth' as we commonly use it except in the sense that something supernatural is grammatically attributed. This sense of truth could be called truth as *test of time*: if we compare within science, say, Newtonian gravity and the string theory, we can see that gravity is truer, and this is because it is an older theory and thus has been subjected to more critique and more test for applicability. The same applies to, say, Christianity or Islam against Satanism or the flying spaghetti monster. But rather than calling something true because it is old, I find a nicer way to put it is that these beliefs are truer because they are *more remembered* and *less forgotten*. The flying spaghetti monster never had the chance to be either remembered or forgotten, so it doesn't compete on the same level. For something to be remembered requires somebody to have a reason to remember it.

As the first example of religious truth, I'll describe a story I recently read in the news. It was reported that in a village somewhere in the world a reincarnated boy had led the village elders to the grave of his murderer, and this was presented as proof of the afterlife. So, the *truth* about whether the boy was a reincarnation of a murdered boy was *empirically* shown by the fact that he led the elders to the grave of a murdered boy. But what sense does such an event make? Well, murder is something that has sentimental pressure to be forgotten: it is painful and frightening to a community and felt like a *senseless* event, and e.g. the mass killing fields of the Finnish Civil War became taboos and areas where children were restricted from going—unholy places. When such an event happens, the event is suppressed into the subconscious; something that is known to exist but that cannot be talked about; and, in a similar way as with psychological trauma, it is also something that is under constant pressure to pop up and needs to be *actively* denied and suppressed (the words 'pressure' and 'suppress' have a common base word). So, after suffering the suppression of a traumatic murder long enough, there is a subconscious wish for it to come out into the open, rather like the way murderers who are being pursued are sometimes seen to help their pursuers by leaving traces, as they subconsciously feel that they have committed an injustice, and that their

PART II. COMMON MISCONCEPTIONS

capture would be justice.[135] And there is no better figure to expose this problem than an *innocent* boy of the new generation: somebody who has not lived the trauma and is untouched by it; only he can *lead* the others to face the traumatic murder, because he will not be a traitor in the eyes of the group that together acted to suppress the bad memory. The elders must have helped the boy and quite literally guided his finger to point in the direction of the grave, but they couldn't say or do it themselves because they were a part of the event. The innocent boy was the most appropriate vessel to obtain salvation from the trauma, and the only thing required was to prove that he indeed was the murdered boy reincarnate. So, the grave of the murdered boy was known to everybody, but the *truth* that the boy was reincarnated brought absolution from the trauma of the murder, since it was shown that his death was not without meaning in the afterlife. The truth of the boy being a reincarnation—the truth of the afterlife—led to the remembering of what was forgotten. As the second example, I will describe the standard process of Christian *martyrdom*, using the Finnish legend of Saint Henry as example. According to the legend, Henry was a bishop in the times of the First Swedish Crusade (around the year 1150) who, while bringing the good Christian message to these barbaric lands, was axed to death by a peasant who was moved to commit a murderous frenzy by distrust, envy and a deceptive wife.[136] The Church retaliated by canonizing Henry, and the members of the next crusade to Finland carried the bones of Saint Henry as holy relics. Between the successful Second Crusade around 1250 that brought Finland under Swedish rule for 550 years and the Protestant Reformation, Henry's bones were actually stored in various churches around Finland as a reminder and object of worship.[137] But what were they a reminder of? —A reminder of the Christian truth of something that tends to be forgotten: that

---

135 This behavior is called *attention-seeking*, and can be witnessed in neglected toddlers and animals, too. A blatantly naughty act is committed in public, in order to attract attention to the perpetrator of the act.
136 This sort of stories are methodically Christian, re-enacting the violent crucifixion of Christ. The Gellért-hill in Budapest is named after the missionary Saint Gerard (Gellért) who met his end at the hands of thankless heathens, rolled down the hill in a barrel inlaid with spikes.
137 A speech delivered by Archbishop of Turku and Finland, Jukka Paarma, in Turku Cathedral on 19.1.2000, http://www.evl.fi/arkkipiispa/henrik.htm [26.12.2019].

your forefathers killed a holy man, just as our forefathers killed Christ. To worship Henry's bones would be to *remember* more clearly and concretely that the chaos of brutal murder could be just one hateful act away: the unspeakable murderer is not a raging lunatic with brain damage but your own fellow man, accidentally led on to the path of hatred; not one of the others but one of us; he could be you and you could be him. The truth about Christ means remembering that Christ was murdered: accepting the truth about Christ on Finnish soil means accepting what your fathers already remember, that, according to folk legend, a bishop was indeed murdered in these parts. And questioning the murder becomes increasingly difficult after one has been shown some bones, as one would need to mock the dead with such claims, further proving the peasant baseness that contrasts so starkly with the crusaders' noble message: "We bring you the truth that your fathers remember but wish to silence: a good man was murdered, and you did nothing but kept quiet about it. Look at yourselves: you're a bunch of shameful murderers! How can you live with yourselves? Now, where is there a free spot for us to build a first church?" And this is the basis of the Christian *social order*; we can justify and tolerate people with different possessions, ranks and lifestyles, but nobody can justify murder, and this is why murder is the theme that needs most emphasis, and hence the remains of murder victims used as holy relics and the most notorious murder device—the cross—as a holy symbol.

The question about the truth of religious claims is not verified by objective standards because they are not objective claims. It is verified by subjective standards; by the question of whether *you understand* what they mean. So, let's talk about *you*, the subject and the second person, and see if I understand you or if I am mistaken. Regarding, say, God, the question is not, and has never been, about whether God 'exists' or not... or, one could say this with the subjective sense of existence; whether God exists *for you* or not. It is a question of whether it *makes sense for you* to speak of God, or if it is the case (about *you*) that it doesn't make sense. And if it doesn't make sense for you, you are not helping anybody by trying to hide your subjective state of lack of understanding by trying to show some objective proof to sup-

PART II. COMMON MISCONCEPTIONS

port your view. For the sake of honesty, you should just admit that you don't understand what is actually meant when such a word is used. That you don't understand doesn't make you stupid: we haven't said anything at all about whether the related religious practices are valuable or not and if you *should* be interested in them in the first place; we have just said that you don't understand them and thus you don't consider such activities meaningful; as we would say: you don't find a place in your heart for such matters. And here is the subjective use of the verb 'find'—"Could you find time for these things?" or "Could you find it in your heart to forgive him?"—implying that one needs to make some subjective *effort* in order to understand. And, given that the matters are familiar to you and the charitable principle that you are a *rational* actor instead of an irrational lunatic, the fact *that* you don't understand shows that you don't *want* to understand, which implies you have a *reason not to* understand; that you are resisting the thought on a rational basis. You are *not* finding sympathy for these things because you have the right to and you are your own master—like Auda Abu Tayi in *Lawrence of Arabia*, you would find such a thing meaningful only if it was your own will and *pleasure*, and nobody is welcome in your territory to tell you what to think. And this means you would first need to see your own *benefit*. I believe this is as far as I can analyse the subjective question of religion: that one will not find understanding where one fails to see benefit. To get benefit one needs to admit need, and to obtain subjective benefit one needs to admit subjective need, and to admit subjective need is to admit subjective weakness. Enter the Christian concept of *sin*: the weakness in everybody. In this regard, religion is a community of admitting subjective weakness and need for support from others; hence the benefit from such community.

Finally, as linguistic analysis is the Swiss army knife of philosophical problems, it can also be applied to problems in religious rhetoric that remain equally problematic for generations. Such as the questions: 1) "Why does God allow a thing that He could prevent?" or 2) "Could Jesus microwave a burrito so it became so hot that He himself could not eat it?"[138] Take the first case; I have heard this desperate question in the

---
138 A variation of "the paradox of the stone" in the problematic of divine omnipo-

II-5. RELIGIOUS LANGUAGE

context of children in particular: Why does God, if he exists, allow innocent children to e.g. die or get sick, whereas he *could* prevent such things from happening? And let me first make some observations about the context of such a question itself: why this would be any more problematic in the case of children than in the case of adults, since, in this theoretical setting, it doesn't involve humans at all but only God? I also find it contradictory that a person who presents the question in a conditioned form ("...*if* God exists...") is asking the question in the first place. He has been told in the Bible that such a thing as God exists, and he seems to take *that* for granted, but proceeds to ask *if* God behaves in such-and-such way... Now, logically, if I told you of a book that reports a remote island in the Atlantic, in which there lives a species of animals that eats stones for food, would you tell me that either it is the case that the island exists or the case that it doesn't exist, and this depends on the fact of whether it is imaginable for an animal species to consume stones? What if the explorer who saw the stone-eating just mistook stone-like peanuts for stones, or what if the animal consumed stones in addition to some other food that was just not reported? Why are you looking to refute a whole narrative based on a detail? And most essentially: why do you think that the question of the existence of an island is dependent on whether animals can consume stones? The doubter would say: "I find it *difficult to believe* that such an island exists, *because* of such logical inconsistency", by which he means that the *story as a whole* is not credible, and as credibility is a subjective quality, what is meant is that the *people* who produced the story are not credible. Dismissing the whole narrative based on an uncertain detail is a common rhetorical tactic to denounce someone. If you parallel this to science, it would mean that you refuse to take presented reports as scientific results at all, but instead produced by *unethical* means regarding science: something presented as science but lacking skill, rigour or virtue required in science; that the results are produced in an *incompetent* manner not worthy of proper examination. If it indeed is the case that one feels this way about the Bible or Christians as a group, this xenophobic prejudice should be brought out for the sake of hones-

---

tence that is Medieval in origin. This variation is from an episode of *The Simpsons*.

ty instead of creating a public kangaroo court in which one toys around with notions that are isolated from their original context: "This God of yours... did he wear a pink hat? (The audience laughs)." So, for the sake of honesty: it is not the story that he finds incredible; it is the people with the state of mind to accept such a story, and that have produced such a story, that he finds suspicious and incredible... and the question about God is just as insincere as someone who says: "*If* I have done something wrong, I am sorry." Now, after this minor side-track, let's return to analyse the first question of why God allows things to happen that He could prevent, and particularly the word 'could'. *Your criterion for 'God' is the Bible*; where in the Bible does it say that God "could prevent things"? *If* you were a Christian and told me that God *does* exist—instead of saying that you are considering whether he exists or not—I might also ask for your *subjective opinion* about God: Why do *you* think God allows such a thing? But such a subjective question is obviously senseless if it is interrupted by the question of whether God exists in the first place; *that* God exists is a subjective condition for the sensibility to ask further questions about God. So, your criterion for God was from the Bible, but your criterion for whether God could prevent things is something else: your own interpretation or hearsay? In any case, the sense of 'God' is confused. And the same is the case with the second question: as in the Bible there is no mention of Jesus microwaving burritos, there is also no mention of God lifting stones. The idea of God doing such things is derived from the metaphysical thought that God, as a creator, must have all the other qualities such a being could be imagined to have; if one can create the Earth, one can also lift stones... but that at the same time would leave open just as many questions, such as why it seems to be the Lord's angels and not the Lord himself who move stones, for example rolling back the stone sealing Jesus' tomb. A metaphysical interpretation of the Bible is no less confused than such an interpretation of the objects of the mind. Another perspective to this question is to note that there is a use of the word 'could' that implies willingness: "Could you lift that stone?" is asked as a test of your strength, and refusing to lift the stone might be interpreted as a sign of weakness. So, if we ask the question of the omnipotence of God in terms of whether he 'could' do this or that, we are missing the

II-5. RELIGIOUS LANGUAGE

question of if he *would* do such things. You can ask a strong-looking man to lift stones if you believe he won't get too annoyed by your plea, but you don't ask a King to do such feats, and this is not because we believe that the King would be able to lift the stone, but because we'd think that the King is so smart, wise and divine that he would not bother with such lowly traits as muscular strength. In the Socratic sense, goodness and value translate to *usefulness*, and *the best* of all doesn't mean somebody who can perform every feat when asked (the perfect tool), but the one who is the most useful; in the sense of people, the one that is the most *capable*. The Greeks had many gods and it makes sense to note that the god of blacksmiths (Hephaestus) is the most capable blacksmith, and the man who asks the god of blacksmiths to "Paint my fence or you're not a god" is not just confused but obviously making a mockery of blacksmiths: he has yet to learn the basics of smithing but acts as if he is more knowledgeable about the expert matter than the best of blacksmiths who are the ones to hold their god the most dear. Socrates and Pistias the armourer agreed[139] that the best armour is said to weigh nothing at all, which doesn't translate to any particular material or physical quality of the armour but solely to the quality of not inconveniencing its wearer; that it greatly *enables* its wearer. Similarly, the Socratic conception of human value is based on enabling the State to make the best use of him: the best man has the most skills and the most capability such that the State is the most enabled to use him for whatever the best purpose is. And if we extend this Socratic sense of *capability as the criterion of value*, via the question of trying to imagine the theoretical extreme of Socratic capability that surpasses our known human limitations, we will firstly notice that capability is not action and we therefore should not be seeing any concrete actions, but secondly, that the most capable of us are ideally not used to perform any actions but to perform governance and guidance of others. We would like to see capable men guiding others and deciding the common questions for groups of men; we would like to see the best of all men sitting on the throne, not doing an awful lot in practice but deciding common questions for the population as a whole. And we would like to see one, better than all men, to be above the King, not

---

[139] *Xenophon*, Chapter X

doing anything at all but just having the King bow his head to him—just as the most important job for a coach is just to sit behind his player in a tournament to oversee his performance. By 'we' here I mean all reasonable people; if you think that monarchy means dictatorship and refusal to consider the questions of leadership and morality, you have been intentionally and effectively brainwashed. Thus, we have arrived from the Socratic conception of capability to our rather traditional Western Christianity. In conclusion to this piece of analysis I hope the reader has not got the impression that I believe "one is not allowed to ask questions about the divine", that I am trying to present the idea that as a general answer to religious questions one should just stop asking them. On the contrary, religion *is* a realm of subjective questions. But just as, within human communication, there are people who treat other people with contempt, there are questions being directed towards religion that are not only confused and anti-intellectual, but show *contempt* in *assuming* the *uselessness* of religion, and proceed to make a rhetorical mockery of it; questions that are not genuine but sarcastic in nature. It is exactly these questions that are *useless* and thus, according to Socrates, worthy of contempt. I am not assuming the value of religion, which I find very open to conversation and debate, but I am assuming its existence.

II-6. The Spiritual World

The spiritual world is born out of our linguistic subjective need; our need to exist in interaction with subjects. We have an intrinsic wish to love and be loved, but no one can just 'love', one can only love some*one*; no one can just 'follow' (in order to live meaningfully), one can only follow some*one*, and so on. This behaviour is primary and uniform to us humans and preoccupation with objective intellectual things is a secondary and less common trait. As all people experience emotions but some are more aware of themselves experiencing them than others, some people are also more given to spiritual causal explanations than others. The profound factor in play here is *trust*; trusting another person is an impossibility for some individuals yet a necessity for others, and this is related to how much control over one's *own* environment one wants. The capability to trust is a universal human trait, but incapability to trust is the general basis of different forms of neuroses that relate to the different ways the subject tries to console his lack of trust, and also certain other blocks for one reaching happiness, but then again naive trust very easily leads to trusting the goodwill of someone who actually doesn't have any goodwill. Trust is very closely connected to empathy and one's willingness to trust another is emotionally related to one's experience of emotionally understanding another. Thus, feigning emotions is a very commonplace method used by many people to substitute their incapability to trust another with seeking control over others through *their* trust. This is learned at a young age through the parental relationship, and on the level of society takes the elegant form of what may well be called 'social theatre'.

From an emotional point of view the problem of trust is a matter of whether the subject is capable of trusting another person at all, but from a practical point of view it is a matter of *whom to trust*, and reaching certainty in this matter requires both empathy and training in recognizing the motives of others from their behavioural patterns, which can occur fully subconsciously. In the context of philosophical thought the incapability to trust takes the form of what we call philosophical scepticism or agnosticism, and it is especially interesting to notice how dominantly this philosophical position is announced among scientists. The word 'scepticism' is used in a perfectly valid setting as an attitude targeting presented information, in a sentence like "I tend to read the news with a degree of scepticism" or "I am sceptical about the presented promises", and in this meaning the doubt targets the motives, truthfulness and accountability of the subjective party presenting some information. But this sort of philosophical scepticism (universal doubt) should correctly be seen as *incapability to trust* since because of its universal nature we have not control over it, albeit that most of the announced sceptics would probably see their position as being a result of personal choice. It is not a choice but a necessity, and this experience, which could be called "sceptical self-deceit", corresponds perfectly with the emotional consolidation someone experiencing lack of trust seeks: an experience of control and power. The sceptic might feel he is in control through not being committed to anything particular, but his very determination to remain uncommitted leaves him unable to see his *actual* beliefs. He takes for granted several scientific claims but would universally doubt claims of a different kind; claims of a different language. If the sceptic would—instead of categorically denying any kind of faith—find the willingness to take a look at what *he* actually subjectively believes in, he might well become aware of the *personal* nature of his determination for lack of faith, emerging out of an unwillingness or incapability to trust, and to which the *ideological* scepticism is rather a comfortable cushion; an ideology to enforce his personality in this regard. In a similar way, radical feminism might typically serve as a psychological enforcement to a woman of weak female identity and often with a universal fear of men. The sceptic might manage to hide this from his awareness by believing that his committed beliefs are something he *knows*—in contrast with things generally considered as "matters of faith"—which creates the sharpest contradiction, with the sceptic making himself believe he has remained uncommitted. *Knowledge* is not a subjective faculty as faith and certainty are; it makes complete sense to ask about the degree of one's certainty: "Are you absolutely sure?" and to ask: "Did you know such-and-such?", but no sense at all to ask: "Do you know such-and-such with absolute certainty?", because

II-6. THE SPIRITUAL WORLD

the only case in which a positive answer would be sensible is if 'such-and-such' referred to a logical tautology, but there doesn't exist a practical situation in which presenting this sort of question would make any sense.[140] Knowledge implies truth, and truth is not a thing with subjective degrees of certainty to it, but something that requires some kind of external verification to determine whether something *is true or not*; whether the claim is to be believed or not. In order to use the concept of knowledge meaningfully, the criterion of knowledge needs to be shared and objective: there is never a reason to ask oneself: "Do I know this?" although there exists a certain figurative use of language used in a similar way to "Ask yourself..." which has a different meaning, since it never implies uttering any words and thus relates to a different praxis. Essentially the same point was raised by Wittgenstein about the non-sensibility of "I know I am in pain".[141] So from the subjective perspective, *knowing* something boils down to a subjective process of verifying and criticizing the matter before believing it—and believing it makes it *true*. Of course there is variance between people in terms of how much and in what form they rely on the external verification: a diffident person seldom admits to knowing anything without someone else confirming it first, a scientist admits to knowing something only when he is familiar with the related scientific theory, and so on.[142] So, clearly, knowledge, instead of being an alternative to faith, in itself implies faith, and the sceptical self-deceit operates in the misunderstanding of the subjective emotional problem of whether the subject himself is allowed to experience trust and faith as a problem of whether his objective statements can, without a possibility for error, be true in reference to an objective framework such as the scientific system.[143] *To claim* knowledge over something means *to believe* that this thing

---

140 Here we must remember Wittgenstein: the meaning of "to know" equals how the concept *is used*; not whatever kinds of uses we might technically construct with the grammatical object.
141 Pain, like any other abstraction, has a subjective criterion: the sensation of pain.
142 A so-called average person admits to knowing things when he simply is familiar with the use of the concept in question, without first checking his basis for his understanding. Reaching subjective confidence through becoming aware of the basis of one's knowledge has from the times of Socrates been the motive of philosophy—and expressed in this form, highlighting *knowledge*, in Socrates' life work.
143 This, of course, is never the case since the whole of science is based on a self-correcting *hypothetical* method.

PART II. COMMON MISCONCEPTIONS

is true, and this belief has no degree of certainty to it, as this would logically break the concept of knowledge. And to believe something simply means to exist in a state of not questioning. Since the sceptic is characterized by his *disbelief* and not his belief, the question about scepticism is the question of *what* he chooses *not to* believe… to claim 'universal' scepticism means to claim 'no belief', which is a contradiction in terms, and what a person like this is likely trying to do is to justify his unwillingness (or incapability) to believe *certain* things with an ideology that supports this by claiming not to believe anything at all. Now, Kierkegaard mentions[144] that "to believe nothing at all is the very border where believing evil begins", which can be seen to correspond with the sceptical determination for disbelief resulting from lack of trust, since willingness to trust another requires using one's empathy, and the ethical change to turning one's back on empathy equals the path of evil. The process involved in becoming evil could be described as the subject being coerced to accept something fundamental against his will and against his sense of justice, which breaks his moral foundation provided he already has one. All things called 'good' are things for which the subject willingly and out of his own initiative takes responsibility, and this is something that evil people call naive, but since all children are born with intrinsic trust, faith and hope even evil people must remember that they once had this quality themselves.

Also, considering the objective and shared nature of knowledge and scepticism, it might be noted that the problem of knowledge and scepticism wasn't originally a solipsistic problem, targeting one's own observations, as the first sceptics, the Pyrrhonists, were not sceptical over their own observations but rather shared Wittgenstein's concern over the basis of *meaningful language* among people, as it is clearly the case that humans vary in experience, senses vary in reception, cultures vary about values, and so on. Scepticism later—and within a context of philosophy as a study instead of philosophy as an existential school of living in a particular way—shifted away from this everyday problem of doubt to a setting similar in nature to the problem of how reliably one can tell one's own degree of drunkenness. It seems to me that the sen-

---
144 Works of Love

II-6. THE SPIRITUAL WORLD

sibility of doubt shares the problem that surrounds all sensibility and language: in order for it to be sensible to doubt something, there need to be *valid* grounds for error, but what sort of grounds for error can a solipsistic investigation produce in one's subjective certainty apart from the fact that one might exist in a state of being certain, or its opposite, a state where one has doubts? Valid grounds are valid because they can be shared. In a particular existential state I am prone to instinctively rely on my immediate impression instead of doubting, yet in another sort of state I can see myself doubting or constantly suspecting, to the extent where I am forced to tell myself that I must make a decision instead of remaining permanently in a state of insecurity. I can relate the sensibility of these types of subjective behaviour to different situations: in a badminton rally one must decide fast, and the best performance is given when one is in a state described as "flow experience" where there is no separate state of conscious decision-making, yet when one is thinking about a major purchase it is said that one should at least sleep on the decision; to give enough time to take all practically related options and possibilities into consideration before making the decision. Taking a concrete example from badminton, which is a game where there is very little time for conscious thought during rallies and the shuttle travels relatively slowly when hit in an upward direction, there are two observable common phenomena in players' behaviour during rallies: 1) indecision, where the player is unable to decide whether to hit the descending shuttle or leave it untouched as it seems to be landing close to the boundary line, resulting often in a late attempt to return the shuttle and a poor quality shot or even a failed shot, and 2) assuredness that the shuttle is going to land out and the player showing this with a gesture such as a shout or a fist well before the shuttle actually lands. Both phenomena are commonly witnessed in both novice and experienced players. Regarding case 2, novices are prone to try and return any approaching shot played to their general direction, but experienced players can become adept in making the clear decision to leave the approaching shot unreturned with a reaction time of just milliseconds with a very high likelihood of the shuttle actually landing out. It is rather astonishing to watch a player retract his racket to leave the flat drive shot untouched that was

PART II. COMMON MISCONCEPTIONS

played directly towards him from 3-4 metres away and approaching at some 100 km/h, and to then watch it land 5 cm out from the baseline—and to see the player perform this consistently instead of it being a lucky accident: the player *saw*, in that reaction time and with more or less clarity, that the shuttle would land out of the baseline, which he can't even see as it is located behind him. This is a very particular skill that seems to resist understanding of both instinctive action—which in badminton always would be to hit the shuttle: the approaching shuttle 'invites' one to hit it, and the beginner without exception hits it without thinking—and knowledge and decision-making, which we might like to think take some time to process, applying the model of thought where language corresponds with thought, as in: "I see the shuttle approaching. Should I take it or leave it?" This skill is clearly related to the player having clear thought and being comfortable with their basic ability to return the shuttle and being comfortable with the variety of possible actions by their opponent, instead of the novice player having to be fully prepared for anything with no reliable preconception or expectation of what the opponent might do (and this insecurity is exploited by a more experienced opponent through using deception). But looking at both cases 1 and 2 together, this is an interesting context to apply the concept of knowledge: it doesn't make sense to say the player *knows* that the shuttle is going to land out before the shuttle has landed, which will provide the objective criterion. Before that we can only say the player is either certain or undecided, which is very clearly observable from his actions that can be seen to show hesitation or full assuredness. Probably a modern (and by modern I mean wrong) way to explain this, as a theory of the mind, would be to apply mathematical or computational language and to say that the player is somehow performing estimation based on the observed trajectory of the shuttle, and this indeed is how one would approach the problem if one was able to observe the situation in slow motion, e.g. on video. But to call that estimation is just using a metaphor from the concrete mathematical or programmatic methods of performing estimation and transferring this to the context of the language of the mind. In practice, firstly, there is no experience of estimation taking place in the player's experience, as there is when a person is performing mathematical estimation, which is a more or less conscious thought process. Secondly, even the top players are consistently seen to show signs of hesitation instead of a process of calculated estimation, and one would expect them to be most adept in this skill. Maybe I could characterize the related experience by saying that for a brief moment it can look like the shuttle is going to land out, but suddenly after a moment it can look like it is going to land in instead, as these options—in or out—are clearly the options of interest, as dictated by the rules of the game—otherwise the whole question would not be relevant. Coaching emphasizes moving before thinking; always moving; the time window to start moving is short, after which one will be late, and during this movement one is able to determine if one is to actually hit the shuttle or to let it land. As a player, in my experience, I am looking and focusing on the problem of whether to hit the shuttle or not from the already established perspective of whether the shuttle is going to land in or out, instead of looking at it as a problem of determining the trajectory of the shuttle. Rather it seems to me that this skill is related to having seen a large number of shuttles launching from the opponent's racket to quickly determine that the shot initially looks like it will fly out of the boundaries. In the next step I can take another look at the shuttle and maybe also a look at the boundary line, and try and confirm whether the shuttle *looks like* a shuttle that is going to land outside that boundary, the skill of which is also related to having seen a large number of falling shuttles to get a feel of its actual landing place. Actually, it is just the observation of the shuttle leaving the opponent's racket; angle combined with speed; certain angle+speed looks valid, looks like it will go out, and I will call 'in' or 'out' instantly based on this brief observation. And shuttle damage betrays the player here; a damaged shuttle may fly a shorter or longer trajectory than an undamaged one, and here one is able to adjust one's expectation rationally if one notices, from its feel, that the shuttle is too fast or too slow. I find this sort of process closest to the experience of determining if a shuttle is going to land in or out, and as such, it is related to experience and being exposed to many practical situations of observing launching and landing shuttles and thus having psychologically associated visual sensations of flying shuttles with the results of shuttles falling close to boundaries. Within this

PART II. COMMON MISCONCEPTIONS

experience my process of guessing if the shuttle is going to land in or out is more educated than for some and less educated than for some others. Also, the experience of certainty in this guessing activity is a subjective quality that can't be shown to result from any objective phenomena, and as such, I would rather relate it (and in badminton discourse it is related) simply to "what sort of day" (good day/bad day) I happen to be having at that moment; players make good choices on a good day when the mind is clear. And this perspective to knowledge and certainty here is in sharp contrast with any mathematical or programmatic loan model of estimation. Also in badminton coaching there exists no conceptual approach to this that could be taught to a player to overcome such insecurity; no technical or tactical instruction (which badminton training is otherwise full of), mind-trick or mental rule to help the player become more comfortable, to be able to better predict their opponent's actions or determine if a shuttle is landing in or out. The players are simply trained to play against different opponents in different environments to get more experience but cannot be trained to reach a subjective state of certainty. And one might think that if one plays and trains badminton all one's life, like for example world former men's singles player Lee Chong Wei, one would learn to overcome the state of doubt regarding such situations, yet, one can observe Lee very often troubled in a state of indecision (case 1) and losing a point simply because of this difficulty.

There is not, and will not be, an objective criterion to use to come to the subjective state of certainty. But there *will* be objective criteria to determine whether my statement of *knowing* something is true or false, and *those* constitute the basis of the sensibility for another to doubt my statement. Firstly, there will be all sorts of ways to check whether my statement is true in an objective sense. For example, given that I stated that I know there is a church behind this wall, it is possible to check via some objective means whether there indeed is a church behind the wall. Secondly, there exists the possibility to question the subjective faith implied by the meaning of 'knowledge' as it is used in language: whether I myself believe at all in what I am saying or if instead I am, say, consciously lying or just making up statements without a real commitment to what I am saying, or as a another option, if I am saying "I know" in order to convince and to hide my insecurity. And thirdly, there might be a valid reason to suspect that I am stating objective facts that I believe in, but I am being biased and omitting some contradictory similar facts, which is called a conflict of interest, and implies a subjective incentive to favour a particular political outcome. And this indeed is the fundamental problem in contemporary politicized science: politicians, journalists, commentators and even scientists are cherry-picking positive factual evidence that supports their conclusions and omitting the negative evidence, and justifying this cherry-picking on political non-scientific terms, meaning the controversial political position of the origin of the negative evidence. *These* presented perspectives are the *valid grounds for doubt*, and one can see that by 'doubt' here I mean, not doubting the truth of my experiences, which doesn't make sense, but to doubt the truth of what the subject is saying, either from an objective or a subjective standpoint: the problem of the reliability of my subjective qualities behind a statement exists in a similar way as knowledge and certainty. Also, what can be seen of the subjective capability to reach a state of subjective certainty, also in the context of the badminton example, is that it is related to one's trust in one's own capabilities. In the original human habitat humans were exposed to changing situations in hunting and warfare, in which one might need to fight or retreat, and it makes sense to weigh one's own capabilities; whether one is fit for the task at hand (take courage) or whether one has bitten off more than one can chew (flee!). It makes sense to weigh chances and possibilities both individually and collectively when faced with a fearsome task, and this takes place before the event, such as while stalking prey, preparing to enter unknown territory or planning an attack on the enemy, and often collectively as a group. In warfare (and business, competitive sports and bad marriages) these functions are further developed into formal tactics and strategy. But this subjective capability of doubting one's own capabilities, triggered by fear, can be witnessed as a constant and dominant activity in a neurotic person: rather than having fear of unknown territory, fight or enemy, the neurotic lives a constant *social* fear and a related uncontrollable fear of being incapable for whatever task might be at hand. And this is because, unlike fear arising in a nomadic or primal habitat that is related to particular events and where the individual receives powerful group support, social activities are a constant and static individual requirement of a civilized society, and people are fundamentally existentially alone in those situations. Thus, unlike in a primal context, the capability to overcome fear, *courage*, becomes a solely individual skill in a civilization that one can in one's life develop or leave undeveloped yet still be socially accepted. In primitive societies men are required to prove their capability of showing individual courage in extreme situations before being accepted among hunters and warriors who have to rely on each other during the hunt or the battle; they have to prove psychologically that the social requirement to act for the benefit of the group will not be dominated by their need for personal security. And this primitive male rite clearly is an *ethical* requirement; a requirement to show socially responsible behaviour instead of relying on security provided by others, as a potential coward will prove not only useless but extremely damaging to the team effort where responsibilities in hunting or battle are shared, just as a weak link in a chain risks making the whole chain useless.

Since the sense of a concept is dictated by its criterion, one can see that 'existence' has multiple senses. How do I verify the existence of everyday objects, such as: "There's a laptop on my lap"? To claim that this is just a matter of my senses is very short-sighted: if I didn't know what 'laptop' means I could never utter such a statement (accidentally producing similar sounds isn't uttering). I have learned 'laptop' to mean a subclass of computers and so on, but this doesn't give me the certainty to name something I see 'laptop'; if I had just theoretically learned about laptops but never seen one, I would be curious to look at a so far unidentified object and wonder whether *that* is one of the laptops I've recently learned about. My certainty comes through both knowing the concept on a theoretical level and also having practice in working in human interaction where the concept has been used, and of these only one is actually necessary in order for me to use the concept correctly in most cases. Also, for children and for language-learners, this process is often a straightforward Augustinian association. Taking my background of experience into account, if someone asked me: "Is there a laptop on that seat over there?" my criterion would be my senses. Yes, I could right now be dreaming or affected by an evil operator and so on,[145] but even if this was the case I would resort to my normal sensory criterion. It could also be the case that the person asking me the question is not himself interested in whether the laptop is really there but, as my teacher, instead wants to see if I understand 'laptop' correctly, but still his expectation of my criterion would be the same. So, in many cases in which we *use* the concept of existence, the justification for using the concept correctly comes through the *sensory* criterion, which defines a particular sense of existence. The evident second sense of existence is the existence of logical or mathematical relations, as used in mathematical language e.g. in "There exists epsilon greater than zero such that ..." in the case of which the (ultimate) criterion is the mathematical proof based on the pre-existing mathematical concepts. Say, "there exists an irrational number between every two unequal irrational numbers" relies upon a number of existing mathematical concepts ('there exists', 'irrational number', 'between') and the method of verifying whether it actually is the case is by using existing mathematical theorems along with logical-mathematical methods of proof. I will not address here the highly interesting matters of mathematical methodology and certainty but just present the philosophical result that mathematical existence simply means something totally different from sensorially verified existence. The concept of existence that has been adopted in mathematical discourse has originally purely practical reasons of understandability through practical similarity, since the praxis of the 'discovery' of mathematical relations is, from the perspective of the explorer, somewhat similar to the praxis of the discovery of new features of the material world, such as new continents, new species or new celestial bodies, namely in the sense that mathematical discovery applies *in*sight whereas traditional discovery applies sight. However, grammatical similarity like this is prone to provoke philosophical confusion, and it is not uncommon for mathematicians

---

145 Descartes' methodological-sceptical idea of evil operator (revitalized recently by the movie *Matrix*) carries the totally unrealistic assumption that people live in their dreams the same way they live normally; I e.g. very often have dreams with a strong premonition of events and occasionally perform unnatural stunts.

to believe their investigation targets "the structure of *the* world" (or something similar), which, however, would be correctly put as investigating "the structure of *a* world", since 'world', as applied here, refers to a *grammatical* world of discourse, or, in terms of Wittgenstein's *Tractatus*, the structure of *his* (the mathematician's) world bound by his language.

Accepting that 'existence' can have multiple senses, we can now get to the problem that the idealist scientist must face with hatred,[146] which is the large ratio of people around the world happily accepting the existence of God or the existence of other spiritual subjects he understands as being accepted with similar empirical evidence (none). The *empirical* nature of the evidence needs to be emphasized, since the people he detests the most—religious fundamentalists—report evidence of the divine that they are unable to produce due to its private nature, such as "God told me such-and-such" or "I have seen God". Now, should we ask the spiritual witness: "Did you *hear/see* God?" he might affirm this. But should we use our skills to pursue him for the meaning of this hearing or seeing, he would (ultimately) submit to the private and *non-sensory*[147] nature of the experience that commonly designates religious experiences. It is not a mystical coincidence that in the majority of cases of witnessing a spiritual being there just happens to be nobody else around to witness it, but rather it is the case that there exists a whole discourse of non-sensory experience with expressions like "I know Peter is dead but he exists *for me* (as real as he ever was)", "I saw you in my dream last night", "You need to listen to yourself before you rush to act" or "In psychosis I would see twisted faces". The discourse borrows the same words we use when discussing sensory experience due to their similarity in private experience, yet an experience of non-sensory observation lacks the possibility for verification that an experience of sensory experience has: in most cases when we would hear something in a

---

146 He will hate it and call it stupidity, weakness of mind or obsolete science, because his ethics refuses to accept it.

147 The word 'extra-sensory' is somewhat misleading, because it implies a phenomenon to be *caused* by something that is *outside* of our objective framework of causes. It is clearer to say that those attributions fail, rather than to say that something is missing.

sensory sense we would have all kinds of means to objectively verify its objective (shared) reality, such as recording or testimony from others. Then again, non-sensory observations have an often easily distinguishable characteristic of being bound to the emotional life of the subject, generally correlating with his wishes and fears. Thus, to claim that the targets of non-sensory observation *don't exist* simply serves to show that the person presenting the claim either doesn't understand the sense of non-sensorially verified statements or is intolerant towards such. Rather it would be correct to say, after their solely private criterion, that they exist in a subjective sense of existence. Nevertheless, both the spiritual witness and the idealist scientist make a major mistake in misunderstanding the subjective, non-sensory sense of the observation: both take the reality of the target of the observational experience *to mean* reality in the sense of sensory observation. It is OK to be somewhat confused, that is the essence of life for us all, but it is not OK to choose to remain confused by refusing clarification.

One might claim that the dichotomy between sensory and non-sensory observation is not tenable due to our incapability to distinguish between them in our experience. However, this would be equally confused as it would be to interpret that because of that we cannot be certain if our experience is a result of being awake or dreaming would result an impossibility to diagnose psychosis, although this does pose a major challenge often depicted in works of fiction. Even though dreams are described as involving a varying sensation of reality and we might sometimes experience dreams that feel particularly real (as opposed to dreams where we have the sensation of being an external viewer of events), surely after waking up we take a look at what had happened: we realize that we have been dreaming and we might try to better recall the dream or interpret it in terms of real past events (often events that occurred the previous day) or our emotional life (our wishes and fears). This event of waking up will simply cancel our interpreting the experience in terms of sensory reality and put the experience in the right perspective: a non-sensory experience. Should this event never occur the person would in practice be diagnosed as psychotic, and the resulting disconnection from reality involved in real psychosis can (in theory) be captured in terms of distinguishable subconscious emotional causes given that the patient is willing to cooperate. This is the theme studied in *Rosemary's Baby*, where an emotionally submissive mother's maternal fears of losing her unborn child develop into paranoid fears about a malicious arcane cult set to steal and abuse her baby. The same applies to religious non-sensory experiences: for example, the subject can be somewhat conscious of his unhappiness as a result of the life he is leading (his actions) yet be incapable of consciously changing this due to his actions being a result of his ethical nature (the way he thinks) containing an internal conflict he is unable to solve. He might even consciously search for practical solutions, but in vain. Such a situation with a strong wish for a change but inability to practically produce such is particularly, as it were, fruitful ground for religious experiences, and often people turn towards religion in search of a resolution to internal conflict. Avoiding religious examples for the sake of clarity, let's take as an example a man who has led a somewhat rowdy lifestyle (resulting in suppressed guilt for having treated other people badly) and experiences a spiritual observation depicted in the popular country song 'Ghost Riders in the Sky' in which the ghost of a wicked fellow cowboy, doomed to ride forever trying to catch the 'devil's herd', delivers an ultimatum to an old cowboy to change his ways or to face the prospect of joining the gaunt and mournful ghost riders herding the devil's cattle forever.[148] With this interpretation of the song and the given conditions for the man's spiritual experience, the correspondence between the man's subconscious wish for a change of lifestyle and the emotional result of yielding to the command presented by the spiritual subject should be quite obvious: now you are (existentially) where you can choose to *always* be different or *always* remain in the same guilt/shame you already experience. Now, we might feel compelled to ask the question of whether the man was—while having the experience—capable of distinguishing whether the observation was sensory or non-sensory. Taking the previous dream example we might notice how the question is actually completely misleading regarding the meaning of non-sensory observation, since he will—not being psy-

---

148 The story probably has its origin in the Book of Revelation, but I can read that similar Norse and Germanic myths exist.

chotic—snap out of the experience after a while and wonder if he was daydreaming or if e.g. others saw it too, and he has many means to try and find this out. But most importantly, the epiphany might have concrete emotional effects on the subject corresponding to the emotional effects of the inter-subjective event the observation symbolizes to the subject, often resembling psychological archetypes. The effects can be of the greatest *ethical* importance to the subject and can encourage the subject to make an ethical change with the same subjective means a human can use over another through e.g. warning, raising a question, commanding, provoking and so on.

The dominant role of science in modern society in advocating empiricism (sensory observation) over the spiritual has brought a dramatic change in the form of society, with the favourable political effect of diminishing political argumentation using religious arguments—an activity that can never be philosophically grounded due to the private nature of religious experience. The overall pre-eminence and the justification of the use of the empirical method in both science and law can be attributed to the fact that basing one's judgments on *objective* empirical evidence is superior to basing them on 1) personal intuition or 2) the testimony of another—both of which are general human tendencies—and this is because a method that operates on *objective* evidence will work hand-in-hand with the cultural objective standards that produce a shared common ground of interpretation and discourse, and thus is less susceptible to misinterpretation and error. However, such a method is no general solution to the acquisition of knowledge, because of its inability to communicate the subjective, and should instead be correctly seen as the smart alternative to replace "hasty jumping to conclusions". However, the current commonplace close-minded scientific idealism that attacks the spiritual with misleading or false philosophical arguments—like an anti-labour-movement elite determined to counter the Marxist workers from the comfort of their institutions and on the level of action instead of rhetoric—has a counter-effect on society, reducing the general feeling of security through its hostility towards a natural basic faculty of an ethical subject. As an example of the nature of modern times, a highly popular book written by a ground-breaking expert in the fields of ethology and biology purports to teach us that religious faith is a delusion and 'qualifies' as insanity. Let me draw a parallel: consider that a scientist goes home from work and, when his lovely wife tells him she loves him, he demands that she presents evidence. When his wife tries her best to do so, by explaining how she feels and the things she has done in order to show her love, he responds by showing how all those deeds can be explained through the wife's other qualities, and that her insistence on the claim that she loves him qualifies as insanity. The scientist would thus mix his empiricist working method with discourse that is outside his work: there simply is no requirement to present any evidence for one's claims outside scientific communication and courts of law, which are organs of society designed for very particular purposes, but it is a reality that a great number of testimonials from emancipated ex-wives contain confessions of having submitted to ludicrous requirements used as tools for abusive emotional control. From an intellectual perspective, such a claim about religion can be identified as being simply provocative in nature rather than being a serious claim, as it is so ludicrous and detached from all sense that no philosopher in history would take it seriously.[149] Rather it is a challenge and a ball thrown to philosophers and philosophy in general by somebody who likes to build a career out of public debates that are entertainment for the masses, asking us to step into the arena that he himself has already built. It is a taunt with the essential implication that scientists have inherited the Earth, and that both religions and philosophers should pack their bags and buy a space shuttle from these scientists so they can get off the planet and stop everyone having to endure boring Sundays. A scientist doesn't need any thought to make such claims, and essentially, while making such claims he is not acting in the role of a scientist.

In modern public discourse it is striking how we can easily talk about groups of people but we don't really have a capability to talk about the subjective, except in an impersonal way, such as in a newspaper article

---

149 I believe this is a strong claim, considering all the things philosophers have ever said. For example, Nietzsche symbolically saying "God is dead" makes a lot of sense because he is also saying that we killed him; not that he is imaginary.

II-6. THE SPIRITUAL WORLD

or in online discussion, and from the perspective of psychologizing groups of people—classifying them as mentally defective—instead of trying to understand them. Therefore, it seems to me that many people carry high prejudices about groups but are barred from expressing them, which naturally causes segregation. In Europe there is a long tradition against racial segregation, but segregation in other than racial terms is rampant.[150] Psychologizing religious people appears to be a fair thing to do, as I read about such silly attempts often; so, I would like to psychologize atheists in turn, because if the conversation is focused on the defects of one party only, the other party can appear better than they actually are, in the way that a person walking a small dog appears taller than a person walking a large dog. Also, to me personally, whenever I experience other people as disturbing or a nuisance, the thing that helps me the most is to try and imagine what a nuisance I myself must be to others who don't share my weird personal world and have social expectations that conform more to general norms… and to remember that I actually enjoy being this individualist nonconformist nuisance and would not like to change. Now, the atheistic refusal of religious language is expressed as the refusal of the existence of, say, God, spirits or demons. But this is actually meaningless, because religious people report *subjective knowledge* of their existence. What the refusal actually means is to refuse the *validity* or *importance* of religious language; to say that it makes no sense to say such things. Commonly, atheists 'argue' this using sarcasm, making fun out of some religious bad examples, which well illustrates the demonic nature of the refusal of religion, which has a spiteful tone to it. Consider if an individual is haunted by demons, by which I mean the sort of behaviour and emotions widely portrayed in art, where an individual struggles with his conscience and with e.g. feelings of guilt and remorse. Let's call it a recurring bad dream, so that the atheists can understand, such as the dreams Ripley is having in the movie *Aliens*; dreams of space

---

150 To me it is obvious that this behavior on the part of newspapers has a pattern and thus is politically motivated: religion, nationalism and traditionalism are 'out' and considered old-fashioned, and multi-culturalism, anti-traditional marriages and religious hatred are 'in' and considered modern. There is no controversy about the fact that a development of federalization is on the way in Europe. From the perspective of those who wish to see a federal Europe, traditions, national institutions and religion are standing in the way.

monsters that killed her space crew that others haven't seen. Therefore, she knows (has subjective certainty) that they are real and others can only be sceptical and say they have no evidence. Her dreams recur due to her guilt over losing her crew and because of the danger of the monsters. Now, would the right way to help her be to tell her that the monsters don't exist or that they didn't kill her crew? To say such a thing is demonic, because you are siding with the demon/monster (this indeed is the case in the movie). Essentially the haunting is related to guilt and remorse, and the symbolical dreamy imagery is secondary, yes, but to say that to speak of such things is *not valid* is to say that the person's *conscience* is wrong. Compare this to where an individual is bullied by a group of other people; if you ask the bullies, they will deny the bullying, and if they are brought to admit it, they can't justify it... they'll say they are sorry because they realize they have no justification: the circle of evil is such that you have been bullied, so, now you do evil likewise but can't justify it. They'll say: "No, we were not bullying... ok, we were bullying, sorry." In order for someone to be able to bully like that, they need to accept and participate in something they can't justify, by repeating to others the humiliation that once was done to them. To be able to participate, one needs to silence one's conscience; the moral problematic of whether what is being done is justice or not. So, would it be too much to say that the atheistic denial of religion is a similar nullification of conscience? If I was Richard Dawkins I would not hesitate to make such a generalization, but instead I feel I really don't know all atheists that well; I just hear quite a few of the things they say. It would be hasty and unfair to speculate on such dramatic personal aspects of groups of people, not being their trusted psychiatrist. I believe atheists can be (and are) moral actors, but there seems to be something particular and personal that takes place in such a subject's life and makes him lose faith. The fictional exaggerations that come to mind are Javert in *Les Misérables* and Pasha 'Strelnikov' Antipov in *Doctor Zhivago*, both of whom are characters that shun normal family life for a solitary existence and focus on their careers, in which they succeed brilliantly due to their will, persistence, determination and capability for ruthless brutality. These characters portray a personal bitterness leading to a determined denial of humane empathy and pity, in turn replaced by a stalwart and ultimately false faith in idealist justice—justice without a personally announced faith in something beyond that system; justice that conforms to a *system* of justice (in the case of Javert, the law, and in the case of Strelnikov, the communist movement) but separated from the self and thus separated from the responsibility of their own actions. These stories depict a very similar character as do all mobster stories; an inherently good man who had to face the dangers and terrors of life, and becomes 'a baddie', implementing the same false justice as the people he initially hated, and does all this in the name of an ideology that exists only to protect the subjective world-view that is built around the hatred that began when he first lost his faith. As other fictional examples that would follow this "eternally vengeful because angry at God" theme I could give Salieri in the movie *Amadeus* and the Coppola adaptation of *Dracula*. Let's also be clear that these characters are fictional extreme developments of particular personalities deliberately made into such by their writers (as is the style of any good fiction) and being an atheist doesn't make one Strelnikov. But among real-life characters the libertine priest Aleister Crowley, who was on a sort of mission against morality and religion, was similarly described by his several biographers as portraying high courage, skill, energy and willpower, while being exceptionally capable of cruelty. 'Will' was a sort of transcendent theme in Crowley's thought, which, in my opinion, clearly conforms to the theme of rebellion against morality: "Do What Thou Wilt" instead of having to be bound by morality. It is interesting to note how the open hostility towards religion, together with an open favouritism towards science, is a recurring theme in the thought and particularly actions of our 20th-century ethnic cleansers such as the Nazis and the Marxists: Lenin, Stalin, Mao Zedong, Pol Pot and so on. People who don't find this worth noting would likely respond by citing Christian atrocities that likely will predate the Protestant Reformation or be classified simply as 'Christian' under the Reformation, which is a bit funny in a world where atheism didn't exist (the whole concept originates from the 16th century) and that was divided between the battle between the Christian Reformation and the Christian Counter-Reformation. As a consequence, such a defence will effectively blame Christianity for any atrocities ever committed... where instead a solid response would use 20th-century, or, say, post-Reformation Christian atrocities as a point of reference—referring to a point of time where we lived in a world in which such a thing as atheism existed. Just take a look at in Hitler's speeches where he commonly referred to God or deistic themes in order to gain people's support, but in a flash after the Nazi takeover targeted any Catholic political and charity organizations, together with minority religions, with bans and imprisonment unless they expressed explicit support for the Nazi regime. There we have a living example of an opportunist who will attest to anything to gain popularity and hence power, which makes it safe to assume that such people existed centuries back. But these people would not have been called Christian in the way the word was used at the time, referring to a way of (subjectively) existing in a Christian way, contra to how the atheist argument from Christian atrocities would use the word simply as an objective classification, such as by e.g. being born to a Christian family. Thus, such an argument reduces to an error in mistaking the subjective and objective meaning of Christianity, as such errors generally tend to do. All in all, in all these examples we see a refusal of Christian morality—the moral norm and foundation of social order—that is done due to *personal* loss with a theme of loss of innocence: someone feels that the world has treated him badly and sees *justice* in returning the disservice. It seems to me that this sort of personal experience of false justice is required for one to be capable of cruelty in an unempathetic manner, which is something people in general are not, but instead their angry emotions will be held back by their moral feelings and their empathetic capability to equate their actions with the actions of others.

II-7. The Social Nature of Religion

In the philosophy of Kierkegaard, a religious existential mode (one could also call it a basis of reasoning) is something that is possible to achieve after first adhering to an ethical existential mode. A mere reference to God or going to church doesn't make one religious, but the Kierkegaardian concept of religious existence describes a state which is possible to achieve and which has certain characteristic features. This is essentially an empirical statement and not mere attribution, but then again, as a theory it cannot be verified since it targets the subjective—thus Kierkegaard would present it in his own described manner of religious humour: "Here is what I've thought of the matter, there you go! You might not agree with it or you might not even like it, and for this difference in our existence I must thank you for the mirth it has brought me!" As ethics equals all purposeful subjective change, religious existence is also evidently something that requires an inner change, which complies with a body of testimonial evidence we possess from people who have become religious. Then again, the difficulty of religion as a topic arises from the personal subjective nature of the *reason* for one's religious devotion and the fact that religion repeatedly visibly leads to irrational behaviour *in objective* (causal) *terms*, and here can be seen an interplay of reason vs. cause. It is easy to take as "negative evidence" that a religious person might attribute to a divine mystery the reason in cases in which an objective cause can be seen. As a simplified example, a religious person might interpret that the reason (God's reason) for him not catching fish was the result of some subjective religious deficiency, such as earlier committing a sin, but a bystander might interpret as the cause of his failure the fact that he used the wrong bait, since the bait used can be causally seen to affect fishing success. Yet to interpret this as somehow contradictory is a simple grammatical (logical) mistake, since adhering to an empirical method, thus letting oneself be convinced based on objective evidence, in itself rules out the possibility of religion. The religious person simply in his life has *chosen* to adhere to a subjective reason instead of objective cause, and this choice has changed him ethically. As our society exhibits a cynical disdain towards religions to an extent perhaps never before seen in history, religious motives often interpreted only through negative examples like the one above, in which the application of causal logic would yield more effective results in objective terms, dismissing both the ethical and any subjective repercussions.

The Kierkegaardian ethical stages are not very complex in theory; it's just that in the modern academic world they are pointless because academia is not interested in life in terms of wanting to make it better. I believe the stages involve the subject's awareness of his own subjectivity in a Socratic sense: it is knowledge of one's own limitations, acquired via developing an external perspective to oneself.

1) At the initial stage, which Kierkegaard calls *aesthetical*, the subject is not aware of himself at all; he does not dare to look at himself, so to speak. His life involves chasing aesthetic pleasures without restraint: he sees something he wants, and he cannot help himself; he must try and get it or feel incomplete while restraining himself. Let's call what the subject is looking for 'love': tonight, the aesthete thinks that love is in German imported beer; tomorrow he thinks love is in staying home on his couch watching sitcoms. This is the life and Western lifestyle that is being marketed to us by the pleasure industry by people who do that for a living—the marketing experts scout people's pleasures and think of how to attack them. As Kierkegaard says, most people never pass this stage of development. Also, there is a form of civil behaviour that is aesthetical: the subject acts according to certain norms because of how it looks: behaving nicely, as one's parents have taught. Such a person will never stand against political forces, because such action would be causing a disturbance, which is never aesthetically beautiful. If met with opposition without a chance to stay on the winning side, he will silently change his views instead, because he is lacking the perspective on himself to see the shame of this action. And because of the possibility of having to change his opinions, the aesthete cannot make a strong commitment to any form of thought and cannot present personal reasons for supporting a thought (he might present convenient reasons he has heard from

others). Avoiding shaming himself in the eyes of peers will remain a constant motivation for the aesthete.

2) The second stage Kierkegaard calls ethical, and I believe it is initiated by developing an external perspective on oneself. As looking at oneself is a subjective quality, I define it loosely as the difference between the man to whom his friends says "Look at yourself!" and the man to whom his friend doesn't feel the need to say such a thing—and this implies there is something the person obviously doesn't see about himself. Whereas initially the subject simply looks at the external world and doesn't consider the consequences of his own actions, at this stage he is met with guilt or shame regarding shameful actions such as saying things that he can't defend and behaving in contradiction to his own outspoken opinions. Therefore, the subject adopts a position on himself as if he would look at himself through the eyes of others, and by this I mean a *civil* perspective, incorporating to his thought the expectations that others impose on him. I use the word 'civil' to stress that superficial adjustment to the expectations of a *group* is a central feature of aesthetical existence, but this is exactly what the subject casts aside when taking the step towards independence when entering ethical existence: the opinions of the group are rendered meaningless as the subject incorporates a broader scope of civil duty. In ethical existence, the civil becomes a *personal* duty: for the subject it is *correct* to act in a civil manner, because the only alternative is to live in guilt or shame. This shame is, of course, subjective in nature, and because of this ethical behaviour is a *mode of existence*; doing things in a certain way, a way that does not lead into subjective shame. This is sometimes called self-respect—behaving in a way that would be deemed respectful by others. The ethical stage is in absolute contradiction with aesthetical existence where the subject essentially doesn't act (civil). But also, at this stage the subject acts out of a subjective necessity of acting—because not acting is wrong—and therefore doesn't pay so much attention to the outcomes of the action or to the motives of others.

3) The external perspective on oneself changes the subject to an existence where, via his actions, he represents ideals that purport to bring

PART II. COMMON MISCONCEPTIONS

about political change. But such existence causes two problems.[151] Firstly—simply the motive of bringing about political change doesn't mean that the goal is either right or achievable with the means available to one. And secondly, the black-and-white act of condemning a group, via the principle of one's actions having to be in accordance with one's opinions, equally justifies others condemning one. Whereas ethical existence is initiated by starting to look at oneself, religious existence is initiated by starting to look at *the outcomes* of one's already subjectively incorporated initiative. In parallel, ethical existence is about being passionate about making change, but religious existence is about how to make that change most efficiently. And here one can see the grounds for religious moral themes such as *compassion* and the Christian principle "Judge not lest ye be judged". The mode of action for Jesus Christ or Mahatma Gandhi can be seen to be fundamentally *defiant* but at the same time compassionate: resisting provoking the anger of the opposition and so providing them with the justification for their oppressive action towards one's hostility. Jesus taught to love one's enemy first and foremost, as the enemy is the one that requires the most compassion as they are being targeted with one's active resistance. Gandhi developed this idea into his principle of non-violent resistance. These themes are in Christianity depicted via the concept of God as the uniting force that is higher than Man and society. For these people, love is a *method*.

Kierkegaard's ethical stages each relate to a level of social consciousness; consciousness of the personal, society and God. Consciousness of the personal can be translated to egotism and the cult of the person; consciousness of society to idealism and consciousness of God to a group of themes relating to the totality and historical unity of society over generations. I find consciousness of the personal particularly interesting because of the prevalence and dominance of this type of existence. In this existence, the subject will not think in terms of universal values that bind him to others on equal terms, but via *personal narratives*, where he himself is the star of the story, and others are seen as other characters with particular predetermined roles the

---

151 Both these problems are excellently depicted in one of Bob Dylan's lyrical master works 'My Back Pages', 1964.

II-7. THE SOCIAL NATURE OF RELIGION

person unconsciously assigns to them, that, in turn, amount to prejudice, and determine how the subject (unequally) treats them. They can be treated as targets of admiration (heroes), targets of disdain and hatred (antagonists), helpers, advisers, relatives that he simply needs to cope with, or simply casual unimportant roles that need no special attention. These roles exist *in relation to the subject himself*—they are to him the role they play in his life—and the subject can become annoyed when others fail to satisfy these subconscious expectations. It is a very interesting phenomenon that famous actors often report that when people come up to talk to them, they speak to them directly via the characters they are known for—the roles that they play in these individuals' lives—and the manner in which they approach can be blatantly disrespectful if the role happens to be antagonistic. A particularly interesting phenomenon is the behaviour that is directed towards people whose status is beyond comparison, such as rock stars: they may display admiration and deference, similarly as in the presence of a powerful figure, but this admiration can turn into its complete opposite, intense dislike, without any change in the behaviour of the target of admiration. This sort of admiration can be traced to a wish to be in the presence of, and to be associated with, a person of status and importance; it is reaching for the *cultural status* of the target of admiration, who has a role in the subject's life that feeds him with something desirable; as we say, the admiration "works for him", and the person doesn't need to do anything for his role to change in the subject's life. This kind of relation changes from admiration to contempt and hatred simply if the important person does something to annoy the admirer. This relation is completely different from the *respectful* admiration we feel towards people who outrank us in the skills we wish to possess and that will not change status depending on how the target of admiration acts; his actions will be interpreted as the actions of a superior and understood as something that might be beyond the understanding of the lower ranks but has its reasons nonetheless.

Let's examine Kierkegaard's ethics and also take note that in the case of all of these *institutions* the related subjective thought is susceptible to *profane perversion*, where the original subjective motivation is lost

PART II. COMMON MISCONCEPTIONS

between generations, and which is possible when the mode of action is ritualized, as the subject performing the ritual need not be subjectively motivated to its purpose. By profane form I mean there exists a model according to which the individual is supposed to act, but the individual doesn't possess the subjectivity to properly assimilate this role. Instead he acts accordingly but doesn't relate to the role; his action is subjectively reluctant and he lacks the willpower to stand up against it and to free himself from this role. The individual who is being forcibly brought up in an institution, for example someone who has a strict Christian upbringing, will strive towards excellence in the formal standards of the institution—the rituals—without developing the subjective motivation for doing so. It may, however, happen that success in the rituals, and the external approval he receives for this success, develops into an identification, a matter of pride, and the standard against which the subject evaluates his actions. I will try to capture the some features of these levels of existence in in the following table.

MODE OF EXISTENCE	1. AESTHETICAL	2. ETHICAL	3. RELIGIOUS
PASSIONATE FOR	personal asset and hedonism	ideal of correct action	morality
INSTITUTION	aesthetic	movement	moral
FOCUS	getting attention and acceptance	cause, courage	honesty, method
PROFANE FORM	narcissist	fundamentalist	false prophet

An aesthetical institution is one where somebody influential has undergone ethical change and left an aesthetical tradition; a *style of beauty*. The profane manifestation of the three existences involves a person who will be personally motivated to excel in the external standards of the related institution—as the fabled Narcissus fell in love with his own image, so are all three of these in love with the image of themselves as the public image of the heroes of the institution in question. Another way to describe this is that the profane achievement is to excel in the standard *literally* (in itself; on a conceptual level). For example,

II-7. THE SOCIAL NATURE OF RELIGION

our modern conception of a beautiful (aesthetic) body is a *slim* body, as slimness represents the ability to show self-control in a world abundant in fattening food. The profane aesthete takes slimness as a goal in itself, detached from its origin as a representation of a subjective (spiritual) quality, and will ritualistically form his/her appearance to more and more slimness, eventually to a degree repulsive to many… and this development wouldn't be possible unless the aesthetic of slimness wasn't *institutionally* constituted by the beauty industry. Only once the concept of slimness exists as an institutional value can there be people who will take this concept literally in their efforts to aesthetically gain attention and acceptance. Below I attempt to describe the profane variant of the Kierkegaardian modes.

1) The obvious Platonic archetype of the perverted aesthete is Kierkegaard's beloved Don Giovanni. Mozart's opera immortalizes the legend of the ultimate egotist and narcissist, to whom every single action committed is an act of using other people as a device for his own personal pleasure.[152] The development of this character involves ritualization of the aesthetical: the pleasure-seeking, which for normal people is something we call a human weakness, becomes a ritual. Don fully employs the contemporary institution of beauty—poetry, lyrics, aristocratic position—in his efforts to charm his victims. He *identifies* with the *role* of a seducer and a pleasure-seeker and strives to become the greatest and most beautiful seducer, heroically performing actions that such a character would be *expected to* do, instead of the things that would actually bring him pleasure. And Don's servant, Leporello, keeps a book listing his seductive conquests and thus records his legend. This might be characterized in psychological terms as attention-seeking behaviour via his hedonistic antics, like a servant for the Devil. In the real world, the role of attention-seeking, hedonistic narcissistic perfection has been played by many pop stars since the coming of TV changed the music industry from a role

---

152 The nature of Don Giovanni as a man is well summarized looking at him in Scene 5 of Act II. Having escaped his pursuers (who seek to bring him to justice for murder and rape), instead of showing penitence or guilt, it pleases him to throw himself a small private party in celebration of his own victory. At the party he uses his only friend to serve him a grand meal (the friend is starving) while the orchestra plays for his entertainment.

PART II. COMMON MISCONCEPTIONS

of storytelling to something that combines music and stage act with theatrical themes. David Bowie might have been the one to first draw inspiration from the haute couture industry; quickly following him, competitive male pop stars all turned feminine, preoccupied with the body, the promiscuous and the theatrical. Bowie has in interviews described identification in his public fictional personae over his own person. I believe the narcissism of our age is largely the result of TV and the Internet as an audio-visual media norm: as narcissists live for adoration, TV creates a setting of visual hypnosis where the viewer is separated by distance from the actual life of the object of adoration, and is presented with only a chosen façade of it. Like monarchs, TV stars are only seen from far away and they dress glamorously to elevate their position via mystery and myth. But the culture revolution that TV brought into music resulted in libertine behaviour; the seriousness of the Christian moral struggle was cast away and it became fashionable to be promiscuous and immoral.

2) The ritualistic development of strictly ethical thought is depicted in the classical activist or fundamentalist, and can be characterized by subjective thought where a group of people or a form of behaviour is deemed bad and an alternative is deemed good, which reflects the form of an ethical ideal that encourages a particular type of action. Fundamentalist thought is absolute polarization without critique; the fundamentalist blames bad people and strives to look like one of the good people in front of his peers; he mindlessly plays the *role* of a pawn of the ideal. Where an ethically existing person feels the need to take action but can see many alternative forms of action which present a dialectic and problematic of approach, the fundamentalist is an individual with personal guilt enforced by the movement, and instead wishes for a justification for a dire act to better fulfil the external standards of ethical action: abandonment of the self and utmost commitment to the ideal—"Just guide my hand, tell me what to do". Fundamentalism is not a result of group action, but a personal struggle that involves belief in personal *salvation via revenge*, and the polarization of thought serves psychologically to justify actions that are a resolution of experienced guilt. This is the same type of guilt that

in a religious context is confessed to the priest, and that is seen to be absolved by divine grace. The priest may traditionally issue penance in the form of prayers or other actions to reach the sinner's sense of justice, where he needs to do good as a just punishment for the bad actions that he feels he has committed. When asking for absolution, the individual is placing himself at the mercy of an experienced superior, and at this moment it is critical, in terms of what sort of action he will take, whether this superior will be a man who believes his sins can be forgiven without him having to commit illegal acts. This sort of unquestioning behaviour is expected from a soldier, and in wartime the problematic of the legality of action doesn't exist and polarized thought is enforced ('brain-washing') in preparations for war. A more closely Western example is the militant feminist.

3) Consider a man who strives to excel in fulfilling the formal standards of a moral or religious institution yet hasn't himself evolved above the aesthetical level of seeking personal pleasures. Such a man could best be called a false prophet or Anti-Christ. Any institutions carrying moral virtue—the skill of knowing how to do things the right way—are a fruitful basis for such, such as the religious institution, the institution of wealth or fame, or, say, the medical institution, the academic institution and so forth. The more the virtue of the institution becomes a mundane ritual, the more the institution becomes susceptible to takeover by corrupt individuals that don't share the spirit of the institutional founders. A false prophet is an individual who closely studies the rituals of virtue in his profession and strives to excel in performing them in a manner that externally satisfies the expectations of others, but fails to learn their function apart from gaining external admiration for skilfully performing them as a member of the institution. He will then fully take on his role as a member of the institution and be vested with the powers of the institution, but cause nothing but great harm, lacking the qualities of virtue that the institution has been established to maintain.

Our modern world is oriented around both objective information and the self, and because of this, religion and religious institutions are not seen as automatically valuable. Not that the rabble would necessarily have seen them as valuable in the past either, but in those times there was no marketing industry to actively encourage people to portray their selfishness and lack of wisdom. I suggest using a solely *functional* perspective when looking at religion; asking: "What function does it serve?" or "What does it exist *for*?" and to remember that, as we know, religion operates in the subjective, personal sphere, which is the same sphere where our questions 'Why?' are answered teleologically; with a *purpose* instead of a cause. You could describe the concept of functionality with the concept of purpose: to ask what is the function of the clock on the wall is to ask for its purpose, and to further ask for the functionality of clocks in general, is to ask for the purpose of the existence of clocks and not *how* a clock functions. The concept of a *function* is something that originally served a *design perspective*: the designer *defines* a function in order to serve a particular purpose and from the functional perspective the technical implementation of the function is not important. In computing, the software designer or architect specifies the function by defining its interface, and the function can have many implementations that are, of course, to be implemented as effectively as possible, but the interface specification of the function defines its functionality from the perspective of the system: the designer has a particular purpose in mind for the function, and others can implement it according to the specification. To understand the functionality of religious institutions or religious concepts, one needs to approach them from the perspective of them serving a purpose or function in the subject's life. And very importantly, the same applies to any considerations about whether the subject is being religious in the *correct way*, as we know that there is a way of using religious concepts that seems awkward to us and gives the impression that the person is not being, as it were, truly religious. In order to make any evaluations about this, the concept of functionality and purposefulness is the correct method of evaluation instead of, say, empathy or empiricism—that we don't have any *evidence* of God doesn't really explain why people choose to believe in him, and to explain this via somehow inferior capabilities of thought is just *ad hominem*. Returning to the function analogy: the architect who specified a function doesn't need to implement it and doesn't even need to know how it is implemented;

II-7. THE SOCIAL NATURE OF RELIGION

he can test its functionality as a 'black box' by writing acceptance tests, where for every function specified he writes a set of tests that verify that a desired output is returned with a specific input and within an acceptable time limit. The function implementations that pass these tests are considered an acceptable solution with complete disregard for what the actual solution looks like in terms of code. In order to be able to evaluate function/purpose, one first needs understanding about the purpose of religion and, within a particular religious discourse, the meaning of the various symbolical expressions from the perspective of subjective purpose. Religion is a symbolical language about subjective purpose. The perspective of functionality forces us to nullify personal considerations; as an example, some people see history lessons as boring and some people see maths lessons as boring, and this boredom is because they don't identify with the function of those activities. Only by reminding them of the functionality of maths lessons can we make somebody who dislikes them remember their purpose. A good study of the purposefulness of beliefs is Kurosawa's movie *Dersu Uzala*, which is based on the memoirs of Captain Vladimir Arsenyev, and portrays a nomadic Siberian trapper who has reintegrated himself into a harmonious natural existence after an earlier marriage. For Dersu, the Sun and the Moon are people, because they are important, as nothing can live without the Sun (and the Moon is obviously indispensable for providing light and assisting navigation at night). Dersu believed that his worsening blindness was caused by him shooting and wounding a tiger, and this makes sense, as the tiger is a rare, dangerous and majestic animal, and this act disturbed nature's harmony: he was right to be fearful for his action, and deserved to be punished for it. Dersu is a character that has ethically *chosen* to live in *nature's* harmony, as his livelihood is nomadic trapping, and this existence is functional for him as it allows him to fully develop skills necessary in nomadic life. The genius of Kurosawa is to display this existence that contradicts urban standards but in a way that forces one to subjectively admire it.

A good example of the importance of religion is warfare. It is easy to imagine that historically the first two structures planned for a new city would be those related to defence (walls or fortifications) and a place

PART II. COMMON MISCONCEPTIONS

of worship, but why is that? Let's focus solely on the subjective and dismiss any idealistic ethical speculations; let's admit that 1) war is necessary (we are a highly aggressive species) and 2) the lack of defensive precautions provokes hostility, similarly to how weak individuals are picked on at school from day one. It should be noted that from the subjective perspective, war is always something that is forced upon one, even though some young souls who call themselves 'pacifists' claim that such issues don't involve them because they don't believe in them, just as some young souls calling themselves 'atheists' claim that religious matters don't involve them because they don't believe in them.[153] Everyday pacifism is nothing but a rationalization of cowardice, and similar to atheism in that it effectively means just disassociating oneself from the related problematic. Both the atheist and the pacifist wish to say: "It is *their* problem, not mine", yet the problem (war/religion) quite obviously involves everybody equally and what the atheist and the pacifist are expressing is their personal discomfort with it. The standard everyday idealism of supporting causes such as pacifism or democracy is not really idealistic thinking but just an assimilation of the liberties of a modern society. If you are enjoying the freedom of not being forcibly drafted into the military, you may justify your choice by calling yourself a 'pacifist', but this doesn't entail any thought at all. One could call this pseudo pacifism. There *is* a type of pacifism that is intellectually grounded, but that will have its place in a particular time in a society; a time of internal oppression that is to be fought by means of a pacifist social movement that is also determined to bring change— not a time when a country is under an external threat. In such a case, pacifism is a valid component of a particular higher strategy that in itself is a defence plan and an alternative to forcible defence. Coordinated civil disobedience is a form of civil warfare. Also, if you are sceptical of certain commonly presented ideas, that doesn't make you a sceptic in idealistic terms. It just brings out your incapability to trust certain things and is the rational justification with which you excuse this incapability. It may be noted that atheists often try to present their

---

153 Children and adolescents learn their existential options by rebelling against brushing their teeth, taking baths, going for walks, visiting their relatives and so on. It is childish to detach oneself from responsibilities by saying one doesn't believe in them, but when we get older, we realize their importance.

position as neutral fact or knowledge instead of belief, but the fact that atheism *is* essentially a latent *belief* that there is no God can be clearly seen in how atheists respond to religious terminology. The intellectual basis for the existence of God is similar to the basis for the existence of *numbers* as there is no empirical evidence of them but just extensive use of related language. Despite this, atheists have no problem applying mathematical language whereas they have a major problem participating in any discourse applying religious language (agnostics don't generally have this problem)—because the attribution of religious ideas contradicts their own *faith* about such matters. I doubt that there exists any other form of atheism except the type of the refusal of *bad* religiousness; the *refusal* of a *stereotype* of a person who is supposed to act morally according to his institution but is not doing so. Atheism is essentially the refusal of religious hypocrisy; e.g. Dawkins is arguing that US congressmen generally are hypocrites while reporting themselves as religious, and in fact some of them must be lying when they say they are religious.[154] Regarding the *argument* that somebody is lying, one should be moral enough to point out that it is common to all *unjust* systems of justice to assume somebody guilty and to ask them to prove their innocence. An accusation of lying is arguing *ad hominem*; for justice, one would need to assume innocence and show lack of credibility with facts.

In both ancient and medieval times, the armies of settled cities[155] carried with them a portable altar and the paraphernalia for necessary rituals in order to consult the gods on important decisions, such as choosing the right day to attack. Armies are highly functional entities that carry only what is absolutely necessary, and this reflects the absolute importance of religion to the functionality of the army. The function of this was not so much to convince the military leader, who was an informed strategist with experience and theoretic knowledge about the causal effects of different strategic moves, but to convince the religious men in service, as they were the ones with their necks on

[154] Dawkins said this on *Real Time with Bill Maher* on Oct 25, 2013.
[155] Nomadic tribes didn't have altars, which by nature are stationary and therefore contradict the concept of nomad. Portable altars are for peoples that live in cities and have rituals bound to the use of stationary altars.

PART II. COMMON MISCONCEPTIONS

the line and needed to believe in victory in order to be able to go to battle at all. The dread of combat will in practice immobilize someone without faith (at least if he is distanced from his comrades in battle), since he will fall to a natural primitive mode of self-protection. So before going into battle a religious soldier needs to know, firstly, that the gods are favourable to the commonly shared cause, and especially so on the day of the battle. If this is not the case, a suspicion might arise that the gods are preoccupied or displeased with that particular side. Secondly, there needs to be a promise that death for the cause favoured by the gods is glorious and rewarded in the afterlife. Some might interpret such a functional perspective to religion as altogether diminishing the value of religion, since one might be tempted to see such rituals (instead of gods) as the cause of people's religious faith. Again, this would be a misconception: what is passed on to people through such religious promises is the subjective *reason* for fighting. One can see that a soldier already knows he has no option except to fight, so there is no reason to give him spiritual encouragement to march into battle. If he does not do so, he will be punished by a humiliating death or the eternal shame and homelessness of a deserter in exile—but the religious promise is: *if* one fights with courage instead of cowardice, *then* paradise awaits.[156] The men are shown that there is a good chance of winning, and also that war heroes are hailed in the afterlife, and because valour is subjective and therefore nobody can force a man into displaying it, the situation is ripe—the stage is set—to allow an *opportunity* to show spiritual potency. Similar psychological coaching tactics are standard in any sports, especially ones requiring high endurance, and involve e.g. promises and compliments or threats to the ego. This functional spiritual process by no means involves a *lie* from any

---

156 Henry V; Bourbon encourages his comrades to fight on:
"*Shame and eternal shame, nothing but shame!*
Let us die in honour: once more back again;
And he that will not follow Bourbon now,
let him go hence, and with his cap in hand,
Like a base pander, hold the chamber-door
whilst by a slave, no gentler than my dog,
His fairest daughter is contaminated.
...
The devil take order now! I'll to the throng:
let life be short; else shame will be too long."

II-7. THE SOCIAL NATURE OF RELIGION

party: men marching to war are not lied to that the afterlife awaits men of valour. Instead it should be seen that without such process an army will likely be *unable* to march to war, and the details of how the related rituals are carried out are the result of a longstanding tradition that evolves just as methods of warfare evolve. You cannot imagine an army marching to war without such a promise; there are no atheist armies. Whenever the divine reason to go to battle has not been God or something else grammatically regarded as a separate subject, it has been the divine ruler, such as a despot or monarch, who simply has played an equal spiritual role. The majority of people have always regarded it as self-evident that the emperor is not an emperor *without a reason* but whatever the reason might be, one must exist—otherwise he wouldn't be emperor. An absolute requirement for the possibility of monarchy has been a divine façade: the calm, virtuous and royal face and the glamorous clothes and settings of royalty. This image has contrasted (and still today does in tabloid world) with the wretched filthy struggle of the poor, making their relation to the divine apparent through carrying the visible signs of *sainthood*. Forgotten are the details of inheritance of power which often involved bloodshed, murder, trickery and betrayal. Regarding faith, there needs to be a reason to believe, and this means that faith must be rewarded by a positive outcome. This is why a prophecy that does not promise a positive outcome is not credible, and this has nothing to do with objective probability but is just an inherent property of subjective credibility. Why believe somebody who won't promise success? He is no leader. A credible prophecy is one that people will wish to believe... and this sensation of wishing to believe is the same as we feel when we wish to escape a nightmare by disbelieving it and waking up, and why we wish to stay inside a pleasant dream and never wake up. This is why alarmism in general is not credible; there is no reason to *believe in* a negative outcome because nobody would follow anybody into such a fate.

Expanding the functional analysis on religion, one can see a relation between nations' political conditions and the form of the adopted religion. First, let's take note that there are no societies that have no religion. Secondly, let's agree that the existence of religion also means that

PART II. COMMON MISCONCEPTIONS

the religion is serving a function for society, instead of existing without a function, and our attention should be directed towards the analytical question of what that function is. Here, anti-religious thinkers typically diminish the role into negativist characterizations such as something like "giving comfort" or "providing security by routine" (as institutions do to the institutionalized) or "providing comfort against the fear of death". However, it is much more fruitful to analyse the language used in religion rather than make wild guesses about the emotions religious people are experiencing, particularly if one has no experience of such emotions and thus has no data to make any empirical analysis of this sort. One thing worth noting is that the unknown and unseen, and thus the dangerous and dreadful, is attributed to the divine. This can be seen in e.g. globally uniform worship of the Sun and the Moon or interaction with wood-spirits in an environment that is bordered by woods, for example. Interestingly, the word 'heaven' has persisted in Christianity to be understood in a symbolic sense, although before the modern exploration of the atmosphere it must have been concretely understood as a place in the sky. An interesting fact is the persistence of reported UFO sightings and the widespread belief that the US government is withholding evidence about extra-terrestrial life (according to some polls around 80% of the US population believes this). One should take note that UFO sightings are related to events in which people concentrate on staring at the sky, so perhaps the tinfoil hats believe because they want to believe, as the iconic slogan of the successful TV series (The X-Files) states: "The truth is out there; I want to believe." The modern SETI advocate is like the man in ancient times who stared at the sky waiting for God to come, spending his time looking for intelligence from outside the Earth. Now, it seems plausible to me that certain Biblical themes[157] align with astrological themes, and one can universally see religious symbolisms incorporating 1) astrological themes and 2) themes of humans and animals along with everyday objects. This shouldn't be a surprise, as such symbolism appears highly functional, and in ancient times the movements of stars and constellations were observable, regular and useful forces to be used in establish-

---

157 such as the date of the birth of Jesus close to the winter solstice, 12 disciples, as there have been 12 major constellations in many zodiacs, and a strong relation with the theme of light

ing a connection between seasons and agriculture, such as predicting the flooding of the Nile in Egypt that all human life was dependent on. It makes a lot of sense to see the movement of constellations as a divine force that precedes seasonal effects. In fact, not only does it make sense, but the man who came up with the deistic theory to accurately predict the Nile from the constellations should be hailed as a genius and prophet.

Another important factor to note about the function of religion in relation to society is that the separation of religious discourse from politics is only possible in a situation of stable foreign policy: a country in war needs a united religion. The link between upcoming disaster and the requirement for religious commitment can be seen for example in the recurring form of religious agitation called 'doomsaying' (warning about an upcoming disaster and offering spiritual salvation) and the common phenomenon of prayer and rituals in the event of disasters. Similar behaviour is also apparently observable in chimpanzees. Simply put, *Homo sapiens*, albeit possibly distanced from the need for the safety of religion in a time of peace and living in a secular state, turns religious when endangered. Another thing is that religious *compassion*, along with the theme of universal brotherhood, being *the* central theme in all major religions, is not functionally necessary for any civilization but only for a civilization in developing diplomatic relations beyond trade. The natural central social unit for *Homo sapiens* is the family, from which the social unit is extended to a unity of multiple families, forming a larger society (a nation) with a joint government, which, in turn, forms the link between society and the divine. One can see that in primitive societies the form of the religion supports the functionality of the tribe by functions such as supporting men to be courageous in battle and forbidding entry to unsafe territories. Those functions emerge as religious themes that are introduced by a trusted medium, such as a holy man, and essentially involve both the internal affairs of the tribe and the relationship of the tribe to its exterior. A holy man is somebody who is so important to society that, instead of thanking him in a traditional way by reciprocal gift or favour, must be thanked with blessing, because the service is acknowledged to be greater in value than one

PART II. COMMON MISCONCEPTIONS

could return. Whenever the holy man presents some rules or rituals of behaviour, he is required to tell *why*, answering to the spiritual needs of the people and offering a solution to a real problem, and this functionality can become twisted and turn dysfunctional only temporarily in terms of abuse of power (a non-successful holy man in practice loses people's trust and is replaced). Now, one can see that a village with a single government has no need for an ideal of compassion, since in a spiritual sense all people in the village are treated as a single unit. Also, establishing trade is quite possible without a compassionate ideal; just because a tribe doesn't fear, worship, kill or eat a group of outsiders encountered doesn't mean they need to respect them as equals, but only in terms of business. The ideal of compassion becomes a requirement only after diplomacy has reached the level of *joint government*: when a nation is required to accommodate natives of another nation, or when a part of a nation, such as a colony, aspires to attain independent government. The latter was the case in the stories of both Jesus of Nazareth and Mahatma Gandhi, both of whom preached compassion between *men* regardless of customs or local religion, essentially in order to unite mutually warring tribes against a common oppressor, thus providing a setting in which allowing compassion and brotherly love to overcome personal needs is the only practical choice. Furthermore, this prophetic unification under a single leader is the distinctive feature of the Abrahamic religions (the name 'Abraham' derives from Aramaic 'abir', meaning a chief, and 'ham', meaning people; it is not necessarily the name of a real man but the name of a legendary man). The success of religions advocating compassion in the evolution of world religions is to be interpreted such that the spiritual theme has proven politically valuable. The necessity for the spiritual ideal of compassion, both on the level of the subject and on the level of society, can also be derived simply from these two facts: firstly, one is to co-habit with people who have differing beliefs, and secondly, one is to treat them as *men* instead of animals,[158] savages or simply trade partners. This is because empathy and related compassion are natural traits and their dismissal will result in guilt, which is a higher wisdom and God's law in

---

158   In the movie *A Man Called Horse*, a white man is captured by Red Indians. His captor initially calls him a horse, before he eventually integrates with the society via relevant initiation rites.

II-7. THE SOCIAL NATURE OF RELIGION

major religions. A recent example from Finnish news: a mother killed her five babies. This made people say: "I simply can't understand", and this is obviously because life and motherhood are holy in a Christian society. Such an event makes people speechless, because such events are unspeakable in terms of Christian values. But it should be noted that killing babies is a normal thing for canine mothers, and used to be a normal thing in ancient societies, until life became sacred—so, the question is: what can't you understand; what is there to understand? What would you say to a mother who kills her babies? Would you tell her what she did was wrong? What would you present as the reason in the light of which what she did was wrong? Remember that you can't vocalize such a thing, since you are speechless, but *symbolism*—speaking by means of a symbol—is a good tool for the speechless. The crucifix is essentially a *reminder* that a society without God is capable of murdering even the best of them all: the son of God. It is a reminder of one particular murder to be remembered by everybody.

Another observation that can be made is that, in practically any field of life, the most virtuous experts tend to have a completely subjectively absorbed perspective on their art, either in the form of confessed religion or some other form that can be seen as having religious qualities, as it is said that "In great things eccentricity is seen as genius, but in small things only crazy". Understanding the subjective nature of faith, one can also see how it is so easy to understand that one cannot alone pioneer where one doesn't believe. Where the subject's ethical devotion separates him from the masses, such as where adhering to an ethical movement creates a dichotomy between the movement and the masses or where one's nationalistic devotion separates the nationalist spirit from outsiders, it is the case that the subject's religious devotion further separates him from everyone else. A person ethically adhering to an ideology is seen to derive his reasons from the ideology and at the same time to expose himself to criticism targeting any contradiction between his ideology and his subjective thought (one is expected to live as one preaches) and criticism targeting any confusion in the concepts used in the idealist argumentation, and the most evident grounds for criticism towards ethical movements is their tendency to

PART II. COMMON MISCONCEPTIONS

condemn political groups outside their ideology, subjectively contradicting their ethical motive to eradicate injustice. But a subjectively religious person is, however, seen to derive his reasons in a subjective way that excludes any possibility for criticism. Also, as Kierkegaard observed with unrivalled perception, the concepts of *irony* and *humour* directly relate to these existential modes. Firstly 1), irony is only possible in ethical existence as it involves a dichotomy between the ethical and, as it were, the non-ethically existing 'aesthetical' mass. It seems to me that the case with ironical connotations is that they involve observations that contrast with the ethical (how everyone knows things *ought to be* within the addressed group), for example when the lecturer says "How lucky we are that Peter has left aside his important tasks to join us" when Peter is known to arrive late in class due to oversleeping, or: "Our dear neighbour just visited to remind us about the importance of peaceful coexistence" when the neighbour is known to be grumpy about the slightest noise. Or "I just bought the world's tastiest water: $4.90 a bottle!" As such, irony functions as a friendly way of expressing ethical concern over action or e.g. a form of thinking that is natural but doomed to failure due to higher justice: in the case of Peter, a student needs to be in class, on time, and falling short of this requirement will lead to retribution. Irony is strictly distinct from *sarcasm*, which shares similar forms of expressing things through opposites, but which is hostile and doesn't relate to anything genuinely ethical. Secondly 2), what Kierkegaard called 'humour'[159] is only possible in religious existence and involves a dichotomy between the ethical and the religious (what is subjectively accepted through subjective reason), such as "The reason we wasted all that money but still lost that battle was so that we could learn exactly this lesson"; "All these struggles would seem to be in vain if we didn't know how valuable they were for our salvation"; or "I'm happy that we're packed like sardines in this train because it is safer as we can't fall down". This sort of statement illustrates that the most difficult things can only be faced with humour, and this kind of humour can be described as a successful psychological strategy to cope with subjective disappointment, and at the same time, a social strategy to avoid

---

[159] One of Kierkegaard's alter egos, the author of *Concluding Unscientific Postscript*, Johannes Climacus, calls himself a 'humourist'.

II-7. THE SOCIAL NATURE OF RELIGION

conflict by not hurting feelings. The role of psycho-social *acceptance* is key in both irony and humour. In the case of irony, the acceptance is *social* in nature—acceptance of the breaking of social norms. In the case of humour, the acceptance is *personal* (or "humane")—acceptance of expressing the humane weakness. This relates closely to the Kierkegaardian spheres of existence. An ironical atmosphere, but one lacking humour, is an atmosphere where breaking social norms is accepted (considered funny), but expressing human weakness (fears, incapabilities, wishes, desires) is, as it were, beyond the pale and makes others feel uncomfortable. But the even more depressing atmosphere, due to related psycho-social tension, is one where breaking social norms is not accepted because an ironical perspective is missing: a person breaking norms (acting stupid) is not accepted via irony and the understanding that this sort of thing happens to everybody at some point. Instead the person is sneered at and is in danger of losing social status by such behaviour. The capability for a certain type of humour equals the psychological capability to accept related phenomena without having to deny their existence. For example, in order to make jokes about death one needs to psychologically accept the necessity of death, or in order to joke about one's own inadequacies one needs to first accept their existence. Kierkegaard noted approvingly about Socrates that he held his ugly appearance as highly favourable because it repelled false love and friendship—people loved him for himself, not his looks. What is subjectively accepted in a religious perspective is something the idealist struggle against can be seen to be futile: when the fight is lost, one cannot be useful in any other way other than learning from the loss, and a person who is not ethically committed will never even risk entering such a situation of personal loss. Thirdly 3), as Kierkegaard mentioned, religious faith itself is immune to any forms of humour, as it is the highest mode of existence. The ironical perspective often targeted towards religions should be correctly understood as targeted towards individuals as representatives of religious institutions, the actions of whom can be pointed out to contradict the religious ideals maintained by their institution. Religious institutions and subjective faith are two totally separate things and relate to each other only in the sense that some subjectively religious people (saints) have played an important role in the birth and the form of religious institutions. The phenomenon occurring in the formation of religious institutions is exactly the one in which the attempt to reproduce the ethical through doctrines produces political doctrines. All in all, a possibly very good formulation for both irony and humour—as it were, all forms of humour beyond just cutting ridicule—is the *motivation to present negative things in a positive light*, and the skill to do such a thing is called a *sense of humour*; the difference is just in the ethical mode; the scope in which the things are experienced as negative. I will try to once more capture these in the following.

1) Sarcastic: reversing one's personal disappointment. Such as "Oh, you treat me so badly, you're such a nice friend!" or "Of course it started raining, this is just great!"

2) Ironic: reversing the audience's disappointment in the face of events that could have turned out otherwise. Such as "The train is punctual, as always" (when the train is late).

3) Humoristic: reversing the audience's disappointment over things that can't be avoided. Such as "The plants are loving it!" (when it starts to rain); "He is now in a better place" (of a deceased person), or "We know that our company's revenue made an all-time low last quarter, which brings us to the best possible place to change our course."

Thus, the skill of irony/humour is to accept undesirable things as funny, and the capability for the skill relates directly to one's subjective capability of dealing with such matters in oneself. The skill of irony is the skill to present *ethical dissatisfaction* in a positive light. But the tight coupling between religion and humour can be seen in that there are things, such as wars, diseases and so on, that cannot be presented in a positive light without religious language, and the necessary preconception to be accepted for the availability of this perspective is that those things are necessary and meant to happen. The distinction between irony and humour seems to be that, in irony, something that could have been avoided—such as wrong actions—is accepted, and in humour, the thing that is accepted is something that is unavoidable (death, war, famine...). Probably the most obvious example of humour is military humour, which can be easily characterized: the more subjectively intolerable the task one needs to undertake, the more humour is socially used in its support. Superiors will give onerous orders and add fuel to the fire by presenting them as delightful rewards, and comrades will take any opportunity to cheer and mock one's subjective misfortune. The orders are subjectively painful enough to be unbearable without humour, which will ultimately help the individual to overcome the pain and discomfort. The efficient soldier is one who carries out his orders without subjective resistance. Someone who claims to see beauty in, say, art, craft, sport or such, but fails to see beauty in an efficient soldier, hasn't yet come to understand these arts in their subjective sense. Fearless soldiers provoke exactly the same human admiration that is akin to martyrdom; where what is admirable is one's skill in casting away one's personal wishes for the greater good.

An aspect worth noting in the degrading West is that *animism* is rapidly replacing secularized Christianity. Worship of animals is the common denominator of non-organized primitive belief systems around the world, and a likely and suitable degeneration from organized religion; it is just that for some reason these modern cults are no longer called worship despite having all the features of worship. The modern Western animal of focus is singularly the dog: a society worshipping the dog would be expected to place dogs on a pedestal and to have their daily lives revolve around this ritual. This is exactly what happens when people take pictures of themselves (selfies) with their expensive cameras; they systematically include their dogs in what they wish to show about their lives, for the same reason as they would with religion: to show that the value is so strong that a newcomer to their lives will have to accept it (in religions, conversion may be required for marriage). Life revolving around such a pet gives meaning via a daily routine imposed by an authority, similar to the way that small cults, such as Hare Krishna, typically employ their members; dogs need to be taken out a certain number of times per day, their fur groomed, nails clipped, etc. Now the dog is sick; now the dog needs to go out… do it! The dog is the authority, and is the whole function of this exercise, as everybody needs the safety of authority and in the case of the West the authority of God has been lost. They take them to dog shows and agility events and immortalize them in paintings and statues. They take their dogs into their beds to sleep with, similarly to how one would have one's altar or crucifix in one's bedroom for nightly comfort—an activity that would surely have been considered unhealthy in a society just a generation ago when dogs wouldn't generally be allowed inside the house except for particular reasons. For me it is personally difficult to understand why civilized people would worship the dog, a lowly and disgusting animal—Muslims tend to see the dog as ritually unclean, which makes a lot of sense due to some specifically canine habits and that dogs in poor countries can carry rabies. But this is likely explained by the dog's loyalty and companionship—this is the everyday quality of social acceptance and harmony our Christian society has lost. But not only our Christian society; Japan is probably the best example of a country with a dog cult that leaves us Westerners far behind in demonstrating what a dog owner is willing to do in the social competition of portraying his love for his pet. In Japan the number of people identifying as religious has dropped dramatically, which likely relates to the introduction of State Shinto followed by its abolishment by means of the atomic bomb. For a Christian his God, likewise to a dog owner his dog: he is the one friend who never abandons you, the one you can always rely on when all people fail you. What is not seen here is that in the relationship between a dog and a human, the weaker party is required to please and show loyalty; the relationship is not one of equals. It resembles the relationship between master and slave, where the slave depends on the whim of his master for his whole life ... our dog owners even get their 'best friends' neutered. It is obvious that the dog, here, is an *idol*—an object with spiritual qualities—and not a dog to protect the house or hunt the birds; this dog is the ritual representation of companionship morality. Without any empirical data I can say that a negative correlation between reported dog loving and religious identification is obvious, because the love of a dog is a replacement for missing spirituality. And by 'religious' I mean moral religions; cults, such as said Hare Krishna or, say, scientology, typically offer spiritual routines in an authoritative setting and actively seek out new members, but lack any sound moral reasoning or philosophy behind their codes of conduct. Cults are always open for those who miss communi-

II-7. THE SOCIAL NATURE OF RELIGION

ties and/or spiritual themes but who reject religious morals; no need to confess anything, money will often do just fine.

Modern atheists attack religion by cunningly employing a repertoire of simplistic rhetorical devices that lose any intellectual interest after being exposed as mere illusion, using classical fallacious tactics or woven from the mysterious fabric of science. In fact, I believe no atheist could take on any *intellectual debate* where it is also expected to charitably take your opponent's view at its face value; wherever we see atheism in an intellectual form, it is always some stage act by cheap illusionists. But I will take a look at a few common arguments against religion.

1) I often hear the argument that *a religion; say, Christianity, should be proven to be true*, which is odd, since the existence of a religion in practice means the existence of religious people—which is hardly doubted by anybody—and the existence of religious people already implies masses of available testimonials to support it. It is just that for some reason the presenters of this argument don't want to go and ask these people if it is true that God exists or if they're perhaps unsure or telling lies. Consider being born and living on a remote island with a tribe. One day the village holy man suddenly reports in his portentous manner that a massive storm is about to come and urges the villagers to pack up and head for the mountains. Yet you can see no evidence of it happening. You check everything; the sky, the sea, feel the air, but everything seems normal. You ask the holy man if he is sure that the storm is coming, and he responds that he saw it in his dream as clearly as daylight itself and there is absolutely no question about it. If you still feel inclined to doubt the holy man's conviction and word, you might take into account that storms are something that vary in magnitude and there might be storms greater than what you have ever seen, but secondly, that the holy man is older than you, has lived through greater storms than you and has significantly better practical experience in weather forecasting. He is known to have exceptional powers to predict future weather from observations of minute details, in the way that experienced trackers can tell the paths of animals from minute trails they leave in their path that are

completely invisible to untrained eyes. But a person methodologically subscribing to empiricism will disregard this practical expertise, and in the context of the example, this approach would endanger his life by ignoring the wisdom of the fathers and forefathers.

2) An even more odd argument that I often hear from scientifically minded people is that *religious faith is fundamentally easy because all one needs to do is to assert one's faith*; but all this confused view works to say is that assuming (creating hypotheses) and lying (make-believe; making somebody else believe what one doesn't believe) are both easy things for many people, which, I believe, is not essentially doubted by anybody. But to look at this more closely, *assumption* should correctly be seen as the initial subjective state of a person *before* he starts to think further about what he is seeing, and the scientific hypothesis is the collective formulation of an assumption that is made before testing it with observations. It is rather this assumption that is *easy to state*, as a stated assumption or hypothesis bears no consequences whatsoever as one can always respectfully admit false assumptions with "It was my assumption but, thanks to you, it is now proved wrong". And this is in strict contrast with attesting faith, which is the strongest form of social commitment to one's words: to attest faith in something and then take it back tomorrow will lose the person all his respect; he will need to withdraw *the basis* of his thought and existence; the base of all his arguments. When it comes to lying, we give lies labels like 'harmless fibs' or 'white lies' to portray the subjective ease of succumbing to lying; the ease of saying something without taking the effort to consider the consequences of one's words. But assuming or lying do not have anything to do with the phenomenon of religious faith, any more than they have to do with any other social phenomenon that the person presenting the argument of ease fails to understand, and it takes a very fundamentally conditioned person to say such a thing; conditioned to have a perspective on groups of people that fundamentally excludes their humanity. I think it's understandable and human for one to see people via the groups they belong to as having certain characteristics, but to see any social group of people as not believing what they say or

meaning what they say is, in Christian terms, to say they don't have a soul; the Christian soul being the basis of subjective integrity and capability of morality that distinguishes people from animals. The immoral consequences of such an argument lie beyond comprehension: "I don't find it easy to lie, but since you do, what does that make *you*?"

3) A third confused yet common argument is one about the *usefulness* or *need* for religion, presenting religion from the perspective of consumer choice, like the question of whether one needs to buy laundry detergent or if one could do without this purchase at this time. It is easy to observe in a modern society that religious behaviour is a phenomenon present in some people and not in others, and the rather late secular movement in the West has succeeded in guaranteeing full citizenship and judicial status for people irrespective of their religious status (freedom of speech and religion). But taking a look at the socially unifying function of religion as a necessity for a tribe, let alone a civilization, to *survive*, one can identify modern secular thought as a rather late development born in the security of the modern university, which in itself originates as a *union* (the original Latin meaning of *'universitas'*) of monastery schools. In Europe, monasteries were places of study for Christian virtue, and they were used as a basis to provide free education for children. This was initially by autonomous rule, but at some time in the 13th century there was an administrative reform that conferred independence on the union of monastery schools from state and local government. It is easy to naively disassociate science from religion and ignore the fact that it was the *social order* provided by already existing Christian society that allowed the emergence of a union of independent units of study and education to be born *on top of* an already existing society that next wanted to advance to a level of educating children in a unified manner. And this unified nature, started by a need for independent administration via the power of a union, is the basis of the unified nature of the scientific system with standards of comprehensibility, publicity, peer reviews and so on, and the existence of this whole system relies on the social order of a society that is established to support such a function. In Finland, the social order and e.g. general liter-

acy required for an organized society was achieved by the Swedish government sending educated Christian scholars to both enforce social order and to teach literacy, and this enforcement of order was achieved by example, theoretic knowledge and applying various penal techniques for insubordination. Now, the question of whether religion is *necessary* is basically taken as a *subjective* question of whether a person needs religion, which means the question of whether a person needs to subscribe to religion and gain a certain status in society through this action. It needs to be this question because this is the only historical (non-utopian) point of comparison: comparing to a society in which one previously did not have this option. Yet this subjective question of need is, in the argument in question, mistakenly applied to the objective status of religion, whereas it could rather be seen that the existence of religion is something already presupposed as a constitutional factor in the social order providing the system of science and free expression that allows one to ask such wild questions without being e.g. somehow punished or considered a lunatic (by many). Yes, *one* doesn't need religion to live and die, and, lately, to be accepted in society. But since the arguer is obviously not referring to Western history with its Christian social order, he should be expected at least to demonstrate plausibility by showing a real-world case of social harmony without religion to use as an exemplary model to take such claims into real ethical consideration. If we don't want to follow Jesus, then whose example shall we follow?—And please don't tell me that we, as a people, don't need to follow; on any day you can witness the masses buying what their TV tells them to buy, looking the way their TV tells them to look and going to the events that their newspaper and friends tell them to go to. Yes, it is a bad argument to justify Christianity by its history, by saying that because the West has always been something (Christian) it also needs to remain that thing. But it is a far worse argument to say that because Christianity is not justified by its history, it is unjustified or unnecessary, and to omit the whole question of social order in one's idealistic speculations about the future society. That is raging lunacy and a sign of a death-wish. To summarize, every atheist is latently religious, since one cannot be an atheist without living in a society that has a social order that provides

II-7. THE SOCIAL NATURE OF RELIGION

the freedom of speech/religion to claim atheism. One needs to have religion to deny it—to put the 'a' in *a*theism—and a society cannot be born without religion because religion provides many of the functions necessary to its survival. The right to be an atheist is like the right not to be conscripted during a time of peace: a right to disassociate from the everyday function of a critical organ of society, and to leave its upkeep to dedicated professionals. Atheists take the Christian moral base beliefs but don't confess religion. This means taking the security of the moral framework and social order as an asset but refusing the responsibilities by identifying with this framework.

4) A fourth argument I would like to scrutinize is the one that says that *the existence of God equals the result of people's belief in it*, which is to say that religion boils down to an emotion. This is a very popular misguided view in our time and reflects our lack of subjective understanding and the tendency to reduce subjective phenomena to emotions; basically, the irrationality that is idiomatic to women. Following this, if there were no believers, there would be no God, and the conclusion would be reached that *God is man-made*—opposite to what the Bible teaches, which is that man is God-made. Let's first look at the scope of this argument via the fact that practically any given religion incorporates a creation myth, and the argument is applicable to any of these religions, therefore countering their myths. So, the wielder of this argument is not only countering Christian Genesis; he is countering what is holy in any given culture; against the beliefs of the whole world, that is, the original cultures. So, one might describe this argument as rather hard to swallow. Secondly, it follows from this argument that we need to take the existence of God as the status quo and atheism as the, as it were, new direction this argument is promoting. 1) The existence of God follows from faith; 2) people currently *do* believe, and 3) therefore God currently exists. From this starting point, this argument implies that God can subjectively be made non-existent by renouncing one's faith; by *saying* one doesn't believe in God. Now, what does it *mean* to say one doesn't believe in God? It means that one is claiming to remain unaffected by the matters that fall under the problematic of Christianity. To take an analogy, consid-

er riding a motorbike and telling yourself you are *safe* to go 200 km/h because you *don't believe* there are any obstacles on the road, whereas the sign says 'max 40', strongly suggesting that others seem to consider the road safe only at that speed. You are exposing yourself to quite a high level of danger, unless you have clear knowledge of the condition of the road, e.g. having covered all of the road on your ride yesterday … and this lack of safety won't apply to whomever is declaring this argument; that is, unless he also addresses the individual human problems that Christianity is currently serving as an answer to for those with faith, and provides alternative solutions to them. To declare you don't need religion means you don't need the *safety* of Christian traditions, such as marriage, burial, prayers, Christian rituals, etc. Now you might feel that way for some time, and you may never change your mind, but you haven't yet *proved* that you don't need such safety; you've simply used your freedom of speech to declare it. I was once told that "Religion is just the answer to fear of death, and I am not afraid to die". Here, what happens is that the speaker declares that they have conquered the problematic of religion by showing courage against it, and the answer to that is to point out that to *say* you don't need religion doesn't mean that you don't need it, only that you apparently *believe* you don't need it, and declaring this doesn't (yet) have any ramifications on your life. To prove this quality, *you* must address these ramifications one by one. And here we can observe that this belief doesn't have an institution to validate your commitment to it, which essentially makes it an ideology; there is no atheist institution that would evaluate whether you fully understand what you are doing. It's like whenever somebody calls atheism a religion; how could it be a religion since it is missing all of the institutional features essential to all religions and there is nobody to validate whether you are committed to what you are attesting your faith in? To say one doesn't believe doesn't require any faith, as it doesn't imply any commitment to anything apart from your own individual life but is simply the application of extended freedom of speech in an individualist society. Therefore, ultimately, this argument loses any credibility, and belongs to the category of assertions like "I can eat 50 eggs" without having shown this capability in practice. But why should you eat 50

II-7. THE SOCIAL NATURE OF RELIGION

eggs? To show that you can, of course. To universalize this claim into the form of "anybody can eat 50 eggs if they want to" is to declare the foundations of an ideology where such behaviour is seen to be somehow desirable, essentially meaning "people should eat 50 eggs just to show that they can", translating to "people should not believe just to show that they can". And here we will have to address the motivation of this task: What is the desirable change in society brought about by the commitment to such an ideology? Why should people not believe? And here, essentially, one should notice that this is a completely different question than the assertion that God is man-made, which has the appearance of a philosophical or a scientific claim on the level of surface. To claim that one doesn't believe is a provocation and a challenge of norms, and its universalization, that if nobody believed, we'd have no God, is a classic idealist assertion in the same class of assertions like "if nobody ate meat, animals wouldn't suffer" or "if everybody stopped smoking, everybody would be healthy", and then showing one's own capability to perform these feats in their own lives. These claims are to be met with a counter-question: Why do you think that people eat meat, and why do people smoke? To answer this question by saying that they do it because they're ignorant or stupid is not an answer at all to this problematic; people have their reasons and for those habits, and if you simply call for their extermination without understanding or even listening to the underlying reasons or causes, first of all, you are wrong, but secondly, you are not dealing with the issue in a respectful or intellectual manner, which translates to a rather poor expectation for the success of your agenda.

5) A similar argument I hear is the psychological argument that religion is something we humans invent in our minds as a protection, and that this need for protection is somehow just conjured by our minds, and it is possible to emancipate ourselves from this need by disbelieving it. This is again warped logic, as it is rather atheists who consistently escape *the reality* of religion into psychological rationalizations. A typical atheist is somebody who rejects religion due to its perceived injustice, for example, because they are unable to understand why God lets babies die or get sick, and this reaction, as I

see it, is understandable and human. But the injustice rejected here is not psychological, imagined injustice, but *real* injustice involving death and sickness! Rather, if religions were only conjurations of the mind, there would be no reason to reject them as unjust, but to view them objectively as potential belief systems. If we are indeed getting psychological in our argumentation it needs to be pointed out that what causes the denial is the cruel reality of the world, which in the case of the denialist is blamed on religion. At the same time, the same thinker is conjuring up an alternative system as a rational option to this religious system that he perceives as unjust... and projecting this mental conjuration on the religion, which makes no sense, as religion is indeed real and this conjuration is not. He will say that the religious imagery and symbolical systems are psychological, imaginary things that only have their power as long as people believe them... but he is ignoring the fact that they are not imaginary but real; the Christian world is full of churches, Christian writings etc. that are real, and on the contrary it is atheism that doesn't qualify this reality to any extent. This makes perfect sense, because religions precede atheism in history, and there is a clear explanation for that, because atheism in practice is just an exercise of critical freedom of speech which is made possible by a social order that first needs to be established somehow. So, ultimately, the psychological argument that religion can be escaped by disbelieving it, fails, as the atheist himself obviously can't escape it but simply resorts to a hypothetical explanation by saying "*if* everybody would disbelieve, then..." where there is no reason to expect that condition to be satisfied... and it is indeed this mental activity that is a utopian conjuration of the mind, against the observable yet deniable reality of religion.

6) One more common argument I hear is that "The world has many religions and they all claim to be the only one that is right. This is contradictory, and they can't all be right." This argument aims to show inconsistency in religions, as if religions ever tried to be mutually consistent like scientific disciplines. Here we see the role of belief in juxtaposition with knowledge. Contrast these sentences: "Anne believes there is a burglar in the attic making noises" and "Sarah believes there

is no burglar but a cat in the attic making noises". No contradiction here, but if you replace the word 'believes' with 'knows', you'll have an immediate contradiction, as knowledge is an objective faculty, and two contradictory statements can't be *true* at the same time. Knowledge refers to a belief that is also true, which means it can be proven and shown to be true, and it is not thinkable that one would go to the attic and show that there both is a burglar and that there is no burglar there. It is unthinkable due to the logic of these expressions. But if someone says he *believes* something to be true, nothing is said about what other people should believe regarding the matter. In fact, atheists, who will likely enjoy presenting this argument, rather think belief is in general bad compared to knowledge, which is of superior quality, and these same atheists would say that because beliefs are subjective, they are the cause of disputes, fighting and war. But what a contradiction here: of those who say they believe and those who say they despise belief and promote knowledge, it is only those who promote knowledge that are likely to think that others should change their beliefs to comply with their so-called knowledge. They are the ones who *claim to know*; theists—real believers—are the ones who admit they don't, and therefore are bound only to believe. So, which party is the more likely source of dispute?

The question of secularism and secularization is worthy of inspection in itself. A reply I have commonly heard to the position of secularism as a rather late development is that latent atheists have always existed yet not been allowed to speak out. But this is not actually true, as the word 'atheist', from a social perspective, denotes somebody refusing religious discourse. Such people have not existed in a world without secular discourse; without a *linguistic* group where it is allowed to deny God in an intellectual manner. The word 'godless' would commonly refer to lack of morals and social outcasts (as God was seen to bring people together), and associated with thieves, bandits or such, and the alternative form of nonconformist behaviour would be some form of heresy; alternative forms of worship. Secularism, however, is

PART II. COMMON MISCONCEPTIONS

a movement of the extension of rights within an already existing social order, bringing about the *right* to separate oneself from society's religious function, and as such it is absolutely certain that secular ideas can only be held by a social minority without the collapse of social order, since the existence of such a movement already implies a society with very high leniency towards individual rights in contrast with an expectation of social uniformity and duty. Consider a thought experiment: a society creates a freedom called "daily free time", and first it means, in practice, just the freedom not to participate in the daily sermons for one minute per day. After a while this freedom gains popularity, and by active lobbying, the individualists are able to extend this freedom to two minutes per day. Following a similar process of *extensions of freedom*, daily free time soon means you can have the whole day of free time to yourself. But there is some problematic about what exactly people are allowed to do in their free time and what they are not allowed to do, and they decide to clarify this in a document called the bill of rights, and they choose to appreciate the existence of this freedom by the symbol of a big flag that is erected in the middle of the city. First, the bill of rights contains the right to smoke a cigarette and to visit your home during sermon breaks, but, as daily free time extends, so also does the bill of rights extend to cover more activities considered permissible. Young idealists emerge to demand more freedoms, giving rise to a slippery slope on which all signs indicate that there will be limitless freedom in the future. Now, one day, the question arises: should the bill of rights give people the freedom to burn flags? This brings about a problem: what happens if one burns the flag in the middle of the city? Will everybody be free after that, now that the whole concept of freedom is gone? And the answer is clearly negative: society will not be elevated towards freedom, but instead will fall back to its original conformist and authoritative state; it's just that the free time allowed to express one's rights will be gone. Here one can see the immediate danger of thoughtless libertarianism, where the principles of liberty are not understood or appreciated but taken for granted; if one dislikes authoritarianism and considers the extension of civil liberties a human achievement, then one is also to appreciate this achievement by paying respect to the work by one's predecessors that has pro-

II-7. THE SOCIAL NATURE OF RELIGION

duced the basis that constitutes these liberties. These people *fought* to achieve them... but what was it that they fought? They fought a world in which living in the security of a city, protected from the teeth of wolves and bears, the knives of bandits, marauders and highwaymen, and the spears of invading armies, translated to submitting to the rule of man by the city's governing bodies. Flag-burners should reacquaint themselves with the realities of such a world, but most importantly, we should acknowledge that atheism is an intellectual exercise of one's granted freedom of speech; the atheist is refusing an existing system, and the religion-atheism debate is not set on a stage where one is able to choose which one is right but on a stage where a commonly adhered system is being intellectually criticized and rejected by the atheist. The supporter of the existing belief system is *committed* but the atheist is not; he is arguing from the cover of not having to commit himself to anything, this cover being provided by the existing system via its freedom of speech. This is why the most popular atheist arguments or works can only succeed in persuading people into disbelief, and no system can be built upon such a ground.

Now, *secularization* is a theory advocated by many (and predominantly outspokenly atheist) social theorists, which presents the differentiation between religion and government as a sort of natural law advancing along with modernization. Secularization is associated with being modern, which makes rule by religion and tradition old-fashioned. And this sort of movement can indeed easily be observed, comparing, say, Eastern traditional societies to Western secularized societies. But to consider the phenomenon as a *natural law* is to simply disregard its constituting basis where the university, as the breeding ground for modern technological innovation, is an institution having been allowed to form as a unit of independent government of originally Christian schools. The *motive* for the secularization in universities has clearly been *tolerance* towards difference in a world that is experienced as increasingly multi-cultural, which is a Christian virtue in itself. Old universities have recently been working hard to remove Christian references from their mission statements, insignia and so on in order to achieve a higher level of tolerance, experienced as a sort of next step in development. But the removal of such references doesn't invalidate the fact that the institution is a product of Christian social order and that the functionality of the institution still repeats the Christian values that it has been founded on; what is removed is the enforcement of those values on students, staff and produced work, and also the capability to present work produced by the institution under the flag of Christianity. And this direction can be expected to invite at least two sorts of social phenomena: 1) erosion of the institution's constitutional values via barring their expression, and 2) conflict with the competing values brought from other cultures that the new formally secularized system is supposed to better tolerate. These two phenomena are the most pressing social issues in modern Western society, not just within universities: the erasure of religious discourse removes the capability to recognize the constituting values people subscribe to and makes it impossible to talk about them and thus identify with them. This results in the opposite of what was intended; instead of increased Christian tolerance on an organizational level the world becomes increasingly intolerant on the level of society, as people no longer identify with the virtues of compassion and tolerance that are fundamental virtues for Christians, Buddhists, Hindus, Muslims... but not atheists, since atheism doesn't constitute any moral codes. An argument I have heard is that secularization is something that "seems to" follow from modernization, as it is an observable phenomenon in advanced countries. I would rather argue that the phenomenon appears in *democratic* countries: as democracy means equality of all and equality of minorities, it is an understandable democratic goal to eradicate symbols of *social class* in order to advance the equality of minorities. Secularization just happens to involve the blind assumption that religious symbols are symbols of social class, whereas they essentially are symbols of social order. Then again, I fail to see any basis for the idea that in the future religion would become more of a personal choice instead of a social organization; we can already easily verify that the lack of moral social frameworks has resulted in Westerners identifying with values that do not represent individual choice any more than in a religious community, but the product of subculture identification and heavily influenced by commercial marketing. Religion, by nature, *is* not an individual

II-7. THE SOCIAL NATURE OF RELIGION

choice but a communal institution with particular rules of conduct and, on the level of the subjective, a matter of whether the individual identifies with it or not. The same is the case with all social identification: one doesn't *choose* what to identify with; rather one's identity is something to explored and confessed on the level of the subject and existence, and people can in practice have serious difficulties with their identity, afraid to "be themselves" under constant and multi-directional social pressure. Identity is a very interesting psycho-social phenomenon; a strong identity, meaning a stable role in society, translates to independence from external evaluation, and it implies comfort and security that are achieved by self-awareness. Religion, globally, is probably the strongest source of identity, and in good times people are to feel more individual freedom from such institutions, but when the times get worse this will be seen as a very sharp movement towards religion in search of group identity; it is the underlying safety system, like the parents of a teenager who can be predicted to return home precisely on the day when the money runs out. All in all, if one fails to foresee this outcome from simply analysing secular arguments, the theoretical basis of secularization—as a process of 'natural' development that involves the functional emancipation and separation of the state, economy and religion—has obviously already proven false in practice, since the West is facing a very sharp shift in the direction of less freedom for both the state and religion on account of its attachment to solely economic values.

A religion *cannot* be born out of nothing, and it is impossible to make a person believe with, say, bribery or the threat of violence; torture victims generally submit in order to escape harm, but will later admit they were forced to say things they don't believe, and such a person would never continue to pass on the lies he was forced to utter. As religious faith can be born out of the human quality of desperately wanting help, a religion can be born out of a people desperately wanting help, combined with a leader stepping out to fulfil that role. In the case of the Bible, the people of Israel, mostly of colourful pagan religions, were under fairly recent tax slavery imposed by the Romans. Such a situation will create anguish and mutual disagreement, a sort

PART II. COMMON MISCONCEPTIONS

of controlled chaos, and such people will gradually lose their original faith but will not give up hope. First they will believe: "Someone will stand up and put an end to this horror", and when this doesn't happen, the hope will degrade into a fainter form: "One day someone will come and put an end to this horror", and as time passes by and this merges with legends, a shared hope will be jointly communicated: "As our wise men of the past prophesied, someone will come and put an end to this horror." They will wait for a *messiah*, a leader appointed by God (such as a Jewish king traditionally anointed with oil), because it is evident that the ruling power will not appoint a leader to help their people, and it is an unacceptable thought that God has forsaken them to such a bleak fate. They will start looking out, especially for newcomers, asking: "Could *he* be the one?" This creates an atmosphere in which somebody is expected to stand out from the crowd, and the one who does so is expected to present the tools to solve the situation that has seemed so insoluble that it has been met with group submission for a long time. All traditional solutions have been discussed hundreds of times, but all of them come to nothing because people who are segregated cannot stand up against an armed oppressor that can easily overpower and publicly execute any subgroup that dares to try. Enter Jesus with his message: "Love God, whose children we all are; love your neighbour and your enemies, too." Functionally: a common God will guarantee united tradition and afterlife, loving one's neighbour will guarantee effective unification, and loving one's enemy will eliminate violent outbursts on the path to developing a unified nationalist mentality. Functionally the message conveys just the tools needed, and the difficulty from that point onwards is to believe the messiah will stay true to his word and not betray his own people. Now, in the same way that a person going on hunger strike (a method used by Gandhi) will symbolize people's conscience by going through such personal agony, Jesus would take the blasphemous role of a messiah, punishable by death, and take the people's sin—of succumbing to a futile fight against their neighbours and rebelling against the known oppressor—on his own shoulders. His self-chosen fate against the greatest horror imaginable would now represent the future and unity of the people who followed him, and his success in overcoming the worst sort of fear would represent the ultimate ability to overcome an injustice of any size with the message he preached. Thus, the Lamb of God voluntarily dying on the cross is proof that a man is able to face even death for justice alone, and the mass of people following him makes it sensible to follow his lead, because the oppressors cannot kill such a large number of people, especially because this would remove their own income from taxes. After Jesus' success, what is left is to spread the word that a way to overcome oppression has been found to exist, and it is the way that Jesus showed. It has been shown that one man can walk to his death for justice, and if thousands will devoutly follow his example, the oppressor will be met with real resistance. Surely this is Good News for anybody to hear: a new messiah can only come in a world filled with hope and expectation. Jesus took this and turned it into faith in Him. And absolutely and unquestionably this is a *true* story regarding Jesus' achievement, yet e.g. the birth of Jesus is obviously symbolical in nature: the long-awaited martyr emerged and brought freedom, which equals the beginning of a new world and the year zero, and his followers wrote his legend in a very similar fashion to e.g. the martyr legend of Socrates—we erect statues and write songs to honour great people. The story must be true because it is unthinkable for somebody to just "sit down and write" such a story out of simple entertainment and reach a cult following with a piece of entertainment—which is a joke of a perspective atheists are seen to repeat. Such opinions, that the story of the Bible is a simple fairy-tale, are cultivated by people who in their cynicism don't take the *status* of a religion seriously: they don't ask how such a story would become a religion; they don't ask the question: "How did it come to be that somebody wrote a fairy-tale, handed it to people and they started worshipping it?" You can't create worship even through the most extreme means of coercion; even if people were forced to worship a fairy-tale under the penalty of death, they would not worship it but just pretend to do so—they would not read the book to their children in the evenings after the daily masquerade was over. So, it might be that Jesus' disciples would spread the message, which becomes legend and develops parts that are untrue in a factual sense, and this is the case with all legends, such as the legends about famous rock stars that arise from stories told by their roadies. Stories of turn-

PART II. COMMON MISCONCEPTIONS

ing water into wine and curing the blind are obviously such innocent additions that add to the miraculous importance of Jesus and reflect his respect. Parts that are historically untrue (unknown) but symbolically (functionally) true are added because of their appeal in story-telling: the person telling the story will sound more interesting as the story becomes more unbelievable but told with absolute seriousness, as the story-teller has witnessed the events himself and knows that the main part, constituting the message of the story, is true. And then at some point, somebody makes the effort to interview these people and writes all these stories down into a written collection. In Finland, our national epic Kalevala was written in the 19th century by such a man that devotedly collected living legends into a single story, driven by a nationalist spirit. That's why the book is epic: it is living tradition and living real beliefs collected.

Religions can be seen as similar to political *ideologies* in several integral respects—by ideologies I mean political opinions of groups that use idealist argumentation, which is a distinctive type of argumentation and characterizes the Kierkegaardian ethical mode of existence. If one is able to forget the metaphysical perspective that the 'idea' in 'idealism' refers to the concept of a metaphysical object (as it is often characterized), one might notice that there is no difference in use between the concepts of seeing an idea (in one's mind) and believing in an ideal. Religions and ideologies both have an ethical motive aimed towards change in society, and they publicly invite members by means of ethical arousal and agitation. They both create an atmosphere in which members are hoping and waiting for the change to take place, and observed phenomena are interpreted to signify the change. They create a body of related discourse that functions as "the message", the adherence to which, through rituals, identifies group membership. During their birth in a favourable political atmosphere they are led by powerful individuals that are worshipped as heroes within the movement but may be left in an authoritative position disconnected from the original political context, such as the Christian Church and Eastern Communism. The same quasi-religious phenomenon occurs in any social field of life, where powerful ethical leaders introduce some practical dogmata that they regard as ethically important, and others mostly follow this authority. These dogmata can then become "holy traditions" to followers whereas those who introduced them might have intended them to be just simple and practical rules. The aim of all ideologies is to change social injustices by referring to how things would ideally be if the unjust status quo were overturned, and one cannot really perceive an ideal without its counterpoint in existing social injustice. Therefore the 'ideal' in 'idealism' can be seen as a reference to an already existing injustice, and thus *ideologies are reactive in nature*, which explains the very commonplace tendency to think of ethical-political matters in terms of opposing political movements, such as "Capitalism can't be wrong because socialism can't be right" or "You cannot escape your own destiny. You must face Darth Vader again. – I can't kill my own father. – Then the Emperor has already won. You were our only hope." This polar nature in the subjective understanding of having no other option except to choose one's existence is shared with religions in the stories of both Jesus and Buddha, and is a definitive feature of all Christian testimonies that work to portray the subjective element of becoming Christian. The idealist question is of the form: "Why does *this* happen and nobody cares or reacts?" However, religions differ from ideologies in the sense that the motive of a religion is to cause *inner* change, whereas the motivation of an ideology is solely to change society through action. Therefore, ideological discourse applies objective language and communicates its aims in a concrete manner, whereas religious discourse is always *symbolic* and related to the subjective. Both idealist and religious movements can commonly be observed to ultimately invite characteristics that contradict with their original ideal: there tend to appear both idealists that condemn people based on their subjective beliefs instead of their actions, and religious authorities or advocates that condemn people based on their actions.[160] The characteristics are acquired as a by-product of their political authority, since they openly invite members, some of whom relate to them through institution and group membership rather than the ideology. Another thing that should be noted is that the national

---

160 Since religions advocate subjective change, in all religions, what condemns one is something subjective.

PART II. COMMON MISCONCEPTIONS

implementation of communism in the East was a classical coup via revolution by using the theory of Marxism-Leninism to address workers. Communism is doomed simply because its principle of common ownership is based on *idealist theory*. The whole concept of 'common ownership' is an artificial one; a concept born out of the refusal of 'ownership' because of the negative effects attributed to it. What the concept of common ownership works to idealistically reject is the territorial behaviour common to territorial animals. Simply taking a dog for a walk and observing its behaviour should make it obvious that threatening other dogs and spraying his urine over theirs is the natural element of a dog—in contrast with the restrained and unnatural life of a dog confined to a human's apartment. If one doesn't like the word 'natural' because it is sometimes used incorrectly,[161] one need simply to ask: what *should* the dog do instead of such behaviour? Similarly, simply watching a group of toddlers in a playground will show a keen observer how an envious toddler boldly comes and grabs the toy of another, declaring it to be his for a moment, making the other toddler cry before discarding it. On a cultural level, Asian cultures have always contrasted with the West in terms of communality, and a good Asian person thinks unselfishly in group terms, but with different results than what one might expect from a communally functioning society: there is no Asian country in which this sort of thought can be seen to have developed an egalitarian society without oppression—themes that can be seen as the motivation behind communist theory. Quite the contrary: modern Asian countries are following the Western lead and enforcement of human rights. But against an idealist, to say that something, such as ownership, is natural, is never an argument: an idealist sees effects that are bad, and to question their 'bad' status is in contradiction with his existence. He feels that if e.g. pain and suffering are not 'bad', then nothing makes any sense any longer. The idealist says: "We don't *need to* behave like dogs", by which he means to show an

---

161   Natural fallacy: it is quite a mistake to derive 'good' from 'natural', as in the classical chaos/order-dichotomy nature represents uncontrollable chaos. Whenever someone asserts that something is natural and thus good, I would have to remind them that the predator eats his prey with a feeling of joy, pride and success, and wild nature is full of disorderly chaos and unrestrained murder. This unruly disorder is, as it were, the natural, proto-human state, and a world created out of that which is natural will contain nothing of what we consider good (or evil).

II-7. THE SOCIAL NATURE OF RELIGION

example through his own behaviour, which, due to this nature, leads him into self-sacrifice regardless of the results he thus achieves. But on the contrary, the fundamental problem for a religious person is: *why* is it that pain and suffering are natural; what *sense* does it make? Essentially, for an idealist, the question "Why must that man (or animal) suffer?" is a way of asking his subjective question: "Why must *I* suffer?" He knows that suffering is wrong because he himself doesn't want to suffer, and he has the courage to stand up and fight against it, but he doesn't (yet) ask the question personally but asks it through others and society.

Another perspective on how religion is distinguished from ideology is the public nature of the political ideology that is born out of ethical thought. Religion operates completely in the subjective realm, and in this sense it is very strongly connected to *tradition* and has a related *institution* to maintain it. Like all tradition, religion is usually introduced to a person in childhood and first absorbed without resistance. Although religions involve mythological explanations of the origin of sensory phenomena, such as the world, people, animals, plants, etc., the bulk of a religion comprises lore about a subjective way of living and making choices, which is deemed a moral truth. This introduction in childhood binds religion and tradition together *psychologically* in terms of denial and acceptance. Our adult wish to control our lives conflicts with what has influenced us—the past, the tradition—and when we see our values conflicting with those inherited influences we battle them with denial, and the extreme form of denial turns into a wish to forget who one is. The one who forgets himself is one who is ashamed of himself and wants to forget: in Finland they get drunk and express their hatred of the past by burning churches and tipping over tombstones, to forget the tradition where you have to commemorate your own father and to forgive his sins. So, ideology is essentially rational thought, but different from a religion in the sense that there is no institution to validate related commitment; it is behaviour protected by freedom of speech but essentially *free from commitment, ramifications, responsibilities or guidance.* You can look at it this way: when you are attesting belief in an ideology, you are giving *a pledge.*

PART II. COMMON MISCONCEPTIONS

Some ideological leader might ask you for such a pledge; to see that you are accepted to the circle of a movement by committing to it, so that he can trust you with the practical matters of the movement. Now, what is a pledge? A pledge is a token of security to signify trust between the parties, such as a deposit when renting a motorbike; you trust the lessor that the bike you are renting is up to certain standards, and in return promise that if you fail to respect the trust and wreck the bike, your pledge will be lost to the owner of the bike. When you attest belief in an ideology, you should be wary of the fact that there typically exist people who act as community leaders that can be very powerful figures and expect loyalty from their followers, but there might not be any standards or processes of systematic government to evaluate the actions of these leaders themselves. By committing yourself to the values of an ideology, you are signifying trust in some related community that you see to be in the business of advancing something you find important, but in return for your trust you should require reliable standards to secure your trust. In the case of religions, the existing tradition equals this standard, and by rejecting and battling traditions one will expose oneself to the influence of people who don't operate under the guidance of such traditions. When participating in an ideology, your action is based on a particular moral thought: freedom of speech and the freedom to form unions exist so that democratic people could get together and return the benefits they have enjoyed from a functional and free society to help make this society better by introducing criticism and changes that they find relevant. If this wasn't the case, these freedoms wouldn't exist but we would live under rule by tradition, being quoted ancient texts as the ultimate justification of actions taken. The freedom you are wielding is the freedom to challenge tradition, and any idealist can be asked to accept, along with their justification for their action ("to make the world a better place", "something needs to be done" or similar) the *moral responsibility* to return the liberty received. Now, you should be sure to expect the same moral reciprocity you yourself are implementing to apply to any group or movement you commit yourself to, and ask yourself the question: Since I am pledging my aid to this community, how is the community returning my service? In the case of private corporations this relationship is concerned

II-7. THE SOCIAL NATURE OF RELIGION

with money, and in the case of religions what you receive in return is the safety of tradition, but in the case of ideology, you are pledging voluntary work presumably against a promise of changes being achieved in the future, so your question should be targeted towards the leaders and government (if any) of such a movement: How are they committed and do they identify with *moral reciprocal* thought to serve *society*, as you yourself do? Very common to such ideologies is the tendency to blame any faults on individual groups, and not responsibly accepting that the fault lies with society as a whole, and this is an abuse of one's freedom of speech from the perspective of its purpose. When communism universally fails, all those who believe in it can only say it has been universally badly implemented, which is to say that the leadership was bad. Well, why would it be good if there is no system to hold its management responsible for the promises they make? And what is there to motivate such management, since the ideal of communism is to have no management at all? What is the reward for the managers' extended responsibility over the pawns of the system, as there are no profits or private property?

I am probably not enough of an expert on Marx to say anything about the actual content of his theories. And I have no doubt that Marx is a very serious and skilled economic and social theorist. But considering his influence, with a line of devout followers quoting his theories as holy scripture, it is alarming to find that his way of writing theory doesn't follow a systematic method, which to me implies a state of obsession contra clarity. Take the vary basis of historical materialism, which, from the perspective of the scientific method, comprises, firstly, an observation that the distribution of property plays a significant role in the socio-economic history of a society; secondly, the hypothesis that there are socio-economic laws that regulate the development of a civilization and an attempt to formulate such laws as hypotheses, and thirdly, verifying the hypotheses with empirical observations. As such, the theoretical approach makes particular sense, because the motive for the theory is based on an evident fact as it can easily be seen that the distribution of property affects the development of society, and there is also a way to verify if the prediction actually came true. But

PART II. COMMON MISCONCEPTIONS

when he would further hypothesize that every society follows a transformation from capitalism to socialism and from there to a never-witnessed utopian stage of communism, this is a theory in a fundamentally different sense, as in order to verify the theory the stage of socialism is already expected from society; there is a 'catch' involved: *if you wish to verify whether communism is true, you first need to be socialist.* The premise for verifying the theory doesn't exist—yet—and as of now we only can make a leap of commitment to the fact that it will exist in the future. It seems to me that this hypothesis is shared with all *pyramid schemes*. Pyramid schemes are a class of networking business models that reappear every now and then: people commit themselves to the scheme, the scheme gains publicity and notoriety, then at some point the pyramid collapses and people are left betrayed without their promised profits... and nobody participates in any pyramid scheme for a while, until the latest disaster has been thoroughly forgotten. Pyramid schemes abuse people's greed with a promise of huge profits from a mathematical model of creating a network of people, but one that is not based on reality in terms of actual capability to recruit that many people. At some point the lower-level operatives recognize that they are unable to fulfil their recruitment goals, after which the pyramid collapses from the bottom to the top, the low level being left with betrayed hopes and wasted efforts while the top level makes an actual profit. The logic of a person being recruited into a pyramid scheme is this: "This product and marketing is the future, and soon everybody will be participating. If I am stupid and don't make a commitment right now, then soon I will be left at a lower stage in the pyramid." His friend could challenge this logic: "How do you know that this is the future; how do you know that everybody will be a part of this in the future?" But the pyramid victim's greed comes before his reason: "You can sit here and hesitate indefinitely, but this level in the pyramid is available only now, and if I don't act, I will regret it." Without reason, without knowledge, I choose to trust instead. Why? Because I want the money. The connection to the promise of socialism should be obvious: you can't know the results yet, but just trust this promise; trust socialism—become a socialist—and in the future you'll have more money, just like the rich. It makes sense to participate in a lottery in which you

II-7. THE SOCIAL NATURE OF RELIGION

can see your lot being thrown into the hat and one lot drawn out of many: you can't know the outcome of the lottery but you can know that it *is* a lottery, as you can visibly witness the process. But what about participating in something called "a lottery" where you will simply be told whether you won or not. You won't have any way to verify the method of determining the winner but you will be told to trust it, nevertheless. No person on Earth would voluntarily participate in such a scheme. Consider a theory that says that such-and-such a thing will come true, but only if you commit to the theory and say it is true… this fundamentally is not a scientific theory but rather a *subjective promise*, akin to the work of a religious prophet. It is the polar opposite of a scientific theory in function and the very reason why the scientific method exists as a means to provide objective, non-subjective information. We could say of this 'promise' type of theory: I don't know what kind of man he is, but his promises seem to make a lot of sense *in theory*. Now, both meanings of 'theory' can be seen to have their place and thus neither of them is the 'right' or 'wrong' use of the word; they're just mixed up, confused. And to confuse totally different *meanings* of the word 'theory' in this manner is to display a lack of *philosophical* thought and a lack of intellectual responsibility over one's words; the reader is thrown a prophecy under the label of theory, but no care is taken over whether he would like to see if he can trust this theory or not. Fair enough, but let's consider if Marx could be seen as a prophet instead; perhaps he had subjective ethical insight that is valuable in itself. Then why does he present his insight as theory instead of candidly asking us to believe in *him* only? Why doesn't he, like Jesus Christ, announce that he has seen paradise and those who follow him will get a piece of the paradise, e.g. dwell in the house of the Lord? *Following* is a very particular thing to do, in which one walks the path already laid by another, and if somebody expects another to simply follow him, that person needs to first walk the path himself. To simply believe and to follow Marx doesn't make sense because he is not leading but theorizing as an external observer of phenomena. Rather the theory acts as a diversion in case somebody were to ask Marx what subjective grounds he actually has for his prophetic insight, such as an epiphany, a dream or suchlike; what proof does he have that he actually wishes the best for all

PART II. COMMON MISCONCEPTIONS

people, the best for humanity... But Marx could be easily excused for not having any such proof, because he has written a lot of theoretical work about it that gives the impression of being objective in nature. Jesus didn't say: "This is how this stuff that I am talking about *should* work *in theory*", but instead proved his ethical nature—barring any possibility of doubt by his actions, by becoming the messianic King of the Jews, a position contradicting the authority and absolute power of Caesar and punishable by death. He put his word (promise) together with his action, which was to *prove* his word correct. In colloquial terms, he put his money where his mouth was. Marx would not do such a thing but was working alongside and in the security of an existing societal movement, and to me it seems fair to say that, rather than being philosophical, scientific or prophetic, or providing some intellectually sound basis for revolution or workers' unity in general, the bulk of his writings would simply sound appealing to people already involved in a such a process and would act as a unifying theoretical framework for such movement. That Marx sounds appealing to people who hate the rich doesn't in itself nullify his value, but one should remember how appealing Hitler's rage against Jews sounded to so many, and simply take notice that crafting an illusion that sounds appealing is the standard technique of con artists and illusionists of various kinds. My (Southeast Asian) friend told me a story about a man (a relative) who had fallen under the spell of a local medicine man—witch doctor—who performed black magic, and the story involved the people around the man having curses put on them. Virtually every time the man came to him for spiritual consultation, being distressed by bad dreams, insomnia, stress and other symptoms, the medicine man made the man believe his family was cursed. The cursed state of the family did become self-evident because the man's desperate situation, which drove him to seek advice from the shaman, was affecting his family, too, and thus the family was also reacting badly. All the witch doctor needed to do for his fee was to observe the man to find his weakness and then to "pull his strings", saying just what he wanted to hear: that the man's situation is not his own fault but caused by a curse on his relatives, and not the other way round. Now, let me make a parallel to Marx: the poor proletariat are hungry and ailing—obviously cursed. Marx would not

II-7. THE SOCIAL NATURE OF RELIGION

see anything natural, intentional or meaningful in this state, in the way that Buddha would say that life is suffering or Jesus or Gandhi would work to make human suffering visible. The very starting point of Marxist theory is that the wretched status quo of the proletariat is an unnatural, passing state that resembles sickness or a curse, and is essentially caused by somebody completely different from them: by the rich who own things. He just abstracted this into a form that the cause is not the rich *people* but private ownership, similar to the way car accidents can be blamed on car ownership. And this is particularly appealing to somebody who doesn't own a car; to somebody who will gladly be a vocal anti-car advocate until, of course, he gets a job for which he needs a car. At this point he will become an active proponent of car ownership. But to subscribe to Marx is to obtain complete absolution from any personal wrongs *and* any wrongs committed by one's forefathers. Subscribing to Marx means learning that one is cursed—bearing the curse of the proletariat—but the cult accepts no blame for this curse: the blame is on people outside the cult. And this is the basic formula of all unjust hatred, such as xenophobia and religious hatred: blaming another class for one's misfortune and refusing to share blame.

This sort of work is very dangerous in its way of presenting ideology as scientific or philosophical thought; a sharp knife with a furry pastel coloured handle that looks appealing to children instead of presenting standard warning labels. Supporters of Marxist theory must admit that there are no real-world examples of successful application of such theory, which, of course, they can (and do) blame on the rich capitalists instead of the one who wrote the flawed theory—flawed because it can be falsely applied due to the inability to test it. To summarize Marxist thought: 1) the wretched state of the poor is not caused by the actions of rich individuals, such as bad government, but by the existence of the rich class, and 2) the universal shortcomings of the communist agenda are not caused by the communist agenda but by particular individuals failing at implementing it. This sort of theory is anti-intellectual and particularly dangerous in encouraging revolution and the overthrow of government without providing a viable real-world alternative form of government that would provide grounds to verify the theory. Instead, it offers a theoretic utopian government in a world simply assumed to have overthrown the human institution of private ownership. In my opinion this resembles thought that is fundamentally obsessed with supporting the denial of something—in this case misfortune and human suffering—instead of trying to better understand it, which is the purpose of both philosophy and science. Although typically presented as a polar opposite to *fascism*, emphasizing equality of the working class in contrast with the open authoritarianism and elitism in fascist writings, I see Marx's communist writings as very much akin to fascism in that they function as anti-intellectual propaganda aimed to arouse primal sentiments, and they utilize the *populist* method of presenting the self as an archaic group unjustly *victimized*. The style of writing in the *Communist Manifesto* and e.g. Heidegger's national spiritualism is virtually identical: identifying a looming world-historical crisis in which there will be a return to a historical way of life that will revitalize the deeper human spiritual capabilities that have been wrongly stripped from the people by others, and this will be delivered with the supreme power of philosophy. Both Marx (or Engels, "primitive communism") and the Nazis ("the Aryan race"), in their own occult ways, saw their own ideology as the natural, protohuman existence that had since unfortunately been corrupted (a highly Christian creation myth), and saw their own role, not just as the knight in shining armour rescuing the damsel from the tower, but as the liberator of *peoples*, revitalizing, not just the world, but *all world history* back into its ancient paradise-like existence. Could we even artificially try and devise a more grandiose narcissist dream? In their activities, both Marx and Heidegger were equally engaged in the most radical political movements available; movements that were aiming towards a complete transformation of the world as we know it. In the light of this similarity it sounds correct to me to say that Marx identified his philosophy with the power of the already active communist movement, similar to what Heidegger did with National Socialism. It is a national sentiment of traumatic victimization seeking pride and a sense of justice but without the means to acknowledge the origin of the trauma: instead of self-reflection and acknowledgement, one plays the victim of abuse and justifies furious retribution. And the political outcomes of the application of such thought have been not only bad, but responsible for creating the greatest individual social catastrophes in human history. A Finnish academic recently suggested[162] that the armies of the world should be united for a green purpose; to reforest the Sahara Desert and similar projects. If a real political party suggested something like this, I would suspect that it was a cover for really sinister plans, because such a proposal goes completely against the purpose of any military force. Today, one can say, as the communists say, that communism is a good theory, it has just been consistently wrongly applied. One can't say this of fascist theories because this is considered to be showing sympathy with the Nazis.

Marx would have to be analytically searching for truth in a descriptive, and not prescriptive, sense, in order for me, personally, to call his work philosophy. And his way or argument is to present as a theory what is essentially an ethical ideology; presenting morality, something that *should be*, as a hypothetical truth. But this sort of ideology also differs from any religion, the basic moral frameworks of social order, in the fundamental way that the motive of ideology is to create a more just society by some *external* (objective) *standard*, such as equality or a better distribution of wealth, whereas religions aim towards moral harmony by *subjective standards*, which is reflected in religious symbolical expression as the justice of the *afterlife*. The afterlife, whether heaven for Christians or the next life following reincarnation for Hindus, doesn't only refer to what happens after one's death, but it is the symbol of what happens if one lives in a particular way, and is always presented in the context of a choice of a way of life. It is the objectivity of society contra the subjectivity of the afterlife that, on the level of argument, makes the commitment to an ideology essentially a question of "How do you want to (morally) act?" and the commitment to subjective faith a question of "How do you want to (morally) feel about your actions?" And this fundamental subjectivity is what makes religious people appear child-like: like a child, the religious person is content

---

162   Eero Paloheimo in http://www.helsinginuutiset.fi/artikkeli/351946-maailman-suurin-voimavara-on-vaarassa-kaytossa-tekniikan-tohtorin-vetoomus-keraa [26.12.2019].

with his subjective assurance of having acted in the right subjective way; in a sense separated from what actually takes place in society. Now, the fundamental deficiency in the morality of ethical ideologies is that they don't actually aim to create *moral people* who would behave in a moral way, but they aim to change society in a way that reflects the ethical thought of a part of society, and are used to spearhead a movement that in itself aims to change society instead of bringing it into harmony. For example, *equality* has been accepted as an ethical foundation in the West, and this has happened because of the established inequality within society where a change has been seen as necessary by a part of society. But as the ideology it is, equality has been separated from its Christian/Stoic origin of what morally constitutes equality: the natural brotherhood of people, where 'brother' is a metaphor for how things, such as food, property or responsibilities, are shared within a family. Equality in itself was once a rallying cry for changing things for the better, but because this slogan in this form is not a religious concept but a moral derivative of one, it has no power to create social harmony but just social change. Now, at a time when Western systems have been considerably changed by the concept of equality, the concept is being used in a violent manner as a tool to create social disharmony by attacking the original religious functions of society which constitute social harmony. It is doing so basically by extending the concept of equality as brotherhood to the abstract concept of freedom and equal rights, which is something that was never meant by 'equality'. Freedom and equal rights, in the sense of brotherhood, can be seen to imply that nobody has intrinsic authority over another member of the family, but the fundamental part of the metaphor that is contemporarily omitted is that brotherhood also means *being bound to the same fate*, meaning that the collective freedom goes hand-in-hand with the collective responsibility over the whole family, which is a completely different relation than simply equal rights. This family justice is very warmly depicted in the Finnish classic novel *Seven Brothers*, where the family of brothers, being bound to equal fate in a joint life in a harsh land, at times had to resort to disciplining a dissenting brother with a collectively decided warm and brotherly beating—something that modern equality rhetoric would condemn. The social advocacy of equal rights

II-7. THE SOCIAL NATURE OF RELIGION

separated from an experienced shared fate has in Western countries become a tool for deliberately attacking the religiously based social constructs that maintain social harmony and the continuity of shared values over generations. Such activities include e.g. advocating equality of sexes (feminism) to deny the expression of traditional sex roles, advocating equality of marriage to extend the concept of marriage to sexual minorities unable to procreate, and advocating "equality of religions" via attacking Christianity.[163] These anarchistic movements generally reflect restlessness and disappointment in the status quo of justice and social order; the general way for the social human to express dissatisfaction is to blame groups of people for experienced injustice, and in the West that blame currently lies on religion and its experienced inefficiency in maintaining the justice and social order that everybody needs from their society. Religion is experienced as an old-fashioned and ineffective system of restrictions in a very recently emerged global information society.

One way to look at the difference between ethical and religious thought is to consider that religious thought includes a second perspective (as in the Kierkegaardian 'double reflection'). Ethical existence is based on the primary role of action in relation to thought and correct understanding, and from this perspective a one-sided ideology is adequate. Because action is primary for the idealist, he thinks in terms of "Everybody should be doing such-and-such", and a person who takes the initiative to do this is good, and a person who knowingly refuses is bad. Whereas idealist thought rewards any action towards a positive goal, religious thought differs from this in terms of *adding* a perspective of *result*: whether the actions initiated will yield the desired results; for example, whether condemning or punishing an offender will yield the result of curing him of his offensive actions. These sorts of questions are not handled in any proper way by idealist thought, but conclusions are always a part of trying to sum up the pros and cons of a particular solution, while being conscious that they may not be comparable; the

---

163 Symbolical attacks on Christianity include campaigns, mock constructs such as the "Satanic Church" to question the institutional role of Christianity, and symbolic deeds such as the US-affiliated agent provocateur group Pussy Riot cutting a large crucifix down with a chainsaw.

idealist takes the role of a judge who has the responsibility for such judgment, but this in fact contradicts what can intellectually be seen as a capability to judge another person. In Christianity, passing judgment is in itself met with refusal, as far as I can see, for two reasons. Firstly, there is a fundamental moral issue in passing judgment over a person without knowing his motives (a person can lie about his motives), as it is impossible for a person to honestly condemn another person because he adheres to motives one justifies in one's own life. Hence the principle "Judge not lest ye be judged", which guides one not to pass judgment, as the judgment for actions based on a motive implies universality, but it might be that the dismissed motives of the condemned were similar to ones one oneself might adhere to. Not to pass judgment guarantees a clear conscience. Secondly, even if the condemned was knowingly breaking principles and laws, and would find his sentence rightful, condemnation will save society from the threat of a villain, but only *mercy* has a possibility to heal him. Neglected children can be taught to reciprocate love by being given lots of love and freedom, and this applies also to adults. Religious thought takes the step of *wisdom*: even if it would seem the right thing to do from a certain perspective, why do something that gives no results? When a person is dying and the desperate family turns to the priest, he in turn speaks of the beauty of the person while he lived, and the beauty of the afterlife. This is because religious thought takes fundamentally seriously the futility of trying to affect things that cannot be affected (death) and uses every effort to target the imagination towards what *can* be helped: the hearts of those whom the death of a relative hurts. By *deliberately choosing this perspective*, religious thought can help the family to see *purpose* (meaning, application) in what can be seen as meaningless and arbitrary. From a functional perspective, the meaning does not come from *what* a particular scripture claims a particular divinity to have said, but it comes from the fact *that* such a thing has been said, and similarly, the meaning of death does not come from *what* a priest says, but it comes from the fact *that* he says it from the religious perspective; *that* there are such things as good motives and an afterlife. The meaning of death is in the *religious perspective* to it, the role of the priest is to remind the grieving family of this, and the purpose of religious *faith* is to

II-7. THE SOCIAL NATURE OF RELIGION

remember an impersonal, larger meaning when one could otherwise be paralyzed with grief at one's personal loss. Thus, the functional role of religion can be seen to bind a society together in a manner that surpasses individual life, and religious perspective and discourse are most needed in matters that are the most difficult for an individual, such as letting go of relatives at the time of death, founding a family in order to raise children, making changes in a life that has gone wrong due to self-deception, going to war, and similar acts.

Another very clear way to distinguish religion and ideology is to take note that *religions have always been* but ideologies come and go and are rather crafted in support of a political purpose that befits the moral sentiments of groups of people. I find this argument the most powerful one in asserting the necessity for religions. The atheist argumentation needs to be turned upside down by taking proper note of the concept of *freedom of religion*, which, like all freedoms, is something granted by the existing society that is *in control* of the phenomenon in question, in this case religion. As a parallel, there can be no "freedom of opinion", unless this freedom is a freedom from something; in this case, the control of public speech to protect the government from slander. So, similarly to all democratic freedoms, freedom of religion is something given *for a purpose*, which is to accommodate differing religions and to abolish justice systems that are based on religious, subjective language instead of objective evidence. And as with all democratic freedoms, if the spirit of this freedom is not respected, it will be revoked, which in the case of religion would mean that if more and more people turn non-religious, this will naturally lead to the reintroduction of religious authority by force. It is easy to speculate how this could happen: the atmosphere of lack of moral rules and rampant moral degradation causes general disgust, which in turn makes religions or sects with more authoritative practices appealing to people, particularly people with a weak identity that crave the protection of a strong group identity. In the same way that a country in need of protection will elect authoritative leaders, the religious groups of choice will be authoritative ones; ones with openly condescending or hostile attitudes towards the moral matters that are experienced as problematic, and ones with more total control over the life of their members. People will voluntarily give themselves to authoritative moral rule and find a stronger identity within this social framework; those who are weak and lost will finally feel empowered by being a part of a movement that answers to their experience of lack of justice and need of proper rules to set things straight. In the West this might mean the rise of more fundamentalist Christian sects, or the rise of Islam, which is known for its tendency to have fundamentalist rules. The other aspect to this is to take note that the common rational aspect that "a man needs religion" is actually misleading as it presumes that man *is free to choose*; a parallel is the common left-wing thought that takes democratic freedoms as-is, instead of understanding that they have been granted for a purpose. This is a form of declarative rhetoric that essentially takes "man *should be* free to choose" and presents this in the form of "man *is* free to choose"... and makes the non-existent existent using this rhetorical device. Now we can see that, in fact, man is free to choose his religion, but we need to also ask: what is the purpose of this freedom? As mentioned earlier, the purpose is, or was, to abolish religious rule; to abolish subjective and arbitrary justice systems. But we don't really have these systems in the West any longer; the feudal king's private justice system has been replaced by evidence-based courts of law that enforce human rights. This essentially means that there is not much need for the freedom; it no longer exists to create justice but only to accommodate different religions, but for what reason? What reason is there to invite, say, two religions to the same country, when the values and practices of those religions are known to be mutually exclusive? Wouldn't it be better to continue having a justice system that is separate from religion; to treat minority religions equally, but to base various domestic policies and immigration policy precisely on religion; to bid immigrants welcome if they share our values and to support conversion?

Superstition, however, is different from religion in the sense that, albeit functioning in the service of a subject's spiritual needs, it doesn't in itself serve a political function and doesn't thus have a social perspective. The similarity of superstition to religion is that it occupies the same realm of subjectivity: something that involves personal wellness and something that can be learned from skilled individuals who possess wisdom in the related arts. The major difference is that the tradition and discourse related to a religion is always tied to its social context and not simply personal wellness, such as bringing good fortune or good health or protecting from harm: in a religious context, the subjective skills passed on with the tradition by nature concern the whole society through the shared practices and language. Thus, the governmental religious tradition starts to evolve into a form that is distinguished from surrounding superstition, and this evolution further separates the related discourse via e.g. separate gods and rituals. The life of this shared religion differs from surrounding superstitions because of its ethical nature: unlike wandering fortune-tellers motivated to cash in by telling tall tales, or old ladies motivated to continue a family tradition, the holy visionaries, prophets and such people are 'winnowed' into their institutional roles by society because they have gained society's trust. Thus, the separate nature of a religion contra superstition is bound to the tradition of shared wisdom within a context of a living society, gathered by people ethically concerned about the welfare of society instead of simply individual assets or the assets of their family. It might be correct to say that our cultural concentration on *wellness* is a replacement for superstition that is marketed to us via advertisements instead of fortune-tellers or snake oil salesmen (albeit that "wellness products" are often seen to be advertised with terminology that can easily be described as hocus pocus). Our advertisements lure us into wellness, and they appeal because of the un-wellness we experience due to social problems. Our concept of wellness essentially means individual wellness where others are unwell: "Don't be un-well! Be well!"

Whereas the context of all ideologies is society, the context of all religions is the subject. This perspective brings out the coexistence of both religion and *art* in the subjective realm, affecting people's emotions. One way to present the difference is to say that ideologies work to point out *what* we should do (because of social outcomes), but both religion and artwork to point out *why* we should do *it*—whatever that 'it' may be. Then again, we have classes of pathos without an implied ethical message, such as *bad art*,[164] entertainment, advertisements or propaganda. The central difference between such activities and religious pathos or art is that they don't appeal to our *empathy*—our distinctive ethical faculty. Then again, *how* this works cannot be explained: for example, one could try and describe the Christian icon of the Madonna to signify that holy Jesus (however he is to be understood, my personal opinion makes no difference) was also a child once and loved his mother—just like the rest of us. But I can tell that such a description really has no basis and to back it up with some sort of theory that tried to justify it by referring to particular features of such artwork would cause a conflict with the interpretation of other religious art. Also, such description says nothing at all in an objective sense: a perfectly valid counter-question is to ask: what does it *mean* to point out that Jesus was also a child once? In *my* life, such emotion that can be signified by the love, trust, hope and security of an infant, is very important, and through *my* life, I can relate it to what I believe to be personal success in relation to what I have seen in many others. Only with this *prerequisite* can I take note that the Madonna signifies a similar emotion felt by the one who is found by others to be holy. A person with no personal recognition of such experience *will* find such a description meaningless, and taking him seriously as an intelligent human being, trying to enforce or underline the message by e.g. grandiose gestures will achieve absolutely nothing. Also, I can say that the same emotional relation could be conveyed by many other cultural means, and that the key factor for me in finding such relation in the figure of the Madonna instead of some other sort of figure is the cultural status of the particular symbolism. Simply put, I know that there is something important in such work because it has persisted for, as far as we know, almost two millennia, for no reason that would initially strike one as obvious—given that, in world history, pictures come and go in vast numbers. This fact awakes an interest in me to *understand* the symbolism instead of shrugging my shoulders: to disregard such an obvious and central ethical piece of culture in the history of *mankind* would be to declare that I don't need to understand mankind in my quest to find what is

---

[164] Bad art is any work made to look like art, based on the social institution of art, but without a genuine ethical motive.

right for it. And then again, if I wasn't searching for what is right for mankind, I would have no motive to search for such symbolical emotional references from such sources—I would simply make do with any form of entertainment, should I feel the need to reflect my own emotions without an ethical reference. This is why the word 'truth' so often appears in religious discourse—the religious personal *search* is searching for what is the most difficult in ethical sense (speaking of mankind, through history, instead of a personal and local context), through a solely personal hidden method. The definitive antinome for this—whether or not we want to use the word 'evil'—is the search for personal satisfaction through a public political method. The same set-up of personal against political applies wherever we are apt to use the words 'good' and 'evil': good people personally sacrifice everything for the sake of the common good; evil people abuse everything everybody else has ever created for the sake of personal gain. Works of goodness are those in which voluntary responsibility is subjectively taken for others (a group or an individual) at personal loss, whereas works of evil are those where the trust of another individual, or a social institution, is subjectively abused for the sake of personal gain.

PART II. COMMON MISCONCEPTIONS

II-8. Technological Argumentation

The modern world is filled with fallacious argumentation that has its origin in the technological atmosphere created by the emergence of new computational methods. But these methods don't really bring anything new into the picture from the perspective of humanity and Western civilization; they just change society rapidly, and while doing so create new social skill requirements and a general atmosphere of haste where competitive speed in acquiring new information becomes a necessity, and wisdom and understanding become myths. It is quite an alarming popular opinion, particularly among young people, that truth and opinion mean bias (deviance from the real truth, which is science) and that there is wisdom in not having an opinion—fully contradicting a fairly recent state of affairs in Europe where having opinions was a political necessity, just as it had been for the freemen of Athens. And this general opinion reflects the form of popular social argument which relies on new technology and will exploit any chance of grounding argument with the power of new technology that people, and the arguers themselves, fundamentally lack proper understanding about. The arguments made by journalists (who have become less and less professional, or just individual bloggers) simply repeat general presuppositions put forward by scientists that bias their technological views completely in favour of their own work or, worse, financial interests. It is a worthy topic for inspection because 1) these arguments dominate the current debate and 2) not many philosophers have enough technological education or expertise to make sense of the pseudo-philosophical technological arguments.

The philosophical doctrine perhaps most commonly related to the (intentional or unintentional) misinterpretation of statistics is a form of "correlation does not imply causation", called Hume's Guillotine—Hume was quite correct to note that causation is not a result of reasoning at all. Rather it is the case that "Why?—because..." is a fundamental human concept with logically separate meanings, which change throughout our existence. Only one of these is called causation and is

II-8. TECHNOLOGICAL ARGUMENTATION

the historically and subjectively later concept. Taking this further, it can be seen that exactly the same fundamental problem also extends to the concept of *probability*, which is defined as a means to express a "degree of belief" or a "degree of certainty" over something uncertain. We don't actually relate belief or certainty to a degree which means a unit of measurement: take a look at how the words 'believe' and 'certain' behave in our natural language: "Do you believe it? Yes/No"; "I believe this hat belongs to you"; "Are you absolutely certain? Yes/No"; "Are you coming tonight? Certainly"; "I don't believe we can make it"; "I'm not certain but I think so". Now, where is "With 88 per cent certainty" in our natural language? Or "I believe it 85 per cent?" It doesn't exist. Let's imagine how such an expression might be used:

– *Do you believe that there's a Sun, up there in the sky?*
– *Yes.*
– *That may be, but are you absolutely certain that you are not at the moment dreaming, or that you have been misled your whole life, and that what you have believed to be Sun is actually a bright light bulb in a ceiling that you can't see?*
– *I admit: I am not 100% certain. Let's say it with 99.8% certainty.*

Two major things are worth noticing here. Firstly, it is the change in the *problem-setting* of the question that changes the answer as well. In fact, one can imagine many different problem-settings, not just this Cartesian sceptical one, to suit the situation to reduce the experienced certainty, such as questioning the sense of the concepts in question: what is meant by 'sky' etc. The second thing to note is that the choice of number is completely subjective and, from this objective numerical perspective, arbitrary: there exists no method of coming to it, yet here the answerer is tempted to invent one. And why is he tempted? Because he has assimilated a discourse in which he believes his beliefs can be expressed with a degree of certainty: he believes there *must* be a number to express it, and he does his best to give one. But as we see, he doesn't know what he is saying. Now, being an inventor is a respectable occupation in which someone has learned to use his imagination to produce tools, but a person can also invent answers to questions. Children learn this at a young age, and by doing it in a completely in-

PART II. COMMON MISCONCEPTIONS

nocent manner they test their parents' reactions to it. A responsible parent will notice it and react to it but ignoring it can teach the child to believe her own lies. Hume's "no causation from correlation" can be reformulated in the language of subjective and objective by saying that the subjective certainty of causation can never be produced by objective data because they belong to different logical categories. Certainty can be produced by subjective observations, but in a subjective manner, meaning that there is no objective rule that such a thing would happen. Furthermore, the numeric concept of "degree of belief" doesn't align at all with subjective faith, which is either said to be blind or shaky and hesitant.[165] Rather, the concept is a *metaphor*, having its basis in both 1) our reluctance to accept our lack of knowledge, as it is related to insecurity and fear, and 2) our subjective awareness of the inadequacy of the basis of our beliefs; our awareness that we haven't come to such a conclusion via our normal logical dialectic, and that the result is thus in an incomplete state regarding our subjectivity. When we have come to a certain conclusion following our dialectic rationality, we also believe the conclusion, and it brings about subjective existential change. And this process is not a linear process that slowly converges towards full certainty; rather it consists of the logical opposites of rational argument and taking into consideration logical alternatives, and the closest objective equivalent to this process is a *judicial process* where there is evidence in support of logically exclusive conclusions. This fact is also evident when looking at the etymology of the word 'judgment', which is a reference to legal judgment. And just as in a trial, there is evidence in support of each view, and there exists a moral question of if the evidence is being looked at or overlooked in the first place.

The etymology of 'probable' traces back to 'approvable' via Latin '*probabilis*', which was applied to opinion or action. The concept was also used in a legal context, where 'probable' would similarly denote approvable claims as claims supported by evidence. So probable, in this

---

165 A similar observation was made by Wittgenstein about the grammar of future and past events: they don't at all conform to an idea of temporality as an arrow in space.

original sense, means something that is *just* and therefore deserves approval, and here the subjective meaning is evident: nobody would claim to have any quantifiable basis for his approval of an opinion, but might just justify the notion by stating the evidence that he finds convincing. Statistical probability, on the other hand, is an objective tool, expressed with numbers, and the sense of every expression of probability is bound to the data from which it is derived, such as that the average life expectancy for the Finnish population is such-and-such (based on a collected dataset of the Finnish population), based on which the probability of dying at a certain age can be calculated. Only within this strict limitation can it be said that statistical probability is a means to express a degree of certainty: the certainty is strictly bound to the *data*; when we agree that something is probable based on data, we are actually agreeing that we also have *sufficient data*, because probability means approvable due to *justice*. When we detach the concept of probability from this subjective justice to a context where it relates to data that is not necessarily sufficient, the concept of probability cannot even remotely express a degree of belief anymore. It simply is something completely different, a "statistical probability"; a numeric property derived from certain data. It is completely senseless to try and apply this concept of statistical probability in a subjective sense, and the temptation to do so is created by the confused definition of probability: faith and certainty are subjective faculties, bound by the definition to a numeric objective framework. Whenever a person, based on subjective grounds, presents a numeric probability for his certainty, he is not expressing certainty at all, but inventing an illusion to hide his fundamental lack of certainty. He is fundamentally *uncertain* and he is *hoping* that he has it right, so he chooses a high number. Or he might have some subjective factors he is comparing, but whatever output he would produce would make no difference as no method exists to see if his method of producing a number is correct or not. Similarly, if a person says: "Quite probably I'll come tonight", he is fundamentally saying that he hopes to come, and I know people who often implement what they hope to do, and people who almost never do. People differ significantly in how inclined they are to express their hopes as certainties: how much responsibility they carry over the disappointment of

PART II. COMMON MISCONCEPTIONS

the other person they are talking to; in other words, how *reliable* they are. Mathematical theories of probability were introduced hundreds of years ago, but cult-like interest in probability theory, which has had the power to leak the mathematical language of probability into the natural use of the concept of 'probable' as 'approvable', has no doubt been created by the advent of the computer. Now it is possible to actually perform large numbers of repetitions of arithmetic operations, and to emulate a stochastic (non-determined) process by utilizing any of the various methods of generating random numbers in a computer. A program can take a random number as input by invoking an operating system (OS) service that generates one, and the standard method for the OS to implement this is by reading current time from the computer real-time clock[166] and performing a series of arithmetic operations on this value.

The statistical deception makes something that is determined from inside seem determinable from outside, but such external determination makes no sense as it has *no basis for criteria*. Statistics is a *method* of inducing probabilities from datasets—a method that is very handy. So it seems to be the case that this applicability of the statistical method, combined with the computational power of modern computers, has created an illusory situation in which one is not just hoping but expecting things to be solvable with statistical means... and it should be noted that whenever a hope is turned into an expectation the situation is already quite drastic and failure is highly likely. It seems to make more sense to think along the lines that if one makes the right plans and follows the procedure correctly, then one must come to the correct results, and in day-to-day life the actual hardship often lies in being able to follow a difficult procedure; as we often say: "It is easier said than done." So, now that we have these great computational devices, surely many if not most people believe that statistics can produce reliable answers in a better way than before; *given that* the planning (data selection) is correct. But this sort of common-sense thinking fails to notice that in the general case dealing with subjective decision-mak-

---

[166] The real-time clock of a computer is a standard quartz clock that gets its value from the oscillation frequency of the quartz crystal inside it.

ing it is not only challenging or practically impossible but *senseless* to give criteria for how to select the data. The impossibility we are dealing with here is not practical impossibility, like, say, dealing with the question of whether it is possible for man to one day visit Saturn, or impossibility in the sense that many people say things are impossible but they turn out to be possible after all, like a seasoned criminal might say it is impossible for him to change, meaning he sees no faith or hope in changing himself, yet we still constantly hear stories of miraculous personal change in people who had said all hope was lost. But we are discussing *logical* impossibility, arising out of the logical distinction between an objective system and a thinking subject—impossibility of the kind of whether hunger could be painted blue. It is a *philosophical* problem, not a practical or technical one, and to solve it for oneself one must investigate the concepts one is applying instead of wasting resources on chasing apparitions. In respect to chasing apparitions (or chimeras, attributable to Socrates), which both Kierkegaard and later Wittgenstein saw as products of a particular type of abstract thinking, it is worth considering Socrates' thoughts about what madness is and how we talk about it[167]: madness is the opposite of wisdom, and a man who *supposes that he knows what he, in fact, knows not*, is close to mad, yet the masses don't call one 'mad' who is clueless about matters these masses don't themselves understand. Someone is only called mad if he is wrong about the matters they do understand, such as if he thinks he is able to lift a house. The false supposition is the basis of madness, but only a very strong and passionate existence upon this basis would be called madness. Socrates' view is a very enlightening one to apply to the vast bulk of contemporary science: "to suppose what one knows not" scientifically means assuming a questionable work hypothesis, yet one can see that modern science deals with matters which the masses don't find themselves adequate to hold opinions over, so neither will they have an opinion about the madness of such scientists.

Here is a very simple illustration of the statistical deception: we know that DNA tests are almost 100% accurate. So, it seems we should expect the result of a DNA test to be almost 100% reliable. But in fact,

---

167 Xenophon: *Memorabilia*, III. 9.

it isn't; it's no more reliable than the people (subjects) who perform the test, and in a crooked DNA test lab the tests will be completely unreliable. The said statistical deception has been introduced throughout philosophy of mind, cognitive science and even psychology, e.g. as something called "probability judgments". You can understand the lunacy of this whole concept by considering a "probability trial" in a court of law, where the court decides the outcome of the trial based on what things look like before beginning the trial. The thought behind the concept of probability judgment is explained in scientific papers as if in a children's book: the writer presents an example in which a person might be inclined to apply the language of probability regarding a subjective matter, and thus deduces that people make decisions based on subjective probability judgments—philosophical case closed. Now, every time people talk nonsense, there must a latent motive for it, and in order to understand the phenomenon you need to look for the cause in other directions. As in: if your daughter one day phones with nothing to say except that she's fine and just wanted to hear your voice, repeating three times that she loves you and then abruptly ending the call, it really is not the case that everything is fine. So, in the case of such 'science' there must be an extra-scientific motive to produce such nonsense: there must be political and/or business pressure placed on science that wishes such things to be said. I read that in Thailand hospital staff generally are placed under pressure by executives to push for profits, and this affects the choice of procedures, the prescribed and recommended medication and the general cost of the service. But recently undergoing surgery in Finland at a private clinic was an interesting experience because I remember in my state of post-anaesthetic haze that the nurse was very clear to me about two things: 1) I must take painkillers *constantly* and not have a break in between, and 2) I must buy and take daily injections because I am at risk of thrombosis. Now, I happen to know that excessive painkiller intake is a common cause of ulcers, and as I was disturbed about this injection pushing, I did some research and read that according to some studies British middle aged obese female airline passengers who have had a completely different sort of operation than me have a roughly 1/1000 risk of post-surgical thrombosis, which seems only logical to me because they form a general medical risk group. Just I am not a member of this group but I understand very well why they would still push the injections on me: they will in fact be covered by the medical insurance and hence it is not me personally who would pay for them, so it would not be against my interest to accept them. This was just my personal example of what is common knowledge—that the field of medicine has in the West turned into a field of pushing medication, and the motivating force behind this phenomenon is not very difficult to imagine. Medicine is a highly esteemed field because it deals with people's health and lives, and in this area the contemporary statistical nature of scientific information has strong argumentative power. As such, I believe the current status of statistics reflects people's fears in a society that gets more and more authoritative in terms of the scientific institution—in this case, the medical institution and the institution of medical experts. The situation is much worse in the case of psychiatric treatment: people are becoming more and more sick. This could be attributed to stress and other issues, but I believe that the central factor is widely omitted, which is that psychiatry is not trying or aiming to cure people mentally, but to make them fit for work. The rationale for this behaviour is, again, statistical: statistically you cannot know what's wrong with a person, because people are unique; statistically you can simply obtain a probability but no certainty. And the role of a doctor or a psychiatrist has changed dramatically in this respect: doctors are not trying to experiment and specialize in the sense of practising *an art*, but instead are working in an environment totally controlled by regulations and law. The doctors are restricted from trying to cure their patients, but are induced to drug them, prescribing medication with a logic of statistical proportions: like dosing a mixture of nutrients to feed to cattle.

Statistics and fear are directly related, because statistics is a tool to make predictions about *the unknown*, and the unknown is what we generally fear. Statistics is a tool for assessing *risk*, and one should see that the existence of risk implies the presence of *danger* as a sense of ultimate unpredictability, so one should only turn to statistics whenever one is unable either to *understand* or to *trust*. It is a modern controversy and irony that the increased authority of the scientific institution comes together with the trust and expectation that the institution is *trustworthy* and works to protect us from harm and danger, but at the same time the institution doesn't work in a manner that would grant us a feeling of safety but instead has fallen into a mode of arguing solely based on the probability of potential outcomes. There is a related modern movement in psychology, called "positive psychology", involving e.g. psychologist Daniel Kahneman who was awarded the Nobel Prize for Economics for his work on how people behave statistically regarding money and risk. The movement approaches the human clinically as a cognitive machine consisting of emotions or choices that can be calculated and analysed statistically, and the name itself suggests that psychologists can determine *right and wrong ways of thinking* as the positive (and negative) ways. But this cannot essentially be a discovery but is simply enforcing and employing a stereotypical pattern of thought, as this is how many people tend to think; through the concepts of positive and negative. Many people have established ideas about what sort of behaviour is positive and what is negative; it is just that people tend to differ quite a lot on what they consider positive or negative, as these words don't refer to anything concrete at all but are just words used in encouragement or discouragement, typically learned from our parents as they were bringing us up. To be precise: 'positive thoughts' means the same as 'pleasurable thoughts', and to focus on the positive means to focus on the pleasure... but there is nothing stopping us from seeing how e.g. anger, hatred and fear are positive thoughts, as they give us strength and protect us from danger. But what is the most pleasurable to us? That would have to be whatever has been approved or disapproved during our upbringing: whatever has been associated with parental approval, or the opposite; whatever we have been deprived of and secretly coveted. And the generality of this doesn't follow any statistical pattern apart from *norms*: what statistically tends to be approved is the norm, of course; this is the definition of a norm. So, you'd like to discover statistically what people in general tend to find acceptable or agreeable? What's the point in that? Why use statistics? This question is the same as asking: What are the norms? You would understand this if you understood the human being as a psycho-social

II-8. TECHNOLOGICAL ARGUMENTATION

being; we are not random machines but, as it were, machines in the strongest sense hardwired to search for acceptance and approval from our close relations, and this approval will statistically correlate with the norm. We don't do *random* things that just *happen to* correlate with approval; we *actually* search for approval, and are quite excellent at scanning people's attitudes for this approval by paying attention to their words, expressions and body language; and the ones who perform best at this skill are not adults but small children. In the strongest sense *we are not random machines* and the notions of statistics simply can't be used in the context of psychology, unless, of course, you admit you are a moron and understand nothing about humans at all, and by this I mean simply that you choose to regress to use the method of statistics which exists to study *unknown* phenomena. This just means you admit you are not and never will be a psychologist but a psychological moron. Consider if a man hits somebody with a car, panics and drives away, knowing he has committed a crime and there is a chance that he will get caught. The police arrive and get the fugitive's licence number from the bystanders. Nobody knows where the man fled to; his whereabouts are completely unknown. Now, what will the police do? Will they start combing the city or searching from random directions? What would *you* do? I know what the police will do: they will first go to the person's home, where he will most likely be, lurking in a regressive state of desperation (biting his nails). If they fail to find him there, they will go to his parents or closest relations, because these are the people he will most likely go to for help in his desperation. Next, they will go to any of his known friends, as that is the next most likely option. Failing to find him there they will classify the man as wanted by the police and wait for him to show up. Now, why do the police work like this? Firstly, because the police arguably are not morons, and secondly, because a criminal is not a machine but *a human*, and humans are psychologically like this; in trouble they despair and resort to their relatives and close friends for aid. This is how this sort of 'typical' criminal is caught with very few exceptions, and actually the only sort of criminals that evade the police's standard methods are likely either professional, organized criminals or psychopathic criminals, both of which excel in not following normal human psychological patterns and are able to coldly calculate both the execution of crimes and the actions of the police. But now back to our original question of what 'positive' means in psychology. It would mean whatever the subject will experience as rewarding in terms of pleasure, and which would statistically tend to correlate with the norm; the standard against which our behaviour would be evaluated and thus considered positive and likely enforced by our parents. But in Kahneman's case the 'positive' would refer to something called 'hedonics', which could be summarized as approaching the concept of *happiness* with the methodology of statistics and economics. But what is meant by happiness here? We can see that the word itself is already committed to the fundamentally infantile (Kierkegaardian aesthete) conception of happiness as a *hedonism* that, as a serious psychological theory, is equivalent to the rather self-deprecating regression of the neo-Cartesian movement that wishes to revert to something that everybody already knows is old, exhausted and *wrong*. I believe such a branch of psychology deserves no further attention beyond noting that people's subjective ways of thinking relate directly to both their personal choices and their political opinions, and the movement implies that experts can determine right and wrong personal choices and opinions. And to lighten this argument by saying that they can't determine right and wrong thoughts or opinions but they can produce statistical information about how probable it is that they are right or wrong, doesn't save such an approach from the simple fact that it presents the outcome of a statistical calculation against a person's *freedom of choice*. It is the subject's personal choice that in terms of any moral framework, such as human rights or any religious framework, relates to the concepts of right and wrong, and on the level of society, these words relate to his freedom of opinion. Speaking of right and wrong ways of thinking binds us to some very specific test framework, such as gambling or, say, competitive sports, that is restricted in terms of subjective choices, and only within such a framework does it make sense to compare right and wrong simply in the terms of winning. Within, say, badminton, it makes perfect sense to say: "You are thinking about the game in the wrong way", which implies that there exists a mental strategy that could produce better results, and also implies that there is a simple set of rules that can be

II-8. TECHNOLOGICAL ARGUMENTATION

used to evaluate success. But the generalization of such methodology is a clear error and misuse of statistics and can be demonstrated as false with the following simple test which I am willing to subject myself to, involving me and any group of scientists.

1) The scientists analyse me (and my brain) with their methodology of choice.

2) The scientists ask me a multiple-choice question of their choosing.

3) I give my answer.

4) We repeat the test as many times as the scientists want.

Of course, this way I can show that any such methodology has no predictive power; for example, choosing any arbitrary number sequence before the test, and repeating that sequence in the choice of answer, will produce a predictability that converges to zero. Unlike in the case of clandestine observation of people's consumer choices or, say, the choices in the prison lunchroom where they only serve one type of meal, in this test I essentially have the possibility of *choice* for giving a right or wrong answer. The generalization of such methodology is strictly limited to a context where people are expected to be *unopinionated* (because they are unaware of the experiment), and the application of any such results from outside this context implies a violation of *freedom of opinion*. The error itself traces back to the underlying cognitivist approach that humans are cognitive machines, which is a simple attribution with absolutely no foundation. Not only that, but it is rather dangerous considering that a class of scientists and other authorities are allowed to determine the right and wrong of these humans that are machines: *if all* humans are such machines, what gives any party the *right* to determine human morality using this hypothesis, as no machines have such rights in society? This error can also be seen to reflect the desire to overlook the subjective human quality which constitutes choices and opinions, which, I believe, just reflects our desperation under the pressures imposed on us by society where the roles of authority have changed.

Somebody wants to call subjectivity statistical for reasons that are

PART II. COMMON MISCONCEPTIONS

not scientific or ethical. And I can relate this to the general feeling of lack of certainty that makes statistics an attractive choice that seems to hold the promise of reduced possibilities for choice. But scientists are at least expected to be civil workers, carrying expectations and responsibility in exchange for both their funding and their trusted role in society, and therefore their behaviour can't be justified based on their personal or collective sentiments. The current lack of control within science, which rampantly applies an unscientific work hypothesis, should also be approached from the perspective of corruption. The scientific community used to be substantially smaller in scale, but it has exploded to an unprecedented size. The number of doctoral dissertations accepted annually in the US rose from around 1000 at the beginning of the 20th century to around 45,000 at the beginning of the 21st century, while population of the US itself only roughly quadrupled in size in that period. A similar trend exists in other developed nations as well. This shows that the relative number of academics in developed nations has not just risen but exploded, by a factor of over 10 in the US. Now, given that academia is a normal political system with self-governance, one must understand that a nation of a modest size is able to maintain its economy due to the ability to control its inner politics, but such modesty is not the virtue of a super-state, which will deplete its resources and find itself hungry for expansion. The expansion of a state through war is not justifiable by argument, as it contradicts our empathetic moral basis, and any state is unable to enter a war without a provocation of some sort that overrides rational justification. Similarly, the expansion of science is not self-justified, as scientific research needs to serve the true needs of society. So, a super-state—without exception—enters a war through a forged political provocation, and so also must the political pressure to expand within an overgrown institution find its release through bypassing moral integrity by some form of trickery. Suddenly, a mass of scientists have emerged who wish to push scientific research with unclear terminology, and the mass creates political pressure on academia with the result of that, instead of proper critical scrutiny to form a consensus over the terminology, the relevant authorities are forced to give in and say: "It is a difficult matter and my personal opinion doesn't matter, since I am not enough of an expert to argue it." The respectability of science is in decline: in science things look true for a while and are confirmed by multiple researchers so that a scientific consensus is reached. Findings are even printed in textbooks, but suddenly they become highly questionable or unclear, again in the light of evidence from many researchers. According to an article in *The New Yorker*,[168] this effect doesn't yet have a name but occurs in multiple fields from psychology to ecology and is strongest in the field of medicine. I believe this indicates that academia has grown to such a size that it has lost its capability for effective self-scrutiny to target its motives and thus confirm its morals. Instead academia, which traditionally has enjoyed functioning self-governance, has fallen into internal conflict that damages it and cripples its ability to form judgment. Maybe it is the case that the success of science until sometime in the 20th century encouraged us to invest highly in it, and now we have an over-sized investment in science overall, and the separation and conflicts in modern science resemble the fight of the siblings over the fortune of a dead father. Or maybe science has simply detached from the conception of scientific *discovery*, because discovery implies something that exists undiscovered: maybe science was like a gold rush but the gold has now been discovered and mined. Maybe a similar thing happened to science as lately happened to lake Inarijärvi, the third largest lake in Finland, which was stocked with a variety of fish such as vendace (Coregonus albula) starting from the late 1970s. This drew in commercial fisherman. After the local authorities permitted commercial trawling, in the hopes that fish tourism would benefit the municipality—against the vocal warnings of the local fishermen—the lake soon ran out of stocked fish in the early 1990s. To make things worse, alien bacteria from the hatcheries wiped out the original salmon capacity of the lake. The aftermath of the disaster left the lake empty of fish and the local rural fishermen without a livelihood for a decade. Or perhaps the ethical expert institution of science has just been tainted by the pressures of having to show a financial return. Perhaps there is a similar situation to one I have witnessed in the IT industry: an active resistance to show the investor and customer of the produced work

---

168   J. Lehrer, 'The Truth Wears Off—Is there something wrong with the scientific method?', *The New Yorker*, 13.12.2010, http://www.newyorker.com/reporting/2010/12/13/101213fa_fact_lehrer [26.12.2019].

PART II. COMMON MISCONCEPTIONS

the true status of the work in progress because in the original request for tender one was pressured into quoting a price that was overly optimistic. Maybe we have enough scientific information for the moment, and maybe we should expect our greatest minds to end the current information age and show us the way to a new one. I personally don't know what form that age might take, but I do know that the modern mathematics-inspired human perspective and computer mind-body analogy is a rediscovery of Descartes, who brought Western thought from the Christian medieval period to the modern period by realizing that the actuating human force might actually be inside a man's brain instead of God in heaven dictating the fate of all his children. This gives us the hope that perhaps the next realization could be the rediscovery of something that was created *after* Descartes, and something that follows from this Cartesian realization of individual freedom and agency as rational human beings. I have this hope because there exists the alternative that beyond Descartes we revert all the way back to medieval times, to a world where experts and machines take the role of God and the medieval church in dictating the fate of men.

The role of computer networks as a sudden innovation is so immensely huge that most large-scale 21st century global issues can easily be seen as leading back to it, one way or another. It is just that such an analysis is not very interesting, apart from the fact that it reveals that quite large portions of people's social life and political awareness are now in the hands of private corporations that operate alongside or outside governmental legislation. A good way of considering the use of technology as an argument is to look at its argumentative power as a token that is in the hands of an authority one is dependent on. The technological argument: "The computer said it",[169] is a fallacy but a very powerful one, and I would liken the use of computers as an argument to the use of a *sceptre* in past days.[170] The object was held by royals while they

---

[169] The TV show *Little Britain* coined a popular catchphrase: "Computer says: no", which portrays the common policy of institutions, such as banks, to use the computer argument to justify their arbitrary, non-negotiating behavior.

[170] Dr Patrick Moore, in a testimony against the bad science behind man-made climate change, referred to computer models as *crystal balls*, when used to predict the future. This is also an apt reference.

talked, as the symbol of arcane and ancient power, just as computers today hold arcane wisdom related to how they are built; the contents of a computer and the related programming in the software that involves years of work by highly trained technical experts and innovators. Nobody seems to know how computers work, and therefore there is the preconception that information produced by computational means must be infallible. It seems that mysterious objects become instruments of power in the hands of authorities, and this power is of the nature of *desiring* to hold the object. This behaviour can be observed even in toddlers: a toy held by a toddler easily becomes an object of desire to another, and toddlers readily fight over toys. This relates to a comment I heard a mother make recently: she told me she was looking to buy a particular toy because her son wanted it as so many other kids have it. A rather mundane comment, I'm sure, but it is exactly the most everyday things that are easily missed: desiring an object seen in the hands of another is so normal and primitive that the susceptibility to it has developed in us before the conceptual language with which we are trying to grasp it. And just like the ancients listening to the powerful king wielding the sceptre, or the tribe listening to the pronouncements of their witch doctor, we take for granted what is presented to us, as *arcane wisdom beyond our reach*. The only thing that needs to be said to persuade somebody of something is that it is the result of computer calculation: people *will not* argue against that. It is a power argument, and thus very useful for the purpose of persuading. The stakes can sometimes be enormously high: cherry-picked computer calculations and hypothetical data models have been used, predictions failing completely time after another,[171] to internationally ground the argument for anthropogenic climate change, which has given rise to policy changes worth billions or trillions of dollars. Hand-selected calculations and hypothetical data models were used in the official report to explain why three skyscrapers suddenly collapsed with near-free-

---

[171] The news article mentioned below features a graph by Prof. John Christy, University of Alabama, that plots "the world's most respected computer forecasts of our planet's temperature since 1980" and shows how 36 out of 38 forecasts were "monumentally wrong". D. Rose, 'World's top climate scientists confess: Global warming is just QUARTER what we thought – and computers got the effects of greenhouse gases wrong', *Daily Mail*, 14.9.2013.

PART II. COMMON MISCONCEPTIONS

fall speed in New York on September 11, 2001.[172] The defining event of the 21st century launched an international invasion of the Middle East persisting for almost two decades, and aimed to expand Western control in terms of natural resources (not only oil and gas...) but also things such as the economic foundations of countries in terms of ties to Western currency and banks. No shame or apology has been expressed regarding the event, such as taking the blame for allowing the US air defence system to fail in its task of protecting American citizens. Nobody in charge has been held responsible; rather, what has been shown is pride and leadership in a global effort of war.[173] Looking at 9/11, I would observe that when we *witness* a terrible event unfolding in front of our eyes, we don't think critically and ask questions but we react humanly and instantaneously based on the assumptions we hold. If I ask people what they think about 9/11, they tell me where they were when it happened and ask me where I was at the time. This is the scope of our political interest: what immediate impact the event had on us. People seldom think about the bigger picture. The story behind 9/11 is controversial, but it is also a taboo subject, so it is likely that the full facts behind the event will not be made public and the relevant documents will be classified until such a time that any national security issues are longer considered sensitive.[174] The latest scandalous US revelations span back to the Vietnam war as the CIA documents about the clandestine bombing campaigns in Vietnam, Laos and Cambodia were recently revealed; bombings with *direct* civilian casualties somewhere

---

[172] Due to the nature of the publicity of this event, most people don't know the facts even to the extent that there were three collapsed buildings hit by two aeroplanes, and that the collapse of the buildings was attributed to fires. No skyscraper has ever before in history collapsed as a result of fire, and the WTC towers were specially designed to withstand passenger jet impact.

[173] This is not to say that 9/11 was in any way wanted or welcomed by the USA but just that it was very useful for a particular type of interest, as many of the related think-tanks look outside the morality of that particular event or the morality of any crisis events, looking at them from the perspective of business opportunity. Think-tanks operate outside of politics and are thus able to take such a stance. If you look beyond the morality of the event, you can easily see that it was highly profitable for any interests that profit from US or Western invasion of Middle Eastern countries.

[174] Two thirds of the 9/11 Commission material—~15 cubic meters—remains classified in National Archive. (S. J. Paltrow, 'Exclusive: National Archives sits on 9/11 Commission records', Reuters, 8.9.2011).

II-8. TECHNOLOGICAL ARGUMENTATION

between 100,000 and 600,000 lives. You can't reveal these sorts of atrocities to the public as the public would never allow such a war to persist. But these figures are the legacy of presidents Johnson and Nixon who don't need to worry about accusations of genocide at this point, 50 years after the events.

In the middle of all technologist argument is the concept of *information*. I believe this concept requires a rewrite in order to demystify it: we need to separate the computer scientific concept of *data* from the human communicative interest of *informing*. Information is communication, and what is being communicated is something a human might say, which is essentially always an opinion, and even the act of communicating it is an ethical choice. In relation to providing information, data should be regarded as a *medium* of information, similar to the printed word, tapes, CDs, DVDs and so on. Data is a tool for communication, and it surely makes no sense to look for the constitution of communication in the brain but simply in the medium of communication. Then again, the mystical nature of data processing—programming, the interest of computer people—should be demystified to exclude implications that the "language understood by computers" is related to computer thought. Both programming and computer use are performed using languages because humans are linguistic creatures, and the rules of using computers, whether as end-users or the ones writing their controlling logic as programmers, are written in human language because computers are used in human collaboration. Say, a Chomskyan context-free grammar is a grammar, not because *a computer* understands it, but so that a *fellow computer scientist* can understand it. Computers don't 'learn' when we command them, via programming, to store or display information according to some innovative rules; the user might learn something. When producing such a software, we are not informing the computer; we are informing 1) the user, via the functionality of the software, and 2) the fellow programmer, via using a programming language and programming methodologies to produce readable code, and any programmer knows that unreadable code compiles and 'works' but is unmaintainable and therefore worthless junk. As Wittgenstein said, the Turing machine doesn't calculate, but it is

PART II. COMMON MISCONCEPTIONS

humans that use the Turing machine to calculate. And I believe this clarification is all that is needed to enable a return from the mystical and inherently regressive spirit world back into the light.

The fallacy where a subjective justification is derived from objective events ("ought from is", naturalistic fallacy) is by no means alien to technology. Rather it is so astoundingly common and every day that it is actually difficult to see; in fact, the question might be more easily reversed: are there many actual cases of arguing for the use of technology with some other argument except from saying that you need technology because others have it, too? Although this does happen, we don't so much argue that investment in technology would make you famous or smart (nerds are unpopular and make unsuccessful choices); make you appeal to the opposite sex (nerds are uncool); give health and long life (nerds are unhealthy), and so on. The nerd was for a long time a comical stereotype in movies. The relation between technology and success is always tied to the idea that being tech-savvy is smart because it is *modern*, and it is smart to "stay on top", which means not falling behind with trends, being quick to adapt to the way the world *already is*, and essentially not to problematize how the world should be. This concept of *smartness* is a standard conception of intelligence in Asia, where our Western freedoms and the concept of human rights essentially don't apply, democracies are shadowy copies from our Western example, and *moral* questions are not considered universal or civil. With this way of thinking we say that smart people get rich because their wealth proves that they are smart; we don't think about whether it is smart to accept this judgment, but have already accepted wealth as a measure of smartness and committed *petitio principii*.[175] Similarly,

[175] Incidentally, a major newspaper recently featured this headline "The rich are more intelligent than the poor—Why?" referring to some studies from Finland, Princeton and Harvard, that found that stock ownership and intelligence correlate, and that low IQ can result from poverty. Here, the Finnish study found that success in IQ tests correlates with stock ownership, which was interpreted to result from the fact that intelligent investors *understand* that stock ownership pays good dividends... which shows that the designers of the study *believe* that owning stock is an intelligent thing to do and only a stupid person wouldn't want to own stock. And this makes it rather dubious to try and present such studies as tests or experiments: the study presents IQ as the measure of intelligence, but at the same time works to redefine intelligence in terms of wealth, which can be read from the

II-8. TECHNOLOGICAL ARGUMENTATION

when somebody says that it is smart to have the latest technology, it is noticeable how this argument has a sound of *threat* to it: you *better* have it, *or else*... the smartness of such an action is not to be debated but accepted due to prudence. And to truly understand what has happened here, and why it sounds similar to Asian thought, is to recognize that we have just exited the ancient Western tradition of dialectic; the tradition in which parties present intellectual arguments in defence of their position in order to resolve conflict, which assumes the position of the speakers as *freemen*. Such dialogue is not argumentation about the role of technology at all, but of a different tradition where the words don't matter as much as the relationship between individuals, and in which the Zen master's lesson of wisdom can be in the form of bashing your head with a stick instead of rational argument. And with complete respect to Eastern traditions the philosopher must simply point out to the Westerner that it is useless to do what he is doing; trying to argue where there is no argument. There are two paths here: either not to argue at all or then to accept that *ad populum* is a fallacy, and to argue correctly instead. They are separate paths and, who knows, perhaps the West will take the path of accepting the obvious modern overlords, global money and technology, as an omnipotent authority that cannot be questioned or accepted. Technology is commonly taken as a value in itself, as a phenomenon that has given birth to some things that are perceived as necessary or at least important, or as something the emergence of which is seen as a natural process. But what most people fail to understand is that throughout the whole of history the course of technological development has taken the form that *technological innovation takes precedence over technological need*. At no time in history has there been a moment when a technology that doesn't exist has been deemed necessary; on the contrary, innovators or inventors, who have varied in term of skills and funding, have usually been personally motivated to create novel technology that works via the process of moving from idea to a testable prototype, and only after

underlying assumptions. High IQ correlates with a completely arbitrary number of other things, too, apart from wealth, so why go to all the trouble of bringing in statistics and why not simply say that the researchers *believe in* wealth as intelligence, and to honestly bring out the irrationality of this belief, as it contradicts their own criterion of intelligence as IQ. (M. Pettersson, 'Rikkaat ovat älykkäämpiä kuin köyhät—Miksi?', Helsingin Sanomat, 9.6.2014) a successful launch of such a prototype have others become interested in putting the design into use. One can say that before aeroplanes or flying devices people dreamed about flying because they saw birds doing so, but nobody would have seen such an activity as necessary apart from certain daredevil innovators who, as it were, had nothing more necessary in their lives to invest their time in. Such people would also generally have been deemed rather crazy. It's tempting to submit to the fallacy of deriving the necessity of technology from its existence from a simple thought experiment looking back to the lives of people living in, say, the 17th century, and considering how they might have been able to live in the first place without modern commodities: of course they lived and possessed skills that we don't possess that helped them in their time, and thus such superficial thought boils down to nothing more than a lack of understanding of a way of life that is alien to us. It's ironic that we look at what the people of the past didn't know how to do and *didn't need to do* and contrast it only with things that we know how to do and need to do. It might be more honest to compare past ways of life with the things we know how to do today but *don't* need to do, such as shooting people or dropping nuclear bombs on them or spending one's life in one's room playing video games. Why do we look back on historical people who seem alien to us yet deem them inferior to us, and at the same time write wishful fiction about extra-terrestrial alien life forms that are consistently deemed superior to us; why don't we want to learn from our ancestors but from creations of our own fiction? What more is there to such pride in the face of the unknown except an effort to justify one's own status quo by the fact that there is nothing that can be done about it, and then escape into fantasy? Why do people believe that we cannot affect the wheels of technological progress while at the same time they argue fiercely for other political changes? The modern technological argument is of the form: "Wouldn't it be great to have *this* sort of technology in the future?" The technological argument tries to create a need that doesn't exist, and makes a promise to fulfil that need, but doesn't create any form of material commitment to such a promise. What we should do is counter the argument with the question: "And what commitment will you give to prove you will live up to your promise?"—after all, every bank de-

II-8. TECHNOLOGICAL ARGUMENTATION

mands this guarantee when giving out loans. The fact that technological argumentation involves humans and human lives but doesn't involve human commitments from the executing or implementing party, makes technological argumentation *immoral*. It is argumentation that simply disregards moral questions and views them with disdain. And this is an integral part of the appeal of such arguments: the morality of pondering whether the choice we are making is right or wrong will appear *weak* against the *power* of being able to make decisions that affect many people. Morality gives way to the question of courage and leadership: will you have what it takes to grasp this opportunity? And this explains the phenomenon that whenever there are no *moral codes* and there is a choice between a moral solution and a technological (or, essentially the same, *medical*) solution to some particular issue, the technological solution takes precedence and the moral, personal, ethical solution loses. People don't behave morally unless they are united by some sort of a moral framework (a religion), and in the absence of one, the choice between a technological solution and a moral solution is a choice between appearing strong and showing weakness.

The standard technologist argument is efficiency of some sort: something is said to become more efficient via the replacement of human labour with a technical solution, for example that the treatment of patients is to become efficient by replacing existing treatment with drugging. The initial thing worth noticing is that the same yardstick, efficiency, also defines a good *weapon* and a good *hit man*—efficiency doesn't make any commitment as to whether it will be used for good or evil. Next, it should be noted that such argumentation typically uses indirect deception by referring to statistical data that is pre-selected. Just imagine how easy it would be if, instead of paying one company for a statistical study involving 5,000 people, you paid 5 companies for 5 statistical studies involving 1,000 people and cherry-picked the one with most support for your argument. To give another example; roughly a third of actual medical studies on depression drugs are left wholly unpublished—usually because the results of the study fail to please its funder.[176] But the argumentation itself typically commits certain errors.

---
176 Pertti Happonen, M.D., head of Finnish Medicines Agency, in the TV documen-

PART II. COMMON MISCONCEPTIONS

Firstly, the *change of norms* is never considered in argument. What is argued is that things become easier, but what is omitted is that when people are using the technology, humans are *expected to comply* with the technological standards, and this might have the effect of making things particularly difficult. Technology is always introduced as a new tool and possibility, but its role in forming norms and expectations is not considered. And once the new technology has established itself, if we ask whether the new technology is a good or a bad thing, we say 'good' and deduce its rightfulness from its existence, because, as we say, we "couldn't imagine life without it", by which we mean that our memory is limited and the living standards we have to comply with also limit our imagination. Secondly, the *efficiency* is argued using subjective terms but implying objective criteria. Cellular phones are an obvious example: it is easy to argue that their use makes society more efficient because people are more easily *available*, which could be interpreted as efficiency of communication, but here availability is somehow expected to relate to a measurable criterion of being able to initiate communication with somebody.[177] Availability is not a *measure* of *how quickly* a person can be expected to be contacted when necessary. Rather, availability is a subjective quality that somehow relates to the experienced ease of communication. But, for example, people who can be contacted but who refuse to communicate can't be considered available, so the ease of initiating communications is not a criterion of availability. Mobile technology has in general made people much less available; 15 years ago, I would have talked to an unknown salesperson calling my mobile phone, but this doesn't happy anymore because people who I don't want to be contacting me are contacting me. It is said that people have much less time for each other, which means they are less available to each other. Another way to look at this is to recognize that our interpretation of availability changes along with the change in the norms of availability: availability used to be interpreted as the ease of initiating communication because physical cable telecommunication was used predominantly in the context of family and work,

---

tary 'MOT: Masentavat lääkkeet' ('Depressing Drugs'), Yleisradio, 26.5.2014.
177 The initiation of communication is reflected in the Nokia slogan 'Nokia—connecting people'. Connecting is what manual telephone switchboard operators would do before the automation of this connection procedure in mobile networks.

in which people were naturally motivated to communicate. Calls were rare and more expensive than today, and the motivation of the people who made them was presumed to be strong. When people are more easily connected over telecommunication, our interpretation of availability changes to include also the motivation to communicate. The third standard error in argument is the *cost-effectiveness* of technological solutions, and here, what is not taken into account is the development and maintenance costs of new technology: in sci-fi when we see spaceships, we don't think about the material costs and what it must take to produce so much steel, but rather directly extend what we have seen in actual space shuttles and large ships into fantasy. There exists a strong motivation to minimize the expected costs of new technology, and in the IT business, the development time and cost estimates are always lies because projects are typically allocated through the process of tender (which is supposed to minimize negative business practices such as nepotism), and it is not uncommon to see project plans and progress charts manipulated before being shown to the customer to portray more optimistic progress indicators. So, the cost-effectiveness of a technological solution is not a standard but an ideal that is used in marketing the product: it should save you time and resources if you use it right—and similarly, "it will save you money if we can build it right". It is *possible to imagine* that it saves time and resources, and the rest is up to the marketing to make the customer say 'yes'. These are arguments that are used by the solution providers to seem appealing in the eyes of potential customers, but they don't involve the fundamental question of the necessity of technology in the first place. The need to come up with better and better technology is related to the intense competition of the marketplace: in your market area, better technology can bring your company a competitive asset over your competitors. In this sense, technology today is in the same role as where the motivation to build mechanical devices originated: the job for the king's inventor was to develop innovations and mechanisms of war. So, from the perspective and context of a company within a particular line of business, the question of the necessity of acquiring new technology is legitimate and can be likened to the questions of how nations should handle their military readiness and overall military strategy.

PART II. COMMON MISCONCEPTIONS

Therefore, the question of acquiring new technology is related to the question of how much one needs to be prepared to compete with rivals using that technology. And war in itself—as we learn in the schoolyard, can observe in chimp packs and have learned from, say, Spartans—is an activity for which one should, without a shadow of hesitation, be ready, but in which the overly aggressive tend to gain momentary victories but to lose completely in the long run. These seem to me to be the alternatives regarding technological progress altogether; in a competitive society, aggressive traits are likely to win unless there's defence in place.

Another insightful perspective on the process of technological acquisition is the dramatic concept of *deus ex machina*. The concept refers to a playwriting anti-pattern with ancient origins: being unable to bring the plot together using the tools already existing in the plot, the playwright uses divine intervention as dramatic device (another familiar anti-pattern would be "...and it was all just a dream!"). 'Machina' refers to the mechanical device that was hidden behind the stage set and used to hover the *deus* above the stage; so, the concept effectively means "bringing in the god, using the machine". The result no doubt appeared impressive on first viewings, but the pervasive use of the device soon aroused resentment among scholars who saw it as a cop-out from the challenge of resolving a play using the logic incorporated in the already existing plot elements. Now, one can liken *deus ex machina* to our practice of acquiring new technology, because 1) *deus ex machina* is a problem-solving device for a playwright, just as our technology is considered to exist or to be acquired primarily for problem-solving purposes; 2) in a similar way as with modern new technology, the *machina* is also a mysterious and impressive technical device, which essentially is unknown to the viewer, and 3) *deus ex machina* is a *complete* solution to the existing problem: the playwright can in practice omit any existing logical requirements or tensions and literally apply divine power to overcome his challenge. Whenever companies make decisions to acquire new technology, a good salesman markets his technological solution as a complete solution. At the same time the decision gets the management off the hook: instead of dealing with the issues known to exist, the manager making the decision chooses to spend money, not personally owned by himself but by the company, and in practice wipes out any need to face those issues again in the near future, since "now we have the new machines". And this is not at all a claim that companies don't need technology, but a remark that it is exactly the *mystery of the machine*—the *hidden* machine behind the stage set—that is dangerous because it makes the "Let's buy what we don't know" argument lucrative to the audience. *The mysterious* is naturally associated with a sense of completeness and divinity; if one is not particularly competent in critical thought in order to clearly tell what one knows and what one doesn't, the mysterious naturally aligns against our hopes and wishes: "Maybe *this* could be *the* solution?" So, *deus ex machina* can be seen as a type of *fallacy*—an attempt to divert attention—and one that is different from a *sceptre* in that it is not wielded by the authority but is something apparently disassociated from the authority. It is a means to literally wipe out any existing issues with a swift divine stroke—one utilizing the mystery of technology.

Consider the idea of replacing a missing human limb, say an arm, with a robotic one—a standard technologist dream. This idea is of the type that we don't know how to do it, but we can imagine doing it because we have an idea about what sort of mechanisms can be manufactured and operated, and we have a tradition of fiction that portrays such devices. The reality about hand transplantation, using the hand from another person's body, is that the *survival* of the transplant for a duration of *one year*, before ultimately being rejected by the patient's body, is considered a major success, and the primary function of the transplant is cosmetic, meaning that the hand won't work. I have no categorical argument against the idea that a technology might be discovered in the future to achieve mechanical implants of this kind, but what is interesting is simply how we talk about the future. The fiction seems to invite people to jump to the argument that we don't know how to make such devices *yet*, as sci-fi typically portrays the future, and technologists' dreaming aligns with the role of fiction as a work of imagination: *in imagination* the borders of fiction and science can be removed. The jump from reality to imagination and back is easy

PART II. COMMON MISCONCEPTIONS

and requires no work or skill whatsoever; nutcases excel at it! But secondly, it is a particular *kind* of imagination that is akin to performing incredible feats in dreams, such as flying or jumping onto the top of a building. It is a dream about acquiring personal traits, something like the way chefs often say they wish they had an extra pair of hands, and as such, a standard pseudoscientific theme. For example, in the movie *The Terminator*, the anti-hero cyborg had mechanical eyes so he could see in the dark, which answers to the human desire to acquire this sort of ability, as we are often in situations where we can't see well enough. He was also a very strong, fast analytical thinker; fearless, unable to cry etc.—all these qualities corresponding to our tradition of heroic fiction. As another example, in *Star Wars* or *Star Trek* people can fly, discover planets and space, fight with laser weapons... all known themes from children's play and dreams. Sci-fi themes portray technological *extensions* of physical and mental human capabilities that intrigue us because we often dream about such things. From a critical perspective, the space flight in both *Star Wars* and *Star Trek*, which has become a space sci-fi standard, is a quite ridiculous extension of atmospheric aviation with ship designs including wings despite supposedly occurring in a vacuum and apparently sitting stably in space or travelling along straight trajectories at constant speeds, unaffected by gravity. In reality, everything in space is in constant high-speed motion due to planetary gravity fields and lack of atmospheric drag, and trajectories of objects are affected by planetary masses and distances that affect trajectories following the inverse-square law. Even a low Earth minimum orbital velocity for a stable orbit would be around 29,000 km/h, and a higher orbit requires higher speed unless shifting to another planetary orbit. This means that the minimum speed to be in space in the first place is a speed that will take you round the Earth in 90 minutes; increasing your distance from Earth requires a speed increase and shifting to another planetary orbit requires a speed decrease. It would make sense for space ships to have wings if they were what we call single-stage-to-orbit[178] spaceplanes, which are something we have

---

178 A single-stage-to-orbit (SSTO) plane reaches orbit in a single *stage* which means it doesn't jettison its atmospheric stage to lower its mass. Real, existing orbital solutions all need to do this at least once; several two-stage-to-orbit examples exist. An atmospheric stage consists of (ultimately empty) rocket fuel containers, at-

II-8. TECHNOLOGICAL ARGUMENTATION

so far been unable to construct but that in theory are possible; however, sci-fi movies don't depict our ideas of realistic orbital spaceplanes. In our dreams, instead of dreaming completely alien things, we tend to extend what we already know by overcoming restrictions and limitations. And this motivation behind fiction is completely different from science, which aims to produce theoretical and universally applicable knowledge. The problem with technological argumentation is not the question of *if* such things could, possibly, be done in the future, but the problem is about what made us come up with such an argument. Technology doesn't evolve via chasing dreams and never has done, apart from the works of innovators and inventors who, while immersed in their work, might dream about such things and find inspiration while doing this—and this is a common technologist reply: if nobody ever dreamed of such things, we wouldn't have any innovations. But an innovator cannot *argue* that *he* is able to produce something that others can only dream about; he needs to *prove* this by producing it, and while doing such work, he is not doing *science* but working on a design, similarly to an inventor. Science is a collaborative organ that receives public funding, but such work would be a suitable project for private funding. If one wishes to call such project a *research* project, the only thing that is being researched is *if a man* is capable of such a feat; producing such a work. And thus, what is being researched reduces simply into subjective excellence, which has never been the aim of scientific research; the objectivity of science is a higher motive. How this has been working in computer science is that the researcher studies a new technology; say, speech recognition, and at the same time produces software that recognizes speech. This process is called research in speech recognition; research in the technologies of speech recognition. The research usually consists of the application of already existing

> mospheric *wings* etc. that are no longer required after exiting the atmosphere. An SSTO plane that survives into orbit could effectively use the wings in atmospheric re-entry to brake into atmospheric flight instead of just cooling the uncontrollable fall with a heat shield. In short, the difficulty of building an SSTO plane is in that jet propulsion is significantly more fuel-effective than rocket propulsion but stops functioning when reaching an altitude where the atmosphere ends. In contrast, rocket propulsion, though powerful and not needing an atmosphere, consumes so much fuel that this largely determines the weight of the full vessel, and, when empty, the rocket fuel containers and engines become simply unnecessary weight.

PART II. COMMON MISCONCEPTIONS

computational patterns, such as algorithms and data structures. So, the sense of such a study being research is that there exists a potential application domain, speech recognition, in which there is 'room' to develop practical applications by applying existing methodologies, and what is produced is more efficient methods to apply those methodologies in this particular application domain. So, effectively, such research is developing methodologies that are applicable for practical applications within a particular domain, which could be best paralleled to industry by comparing to the production of, not nuts and bolts because they have already been discovered, but nuts and bolts that best suit a particular use, such as building bicycles. And this sort of study is already in quite a marginal domain regarding the function of science because it is married to the industry it serves. Core computer science, consisting of the models behind the nuts and bolts that are accepted to be the most efficient way of performing a particular function and that are being reapplied again and again, is quite old, often dating back to the times before physical computers.

So, what about the frequent assertion that "robots will replace people on the labour market"? The motive behind this statement can be difficult to identify, as it is not science or anything at all, really... so, why is this rumour so persistent? Well, it might be manufacturers of robotics who are putting out this somewhat speculative information in the guise of actual news. The argument that people in the future may be replaced by robots calls into question the position of the labour force and portrays them as a redundant or replaceable alternative to superior machine labour. This development and the related phenomenon of the computer-dominated second industrial revolution are similar to the development of fascism, which essentially was a development that rather quickly followed the first Industrial Revolution. The word 'fascism' is thrown around more than it deserves, but we should note that fascist theories were something developed by factory owners who had made significant investments to acquire industrial machines and were thus strongly motivated to try and position the human labour force operating these machines in the most effective way to serve their manufacturing goals. The correct way to look at fascism is to see it as a

II-8. TECHNOLOGICAL ARGUMENTATION

technocratic ideal. In this early fascist perspective, the machines were *financially* greatly superior to the workforce (the major investment), and the romantic fascist ideal was a reflection of men as effective extensions of production machines: hordes of men as uniform machine-like malleable collectives saluting their masters with slogans, not to mention the mechanized warfare of the time. This dream is closest to reality in Japan, where companies hold the exhausted labour force in an iron grip, and the idea of dying for your lord or emperor has been effectively transferred to corporate employees dying for their companies. It would not surprise me if there were captains of industry in the West who harboured similar hopes for the efficacy of their labour force in the West—only the outright expression of traditional fascist ideas is a strict taboo and the Nazi reference or allusion serves instead as a branding tool in political discourse. The mentality behind spreading news about modern technology: machines are better than you—because 1) they are more expensive and 2) one tank or an armoured car can outweigh several men. So, do your work well or be replaced like a machine; money can buy either. But it is worth noting that the Industrial Revolution differs from contemporary times in that it actually saw factory workers as expendable machine cogs; a machinist losing a limb to an industrial accident could end up having to pay for the loss of revenue caused by having to stop the production line to rescue him. This contrasts with the modern sensibility: we are actually hyperconscious not only of bodily harm but of any kind of experienced mental harm another person might inflict on us. We are lazy, overweight and entitled to abuse our bodies to the extent of looking terrible in the eyes of others, and the whole idea of having to punish our body ourselves in the form of sport, or having to endure physical pain or stress in any form of social activity, is a human rights violation to us. We will be sure to employ every right to its maximum extent, but not only that, we will aggressively shout for more rights. We lack identity and are insecure about ourselves both in mind and body; in lay terms we are 'pussies'; a common pattern is to act entitled, get snubbed, then rally sympathizers to attack the wrongdoer. As in the early days of industrialization, modern machines also pose a risk of accident which creates a rather serious security concern. Not only will a company investing in the machine need to cover the in-

PART II. COMMON MISCONCEPTIONS

vestment, maintenance and development costs, but as employers will be responsible not only for keeping the users or machine operators safe but also training them. And often modern machines don't last very long; their hardware lasts longer before the need for update, but the software tends to update in short cycles to improve efficiency and to fix errors that often are present in a product that is hurried to the market to win sales from competitors. In any consumer hardware products, such as mobile phones, network routers or printers, severe internal faults, such as memory leaks or segmentation faults,[179] are rather common, due to hurried development and lower production standards. It is exactly these types of errors that are difficult to reliably capture by standard testing; eliminating them would require a higher production standard where critical memory-accessing code would be subjected to more expert attention. These sorts of faults are serious enough to randomly crash the system. A software vendor always offers updates that fix these bugs but will never openly tell the consumers something like: "We are sorry but the earlier version had a fault that will in fact crash the whole software once a day or so." Having seen tens of IT companies from inside, I can say that it's a shameful and well-kept business secret that some critical piece of code sometimes just happened to be written by only one person and the rest of the developers refuse to touch it with a bargepole as they find themselves unqualified for the task, and in the worst case the person who wrote the code is no longer in the job and cannot be reached. Despite this, the code is being reused without full developer understanding of its function, and when asked if it works or not, people will say yes, and when asked if they are 100% sure it works, people will say that all we know is that it seems to have worked so far. It needs to be taken into account that when we are shown prototypes of machines developed by a team of researchers who have been able to work the relatively small codebase of control code by themselves,

---

179   A memory leak is a bug where the programmer fails to release the dynamic memory resources reserved for an operation after finishing with the operation. This will cause no visible ailment while slowly depleting the system's available memory... until the memory starts running out, when the user will likely witness unexpected behaviour such as slowness, and the ultimate crash of the system that has run out of memory. A segmentation fault is a bug where the programmer tries to access an incorrect memory address. This will either immediately crash the system (if the memory is protected) or cause completely arbitrary behaviour.

II-8. TECHNOLOGICAL ARGUMENTATION

they have not been subjected to the problems of mass-production that become evident as soon as such a product is commercialized... and this is to say that any commercial product will have to admit a possibility of malfunction due to software error.[180] Considering the safety of large robots, one needs to understand the consequences of possible malfunction, the safety of consumers or machine operators, and the fact that in contemporary society it is no longer possible to run cowboy machines that theoretically can pose a safety risk to people; nobody will agree to use these machines or be subjected to their operation under the risk of malfunction. All in all, our technology is simply so bad in quality and reliability it can never be considered as a viable replacement for a human work force. And these sorts of concerns are typically not addressed at all in futuristic projections about a society run by machines; rather these fantasies are always based on an idealistic image of what machines could be but in practice never are. The visible reliability of our machines (say, a website) is constantly and uniformly backed up with lots of human labour, but this part remains mostly invisible to the consumers.

Yet another feature of modern technology is its role in shaping public space. Looking at world today, we can see that it is much more "efficiently connected" via technological means over the Internet and mobile networks, but this affects the underlying social fabric in many ways. 1) The first thing to mention is that while people have more freedom in connecting with their social groups of choice, this allows for much more social behaviour that is completely uncontrolled. When the police or other security providers carry out their safeguarding activities in a traditional setting, they tend to monitor the places that are usual or expected locations of undesirable or criminal activity, because it is rational to think that *if* some *typical* group, such as teenagers, the homeless, drug addicts, bicycle gangs or such, *would* like to get up to mischief, they would choose exactly a place that is out of plain sight. Performing this kind of normal safeguarding activity is a bit like

---

180 This is well depicted in the movie *Robocop* where an R&D team introduces a law enforcement robot that in a demo session accidentally brutally kills the first volunteer test subject. The team explains that this happened due to 'a glitch'.

PART II. COMMON MISCONCEPTIONS

cleaning a room properly: in addition to mopping the floors, you have to check the places that gather dust because they are accessible by dust particles but are out of sight. Forms of *organized* crime are instead exposed by gathering intelligence through informants and undercover agents, and this method is based on the nature of organized crime as criminal networks that are identifiable in structure despite the difficulty of obtaining incriminating evidence of their known illegal activities. Now, in addition to the obvious fact of better connectivity of criminal groups, such as the common big city sight of car thieves operating in teams using an active mobile connection, it is the nature of online social networking that completely new groups form, with the group members located mostly in their homes but sometimes also meeting up in person to carry out their common activities. These kind of groups are an explosive new phenomenon especially among young people not yet in full-time work, and while most of them are harmless in intent, they are in practice uncontrolled and unpredictable from the perspective of both society as a whole *and* of law enforcement. This situation represents an open invitation to extend activities in illegal directions, and this means these are new forms of *organized crime* that in fact won't be exposed by just traditional monitoring of the streets. 2) The second major social change that technology has brought relates to the expression of personal opinions, which has altered dramatically as the norms of communication have shifted towards forums that are technologically governed by private institutions. People who meet online, instead of in traditional settings, are subject to very different rules of public opinion. An important aspect of such communication is that expressing opinion is not organized: anybody is allowed to talk, which contrasts with group communication in a traditional setting in which the only ones who are allowed to talk out of turn are the people with some interesting knowledge about the subject matter. Traditionally, at the end of university lectures there is a time window of, say, 10 minutes, during which the lecturer can address *public* questions, and he precedes this by encouraging people to ask freely, saying that no question is considered stupid. In reality, however, free questions are often 'stupid', in that they do not tend to bring any relevant information into the ongoing discussion. Another feature is that online discussions tend to explode into violence as individuals are not present as humans but behind some sort of online user profile and can therefore easily be experienced as not quite human: cold, calculating, untrustworthy, malicious. Think about attending a lecture in which the speaker is not visible to the audience; there would be constant suspicion about both his intents and identity. When there are no gestures of communication to interpret and the speaker is unknown, a very reasonable primal behaviour is distrust and fear of threat: when cities started to develop and to offer people safety from surrounding hostile environments and outlaws, anybody arriving at the city gates was made to identify and present himself before the gates could be opened. Then again, people often don't even consider that their online conversations are being recorded, which I feel is an infringement of people's privacy, given that people don't understand these underlying facts. These recorded online discussions, or any discussions that are expected to go on the record, should not be included when discussing the topic of *freedom of speech*, which is a *political right* implying a setting in which a person first forms his opinions and then consciously chooses to express them in a public statement. I believe the right thing to do would be for governments to step in to protect the rights of their citizens from the owners of these social platforms (corporations) that will exploit people's wish to communicate, and to clarify people's rights and responsibilities, which have been muddled by technological change.

PART II. COMMON MISCONCEPTIONS

II-9. Computationalist Science

The world has been dramatically changed by computers in a multitude of ways worthy of proper inspection, but here I will only address the issue of their incorporation within natural science. It seems to me that this change is the effective reason behind the dominance of natural science in the whole of contemporary science, and it has also given birth to novel 'disciplines' like cognitive science and artificial intelligence (AI), and directed great hopes towards neuroscience. These new hopes are related to the advent of novel research methods using data models that are able to produce a novel kind of information, and not because the fields in themselves have some importance in e.g. producing answers to important scientific questions or producing the means to create something useful. At the same time, the modern world-picture is littered with technocratic base assumptions that are just silently accepted because everybody knows the media reality is enabled by hundreds and thousands, or even hundreds of thousands, of computers that in practice are server machines that host the information the media delivers to us. This new technological reality has challenged many of our fundamental beliefs, to the extent that we don't know whether they are true anymore, and it has brought new beliefs that are so novel we can't trust them either. The result is a world in which the sense of reality has been to some extent lost. This challenge has never been an *intellectual* challenge, but a challenge of the *power* and *authority* that the application of modern technology has brought to those who wield it. This new reality is rife with scientism, and routinely promotes scientific discoveries and arguments as *truth*. This trend has been so powerful that it has caused even successful, reasonable people to consider whether there is a need for philosophy any longer; whether we are living in a new post-philosophical era of science. And this is a deeply warped and perverted perspective of truth. Science doesn't possess anything related to truth; a person's truth derives from his reason, and here we have the four types of reason, of which science (in the contemporary world) deals only with the causal objective-objective sphere... yet it is the person's subjective sphere that is primary to him, and a

II-9. COMPUTATIONALIST SCIENCE

person's subjective justification, following his moral sentiments, is his primary interest in truth. Whenever science is referred to in argument by the media, it is through scientistic rhetoric, applied by *a person with an opinion*; a person with a subjective opinion is telling others they should apprehend his subjective opinion to trust science. And this borrows its sense from a tradition from the era of industrialization where scientists would create actual new innovations and inventors and factory owners would put these into practical application for the good of the GDP and the glory of the industrialized nation—this is the world where this sort of media behaviour was meaningful. But why do we do it today; who actually benefits from publicizing even the smallest and most insignificant scientific preliminary (and statistically likely to change) result as the final truth that will likely change the world in the next couple of years? This is not the future; it is a horrible reality. If science itself is solely objective and omnipotent, why does it try to feed off popular opinion in this way? If science was indeed this powerful, we would see it constantly criticized and not needing to enforce its position by controlling people's opinion over it.

Alan Turing attended Wittgenstein's lectures in Cambridge. His ideas about whether a "machine can think", determined after his proposal in 1950 by the Turing test that has since been adopted by entire line of academic study called artificial intelligence, no doubt would have appalled Wittgenstein who remarked on a few occasions[181] that the impossibility for a machine to think is logical and not empirical in nature. These ideas managed to slightly surpass Wittgenstein, who died in 1951, but he managed to write a remark or two about Turing machines. He wrote that Turing machines are not calculating machines but calculating humans,[182] a statement that is obviously targeted at correcting the language constantly used then and now by people associated with computers that imposes an active subjective (spiritual) quality to something that is essentially a grammatical rule; an object and an instrument. Turing machines are theoretical constructs that operate by

---
181 The Blue Book, The Blue and Brown Books, Blackwell, pp. 16, 47; Philosophical Investigations §360
182 Remarks on the Philosophy of Psychology §1096

PART II. COMMON MISCONCEPTIONS

changing their state based on their current state that contains tape input, and Wittgenstein's critique was targeted at the inclination to say that the machine itself performs the calculation.[183] His motive for this could have been that he was aware of the age-old reasons behind such language use, depicted e.g. in the story of Frankenstein, or Prometheus, as the original name of Mary Shelley's novel commemorates. The critique is not to be understood to be directed at the grammatical form of inanimate objects as grammatical subjects, but rather at the danger of getting confused and reaching for non-existent results through not being clear about subjects amidst the creation of a novel language. The sensibility of the Turing test (which posits that a machine is intelligent if it succeeds in being indistinguishable from a human when conversed with via a text console) is easily refuted: for the sake of argument, let's imagine that a machine, such as AI chat software, passes the Turing test and thus earns the label of intelligence; let the AI people throw their hats in the air for having created an intelligent piece of software. Now, what can we do with such software? Can we transform it (him) into, say, medical software? Since a software passing the Turing test, constituting the hereby accepted proof that a piece of software *can* be intelligent, doesn't make *all* machines intelligent, the right question is: what is the criterion to determine the intelligence of a piece of software? And the answer is: that it passes the Turing test. Now, if somebody somehow transformed the intelligent piece of software into something other than the chat-bot it is, such as a medical software to which you would input symptoms and it would output a diagnosis. Would the new software pass the Turing test? The answer is negative, given that cheap tricks are ruled out, such as somehow including the original chat-bot in the new software bundle.[184] After all, a doctor is not a chat-bot, and the Turing test measures intelligence in terms of textual chatting. The Turing test argument would need to be extended by attributing the intelligence, not to the software as a whole, but to some property of the software, such as a particular computing meth-

---

183 He gave a parallel to an imaginary "racing game" that borrows the idea that a racing driver is receiving verbal instructions that have their sense bound to certain situations.

184 One could make a piece of software that includes both the Turing test-winning chat-bot and, say, a car-racing game, and extend the awarded attribute of intelligence to the software, calling it an intelligent car-racing game.

odology applied in the chat-bot, such as heuristic searching of textual fragments from a database, but this would not make sense any longer, as this doesn't flatter our understanding (concept) of intelligence but rather our understanding of searching. This reveals that the notion of machine intelligence does not comply with our understanding of intelligence in general, since an intelligent machine can only perform its predestined function of outputting textual answers to textual questions, and cannot be applied to a novel environment—which is exactly the basis of our traditional notion of intelligence: ability to perform successfully in a new environment. But there should be nothing unexpected about this, since the Turing test was formulated before any physical computers existed and before there were any real-world applications for computers; it was a time when producing language was popularly seen as the mark of intelligent life and what they had at hand at the time was just the idea of a machine of input and output with seemingly limitless possibilities, and any actual researched methodologies of producing language with a computer were unavailable. By the knowledge available at the time the Turing test criterion is understandable, and what Turing formulated should be seen as a challenge for future computational research rather than a serious philosophical concept, somewhat akin to the way famous mathematicians have had the vision to formulate conjectures they themselves have been unable to prove in their lifetime. Turing was no philosopher and didn't spend a single minute pondering whether his acquired conception of intelligence was correct or not; he would work in the way of a natural scientist by setting empirical standards to this question.

The power of the *theory* of Turing machines is in that they *can* be physically realized. This is why we would like to prove computational problems using Turing machines instead of some other sort of formal mathematics; we show theoretically that the problem is solvable via emulating the a step-wise behaviour of a machine with internal logic and a tape for I/O, and also prove that there is no theoretical difference in whether we use one or multiple tapes. These theories of Turing, along with many others, would give birth to the actual physical realization of these machines towards a computer processor with internal registers, arithmetic-logical unit, and access to a form of external memory. This model would stabilize as the form of a digital computer, giving rise eventually to extensions of this theoretical model. All computer software are algorithms that are run on the computer processor that, in turn, follows the basic idea of a Turing machine. But the language we use about running tasks on a computer is designed for our convenience, e.g. "Let the computer calculate that" or "Let's ask the computer". This language has been used throughout the whole brief history of the computer, and a central concept has been an idea that *the computer is intelligent.* I like to say I am not very intelligent because I like to compare myself to people who are more intelligent than me, but what does it mean to say that a computer is intelligent? Intelligent compared to what; compared to whom? We would probably answer that we are trying to build a computer that is intelligent... and the point of reference here would probably be the same as when building a calculator: the machine is able to perform *a particular task* more efficiently than a human. Computer software and likewise computer hardware should be understood as mechanical creations of their designer's mind and intent, and any impression of their 'intelligence', or an impression of other subjective qualities, is related to their role in their actual use *replacing something traditionally performed by a human,* similar to the way a calculator can be used to replace simple mechanical everyday calculations. Certain software functionalities; say, a web browser functionality that adapts the browser user interface according to the user activity, have been called 'intelligent', but this is solely because in the case of a traditional web browser any user interface adjustments need to be performed manually by the user. Thus it may be said that the inclination to call a software feature intelligent borrows from the intelligence required by the user to perform the same task before the new replacing functionality, and also any person inclined to call a feature intelligent needs to be aware of how things were done before the new feature became available. It is noteworthy that supercomputers have been used to run software to perform highly complex and intensive calculations far exceeding human practical capabilities for decades, yet they were, quite rightly, not referred to as intelligent due to the different nature of their typical application—running repetitive tasks requiring intense processing capabilities. This notion of machine intelligence seems clear enough, but just take a look at how the word 'intelligent' has functioned within the study of AI: researchers have no doubt experienced the "presence of intelligence", been struck and puzzled by it, but interpreted it in a metaphysical sense as something like a shadow or a glimpse of "true intelligence", and in their inability to reach it with current means they desperately concluded that achieving this requires more research or more computational power. The AI grammatical metaphysicism runs so deep that it is present already in the word 'automaton', which means 'self-acting', which literally suggests that a machine could work on its own, whereas no machine in reality is known to do such a thing but is more or less built by a company, plugged into a power source, started and stopped by a person and routinely maintained by a person. An online dictionary definition of 'automaton' says the word denotes "a moving mechanical device made in imitation of a human being". I think this is accurate, as long as we keep in mind that to imitate a human being means to imitate *the function*, not the appearance, of a human being. However, for this purpose the word 'automaton' is misleading as it falsely attributes human qualities to a machine, such as a vending machine, that essentially is completely dependent on human labour and in no way responsible for anything relating to its operation, as we would expect from the human being the machine essentially is imitating and replacing. AI freaks tend to ask questions like "Would we project our emotions onto these machines if they actually looked like humans?"... as if they were living in a dream and persistently wishing to stay in the dream and not looking at what machines *actually are*. All the information they want is very easily available, on the table, ready for reading and inspection, clear as daylight. It's not their fault; they have been misled. The whole field of computer science is *littered with* terminology that works to maintain confused futuristic visions. But why? We need to look at *the naming tradition of natural science*; suppose a scientist wants to call a particular feature of computer software something arbitrary, say, a 'mind-blower'. The only thing he needs to do is to decide and define a set of conditions that functions to *empirically* determine if some software is a 'mind-blower' or not. Then, if it manages

PART II. COMMON MISCONCEPTIONS

to highlight something that in theory might yield practical results in the future (not necessarily in the near future) it will be happily accepted by the community as something novel and interesting, and they will together celebrate the 'discovery' of 'mind-blower' software. This kind of naming, of course, is abominable from a rationalist philosophical perspective, since it conflicts totally with how natural language normally evolves. Concepts created this way actually are to be understood as specialized expert concepts and should be very strictly separated from having *any connection whatsoever* with the meaning of the natural language concept that was used as inspiration when choosing the specialized concept, apart from a practical connection related to a particular area of life. Consider if we found a strange object and didn't know how to use it... in this case we would likely name it according to how it could be used. If we found a sharp rock, we might call it a grass-cutter. The case of AI could be called anthropomorphising of methodologies, akin to the way constellations were once named after animals because it helped people to recognize them. Nothing wrong in that, right? But what should we call it when grown men know precisely what an object is but then they start to call it something else? Take a machine-intelligence software, say, a chess software, and start calling it a chess player, based on the idea that it is performing the function of a chess player. Isn't this exactly what happens when a grown man buys an inflatable doll, from a shop, with money, inflates it, and starts to call it a woman? Or when a teenage boy decides that his desire to be a woman (his psychological identity) is stronger than his feelings about being a man, and starts to dress up as a girl, to call himself a girl, and to insist others call him a girl, too. What happens here? It is a regression of the mind; there is a desire that wishes to be fulfilled, but isn't, so the person starts play a game in which the desire is fulfilled. Because he is unable to fulfil a desire that conflicts with actual life, he is comforting himself by actualizing his fantasy. To put this in the correct moral perspective; it is acceptable to call something by a comforting, practical name, when you *don't know* what it actually is, but it is no longer as acceptable when you *don't care* what it actually is. That is to be considered fetishist. Is actually incredible how we can have this kind of attitude in science, whereas, in other important areas of life such as in the military context correct naming and terminology are highly emphasized in order to rule out the subjective; to remove any subjective attachments we carry in connotations when using comforting, pretty names for things. This is because any misunderstanding about what things are called could be a matter of life and death; in the worst case the fate of whole units might be at stake. So, it is ruled out, and the use of strictly technical, correct terminology is enforced. The same requirement for terminology would apply in, say, an operating theatre: the surgeon can't say "Hand me the cutter-thingy" when he actually means a scalpel.

Consider if a natural scientist should create a theory about, say, *cats*, according to which any construct that satisfies certain criteria, say, furriness, having whiskers, hunting at night, etc., all identifiable or measurable with certain criteria such as a form of data input (and then would advance to create a computer software that satisfies those criteria and further claim to have shown that software cats exist), and furthermore consider this theory gained wider recognition and acceptance. No matter how influential the theory became, whenever a housewife utters the word 'cat' she will not *mean* cats in reference to the new theory but cats in reference to the linguistic practice: how the word is used in real life. She is *unable* to mean cats in reference to the theory because she is unaware of the theory. It seems quite impossible that the expert concept would ever surpass the original word in linguistic practice as long as real cats exist in houses, because housewives will be coming into direct contact with cats, and when asked what they mean by 'cat' they will point to a cat or a picture of a cat, and/or give descriptions of cats they know—not through the theory, but through their practical life experience with cats. The concept will remain an expert concept with a clearly distinct meaning. As a real-life example, 'machine learning' is used to describe iterative algorithms with a modifying execution pattern between iterations based on an internal volatile dataset, and in practice such algorithms have an application in a context where the programmer is not aware of the actual input beforehand but is able to determine parameters that capture the form of the data and to determine by rules how the internal dataset and the resulting algorithm execution should be modified based on the input in order to reach the purposes he has in mind. So, the relation between 'learning' and the functionality of such an algorithm is in that iterative algorithms normally function in a static way but the internal modifying dataset makes the algorithm functionality change between iterations, based on, as it were, what it has learned so far. It's such a convenient word for describing a class of algorithms... but such a linguistic trap for others who don't understand the theory and functionality behind such an algorithm. It misleads them into thinking that "computers can learn" and be led to the slippery slope: "At time t_0 computers couldn't learn and at time t_1 computers can learn to some extent, therefore there exists a good reason to expect that at time t_n computers will be learn exactly the way that humans do!" The average man naturally thinks that since we're speaking about learning and the people who do that are scientists, this must have something to do with learning in general, and as if this weren't enough, most of the scientific world is equally confused, or if not confused, refusing to take responsibility for clearing up the conceptual mess that contemporary natural scientists have created. This is very understandable because they lack a financial motive, as a great deal of computer scientific research funds come from outside academia, from businesses or organizations that ultimately do business with the end-users of the software that the new innovations help to produce. The research needs to be marketed with exciting words.

The correct way to avoid the confusion related to *software,* and to get the correct picture of the logical application of language related to software and computers, is to understand software as an algorithm of machine instructions written in a language comprising commands that are members of the hardware instruction set of the machine architecture, and the purpose of the software as to, by commanding, use the machine apparatus as a tool for some human task. Some clarification is needed about what actually is meant by a piece of software; do we mean a full product, a locally installable application bundle of a product, or just the software code? the word acts in juxtaposition with hardware, which means physical computer components. We could as well say 'application' or 'computer program'. The purpose of software

II-9. COMPUTATIONALIST SCIENCE

is to automate tasks, which means having tasks done more efficiently with the aid of a machine, and the formulated mission of computer science (repeated like a mantra by professors during my computer science studies) is to answer to the challenge: "What tasks can at all be automated, and what is the most efficient way to do it?" Here 'task' is obviously a reference to a *human* task. Software code is an expression in a formal programming language. An important thing to note is the use of active verbs in describing machine functionality, which is related to the designer perspective: for example when someone says that a machine component 'understands' a language, he means that the component has been designed to function in such a manner that you can 'say' things to it and get a response. Such use of active language has always been standard in engineering: instead of saying: "I placed this bolt here in order to prevent this hatch from opening" the engineer says, "This bolt prevents the hatch from opening". Now, in an effort to bring a bit of clarity between different worlds of naming and meaning, a computer scientist might *very succinctly* (this is complex, complex stuff) explain to a philosopher that the processor of a modern digital computer is a highly sophisticated physical realization of a multi-tape Turing machine that, instead of the tape used by Turing machine, uses different types of memory realized by various means of storing digital data, such as static logic gates, capacitors, magnetic fields and laser-manipulated dents on material surface. These storage media are made available to the processor through the motherboard architecture: built-in chips in a static manner, modules and storage peripherals in a dynamic manner. The language read by the processor on one Turing machine tape is a sequence of processor instructions called, among other names, an 'executable program'. A single instruction may involve one of the following:

1) reading data from or writing data to any of the tapes,

2) performing arithmetic—a static data manipulation operation— using the processor's arithmetic logic unit (or floating-point unit),

3) performing a system call to access any other functionality provided by the motherboard architecture, such as the real-time clock, network controller, sound controller etc., or

PART II. COMMON MISCONCEPTIONS

4) jumping to another specified location of the executable program by moving the reading head on the corresponding tape.

The word 'data' here is a simplification of something the manipulation of which physically occurs using the processor registers (internal fast memory banks) which vary in design between processor architectures. Because of this variance, both device drivers and code compilers—software components that handle translating any data produced by the software programmer or a peripheral device to compatible representations in the processor registers—are separately designed per processor architecture (and this process causes the limited functionality of old software on a new processor architecture). Nevertheless, all this functionality is in theory presentable as one astronomical Turing machine state transition function where e.g. the arithmetic logic unit consists of a huge static set of transitions and the set of primitive data types requires an exponential amount of separate transitions, and this makes the Turing machine a simple yet effective theoretical model also for modern computer science. Furthermore, the computer physical architecture provides a base for an *operating system* (OS), a big set of interrelated software designed to be run on computer start-up, that, in addition to providing a basic user interface to the computer (graphical interface or text-based command interpreter), provides a set of services (application programming interface, API) that translate into hardware-level operations using the device drivers provided by the operating system in a dynamic modular manner, and memory allocation to provide access to available dynamic memory; that is, physical writable memory not already used by the OS itself. These OS services are the single route between everything that occurs between *(software) applications* and the computer hardware and are a basic feature of every computer in the context of which it is sensible to speak of software applications, including e.g. web servers, supercomputers and cellular phones. Applications, in turn, are the main context of discussion whenever one is speaking about the possibilities or limits of computation. An application consists of executable program code that, in turn, consists of low-level machine-language instructions that instruct the particular processor architecture, and optionally data files storing related information. When an application is executed, or *run*, often by user command, the OS copies the executable program into memory and passes its execution to the processor, after which the processor follows the given sequence of instructions (code) and OS services remain available to the application during its execution. Applications, in turn, are created by software programmers in a process that involves writing a sequence of operations (or a set of rules) called program *code*, that logically defines all the functionality of the software, such as requesting memory allocation from the OS for required run-time memory, reading from allocated memory, files, devices or user input, writing to allocated memory, files, devices or screen, and so on. Also the code strictly defines, through its inherent logical structure and logical constructs available in the programming language (such as conditional statements and repetition loops), the program execution sequence, making it dependent on both programmer predetermined logic and programmer determined rules of functionality related to program input during its execution. Code is, in most contemporary cases, written using a high-level programming language that contains operations on a higher abstraction level, as it were, closer to the programmer than the OS. This code is then translated into an executable program—the sequence of processor instructions—either as a pre-processed separate step (compilation), or at the time of its actual execution (interpretation) by processing unary instructions by first translating and then executing them. Contemporarily, the execution environments of many applications have become more complex, providing another abstraction layer between code and the OS, called a virtual machine, but the essential difference in a virtual machine approach involves a combination of both compilation and interpretation in order to achieve application portability between processor architectures by modularizing the related problem area to the development of the virtual machine instead of the application. This same idea is the theoretical outline in the modern development called hardware virtualization, in which, more or less, computer hardware is replaced by specially designed software that, in turn, functions as an installation platform for an OS, and further to its applications, creating a total layering of hardware→OS→virtual machine→OS→application.

PART II. COMMON MISCONCEPTIONS

Now, a piece of software functions along the same logical principles of Turing machine as the processor does, containing the OS services as corresponding tapes and a set of state transitions predetermined by the code. Since everything running on an OS, including the OS itself, is an application, the whole totality, no matter how many applications are run layered or in parallel, is, in theoretical terms—and without any controversy within computer science—equivalent to a Turing machine, and physical differences regarding e.g. processing power, amount of memory or screen resolution, provide no theoretical change to this outline. This is as computers were at the time of their birth and their evolution has brought no change whatsoever to these facts, despite quite dramatic changes in their physical size, potential fields of application and types of peripherals, and the huge change their surrounding world has undergone as a result. They are realizations of the Turing machine, the theoretical machine that was great because it could be realized, as it was founded on concepts such as head and tape. The concept of *parallelism*, which might sound like a potential change in the limitations of computing, doesn't present any logical change in this sense. Parallel and distributed computing, *from the OS perspective*, means two things: the capability to execute multiple parallel applications on a single OS, and offering individual applications a platform for managed multi-threaded execution and the related services. An application may request a number of new threads of execution to its use, and the execution of parallel threads on a single processor is managed by the OS and performed by "scheduling", in which the OS schedules each thread a tiny time quantum (e.g. less than 200 ms), and controls their execution by swapping the thread of execution based on the quantum: one thread is given a quantum of execution time in turn while others wait for their turn. Recently, apparently due to changes in the prices of physical components, multi-processor computer architecture is becoming common despite being a dated innovation, and the only change this architecture brings is related to performance: the OS is capable of employing multiple processors in the execution of parallel threads instead of sharing a single one between them all. But, essentially, both features of parallelism have been supported as a standard feature of operating systems for decades. *From the application perspective*, parallelism is correctly seen as a methodology to increase software performance on particular occasions. In practice, a potentially crucial performance gain is possible when the computer processor, using a model of a single thread of execution, would need to wait for input and/or output (I/O) from any system services, such as memory or peripherals, and could instead be assigned to perform some other tasks during that wait time using a model that employs multiple parallel threads. This requires the distributed nature to be programmed in the application by having it request available OS services and having it control the execution of threads by ensuring that they don't produce any unplanned conflict when accessing shared resources, such as memory space, data files or peripheral I/O. Also, the concept of parallelism is applied in the meaning of distributing the application between multiple operating systems and computers using networking. This is standard in e.g. public web services such as web-based search engines, privately hosted web services such as websites or e-mail services for private organizations, and online digital entertainment. Also in this case the parallel nature of the application is a fundamental development challenge in software design: for example the Google search engine doesn't 'automatically' scale to thousands of servers, but the seamless user experience independent of geographical and Internet location is achieved only by countless thousands of hours of high-level expertise, careful design and functionality hidden from the service users, that involves developing the distributed management of the gathered, analysed and served data. As such, the challenge of distributed application design over multiple network servers both in theory and practice is equivalent to the corresponding challenge within a single OS, the main difference being the communication over computer networks instead of directly accessing the OS provided services, which poses a design challenge, since networking is slow, unreliable and unsafe in comparison with direct access. Another difference related to services available to a large group of users is the increase of points of user I/O, which is reflected as an increase in the number of Turing machine tapes.

The point of this review of computation fundamentals is to point out that all forms of computing obey the same basic principles: the Turing

PART II. COMMON MISCONCEPTIONS

machine along with its state transitions, as described by computer scientific theory, are physically realized using electricity and hardware components. Failure in any of the software or hardware components produces similar results as jamming a factory machine cog with an iron rod. Then again, software is something *designed* by its creator to produce certain functionality, and software testing is a process of confirming how well the actual implementation corresponds with the design. Any deviations from intended plans are considered software faults (bugs), and, when found, are classified according to severity. And these basic computer scientific facts are not in the least controversial among the people who understand anything about computer science and computer systems as engineered and controlled entities, who are those with the greatest expertise in these matters: theoretical computer scientists, system architects and various experts. But, unfortunately, this rules out many types of pseudoscientific opportunists and virtually all tech journalists (who know that the general public are completely clueless about all this). Now, it is worth asking the question whether anything 'novel' can occur in this process, and it can be noted that a piece of software can handle nondeterministic functionality via e.g. random number generation or user or peripheral input, but the input values from these nondeterministic sources are always placed in variables set by the designer and used with an intention and manner set by the designer very similar to how factory machines might work: imagine a factory machine that collects raindrops that fall in a nondeterministic manner, but the designer of the machine has set a mechanism to trigger when the water reaches above a certain level (or a certain weight) in the collecting device. This is exactly the kind of novelty to be expected from a piece of software; the software doesn't actually produce the random event but contains static programmatic rules for how to respond to them, and in this sense the novelty can be likened to the functionality of a simple thermostat that responds to temperature in a static way by changing between two states.[185] So, the novelty of randomness, as it were, is not actually produced within the software, any

---

185 John McCarthy, who first coined the term "artificial intelligence", explicitly saw no problem in calling thermostats intelligent, which might say something about the linguistic atmosphere surrounding early AI discourse, but the problem is that this discourse is still alive.

II-9. COMPUTATIONALIST SCIENCE

more than a street light system with a magnetic sensor under the asphalt that responds to passing cars can be said to produce something novel. Software, if it functions at all, functions *exactly* as it has been designed to function, and in cases of exception to this the software fails (crashes)—apart from lucky accidents that are still deemed software faults. All software is designed by humans and run on computers that are started, stopped and maintained by humans, and any exception to this is undesired and in practice causes panic, chaos, lost data, lost money and lost jobs. Similarly, unlike with robots in science fiction, should a piece of machinery ever start working unpredictably, we would not greet it with love and compassionate feelings (this is exactly the key romantic fairy-tale element in science *fiction*) but rather with horror and forced shutdown by any means necessary, just as one would do in a factory if one of the machines malfunctioned. What is necessary is immediate shutdown to avoid further damage. In fact, this fundamental fragility of being destroyed by just a misplaced bit of code in a space of gigabytes of data, together with the absolute requirement of security in whatever we expose our citizens to, will effectively contain the application of any larger robots inside controlled industrial facilities for all eternity. They cannot be realized in any environment where they can be somehow manipulated. In terms of responsibility, either the user or the manufacturer of the machine shall be liable for any damages for the misuse or malfunction of the machine. In the case of a company manufacturing robots that are to some extent human-like, we would place that company under extremely high levels of scrutiny, requiring total visibility of the principles of operation of these machines that we trust our own security with. This in turn would strip away any fantasy or sense of wonder related to these machines, which ultimately are simply a marvel of human engineering, and in this same sense robotics has already been a living reality for a long time. In the case of all computers, a human causes one to start, in the event of which the computer components connected to the internal power source running on AC power, including the motherboard and cooling systems, start up, and a signal is passed to a small program located in a motherboard static memory chip that determines how system devices such as the processor, memory modules and connected devices are

PART II. COMMON MISCONCEPTIONS

used while the computer is running, and from what physical memory location the processor should take as input the first application (the OS boot loader), which determines the trail of execution from that point forward, in practice starting up the OS. The program then tests and initializes the system devices, and in case of success, executes the boot loader from the specified location. What happens after this is solely determined by the designers of the OS and any run applications, apart from user-initiated hardware calls, such as moving the mouse or pressing the shutdown button, that are received as OS input. Any unexpected deviation from normal hardware functionality, such as a drop of water producing a current between two isolated conductive wires in an electronic circuit, is likely to have catastrophic consequences, just as jamming a machine cog can jam a production line in a factory and destroy any material currently under production—a reality that fully contradicts the fictive image of worn-out technology first popularized by the film saga *Star Wars* and obviously modelled on motor car culture and analogue mechanical devices. In addition to hardware errors, software errors are classified in the software code, and while some error scenarios are recoverable and minor, some are considered unrecoverable or fatal. From the programmer's perspective, an unrecoverable system state means that a quick shutdown is desirable, because correct configuration cannot be determined, behaviour will be unpredictable and delaying the shutdown means just causing more harm. The correct program action at that point is to raise (throw) a fatal error that causes application shutdown. Examples of fatal system states are the crash screens of various OSs, such as the notorious blue screen of Windows or Linux core dump. Thinking of AI, if a computer could "keep itself on", these screens wouldn't exist, because the OS developers would surely circumvent this highly undesirable situation that causes user rage if there was a practical way to do it. Fundamentally, everything related to computers and software clearly is a tool-oriented human process no different from e.g. building houses or mining for minerals, apart from the historically novel level of complexity in terms of the layered application of the results of sophisticated expert work: every hardware and software component involved is the result of a marvellous history of expert development. Hence Wittgenstein's critique: Turing machines are not machines but humans that calculate. This, however, hasn't been enough to satisfy the hopes of AI research to achieve "true intelligence", but the concept of *intelligent agent* was coined to give the impression of independent functionality. This, naturally, has nothing whatsoever to do with human intelligence or whatever we might mean when talking about animal intelligence—the only relation being that somebody personally liked the word enough to choose it, instead of, say, the name of his pet, as a basis for coining a new concept. "Intelligent agent" simply relates to an approach in software design that contrasts with the traditional modular model, but that by no means differs from said common principles of computation. Furthermore, the very same terminological sleight of hand, where a word applying to humans is mixed with the functionality of software, has been in play every time some AI field of research (such as chess, chat-bots, expert systems, neural networks, genetic algorithms…) has gained fantastic features and has succeeded in hyping results that somehow in technological sense breach the possibilities of forecast. It also would seem quite obvious to me why it is 'intelligence', and not e.g. 'humanity', 'life', 'soul', 'spirit' or such, that becomes the unicorn horn for, among many others, AI scientists: as aesthetics is the footprint of ethical change, intelligence is an aesthetical value for a scientist who has undergone an ethical change to become one. Intelligence is what such a scientist personally reaches for.

Now, an AI scientist could (and would) argue that the conceptual analysis I have presented here does not rule out the *possibility* of artificial intelligence; that it is still possible to dream of machines performing human-like tasks and doing whatever he sees people doing. This is true, but what my analysis targets is what has been meant thus far by the concept of artificial intelligence. My analysis is targeted at a specific (pseudo-?)*scientific* programme that posits something that is essentially meaningless in a scientific sense. And first supposing something that is contradictory in nature and then saying that the opponent has not presented a valid argument for "Why not?" is not valid argumentation, since the burden of proof lies in the hands of the people who have presented the initial argument. It is a similar case of inverted argumentation as that often applied to gay marriage, where the argument is that our current marital institution violates human rights and the people opposing gay marriage must prove why the current system should *not* be changed. This is like requiring a person on trial to prove his innocence. The position that the current institution violates human rights is contradictory on some account, which is easily shown, but it still often happens that a person who is ethically committed to a certain goal for some reason refuses to let go of his goal, and instead starts to make a noise and to *persuade*, and at this point the question is beyond intelligent conversation but what is at hand is a political movement without an intellectual basis. Consider the claim "Machines could be able to think": what does it mean? Thinking, as obviously is meant here, to make any sense at all, is something attributable only to living beings, and machines are not living beings. So, the logic here should be like this:

1) Machines could be able to think.

2) As thinking is understood here, only living beings can think.

3) Machines, as understood here, are not living beings and cannot be made into such.

4) Contradiction → 1. is false.

Otherwise, *if* we accept the contradiction, we know that *ex falso quodlibet*: any conclusion from this premise is valid and the Pandora's box is literally wide open. It is not any more logically valid to say that if machines could be able to think, we should study them and try and build one, than to say that because they could be able to think we should immediately cut any funding for such efforts as such computers will be an immediate threat, because ultimately we don't have a conception of what such a thinking machine means. Any such speculation will be totally groundless because the premise is contradictory; albeit that it is marketed as something that we don't *know* because we have no evidence. But the premises listed here we *do know*: man cannot make life, as we understand it, out of machines, and the concept of intelligence has, before Turing's formulation of another concept of intelligence, been sensibly applied only to living beings. But in a similar way to children, who don't want any limits, natural scientists don't take such logical restrictions of concepts seriously, because they believe they are allowed to call anything by any name, as long as they can set out some sort of criteria by what is meant, whether it is contradictory or not. It should be the philosophers who are pointing this out, but this has not tended to happen, which, I'm sure, has a lot to do with where such natural scientific study gets its funding: technology manufacturers who are big in consumer markets.

The kid brother of AI, *cognitive science*, is another bundle of conceptual confusion; an interdisciplinary field made up of scientists united by what seems more like an interest in conceptual vagueness than the opposite: having traditions firmly rooted in natural science. I see cognitive science taking advantage of the fact that the current situation of computational expertise is polarized to a particular scientific group that applies specialized terminology in a liberal and unrestricted manner without proper critique. The very grounding hypothesis on cognitive science, that *the mind should be understood through computable mental representations*, is not philosophically tenable,[186] but this is not understood or considered by cognitive scientists. A scientific hypothesis should be such that one is able to test it, as Popper has famously argued, and one should see it as obvious that the cognitivist hypothesis is ultimately untestable: who could determine what is the right philosophical perspective from the standpoint of science? A philosophical perspective is one that applies to the single subject only, and in order to know a perspective one needs to apprehend it and live it, and only the subject that has tried multiple perspectives is able to compare between them, and after that it is up to others to decide whether to give this subjective appreciation any value or not. But this subjective style of choice is fundamentally the opposite of what natural science means by testability and also the opposite of the very ideals of natural science. In this vote the one who knows only one perspective is serving a solely political—not an expert—function, and obviously the hypothesis has been approved under pressure by vote by loudest voice. Yes, anyone can agree that we, as it were, picture things in our minds, and can re-

---

[186] This is pointed out at the beginning of *The Blue Book*

PART II. COMMON MISCONCEPTIONS

member and repeat the visual aspects of things we have seen and often have dreams of a strong visual nature, but in order to produce a sound basis for *meaning* one needs to expect a shared criterion, such as the traditions and practical cases of human linguistic interchange: the *use* of language. I will demonstrate the senselessness of the theory of mental presentations with an example owing somewhat to Wittgenstein in originality. Suppose I am in a room with another person and I would like him to hand me the bottle of water that sits on the table. I will say to him without looking in the bottle: "Give me the bottle!" and he gives me the bottle. Now, what did I *mean* by the word 'bottle'—what was the meaning of the word 'bottle' when I used it? Since I didn't look at the bottle, one might be inclined to reply that the word 'bottle' refers to the mental image of the bottle in my mind. Good. Let's repeat the test such that I am sure not to *think* of a bottle but instead focus my eyes on the bottle on the table itself, and furthermore let's replace my request with "Give me the, um...!" accompanied with a gesture of looking at the person, raising my eyebrows and extending my open palm towards the bottle. With this gesture I manage to get him to hand me the bottle. It should be pointed out that this kind of language use, in which we don't imagine anything but rather act in response to actually looking at something, is very common: there are situations in which we simply have no time to think but respond immediately at the sight of an object, and situations in which we are about to say something but are unable to finish the sentence without resorting to external observation. Actually, since both I and the other person are able to see the bottle, I might equally well choose either to utter the word 'bottle' in my request or to replace it with my gesture. Actually, if we want to think that the private sensation is most important, considering that I e.g. just entered the room and was very thirsty and then noticed the bottle on the table, it would make more sense to claim that my request is more closely connected to my *thirst* (my intent; the thing I had in my mind) rather than that I conjure up a mental image of a bottle first and then formulate the sentence that forms my request. But consider the case at hand, with me gesturing towards the bottle—what did I mean by 'bottle' or the '...' that accompanied gesture? Doesn't it feel a bit far-fetched to think that I'm meaning the mental representation of the bottle? And if not, what representation did I mean? Suppose that that particular water bottle is of a brand I have never seen before. If this is the case, which bottle representation does my word/gesture refer to: the representation of that particular new bottle, some old bottle I have seen before or perhaps an abstract idea of a bottle? The first case would mean that the mental representation equals the visual experience of the bottle, the second case would mean that what I meant has nothing to do with the particular bottle on the table in the example, and the third Platonic case probably doesn't seem so appealing in this industrial age but in any case raises the question of how the abstraction of a bottle ends up in my mind in the first place and the question of how I connect the bottle on the table to my mental representation of an abstract idea of a bottle. What if the person responds: "Do you mean this bottle of Evian?"; I would have to respond "Yes, that bottle on the table", since I don't know if it is Evian or not. After that we ask that person: "What did he *mean* by his gesture?" and the person respond: "He meant this bottle of Evian"... would we now contradict this by saying: "No, no, no, he meant a mental representation of a bottle in his mind." He would have to respond with: "No, he meant this bottle on the table, I am very sure of it", and he would be very correct to do so; to claim anything else is sheer lunacy. All of the cases seem rather absurd and there really is no need to pursue them further and show that any post-constructions will ultimately not appear intellectually satisfactory.[187] It is more sensible to say that in this test by my word/gesture I meant the bottle on the table and not the mental representation, and this will result in a contradiction between whether words refer to external objects or mental representations. However, what is common to both these tests and totally unproblematic was that I successfully used language in order to achieve something; namely to get the person to hand me the bottle, and this language use indeed is the only identifiable basis for meaning that doesn't result in the necessity to back it up with complex or verbose theories that in the end fail to satisfy the original problem with an explanation. I, for one, instead think without contradicting myself. This means that meaning simply does not reduce

---

187 Such an approach is equivalent to cleaning an apartment by pushing the dirt from one place to another and finishing by getting tired or reaching a diplomatic agreement about the location of the dirt rather than achieving the original task.

PART II. COMMON MISCONCEPTIONS

to mental representations but is essentially a linguistic practice.

In the correct Popperian sense, the logical possibilities to refute a scientific claim constitute the power of the claim, given that it is supported by evidence. This is the same as saying that the more unbelievable a claim is and the easier it is to think of ways in which the claim is not true, the more powerful it is and the more scientific value it has, given that it can be proven with evidence. The strongest example would be to claim that the Earth revolves around the Sun, in a world full of evidence to the contrary. By contrast, a claim that cannot be refuted by any evidence is not a scientific claim at all and has no scientific value. Say, the thought that there is God in heaven is a basic tenet of Christianity but a scientifically worthless claim because of the nature of God and heaven, which are beyond the capabilities of verification or refutation by evidence. For example a common pseudoscientific claim, that wireless Internet routers cause restlessness in children, is a very weak scientific claim because of the lack of possibilities to refute it, and furthermore, one can see that in its credibility it can be placed in the same category as many other similar claims, such as that the restlessness in children is caused by the monsoon, changes in solar winds, changes in Earth's magnetic fields, changes in local bacteria types or levels, changes in emotional atmospheres, and so on. Such a claim would have the same scientific credibility as religious claims, and the ultimate difference in credibility between pseudoscience and religion is *tradition*—the difference between scientifically untestable beliefs that are held by a superstitious few, and beliefs that can be seen to be the wisdom of millennia. And here we see an unscientific criterion that could be called "the test of time", and the limits of empirical knowledge which doesn't consider the subjective and traditions. Consider the subjective question of what the best type of hammer for hammering nails is. Scientifically one could test the qualities of the hammer from different perspectives: its weight and shape, applicability to common nail types or other tasks. It should be noted that these types of tests would in themselves be implied by the tradition of hammering and the tasks that one would be expected to do with a hammer. But probably the only other thing the scientist could do is to compile statistics about people's opinions on hammers, and such statistics would have to target scientific neutrality, but what good would that do? Neutrality is not goodness, but the loss of any subjective information. What we want to achieve is to find the best type of hammer, and here we should simply ask the opinion of the best smith or carpenter, and if he proudly tells us that the hammer of his preference is a type of hammer that was used by his father and grandfather, this piece of information is not just a random piece of history, but valuable information about the subjective preferences in a line of tradition regarding the particular subjective expertise. From the perspective of the scientific method, of course, subjectivity is a vice, but from the perspective of life, using the scientific method in search of subjective answers is folly. Whether a question is subjective or objective in nature can be determined by linguistic analysis by asking for the criterion—in the case of "good hammer", asking for the criterion of a good hammer—but from the perspective of scientific methodology, a question can be called an objective question if there exists a logical possibility to produce objective evidence to refute it, and only in this case is it interesting to present objective evidence that supports it. Questions that cannot be refuted by objective evidence are subjective, and it is by no means implied that one should follow traditions in all subjective questions, but simply that *regarding subjective questions tradition is one's best information resource*. Regarding the objectively untestable question of whether wireless routers cause restlessness in children, the subjective nature of the question is in the worry about whether some measures should be taken, and here the best information sources are one's traditions. If one doesn't have traditional wisdom about what generally causes restlessness in children, one might e.g. consult other parents or study the matter from this general perspective of restlessness in children, instead of rushing to attribute a pseudoscientific cause for the phenomenon. If children are restless, first one should consult the grandmother, who can tell if there is some change in how children today are being raised, because she has seen two generations.

When cognitive science studies "the mind" (or "consciousness") it is stepping directly into the pitfall of attributing the universally myste-

PART II. COMMON MISCONCEPTIONS

rious nature of the intersection of private experience, language and observation into this object called "the mind". Without giving proper and serious thought to what causes that mysterious nature every cognitive scientist rushes to be among the first to apply these great new computational theories and related algorithms to that mystery and with absolute certainty manages to produce nothing novel in solving the mystery for themselves or anybody else. And how can they achieve this while giving even the impression of a basis of serious thought? Naturally enough, by searching backwards into the history of philosophy for a renowned philosopher whose thought complies with their aims of being able to make a living by conducting research, finding one in *Descartes*,[188] and raising this fellow to the status of sage. Descartes' mind-body dualism complies perfectly with the cognitive approach, as he saw the body as a mechanism operated by the mind (via levers located in the pineal gland, as he speculated), which reflects the level of understanding of human anatomy at the time, where an anatomist would identify bones, muscles, tendons, nerves and so on as being somehow linked to the brain by the nervous system and supported by body tissues and fluids. More problematic biological discoveries to challenge a mechanistic approach, such as cells, membranes and chemistry of the body, genes, and details of the nervous system, were introduced after Descartes, and pose significant issues for anyone claiming that the body is a mechanism. Such a model can be countered by contradicting scientific evidence discovered after Descartes' time. Of such evidence I give the following examples.

1) Neurology hasn't been able to locate any distinct control centre in the brain, as Descartes suggested. On the contrary, simple reflex action is initiated without the nerve impulse ever reaching the cranial part of the brain but just the grey matter of the spinal cord, and then again, certain areas of thought have been seen to correlate with brain activity in specific parts of the brain. In a model of the mind operating the body, the singular experience of the mind, call it, say, consciousness or individuality, would be expected to correlate with a

---

[188] In this process we have degraded in problem-setting back to the early modern period, slightly surpassing the Middle Ages. I am sometimes told that Wittgenstein and Kierkegaard were products of their respective eras... in which case, what about Descartes?

II-9. COMPUTATIONALIST SCIENCE

neural unity.

2) Infection clearance and wound healing, contrary to being processes initiated by the brain, are shown by modern science to be completely biochemical processes. Only the related pain involves nervous signalling with the brain, which can be seen as functional in producing a reaction to protect the wounded area of the body in order to provide a cleaner environment for the wound to heal.

3) Contrary to limbs being predetermined parts of a mechanism, animal gene manipulation experiments have succeeded in e.g. manipulating the types of limbs developed by embryos.

Given the approach that the mind controls the body mechanism through the brain, these examples highlight features that are not attributable to any known mechanisms. But this does not bother the cognitive scientist at all, as after all his quest backwards in the history of philosophy was to find justification for his own methodology, not to find an answer to the problem of the mind. And so, this half a millennium old philosophical approach has launched an unsuccessful yet excitingly marketed search for neural correlates of the mind, flattering the imaginations of its funding organs with images of dream-collecting machines and the like. Some explanation for the lack of success might be found in that the Cartesian cognitivist will ignore his own sage's thought in that Descartes believed that God created Man and that God is a perfect being. But ultimately, the problem of the mind is a conceptual problem and such problems lie in the domain of philosophy, not new scientific theories or computer software. Academia is in crisis.

Finally, many sciences, such as neuroscience, are gaining a great boost from computational methods providing a new approach to apply mathematical and statistical models together with modern results, which gives such scientists the credibility to apply the "we're just one small step away" argument, as old as science itself. Anyone who denies that the mind is produced by neural activity is snubbed because events in experience are shown to correlate with neural activity. That *cum hoc* fallacy manages to give computational neuroscientists adequate grounds for adopting the computationalist approach towards the brain

PART II. COMMON MISCONCEPTIONS

to study "the nature" of concepts that belong to the domain of the humanities, and there seems to be no restriction on this: 'consciousness', 'knowledge', 'normativity'... For example, the atmosphere allows the research of computational-statistical "causal models", in which a valid research question can be one such as: "How do people construct and reason with the causal models we use to represent our world?"[189] This is fundamentally insane and means absolutely nothing. The atmosphere is such that a scientist can just come out and say: "Men reason with causal models", or "Language is a digital and infinite biological system"... lines that *mean nothing*, and continue that line of thought into any wanted direction of research by technical means; no holds barred, no academic organ will stand in the way by pointing out the absurdity of what is being said. The senselessness of such a sentence can be seen directly in that reasoning is a subjective faculty and any theoretical models are objective, but to get to the root of the problem one must dig further to find that, firstly, the intended meaning of 'to reason' here (along with other dispositions of the mind) is assumed to be computational processes, and secondly, 'causal' here means any model, diagram or such, that has been constructed in a particular way, namely by e.g. naming some elements 'causes' and some 'effects'. Let's first note that the claim that dispositions of the mind are computational processes is a simple assertion (a work hypothesis) with *no* grounding philosophical argumentation, and thus equal in *credibility* to asserting that the dispositions of the mind are, say, hierophant balloons. It is an assertion that, because it can't be validated or refuted with evidence, is essentially ludicrous in the same way that it's ludicrous for a man to consider his wife a hat. The same is the case with the claims that causality is a model, or that language is digital. But could we *try* to understand what it means to make such an assertion? It means *commitment to a methodology*, which, in the case of causality, is commitment to the statistical methodology that underlies the concept of causal models, or, in the case of language being digital, the computational methodology. It can be translated into meaning: "I want to study mind/language with a statistical/computational method." And secondly, let's

---

[189] This is the problem setting in a book *Causal Models* published a few years ago by Oxford University Press.

II-9. COMPUTATIONALIST SCIENCE

note that the sensibility of computationalism is grounded on the hypothesis that our computational models are somehow physically constituted in the brain—in the same way as the sensibility of Turing machines is our capability of physically realizing the related theory. Now, Wittgenstein gives[190] an intriguing thought experiment regarding the language of the physical constitution of thought. Consider an experiment where the subject has a 'window' to his own brain—he called it a 'mirror' but it is better for the thought experiment for this to be as vaguely defined as possible. The subject will now have two separate experiences: 1) the introspective experience of his own thought, and 2) the experience of his observation of the activity in the brain. Now, let's ask the question: "Where is the thought located?" Let's assume that the 'window' is located on the table. Will the subject point his finger to his own head or to the window on the table? *If* he points to his own head, then he means thought in the same sense as we mean for example 'pain', and to show the related difficulties here (which Wittgenstein studied at length) I'll simply make two remarks to point out the non-physical nature of the pain experience: first, both amputees and people born with congenital deficiencies typically report pains that are located in their non-existent limbs, in a space of thin air outside the physical body ("phantom pain"), and secondly, heartache is often reported to be the feeling of the other person's pain. And I know many people would like to say: "No, it's just physical/neurological pain but experienced", which is nothing but an assertion with some confusion in terminology, as experiences logically are not physical. But then, *if* the subject in the experiment points to the window instead, then he means the window of observation and experiment to the physical/biological processes that take place inside the brain at the same time as thought, and here we see why the 'window' needs to be vaguely described: all the results that we derive from using the window are related to what sort of window we choose. Currently, the interest is to study the neurological processes in the brain, and I think in principle there is no problem whatsoever in studying the relation between neural activity and thought. Wittgenstein explicitly denies meaning that to say that the thought is located in the brain is by itself senseless, but he uses this

---
190 *The Blue Book*, Blackwell, p.8

PART II. COMMON MISCONCEPTIONS

experiment to show why the expression is bound—by its criterion—to a *particular* meaning, and that in this context these meanings tend to get confused, which is why he suggests that one refute the question of the locality of the thought as senseless. The problem is the sort of metaphysical thought that considers neural activity to *be* thought, in the same sense as my experience of my own thought is. I concur with Wittgenstein and suggest refuting the question of the locality of thought altogether, and instead changing the terminology: on one hand we have the (subjective) introspective experience of thought, and on the other we have the (objective) empirical observations of thought, and as we notice the difference, we also notice that the nature of the empirical observations equals our research hypothesis and methodology. So, I would rather demand more accuracy and refer to the observations from the "neural window" the *neural basis of thought*, just to point out that there is a lot more to thought than neurons and that we don't *have to*, and we shouldn't, commit to a single approach; for example, we know that the *chemical* processes in the brain don't behave in a mechanistic manner yet they affect neural activity. This clarification that Wittgenstein presented, before the observable craze in computational neuroscience that followed the Nobel prize-winning Hodgkin-Huxley physical neural model in 1952, was well timed, as he didn't just predict what would happen but he literally and concretely solved the problem before it emerged. Unfortunately, this wisdom was forgotten. Now we have computationalist cognitive sciences and neurosciences that don't make proper linguistic distinction regarding thought and therefore run up against the wall (against the boundaries of language). They don't notice, and we don't notice, that the appealing nature of the results that they derive is derived rather from their choice of research methodology and the related attribution. On a general level, is it any wonder that researching thought *as* neural processes will produce the *image* that thought *is* neural processes? Is it surprising that if you study the mind *as* processes, you will also come up with the idea—nestled inside your conclusion—that the mind *is* processes? If you think this is an exaggeration, go and ask those scientists; they will tell you "We believe that thoughts are neurological processes" or finesse this slightly by saying: "We believe that the best way to study these things is

II-9. COMPUTATIONALIST SCIENCE

to make this assumption", and you will feel awkward when a person, who is literally being paid not to believe but to experiment instead, tells you that all of his work is based simply on what he believes. He believes it is the best way because he is a member of that club, of course, but will he be ready to scrutinize this basic belief and to ask why it is the best way? Likely not. And when we follow the scientists and take thought to be neural processes, we are following what they believe but what has nothing whatsoever to do with science: a simple assertion and attribution; a dogma and a principle.

Then, for example, Chomsky, a celebrated modern linguist and a fundamentally influential figure, postulates the grounding basis of his theories for human computational linguistic capabilities with simple occultism, saying that it must be that the brain has been organized the way he suggests during evolution by a mysterious force that might have been a cosmic ray shower or a divine architect. And given Chomsky's renown, we can honestly say that this is the best our modern minds can come up with—something a medieval alchemist might have conjured—and it strongly represents the state of what is considered philosophical and thus forming the intellectual basis of our standards for science altogether. Throughout the history of Western science it has been standard that if somebody finds it appropriate to speak of something with the aid of a metaphor (such as a computational process), he is expected to explain the sense of such a claim in a way that leaves no doubt about what is meant by the new concept. But what has happened here is that the discussion around AI, a quasi-religious academic discussion between 1950 and 2000, was lost by the academic philosophers by majority vote, since the phenomenon of the digital computer has been so new, complex and interesting that enlightened computer scientists and natural scientists were able to win the argument in the eyes of the masses by resorting to their knowledge of this new technical science that academic philosophers simply didn't possess. There suddenly appeared masses of academics with a similar wish to call humans computers. And now we've got to the stage respectable newspapers publish frequent articles explaining that computer 'robots' (simply a science fiction term) are becoming members of society and that some quoted neuroscientist has opined that their team is just about to overcome some final frontier to make this possible, usually with the suggestion that more money should be made available to do so—this message being the sole function and purpose of publishing such an article, which otherwise conveys no scientific results or content whatsoever. But this is not enough, now respectable newspapers are quoting scientists saying that AI software has become self-correcting[191] (we know this is impossible) and robots will soon replace the majority of the work force.[192] The insanity of such claims can only be explained by the fact that they are intended to cause a particular effect, such as more panic in the job market. This is obviously news that can take no closer scrutiny. An error of this magnitude, where such argument is possible in the first place, could aptly be called mass psychosis, defined as the psychiatric state where a group of people are chronically unable to distinguish dreams from reality. This has happened at the same time as philosophers have been cast out of the discussion as old-fashioned—of course I am not implying these two things to be causally related. Since Wittgenstein there have been no philosophers skilled and authoritative enough to break down such language with proper linguistic analysis (the definitive argumentative tool), but AI counterarguments gaining recognition haven't been strong enough. Quite probably there have been many capable thinkers revolted by the direction the world has taken, but since they have been a part of the academic institution that at the same time guarantees the authority of both them and their opponent, they have chosen not to saw off the branch they are sitting on.

The study of intelligence and consciousness seem to have functioned as the main trunk of the tree from which different modern disciplines have branched, and indeed from a Wittgensteinian perspective calling for full accuracy and awareness regarding the meanings of concepts, a modern scientific book about consciousness with proper academic

---

191   J. Markoff, 'Brainlike Computers, Learning from Experience', 28.12.2013, The New York Times http://www.nytimes.com/2013/12/29/science/brainlike-computers-learning-from-experience.html [26.12.2019].

192   J. Markoff, 'Skilled Work, Without the Worker', 18.8.2012, The New York Times http://www.nytimes.com/2012/08/19/business/new-wave-of-adept-robots-is-changing-global-industry.html [26.12.2019].

references may not considerably differ regarding either soundness of problem-setting or style of writing from a book about consciousness put forward by the Hare Krishna movement. Taking a look at intelligence and consciousness, one can note their similar role in that they both refer to mental qualities that are quantitative, and taking a precise look at why they are quantitative reveals that their quantitative role signifies *moral responsibility*, as it is the subject's degree of both consciousness and intelligence that determines how responsible the subject is for his own actions, and thus how guilty he is. I personally have always made an effort to try to become more conscious (or aware) of what is beyond the ordinary things that we see, which translates to my interest in truth and philosophy, which, in turn, translates to striving for a better position to judge and determine my own actions, and via this, naturally, a better capability to act responsibly and to guide others to do the same. I have my own personal-historical background to this, which makes it easy for me to understand another person's effort towards excelling in intelligence and consciousness that just takes a different path from mine. But what I don't understand is why such mental qualities are studied *via natural science*, as they are clearly and distinctly, probably more so than many other mental qualities, *psycho-social* qualities, the study of which is firmly rooted in humanities, as they involve an ethical perspective. Now, *pseudoscience* is where something is presented as science, working to enlighten a phenomenon via producing plausible conceptions of it, but instead it can be identified as having shortcomings, and I'll mention here the two important ones.

1) In the case of a pseudoscientific claim, the person making the claim can be identified to be motivated to personally *acquire* some subjective qualities for himself, or, say, to be trying to avoid bad things happening to himself via attribution of something that is not scientifically defined. An obvious example is the climate change movement that presents itself as science but is quite obviously motivated by a fear of the end of the world and thus the desire to stay safe and not to be afraid. But let me give another example via something I've read about recently in the news: some people believe they are allergic to electricity and are angry at uncaring doctors for not accepting this

PART II. COMMON MISCONCEPTIONS

modern new allergy. Their claim initially sounds plausible because we are living in times of prevalent pervasive wireless electromagnetic communication. But one can first note that allergies are reactions of the immune system to *substances* called allergens, which electricity is not, and secondly, the argumentation to prove the allergy is based on reactions that are self-experienced. Hence among those who claim this there is a motivation of safety and cure to one's own conditions. I chose this "electricity allergy" simply as one example; eccentricities described by patients or their parents easily get diagnosed as psychiatric conditions (e.g. autism, Asperger's or bipolarity), and some health service consumers visit one doctor after another until they reach a satisfactory diagnosis—one that essentially psychologically works to alleviate their fear of social humiliation, and confirm their belief that there is really something wrong with them (hypochondria). These fears used to be alleviated by spiritual means, when one would confess one's hidden fears to a priest, but not today; the poor individuals find no other escape than the comfort of being officially labelled sick so that they don't have to live with the fear that their individual eccentricities will bring them unforeseen social harms. It is very human for an individual to have such fears, but, unfortunately, the society we live in is not very caring and doesn't provide a service that will officially grant them love and acceptance, and tell them they are good enough and valuable members of society despite their social shortcomings. Instead we will give them the a fundamentally inhumane label of being born with a defective brain, as if they were a replaceable motor car manufactured with a faulty engine. If they admitted how they felt, they'd not be understood but either treated in a non-effective manner or determined to be ill and treated medically. But regarding the actual claims, such as that the cause of particular pains or behaviour is latent electricity, or that the cause of, say, social shortcomings is a defective brain; the pseudoscientific mistake happens where we are looking at objective methods of producing information for subjective phenomena, and are bound to the common motive of helping people to somehow become better, such as forms of medicine and therapy. These are motives that by nature don't need to be established on scientific concepts but are that by nature via our scientific institution of medicine. You can help another's back problems by practical methods such as massage, and often people find that psycho-social issues are alleviated just through the experience of being taken care of and helped to overcome undesirable psychological states. This practical social need of helping people is completely distinct from any scientific motives, yet pseudoscience is something that confuses these motives. Hence the word *pseudo*science; 'pseudo' meaning a lie, the lie being posing as objective science instead of honestly presenting itself as a sort of movement, an association or similar, consisting of like-minded people with a belief. This reaching for the subjective realm via objective means should also correctly be seen as occultism; the actually targeted subjective realm being presented as something 'beyond' the objective methodologies—beyond as in *super*natural or *sub*conscious. And this is not at all to say that the miracle of life and the mystery of conscious experience are not absolutely interesting and fascinating, but just to point out that if one doesn't feel the need to focus on the sense of what the experience makes one inclined to utter about it—in terms of how the concepts used have been used before and thus how the acquired knowledge will be passed on to a reader—one will be inclined to utter nonsense.

2) Pseudoscience typically mixes with an *ethical ideology*, which implies that the subject has unidentified ethical motives in the background. It is by no means wrong for a researcher to have ethical motives, but if he can't himself distinguish where he is forced by the ideology to see things in a particular light, his observations will contain bias. An ideology can be distinguished from scientific theory and scientific thought by the key feature that *negative evidence* should be the most important thing to an empirical scientist. Because the scientist is essentially *postulating* a theory—saying: "Let's assume *this* is true"—his main attention and activity should go into efforts to *revoke* his theory, *not* to *affirm* it. Why affirm something as true if it is already postulated as true?—No, the point is first to postulate it as true and then work to revoke it. This is because the nature of something can be best described via how it differs from other things. Let's say I buy a Napoleon hat and a jacket, learn to wear my hand

PART II. COMMON MISCONCEPTIONS

inside my jacket and to speak of myself in the third person with a strong French accent. Then I make the claim that I am Napoleon. Fine, there are certainly similarities and we could for example put me on a stage where I could address people and ask: "Who am I?", to which they would respond "You're Napoleon". Now is this method reliable? Hardly. And why not? Because I am not Napoleon; it gave a false positive. But why am I not Napoleon? Because I only need *one piece of negative evidence* for this; say, just to point out that Napoleon was born in 1769 and I was not, and hence I am not Napoleon. It is very easy to point this out via just looking for the most obvious negative evidence. Ideologies differ from this activity in that negative evidence is not considered fatal to such a theory... because it is not considered. Rather, the mark of an ideology is that the more negative evidence there is, the more the idealist will passionately disregard it and concentrate his attention on the positive; the more capitalist the world is, the more communism is considered necessary by those who subscribe to it. This brings about a very visible phenomenon in society: whenever we see a very vocal and highly publicized defence of some particular value, it means that there apparently is no scientific evidence available to make the case as a rational argument, as there is a need to make a passionate case by appealing to emotion.

Both cases 1) and 2) point to a mistake where the subjective (acquiring subjective qualities for oneself or the world as an ethical goal) is being approached by objective standards—scientific standards. On a social level and especially in the modern information age, the problem is that the scientists holding common views are able to form cliques and schools with like-minded scientists despite the fact that the things they say would only be meaningful within those groups of people adhering to shared work hypotheses. There is no academic organ to validate wildly formulated research proposals, as traditional academic philosophers have been successfully superseded by the union of natural scientists and like-minded academic philosophers, and given a space in their underground chambers to study their ancient scriptures in peace in exchange for a daily meal. Academic philosophy is divided, with no communication between the parties.

II-9. COMPUTATIONALIST SCIENCE

The most alarming of all pseudoscientific issues is contemporary "climate science", and it's possible to note that *environmental alarmism* in itself bears the mark of pseudoscience, because the motive is directly related to people's fundamental need for safety, rather like the common pseudoscientific themes of fears of ghosts in places with a scary atmosphere, electromagnetic radiation, government secrecy about scientific facts such as the existence of extra-terrestrial intelligence, telepathic interference, the health effects of diet and various digestible or applied substances, and so on. When people's feeling of security is compromised, they change from rational thinkers to a mode of thought where one simply works to confirm one's fears instead of critically considering the sensibility of suspicion. I too tend to think in a similar irrational manner when I experience thoughts of suspicion and distrust; in my life I have harboured suspicions that, once my feeling of security was restored, seemed irrational and absolutely out of character for me. This felt rather shameful because I tend to mostly rely on reason in my life. This is why people with a pressing need to make a living have long found profits in exploiting other people's fear by providing services such as fortune-telling, miracle healing, talismans and aphrodisiacs, child safety products and even funeral plots. It could be said that wherever fear exists good business can be done in exploiting it. It is possible that we will all be killed tomorrow by a stray meteorite smashing into the Earth, but this fear by itself doesn't justify scientific research that simply works to confirm this claim by interpreting astronomic observations in the light of this claim. On the contrary, *fear* is *the* subjective phenomenon that causes all irrationality. In the old days good and responsible men were expected to show courage and capability for rational thought under dangerous circumstances, and panic was something expected from women and the weak minded. And in the case of environmental alarmism the correct alternative to such sentiments and alarmist arguments is simply *adhering to the scientific method* that has been developed in the effort to protect rational thought from well-known human weaknesses of the mind: 1) observe a phenomenon, 2) develop different theories to explain the observations, and 3)

PART II. COMMON MISCONCEPTIONS

try and collectively determine which is the most credible explanation. In the political practice regarding environmental alarmism this process is heavily manipulated by lobbying for the support of theories and publishing them as scientific truths instead of letting them become scientific truths via the normal process where unsound research is scientifically refuted by academic peers. Environmental alarmism has a colourful history, with ice age fears, warming fears, stratosphere cooling fears due to greenhouse effect, ozone depletion fears, fears of sea level rise... I am no expert, but it seems that the Gauls' fear in Asterix, that the sky would fall on their heads, is still alive and well in the 21st century. I would simply like to draw attention to the scientific status of these claims in their respective times, since it makes no difference whether the related theories are produced by scientific organs or fortune-tellers because such theories have always been of an untestable quality in their context of application. Also, they are in practice tested in small-scale isolated environments or, nowadays, with computer models based solely on assumptions. If they are produced by scientists it is thought to be too challenging to question the authority of scientists in these matters. But this shouldn't be too difficult, and rather it seems miraculous that scientists hold *any* credibility regarding such issues, because *all* of these scares and fears that put forward some deadline after which all hell will break loose are no different from every doomsday scenario in the history of the world so far. You can call it a divine miracle, guidance or whatever, but miraculously the world we live in has not ended despite such a prediction being made by countless doomsayers that eventually died of natural causes in spite of their worst fears. And in the case of global warming it is a very embarrassing situation to have all of the tens of respected computer climate models that UN has used in its drafting of policies proven wrong simply because the debates have endured long enough to witness the falsity of the predictions by real-world data. This shouldn't come as a surprise to anybody who understands the pseudoscientific nature of such claims as fear-induced untestable irrationalism, but of a style that is portrayed as science and thus manages to appropriate authority it doesn't deserve. A study found that, in the case of climate change, if the *abstract* of the scientific publication was written in a style containing *narrative elements* (using a determined set of narrative indicators), this led to a high number of scientific references to this publication by other scientific publications.[193] This outcome indicates two things: firstly, narrative elements in the research setting of a natural scientific study is an indicator of poor quality, and secondly, the fact that the correlation occurs with the abstract of the publication implies that the abstract itself is meaningful in predicting incoming references, which in turn implies that some of the referrers read only the abstract of the publication and no more. Global warming, or climate change, is a *radical ideology* in which reality, truth and failure are systematically ignored in favour of the *fundamental necessity* incorporated in the ideology... and actually it is more radical than communism because communism predicted only that the world would inevitably develop towards communism, not that it would die altogether, as the climate alarmists claim. This alarmism is of the sort that calls for the most drastic measures to curb it; of the sort found in misguided people who follow crazy and dangerous cult leaders. I once heard talks by two individuals passionately explaining how cities should be planned in the future: the first gave a lecture about how to minimize earthquake damage in city planning by using statistics more effectively to decide the locations where cities are built, and the other gave a lecture on how flood gates should be better planned in cities to avoid flood damage. As a Finn, I myself could share a lot of historical wisdom about how houses should be designed and built for efficient heating. But this event made me realize that people are very afraid of the unknown in the face of increased global awareness, and the high level of alarmism is a general fear reaction to this. And this fear is currently being abused in global policymaking: in their fear, people turn to the authorities for help, and just as the two alarmist individuals described above have their personal ideas about how to improve disaster readiness, the influential people behind global policymaking are using the fear as an opportunity to bypass scientific rational thought and to push the solutions that will bring them personal profit. The Antarctic ozone hole scare managed to create a global ban on the production of CFC products and after that

---

[193] A. Hillier, R. P. Kelly and T. Klinger, 'Narrative Style Influences Citation Frequency in Climate Change Science', PloS One, http://doi.org/10.1371/journal.pone.0167983.

the problem disappeared, but more ozone holes have since been discovered over the Arctic and over Tibet. The logical scientific conclusion would be to say that CFCs were not the cause of ozone holes or that ozone holes are not dangerous, but who would return to defend a thesis that was not testable, provable or disputable in the first place? Rather what happened is that the ozone hole theory was maintained in alternative forms, such as that CFCs weren't the cause or that they were the cause but something happened in addition to create new holes (the trick of blaming an unrelated third party) combined with the new global warming scare, which shows that the real nature of these claims is political and pushed by lobbying groups that see any scare theories as political fuel, and this manipulation of science will take place as long as it can be seen as profitable business by the people who create it. Rather than looking at vague or preliminary scientific evidence for a yet another predetermined environmental dystopian scenario and listening to the accompanying neurotic lecture that, as is typical with pseudoscience, establishes its critics as enemies, one should take a good look at how lobbying groups receive their funding, and determine the motives behind such politicized science. In the case of global warming the manipulation of the scientific process seems to extend all the way to the level of manipulation of the computer models that produced the data that grounded the formation of UN policies and panels—if not as a demonstrated fact, then at least as a well-established suspicion. And the manipulation of public opinion is full-scale information warfare and widely reported systematic harassment of political enemies with features familiar from high-stakes election campaigns and wartime diplomacy between countries. The lobbying experts and PR agencies involved are masters of the art of creating a credible environment for their claims. But most of all, I would be delighted to see somebody list all these historical scientific doomsday prediction failures and say something conclusive about the current human capability to scientifically understand weather and climate as a phenomenon, or at least to make a clear case for the general reliability of our scientific capability to form correct theories about novel observed phenomena, such as ozone holes or warming periods. The Earth's ecosystem is a fundamentally complex phenomenon, but modern scientists have completely lost their humility in trying to create predictions about its behaviour—instead of being happy about small scientific victories they want to jump to grander conclusions, failing time and again but refusing to look at their failure. Now, there is a standard technique used in the dominating 'agile' software development project model Scrum, in which work is produced in a cyclic process with a relatively short interval. The technique involves tracking and graphing the development team's cost estimates (estimates about how many working hours and how much work complexity it will take to develop a needed piece of functionality) for each development cycle against the actual cost outcomes, which essentially produces information about the reliability of one's estimates for each development cycle and over the evolution of the whole software product. At the same time, during each cycle, it teaches one how to correct one's estimation process and steer one's estimates towards more accuracy. Another similar method is the statistical estimation of margins of error in e.g. election outcome predictions. In IT, the Scrum model dominates because it provides a practical solution to the longstanding software development problem of communication between the customer and the provider, which is similar to the relationship between an apartment owner and an interior designer: the customer needs to invest a lot of money in something that he only has a vague initial idea about, but an interactive process between the provider and the customer will produce much better results in terms of customer satisfaction than trying to agree on all details and costs before the actual work is started. So, the solution is interaction and *visibility* in the development process. The relationship between the IT customer and the IT provider differs from the relationship between the public (the financier) and the scientific institution in the sense that science is an enterprise that is not meant to produce anything directly valuable, but the relationship is similar in the sense that both science and the IT provider are producing expert knowledge and the financing party needs to place significant trust in the providing experts. This required *trust* makes the position vulnerable because, for this very reason, it is common knowledge that in the cowboy-like world of IT, coders and IT houses won't produce products that don't break, but they come up with the products quickly and in

PART II. COMMON MISCONCEPTIONS

such a manner that *if* they break, they need to be fixed using the tools they themselves provide.

I am not promoting cancelling the scientific program, but I believe the modern scientific institution is a failure. The existence of this institution is justified by tradition and history ("If we didn't have science we wouldn't have these-and-these innovations"), but this historical perspective is consistently missing political aspect. Looking at the world where science made its breakthrough as an institution (academia, the university), one can see that science stood with the revolutionary values together with art, and these were the new values for the liberated Europeans. Science liberated the individual via a collective, institutionalized formation of truth, and brought an end to evil times of feudal clan existence, raising Europe to a new age of civilization. Hail science for that but look at the science today! The institution has been bought with private money from corporations that, in these modern times, represent exactly the papal and regal power of the times of the origin of the institution; the powers science was to abolish. A study from 2005[194] notes that most scientific results are false positives and soon refuted by further evidence, and this result is predicted by small sample sizes, small scientific effect of the finding, the lack of preliminary studies in the same field, flexibility in method, financial interests in the field, and having several scientific teams involved in the scientific field. A credible explanation[195] is that researchers simply "hack the p value" by manipulating their data after seeing it. This is because $p \leq 0.05$, statistical significance, is the *de facto* measure of research success in virtually any field, and researchers are tempted to manipulate their datasets until the magic number pops out of their computers. This is, of course, an expected result when you declare that statistics equals truth. I believe the biggest argument in favour of our empirical science has been that it is *based on objective evidence*, which would categorically make it a favourite over any system with degree of subjective results.

---

[194] Ioannidis, J.P.A. (2005) 'Why Most Published Research Findings Are False', PLoS Med 2(8): e124, http://doi.org/10.1371/journal.pmed.0020124.

[195] Geoff Cumming, 'One reason so many scientific studies may be wrong', The Conversation, October 6, 2016, https://theconversation.com/one-reason-so-many-scientific-studies-may-be-wrong-66384 [26.12.2019].

II-9. COMPUTATIONALIST SCIENCE

But this is clearly not enough because evidence can be subjectively manipulated, and in a huge system that is based on evidence, evidence can be manipulated on a huge scale, giving the impression of objectivity.

Science has failed as a multi-national system of truth, because it fails to produce truth. The meaning of *truth* is not as simple as being just the result of science; nor does the word refer to simply a belief. Truth is to be revealed, which means that there already is something relevant to be discovered, and this very clearly is a political function. This aspect explains why modern scientific discoveries are so bleak; it's not at all because "everything has already been discovered". It is because the discoveries are not politically relevant, as there doesn't exist any wish to be relieved ('relevant' means 'relieving'), apart from the private interest of the political benefactor. The discoveries fail to reveal. Then again, looking at our actual political wishes relating to science, we find that the things that are most anticipated—via the argument that "very soon such-and-such will be happening"—the most visible ones are the anticipation that workers will be replaced by robots and the anticipation that the Earth's climate is heading towards doomsday. The idea about robots hasn't changed in 70 years but is much less credible now, as we know so much more about computation yet our predictions about workers being replaced are calculated with much less credibility, as all such predictions typically leave out any material or maintenance costs and just use the age-old idea that when dealing with robots everything just happens automatically like magic. Then again the anticipation of climate doomsday, to a large extent analogous to the expectation that our workers will be replaced by machines, is not credible simply because it is a catastrophe scenario, and *credibility* translates to "a reason to believe", which such a scenario fails to provide by default. Who would like to believe in a great catastrophe? Anybody can paint grim scenarios, and also take note that multiple predictions of the end of the world have failed to come true. Therefore all these models that predict imminent destruction must all be false, and indeed have turned out

PART II. COMMON MISCONCEPTIONS

to be, but what has been wrong is not only the system that produces such predictions but also our faith in this system that seems to be set to produce truth but produces fundamental lies and fails to address this problem. Our wishes (expectations) about scientific outcomes are failing, which translates to the fact that the neutrality of science has been compromised by politics and ideology. What we would wish to be the truth and reality, in fact turns out to be untrue by objective study, and this means that we are trying to use science for something it is not meant for in the first place. Science is not suitable for ideologies and politics that by nature deal with matters that *are not* but that *should be*, and the correct question rather is: Why is it that political and ideological desires, funded by immense quantities of money, work to *pretend* the form of science? The answer to this question is that science is the modern day's religion in that a scientific claim has credibility in the eyes of the 21st-century masses, but just lacks any relevant qualities of a real religion.

Finally, let's look at what we, as a society, *need science for*. Why do we fund research and not spend this money on something else instead?

- You might say that we need science to help, as we might find cures for presently incurable diseases and ways to help the sick. The truth is that modern medicine is mostly letting psychiatric patients die without cure, or, at best, uses them as guinea pigs for more science... and this is just the case with those who seek help. Defunding scientific research in medicine won't affect the functioning of hospitals and care facilities, it will just stop them from using live humans as guinea pigs. Let those funds be spent on helping people instead, for example by hiring and training more staff, to provide the help we agree is necessary. The point I'd like to make is that our medical institution is obviously not evolving in the direction of helping people more. Rather the development is towards things such as 1) prescribing more drugs with less control over whether those drugs help, 2) dropping groups beyond the of help altogether, and 3) legalizing irreversible body mutilations for the purpose of personal pride and vanity (sex changes). We have increased the scope of people's freedom to decide about their own things; moved them away from governance. In some cases, we wish to stop talking about specific conditions as sicknesses, in a wish to alleviate the person's suffering by doing so. However, as sicknesses can be seen to be best defined as all things that need help from the medical institution, if we don't see these conditions as sicknesses, then they fall outside the responsibility of society, which makes sense as a part of the general development where people are left alone with their own problems. As a society, this is not helping people but ignoring them. People don't easily admit to needing help; as an example, in my own case I delayed my shoulder surgery for almost 2 years, just ignoring it and letting the condition get worse. Many people persistently deny having anything wrong with them and need their family or friends to strongly advise and direct them to seek help, sometimes almost physically dragging them to see the doctor. It is not just that people don't necessarily admit or notice that they need help; it can be that a person feels he wants to die and doesn't see a reason to live, that he is on the verge of taking his own life while possibly not showing this for the sake of pride. The next step in this development obviously is officially accepting euthanasia, which would drop *any* groups with suicidal thoughts outside society's care.

- You might say that we need science to understand humans and our lives better. I'd reply to that that both our philosophical and psychological knowledge have very considerably degraded already due to our concentration on natural science, which is so heavy that related methodologies have been forcefully transported to the humanities. In philosophy we are degenerating to a point further back in history than Descartes, but in psychology all they seem to do is to study the brain, searching for Descartes' magical little elf that pulls the strings, and the results typically do nothing but confirm folk wisdom. One might note that folk wisdom is often thousands of years old, and the fact that science is now confirming such knowledge means that our ancestors are ahead of us since they knew those things while we are still in the process of confirming them. So, it seems to me that natural scientific psychology has quite a low chance of helping us understand ourselves better, as it persists in using methodologies based on a dualism that has long been shown to be problematic and unstable. Wittgenstein said a long time ago that the mind is not in the brain. It's important not to dismiss that problematic but to change or stop doing what you are doing; you are not on intellectually solid ground anymore. The mind is not located in the brain any more than thoughts are located in a book, and nobody in history has ever looked in a brain (listened to a brain, smelled a brain...) and observed one thought or mental image, which we would expect experts to be capable of, in the way that a composer can read another composer's score and hear the music, or a programmer can read another programmer's code and explain in detail how it will function. All they can do, and they do it very proudly, is to come up with the suggestion that "with some certainty" this brain pattern will result in such-and-such behaviour.

- You might say that we need science to help us get better at catching criminals. I'd like to point out that modern facial recognition techniques, despite possibly having cool consumer application potential, are being applied in building a society that works to control normal citizens or potential petty thieves, while at the same time the same system fails to catch crimes of the largest scale. These larger crimes are in practice corruption, economic crimes, identity crimes and so on, and they can't be controlled via scientific means, as they involve policies and living people who implement those policies. One could perhaps devise a computer system that large banks would have to apply, which would recognize and report money laundering as serial multi-account transactions involving large sums. However, such a system could easily be decisively deactivated or modified to make it ineffective. In another example, we have been able to produce reliable DNA test methodologies to better determine the identity of people through forensic evidence or e.g. tracing their ancestry, but at the same time the news can routinely portray authorities whose identities are completely unclear, as they omit any necessity to provide birth records, birth certificates or, say, the graves of their alleged parents. I think advanced scientific means of determining people's identity have no use if the elementary means of identification are ignored. In other words, fake news can produce fake people. Regarding the question of whether science helps us to better identify criminals, let it be noted that the FBI has admitted to routinely fabricating forensic testimonies, and it is precisely the expert nature of the forensic science that has allowed systematic abuse to be passed off as "bad science" instead of bad people and corruption. This is to say that science doesn't "help us" but science equals methodologies that are always *applied*, and in the FBI forensic scandal case it was precisely science that helped us better hide a flawed system in which testimonies are not just opinions but involve scientific procedures that are much more difficult to investigate for flaws. Looking at a person, say, in the news, it will be quite difficult to determine that the whole person does not exist, by which I mean that the person is not who they say he is; his *identity* is questionable, and the problem of detecting crime relates to *identifying* a person. With natural science, one would need to produce evidence that something doesn't exist, which doesn't sound like a very successful project. Identifying people is done by means that are scientific only in the sense of applying specialized methodologies, but essentially it involves comparing identification data with existing records of people's identities. If this institution is flawed, science has no power whatsoever to affect identifying criminals, but it might well contribute to the contrary.

- You might that say science could develop more efficient forms of energy for mankind to save energy in the future. Here I'd like to point to statistics[196]: in 2000, the world total energy production was roughly 10 Gtoe (billions of tonnes of oil equivalent), while the energy consumption was slightly under this, about 9.8 Gtoe. Since then, all sorts of fantastic scientific developments have taken place, mankind has developed to a new level, and production has risen to around 13.8 Gtoe. Where is consumption, then? Slightly under this figure, at 13.4 Gtoe. If somebody is saving energy, it seems it is not mankind. And it is also likely that if energy is produced more efficiently, it still won't be saved but almost certainly consumed. The argument presented here is that energy needs to be 1) produced more sustainably and 2) consumed more efficiently... but I don't follow this logic; if we say that preserving our planet is important (sustainability), isn't the obvious

---

[196] Global Energy Statistical Yearbook, https://yearbook.enerdata.net [26.12.2019].

solution that energy needs to be produced more lazily? Regarding 1), if we want to desist from overharvesting our planet, this is a political motive, not a scientific one. But regarding 2), how would inventing more energy-efficient products—appliances and such—reduce the ratio of produced and consumed energy, which seems to remain the same? If it didn't stay the same, that would be called overproduction and would be tackled by increased sales, discount sales or such... the average consumer could have two energy-efficient microwave ovens instead of one. Would you expect him to feel guilty for using too much energy? What I do know is that the Nazis tried to ban smoking—a consumer choice—by influencing people's attitudes with radical racial ideology and policies enforced on soldiers. After some success in achieving a decline in smoking the war ended, after which smoking exploded via black-market products to double or triple the pre-war levels. In general, it seems that possible results achieved by radical ideology are fleeting at best.

PART III. SOCIO-POLITICAL ANALYSIS

In this section I turn my attention to the society. I try to theorize a bit about what I think about the base of a society, and then turn my analysis into current issues and what I see to be the future direction. This section was painful to both write and edit, as looking at the state of our society is painful overall. Because of this, people have mostly isolated themselves in opinionated bubbles, and will actively ignore political issues and react emotionally to them, as many people possess alarmingly few mental tools to deal with differing opinions. The state of freedom of speech is terrible, and the idea of banning speech is constantly present. People are split into camps, and the gap between the camps is widening. I don't blame them. I see our society as not only full of problems but worse than that: on a course that will lead to something novel that we haven't seen since the Enlightenment and that I never believed I'd see, growing up as I did in the world I was born into and with the values I still hold but take no pride in expressing any more, as they have become instruments of evil. The institutions we have created to avoid war and promote equality and common rights have become agents of creating instability, injustice and inequality. Due to the change of political setting, I have had to rethink all the values I used to take for granted, and to switch political camp to react appropriately to modern problems that I believe are best solved by thinking in a different way. I have heard many similar stories from others. Day by day the news just gets worse, and the bizarre and ludicrous establish themselves as norms in an overall sinister descent into apathy and decadence. It is painful to watch, yes.

However, I am a big boy: I am not just an optimist, but also find myself looking at what is going on very sympathetically. You have to make yourself very strong to be able to take things like an adult, and if you can do that, I think the best way to change the mind of someone is to understand them. But an inevitable and sad truth should be stated very clearly: bad things also need to be pronounced—admitted—in order to be dealt with. No understanding or punishment will help somebody who refuses to look at himself. There is absolutely nothing that will help him. The thing we are the guiltiest of, as a society, is *ignoring* what is going on, and being unable to talk about it. We are living in times where those with the greatest desire to speak the truth are hated the most, but we must resist this, and we must bring truth into the light, even if some people are offended or, say, disgusted by it, and even if our governments take the side of the offended and feel that respecting the right of people not to be shocked by truth is more important than truth itself. Apathy is understandable, because we feel that the pain of looking at what is going on is worthless if there's nothing we can do about it. That is something we must all resist, and we must understand that coming into a correct understanding itself is a good action that will have positive consequences. We must see truth as the highest value. If freedom of speech simply vanishes one day, we must remain positive that freedom of thought still exists. One must not join those who do not care, and one must take pains and strive towards correct understanding, using both one's mind and heart.

III-1. The Basis of Democracy

Homo sapiens tends to settle down, and while he does so, there are two significant features of his existence: 1) he finds comfort in *religion* and 2) he starts to create *culture* via *art*, the role of which is essentially to communicate the ethical values that are necessary in a settled existence and thus to impose social harmony to make this static way of life possible over generations. The word 'culture' derives from 'cultus', meaning cultivation of land, which is also the basis of 'cult', meaning worship. Can monkeys have culture or worship? No, because the words 'culture' and 'cult' both post-date cultivation that is beyond monkeys in development.[197] Regarding culture, one should understand that by nature it is something that is meant to help us coexist in a *settled manner*, in contrast with a nomadic existence where conflicts can be resolved most easily by just avoiding other people ("I'll go this way, you go that way"): you don't need to move your house to get out of the way of another. The same applies to worship: only settled humans build altars and places of worship. The ethics of such a static existence reflects morality, which, from the perspective of the persistence of society is *interpersonal harmony* where one fully comes to an existence where another human being is not considered an enemy: in order to settle down one needs to

[197] Just to make it clear: there is no philosophical way around this etymological relation. If you e.g. try to break 'culture' C into some set of constituent features $C=\{a,b,c\}$ (what I write here applies to any such set), you essentially are not talking about culture any longer but about these a, b, c that *you* have declared to be essential, and your analysis will fail for the same reasons that you may believe a good disco party can be assembled simply by herding a group of random people into a room and adding a disco ball and some disco music. Yes, that can be done *if and only if* these people have certain social qualities that are already presupposed where we might imagine that it would be a good idea to try and throw such a party. You will also find that these qualities are subjective in nature and bound to the cultural value base you yourself have already assimilated. One way to describe this relation is to declare C a *holistic* quality where the whole is seen as 'more' than its constituent features a, b, c, but the right way is to understand that those features are only constituents because you, for some reason, regard them as such. If you choose to call a human a set of organs, do you mean by this that you are in a position where you can manufacture humans? The correct way is to understand that this mechanistic compositionality is an *aspect* of bodies (doctor), cultures (cultural analyst) and so on, and as an aspect, it is bound to the viewer, too. The enlightened viewer has various aspects at his disposal; as a philosopher, change your viewpoint and the problem will disappear.

exist in such a way that others are not considered enemies, or otherwise one is better off having a nomadic existence. That God represents morality and truth means that a harmonious, settled existence is the highest ideal for such a society. But this is not the only form of human existence; instead, as we know, human nature is both good and evil, and a moral existence is rather one where a person advances in stages, in a similar way as one advances in one's work career in stages, or how one advances from courting to marriage in stages. From the subjective perspective, this can happen if one is brought to find wisdom and peace in such existence and is not scared off in favour of doing something else or spooked into simply hiding and remaining inactive, barred from any existential advancement.[198] Even within stable societies there have always been those who are not brought to see wisdom in abiding by society's rules. They can well be considered immoral, but the important thing to understand is that calling somebody immoral can only have an effect if the person adheres to the moral belief system. People who exist outside organized society employ a different system of honour and justice that bears a strong resemblance to that of other pack animals: strength is respected and the relationship with others is strongly guided by practical needs, where submission and obedience are shown in the presence of a superior and any opportunity is used to advance one's own well-being and social status.

If morality produces the social harmony of an organized society, looking at the opposite of morality is to look at its alternative which is found in our biology; the logical opposite of 'moral' is not 'wrong' or 'bad' but *primitive*. Biologically, man is a social predator (pack hunter) whose hunting is, along with the chimp—our closest relative with a shared ancestor—normally performed only by males. Chimps are strongly territorial and aggressive, hunt in a specialized troop formation and

---

198 I have heard others talk about something I have also witnessed myself; a person leaves a relationship that he experiences as dysfunctional, and meets his ex-partner after a long time... and the reason why he left is still there in the other person, it has not changed. An existential block is something that can easily be seen by others, and most likely by the partner. Such a block is always of a personal traumatic nature; something constantly escapes notice due to related traumatic experiences.

III-1. THE BASIS OF DEMOCRACY

kill other members of the species in violent territorial disputes. Chimp social order is formed by aggressive males competing for pack leadership, and the rest of the pack siding with leaders of choice and settling within the frame of the peace that follows the leadership changes. This behaviour is not general ape behaviour but contrasts with both bonobos, who are non-aggressive and matriarchal, and gorillas, who tend to harmonize under a single mature male in a relatively non-territorial existence. The difference in behaviour reflects diet: omnivorous chimps, like humans, are pack hunters, whereas bonobos are predominantly frugivorous and gorillas predominantly herbivorous. Diet, in turn, reflects the physical constitution of the animal; the carnivore and herbivore digestive enzymes differ from one another in a manner specialized to the respective diet, and the animals exhibit recognizable external characteristics such as the carnivore's pointed teeth and the herbivore's strong jaw muscles and considerably longer digestive tract. The omnivorous *Homo sapiens* has physically specialized to e.g. cooking his food, thus reducing the need for fangs, yet his social capabilities and behaviour clearly reflect the pack-hunting chimp that needs to fight competitively for food and existence. Now, we can see that the human plastic phenotypic characteristics have adapted to a social and physical existence that is very different from our natural environment, but in the same way that our dietary system is adaptive yet has obvious limits to its adaptive capability in terms of what sort of food we are able to digest, our social behaviour is also limited in terms of how much adaptation it is, as it were, humanly possible to make. When this limit is exceeded, accumulated barred primitive behaviour bursts out as acts of uncontrolled violence (passive-aggression). As chimp relatives, violence is in our blood, and reducing it in a society requires inhibition. This genotypic human behaviour is something that is completely dismissed by a lot of idealist social theory, such as women's rights advocacy but also any theory that expects that people can just be moulded into a theoretical ideal; such thought for one reason or another tries to be moral without paying attention to human well-being. It also means that the world anywhere outside organized society (as signified by the existence of religion and culture) can be expected to be unstable due to territorial disputes and almost exclusively male dominated. Also, this is the correct framework to interpret, say, incidents of random violence or rapes; they are not crazy in the sense of being unexpected but rather can be understood by understanding the primitive human. They are psychological events where the person stops abiding by the social norms that are restricting him from realizing his primitive existence. Like the sexually restrained chimp, he will be sneaky and try mating when the pack leader is not vigilant. In a primitive animal pack, the sexually restrained beta male has the option to either challenge the alpha male or to attempt to satisfy his urges while the harem is left unguarded, so, why would the human male, who is sexually restrained but unrestrained in terms of conduct, behave any differently? Rather, outside organized society, humans everywhere form packs of some kind, such as gangs, tribes or clans, and if you understand the human, the behaviour of such groups is predictable, not crazy or wrong. To the moralist I would like to say: you would do the same if it was necessary for your survival, and if you insist that you wouldn't, this simply shows how far you have distanced yourself from your primitive existence by submitting to the various social codes of an organized society. If intelligence means capability of success in a novel environment, it is not the primitive man who is beneath the moralist in intelligence; rather it is the moralist who has degenerated in intelligence by letting go of his primitive existence, because a novel environment is more likely to reward primitive than specialized human qualities. Now, apart from fighting or trading with outsiders, primitive human activities also involve many social traits that relate directly to social hierarchy within the group and that are shunned within an organized society, such as the following.

- *Enforcing status* is the behaviour performed by the dominant individual, through which symbolic acts induce submissive acts by others. In animal groups this means physical violence, and higher animals have many gestures and acts for threatening before an attack, such as showing teeth, flattening ears and miming bites (e.g. dogs and horses), approaching with rear end first with possibly cocked hind legs (horses), and the alpha chimp can display power by making a noise, throwing rocks, bashing trees with sticks, etc., in an effort to show what a possible confrontation with him is likely to involve. In modern

III-1. THE BASIS OF DEMOCRACY

human communities, this likely consists of verbal violence in forms that range from harmless nicknaming or minor social challenges that resolve in domination, to systematic harm against a challenger that can target the public image and reputation of the individual. In modern communities, social rank can be enforced by much more complex patterns, whereas in primitive societies it is a more straightforward display of physical power, wealth or other capability that calls for respect.

- *Flattery.* Flattery is an act of seeking the approval of a higher-ranking individual and hence personal social elevation. Many social animals show flattery in a behaviour where the animal directly mimics the actions of an individual of higher status. This can directly be seen to be reflected in e.g. a lower-status individual siding with the dominant one in disputes (the dominant dog barks at, or bites, another dog, and the flatterers side with him by repeating the action), or in how bird flocks manage to fly in a uniform manner by instantly repeating the actions of the alpha bird. The action of following/mimicking typically triggers approval from the higher-ranking individual; the follower is under his command. Humans communicate with language, so, this behaviour also forms the basis of doing what somebody says. In human social groups, the words of a dominant speaker are received with respect, no matter whether they bear any truth; if an individual of high status were to say something controversial, few would dare to express their concerns and many would concede that "he must have his reasons", whereas a lower-ranking individual would have any and all of the weaknesses of his comments directly exposed to potential ridicule, depending mostly on whether the dominant speaker sides with him or not. Most of the speakers in a group choose their behaviour based on the actions of the dominant speaker. Mimicking is not the only form of flattery; toadying up to authorities in various ways is an attempt to gain status via their approval, and in a male-dominated society the obvious way for women to considerably increase their social status is to succeed in portraying sexual and spousal competence to a man of high status.

- *Violent coup* is a planned takeover of an authority position. With chimps, in a successful coup the old leader is killed unless he manages to escape. In ancient human power struggles, a violent coup also involved the killing of the family and the close companions of the old leader, to prevent longstanding vendettas. A clan existence typically involves persistent blood feuds in many directions where the losses from enemy attacks are accepted by the whole society to protect individual families from vendetta.

Wherever the social order of our organized society, comprising religion, laws, law enforcement and norms, fails and groups of people are formed outside its reach, the resulting social order to replace the old one can be found by looking at human social behaviour from the perspective of human as a pack animal. Whenever the sense of justice is not bound to the morality of society and its underlying religious belief system, it will be bound to what is called an *honour system*. The concept of the honour system is sometimes applied to highly Christian values such as virtue, sincerity, fairness, truthfulness and so on, which reflects the moral system of our society. But honour systems are not bound to this morality; honour systems are rather *competitive* systems, where the honouring behaviour is triggered by showing competence, honourable conduct is required for unity in social competition against some other group, and, in a similar way as with religions, the honour functions to counter individual needs and desires for the benefit of the group. I give a few examples.

- Gang honour: public insult requires public retaliation. This is to prove individual loyalty to the gang that, again, is in persistent rivalry and feud with other gangs.

- Competitive sports have specific codes of honour that reflect the codes of battles in ancient times. These work to portray a competitive image towards rival groups: for example, the honourable defeat of an individual does not imply group defeat, and one is not to shame the group in individual defeat. On the other hand, forms of combat, such as fencing or pistol shooting, are arts of their own, and someone learning fencing will learn fastest by observing the masters. The practitioners of a particular skill or sport would form a guild or similar organization that would introduce honour codes for the skill, the function of which was to protect those learning the skill from receiving inferior instruction. So, here the competition is between the true skill or art form that makes one an excellent, say, fencer, and immoral fencing trainers that try to gain fame, students and income by teaching the art while lacking adequate skills.

- A woman's honour means not presenting herself to a man before marriage and the related family arrangements, and breaching this will bring shame to the *family*, which is the socially competitive unit. For established families, virgin daughters are capital for opportunities to enter into good family unions and fortune.

- Honouring the dead refers to honouring what the deceased have died *for*—which group their life work represents, to which they contributed, which, again, works to politically compete with some other group.

- The *omertà* code of silence, employed by Mafia-style organizations, exists to enforce loyalty to the criminal organization, which is in competition with the authorities.

That these codes are rules of conduct that are bound to the functions of a *particular social group*—instead of being constantly applicable moral laws to convey universal justice—can be seen in that they are only enforced in terms of *public* behaviour, and that they are not backed by any rationale, reference to conscience, or such. They relate to the *public image* (face) of the competitive unit that, in its competition, will benefit from *showing strength* and *not showing weakness*. This is why honour systems will not promote universal openness, honesty or truthfulness, but often encourage quite the opposite, as disguise and deception are integral features of competition. One could say that the measure of honesty or truth in an honour system is in integrity and loyalty (staying true) to the good of the group—the competitive advantage of the group.

Loyalty to a particular competitive group can, from the perspective of the subject's social behaviour, be seen as the alternative to *moral* behaviour that would involve *reciprocity*. Consider if somebody did something wrong by certain standards, and we had to think of a suitable punishment for him—we are asking the question: "What is *justice* in this case?" In a reciprocal moral framework, the problematic essentially *involves us*, because we will ask, among other questions that become complex due to their introspective nature, whether we would accept such a punishment on ourselves for committing a similar error. Now, contrast this behaviour with the behaviour of such a competitive group; from our perspective, the punishment should be arbitrated by the group leader(s), and should we wish to intervene with the process of enforcing justice, this would be interpreted by the same standards as with the original perpetrator: we are also being disloyal to the group. But look at the problematic from the perspective of the leader who is personally not involved in the wrong-doing: in his decision to enforce justice, he needs to consider two things: 1) the persistence of his own authority, and 2) social balance; that people won't be too upset about the decision and try and challenge his power. So, the question of justice is completely different for him than for the others in the group, and, in itself, doesn't involve any morality. Morality can be brought to override mob rule, where one is loyal to arbitrary authority, only via the example of somebody who takes a stand in ethical action and says that the morality of family and brotherhood should be extended to where one is not personally involved: "He who is without sin, cast the first stone." It takes a particular ethical movement to bring morality into commonly applied justice and law that, in turn, will create a social order that is something other than a battle between rival gangs and clans; to bring together, in the shared concept of justice, the reciprocal moral conceptions of the people and the wish for social balance by the leader, that, by nature, are not in this state but highly distrustful to one another.[199] To understand the relation between morality and society, it is most crucial to note that this harmonious existence between rulers and people, where rulers subject themselves to law and morality for the appeasement of the people, and people, in turn, are appeased

---

[199] This union is memorably depicted in the handshake finale of the movie *Metropolis*.

III-1. THE BASIS OF DEMOCRACY

with their status as being ruled over instead of plotting coups, is a *delicate state*—called a *social contract*—because it involves *trust* that, in turn, is susceptible to abuse. Humans are not sheep by nature, and it is not a natural (primitive) human state to live in a society where one can expect rule by morality. Wherever there have been attempts at social moral theories, they seem to expect a stable society or morality as some universal law, and don't consider the relation between these two elements. If we take the notion of a social contract, one should understand that contracts and agreements, by their nature, are not something morally binding (they can be legally binding if such laws can be enforced), but things that are honoured due to the competitive asset of the union reached by the agreement. Another way to present this is that contracts are binding as long as they serve the interests of the stronger party, as breaching them will aggravate the opposing party, and this can be potentially dangerous or then not, which is a matter of power relations. One should understand that the concept of social contract is not made any weaker by the fact that no such formal contract exists, and this can be explained by the fact that contracts are not morally binding but just formal devices for communicating intentions, which can as well be achieved informally. If the rulers and the people abide with such a balance, then a contract can be said to exist in a similar way as when two warrior parties meet and their envoys negotiate. One party says they will move in one direction and the other will say they will move in another direction and as they leave both parties signal respect to one another—there's no formal agreement and even if there was one, it would have no power as morality is not involved here but just mutual assent by sharing intentions. The word 'agreement' would refer simply to the observable result of whether both parties respect their signalled intention; if they seem to do what they said they would do, then they agree. Similarly, if a contract between two parties is breached, the question whether any third parties give a damn is a question of their private relations to the first and second party. Since an agreement is private in nature, the details of the events that follow after the breach of the agreement can be written from the perspective of the competitive good of the victor: they can stage a public story for the moral justification of the breach, and this perspective will morally

PART III. SOCIO-POLITICAL ANALYSIS

bind the audience. The deceived party will appear careless and stupid, and there is no moral outrage as no moral codes are broken in a contract breach.

The democratic question reaches far beyond the problematic of devising a system that would make all people heard. Rather, the fact that all people are made to be heard is far less relevant than the feature of democracy that in contemporary life is simply overlooked; we could easily create a democracy in which not all people are heard but the votes would somehow be randomly selected from among the population. This might sound like a modern idea but it is an ancient innovation, as the Greeks used a machine called *kleroterion* to randomize jury selection on the spot so that members couldn't be influenced in advance. Furthermore, the Greeks seem to me to have been much more aware of the problematic relating to governance. The problematic is best illustrated with an excerpt from John Stuart Mill[200] about the historical development towards democracy in Western thought:

> *By liberty [in ancient Greek, Roman and English thought], was meant protection against the tyranny of the political rulers. The rulers were conceived ... as in a necessarily antagonistic position to the people whom they ruled. They consisted of a governing One, or a governing tribe or caste, who derived their authority from inheritance or conquest, who, at all events, did not hold it at the pleasure of the governed, and whose supremacy men did not venture, perhaps did not desire, to contest, whatever precautions might be taken against its oppressive exercise. Their power was regarded as necessary, but also as highly dangerous; as a weapon which they would attempt to use against their subjects, no less than against external enemies.*

The necessity for governance in a civilization comes together with a healthy fear of the abuse of that privilege, and the governance is originally and historically initially accepted, but with heavy precautions taken against its abuse, and not out of desire or pleasure, but out of

200 *On Liberty*, Chapter I—Introductory

III-1. THE BASIS OF DEMOCRACY

practical necessity. To call it a necessary evil would perhaps do it justice. Mill continues:

> *A time, however, came, in the progress of human affairs, when men ceased to think it a necessity of nature that their governors should be an independent power, opposed in interest to themselves. It appeared to them much better that the various magistrates of the State should be their tenants or delegates, revocable at their pleasure. In that way alone, it seemed, could they have complete security that the powers of government would never be abused to their disadvantage. By degrees, this new demand for elective and temporary rulers became the prominent object of the exertions of the popular party, wherever any such party existed; and superseded, to a considerable extent, the previous efforts to limit the power of rulers.*

So, the shift to a model of democratic thought has evolved through the initial acceptance of *contestable* governance to a model where the contestability was maintained in the possibility of freely revoking the governing privileges of individual magistrates. Mill continues:

> *As the struggle proceeded for making the ruling power emanate from the periodical choice of the ruled, some persons began to think that too much importance had been attached to the limitation of the power itself. That (it might seem) was a resource against rulers whose interests were habitually opposed to those of the people. What was now wanted was, that the rulers should be identified with the people; that their interest and will should be the interest and will of the nation. The nation did not need to be protected against its own will. There was no fear of its tyrannising over itself. Let the rulers be effectually responsible to it, promptly removable by it, and it could afford to trust them with power of which it could itself dictate the use to be made. Their power was but the nation's own power, concentrated, and in a form convenient for exercise.*

PART III. SOCIO-POLITICAL ANALYSIS

This indicates a pressure towards a change of rhetoric having followed the shift in thought, to undermine the problematic of governmental authority and the related trust, but which was then subjected to due criticism:

> *It was now perceived that such phrases as "self-government," and "the power of the people over themselves," do not express the true state of the case. The "people" who exercise the power are not always the same people [as] those over whom it is exercised; and the "self-government" spoken of is not the government of each by himself, but of each by all the rest. The will of the people, moreover, practically means, the will of the most numerous or the most active part of the people; the majority, or those who succeed in making themselves accepted as the majority: the people, consequently, may desire to oppress a part of their number; and precautions are as much needed against this, as against any other abuse of power. The limitation, therefore, of the power of government over individuals, loses none of its importance when the holders of power are regularly accountable to the community, that is, to the strongest party therein.*

This is to say that the problematic of trust towards government has never disappeared from within the problematic of democracy, but we can wonder at its complete modern absence from Western democratic discourse. Mill's book is a historical relic as is the adherence to such thoughts as a democratic ritual and *tatemae*. That governmental offices are by nature revocable *at pleasure* is a foundational democratic principle along with the metaphor of MPs being *tenants* or *delegates* of the people, but the people have lost much of this authority over their MPs due to the interoperation of business and media power behind the closed doors of government, and are gradually losing more and more of this authority. The formula is hardly front-page news because it is so mundane and common that it evades proper inspection: money buys power in terms of visibility for manipulating public knowledge and opinion regarding politics, and in terms of lobbying politicians to support a desired political outcome. The problem of 21st-century pol-

III-1. THE BASIS OF DEMOCRACY

itics is not the problem of the correct form of political government, because what we are seeing rather illustrates that, regardless of what happens with other forms of government, *even* the democratic system is vulnerable to systemic abuse. Even if we reapplied the Greek *kleroterion* to randomize decision-makers, the highly powerful and politically aligned groups outside the government will target the weaknesses of that decision-making to push their political agenda and will likely be successful in doing so. Democracy was devised in times when such forces didn't exist to any identifiable extent that would be threatening to the system; or, rather, the idea of democracy wraps in itself the idea that the government is also capable of affecting such groups. A true idealized democratic government would be capable of addressing economic inequality, which in the modern global world is not the case with any of our existing democracies. Therefore, what we have is a relic of a democracy that is deteriorating rather quickly under the dominance of globalized economy. The idea of a people-controlled democratic society, which lives in the hearts and minds of all people and in all political rhetoric, is on an inevitable collision course with publicly uncontrollable global economic power. A major study[201] states that the USA is not a democracy but an oligarchy, based on extensive comparison between 1) enacted governmental policies and 2) the expressed preferences in policies of different social groups such as average Americans, affluent Americans and different special interest groups. The study finds that the illusion of American democracy serving the interests of voters is created by mere coincidence: sometimes policies favoured by voters are enacted ("The system works!"), but this is only because they also happen to be favoured by affluent Americans, lobbying groups or special interest groups. Statistically the enactment of policies correlates *only* with *wealth*: the wishes of corporations and business and professional associations.

Let's look at democracy from the perspective of it being a contract where those who are being governed are considered tenants of the

---

201 Z. D. Boren, 'The US is an oligarchy, study concludes', 16.4.2014, *The Daily Telegraph*, http://www.telegraph.co.uk/news/worldnews/northamerica/usa/10769041/The-US-is-an-oligarchy-study-concludes.html [26.12.2019].

government and, instead of restricting the powers of the government, have entrusted updates to the system of government to the government itself. The reasoning behind this social contract is that in exchange for their *loyalty* to their leaders, people can expect safety and rights that the government is expected to maintain. As we are speaking of a *contract*, it is important to understand that the idea of a contract will make neither party—the government or the governed—regard the responsibilities implied in this contract a *moral* obligation. Many would like to claim that it is indeed a moral obligation, in the way that, for example, European politicians make claims that Europe has a moral responsibility to intervene in individual member countries' affairs (these crocodile tears surface in news whenever bad things happen in individual member states). What they actually mean is that it *should be* a moral obligation, which may sound similar and not feel like much of a difference, but one should understand that the difference between a descriptive and a normative claim is the difference between the statements: "That man is not beating his wife" and "That man should not be beating his wife". The said claim can be countered by observing the *de facto* moral behaviour of people who live in a democracy: in practice, people show loyalty to their social groups instead of behaving as opinionated and active democratic citizens, and will actively blame the government and politicians for experienced problems, disconnected from a sense of responsibility as active citizens. But what does it mean to say that honouring the social contract *should* be a moral obligation? The answer is very simple; what one is saying here is that one should feel membership of a larger group than just oneself, that one's nation, or maybe even the whole world, constitutes one group to which one has a moral obligation. But let's think about a democratic nation in terms of its political groups; in a multiparty system it should be the obvious case that different parties have different agendas, and parties are in direct competition against one another for political power. Economic competition forms another area where individuals or companies are in direct competition against one another within market sectors. These are not moral systems, and the honourable behaviour in the rivalry that is involved is due to the related honour system. So, again, why does one say that one *should* honour the social contract? The example that

III-1. THE BASIS OF DEMOCRACY

we have of this sort of system is Christian morality, where we say that one should love one's neighbour, because it brings the asset of going to heaven instead of hell after death. *All* Western democracies are, historically, deeply Christian, and such a system has simply been crafted under the expectation that we, as a nation, *are* unified under God. And this is the only *sense* there is to say that one *should* be a good citizen in return for good governance; that the relationship between the citizen and his government is reciprocal and moral. Today we see the role of Christianity diminishing in people's moral thought and being stricken from our political institutions under the slogan that "religion and government must be separated", and it is being replaced by, most visibly, economic values. At the same time, we see the social contract being trashed with a drop in general political interest, the support figures for political leaders, voter turnouts and so on. This is no coincidence at all but just the result of the situation where the morality of religion is not given its due value: morality is subjective, which makes it hard to see, so to many people it seems that religion is not needed. This problem particularly affects people who are angry at religion, because we humans are known, when we are angry, to dismiss the value of things that in reality are valued, and to say things that we don't really mean. This thought that likes to attack one's own domestic moral system is *immature*, by which I mean that it still *always assumes* the related moral base values but just neglects to look at their source and at one's history. I would compare this to domestic violence where someone attacks his spouse in anger and in a state where he is oblivious to the reasons that originally led him to marry. He will later recant his words. But essentially I find it quite amazing that in the modern world we can live in such a situation of expected social control and authority, considering our history. It may seem modern, but actually it is rather absurd and unnatural because of the lack of recognition of our history and our animal nature. We simply take our organized, controlled society as a given and don't understand that it is a carefully and painstakingly crafted model that works only with a certain idea or spirit behind it, and if it is not honoured, it will surely collapse back in part to the more primitive modes of human existence.

PART III. SOCIO-POLITICAL ANALYSIS

The parties of the social contract—the governors and the governed—are largely the basis of the development of the political left and right wing, where the right wing represents established forces of government and the left wing represents change, often taking the anarchistic goal of simply shaking up the system or breaking the establishment. Historically, the left and the right trace back to the French Revolution and depict whether loyalty was to reform or the established monarchy and have developed some typical characteristics that reflect this underlying thought. A rough characterization of some typical features is shown below.

	LEFT	RIGHT
GOAL	Reform, change	Conservation, resistance to change
CENTRAL VALUES	Equality of social groups	Traditions, protection, order
CONCEPTION OF ORDER	Empathy, acceptance, social harmony	Tradition, competition, rule by the strongest, loyalty
CONCEPTION OF EQUALITY	Material equality	Transcendent equality, traditional honour systems
TYPICAL PROPONENT	Junior	Senior

There are occasions when the balance of power seems opposite (the right wing seems to wish for reform and the left wing seems to represent more established values), and these occasions should be interpreted as populist developments where the established elite is scheming to masquerade as a people's front. The rich and powerful have many ways of manipulating the political stage to create an appearance that ultimately plays to their benefit, particularly by financing public provocations that arouse hatred or compassion in the weak-minded masses. The dominance of left-wing politics in the 21st century is due to

III-1. THE BASIS OF DEMOCRACY

globalization, which is a large-scale political change, and the left represents change and progression. It is not possible to *become* globalized under either conservative or nationalist politics; the only way to do it is to be both liberal and globalist. Both conservative and nationalist opinions are attacked so strongly by the globalist movement that they are trying to get such opinions banned as hate speech in virtually every area of life. And this is, of course, all to the advantage of the globalist agenda of uniting the world under the same rule. The information society has created new venues of advertisement and manipulation with images: images of love, compassion, tolerance, happiness, puppy dogs' eyes, suffering children are much more pleasing to the shallow moral eye than images of the stony faces of officials, sales clerks or truckers that go to work every morning to keep society's base structures together. When people have been politically disarmed as a mass, as a mass they will be susceptible to poverty porn, which is the main vehicle of pushing the guilt-ridden 21st-century people towards globalist (anti-nationalist) values. It is in the nature of men that power is always seeking to rule over others, and those who are weaker will seek to unify and overcome the power if they find themselves on a collision course with it. It is in the moral consciousness of men that when a ruler grows powerful, this power also brings about responsibility and the expectation that one will take care of a larger domain. So, even though in any strategic game setup the one who is able to accumulate resources needs to then try and work out how to benefit from the extra resources he is unable to consume directly, our moral sentiments generally allow groups or individuals to become socially powerful, as long as they care for their surroundings and use this power in such a way that the benefit of the group is moderately in balance with the benefit the group brings to others around it in terms of social assets such as services, stability, protection, benevolence and so on. Alongside the social contract and the laws that govern the people within a society, those in power and rule are not in practice bound by the same rules. There are no such rules that apply on an international scale, and any dreams of establishing such rules should immediately be translated as dreams of expanding one's own rule over other countries. This is simply because there are no laws without law enforcement, and this also applies to religious

PART III. SOCIO-POLITICAL ANALYSIS

laws that preach their reasoning using a symbolic language that reflects the moral sentiments of a people. Understanding the left and the right is important, as modern democracy must be correctly understood via its history as a development that in its primitive stage was simply the relationship between the city that offered protection from bandits and its citizens, which agreed to follow any rules set by the city in exchange for this protection. If, for example, today some left-wing thinkers criticize countries for imposing apparently arbitrary rules on individuals, it should be remembered that city states had powers to punish and exile their citizens, and they used these powers on the troublesome. In order for a criticism of society to be successful, it always needs to contrast the status quo with actual history rather than with an imaginary utopia; it needs to point out that something used to work but doesn't work any longer. Comparison to a utopia is a mechanical process where one 1) doesn't like something and then 2) imagines its opposite and presents this as the desirable state. Dystopia, however, is a much more useful critical tool; in a dystopic scenario one is not presenting a solution but just pointing out a possible error in current development, and if the dystopia is revealing, this means that the criticism is accurate. Creating a successful dystopia displays historical understanding of how ideals or choices lead to societal progression.

Historically, we Westerners have the Abrahamic idea that we will religiously and ideologically yield ourselves to and follow a leader who is also just. And this immediately presents two aspects of justice: what kind of people we accept as leaders, and how we expect them to judge us. 1) The first question is about what kind of people we accept as leaders, and I believe in our modern world this question is to a large extent being ignored in favour of the second question. Our ideal of a leader is portrayed in our legendary religious leaders who were fighters against oppression; selfless men who put social justice even ahead of their families. That is the ideal, but the majority would settle for letting the king be king, unless the king somehow goes bad, and I think the limit to this is when somebody owns an amount that is considered to be *excessive*, and excess is not determined quantitatively but in terms of how the resources are put to use; who they are used to benefit. It shouldn't matter

III-1. THE BASIS OF DEMOCRACY

how great the empire; the people will be proud to live in it if it is well governed, and thus it is completely wrong to determine a good society in socialist terms of everybody getting an equal share. Rather I believe the correct justice and equality that everybody can understand and relate to is that *those who have more resources also have more means, and as they have more means they are also expected to have more responsibility and to show benevolence in their actions*, and if they don't fulfil this responsibility they risk being unpopular and the gap between the masses and the leaders will grow too big. To verify this just look at how aggressive street bums act: they ask you for a cigarette, and if you don't give them one they curse you, because they consider you have a level of excess compared to them but you refuse to benevolently share. Street bums might be rude and a nuisance, but their conception of justice is actually universally understood on all levels of society. The abusive bums simply want the one with higher status to share just a little of what he has... and in their morality they determine whether he is a good or bad person based on this behaviour, as their miserable lives are in practice hanging on a hope that perhaps some goodwill and justice still exists in this world of the cold shoulder. Looking at, say, gender equality or "sexual equality" (whatever that means), our Western society is performing very well, as men, having more means in society, are also behaving very benevolently with respect to women, and similarly society has made a very clear turn not to condemn sexual minorities. But in terms of money we do rather badly in terms of justice; those who have money tend to compete aggressively for more private wealth, hide it, and keep it for the sake of private indulgence in luxuries and the vices of an over-indulgent life. Our world can be seen to do quite well in many respects, but justice is not one of them. 2) The second aspect of justice is about what kind of judgment we expect from those we have accepted to rule over us, and it is this question that seems to gain all the attention while the first one is ignored. Here *we would like to see judgment where members of society are not being discriminated against but judged equally*, for the benefit of the whole of society. And because of our ignorance of the first aspect of justice we tend to try and enforce this "earthly equality" in terms of laws and rules; we are trying to create a society where things would just objectively *be equal* instead

PART III. SOCIO-POLITICAL ANALYSIS

of the equality being a subjective quality of our governance, which is the only context in which it makes sense; equality is an ideal to be enforced by systems of justice and not the empirical world. Equality in subjective terms is much more difficult to determine; it would effectively mean that courts make decisions likewise kings who see the correct place and purpose of everybody in society and use their infinite subjective wisdom, and also authority and respect, to reach a satisfactory judgment, just as a good head of a family would make decisions in the best interests of the family. This aspect is what we have attempted to characterize in our conception of human rights; it is a collection of principles, stated as rights, and meant to be a framework of subjective judgment for our system of justice and not an objective measurement. And it is important to understand this, because subjective things are impossible to assess objectively, from which it follows that something can look like a human rights violation and not be one, and vice versa. Whenever somebody alleges a human rights violation, he effectively means that somebody is not being treated justly according to some principle of human rights, but this is meaningless unless he can point out how our system is acting in discord with the principle, such as by some particular official stepping over the boundaries of his rights as an officer. I am pointing this out because there is so much appalling argument from "human rights groups" that simply uses human rights principles on the level of rhetoric and outside the context of the application of law, that tries to seduce people into grassroots activism via pointing out human rights violations, as if the correct application of human rights could simply be deduced from these principles using rational logic in one's mind. Rights are not rational principles but something that requires interpretation by the system of justice and produced in the form of legal precedents, and their reception, producing information for later similar cases.

III-2. Democratic Developments

There is a distinction between freedom and rule in human existence, present from the start of our life when we try to move around on our own yet are required to quickly revert back to the comfort and safety of our parental governance. The best way to understand the nature of these qualities is simply to accept them as basic human attributes; forms of behaviour that humans tend to demonstrate. The analyst in particular should free himself from any ethical associations that are easily carried over from our political-ethical beliefs and accept that humans will be to some extent free and to some extent governed by authorities. These are the two human forces that affect our sentiments of justice.

The distinction between authority and freedom—liberty and governance—is probably the most distinctive difference between life in the East and the West. Historically it is most important to understand that the Western state is a rather late development, and I believe the key factor that allowed the West to develop this way was the union of monastery schools, *universitas*, gaining independent multi-national government, which later on allowed scientists the ultimate power to challenge the Christian tradition. When Galileo muttered his legendary "And yet it moves" in ultimate defiance against the Roman Inquisition, this was made possible by the existence of a *multi-national* institution of science (with Galileo corresponding extensively with scientists abroad) to perpetuate this legend, which would *ultimately* collectively conquer resistance from the authorities. Had there not been such a multi-national body, we might remember the legendary scientist as Galileo the Mad, imprisoned and ridiculed for his advancement of some hypothetical Prussian system over God and good governance. The Pope failed in his efforts to stop the internationally unified scientists, empowered by the innovation of a mechanical printing press, that challenged his authority, and the balance of power shifted away from the Roman Catholic Church, making way for both new protestant forms of Christianity based not on authority but equality, and a reinvented Greek democratic system to challenge existing monarchies. This shift in the balance of power led to local revolutions in favour of both egalitarian political systems and successful protestant movements all around Europe separating religious institutions from the demeaning contemporary practices of Roman Catholicism. In terms of the East and the West, this historical development of changing the balance of power to overcome tradition is the only distinguishing factor, and in modern democratic discourse it should be understood that modern democracy is the historical Western answer to the authority of tradition and in itself a collective Western *cultural* achievement, not some arcane remedy that could be exported or sold to Eastern countries that experience their own clashes between freedom and authority. We Westerners have our legends tied to religious heroes overcoming authority via defiance and sacrifice. The independent status of Western academia—the system that once played a key role in our shift from tradition to reason—is already in a fundamental crisis under the sway of recent developments in the global economy, and our system is very broadly producing pseudoscientific results that misuse the authority of the system. Conceptually, this doesn't differ from the actions of the medieval Roman Catholic Church which, in a state of hubris from gaining more authority, became more and more hypocritical in a process where the practices were ritualized and in themselves became instruments of power used by the ruling elite. Sacred concepts that once related to redemption and the afterlife within the subjective soul became earthly rituals where the Christian redemption from suffering literally meant redemption from penal practices. Such a development reflects the ancient wisdom about what power does to individuals—it does it to institutions as well. Perhaps academic concepts could be reinterpreted: e.g. academic freedom could mean the privilege to receive an academic education that will be available only to the wealthy and fortunate. We regard democracy as an achieved milestone on our way to greatness and are so proud of this achievement that we have started to reinforce this thought by thinking that other countries should be democratic, too. This behaviour of reinforcement is a sign of neurosis and panic-like fear (Freudian anticathexis): an underlying fear of appearing dirty can be reinforced in obsessive cleanliness, and likewise, an un-

III-2. DEMOCRATIC DEVELOPMENTS

derlying fear of being undemocratically governed can be reinforced with obsessive democratic thought. It is also a form of toadying to an authority that is posing as democratic: in any group, the one who needs to work the hardest to impress is the one who is lowest in rank, just as in the military where the lower in rank salute the higher and do the most visible work. But the saddest thing in cultural investigations is to find "democratic thinkers", people who believe Western democracy would provide a solution to the issues of the rest of the world, who have no vision or appreciation of the traditional cultural and spiritual wisdom of the East. This is a wisdom that we in the West have to a great extent *lost* and distanced ourselves from and currently secretly admire in the East. We long for a life with intrinsic meaning and spirituality, harmony and the collective unity of traditional cultures. And in denial of this secret wish for something one lacks but is barred from obtaining, one is desperately pushed into the senseless and dark argument easily identified as traditional *eugenics*. Such fundamentally anti-Christian (and thus untraditional) and blatantly immoral thoughts are gaining popularity among Western intellectuals and expressed under various themes, such as worrying about something called the "global carrying capacity". Consider, as an analogy to diplomacy, that you and I are roommates, and there's something I don't like about your way of living. The first step for me is to decide whether my discomfort is grounded, and the method for this is to see if your behaviour contradicts with the *norms* of communal life. The common way to check norms is to ask for other people's opinions. Given that your way of living misaligns with *both* norms and my comfort, first I will try to give you a hint, and given that you don't respond, I will speak to you more directly. If you still fail to respond to my preferences, I will communicate to you either by showing the disagreement, e.g. by not talking to you at all, or I will confront you with the issues and try and force you to respond. Now, if we still fail to communicate, it should be understood that empathy (the standard female conflict resolution method) is not a rational option because the situation involves you failing to fulfil the responsibilities you yourself agreed to. So, I will have to give you an ultimatum with related consequences in case you fail to comply. And if you fail to comply, I will implement my threat and show you that I keep my word, and next I will give you another ultimatum with another chance to comply, as you have now been shown that my ultimatums lead to actions and thus I am a sensible and rational person to communicate with. And if you still fail to comply, we are in a situation of disagreement where efforts to communicate have failed, and the next step involves a change of rhetoric where I become very worried about the *carrying capacity* of our shared dwelling. It just means "I'm afraid there's no room for *you*!" Well, we in the West are not roommates with the people in Asia, Africa and so on; to think of oneself in such a position one must already think in a mode that can be called 'globalist'; that we are inhabiting the world with foreign countries as roommates. But this analogy is completely false because roommates share both joint responsibilities to the landlord and the decision to live as roommates, which involves established cultural norms regarding what it is to be a good roommate, and in accusing another of failure to communicate, in the sense of my analogy, one is acting in reference to these norms already with the justification of the action deriving from the implication of breaking these norms. The contradiction in such thought can be seen from another perspective in that such feelings are a mixture of Christian *guilt* over the desperate situation of other people, but bundled together with anti-Christian cynicism about one's ability to help them; one feels the need to get rid of people in order to escape the guilt of seeing them suffer. Christianity in itself is a direct solution to such cynicism as it attributes salvation irrespective of earthly achievements. *If* one didn't feel guilty about not helping struggling nations, one would let them deal with their issues by themselves. And if one *did* feel (Christian) guilt over the suffering of these nations, one would offer them help in a passive manner with no strings attached, like the Church takes care of the poor, and like Jesus would offer salvation to anybody who *chose* to follow him. But globalists don't seem to be talking about their feelings of guilt but simply using such globalist political discourse (an open political discourse of guilt would most likely be taken as hypocritical); yet very obviously the power of such discourse in convincing people relies completely on our Western Christian tradition of such guilt.

III-2. DEMOCRATIC DEVELOPMENTS

One should correctly understand the basic roles of social institutions within organized societies as follows: the institutions of religion (the Church), tradition and private business occupy the private, subjective domain of life, whereas government and civil life occupy the public, objective domain; and within these realms they represent the roles of rule versus liberty. This is shown in the following table.

	PRIVATE		PUBLIC
RULE	*rule of the private* religion, tradition ↓	→	*rule of the public* authoritarian rule ↑
LIBERTY	*liberty of the private* free trade, moral liberty	←	*liberty of the public* civil life, human rights

Modern societal change is represented by the arrows in the table, as follows.

1) The domain of rule changes from the private realm of rule by religion and tradition towards publicly shared authoritarian rule.

2) The domain of liberty changes from public civil liberties, such as public spaces and human rights, towards freedom of private property and unrestricted private life.

3) The private domain changes from moral authority towards libertinism and from restricted to unrestricted private property.

4) The public domain changes from public freedoms towards an authoritarian society.

These movements respectively produce, as an example, sentiments like the following.

- *Erosion of common civil responsibilities* is experienced as reduced common consideration about one another, public property or, say, animals. An experienced decrease in caring increases the efficacy of two kinds of discourse. The first one tries to maintain the civil responsibilities emphasizing civil rights, such as human rights or animal rights, and applies pathetic forms of discourse and discourses of public guilt or shame, where one is socially expected to display common concern over the eroding values. The second kind abandons the civil responsibilities and falls back on a multitude of pre-civil conceptions of justice, such as religious sects or honour systems, and instead of a civil society identifies with religious, ancestral, racial or genetic identity.[202] The erosion segregates people into opinionated camps. People become more pretentious in their efforts to display social status, as their civil status is no longer respected; they compete for social acceptance and status by trying to appear stronger, more beautiful and more knowledgeable than they really are. To fill the void of social concern, people's primary concern turns to personal health and wellness. Voter turnouts generally decline, reflecting the diminishing experience of voting as a civil responsibility.

- *Erosion of moral values* is felt on a civil level as a change in moral discourse to one in which shared values are not implied. This centrally involves different like-minded groups desiring *personal freedoms* as a departure from society and its traditions, and can in the modern West be seen at least in the promotion of business freedoms, freedoms of alternative forms of marriage, freedom to manipulate one's body and freedom of uncontrolled use of the Internet. The promotion takes at least two forms: portraying oneself or one's group as demonstrating civil concern or blaming groups or individuals for lack of such concern. Absent moral values generally predict hedonism and basic parenting problems.

- *Reduced availability of work* reflects the increased liberties of private businesses; the increased competition they face implies more pressure on workers, a higher risk of being fired and higher risk of

---

[202] Nazi allegations ('Argumentum ad Hitlerum') are a powerful branding tool even today. In today's Europe, nationalist parties are constantly branded as Nazis by the media, whereas countries of interest can have actual neo-Nazi movements that are ignored, because they are somehow useful to the EU. Wherever the social order fails, people will fall into a non-citizen identity that relates to ancestry and traditions.

permanent unemployment due to skills not reflecting rapid market changes. Also, the globalization movement in multi-nationals moves both jobs and employees between countries. These functions reflect most negatively on the workers, because companies base their business decisions solely on economic factors, and money, unlike workers, is immaterial. Workers have no option except to be tossed around or to quickly adapt to change, which has the effect of keeping a large group of potential workers permanently outside the market because they have simply had enough.

- *Increased authority of institutions over individuals* can be felt in almost every aspect of society, not only in, for example, increased control in granting public funds, such as social security benefits, and vastly increased rights for law enforcement officials and e.g. security measures in airports, but also as increased reliance on experts and policymakers and e.g. a degraded concept of public space and an increased tendency to be treated as vagrant by simply being present in some public area without an evident purpose. Similarly, in the role of private companies as institutions, we have seen a significant reduction in the legal position of employees respective to employers. An increase in the authority of expert institutions, such as scientists, lawyers, and technological and political experts, is felt as *fear*. Censorship is rampant in online discussion forums, and the suppression of critical voices extends to the media downplaying demonstrations and the forceful removal of dissidents from public occasions. These factors lead to a frustrated polarization of political opinion.

The concept of *liberalism* denotes an ethical ideology in a world that was once dominated by the Roman Catholic and monarchist authority that maintained a balance that contradicted conceptions of justice. Liberalism was the conception founded on the concepts of liberty and equality that constituted the new way both in Christianity and government. In such a world under change, to be a liberal was a highly moral and responsible act in support of the individual rights of all people, and to call oneself liberal was an act implying personal risk against these authorities. But in a world where these authorities no longer exist, but on the contrary, capital in fact constitutes authority, the concept of *neoliberalism* (which advocates trade liberties with accompanied theoretical argumentation—derived from original liberal thought—of how increasing liberties is better for everybody) shouldn't be seen moral, as the commitment to neoliberalism doesn't imply any social responsibility but is an expression of the refusal of any. To be moral requires taking responsibility. In a world where authority and hereditary privilege are held by capitalist dynasties benefiting from trade liberties, one cannot, via subscribing to an ideal, act to *liberate* (as in 'liberalism') from the hereditary privileges and tradition, by introducing more liberty! Then again, *capitalism* is an interesting concept because it is derived from the word 'capitalist', meaning a person with capital, but capitalism is not originally an ideology but its opposite; an expression of disapproval. Capitalism was a description of a type of society where capital holders can thrive. The dominance of the word 'capitalism' seems to derive from its juxtaposition against socialism and thus can be seen to serve an ethical-political function for those who are against socialism, as these two opposites have developed in discourse to symbolize freedom against authority. But the real essence of this liberal freedom of capital is *anarchy of capital*, and the more the world is run by corporate money, the more the world exists in anarchistic chaos. One can also take note that *private property* is something of a taboo due to its history in liberalism and the ambivalence of Christianity towards it: material wealth is to be considered meaningless when evaluating a person, and everybody needs to have the right to free trade, and therefore private property enjoys the same protection as other human rights. This atmosphere has allowed capitalism to grow and flourish; we can't judge somebody for being stinking rich, because we'd be met with the empathetic rhetoric of Christian brotherhood: would you behave any different if you were also rich? Things are bound to turn interesting now that many people are poor and some people are ultra-rich. This has been achieved in a liberal manner but liberalism was never designed for some to get stinking rich, but, on the contrary, to abolish stinking riches.

Culture means social harmony via unification under shared values. And *marketing* is the exploitation of the phenomenon of culture: it

III-2. DEMOCRATIC DEVELOPMENTS

creates mass movement and unification but it doesn't contain shared value. Compare: "*We* should do *this*" to "*You* should buy *this*". In a cultural context the plea ("Please do *this*") is directed equally to everybody and is a form of leadership. As the plea binds its presenter as well as those it is presented to, it is moral. In a marketing setting the plea is presented by the producer and directed to the consumer. The values portrayed in the image don't bind the producer. For example, an advertisement might say you should buy Acne™ Shampoo to look cool and desirable, and the image may be conveyed that the employees of Acne are also using the product, and the owner of the company may even have committed his face to the commercials to bring a further guarantee that this really happens behind the scenes. But since we are discussing products and not ethical values, this doesn't entail any real commitment to prove that he is really subscribing to the product and not just saying so. Say, if you want to prove that you are a shipwright and hold some valuable knowledge about how to build ships, people won't be convinced if you just pose in a picture with ships; they'll want to test your credibility by various means. But to the question of whether you are the user of some product or not no such test criteria can exist as it doesn't relate to any subjective value but an objective product. And hence the bad side of commercialism that is well parodied by the character Krusty the Clown in *The Simpsons*: he typically poses in TV commercials gorging happily on the delicious produce of his Krusty Burger hamburger chain, but the moment the TV camera switches off, he spits out the foul burger and writhes in disgust at the taste. One might say that commercialism has lost its morality along with its technological advance; the image marketed to the consumer and the reality of the capitalism underlying production don't coincide anymore. These two sides are married together but have become distant from one another in the sense that they don't work for the same goal any more in terms of *value* but only in terms of a valueless corporate unit bound together by its form as a corporation within the market economy. If you believe marriages should be held together by love, you should believe this only because you understand that this is a value because it is not a standard but rather an ideal: marriages are also held together by formal means, such as the wealth of one of the spouses, fear of embarrassment and failure, fear of traumatizing the children with break-up, etc. And if you'd like to take a step further and call this *form* of marriage 'love', meaning that "it must be love as it seems to be holding the marriage together", then you have arrived at the concept of a modern corporation: something that we trust must be something *because it exists* as a single unit in the market economy, and units of this kind have carried some genuine value since their role in the liberation brought about by Liberalism. What happens here is the inversion of logic: first the corporation is considered valuable for one reason or another, and it is because of this value that it is considered to serve the economy. At the next step we forget what it is that makes a corporation valuable, and we conclude that the corporation is valuable because it is serving the economy. Originally, the economy consisted of the economically valuable actors, but now the actors inherit their value from the economy itself. The power has shifted from the people and their ethical thought to the economy; the economy has become a power in itself, even though that was never meant to be the purpose of capital. What used to be liberal, because it is designed to overthrow the right of the tyrant to tax and control trade, has now become liberal by definition, and has begun to tax and control individual trade attempts.

In traditional European monarchies power has been justified by tradition, which I find best brought to light in Monty Python's Quest for the Holy Grail, where the arrogant peasant asks the king how he became king, and the king answers: "The Lady of the Lake, her arm clad in the purest shimmering samite, held aloft Excalibur from the bosom of the water, signifying by divine providence that I, Arthur, was to carry Excalibur. *That* is why I am your king!" But looking at the concept of a democratic government as an expert institution of governance, one notices rather quickly that many modern parliamentary democracies have sadly departed from having experts in governance as MPs, and also departed from the question of whether people accept the rules of their governance. Unlike in the Enlightenment, when the ideas of democratic government were crafted, and unlike in the process of the creation of some European democracies, *the modern democratic spirit justifies the legitimacy of governance simply by tradition.* Any ques-

III-2. DEMOCRATIC DEVELOPMENTS

tions targeted to the legitimacy of the form of government are considered very good questions but overlooked in favour of tradition and given the King Arthur answer, and if that doesn't satisfy, they are forcefully silenced. I constantly hear the announcement: "Those who don't vote shouldn't get to criticize decisions", which is not a moral argument but one of authority; a father could say this when he calls up a family meeting. In the old times, the king's guards, or the tribunals of the Church, upheld social order by silencing dissidents in a violent ritual of public shaming involving stocks and rotten tomatoes. In information age the silencing is similarly done by means of public shaming by paid demagogues—such as news commentators—and a reduction in one's social status by losing one's job or office. This sort of demagogue lives by inserting a short hate article about the current Western political enemies between the stream of pointless news in every popular magazine: "How to get a guy in 30 minutes? How to look your best underwater? Why don't we go and get Mugabe, the racist who hates gays?" But take any *real* political questions: Why do we have such low voter turnouts? Why are politicians colluding with business? Why is the media systematically biased? In regard to such questions, the whole West has become a traditionalist society, referring *only* to the tradition of democratic governance in public discourse about governance, or by accepting the current fate of society as being dominated by an undemocratic reality, whatever the power behind that reality is considered to be: capitalism, secret plutocracy, shadow government... The morbid nature of the modern day can be traced to the contradiction between public image and practice: the whole democratic discourse has been born in a strict opposition of tradition and for the reason of defying tradition, but to describe what we see today as an unquestioning and zombie-like acceptance of everything that comes from the tradition of Western democratic practices would be overly kind; it is worse: a hysterical enforcement of traditional ideals of democracy that can be seen to be wrongly applied and in need of adjustment. This behaviour resembles a lunatic driver who, when he notices that he's heading towards a wall, refuses to confront the *shame* of his out-of-control driving but instead steps on the gas pedal. The West has become a traditionalist society that doesn't understand that it is traditionalist, carries a terrible shame it cannot face, and thus actively works to hide this shame. What we see today is not the democratic ideal but the enforcement of tradition that is based on democratic ideals but that has evolved to a state that is completely ritualized and detached from its original motives and justification. It is in the Western tradition of democracy to treat dictatorship as an enemy; surely not in the thought of Aristotle, who saw a king or a royal family as an acceptable ruler as long as they happened to be virtuous.[203] Rather we exist in a state where an absolute authority is teaching us a redefinition of dictatorship, which means nothing at all except "a non-Western country".

The recent developments, alongside the global downplaying of the humanities in teaching and schools, have resulted in fewer politically active intellectuals overall. This is not only related to political decision-making but also to the fact that intellectuals can be expected to become a rarer breed due to the trend of a global decline in general learning skills of children; a phenomenon that teachers attribute to a change in children that have become less attentive, hyperactive and apathetic. And it's not only the children; their parents suffer from similar apathy and also a lack of authority over their children, which directly reflects their own state of detached submission to the authority of modern society. Instead of providing a safe model of authority to reflect the authority of society in future life, parents submit to the whims of their children, who in their behaviour are normally searching for their established boundaries. This in itself reinforces problematic behaviour and leaves them in a state of insecurity, producing children who know no limits. Rather than becoming high performing, self-actualizing and moral intellectuals, such children when they grow up tend to lack the basic skills of personal and social life and tend to clash with the laws of society. The modern difficulties in parenting can be directly related to the trend of disappearing *morality* in society: people feel confident enough as members of society when they act in their everyday lives, as long as they don't break too many rules or deviate too much from common standards... but when it comes to the question of raising children, the problem of whether one's actions are *exemplary* comes into play.

---

203 *Politics*, Book III, XVII

III-2. DEMOCRATIC DEVELOPMENTS

The common parental panic indicates that parents are uneasy behaving in front of their children the same way they would behave in front of, say, their boss at work, which implies that people are pressured towards behaviour that is not a suitable example to their children. Your boss might want you to do your work in a manner that would not be exemplary in terms of professional standards regarding ethics, and I suspect this phenomenon is very widespread. The pan-Western decline in what we call "critical thinking skills" has been blamed on parents being absent too much or the children using too much technology in their lives, but the explanation for the phenomenon is much simpler. There is no need for critical thinking skills as society doesn't acknowledge the need for *critical thought*, which is a very different form of thought from, say, skills required in engineering or science. The word 'critical' has the base word 'crisis', and something is to be called critical when it is of the nature that it can cause a crisis. Critical remarks are revelations that aim to expose something that is not noticed, and their critical nature implies that something so dire is going unnoticed that its revelation could cause a crisis. The term "critical mass" means the number of people necessary to pay attention to the thing that is going unnoticed in order to cause the crisis. The word 'critical' is used in a very similar way to the word 'truth', but it just operates on the level of political opinion instead of subjective belief. It is also similar to the word 'relevant' but refers to politically controversial information. Being critical in thought only means being *politically* critical. Critical methods involve analytical methods such as exposing controversies of thought or hidden presuppositions and political connections behind political language, but also exposing critical information which has been the fundamental purpose for the existence of the media in the first place: if there is no need for social criticism, there is no need to circulate news either; no need for journalists to do the reporting; we could get by more easily with just a loudspeaker for the authorities to communicate to us our daily tasks. Also, critical thought is a skill that must be developed, and if one only thinks and doesn't *debate* and thus expose one's thought to actual criticism, one will develop into a cowardly thinker who only knows how to enforce one's presuppositions and is afraid to come to logical conclusions that entail results that won't find social support. I find it questionable whether such 'thought' should be called thought at all, since it will only conclude what it already latently presupposed when it started, and it often astonishes me how much time some people can take to analyse or comment on an issue without actually uttering anything of insight. I think in this information age throwing abstract ideas around is considered a desirable skill that impresses people with no talent for thought: intelligence is sexy, so it is desirable. Also, criticism is something primarily targeted outwards, but self-criticism is a higher skill. Self-criticism requires willingness, peace and calm to target the self with similar thought as one naturally directs outwards. When a person is agitated, he is not self-critical. The same applies to political discourse, when the diplomatic tension escalates between countries, all self-criticism is suppressed and all interest is targeted in the criticism of the opposition—which Jesus called hypocrisy. Anyway, there is a long Western history of critical thought that originates from the times when democracy was formed and the models of our society were targeted to critical thought; thoughts that needed to be circulated in the form of books and newspapers that were politically critical. But look at the situation today: public critics are actively silenced and political whistle-blowers are declared enemies of the state. There is a ban on criticism and, following this, a distaste for critical thought. The democratic *freedom* required for critical thought doesn't exist today, and thus it is absolutely controversial for a society to try and bring up and train critical thinkers while at the same time making their work impossible. It is information, not thought, that reigns, and the one who controls the information has the control. The overall sentiment of disapproval towards critical thought on the level of society will be passed directly to the children studying such subjects; we are trying to tell them, democratically, to study whatever feels like the right choice for them, but at the same time we cannot hide our general feeling towards free and critical thought that it is a bad idea and a waste of time. It is simply dishonest to try and blame this on the children or their parents: it is the fault of what our society has become, and in order to take responsibility for it, one needs to feel responsible for the whole of society and admit that our escapist lives are being wasted in ill-placed trust in a society that doesn't suit our ideals by any stand-

III-2. DEMOCRATIC DEVELOPMENTS

ards. To look at this correctly from the perspective of *life*—this generation and the next one, *sub specie aeterni*—: we can either start admitting error and feeling responsible for society now in our own lives, or we can pass this whole mess on to the next generation and book the next golf trip to the Riviera because "life is short".[204] But in any case, the mission of trying to pass on the ideal model of critical thought to a new generation in schools has failed because we have taken away their freedom by excessive authority and forgotten the natural relationship between the old and the new generation: the new generation will have to deal with the problems that we have created, and this will create a conflict in the absence of the aspect *sub specie aeterni*. This silencing of criticism is common in traditional societies, but not in democracies.

The overall reduction of intellectuals alongside the development of privatization is logical from the perspective of this sort of society, because intellectuals are not needed as they are of no use in making private business decisions that are based on the behaviour of the global market; instead they have been replaced with consultant economists and business analysts that traditionally are not intellectual civil professions but something developed from accounting, expert work that mostly involves precision in the use of numbers and basic knowledge of business laws. In ancient Athens, both business owners *and* analysts were *metoikoi*, of non-citizen class, and therefore separated from civil interest, similar to the way that people motivated solely by money are a civil development of a servant class only educated to the use of tools. Similarly, in Japanese *samurai* society, merchants constituted the lowest class; lower than lords, peasants and artisans. Today we live the rule of the traditionally lowest class of people: merchants. On the level of societal activity, the behaviour of politicians in which it can clearly

---

204 That life is short is a very successful commercial slogan, and essentially operates on a person's narcissism: that life is short means that the right way to think about life is to look at it from the perspective of your own life only and not the life of your children. Incidentally, "*Carpe diem!*" has been successfully turned into a reverse meaning as a marketing slogan: originally urging people to live in the moment and to trust gods in matters of eternity, the poem by Horace taught not to worry about one's looming death and to turn to magic and fortune-tellers that offer quick salvation. This shortness of life and quick salvation by consumerism is exactly what the modern "*Carpe diem!*" urges people to invest in.

be seen that full truth is never being communicated, has created general distrust towards politics and the rise of populist political methods in Western countries, both on the left and the right. I find nationalist resistance to be the preferable way to resist the extra-national political pressure towards a globalist world, but my worst nightmare is that somebody will find a way to unify the local populist movements into a super-populist globalist countermovement that could once again use agitation to seize pan-European power under military enforcement. Such populism has historically been fuelled with nationalist mentality, and that can't be used for agitation in support of a multi-national entity due to its national nature, so it will look different this time. The mentality is already in the air: the people, distanced from politics and living a secluded narcissistic existence, are angry and channel this anger into feelings of guilt and the need to give up their lifestyle for a common cause. Currently, I see many separate values that all act in support of this same mentality and seem to stir people into passionate expressions of globalist mentality. There is an unsystematic yet surprisingly popular radical school of thought called "cultural Marxism" that I find to be the closest modern equivalent to Marxism (or fascism) as it uses victimization rhetoric and irrationally blames all forms of culture and traditions for social injustices and inequality. It typically uses victimizing and pathologizing rhetoric to brand any social groups that represent such cultural or traditional values as sick and harmful, ultimately aiming to collapse traditional power structures. There is the climate change movement, in which some people have conjured up an end-of-the-world scenario with pseudoscientific rhetoric. There is a latent anti-Christian mentality that is an extension of the left-wing anti-Christianity and multiculturality. There is also military-level destabilization activity: the theoretically Gandhi-inspired works of the late Gene Sharp have been and are being used as texts to teach local dissidents anti-Gandhian methods of destabilizing governments in at least Serbia, Georgia, Ukraine, Kyrgyzstan, Estonia, Lithuania, Belarus, Zimbabwe, Tunisia, Egypt, Vietnam, Burma, Guatemala, Indonesia, Iran and all the so-called Arab Spring nations including Libya and

III-2. DEMOCRATIC DEVELOPMENTS

Syria.[205,206,207] The following quote[208] is by a retired US Army officer, Colonel Robert J. Helvey:

> *Gene's work has changed how we think about conflict resolution. ... There are options other than massive bloodshed and destruction to bring political change. ... We now have an alternative to war as a means for people to liberate themselves from tyranny, to deter would-be tyrants and lesser authoritarian rulers.*

By 'we' Colonel Helvey obviously means the US Army. So, it seems that the US Army has found a successful agitation weapon that is being used to stir people up against their governments, but one that works differently from the way Marxism-Leninism has been applied in various parts of the world as it doesn't contain any revolutionary ideology but simply tactics and the strategy of civil resistance in support of revolution. In the absence of any *international* people's movement that would apply the related rhetoric of democracy against 'dictatorship' or 'tyranny', the movements that have been attracting headlines for over a decade can well be interpreted as representing simply proxy warfare, following the old US and NATO policy of enforcing regime change via destabilization of disobedient governments. Proxy warfare and regime change doctrines are nothing new, but it is worth noting that these new wars gain prominent publicity and the governments targeted for regime change are targeted by high-profile information warfare in the Western media, which manipulates public opinion to accept them. Modern Westerners would not accept a war unless it is against something believed to be a tyranny, in which case their sentiments seem to

---

205 S. G. Stolberg, 'Shy U.S. Intellectual Created Playbook Used in a Revolution', 16.2.2011, *The New York Times*. http://www.nytimes.com/2011/02/17/world/middleeast/17sharp.html [26.12.2019].

206 C. Off, 'Gene Sharp on Non-Violent Revolution', 23.2.2011, CBC Radio. http://www.cbc.ca/asithappens/features/2011/02/23/gene-sharp-on-non-violent-revolution/ [26.12.2019].

207 L. Gray, 'Gene Sharp: How to Start a Revolution', 21.10.2011, *The Daily Telegraph*. http://www.telegraph.co.uk/culture/film/filmmakersonfilm/8841546/Gene-Sharp-How-to-Start-a-Revolution.html [26.12.2019].

208 J. di Giovanni, 'The Quiet American', 3.9.2012, *The New York Times*. http://www.nytimes.com/2012/09/09/t-magazine/gene-sharp-theorist-of-power.html [26.12.2019].

be such that they don't actively oppose it—it is a rather simple formula actually: "war is bad except against a tyrant". I think a great many people I know would subscribe to this thought. So, we have had multiple wars against governments portrayed as very evil tyrants in rather short succession, and it seems to me that any leader in the world is liable to become a hated tyrant in the Western conception; war news is typically produced by anonymous intelligence sources and the media publishes such information against journalistic ethics because this type of news sells the most papers. One can observe that the media uniformly presents anti-government demonstrators as 'terrorists' or 'mobs' whenever the government seems to be favoured, but organized militants, terrorists and mercenaries are called "peaceful demonstrators" when the government is not favoured. One can actually often make accurate guesses about the future outcome of global news stories based on how things are presented in the Western media by noticing whether events are being reported using the vocabulary of 'democracy' or 'dictatorship'. Every now and then a head of state is demonized and shown as tyrannical, and the actions of Western countries shown as democratic in contrast, and this can easily be read as aiming for a particular reaction by the masses: if you understand drama to any extent, you can also predict the plot. Whenever such a thing happens, it can be taken as a prelude to upcoming controversy regarding the matters at hand that will be publicized not by the Western media but by other sources. The masses are kept in the dark and protected by their own willingness to live in the comfort of believing the world is not like this but has progressed in ethical terms since the bad old days, and that the minor controversies associated with these events are produced by malicious and unreliable critics.

Let's take another look at the sentiment that is currently expressed under the climate change rhetoric. I will call it the "climate change movement", though it is hardly a people's movement as it incidentally converges with the globalist corporate agenda in terms of its goals. Rather I'd say it is a machination devised to agitate the radicalized left as useful idiots—a tactic traditionally associated with the radicalized right (neo-Nazis) in Eastern Europe. No serious mind can take any of this rhetoric seriously, and no doubt if this sentiment does not gain a popular foothold, we will see another one with similar themes. It is interesting to look at it from another perspective, namely as an agitation rhetoric that I'd like to parallel with the National Socialist sentiment from World War II in terms of the following features.

1) The 'socialism' in National Socialism was effectively a free ride on the popularity of Marxism, which spoke to the people as an idea of unifying the rich and the poor and via the largely favourable image of the Soviet Union. Similarly, 'climate change' is a smart buzzword because it doesn't really mean anything (the definitions are consistently mixed up in common rhetoric) but it symbolizes change. It is a free ride on the popularity of environmentalism, which is likely the most appealing grassroots rhetoric to modern Westerners who are detached from active politics and in a relatively well-off economic situation.

2) The climate change movement is *totalitarian*. Their wish to impose authoritarian rules on people's live ranges from the smallest purchases by local consumers to controlling the birth policies of nations on the other side of the world. Overall, their solutions to any problems stem from radicalized ideology and a demand for immediate action by imposing rules. The totalitarianism is most clearly manifested in attitudes that wish to ban public speech. As the ideology spans from the micro matters of people's personal lives into the global macro scale, this leaves no place safe and free from public scrutiny and ridicule; no place that one could consider private and where one is allowed to live in whatever way one wishes.

3) Like National Socialism, climate change is a *corporate* and *technocrat* movement from the point of view not of expressed ideology, but in that it is funded by bankers, industrialists and aristocrats. This is highly controversial, since socialism is essentially a working-class movement, but it is to be understood as a scheme where technocracy is masquerading as socialism. Original Italian Fascist theory was devised by the factory owners and it promoted a Parliament run by corporate industries.

4) Like National Socialism, the climate change movement is *author-*

PART III. SOCIO-POLITICAL ANALYSIS

itarian, anti-intellectual and *atheoretical*. One can witness and comprehend a globalist organ to be working and hear politicians and the media discussing things such as European "federal development". Yet there exists no related social theory, just a discourse that says policy-changing actions *must* be taken as soon as possible, and a vindictive mentality where one public comment out of line could destroy someone's political or corporate career. An intellectual movement would be one that promotes a rational choice of a better way of living or organization.

5) National Socialism employed *social Darwinism* (Aryanism). This sentiment is inherent in modern globalism: poor nations are seen as poor because of their inferior quality,[209] and the standard humanist and Gandhian problematic of poverty as a result of social infrastructure is not at all addressed. Instead, modern environmentalists see that countries in a better position should take over the decisions of those weaker nations in order to save them from their bad governance. Also, there is a constant worry over the global carrying capacity, which translates to eugenics. An evident parallel can be seen between modern sentiments towards immigrants—particularly of religious minorities—and National Socialist sentiments towards Jews and other minorities: minorities are perceived as being privileged over the masses, and as *economic waste*. The National Socialist radical implementation of eugenics was inspired by its popularity in the scientific atmosphere of the time, and the implementation of eugenic laws in several US states. The Nazis forced medical sterilizations on half a million people, and the Nazi elite group the SS was racially selected and committed to eugenic marriage and to Hitler, the messiah sent by the God of the German race. Today, we have environmentalist rheto-

---

209 I watched a Danish documentary where a researcher promoted "cognitive capitalism" in a speech about intelligence that was slowly articulated (so that stupid people would also understand) in beautiful British English. He argued based on various empirical data that 1) "cognitive capital"—a country's bright people—is what really drives things, making a society better, and 2) rich countries boost people's intelligence. So, smartness produces wealth and wealth produces smartness. He called it a virtuous cycle... it seems in modern intelligence cycles in logic are virtuous. He said "we think that cognitive capitalism is what really drives things" ... which sheds light on the latent ideological capitalism underneath a scientific appearance.

ric that promotes medical depopulation.

6) All green environmentalism has a similar wish to ban smoking and promote health, as did the Nazis. Personal wellness is a huge value, and it is more so, of course, the more demanding and stressful our work life gets. There is a strong cult of the body, with a strong relation of health and wellness to physical appearance. This stems from the totalitarian attitude where every action and life choice are subject matter for the ideology.

7) Like National Socialism, the climate change movement is *anti-Christian*, which is made understandable by the fact that Christianity is the European *moral* standard. In fact, the whole idea that the world is in danger and must be protected by us people effectively implies that God didn't create Earth, as it is implied that the Earth is not capable of handling humans but we are instead actively responsible for it. Any such thoughts that imply that we are responsible over the whole world are anti-Christian. In addition to the development of secularization, and the attack on the traditional Christian conception of marriage, there is widely reported governmental favouritism towards Islam, which effectively works to erode the European traditional moral basis and to provoke racial and religious fear and hatred, which, in turn, decreases unity and harmony, and increases the power of government. The National Socialist intellectual foundation was built firmly on mysticism and libertine pagan worship of Nordic gods, essentially as a refusal of Christian morals as the solution to cultural conflict.[210] The *libertine heretic* nature of such thought was reflected as an overall depravity of the Nazis which carried a sense of joy from the relief from the restrictions of religious morals that were considered to have failed: heresy becomes appealing when religious morality fails. The Nazi racial hygiene programmes were kept secret mainly because of opposition by the Church, although they were considered interesting in the scientific atmosphere of the time.

---

[210] It might be mentioned that prominent newspapers have published evidence showing that many important Western political figures regularly participate in rituals of an occult nature. But we have freedom of religion, so, if one is interested in witchcraft, secret societies or such occult activities, this is mostly seen a matter of one's personal life and not something for others to worry about.

8) It is the implied Western corporate capitalism that conveys a sense of authoritarianism like National Socialism, because business life behaves in an authoritarian way. EU-minded national leaders are highly authoritarian in behaviour, no doubt originating from the transnational corporate involvement in the high ranks of EU, where corporate money lies in the hands of completely private executive power. Yet the authoritarianism is latent and not expressed in words, and I believe this is due to the Nazi stigma: cold corporate attitudes are allowed free rein, as condemning them as authoritarian is a Western taboo.

So, it seems to me that the modern global West, albeit applying a whole new type of language and facing problems that seem novel, is enacting a historical repetition of the society it ostensibly most detests. And this behaviour closely resembles the way individual people, who are unable to come to terms with their childhood traumas but instead suppress them, tend to closely repeat the behaviour of their parents that they ostensibly detest. To compare with the similarities, there are, of course, obvious dissimilarities, such as the National Socialist *racial* and *national* superiority that isn't, and cannot be, seen in a globalist movement. Modern democratic values are egalitarian in a Platonic dystopian sense: nobody, no matter how unequal in practice, is to be acknowledged as unequal—which effectively bars the recognition of the underlying economic inequality: you are allowed to own so much money that it places you in another class from others, but nobody is allowed to say that such a class-based society exists.

In a power struggle over *rights*, an argument in favour of a right needs to be backed with the power of a social movement; the power to affect people *in defiance* of authority. A developing country will develop in this sense when it manages to apply such movements to change its social system in such a way that the system provides *an alternative to tradition*: for example the social security system has been developed to provide poor people with an alternative to succumbing to traditional means of gaining a livelihood that have been seen to have a negative impact on society as a whole, such as begging, theft, swindling or pros-

III-2. DEMOCRATIC DEVELOPMENTS

titution. The development we see today is a reduction in the amount of help provided to the lower class by these institutions and the increased ruling class rhetoric that from the safety of one's own secured position encourages others towards greater personal effort, which, in the absence of a functioning social system, equates to encouragement of just these immoral traditional means of gaining an income. The unified nature and implied social struggle of socio-cultural movements contrasts sharply with private business interest, and requires ethical individuals with relative freedom, a motive and an inclination to *sacrifice* personal assets for the common good. These ethical thoughts can shift from these individuals to larger groups of people through philosophy and social theory that transform the ethical ideals into political doctrines. One should take a particularly close look at the type of sacrifice that was offered by Marxism-Leninism, which included a lot of socio-cultural theorizing aimed at changing the world. The movement asked people to sacrifice themselves *for the ideal* of Marxism and promised them an end of oppression and the reward of getting to live in a paradise nation. Now, an ideal is an abstract, and therefore, first of all, nobody takes responsibility for fulfilling the ideal; if Marxism-Leninism fails, there is no point criticizing its creator, because he will say that his ideas were just wrongly applied (and this is the interpretation put forward by Marxists today). But secondly, and more importantly, what is offered for the *subjective* sacrifice of giving up one's more immediate plans is a logically contradictory *objective* reward: a better world *for all*, with an objective criterion for what is considered better.[211] This 'promise' takes the following form: "Give up everything in front of everybody, and we will let you know when you've given up enough." This is not actually a promise except in the sense that the acolyte promises to follow the leader, and in this sense it is similar to the agitation cultures of religiously ruled countries. Contrast this with the reward Jesus Christ and Mahatma Gandhi personally promised for the subjective sacrifice of following them: living in a *symbolical* promised land meaning the cleanliness and purity of the *subjective* soul. This promise is of a different kind: "If you choose to *believe me* and to do as

---

[211] The subjectivity of personal sacrifice is depicted e.g. in the Negro spiritual "Nobody knows the trouble I've seen".

I show you by my example and to follow the *way* I am showing, then *I* promise that this way *cannot fail.*" Here there is reference only within the subjective, and the outcome of action can be seen to refer only to the collective success of performing *faithfully* to an ideal.

The whole of civil society can now be seen to be on a course towards annihilation, because it is more and more visibly replaced by the tyranny of a global plutocracy, which we know to represent simply capitalist anarchy on the subjective level of morality or ideology. The only thing that keeps this fact hidden is people's reckless willingness to disregard dangers and to overlook what is terrible. People seem to be very worried in general, but because the subjective has been erased from global consciousness, their worry is directed towards objective observable distractions, such as climate change, global carrying capacity, local politics, immigrants, animal or human rights, and many more. Western civil society is a system originally devised by the ancient Greeks and further refined and developed by the great minds of the Enlightenment, but one that has been crafted by a long history of conflict against *rule by tradition* ("the powers that be") involving the university, trade unions and socio-cultural ethical movements like the racial equality movement, feminism, environmentalism, and animal rights... all in favour of a more unified civil society expressed in the ideal of a "better world for all". What we see today, not in spoken word but in practical action, is the actual increased indifference towards all of these values, and the attack on society is actually coming from the opposite direction than that publicly admitted. For example, we see

- increased racist (attack on "white supremacy") and eugenic (global carrying capacity) opinions while visibly trying to enforce a full-scale ban on any racism, fascism and other 'isms'

- decreased tolerance towards difference in terms of opinion, culture and religion, while visibly trying to enforce an ideal of tolerance

- increased hate crimes towards gays (in countries with gay marriage) while enforcing a tolerant ideal via gay marriage

- increasing wealth and income gap between men and women while trying to enforce policies to abolish the perceived pay gap

- increased objectification of women in sexual attitudes via liberal hard-core porn becoming mainstream, while visibly trying to enforce full sexual equality, and

- decreased valuation of Mother Earth as the source of natural resources as people resort to extravagant consumerism and travel, while trying to uphold an image of environmentalism.

The current situation where political correctness has taken over healthy dialogue can be observed to produce precisely the opposite actual developments than what is desirable on the level of argument. We see the decadent remnants of the societal representation of the Western post-Enlightenment values, hijacked and molested by global corporations; we see global fascism masquerading as environmentalist (the green movement) and humanitarian (corporate philanthropy) public images. We see the Western institutions applying *fascism* with a rhetoric of "there is no other alternative", and grassroots movements portraying an alternative to such development, with both of these movements in fact working in the service of the convergence of corporate power. Environmentalists fly the green flag as a humanist value, portraying themselves as helpers or world saviours, while sometimes quite blatantly doing it for personal profit—I just witnessed an election advertisement from the Green party telling me "Saving the world is good business". Here it might be noted that if you make a profitable business out of doing "good things" then, naturally, your long-time success is laid upon the foundation of preserving misery. In short, a corporation's function today is to make profit by any means necessary, and if a corporation runs out of business, this means loss of profits for the shareholders and it's time to switch CEO. If one looks at the intellectual basis of what being 'green' means, the most fundamental value is that in the economic model, where a consumer uses economic services or commodities, it is the *consumer* who deserves to be blamed for excess and wastefulness, for cutting down the rainforests, etc. The green movement has no intellectual basis; it originated as a grassroots movement in citizen activism of the type that once was exercised as an unspoken democratic responsibility in the spirit of ancient Athens, where one is to be either actively opinionated about matters of the state or to be an uninteresting idiot. It has since, however, been taken over by corporations that lead the poor greens to believe that they can achieve environmental change by doing what these political forces tell them to do. We see a fascism where the spying on citizens seems to be on a far worse level than in any time in history in any place on Earth, with spy organizations (mostly the NSA in USA and GCHQ in Europe) actively monitoring and recording practically all of people's digital activities by having direct access to the largest Internet companies,[212] having laptop users' pictures taken,[213] having the capability to record and store *all* telephone calls of a targeted foreign nation,[214] accessing both mobile phone operator data[215] and user data,[216] and having very sophisticated methods for on-demand spying on Internet routers, laptops and mobile phones.[217] I say "seems to be" because I don't believe anybody has seen any evidence of said spy tech, and the reports could all turn out to be national tech boasting akin to the Space Race in the Cold War. Intelligence agencies are also reported to work to apply various methods to targeted people that have not been charged with crimes, such as discrediting them with planted disinformation, using false identities to get embarrassing personal information and shutting down their communications using computer viruses.[218] A society that can do this will

212   B. Gellman and L. Poitras, 'U.S., British intelligence mining data from nine U.S. Internet companies in broad secret program', *The Washington Post*, 7.6.2013.
213   S. Ackerman and J. Ball, 'Yahoo webcam images from millions of users intercepted by GCHQ', *The Guardian*, 27.2.2014. http://www.theguardian.com/world/2014/feb/27/gchq-nsa-webcam-images-internet-yahoo [26.12.2019].
214   B. Gellman and A. Soltani, 'NSA surveillance program reaches 'into the past' to retrieve, replay phone calls', *The Washington Post*, 18.3.2014.
215   E. Nakashima, 'Verizon providing all call records to U.S. under court order', *The Washington Post*, 6.6.2013.
216   J. Larson, J. Glanz and A. W. Lehren, 'Spy Agencies Tap Data Streaming From Phone Apps', *The New York Times*, 27.1.2014. http://www.nytimes.com/2014/01/28/world/spy-agencies-scour-phone-apps-for-personal-data.html [26.12.2019].
217   J. Appelbaum, L. Poitras, M. Rosenbach, C. Stöcker, J. Schindler and H. Stark, 'Inside TAO: Documents Reveal Top NSA Hacking Unit', *Der Spiegel*, 29.12.2013. http://www.spiegel.de/international/world/the-nsa-uses-powerful-toolbox-in-effort-to-spy-on-global-networks-a-940969.html [26.12.2019].
218   M. Cole, R. Esposito, M. Schone and G. Greenwald, 'Snowden Docs: British Spies Used Sex and "Dirty Tricks"', *NBC News* , 7.2.2014. http://www.nbcnews.com/news/investigations/snowden-docs-british-spies-used-sex-dirty-tricks-n23091 [26.12.2019].

III-2. DEMOCRATIC DEVELOPMENTS

have endless ways of suppressing any anti-authority movement that it deems a serious threat; there is no need for brute force or ruling by the threat of visible violence, because anybody posing a serious threat could be singled out and found at any time of day. The information that we see about these potential surveillance capabilities on individual citizens comes from alleged defectors, and such sources, no matter how abundant, should not be believed while the identity of these defectors can't be established. But essentially, the underlying terror and fear is established on, and feeds on, the same thing that all fear feeds on: the *unknown*—people are kept in the dark and are forced to stay in denial about the steadily increasing evidence of the true nature of such a society. It behaves like a type of fascism yet it is not called a fascist state but a democracy; a democracy so pure and virtuous that it has the right to condemn every other nation, to mock and ridicule them, to impose sanctions on them, to fund paramilitary operations on their soil and to ultimately attack them.

One can look at the *motivators* that determine people's actions *from the subjective perspective* and make a certain distinction between types of motivators. By subjective perspective I mean that I am not describing these phenomena here in a general sense but saying something about their role for the subject. I drafted the following two short, suggestive and probably highly incomplete lists in an attempt to describe these values; the lists are not meant to be read as a suggestion for a naive simplification of human motivation, but the focus here is their separation into the two distinct columns.

Personal motivation	Social motivation
survival	agreement, promise
family bond, companionship	law
truth	money, personal asset
moral principle	social status
religious faith	ideology
tradition	beauty, appearance

PART III. SOCIO-POLITICAL ANALYSIS

The left-hand column lists *personal* motivators, which means that the related behaviour doesn't involve objective standards or involvement from others. The first three: survival, family and truth, are intrinsic and instinctive human motivators. We could argue that a person can, via ethical change, overcome these motivators: one can become apathetic regarding one's own well-being or even life; one can betray one's own family, and one can become a compulsive liar—but all these are extreme psychiatric cases. Moral principles and religion are subjective in nature yet not intrinsic, and it is only after they are established that they function in a sense that excludes choice. Religion can be seen to relate directly to all three: survival, family and truth, in its symbolism, which should explain the subjective motivation also to a person who doesn't consider himself religious. The right-hand column lists *social* motivators, which differ in that they are socially constituted, and, firstly, their upholding requires a social awareness and, in a general sense, social preservation: promises and law are broken, money stolen and ideals forgotten when nobody is watching, and the only social institution to maintain these promises and laws, apart from their social enforcement, is the institution of honour. Secondly, they can also be forgotten or destroyed, unlike the intrinsic, personal human motivations. Some things on the lists might seem counterintuitive; for example, many would like to call money (personal asset) a personal motivator or companionship a social motivator, but this is not true; money is a social differentiator and a means of gaining assets relative to somebody else. Money by itself is worthless and the need for it is argued without a reference to any real values, and the emptiness of money and our inherent willingness to give up money in favour of more subjective values is a standard cultural theme; every now and then you will see people who just give all their money away, to reach for more important and true values in their lives. Also, no matter how much people like to talk about companionship in terms of doing work for the good of the other, companionship is a solely personal need, which is shown simply by the fact that people end companionships and start new ones. The standards of currency have changed time and again in human history, and institutions can function without any interaction via money. Standards of beauty have changed many times and in the modern West they

III-2. DEMOCRATIC DEVELOPMENTS

just happen to reflect the value of wellness,[219] and similarly, beauty is fleeting. I believe another way to compare the two columns is the way shown by Aristotle: the values on the left are good in themselves, and the values on the right are things good for the sake of other things that are good in themselves, mostly ones that are located in the left-hand column. From this perspective, the personal motivation can be seen as primary to the social; for example, you might have to make an agreement in order to survive, but it doesn't make sense to say you are surviving in order to do anything else. All in all, the two columns should reveal that the subjectivity of a motivator also signifies its place within human nature, and as such, as something that won't change with time, and that has remained the same as long as we have written down history. When people, and society, are under pressure, the values in the left-hand column will gain importance while the ones on the right will fail and collapse, to be reinvented in another form later on.

Those who understand the severity of modern developments may wonder whether corporate plutocracy can reach a homeostasis of neo-feudalism. Could it happen that the corporate elite that wield true economic power would gradually develop into a system of visible and accepted leadership? I will consider this option via the perspectives I find relevant. Firstly, an argument in favour of the hypothesis is that the position of a modern oligarch could be better secured than that of a monarch or a feudal lord in the past; if he plays his financial cards wisely, he will only need to deal with his competitors and to avoid publicity, and will not have to worry about losing the trust of his own people, as he essentially has no people to rule over. But the complement of this argument is that feudalism is *anti-democratic*, which means it contradicts people's beliefs of justice, and in this aspect the problematic involves the question of whether people would accept a shift to a formal system with inheritance of power. I'd say the answer

---

[219] One can directly see the relation between social status and beauty by comparing Western and Eastern standards of the beauty of skin. In both the West and the East the tone of skin symbolizes the amount of free time the person has: the Western skin needs to be tanned to indicate lots of leisure time and the ability to travel to warm places, as the Eastern skin needs to be pale to indicate not having to work in the sun.

is negative, and rather it is key to the current oligarchy to be able to work away from sight; high personal wealth is considered a negative trait in the Western democratic mind-set and this fact is rather used to smear enemy heads of state—the personal wealth of leaders one opposes can be publicized to arouse anger. Shadow capitalism involves a continuous imbalance that causes internal political tension, and just like the self-deceiving subject that constantly needs to actively escape the internal contradiction via blaming others, shadow capitalism has no other means to provide unity and to fight internal conflicts except creating artificial unity via some supposed external threat. By definition such a state can only exist in constant conflict, which rules out the possibility of homeostasis. Now, to compare this state with a feudal one where people are bound to accept the feudal lords as their masters: the justification of this status is found in *lore*: the legendary stories of how these masters originally were granted their position by divine powers. In a modern setting, this part reduces to biographies of the oligarchs where the personal histories of these rulers are presented as eventful and fascinating heroic struggles for the right cause. The stories can be interwoven with the political narratives of the time, and people who wish to understand politics may read them to get support for their political views, but they no longer hold the mystical and divine status in which the divine position of the ruler would somehow be justified by gods, spirits, the will of the nation or suchlike. A new monarchy would need to somehow justify its inheritance of money and power in order for the oligarchs to be able to come out of the shadows into public life. And it will ultimately fail to do this, because the whole concept of printed currency rests on the basis that this currency provides equality and liberty via free trade, which is in direct contradiction with inherited power.

Now, in the middle of the terrible global developments, the Achilles' heel of the current financial situation is money, and the power of money is based solely on the fact that people accept it as currency used in trade. People don't want discrimination based on status created by money, because the money hasn't even a trace of justification behind it. There are many historical alternatives to money as currency in terms

III-2. DEMOCRATIC DEVELOPMENTS

of people defending their livelihood. For example, the Indian flag carries the symbol of a spinning wheel because of its role in the political process leading to the liberation of India: the spinning wheel symbolizes the basic human right to use local resources to manufacture one's own clothes instead of being dependent on imported fabric or fabric produced under foreign control, and this generally human conception of justice spans to all people's basic needs for survival such as food, water and shelter. One can present a good argument that companies should produce people's basic commodities, but nobody can defend an argument that people shouldn't be able to provide them themselves and trade them with each other, and this truth is independent of moral systems such as human rights, and the very constituting idea in the birth of liberalism in the first place. The world currently faces a historically unprecedented scale of inequality in the form of financial inequality. It is not unprecedented in the sense of tyrannical brutality imposed on individuals; rather, conditions are better than they used to be for the very poor. But it is unprecedented in the concentration of global control that is above legislation. And in view of the fact that the inequality of money is a social quality secondary to survival or moral principles, it is clear that this situation is not tenable, as it is not the case that the people have grown more tolerant of inequality (quite the opposite feeling is expressed on the level of public opinion); they have just for this current moment forgotten what equality means, having been offered by the propaganda machine an easy mental escape from their own desperate existence to concentrate on minor social issues. The current situation could indeed be seen to bode ill if it wasn't for the fact that it is based on the weakness of money portrayed in its juxtaposition against personal moral motivators; for example, ordering troops to commit murder is possible when the control of troops is based on terror and fear, but it is not so easy in the case of mercenaries who work for money. Money is a very globally popular motivator but a very *weak* motivator, and the financial inequality that is based on this weak motivator has had the chance to grow to its modern extent only because the process has not been visible: money has always worked in the shadows. Therefore, I believe that the birth of a coexisting alternative economy out of the desperate inequality of the current one is just a matter of time and will involve an alternative means of basic trade. But this economy will have to clash with the current one and to be protected with idealist and spiritual means that bind it to the said basic moral truths; it will have to be an economy that cannot work against our moral foundations. Such 'currency' has historically been supernatural and spiritual in nature; currency that buys afterlife, such as Christian following of the example of Jesus, Indian following of the example of Gandhi or Buddhists investing in karma. And such currencies are not crafted by economists or financial theorists.

III-3. The Decline of Morality

The 21st century so far is easily distinguished as an era of eroding morality in the West. Where this can be seen is that religious terminology and language that impose *moral restrictions* on people have vanished from common discourse. The obvious vanished thing is religion, but essentially any language with moral restrictions has been replaced by ideals that 1) are based on and derived from Christian values but 2) don't impose restrictions on people like the original moral values do *in provable (testable) means*. The development can be called modern liberalism, and the expression "wrong type of freedom" suits it well. The proof of being a good Christian is to be tested in one's faith, just as the proof of being a good guitar player is not in believing it in your mind and expressing it in your appearance, but subjecting the performance to audiences or teachers that act as judges. Modern ideals don't require any skill or sacrifice and this is reflected in the fact that identities can be and are switched very easily. They are simply the use of a freedom without any responsibility or consequence. Let's take for example "rock, peace and love". Rock, for a 21st-century person, means an ideal of a certain way of life that incorporates rebellious youthful elements, and these rebellious elements are made possible by the rock movement that is built upon democratic freedoms of expression and opinion; freedoms to look, talk and act any way you like as long as you are not harming anybody. As these are essentially *freedoms* they don't impose any requirements for the person who subscribes to such a value. 'Peace' means using the same freedoms and subscribing to a similar, originally hippie, movement and the ideal of pacifism, which, again, poses no requirements of action but uses the freedoms to publicly refuse certain responsibilities, yet is clearly derived from the ideal of non-violent resistance that is a Christian ideal originating from Jesus Christ and Christian martyrdom. The hippie would shout 'Peace!' but would not accept the responsibilities and consequences of martyrdom—far from it, being rather characterized by laziness and avoidance of responsibilities in general. 'Love', as modernly applied, is derived from the universal, brotherly love that has been advocated by Christians since the earliest times of that religion. It's just that the modern ideal of love doesn't impose the sacrifice of your own personal space and right to serve your neighbour who thinks differently from you, which was the very essence of the love Jesus preached. The modern gay rights activist will passionately promote love as the basis on which two men should be allowed to marry, and will equally passionately say that they have the right to marry based on the fact that they love each other exactly because it imposes no harm on anybody else. So, it is exactly the lack of responsibility—simply the subjective feeling of love— that, in their thinking, constitutes love, and love strictly is not a sacrifice where something is given away for the reason of common benefit. And they would say that this love is a right; everybody should have the right to love anybody or anything they want because of the love. Even if, say, the love was of the kind that is harmful to themselves or their partner. This is very different love indeed from the original Christian love, which would essentially be behaviour that *grants* a right to somebody else, your neighbour, by you willingly giving away your own comfort. So, the essential thing that differentiates modern rock, peace and love from their original ideals is a lack of institution (guild) to test and determine a person's *skill* in these values, and this shows that such a skill does not actually exist, and we are using these words without relating them to a skill. We all know loving is a skill, but when we think about the love that supposedly justifies gay marriage there simply and clearly is no skill related—this love means simply something different than love as we would use the word in the context of a normal relationship. And I can easily point to the error: we have a false conception of language where we reduce the meaning of a word to its related subjective feeling (Wittgenstein's beetle in the box). Therefore they tend to think that when a person says 'love', he means the feeling of love and not *the use* of 'love' that carries along with it much more than just the feeling, this being social responsibilities and expectations to behave in a certain manner that simultaneously act as the criteria to test whether somebody truly loves somebody or whether they are just talking hot air. These social norms are the measurement against which anybody's love will and should be judged. It should be noted that these sorts of discussions about what is true love and how to test true love dominate

III-3. THE DECLINE OF MORALITY

women's magazines and discussion forums. It is such an important topic as it relates to the decision: "How do I know whether I should agree to a life-long partnership with a person whom I don't know completely and who might be deceiving me about his intentions under the guise of love?" They might ask: "Does he really *feel* love or is it just talk?", but this is a misguided question as feelings are by definition not measurable. The correct question is: "Do I have a reason to believe he will act responsibly with respect to *the norms* of love?" Which translates to a two-fold question: "What kind of behaviour or actions should I *expect* from a man in love?" and "Will he *do* what I expect a man in love to do?" These questions are traditionally involved in the process of *courting*, as the couple would be expected to *show in action* their feelings by following the social norms. During courting the major concerns and expectations could be brought to light and the couple could possibly be saved from an unhappy marriage. In a modern society the process has to a large extent vanished and relationships are formed without it, and it should come as no surprise that the amount of liberalism versus traditionalism in a society directly relates to the levels of divorce in that society. If there is no courting to show love, it should be no surprise if newlywed couples don't actually love each other, and by love here I strictly refer to the testable norms of love. It could also be that these norms change; who knows, it might be that we move towards the norm common in developing countries where a suitor is expected to show wealth, and acts of spending on one's girl are interpreted as expressions of love. This conception matches our Christian ideal of love being sharing from your own, but it contradicts the ideal because small gifts from a wealthy man hardly portray sacrifice of one's comfort. If love has little related sacrifice, we should expect that love to be closer to a norm where a powerful man can have multiple wives or mistresses, similarly to how a man with a big or expensive car needs to pay less attention to traffic rules than a pedestrian or a cyclist. And this is of course the norm in developing nations. Or maybe you believe that wealth is a good balancer because it is in the process of reaching equal distribution among sexes? In this case you should check your facts about the way things are actually developing. Our Western conception of love is a moral, egalitarian and reciprocal institution, and if one wants to reduce it to "just a feeling" then this will likely just mean moral regression because of the shift away from the moral institution that is the origin. Our confused wish for more liberty and freedom, in order to achieve more 'equality', will result in an inverse result, if one doesn't already believe in egalitarian Christian love.

The aforementioned ideologies, which don't involve the original moral restrictions that their historical antecedents did, could be presented as a *mundane development* of a *moral* theme of faith. Looking at historical human society, humans have always believed in the supernatural, and this is by no means limited to the phenomenon of religion. We start our lives believing in fairy-tales; believing a collection of stories that sound incredible but that we also cannot explain. We hear stories about people with supernatural skills and supernatural beings such as ghosts. One might expect that due to the advances in science belief in the supernatural would be replaced by a scientific, sceptical, evidence-based worldview. Recent polls[220] from the USA and UK, however, find that around half of the population actually believe in ghosts (42 and 52 per cent respectively). The number is even higher in Asia and even in highly secular places like Japan, and also high in Scandinavia. The prevalence of paranormal beliefs in Asia can be witnessed in the massive popularity of the ghost theme in entertainment. I myself have met a number of people who describe their supernatural experiences to me as proof of the existence of supernatural things in general. This result supports the idea that the scientific and secular world-view is something like a prop or an idealized model of thinking that is held up in our society by the system of science and educated people all around, but essentially something that doesn't seem to transfer into people's minds, no matter how we much portray it as correct or true. Then again, we *know* that *morality* behaves in exactly the same manner; moral people are held up as ideal examples, and the masses look up to them and agree what they are doing is correct and that they should be doing exactly the same thing in their own lives, while consciously failing to implement that ideal in their lives. Similarly, we would listen to a beautiful concert: we admire the ideal skill presented and are moved

---

220 Wen, T. 'Why Do People Believe in Ghosts?' *The Atlantic*, Sept 5, 2014.

III-3. THE DECLINE OF MORALITY

by it, while knowing that we can never do it ourselves. Now probably most people would say that we are unsure whether God exists, as they would probably also say that we are unsure whether ghosts exist; we know that sometimes unexplained things happen and we know that many people interpret these as supernatural events, but now if we were to answer whether ghosts exist we can take two paths: 1) we can say no, and mean that the ghosts literally do not exist as the entities as which they are perceived, but 2) we can also say yes, and mean that the ghosts obviously do exist as they have such an effect on people's lives via their belief in them. Now, a certain kind of person would very clearly give answer 1, but still be entertained by ghost stories: he would strongly strongly support the objective, correct world-view in which there is no room for ghosts, but at the same time he would live in a world in which many of his friends actually believe in such stories, and this would feel to him peculiar and interesting; something he can't explain because their way thinking is so different from his. He was never moved by ghosts because he chose not to believe in them... but why did he do that? Ghosts are not just supernatural characters; there is a clear moral logic to ghosts as they haunt places where something bad has happened or e.g. come to take revenge or to give reward to people as an act of post-mortem retribution or reward. If we take the view that the prevalence of people's belief in ghosts justifies considering this as a some sort of basic human need on the level of belief, people who are completely oblivious to ghosts and strongly refute them on the basis of their supernatural character seem to also be people who consistently refute the whole human sense of emotions that relate to the death of a person or, say, atrocities that take place in some locality. And those feelings simply can't be dismissed as senseless; when people die, we don't just have a strong need, but a *primary* need, to justify and understand what happened, as opposed to seeing the event as a senseless and arbitrary event perpetrated by a cruel and random world. We can't explain death scientifically; an objective causal explanation is completely meaningless when we need a subjective justification: "Why did she have to die?—Well, you see, the lunatic's knife entered her body in the vicinity of her aorta, rupturing the aorta and causing both internal and external bleeding, which was followed by a disruption in the blood flow to her brain..."

PART III. SOCIO-POLITICAL ANALYSIS

Now, if we assume that the historical, human antecedent of answering this kind of question would be something in the form of a supernatural teleological explanation, what do we expect this to be replaced with in the modern world if not religion, or alternatively, ghost stories or, say, occultism? If you say the supernatural doesn't exist, I would point out to you that ghosts or divine beings are still experienced by many people, and I would ask you: What would you suggest as the alternative subjective justification to people for these experiences if not God or ghosts? If your answer is 'nothing', then you are not actually even listening to the question but just ignoring it. Would you also say that crying is pointless because there is obviously nothing observable to cry about; why cry over the lolly that you've dropped because it has already gone. No, you might perhaps say that the reason to cry is related to the feeling and evidence suggests that crying is good and healthy, so you should do it. But if I told you that Jonathan's dead wife was sleeping with him for 6 months after her death and gave him comfort, you would think there is something contradictory to this statement because it relates to something that is not real. What do you mean by 'real'; are the things that we are missing real or are the emotions we are feeling real? Enter the supernatural: where the existence of things is accepted based on the subjective justification that it is *right* that they exist; that they *should* exist. Jonathan's wife still exists, because she should exist, because it is not justified that she is gone. Now we can bring our need to justify via the supernatural together with our moral systems, and see that it is precisely the religious system that offers the justifications in the events of death in the form of the afterlife and the services of a priest, and in a religious world these would be accepted as the alternatives to the ghost stories that we would naturally be inclined to entertain. It is just that the religious system does this in a moral context in which we are united in brotherhood under the same father, whereas a primitive society may view the morality of death in different terms; for example that the dead person angered the gods and was rightfully punished. It is becoming more common for a person to *lose his touch with the cultural element of justification*. He starts repeating the same cultural behaviour but without believing in the justification that it offers, and as he loses his faith in it, he will also not share the related moral responsibilities. The justifications, however, need to come from somewhere, so my expectation is that as secularization advances, the prevalence of these primal spiritual justifications, such as ghost stories, will directly increase. The morality of our justification will naturally also degrade to the same primal level where undesirable things can be accepted to happen without too much concern, as nature is unpredictable and chaotic.

The Finnish news media are littered with egalitarian rhetoric, with heavy use of the term 'equality', but if you ask the simple question "What do you mean by 'equality'?" you are likely to be attacked, because the person using the word doesn't understand it and doesn't want to admit it. And the easiest way to understand why equality is being pushed everywhere is to understand the nature of the concept as a Christian/Stoic ideal related to the history of Europe via the Enlightenment, but one that has been perversely separated from this original meaning of equality in the eyes of God. In this *Christian religious* sentiment, nobody can be seen as an authority over another, because God reigns over all and judges the living and the dead, and therefore a good Christian will see his brother as an equal and won't condemn him out of envy for his superior position or better fortune, or out of contempt for the sins and weaknesses that he shows, which we all show. This equality is *spiritual* in nature, and the modern European feels this spirit in his guts and bones and is holding fast to this absolute basis of equality; it's just that he has forgotten what it means. Not because of bad luck or chance, but due to *forgetting who he is*. The 21st-century European, in any European nation, faces serious issues and problems that he is unable to overcome. The obvious outcome of these developments will be the loss of equality, and this outcome is the highest justice, because Europeans are in a way sleepwalking into this fate, in a state of unawareness. Someone who goes for a walk in the woods wearing his best garments will get his garments soiled, muddied and torn, and nobody in the world will think him unlucky. We will forgive him because he forgot—we all forget—but the essential question is only if he can forgive himself. What was the value of these best garments? How long did it take to sew them? The denial of the shame he would feel, and the

PART III. SOCIO-POLITICAL ANALYSIS

related anger, are the opposite of the calmness of enlightenment and wisdom. It was easy for me as a Finn to agree with a Dutchman the other day that what we both need is a revival of tradition to claim back our pride; but I don't mean simply nationalism and much less national socialism, but the Western spiritual wisdom that spans generations and that we all possess even in our basic concept of equality but just seem to be ashamed of. It seems to me that the whole of Europe has been made to feel shame about the past. And this is senseless because I see no other major shameful thing that individual nations have done except having slowly and gradually accepted an external power to rule over them.

But we don't see surging crime rates, violent attacks and such things... doesn't this mean that people are being moral? No, it just means that people are taking the safety of modern society as a given and acting within common courtesy; they have been to some extent institutionalized not to question the social order, but this doesn't mean they would have it in them to rebuild the social order if it collapsed. The immediately emerging acts of immorality will not be ones that attack the law; rather they will attack the subjective reciprocity of morality by abusing the expectations of moral norms, but without breaking the law unless the perpetrators can be confident they won't get caught. Whatever is not in practice punishable but that is traditionally expected in terms of conduct will be subject to heavy abuse of the norm. The following types of activities will increase:

- Deception via lying and trickery

- Attempts to act anonymously; identity theft where one doesn't expect to get caught

- Disregard of health, such as hedonistic eating habits, lack of exercise and substance use

- Adultery and prostitution, under a legal cover

- Indecent sexual relations or ones that deviate from the norms, paedophilia

III-3. THE DECLINE OF MORALITY

- Unstable partner relations based on a concept of love that deviates from norms

- Gambling, stealing, tricking people into parting with their money

- Pretending a significantly higher social status than one has

- Acts of punishment, such as stealing items from friends, spreading false rumours, slander

- Stalking, deceiving or forcing others into sexual relations, rape where one expects to get away with it

- Reckless spending and living beyond one's means, either by knowingly hurting one's personal economy or by getting others to pay

- Unwillingness to work; attempts to minimize one's responsibilities at work

- Being oblivious to the suffering of others, such as hurting animals or turning a blind eye when one witnesses suffering.

I came up with this list by reversing the Seven Deadly Sins and thinking of actual cases where this might happen or where I know that it is happening, as I myself have often been struck by normal adults' capability to act like children. These are in practice acts of children that exist at Kohlberg's level of no morality, where the basis of one's action is whether one expects to get caught or not. At the same time, they are behaviours that many people today would see as rights instead of feeling that people should somehow be restrained from this kind of behaviour. These people would be the ones who, in a more restricted society, would be inhibited from this sort of behaviour by being forced to follow the norm, despite themselves lacking the sentiments that would produce the norm. They would be the ones of whom we would perhaps say that they are not bad people but are better at following the example of others. The example of others produces the norm but it is the enforcement of the norm that ensures people consistently follow it, and therefore the norm will lose its power after it becomes acceptable to deviate from it. This will have the natural counter-effect that people will also be searching for security from various other communities where moral behaviour is somehow enforced, such as religious sects

PART III. SOCIO-POLITICAL ANALYSIS

or ideological communities where commitment to ideology is seen to compensate for personal-level moral faults. I hear people constantly downplaying the importance of religion, but we don't actually have any institutions that work to enforce—in principle—these behaviours that still constitute our norms; they think they are somehow automatically followed, but what would be their origin if not religion? They *could* have another origin, in principle, but *de facto* they don't, because we, in the West, are Christian. Let's consider then what it would take for us to put in place another moral inspiration to replace religion, as it seems that many people have issues with religion. This new moral inspiration would need to be one that lays out these rules *in writing*, and at the same time in a way that makes sense to people so that they accept them as authoritative, as people will not follow an authority they don't find is working in their best interests. As a religious teaching they make sense, but this will only happen *in a context where the teachers of these principles are themselves also adhering to them*. Anybody who tries to enforce principles he doesn't visibly follow himself will simply be a clown in the eyes of both children and adults. So one can't simply devise a new system; one needs to express this system in both word and action, and to do so consistently so that the whole school is organized tightly around these principles in such a way that a breach of the principles by the teachers will also be punishable. And now if we ask ourselves what it would take to create this kind of a new religion or an active communal system, we can see that the task becomes significantly easier when the system is *not moral*; doesn't promote any principles that would place restrictions on behaviour that new adherents would find confining or difficult to conform to. And this is why we see many cases where somebody has created a new 'religion', say, the Church of Scientology, the Church of Satan, Wicca, Thelema or such, the moral codes required are minimal at best, or, consistently in the case of the pagan religious attempts, completely absent and replaced by something like "Do whatever you want". In luring adherents from the main religion, the successful formula has been to offer something similar with a lot of communal activities, rituals and incantations, a sense of identity, etc... but essentially with fewer restrictions and more personal liberty than what the main religion would require. And thus we can see that the activity of creating a *moral* community or system has been particularly difficult, as such a cult would have to be built according to the teachings of a person who himself is highly moral and who has proved this by his actions and, in the case of our major religions, an actual martyr whose legend is continued by his followers. If this wasn't the case we surely would have already seen the creation of such moral systems by these vocal critics of the main religion.

As empathy is *the* fundamental moral component behind the reciprocity of morality, we have a tendency to understand morality via the idea of *empathetic understanding* where one *identifies with the feelings* of another, mainly via his suffering, and feels an understanding of him and a desire to help him. We tend to think that we are being moral simply by having an empathetic feeling towards the suffering of another person and a desire to help them. This would be the way we Western children of Christianity would easily understand those in a weaker position, such as immigrants, animals or minorities; because I myself will try to avoid suffering, I understand another who behaves in a similar way. But if I do this and conclude that the pity or empathy is the source of my morality, I am ignoring the moral *framework* of values that gives rise to my actions. This sort of understanding is in fact closer to acceptance, and it is possible strictly within a frame where the subject of the understanding feels he shares the values of the object of this understanding, and this would apply to the cases where we consider those who suffer to be innocent and not perpetrators of crimes against our values. If we see that somebody is suffering, but at the same time we don't share his values, we feel that his suffering is his own fault and don't feel this pity, but rather become cold and judgemental and turn away from his suffering. It is exactly at this point where only the truly religious person would feel pity: pity towards everybody including his enemy; universal compassion and pity that arises from a recognition of the universal suffering of people, but that doesn't contain acceptance because the values are considered wrong. Christians would call it mercy; it is where one would otherwise hate and be ready even to kill, but one chooses to forgive instead. We could say that this kind of understanding goes to the next level and is not very commonly displayed. To simplify; in the said case of identifying with the suffering of an innocent object, I am trying to act like Jesus, Buddha or Frodo Baggins, by methodologically using my pity and empathy, but at the same time my attitude towards the suffering is that it is caused by bad people, from whom we good and strong individuals should actively be protecting weaker individuals. But in the correct Christian or Buddhist understanding suffering is not caused by bad people; rather we all are sinners, evil and somehow defective in our nature, and therefore suffering, making others suffer and being affected by the suffering of others are all inherent to us. Thus, when we look at those who suffer via simply our feeling of empathy, we are not actually being understanding but irrational, inequal, anti-intelligent, anti-Christian and hypocritical, because this behaviour that comes under the flag of goodness and caring in fact equals the *moral condemnation* of those who cause the suffering. This can clearly be seen in the modern left-wing understanding rhetoric that is delivered from a moral high ground where the speaker is trying to portray acceptance in word but cannot help displaying fundamental moral judgement at the same time towards to those with an opposing viewpoint. And the source of this behaviour is clearly in our Christian heritage, because we are externally trying to act in accordance with a higher religious-moral ideal, but internally we have not yet understood the nature of suffering; we have not yet understood that Christ, whom we are to follow, volunteered for the cross exactly as an alternative to moral judgement.

The *immaterial* nature of knowledge/information and, say, all modern currency, which mostly consists of bits on somebody's computer, makes it a lucrative target for crime. If you look at information from the perspective of the subject, you'll find that trustworthy people in terms of morality—people who honour granted trust even against personal assets and with some higher rationale—are not very common. Rather, the information world typically relies on legislation where one would need to show that somebody has used confidential information in his possession in order to gain benefit, and these cases are known to be very difficult to solve, as sharing information with others brings mutual benefit in terms of the new immoral business. This has moved

III-3. THE DECLINE OF MORALITY

industry into contract models that employ denial of competition and impose severe penalties for information breaches. These legal threats are due to the difficulty of showing information theft in comparison with, say, bicycle theft. When we speak of information in the sense of private information which is something that can be stolen, to hold information is to do so subjectively; to hold it in one's mind. So, one would like to see the information society complemented with high morality—high awareness of justice regarding immaterial knowledge—to protect modern intellectual rights and property. But this we know not to be the case but the exact opposite of our modern world, which is characterized by immaterial property *and* blatant immorality. The modern world is so immoral that intellectual property must be protected by technical means, not by people's belief that stealing is wrong—simply because to information-age people "Thou shalt not steal" is reduced to a joke. The suppressed looting behaviour cannot be held back by remnants of good manners and some vague idea that causing harm to another human being is somehow wrong, but primarily by the fear of the consequences of getting caught. The technical means employed to protect private information are limiting its access and legal action against culprits. No companies can really refer to any moral system due to the fundamentally immoral nature of a corporation. Due to this lack of moral restrictions, one should expect to see lots of theft where people are able to hide their tracks. It makes perfect sense that globalization first took place via global money, and now there is an attempt to globalize formal authority. Money was first to globalize because it is immaterial and technological: using technology, two parties can talk securely from the opposite sides of the planet, and once they have reached a deal, funds can be similarly immaterially transferred.

In the global world corruption has become somewhat of a norm, and we live an era where public lying and reaching for personal gain are common. I believe the explanation to why our society is so bent on lying is because we are missing the traditional rites and rituals that exist to make lying impossible; we don't really publicly commit to morality and truthfulness like we used to. I'd like to identify two features that explain why democracy is vulnerable to corruption. The first is the adherence to the principle of charity in public debate and the reluctance to publicly address lying. An accusation of lying is considered a personal *ad hominem* attack, and democratic dialectic is completely unable to directly address the issue of lying. Our moral frameworks encourage us to trust others, in order to advance social harmony, but at the same time there are two things that work to do the opposite and covertly reward lying. The first one is the importance of deception in successful warfare, an art fully extended to any corporate entities in their competition for profit. Salesmen and corporate representatives habitually 'bullshit' (consciously mix truth with lies) because this approach allows them to mix diplomatic rhetoric with the intent to both weaken their competitor and portray themselves as bigger than they are in a competitive situation. The determined and successful salesman will scout your character to find out your likes and fears and use this information to their advantage in trying to make a sale to you. From his perspective lying is not wrong but *risky*, as it comes with the risk of clashing with the moral framework of the customer and aggravating the customer so he cancels the transaction.[221] The presence of bullshit means the presence of competition; it will be present in any trade where prices are not already set. Another thing to mention is that calculated risk-taking in general is a primitive *male* trait, so the risk of sales bullshit naturally (statistically) favours male salespeople. The other lie-rewarding area is *professional PR*, where lying is justified via the idea that the subject is professionally representing an institution or entity to project internal unity and a favourable external public image. As we believe individuals have the right to privacy and we don't expect them to publicly reveal humiliating things and also will empathize with white lies told to protect their honour in such matters, we will naturally extend this idea also to institutions and permit them similar behaviour. We would ex-

---

221 The end of the movie *Casablanca* is very inspiring. The corrupt police chief constantly plays both the roles of a moral law enforcement agent and a private businessman, and risks his position by protecting his private (corrupt) business partner against safely and formally complying with a foreign military authority... and the romantic setting of the movie portrays this as the moral choice, as if done in protection of the moral values portrayed by his partner that he doesn't himself share. So, the resolution romantically promotes liberalism and the free market economy: the moral protection of private business under the threat of the immoral military authority of a foreign nation.

III-3. THE DECLINE OF MORALITY

pect a PR manager to routinely handle this sort of task by putting forward statements that embody the company's collective opinion about some matter at hand that will draw public attention. But consider if a company got into a more humiliating situation where the public image needed to be more forcibly protected... in this case the PR manager would need to lie routinely, and this might not be the job for everybody. But this is where professional PR comes into play: the professional PR manager will be well paid for the task at hand; in practice, to ignore the fact that the lies put forward are not white lies any longer but rather a public image completely detached from the consistently humiliating truth about the company's state. On the level of rhetoric, lying is made easy by the objective conception of truth in which truth is considered a correspondence between what is presented and reality, and not subjective truthfulness. In terms of objective truth, lying can be presented as simply inaccuracy or accidental falsity, which can hardly be incriminating.[222] Subjective truth, however, would be testable by assessing the subjective requirement of subjectively adhering in action to the principles that one is presenting. The second invitation to corruption is the acceptance of secrecy in the actions of powerful actors, such as governments and corporations: by allowing secrecy one essentially provides a cover for checking whether presented statements are truthful or not. These features should be the key problematic in creating a society of integrity and harmony, and one could well ask why our society strictly condemns even the slightest physical harm done to another human being, while not condemning secrecy and lying, whereas deceitful words, which have their deceitfulness protected by a policy of secrecy, can cause far more harm. Consider, say, a plane crash that kills hundreds. Let's say that the cause was engine failure, and all the available evidence points to a failure in the engine, but there exists some policy of privacy that bars an investigation into the material cause. Now, the knowledge of the existence of such a policy will surely invite (not cause) the airline and the engine provider to deny any allegations of engine failure, as, firstly, they know that such allegations probably can-

---

222 It is particularly interesting to read news reports of US weapons deliveries repeatedly, and always *accidentally*—according to the reports—ending up in the hands of terrorist parties that, according to US foreign policy and all common understanding, should be their sworn enemies.

not have supporting material evidence, and secondly, they know that even if they were caught lying, this event would not have material consequences but only possibly repercussions on the level of public image. Then again, if they know that this would be the likely course of events in any case if such an event would occur, they might be tempted to plan their business in the knowledge that causing the deaths of hundreds of people is not a big deal, as it will not have repercussions based on its immorality. Therefore, the possibility of secrecy invites the abuse of that secrecy, and this is a natural process in which things may develop in the direction of corruption after the discovery of the opportunity. Secrecy doesn't create corruption but provides an opportunity for it, and opportunities generally invite opportunists. Things have moved on: lying has become a standard act of policy. Corporations always first publicly deny any allegations, and when met with countering evidence, they 'stonewall', meaning silence and refusal to comment, or insist the matter was down to an accident. This is the contemporary standard policy for any high-profile political actor and is being tolerated because these actors hold the power not to change this behaviour.

We are immoral because we don't think about morality, and we see cases of appalling behaviour and look away, because we don't have the framework to comprehend it. But this looking away results in guilt. If I lived in such a way that my actions were to a large degree in accordance to my understanding and my awareness of my own limits, I would naturally have justification for my action and feel content about it. I would not feel guilty for the things that lie beyond my reach. Living like this requires some invested time in contemplation of the justification of one's actions. But if I live in such a way that I am consciously neglecting something, then surely I will not be able to comprehend what I actually am neglecting... and then if somebody tells me I am neglecting such-and-such, I will become unsure about it and agree that 'maybe' this is the case. So, what happens next? Enter various world-saving NGOs to cash in. All they need to tell us is that they support some good cause and we pay, primarily not because we believe in the cause, but because we want to absolve our guilt somehow. In the Catholic Church the priests assign penance for those confessing their sins; this

III-3. THE DECLINE OF MORALITY

might take the form of reciting prayers or saying the rosary. So, there is a rather natural relationship between the feeling of guilt and admitting that we have done something wrong and submitting ourselves to a moral authority who we could trust to be protective of our souls via assigning us a penalty that will help us remember to behave better in the future. I would call this a sacred trust, because it is not just asking for a penalty but essentially trusting our souls to the hands of the authority assigning that penalty; asking for help from our religion in our state of being lost and helpless. And it is exactly this helpless trust that is vulnerable to abuse. A person with a guilty conscience is a sorry being, and susceptible to all sorts of abuse, as any calculating abuser of women knows; typically, childhood guilt is the source of excessively agreeable behaviour. An NGO 'chugger' soliciting donations will walk to you and, while not directly blaming you, simply act as if you should be paying up because you already are guilty. If you stop and talk with them, they will soon insinuate that you bear some guilt. And at that moment, if you feel you are guilty, you will soon be paying. This works because guilt is an emotion and not a reason, and thus is by nature irrational and associative. Looking at my own guilt; there are things that I know I am guilty of, and there are things in which I am not sure whether I am guilty or not... but in the case of these NGOs I know I am not guilty of the things that they are insinuating. But I have the asset that I am conscious of my guilt; a person who is not conscious will be a sucker for the associative guilt trip. There is also something that could be called real goodwill, and that would be distinguished from the mooching behaviours of NGOs by the fact that, firstly, they act silently and without praise for their actions, and secondly, they don't expect anybody to join unless from their own free will. Confronting people on the street in a semi-harassing manner is hardly like this; rather the charity muggers believe their cause deserves as much visibility as possible, which they feel, in turn, justifies their aggressive behaviour about it.

On the current path of modern society with its declining morality and blurred core conceptual framework, it's not surprising that the immoral come out on top. The Ten Commandments are so routinely broken these days that only murder still seems to have a taboo associated with

PART III. SOCIO-POLITICAL ANALYSIS

it. But today's immoral character is not necessarily a murderer; rather, an exemplary case would be a destructive narcissist illusionist who not only cares nothing for morality but is on a mission against it. By illusionist I mean a person who uses make-believe as his main tool for work. A perfect example of a modern-day 'baddie' would be the magician Aleister Crowley, details of whom are listed below.

- Crowley was clearly a classical pathological narcissist with a distorted self-image and delusions of grandeur that were sometimes manifested in hallucinations and out-of-body experiences.

- He had an aristocratic background and an inheritance that gave him a notable status, but no capability of producing any wealth due to a lack of any real skills and personal motives that defy all standard social norms. He dropped out of school after his father died when he was 11.

- Crowley developed his own pagan spiritual philosophy in the form of a secret society, Thelema, which was based on his combined research on languages, practices, symbolisms and rituals, and an ethical doctrine that basically instructed one to follow his will.

- Wherever he settled, he would try and create a personal cult of worship around himself and acquired a group of devout followers with his magical ideas. The victims of a narcissist are typically socially weak individuals who are naturally less suspicious and drawn towards the guidance of a leader-type.

- Crowley consistently made incredible and untestable claims that would justify his self-created symbolisms via visions or other unnatural experiences. Simply put, all the weirdness was there to attract attention and interest, and it would be explained via supernatural means, which makes it impossible to trace them. The display of magical skill was often an orchestrated attempt to gain attention.

- He repeatedly switched country and was expelled from both England and Sicily because of disapproval of his practices.

- Crowley had grandiose goals that were never achieved; instead, social catastrophes were dealt with by prompt escape and change of

III-3. THE DECLINE OF MORALITY

place. Common goals are what bind people together, so the narcissist sets grandiose goals because his psychological motive is to impress and to manipulate others into teaming up to support him in his effort to achieve the goal. Once this core rewarding part is done, the outcome of the project itself loses importance to the narcissist; he might change the goal multiple times along the way to retain the interest of the others involved and to escape doubts and accusations of lack of progress. Precisely because of this quality it is better if the goal is as unclear as possible, and best when it is esoteric, mystical and magical, so that there is no connection to the real world at all to bind the goals to. The shroud of illusion produced by the mythological occult is cast away with the very simple procedure of replacing the word 'magic' with 'make-believe'.

- Crowley tried to take over his former secret society (Golden Dawn) by force, entering their premises and changing their locks (in the same way the Nazis would attempt to seize power by bringing a machine gun to a meeting), and when he failed to do that, he founded his own secret society.

I believe this kind of abusive and dishonest personality would thrive in modern workplaces, because we lack the subjective understanding to uncover the pathological narcissistic character, but also because modern work is fast-paced and people switch jobs often. The word 'narcissist' is often used loosely just to describe a person showing some traditionally selfish or egotistic traits. Real narcissists, however, are illusionists that escape work and reciprocal responsibilities, and place themselves grandiosely above such needs. Instead they rely on their skills to gain the trust of powerful people and seeing what they can gain from that. Because we only look at the objective façade of people and not their subjective character, and because we tend not to judge people's words against their actual actions or achievements, we will be suckers for exactly this sort of man. This is to say that the more narcissistic we are the weaker we are against *flattery*. A modern-day magician would likely be a socially flamboyant individual who works exceptionally hard to impress but doesn't carry out any successful projects within the standards of his field. He will have very few real friends but will be revered within his group of choice, as impressing this group is his sole purpose, and if this purpose should fail, he will promptly escape, then switch group and continue his ways in the new group. He will be difficult to spot because it is painful to doubt the motives of a very popular individual, and he will likely be able to lie not only with a straight face but with good humour and joviality—so that people give him the benefit of the doubt and feel churlish if they suspect him of misdemeanours. In a serious case this kind of person can hide his identity and be ready to flee rapidly if caught, because he believes he has a low risk of getting caught. He may, for example, have fake credentials or have invented a fake history. Therefore in spotting this kind of individual it is key to pay every attention to his *actions* (and reactions) and no attention at all to his words... the question one should ask oneself is whether the individual is committed to what he is saying/promising/promoting or is he *simply trying to impress*? Often others around such an individual have moments of doubt, but they consistently repress these doubts, because if they turned out to be true, this would effectively end the friendship, which they value. Also, in exposing this kind of character one should avoid any kind of confrontation but instead find or record instances where he provides false information and compare it to real information. In the workplace this should be done with discretion and with no intention to publicly discredit the person unless there is evidence of manipulation. And this is the difficult part, because we live in a world of short-term employment and project work, and people's backgrounds are considered personal information; an employer might not have the means to find out whether the information the employee provided is actually true or not. I think in the worst case the employer would need to resort to private investigators to verify the person's work history and credentials; this is where the deception would most likely be found because the narcissist essentially is somebody who avoids responsibility and moves to a different job when outed; he might have previous jobs or communities that have already outed him.

III-4. The Invisible Hand

The real and novel challenge that the West faces in the 21st century is the challenge of the global economy, brought about by certain developments seemingly independent from each other but which, together, have created a very alarming scenario. The first development is the relationship that has grown up between banks and central banks, in which one important step was the world moving from the gold standard to free-floating currency following the unilateral decision of President Nixon in 1971. The freedom from any physical restraints for currency has led to rapid developments in the global economic system, and a situation where the institutions holding public trust and governing authority—the central banks—are in fact private corporations portraying a public image of their role that contrasts with the legislation that governs them, and via their wealth holding massive authority over their own public image. The practical and legal division of roles between banks and central banks seems to be unclear to almost everybody, and it seems to me that the banks themselves like to protect these details as business secrets, as private corporations typically withhold any information related to their business and would only publish such information when it benefits them or they are compelled by law. The absurdity of this confusion about the role of banks is exemplified by the head economist of Finland's Aktia bank, in a live radio programme being confronted with the basic question: "Who creates money and how?", failing to answer the question and calling it absurd.[223] I would draw a parallel here between a computer expert being asked a question about how data is concretely stored in a complex computer system. This could easily and happily be explained and exemplified by any computer expert, let alone the head computer scientist of some major

---

223 The live radio programme was "Mikä maksaa?" by national *Yleisradio* on 25.1.2013; the economist was Timo Tyrväinen and the prearranged guest presenting the question was Ville Iivarinen. I will also translate the programme description: "Mikä maksaa? searches for answers to normal citizens' questions about economy. Where is our money going to? Who ultimately determines the direction of money? What should citizens know about local and global economy?" http://talousdemokratia.fi/?q=node/61 [26.12.2019], http://areena.yle.fi/radio/1811853 [26.12.2019].

PART III. SOCIO-POLITICAL ANALYSIS

organization. The message is: "Don't *you* dare to ask if *the Emperor* has clothes", and the attitude of secrecy and superiority has been enough to motivate long-term mass protests (the Occupy Movement) on Wall Street, which spread to many major US cities and to other countries. Just recently, the Bank of England published an article[224] that aimed to clarify the concepts of modern banking, in which it bluntly admitted that the most common conceptions that people have about the role of banks between people and money are misconceptions, and that these misconceptions are even taught by many textbooks about the economy. Banks have been distributing false information about this. According to the report, money is being created by the bank whenever a new loan is made and is not controlled by central banks in terms of the quantity of loans and deposits but in terms of monetary policies that mostly target interest rates. So, it turns out that modern economic development has been in the direction of (secretly) developing banks into a role of mortgage-granting machines that are centrally controlled, as most people don't have many savings but are granted much bigger mortgages. Also, they can provide their customers with false information about their policies and functions that are invisible to the customer, portraying a 'customer-friendly' image of only handing out money that they have somehow acquired and is already in their possession. To think of money being created upon the signing of credit agreements presents a completely different ethical question; it is revealing that the banks don't want to show the reality, because money was never designed to be created this way, and it seems that banks have grown so powerful that they have managed to change the way money is handled in secret. This is not the only outrageous thing modern banks do; HSBC bank has been reported to sometimes stop customers from withdrawing money unless they provide a satisfactory reason for wanting to do so,[225] and to refuse cash deposits without proof of the money's

---

224 M. McLeay, A. Radia and R. Thomas of the Bank's Monetary Analysis Directorate, 'Money creation in the modern economy', Quarterly Bulletin 2014 Q1, Bank of England, https://www.bankofengland.co.uk/quarterly-bulletin/2014/q1/money-creation-in-the-modern-economy [26.12.2019].

225 G. Stafford, 'Bank refuses to give customers their money unless they can prove a good reason for needing it', *The Daily Caller*, 29.1.2014, http://dailycaller.com/2014/01/29/bank-refuses-to-give-customers-their-money-unless-they-can-prove-a-good-reason-for-needing-it/ [26.12.2019].

III-4. THE INVISIBLE HAND

origin.[226] Such policies obviously work to increase the bank's control over the customers' accounts, and tend to be revoked quickly when brought to the public's attention. Increased control means more opportunity for the banks themselves to use the accounts for money laundering via cycling it between accounts to hide its origin[227]; we know that because of its money laundering policies HSBC is punctilious in refusing deposits of cash from pensioners obtained through motorcycle trades, while at the same time overlooking the monitoring of £38 trillion worth of transactions from places such as the Cayman Islands and Switzerland.[228] The Nordic banks Nordea and Handelsbanken frequently get fined by Sweden over their deficient money laundering policies,[229] which effectively mean that the banks have not carried out surveillance of customers who try to channel funds to hide their origin. And let's not forget the Libor scandal, which involved a group of the largest European banks and resulted in losses to homeowners estimated in the billions because of bank clerks routinely manipulating interest rates for a period of 20 years or so. These stories should prove beyond doubt that the banks have completely betrayed the trust of safeguarding people's money, and are now out of control, being above legislation, with no transparency at all about how they create and handle money. I'm not saying any bank is running a money laundering racket of any kind, but playing the devil's advocate, consider *if* we indeed lived in a world in which a bank was secretly running a racket of, say, £38 trillion... do you think in this case a fine of £640 million is sufficient to make this racket non-profitable for the perpetrator? Moreover, the willingness of banks to give loans suggests that it is profitable

---

226 S. Dunn, "'I've been a loyal customer for 50 years, but HSBC wouldn't take my £7,300": Why banks won't let you pay cash into your own account', This is Money financial website, http://www.thisismoney.co.uk/money/saving/article-2551823/Why-banks-wont-let-pay-cash-account.html [26.12.2019].

227 The standard method of money laundering involves the method of *layering*, which means "a series of conversions or movements of the funds to distance them from their source". See 'What is Money Laundering?', Financial Action Task Force (FATF) website, http://www.fatf-gafi.org/pages/faq/moneylaundering/ [26.12.2019].

228 R. Davies and T. Shipman, 'HSBC let drug gangs launder millions: First Barclays, now Britain's biggest bank is shamed – and faces a £640 million fine', *The Daily Mail*, 17.7.2013.

229 N. Magnusson, 'Nordea, Handelsbanken are Fined for Money-Laundering Breach', Bloomberg, 19.5.2015.

to keep people indebted, and it might be noted that all over the world it is organized crime that runs the racket of granting loans to desperate individuals who are powerless in the face of a powerful syndicate. And this development is just a part of the *privatization* development that involves families; privatization in globalization is the modern form of colonialism and involves somehow acquiring the ownership of a previously locally owned property or resource, and then lending it back to the original owner. Typically, the acquisition price is a fraction of the profits made by this business, because the original owner's desperation is abused in the transaction. The earliest known innovator in this area was Marcus Licinius Crassus, the founder of the first Roman fire brigade around 115 BC, who made his fortune negotiating over the sales price of burning houses with their owners, while standing next to the house with his fire brigade, which would only put out the fire if the house was sold. Modern privatization involves any natural resources, farmland, businesses, etc. The modern banks also seem to be striving to be the first to establish offices in countries where a government has been overthrown by means of war. There is no argument to support such privatization, which effectively creates slavery: private ownership has in the liberal sense been in exactly the opposite role, making it possible for entrepreneurs to do business on their own instead of having to submit everything to a central controlling power. The global ownership acts simply as a relationship in which executive power, which is not actually present but located elsewhere, uses the local branches to make as much profit as possible—no different from colonialism except that the profit is not necessarily made in exports of materials but can be made in the interests of the indebted people, once the country in question has established a bank to trade their local work effort into global currency. After that, the slave-runner gets profits in his own currency from the working hours of his offshore slave. The word 'privatization' is completely misleading in this global context, as it gives the impression of something shifting from public to private ownership. But consider a country where say, rice fields are under government ownership: privatization would mean passing this ownership from the government to certain individuals or e.g. families or unions of the people working in those fields. However, the government selling

III-4. THE INVISIBLE HAND

the fields that belong to a nation to a *foreign* multi-national company is not privatization at all but national surrender. Now, since there is a profitable business for multi-national companies in making global acquisitions, it becomes more valuable for the profiteer the more he can manipulate the price of the acquisition and expected rental revenues. The best profit is made when the purchase is made when 1) the original owner is completely desperate and 2) one will be able to somehow increase the productivity after gaining control, such as by lowering the salaries of workers and increasing their working hours—of course consideration is needed to keep the business running instead of harming it by overexploitation; a smart extortionist will not kill his subjects. And the best opportunities for this sort of manipulation arise in *war*: people negotiating for their properties are negotiating for their lives, and wars tend to end quickly, after which businesses may resume operation but with increased efforts. The outlook towards this has not changed from the times when emperors sent their armies to conquer distant lands; these days the corporate emperors will assert: "We need another war!" and actively promote war until they get their hands once again on the golden opportunities. Man has not changed; it is just that the organization of society has brought humanitarian values into public discourse and moved war negotiations into secrecy. It is not rare at all to meet a person who supports war. But another thing that the global business empires give rise to is harm to nature and environmental catastrophes, because the distant ownership separates the executive power from the local harms that they cause. In addition to the occasional oil spill, the most recent of these developments is fracking, or hydraulic fracturing, which is a rather old technology but something that has been finally employed in this new globalist spirit—and, of course, since it hasn't really been done before, there is no precise way to estimate the environmental harms of pumping hundreds of tons of pressurized liquid into the ground.

The liberal freedoms given to private corporations have developed into a perversion of justice where the freedom of corporations to withhold even the most basic information from their customers trumps the ideals of transparency that we have long imposed on our democratic governments. The intent to rule out corruption and nepotism by insisting on full disclosure has failed in a manner so blatant that it is completely unrealistic to expect any change unless there is a major global crisis. The second major development is the impact of the Internet on global communication. The idea that democratically elected officials cannot meet with representatives of the business world without being subjected to doubts about conflict of interest has traditionally been policed by the media, in the sense that, for example, physical meetings parliamentarians hold with business leaders will be monitored by journalists. Also, legal authorities have had some control over telecommunication connections through the availability of call records. But secure Internet protocols and the availability of mobile technologies have in practice made any effort to try and monitor collusion by means of telecommunications hopeless. If the representatives of business and politics want to confer, they don't have to travel to a remote location under a pretext and worry constantly about arousing suspicion; they will have many means available for holding discreet remote conferences. They will also have many partner organizations available that operate to establish trusted negotiations as a consultancy service under legally binding non-disclosure agreements. This means that for any business or public official that wants to establish discreet connections with other parties, this opportunity is available for a reasonable price. The functionality of Internet networks that manage to effectively hide the identity of their users is publicly well known because the police need to deal with small-scale criminals using those networks to organize criminal activities. However, nothing is really written about the very obvious fact that these networks can be used equally effectively for high-level business negotiations that do not leave a trace, and very obviously the possibilities for the use of the Internet for the purpose of anonymity were exploited long before these technologies became available to petty criminals. This essentially means that any means to identify or monitor collusion between business and officials have gone. But secondly, the Internet has made history of the idea of capital investment where the investor would have to monitor stock markets through newspapers and TV and handle his investments via a trusted agent located on Wall Street. The money-making possibilities for

III-4. THE INVISIBLE HAND

gamblers have exploded with all sorts of available stock market options and automatically triggered stock software that has given financial markets a sort of unregulated no man's land status. And it's not just individuals who do this; the major European banks have been systematically carrying out credit rate manipulation, agents committing and executives overlooking. It is impossible to estimate the damage caused by this, as the manipulation targets the interest of customer loans with their worth calculated in trillions; the fines issued to the banks amounted to hundreds of millions. Then again, the very unity of companies has been severely compromised through at least the following features: 1) both experts and, more essentially, executive officers, regularly switch employers simply for personal business reasons, 2) executive decisions to lay off employees for productivity reasons can be avoided by outsourcing the employees and having the outsourcing company lay them off, 3) companies in practice don't have methods to consider internal problems by discussion; if there is an internal issue, instead of the problem being discussed between management and staff, a third-party consultant is hired to make recommendations for change, and from the perspective of the company's internal dynamic the consultant works for the management instead of the staff. All of these activities work against the basic liberal spirit of corporations, where the sole function of a listed company is to produce profit for its investors, which in itself is founded on the idea that the investors have invested their money in a company that they hold somehow valuable. Instead, the stock market behaves in such a way that investors rapidly move their money from one company to another in search of the greatest personal profit, executive officers switch companies on a fast cycle in search of the greatest personal profit, and there is no mechanism to establish whether the company is actually doing anything beneficial to anybody, as it can have no values in such circumstances. But the most alarming thing is that according to the 'liberal' trend in which smaller companies are being acquired and merged or come under the executive control of larger corporations, in virtually any given field of business this has resulted in the centralization of power to a relatively small number of independent owners; for example the American corporate media is controlled by five media conglomerates. This inevitably produces a monopoly effect because this small group of companies naturally share common business interests and, instead of keeping the market free, can establish collective control over the whole business sector. Formal competitors and enemies can hold joint business meetings to discuss matters of mutual interest in terms of keeping the whole business sector in a collective stranglehold instead of providing space for more competition.[230] This works for their collective benefit because emerging new businesses would threaten to diminish the business share of each participant of such a collective, and I believe this effect in general can take place where the number of competing but market-sharing parties is small and well established enough for a traditional *honour system* to form between these parties. Such an honour system by itself creates a certain trust via honour, and the honour involves sharing values about the *way* of conducting business. An analogous situation might be the way that the ancient Japanese *samurai* lords and warriors would study their adversaries' methods with respect and with a strong preference for having respectable adversaries who could also learn from them, rather than dealing with faceless, unidentified threats that these adversaries also collectively participate in fending off. Such adversaries gain the privilege of being approached with diplomacy instead of warfare, which is the basis of the formation of tribes, clans and nations, and the foundation of the long-lasting and relatively harmonious pre-democratic historical world state of only a few mutually warring national monarchs or clan lords. All in all, these features of the modern market economy are tantamount to saying that the liberal principles that once worked for higher equality and freedom of individuals as workers no longer promote such values, and this issue reaches to the very basis of our legal standards that regulate corporations that are based on the liberal model of a company that consists of a *unified group* or a family *bound to the same fate* that should be allowed to freely compete. The freedom of liberalism has developed to make the concept of a free corporation obsolete, and has diminished the role of such a corporation to a flexible mass that, instead of fulfilling its intended role of guaranteeing the independence of its constituting actors, bends to the will of the subjective business interest of executive

---

[230] Such meetings are portrayed in the *Godfather* movies I and II.

III-4. THE INVISIBLE HAND

power—no different in this respect from the formal practices of the secretively administered Roman Catholic Church bending to the will of its papal executive power.

The European Parliament has been reported to work consistently in a manner where "significant breaches of the rules [are] common" but the MEPs in charge of responding to these audits are silenced with legally binding non-disclosure agreements.[231] The EU also failed its tax audit every single year for 18 years in a row up until 2012 with the "error rate" describing unaccounted money showing an increasing rather than declining trend.[232] Given that these reports are factual, they easily allow one to characterize the EU, as it is today, as an organization strongly affiliated with organized financial crime. But I would expect no better from an organization that contains independent organs of non-democratically appointed executive power, such as the European Commission, and can 'audit' itself in private or to organize investigative hearings on its administration in a form of private confession. The EU has proud goals to promote democracy but it is in itself lacking democratic administration, very much like an institution that promotes a life without sin, but one whose administration itself is in practice beyond the capability of sin, because nobody will dare to ask if they are sinful or not; only the institution is allowed to investigate the sins of the people it rules over. There is a case to be made regarding highly public events some years ago in Kiev, where it so happened that the government was overthrown and replaced by one openly supported by the EU; an event the media later widely blamed on Russia. But the capability for the Ukrainian people to overthrow their government sounds unlikely in the face of the fact that EU aid money was spent particularly on training riot control troops.[233] Now,

---

231 B. Waterfield, 'Scandal the European parliament tried to keep secret', 20.10.2011, *The Daily Telegraph*, http://www.telegraph.co.uk/news/worldnews/europe/eu/8837224/Scandal-the-European-parliament-tried-to-keep-secret.html [26.12.2019].

232 B. Waterfield, 'Audit "seriously undermines credibility" of EU spending', 6.11.2012, *The Daily Telegraph*, http://www.telegraph.co.uk/news/worldnews/europe/eu/9657673/Audit-seriously-undermines-credibility-of-EU-spending.html [26.12.2019].

233 M. Holehouse, 'British aid to train Ukrainian riot troops', 10.3.2014, *The Daily Tele-*

one might expect such humanitarian aid money to be duly used to protect the Ukrainian people's human right of stable government (UDHR Article 28), but the news article mentions that the opinion of the European Commission is that "it is 'ridiculous' to suggest the Interior Troops' job is to protect the government", which should raise some serious questions about what the humanely funded riot troops were supposed to be doing in Kiev in the first place, if not to protect the government and social order. To put it into a moral perspective, one might wish to ask: "Is there anything worse than the violent overthrow of a democratic government?" and answer: "The violent overthrow of a democratic government using money that was meant for sick children." This is a good example of how financial crime and war and murder are directly linked: dirty money can fund wars. As another example, a report in 2013[234] suggested that the EU promote "media freedom and pluralism" as a reaction to media convergence resulting from centralized private media ownership. This is a noble goal because this is a serious issue, but the suggested way of doing this was to place national regulatory organs under centralized control to ensure that national media organizations comply with European values: to create a system of censorship to promote media freedom. Another example is the "transatlantic trade agreement" that works under the pretext of "delivering growth and jobs" but which effectively aims to nullify independent European governments' freedom to control their markets in the face of the "investor protection" needs of transnational corporations, meaning that the corporations can sue governments that resist their products in a manner that bypasses local courts.[235] A leaked document reveals that the European Commission aims to advance the agreement under a process of systemic secrecy. These publicly disappointing but theoretically predictable results of EU behaviour are very similar to e.g. the UN predictions regarding climate change because they are cre-

---

graph, http://www.telegraph.co.uk/news/worldnews/europe/ukraine/10687948/British-aid-to-train-Ukrainian-riot-troops.html [26.12.2019].

234 B. Waterfield, 'Leveson: EU wants power to sack journalists', 22.1.2013, *The Daily Telegraph*, http://www.telegraph.co.uk/news/uknews/leveson-inquiry/9817625/Leveson-EU-wants-power-to-sack-journalists.html [26.12.2019].

235 G. Monbiot, 'The lies behind this transatlantic trade deal', 2.12.2013, *The Guardian*, http://www.theguardian.com/commentisfree/2013/dec/02/transatlantic-free-trade-deal-regulation-by-lawyers-eu-us [26.12.2019].

ated in a similar faulty manner: not with smart, educated people discussing the issues over a round table, but on the level of politics with the feel of an invisible hand. There is a sense that somebody powerful has already made the decision of the correct political outcome and is just using different political methods to advance that agenda, in an atmosphere of urgency and pressure to make political decisions before understanding the related problematic, and, in the case of climate change, with a manipulative tendency "to accentuate or even exaggerate the damage caused by climate change", as one academic study[236] found. And this is very well explained, in the absence of a simpler explanation, by assuming that this is the case; the related financial business decisions have already been made by the concentrated managerial ownership of the relevant businesses—protected by business secrecy. I haven't found any European studies about this, but I would expect that globalization has brought an increasing trend of political party heads enforcing party discipline. Party heads and key figures can be powerful partly due to their ties with industry, and if they are allowed to steer the party votes around their own opinion, this will have the effect of allowing corporate opinion to easily trickle down to the parties without the corporations having to persuade every single MP through lobbying. Strong party discipline is something we would relate to Chinese and communist government, not the modern democracy where MPs are to supposed represent the needs of the citizens and it is common for individual MPs to meet with citizens and to address their issues in their work in policymaking. In Finland, strong party discipline seems unconstitutional but the country lacks both legal precedents and a constitutional court to determine whether this is the case. Centralized corporate ownership is shown by most empirical studies to have a negative impact on transparency and the quality of governance practices, but in order to get a better picture of the extent of centralization of ownership in multi-national companies, one can scrutinize the public stock ownership data to make the terrifying observation that a relatively small group of banks and holding companies constitute the <u>largest stockholders</u> in any of the largest companies in the world, and these

---

236 F. Hong and X. Zhao, 'Information Manipulation and Climate Agreements', 24.2.2014, *American Journal of Agricultural Economics*, vol. 96, issue 3, April 2014, pp. 851—861, http://doi.org/10.1093/ajae/aau001.

companies at the same time are the largest stockholders of one another. This situation is a clear sign that everything is not as it should be. The *first global assessment* of the structure of corporate *control*[237] was conducted only in late 2011, and applied network analysis to determine the indirect stock ownership structure of existing companies which, in turn, is equivalent to control, as shares translate to voices in corporate decisions. The findings were disturbing and confirmed the worrying rumours and fears. Within the network of the 43,060 OECD-defined transnational corporations listed in the world at the time, a *single group* of 737 tightly interconnected (owning each other's stock directly or indirectly) corporations were in effective control of 80% of the whole structure, in addition to which there was a 'core' of 147 tightly interconnected corporations that had control over 40% of the whole structure, and formed a closed circle by having their stock owned almost exclusively by members within that same group. As the study mentions, this is counterintuitive, because "one could expect inequality of control to be comparable to inequality of income across households and firms, since shares of most corporations are publicly accessible in stock markets", and this raises the question of why the markets are not behaving freely, as we might like to imagine them doing. The study acknowledges earlier observations of similar interconnected structures having underlain motivational explanations such as "anti-takeover strategies, reduction of transaction costs, risk sharing, increasing trust and groups of interest". The second intuition the study demolishes is the one that corporate wealth and control would be proportional to each other, as it finds that instead "network control is much more unequally distributed than wealth ... in particular, the top ranked actors hold a control ten times bigger than what could be expected based on their wealth", which means, I believe, that a great number of the core companies in the structure are holding companies with the sole function of holding ownership of shares and thus control over other companies. But there is also something very counterintuitive in the fact that we have only recently found out about this—these corporations dominate our lives in such an absolute manner that walk-

---

[237] S. Vitali, J. B. Glattfelder and S. Battiston, 'The Network of Global Corporate Control', 26.10.2011, *PLoS One*, http://doi.org/10.1371/journal.pone.0025995.

III-4. THE INVISIBLE HAND

ing into a shop one immediately sees an array of brands owned almost exclusively by transnational corporations. One would therefore expect information about these companies to have been widely scrutinized, reported and investigated. So, why hasn't such information been available? Don't we like information, do we lack computers to calculate statistics? It is an interesting trail of investigation how the managements of these companies can be linked to financial groups such as investment banks or dynasties. This is interesting because it makes it a plausible idea that, as I mentioned earlier, the companies in the modern setting are not required to produce anything valuable, as we would like to imagine them doing according to liberal values. Such companies rather function as a front to give the impression of a wide diversity in ownership via smaller stock percentages by individual companies, and to effectively disguise centralized ownership and government of these entities: to provide the cover required to avoid moral outrage caused by the world's centralization of wealth and financial inequality. It is difficult to estimate the true wealth of a dynasty or a similar group of investors that are commonly rumoured to be significantly wealthier than the listed richest people on Earth, but who persistently don't receive any publicity for their activities but rather seem to actively work to hide their ownership and control. It used to be that wealthy individuals were known to be wealthy, but these days the wealth is in globally distributed ownership and well-hidden foreign bank accounts, always basically in an immaterial form. A modern intellectual should understand that groups such as the Jews, the Rockefellers or the Rothschilds can be wildly theorized over by, as it were, amateur thinkers, and the related anti-Semitic sentiment was used for an evil purpose by the fascist rhetoric, but when a group or an institution can be observed to behave in an actively secretive manner, this will quite naturally arouse suspicions and an active rational interest in explaining observations. After all, less publicity equals less regulation, and for any group wishing to test and extend the limits of legislation there will be little chance of being reported to the authorities for financial investigation, as reporting financial crime always requires a separate investigation. The word 'business' doesn't imply that the business is legal, and in the world of business, one can weigh the potential benefits against potential risks even in disregard of law. In any case, public political discussion involving intellectuals, critics, philosophers and so on, has almost vanished or is now confined to a small number of public intellectuals. This is because political decisions are no longer discussed but just communicated, and what is left for the occasional critic and public moral outrage is just the controversial decisions already made, and the critic will find that the more cogent his criticism the more he is met with indirect political resistance involving badmouthing and refusal of publication. Public critics are attacked so fiercely that there are not many who are willing to risk that kind of treatment. Unfortunately, in the contemporary state of the Western media, the major newspapers can, without any real consequences, consistently get away with publishing as news what in reality are provocative opinions of very weak reliability—even information reportedly originating from anonymous intelligence officers. And this leaves the majority of even educated Western minds in a state of total confusion about the reality of world events. Most normal people correctly associate the word 'propaganda' with something bad and related to war, but too many intelligent and educated thinkers still inhabit a world where the word is associated with demoralizing radio broadcasts or leaflets dropped from aeroplanes, instead of the modern reality where most intelligence work, such as sabotage and discrediting using methods such as systems infiltration, surveillance, producing deceptive information ("psychological operations"; "psyops"), document forgeries and identity crimes, is frequently carried out by private intelligence agencies that can equally subcontract government agencies or private companies.[238,239] Private contractors are running and benefiting from US drone warfare all around the world in a "secretive industry worth hundreds of millions of dollars".[240] Corporate agents are able to operate without trace from

---

238 P. Ludlow, 'The Real War on Reality', 14.6.2013, The Stone, *The New York Times*, http://opinionator.blogs.nytimes.com/2013/06/14/the-real-war-on-reality/ [26.12.2019].

239 T. Shorrock, 'A Modern-Day Stasi State', 11.6.2013, *The Nation*, http://www.thenation.com/article/174746/modern-day-stasi-state [26.12.2019].

240 A. Fielding-Smith, C. Black, A. Ross and J. Ball, 'Revealed: Private firms at heart of US drone warfare', *The Guardian*, 30.7.2015, http://www.theguardian.com/us-news/2015/jul/30/revealed-private-firms-at-heart-of-us-drone-warfare [26.12.2019].

the legal perspective, apart from leaks such as hacker groups and individual whistle-blowers that are able to disclose original and incriminating documents. There is no organ with the capability to monitor private intelligence contractors; according to retired US Army Lt. Gen. John R. Vines, there is no "agency with the authority, responsibility or a process in place to coordinate all these interagency and commercial activities [in the Defense Department's most sensitive programs]."[241] It is possible that some corporations are secretly trading spy information, which would give the possibility to e.g. extort individuals based on illegally acquired private data, and secondly, one can't control whether fabricated documents are being actively inserted into news or e.g. the decision-making process of political leaders. The common thought about spying on people is that if you have nothing to hide, you don't have anything to be afraid of, but private intelligence work is not designed to bring to light the truth about what you are doing; rather agents can be assigned to bring out any information that can be used to maliciously discredit you, either by itself or used together with fabricated information that cannot be shown to be false. The FBI recently confessed to prolonged and systematic flaws in producing scientific forensic evidence in the form of false expert testimonies in trials that often led to death sentences.[242] News like this doesn't exactly make one feel that one has nothing to be afraid of in the face of the constant increase of surveillance and authority, but the interesting part is the rhetoric where systematic abuse is blamed on science; the news is headlined "flaws in hair analysis" as if it was the fault of just some methodological lapse in forensic evidence analysis when "[o]f 28 examiners with the FBI Laboratory's microscopic hair comparison unit, 26 overstated forensic matches in ways that favoured prosecutors in more than 95 percent of the 268 trials reviewed". Such clear bias implies that if hair analysis wasn't sufficient to prove the defendant guilty,

---

241   An estimated 854,000 people were holding a top-secret security clearance in USA in 2010. Most of the intelligence work is done by private contractors working in secrecy. The publicly announced US intelligence budget was $75 billion. D. Priest, W. M. Arkin, 'A hidden world, growing beyond control', The Washington Post, 19.7.2010, http://projects.washingtonpost.com/top-secret-america/articles/a-hidden-world-growing-beyond-control/print/ [26.12.2019].

242   S. S. Hsu, 'FBI admits flaws in hair analysis over decades', The Washington Post, 18.4.2015.

PART III. SOCIO-POLITICAL ANALYSIS

I would expect the FBI to fabricate some other supportive evidence.

The state of the contemporary media can, I believe, be mostly attributed to its corporate nature and susceptibility to the previously discussed concentration of global corporate control. This shouldn't be interpreted as a claim that the entire media is somehow directly being controlled by or conspiring with corporations: one should correctly understand the standard conspiracy theory of a global super-entity or cult secretly controlling everything rather as *the simplest theory* to explain observations that don't make sense in the light of our standard image of how the world is governed. Any scientific thinker should actively promote the simplest theory based on the methodology of Occam's razor; there may be little evidence at the point in time when the hypothesis is formed, but the hypothesis is meant as a guideline to steer the process of active research into the subject at hand. The truth can be much more complex and operate differently on different institutional levels. Firstly, the executive level of media corporations has been shown to be susceptible to secretive corporate lobbying, as was revealed[243] to be the case some years ago with the BBC and their executives' position on global warming, which the then-head of news said had impacted a broad range of output. In this case the relevant information, regarding the executive meeting with a relevant lobbying group, was so well hidden that it came to light only after a private citizen challenged the corporation under the Freedom of Information Act in a six-year legal battle. But journalists have an all-time tough situation with the old non-digital way of publication being threatened, resulting in layoffs of thousands and deteriorating work conditions for the rest. A recent study[244] about the experiences of Finnish journalists shows cynical attitudes as journalists have become "errand boys for the news editors" or "assembly workers" and their freedom to choose their own topics

---

243 D. Rose, 'BBC's six-year cover-up of secret "green propaganda" training for top executives', 11.1.2014, *The Daily Mail,* http://www.dailymail.co.uk/news/article-2537886/BBCs-six-year-cover-secret-green-propaganda-training-executives.html [26.12.2019].
244 V. Luoma-Aho, M. Leppänen and T. Uskali, 'Errand boy or entrepreneur? Journalists' expectations of their future roles in Finland', *Central European Journal of Communication*, vol. 6, no. 2, 2013, pp.188—203.

has diminished. Journalists in the study also seem to expect the media business to see future budget cuts, worsening conditions due to digitalization, media convergence and accelerating news cycles, reduced quality of journalism, and a further increasing demand for fixed-term, shift-term, outsourced and freelance work. Global studies on press freedom hide these obvious facts, as World Press Freedom Index 2019 considers Finland to have the freest press in the world after Norway. However, the index bases its ranking on such things as violence experienced by journalists or direct censorship by government or the news providers themselves. Looking at just censorship, what is overlooked is the power of modern journalism in shaping people's opinions via online content with online comments that are typically heavily censored of any opposing opinions. In this sense, the censorship doesn't target journalists but the expression of public opinion that is now free to be shaped by the media houses. Further diminishing the responsibilities of the publisher, many of the 'expert' (paid) commentators are not professional journalists but media celebrities with private contracts or, say, online bloggers who publish only a part of their work under the media outlet's name but the rest as private citizens, which makes their journalist status semi-official and less likely to incur sanctions for ethics violations. The decline in the quality of journalism is actually worse than censorship: the silent unspoken threat of being fired or not having one's contract renewed is worse than a prominent (and legally accusable) censorship organ, as short-term work is not protected by the standard right of any profession where an employer needs to present a valid reason for terminating a contract. The employers can and do fail to renew fixed-term contracts, and if they like, they can even be blatant about it and tell the reason: "you wrote the wrong thing about the wrong thing". This action is very clear censorship but simply carried out in the new corporate media environment. This censorship uses *fear*: the censoring organ won't come and stop you before publishing but just tells you "you have been warned", and one day you might just find your desk emptied. And you might find that if you try to publish something controversial it might displease the publisher because of commitments they have on an executive level that you are completely unaware of. In this case your work might be scrapped without explanation. So, to the question of whether a journalist is free to write about whatever he chooses, the answer is positive: yes he is very free, with the small addition that the publisher retains the right to leave the work unpublished or to pull it from the digital newspaper even after publication, and to put the journalist out of work if he is not happy and to replace him with the next trainee from the queue at the door. Rather than a relationship of employer and employee where the employee has certain legal rights enforced for him by the workers' union and legally included in his contract, this relationship resembles the relationship of customer and service provider. Here the customer is paying to produce something he himself defines, and rather than relying on a particular service provider, he will naturally put the production out to tender to increase quality and decrease production costs. And how do such journalistic service providers compete for businesses? By not competing in terms of the quality of content but on the *quality and price of service*, which, from the perspective of the related business, translates directly to economic values: producing content that 1) is most likely to be read by the consumer, and 2) is done in the least time for 3) the lowest price. These qualities are obviously statistically best satisfied by pornography or nudity that is produced by copying from an already existing source. Another way to look at such service-provider journalists is that their work is motivated by two factors: 1) being interesting and 2) avoiding risks. Regarding political journalism this risk-avoidance produces a neurotic mass effect of political conformity, similar to what happens with people's political opinions when they are around authoritative and powerful figures: everybody will want to conform under the immediate threat of permanently losing their position, and nonconformists are treated harshly. And this environment is fruitful grounds for people who thrive in such an environment: people who like to have influence and to appear strong and opinionated but will have no personal moral commitments regarding the subject matter of their journalism. This enables them to conform to the will of the media outlet; people who will defend the jointly agreed political position of the media company against any of their personal moral sentiments. Journalists interviewed for the study cited above called the modern news commentators "celebrity journalists", and the reference is apt, as modern celebrities essentially are actors who are paid to represent. It is important to understand the business and legal truth behind the image: corporate media news commentators are *representatives of the opinions of their publisher* because in business *ownership translates to control* as stock translates to a voice in every decision. And in order to find out whose opinion is behind a corporate news source, just look at who owns the most shares in it. The role of the news faces resembles that of pop icons, because manufactured pop stars establish their fame on a fake 'identity'—the hard work of their production agency—using images borrowed from traditional bands, singers and songwriters; pretending to write their own songs and to choose their own clothes, views and attitudes. Similarly, a news commentator that has an attitude or political opinion and happens to work for a media company that highly approves of that attitude or opinion, is faking his service provider role in the image of an actual journalist. The only problem with this is that the model exploits the trust of the viewers and readers who take them for journalists instead of corporate puppets. The same exploitation has entered the general content of the news in something called *native advertising* in marketing jargon: native advertising is an ad that takes the form of the media platform, such as a news article. This means that your standard daily news can be full-blown propaganda that has nothing to do with news or journalism but money is being paid to a marketing expert who will find the best way to exploit the readers into supporting the opinion of the financier (the customer). The expert agency can show the customer a catalogue of different ads and some monitored figures about end-customer behaviour that portray the efficacy of the ads as a return of investment for the paying customer, so that he can consider the value of the investment before the purchase. Then again, the real journalists—those who are not commentators paid to represent the opinion of their employer—are completely restricted from presenting their personal opinions and are expected to fully comply with the values of their employer in public. Public deviations from the employer's values are not e.g. discussed in terms of career development but resolved swiftly. There was a time when journalism was ethical and professional, and the journalist was an esteemed professional, but it is very easy to verify that this time is long gone. The profession of journalism is not considered an ethical profession in terms of respect or salary, and the many ethical standards of journalism are followed simply on a formal technical level, in terms of objective considerations such as that sources are accurately quoted. But no modern journalist is expected to do investigative journalism or to follow *any* of the *moral* requirements of journalistic standards, such as (just to mention a few)[245] giving a voice to the voiceless, examining one's own cultural values and striving for neutrality, distinguishing between advocacy and news reporting, striving to ensure that governmental records are made public, avoiding undercover methods of gathering information, making certain that headlines don't misrepresent the article, showing compassion for those affected, and so on. On the contrary, the journalist is forced by his employer to prioritize work efficiency over any of these considerations. It is actually misleading to call such reporters journalists, as they are not following journalistic codes.[246] To understand how there can be such blatant code violation in this particular profession one just needs to understand that modern journalism, as an ideal of neutral journalism as the watchdog of the government in service of the people, is a very young profession with the first guilds founded around the year 1900. The Enlightenment revolutions were followed by an *ideal* of transforming the existing state propaganda press into a *free* press, and this ideal is today supported by laws that guarantee press freedom—a freedom for the press to act against the direct interest of the government—but the motive for the press to use this freedom has always been only private interest, which has been satisfied only via media companies' competition for customers. This is very unlike many professions, like doctors or artisans, where the need for professionals is driven by individual people's demand for professional services. Journalism is a peculiar institution because we Nordic social democrats tend to think that it should be state operated in order to be neutral as opposed to being driven by private interests, but rather the whole

---

245 Society of Professional Journalists Code of Ethics, http://www.spj.org/ethicscode.asp [26.12.2019].

246 The Finnish journalist Saska Saarikoski, working for our largest newspaper *Helsingin Sanomat* and the winner of the 2013 Journalist of the Year award, just tweeted that he knows who murdered Boris Nemtsov, and he implicates Putin in his tweet. I think this transgresses just about all the ethical standards of journalism.

III-4. THE INVISIBLE HAND

meaning of press freedom points to the liberal independence of journalism exactly from the state. Journalism needs to be funded somehow, and if people don't buy the newspapers or the news content, the news agencies will no doubt still take money from somewhere. Maybe the whole media institution should be reinvented from the bottom up by people willingly paying for quality journalism. However, I can't imagine this happening without re-invocation of journalistic ethics by the new media. I tend to think that, similarly to science, the integrity of journalism has been compromised along with the waning of the democratic spirit which essentially was a joint wish to place power in the hands of the people instead of kings and the pope, who were regarded as tyrants. A very intriguing suggestion, at least on the level of a thought experiment, is something I happened to overhear: what if figures in the media such as news anchors, commentators and so on, were required to wear the company logos of their benefactors, similar to the way athletes are required to present their equipment and Formula One drivers wear their team overalls with sponsor logos? We have the statistical formulas to graph the branches of corporate stock ownership behind all relevant benefactors, so why not make this live online information? I believe seeing the same companies behind every single news commentary would correctly dissolve the misconception that the media is free and the trust that is currently being abused because people remember, and wish to remember, the times when the printed word was more expensive and public misrepresentations had consequences. Furthermore, why not make it a legal requirement for companies to, according to agreed standards, reveal the breakdown of ownership of their stock, and have the news presented like this: "Hello, I am Greg from Happy Apple News, 54% Vanguard, 24% JP Morgan Chase". Or at least create a free online service that displays this information. All this information is public, but the problem is that the branches of control are not visible.

There is a constant trend of less and less public visibility in the administration that governs the people, which equals more and more power to our institutions of government. In Finland this can be seen in the trend for cities to move their activities inside owned limited corporations, as publicity and democracy are seemingly considered excess weight. One can identify a directly related and predominant modern phenomenon, which is the *abuse of the expert position*. In this model an expert service that involves trust in expertise is provided by an individual or a private company, but at the same time the provider uses this expert position to secretly create a need for more of this service. All *abuse* generally involves the abuse of *trust*, and practices considered abusive are ones in which a party places trust and an expectation of collective behaviour on another party, and that party uses this knowledge of the trust of the other party for personal advantage in contrast with collective advantage. The implied *relationship of trust* is the general distinctive quality of exactly *seniority*, which again is the distinctive quality of *expertise* in any line of work, and the correct use of the word 'expert' already implies trust; before becoming also a general job title for newly emerged lines of work, the word was an honorary title of somebody who, unless you yourself are an expert in the matter, is senior to you regarding the matter, and his expertise can only be credibly challenged by another expert in the same matter (the same has traditionally applied to e.g. the word 'philosopher'). Due to this honorary nature of expertise it is a status that requires reinforcement and it easily invites challenges and develops competitions and tensions between individuals, as has been the case with honour systems since the early days. The scientific *collaboration of experts* is a rather particular and exceptional expression, because the word 'collaboration' doesn't relate here to individual studies but to the overall fields of scientific study— scientists tend to be in this sense rather hostile and competitive towards one another but to strongly defend one another in matters regarding the status of the whole field, which reflects the honorary nature of science as a field of expertise. And such is the power of expertise in the modern "real world" where information and knowledge reigns, that when the senior expert speaks, others don't reflect or question his words and you can almost feel thunder and shaking ground as you see listeners bow their heads, tremble in fear and try mightily to hide their inferior knowledge and escape the public humiliation that an expert can heap on the ignorant with just a few well-chosen words. Because of this, the words "I don't know" are particularly rare, and I find this to ironically reflect the state of truth, as these words are most attributed to Socrates, the high beacon of truth. Everyone is acting as if they know, even when they know they don't know. They hide their lack of knowledge. In business, knowledge is used as a *weapon of power* instead of our conception of collective and collaborative scientific gathering of new information. And all this expertise, as with all seniority, is in its nature potentially abusive. Consider a private fire brigade being entrusted with fire safety and gaining access to people's homes: while they can help prevent fires starting in homes, they also learn the typical and particular fire vulnerabilities of homes and can exploit this information in secret to cause more fires and gain more business. Because of the private nature of the administration such abuse would go unnoticed by the public and possibly most of the employees, because in private companies the top executives wield absolute power and can control all the information that is shared downwards in the chain of command. And these issues are not questions of morality or public honour in terms of accusations, but the issue is the commonly known fact that *opportunity invites abuse.* The abuse of an institution is something that develops over time through established practices that remain static, trusted and unnoticed; just as dust gathers unnoticed in inaccessible corners of an apartment because such places are not noticed during routing cleaning. Regarding trust, I would like to draw attention to the behaviour of private US-affiliated anti-terrorism companies that exploit the US "War on Terror" and provide anti-terrorism expertise to trusting governments as a consultancy service—there's no need to present any accusations but an intelligent person can just take a look at the model of providing a service by a privately administered company and the trust that the business makes its money on. The dissemination of news about terrorism is a charade; such news typically originates from intelligence agencies, but sometimes it appears originate from the terrorists themselves; say, from an online video. Just think about it: the government has red-alert anti-terror laws that bypass the constitution to protect citizens from the threat of international al terrorism—laws that can prevent any news that is a threat to national security from being aired—but they won't do it in the case of the world's most wanted terror organizations that routinely get high news

PART III. SOCIO-POLITICAL ANALYSIS

coverage on any given day, and actually started getting this publicity after those laws had been passed. The media rather obviously acts in collusion with the government; it is a distinctive feature of information age political rhetoric to wildly publicize acts of terror and to publicly demand political action based on the high profile of these incidents. This is a very dark joke; it is as if these laws were there just to ensure that the terror threat gets news coverage. Because these acts cannot be reliably investigated and the suspects brought to justice, any nation that wishes to maintain a system of justice should first condemn *the act of publicizing* these terrorist acts. It is common knowledge that acts of terror are aimed to gain maximum visibility; therefore, giving these acts maximum visibility should be deemed as supporting terrorism, and the editors of media outlets that do so should be held responsible for breach of national security. Traditionally, any normal and mostly legitimate business might have indulged in activities that were against the law, and in addition, legitimate businesses, called 'fronts', were set up for the primary purpose of legitimizing organized criminal activity, but nowadays one can observe new corporate entities with increasingly vague descriptions of their line of business, such as simply 'consultancies', 'steering groups' or just 'groups'. This is not to point any fingers but just to point out that if somebody would like to perform some of the illegal activities that businesses did in the past, today the formal means for doing so are in practice much easier because one doesn't have to raise suspicions by observed activities contradicting public statements about one's actual business activities. Now, if you look at expert work in itself in terms of it being an *art* (in the sense of 'craft'), the historically esteemed positions have been e.g. doctor, craftsman and architect, but all of these positions are public in their nature, in the sense that the subjective quality of their work can be publicly inspected. This is something that does not apply to private consultancy or to, say, software development—in IT the buyer of bad code doesn't really have the option to complain publicly about his bad purchase, because companies buying bad software will not raise *moral* outrage as their own motives for the purchase are not moral. Business in a market economy is a cruel game where one's actions aim at gaining personal advantage over one's competitors instead of civil behaviour that carries

III-4. THE INVISIBLE HAND

a moral preconception of being beneficial to everybody and that has its roots in a public democratic system. From a moral perspective business loss can rather be getting one's comeuppance for doing something one shouldn't be doing in the first place. All trades employ an honour system with certain distinctive features, such as the following: 1) offering to pay too little is considered an insult on the *skill* of the trade partner, and 2) offering to pay too much is considered stupid and results in lack of respect. A similar relation of rivalry and respect generally exists between competitive athletes of similar level. The only friend who can empathetically understand a businessman is somebody involved with similar decisions—one who is most likely in the same kind of business, and in practice, one who is either his partner or his competitor. And this is the definitive truth about the fundamentally immoral nature of private business and corporations; morality would require empathy and a motive for common good, and no matter how many businesses try and feign this image for their customers by saying "We are like *this*", the truth is that both the legal foundation of a corporation and the brutal competition of business economy dictate that such a thing is an impossibility. Such statements should not be expected to be true in the sense of honesty; they are "corporate bullshit", carefully constructed and calculated statements whose sole purpose is deception. In the battle of corporations, these statements are used as weapons, just as money is used as a weapon. Corporations are not humane; corporations portray an image similar to how nations do in their diplomacy: not based on truth and morality, as children are taught to do, but based on what is most advantageous to them in a setting that is essentially a competition—it is just that in democracies there has been an increased demand for such political facts to be true and not lies, which is because, unlike in other forms of government, in a democracy politicians need to gain the trust of their own people by transparency. Anybody who plays badminton knows how important deception is, and anybody who reads the warfare classic Art of War knows, through the words of a military general and master strategist, that deception is the basis of all warfare; an essential requirement. This should be no news but self-evident; it's not *bad*, it's just immoral, and people should be aware that corporations are just as ready to compete aggressively over their market as they are to deceive their customers into purchasing their products. And this is not to say that corporations are bad, just that they are not people, and they don't come with the expectation of a *moral capability*, which is a very particular human condition. In order to decide if global corporatism is good or bad one should clarify one's fundamental conceptions of morality; who knows, maybe everybody in the world should all compete against each other as families, villages and tribes? At least we have conclusive evidence that this form of existence is possible for humans until some people started talking about such a thing as universal moral issues involving everybody and not just the interests of a group. I would go on to say that the primary challenge our world is facing today is the modern model of private corporation and the resulting loss of transparency of administration of this work that used to be made public through public offices, expert guilds, ethical codes and so on. While trying to maintain high ideals of democratic equality, the public model of administration, originally incorporated in the spirit of liberal liberation from the secretive practices of the Church, has been lost again and replaced by a new wave of secretive abuse, as private corporations are today commonly also doing the dirty work of public offices in a subcontractor role. It is easy to determine that no matter what the future mode of institutional operation will be, the essential thing that would need to change is the visibility to its administration, but so far the movement has been only towards more secrecy, which entails more abuse and less overall control in the direction of the development of mankind.

One could perhaps draft a general rule that the opportunity to create public unions, backed by supporting law, will sprout public unions for public interest, but the opportunity to create secret unions will sprout secret unions for private interest, similarly to how secret collusion has long been a common method for making collective profits in certain casino card games. Wherever there is a financial opportunity for mutual benefit within an institution, there exists a financial motive for collusion, and any established state of collusion within a system of government is called corruption. An institution, in turn, is a much later development of human cooperation than partnerships

III-4. THE INVISIBLE HAND

(seen in primate allogrooming patterns) and barter, and one can see that the social skills required for mutually beneficial partnerships are much more fundamental and widespread than the skill required for holding a particular office. This is why, when an institution is born, prevalent nepotism and favouritism are the necessary *initial* state, and their role can be diminished along the way by increasing independent surveillance over officials through methods like reporting and auditing that, in turn, are backed up by law enforcement. I already mentioned the prevalent economic crime within the EU, which seems to be related to the lack of law enforcement over the surveillance methods. In Finland, for example, the historical state of nepotism within doctors' rights to prescribe medicine has been successfully tackled with increased reporting. But in general I have met with heavy resistance when I have suggested that unreported crime within institutions is an inescapable norm in any country, and any situation where an official is using his authority to make decisions over some area while at the same time financially partnering in some way with a company or an organization that is a major actor in that particular field should be typically interpreted as favouritism. Such corruption betrays the trust and expectations that we place on appointed officials, and officials easily fall prey to it because the opportunity is so tempting. Such corruption creeps into a system slowly, using all the skills of the romantic thieves of old that we all possess and practice in various games in childhood. The intruder—one who can as well be a paid foreign agent, an adventurous hacker type or just a regular employee finding himself bored and unmonitored—uses the cover of darkness, entering the path he knows to be unlit and now unguarded. He peeks around corners to ensure nobody is watching while entering deeper into the forbidden area; if he feels threatened, he can go back and return tomorrow to continue the quest. Slowly, piece by piece, he will learn the vulnerabilities of the system and be in the position of abusing them himself and/or revealing them to the enemy for compensation. The common everyday opportunist could use the discovered vulnerability first for an insignificant personal profit to ensure that his plan of abusing it will go unnoticed. Typically, after discovering this, he would increase the profitability of his abuse, and this happens partly against his own will, because the emerged opportunity contradicts his own moral sentiments. It is common for opportunist criminals who get caught to report relief after getting caught because of the discomfort of being lured by the opportunity into doing what is also known and felt to be immoral. Furthermore, it is my belief that an experience of getting caught is actually an existential requirement for fully developing into moral citizens, but one that in an ideal case happens during one's youth by one's parents that provide the child with a model of social authority—one cannot learn to do right if one is either always restricted from trying to do wrong *or* if one does wrong and always gets away with it.

It seems to me that analysing crime is a challenging venture altogether and talking about crime generally brings an expression of extreme discomfort onto people's faces. I believe this is because it is subjectively difficult to think about such things, as thinking and analysing them is implied in *considering* criminal acts, and the subjective difference between analysing and considering is generally not very clear. Subjectively, avoiding criminal deeds involves somehow avoiding thoughts that tempt one to commit such deeds, and most people wouldn't want to talk publicly about such ideas because of the social association with crime—in many places planning criminal activities is considered a punishable offence. As such, crime is a field of life that most people don't really know anything about, apart from learning certain precautions against crime to incorporate in their lives, and this in itself makes the topic even less appealing, as one would be both restricted from arguing or debating and at risk of appearing ridiculous in the absence of knowledge. And as a final antipathy to hypotheses about criminal activity, it is known that certain psychiatric conditions involve a fear-induced paranoid tendency to interpret social observations from the initial perspective of general hostility against the self, and one might fear being associated with such generally distrusting groups, branded as crazy conspiracy theorists. Due to these difficulties we can easily accept on the level of abstraction that crime is common and pervasive at all levels of society, but due to these strong antipathies both learning and hypothesizing about crime is difficult. Furthermore, the idea of rogue elements inside governmental institutions is a considerably less

III-4. THE INVISIBLE HAND

appealing thought than the idea of rogue gangs roaming the streets at night, and what causes this is not actually our moral expectations about the behaviour of upper or lower class citizens, but that, unlike streets, the functioning of governmental institutions is to a large extent *unknown* territory to us normal citizens, and therefore we *are forced to* grant them a considerable amount of *trust*. We fear the subject matter simply because we don't know anything about it, which means our relation to it employs more trust than matters we can see or are well acquainted with. Yet it is a fact that exactly the trust we have in governmental institutions functions as the necessary cover for abuse within those institutions. I believe that the standard methodology to tackle this problem would be a *policy of distrust* like what a night watchman might apply in his work. He would understand the said problematic and perform his inspection duties by the book and not inspect just the company warehouse back alley because he suspects it could be a potential entrance for intruders, but inspect the whole premises methodologically, because every place requires regular inspection, ideally in a fashion that avoids predictable routines. The central criminal concept that relates to any executive officers, such as companies, governments or, say, media, is *plausible deniability*, which means that one is in a practical position to in one's actions break any laws, norms, standards, codes or expectations, as long as one is in possession of a means to deny accountability in the event of public queries or a criminal investigation. The concept is the legal equivalent of the old Gypsy admonishment: "You can do whatever you want but come home in a police car and I'll beat you proper." In cases of office, "I didn't see it" or "I can't remember" are poor explanations because norms hold officers to guard their posts and to remember their actions, but common methods to produce plausible deniability are for example that many other officials in similar positions can be shown, in the case of legal prosecution, to be guilty of the same breaches in standards; that an urgent matter had drawn the accountable person away from his post; that the officer in charge had been temporarily replaced, or that some general major accident happened to coincide with the event, such as hard disks or archives being destroyed by hardware failures or office fires. Plausible deniability is a methodology for planning crimes, because one can plan actions based on knowledge that there no basis exists for legal prosecution. Legal prosecution works based on evidence, and if one is in a position of being able to control the evidence of one's criminal activities, one has plausible deniability. Both companies and public offices today have lawyers at their disposal to provide them with detailed and recent information about how a potential legal prosecution would proceed; a lawyer doesn't assist in the planning of a crime when he simply provides technical legal consultancy and doesn't need to know about any plans, and in any case lawyers are required to withhold all information about their clients. A lawyer can provide information about both the chances of a successful legal action against the company or the officer and the potential consequences of such action, which gives an executive the opportunity to weigh the expected profits gained from illegal action against the risks of legal consequences.

It is my observation that many normally smart, cool and rational thinkers regress into angry denial when met with a mode of scientific thought hypothesizing over potential criminal causes of things that are not directly supported by the common level of political understanding provided by newspapers, and that are hypothetical because criminal activities by nature are intended to leave no evidence. A person can be brilliant but strictly limited to an evidence-based approach, and the case where one would need to form an opinion over a course of events of which there is no evidence because one could be expected to want to hide the evidence—the basic goal of criminal investigation and attorneys in a court of law—can become overwhelming to the extent of causing meltdown. Natural science operates with evidence, but it doesn't only use evidence, it also creates evidence by experiments and tests. What happens here is that just the thought of secretive elements within government is very threatening to our basic sense of security, and it may be that people who had their personal security compromised during their development find it easier to handle such knowledge without falling to fear-induced irrationality. Everybody knows that governments are involved with secretive elements at least to some degree. Stories of government corruption are ten a penny but trying to talk about it directly is not like chatting about the similarly unknown

III-4. THE INVISIBLE HAND

phenomenon of the weather. Instead, it is experienced as an attack on safety and is met with a neurotic laugh and a swift change of subject, as a friendly response, or with branding or name-calling as a less friendly one. And unlike gossip involving people's personal lives and decisions, which people generally don't like *talking* about but are counteractively highly interested in *hearing* about to the extent of creating an all-pervasive tabloid culture, this is a topic they very seriously don't want to hear about; their reaction is not one of interest but one of covering their ears and going "La-la-la!" Fear has the effect of destroying logic: one starts to either *avoid* the dreadful assumption or to *enforce* it, which disrupts the subjective detachment that is required in applying logic—an objective discipline about subjective matters—without error. Therefore, to be a serious thinker also means having the *courage* to challenge one's preconceptions, and this doesn't at all mean that one should believe any particular popular fantasies (conspiracy theories) about secretive governmental elements, but in order to hypothesize about such elements one needs to have the basic courage for such *hypothetical* thought. And most sadly or ironically, I find that people who most admire the accomplishments of modern science in their expressed opinions are at the same time the ones least capable of said hypothetical mode of thought required in all science. Real scientists are typically thinkers who will not rebut any assumption before considering it in the light of evidence, and after consideration will deem alternative assumptions likely or unlikely in the light of evidence; they will understand the role of an assumption in guiding the direction of the investigation where there is little evidence available or none at all. The work of a scientist ideally involves adhering to an assumption and trying to find evidence in its support, but at the same time using any negative evidence as an effort to correct the assumption and contradicting evidence in demolishing it. In this basic sense the method is equivalent to how a rational person would behave in acquiring better knowledge about any unknown phenomenon: making an initial guess based on what is known at the moment, and then getting more evidence and correcting that assumption as new evidence is brought to light, being less and less reliant on simply a guess, or until contradicting evidence makes further investigation pointless as the initial

PART III. SOCIO-POLITICAL ANALYSIS

assumption can no longer be defended. At this stage one should also take an introspective look at what went wrong in making the initial assumption. The very same method applies to politically controversial topics; where there is no visibility, one needs to rely on assumptions until evidence is available. In science, revolutionary results that change the minds of the whole scientific community are historically commonplace, and one can never deduce the 'likelihood' of a scientific outcome from scientific consensus, especially regarding topics that are known not to have been subjected to much research—research that would produce the evidence to use in the formation of such opinions. Therefore, from the perspective of rational scientific thought, whenever one can identify a situation where a conclusion has been reached about a certain phenomenon without all the evidence being considered, instead of forming any opinions one should instead re-investigate the phenomenon, as the status of missing evidence already implies that the relevant question is a question of interest. Also, it seems to me that the role of evidence in scientific thought, in general, is in its *power to distinguish between alternative claims*. This means that in a situation where we are presented with 10,000 pieces of material evidence in support of claim *A* and no other claims are presented, the evidence really plays no role, and all credibility of the claim derives from the authority of its originator. The authority of science is devious in modern times, as it is customary for e.g. governments to launch investigations that basically take *the form* of a scientific study, and thus give an impression of neutral scientific investigation, but in which they at the same time are in a position to control and decide the hypotheses that are taken under consideration. Science differs from such a charade of an investigation in that the scientific community are freely allowed and encouraged to present alternative hypotheses, and this takes place within the forum of the scientific institution. If the governing body were able to control an investigation in such a manner, it would be honest not to present any evidence at all to the audience, as the evidence has no scientific value, and the process is not a democratic process in which the hypotheses and claims are available for open debate. The result of such an investigation is simply a political opinion with no scientific basis.

III-4. THE INVISIBLE HAND

To comprehend the direction of global development, it is important to recognize and digest some rather sinister facts.

1) Money *still* makes the world go round and no other form of currency has turned up; on the contrary, money has established its sovereign role of currency, reigning over all cultural products that diminish and fluctuate in value, and over any religious or honour systems providing socio-cultural frameworks to maintain social harmony. There was a time when money was considered, as it were, just *one kind of* power, coexisting with values such as family, tradition, homeland, religion, freedom, love, friendship or honour, but most of these other institutions have diminished in power in relation to money.

2) The largest private companies have long been larger than a great number of independent nations in terms of calculated "value added" against national GDP; for example, both Walmart and Exxon are bigger than the Czech Republic or New Zealand.[247] But this fact, bundled together with the reported convergence of corporate control towards the dominance of a single interconnected group over the majority of transnational corporations, with acknowledged motives in risk sharing, increased trust and mutual interests, can, I believe, be seen as evidence for the existence of a global force wielding executive power that financially overpowers nations.

3) Corporate lobbying is an established way of influencing politicians in order to gain a political outcome. Using interest groups and consultancies that act as intermediaries in establishing trust between corporate and governmental parties in a manner that can effectively hide the corporate financiers as a protection from potential legal accusations, together with the standard methodology of non-disclosure agreements, creates a base framework of secrecy for direct personal lobbying that could involve unequivocally unethical measures of persuasion, such as bribery or extortion. Although there is little legal evidence for this, accusations of blackmail commonly emerge in the context of international corporate lobbying. In 2014 there were around 30,000 lobbyists located in Brussels, which is about one lobbyist per

---

[247] P. De Grauwe and F. Camerman, 'Are Multinationals Really Bigger Than Nations?', *World Economics*, vol. 4, no. 2, April-June 2003.

PART III. SOCIO-POLITICAL ANALYSIS

European Commission staff member, and an MEP describes their visits as "very cordial and absolutely threatening".[248] Lobbying in itself is an anti-democratic activity that never had any ethical basis in the context of democratic government, and in Athens jurors and officials were appointed by lottery instead of elections, which separated personal wealth from democratic decision-making. Regarding the plausibility of businesses providing a cover of secrecy for private meetings, I would draw a parallel to the institution of "love hotels", originating in Japan and popularized all around East Asia. These establishments work around legislation to provide private meeting places in the face of the powerful cultural taboo against extramarital affairs, and, in addition to the obvious services, typically provide many conveniences for customer privacy, such as hidden entrances and garages.[249]

I believe the direction of development is not very difficult to comprehend once one understands that the Western development of concentrating and privatizing control is not being met with any resistance; there are no idealistic movements that could challenge the power of money; the active threat of communism is gone, and labour unions are losing power with short-term employment contracts making workers scared to flex their muscles. "American media on Russia today are less objective, less balanced, more conformist and scarcely less ideological" than during the Cold War,[250] and leading international broadcasters concur that "Media freedom has not faced such a concerted campaign of disruption since the end of the Cold War" as the whole of Eastern Europe is subject to regular satellite and shortwave jamming and cyber-warfare attacks on media organizations.[251] Western propaganda,

248 I. Traynor, the Guardian; B. Kuraś, Gazeta Wyborcza; P. Ricard, Le Monde; I. F. Somolinos, El País; J. Cáceres, Süddeutsche Zeitung; M. Zetterin, La Stampa '30,000 lobbyists and counting: is Brussels under corporate sway?', *The Guardian*, http://www.theguardian.com/world/2014/may/08/lobbyists-european-parliament-brussels-corporate [26.12.2019].
249 Referencing similar solutions to American cultural taboos made "Y.M.C.A." an international super-hit song.
250 S. F. Cohen, 'Distorting Russia—How the American media misrepresent Putin, Sochi and Ukraine', 11.2.2014, *The Nation*, http://www.thenation.com/article/178344/distorting-russia [26.12.2019].
251 'Media freedom faces "greatest challenge since the Cold War"', Press release issued on behalf of AEF, ABC, BBC, BBG, DW, NHK and RNW, 5.5.2013, *Deutsche Welle*, http://www.dw.de/media-freedom-faces-greatest-challenge-since-the-cold-war/a-16787507 [26.12.2019].

III-4. THE INVISIBLE HAND

in the absence of the threat of communism, concentrates on negative myths about Russia that revitalize the Cold War era sentiments.[252] The function of propaganda is to make people to forget that a group of people are *human* in the sense of civil society. This is possible because it is human nature to be able to kill; one just needs to consider it justified. Propaganda aims to arouse primal emotions of discrimination. My hypothesis that the Western balance of power will keep on developing further towards the privatization of social capital is not a slippery slope argument from the observable privatization development or an ethical argument from the perspective that such development is right or wrong, but an analytical conclusion from the observable causes of societal change that enables the development, and the fact that there is no plausible political force to change its course. Money simply seems to behave in this way under the legislation and the authority that regulates it. One can hypothesize many corrective manoeuvres for it on the level of legislation, changing corporate and financial legislation, but the problem is a global political problem, and achieving political change is different from presenting good ideas, as a controlling authority tends to use any available means to protect its controlling position. Also it is impossible to me to estimate the Russian and Eastern influence on the internal development of the West, as the battle of global corporate power takes place in a whole different realm than classical battles of nations; such analyses need the support of historical wisdom, but the current world conflict is unique in world history.

There is a grim irony in the double standards applied by the global plutocracy, because the words 'democracy' and 'freedom' are being applied as the tools to oppose tyranny. Plato, by contrast, in a superbly insightful passage of argument,[253] saw democracy as naturally susceptible to tyranny via its excessive freedom. He predicted that democracy would turn against itself by getting "drunk on freedom" and falling to the vice of limitless greed and insatiable desire that ruins oligarchy via its hunger for wealth, leading to tyranny. To him the excessive free-

---

252 M. Adomanis, 'Five Myths about Russia', 2.4.2013, *Forbes*, http://www.forbes.com/sites/markadomanis/2013/02/04/five-myths-about-russia/ [26.12.2019].
253 *The Republic*, Book VIII

dom was tinder for tyranny. He saw that democracy and equality mean the desire for equal authority for all, and predicted many phenomena that we can observe today: the mockery of loyal citizens by "slaves who hug their chains"; parents being scared of their disrespecting children—and old men of younger men—descending to their level, adopting their manners and trying to be gay and pleasant to avoid being labelled morose; complete strangers being equal to both *metoikoi* and freemen, masters flattering their students who, in turn, despise them back; women "marching along with all the rights and dignities of freemen", attacking anybody on their way until the road is clear for them; and people becoming oversensitive and hateful towards all authority, even ceasing to care about laws. Now, the sickness of modern Europe can be seen in both the plutocratic vice of greed for wealth and the democratic vice of desire for personal freedom working hand-in-hand: our powerful nations are leading the march to push Western values— called 'democracy' in rhetoric—to other countries. This relates to the blind greed of the plutocrats behind this movement, but at the same time this move is made possible by the democratic citizens' enthusiasm for their personal freedoms to the extent that they ignore their own laws and democratic history, as invasive and provocative warfare—this contemporary wish to impose sanctions on and to manipulate the governmental structure of independent nations—is so fundamentally undemocratic in principle, regarding the history of Western democracy, that it shouldn't even have to be explicitly declared as a human rights violation.[254] Because modern warfare is so synonymous with information warfare, the main military strategic tool to achieve support for aggressive sentiments in terms of military force is *information* instead of, say, arousal of nationalist sentiments; the appealing rhetoric in the Second World War. Information-based provocation is a planned act where acts of heroism or atrocities are carried out in front of the camera so there is video evidence of them, and this evidence is immediately provided to the media to fuel people's love or hatred. In the latter case,

[254] The Universal Declaration of Human Rights states the following. Article 28: "Everyone is entitled to a social and international order in which the rights and freedoms set forth in this Declaration can be fully realized." Article 30: "Nothing in this Declaration may be interpreted as implying for any State, group or person any right to engage in any activity or to perform any act aimed at the destruction of any of the rights and freedoms set forth herein."

III-4. THE INVISIBLE HAND

this will lead the public to push for invasive measures, leaving further detailed investigation into the event to be carried out later. This might, however, never take place due to the progressing nature of a conflict, or, if it actually takes place, it will receive little publicity and interest because of the unfortunate phenomenon that people—if they can avoid it—don't actually want to memorize any of the uncomfortable events that aroused their anger and indignation. This model of political provocation repeats over and over in all modern conflicts between the West and a foreign nation: video material is fed to the Western news stream and accompanied by allegations targeted towards the political opposition. In view of the misplaced Western trust towards the media, this publicity produces the desired effect of gaining immediate support from unsuspecting viewers. Modern citizens are drunk enough to be easily persuaded by propaganda to agree to the use of violence against other nations because they don't really care about these other nations enough to analyse the news flow critically. They care more about their own personal freedoms in the form of political agendas such as gay rights or legalizing marijuana. These political activities are being pushed with exactly the perversity greedy democratic desires, and that was seen by Plato as a weapon: the chain-hugging slaves that mock loyal citizens are the radical extremist elements—both right wing and left wing—that are being used to create governmental imbalance in independent nations by means of both rhetoric and terrorism. Women who claim but disrespect the rights of freemen are the feminist and gay rights elements that are being used to the same purpose,[255] and the equal complete strangers are the flows of immigration and exodus

[255] There is moderate contemporary pressure towards discrediting the traditional institution of marriage, which, I believe, is equal to the motive to defile statues and tombstones. But because there is no pressure to discredit the burial institution, I believe the motive to discredit the marriage institution is being actuated from an international source: the institution of marriage is the only traditional institution that can be humiliated with international equality rhetoric. The US president is now promoting gay marriage, having flip-flopped from his 2004 view that a man and a woman are married in front of God, which doesn't seem to make any sense, as it is a minority issue and there is a strong and global traditionalist opposition to this idea. We would expect a president to try and increase his popularity both in terms of enforcing his credibility and by promoting globally agreeable policies. This should be interpreted that the president has a motive to become, not modernist, as he is setting an example according to the proud tradition of American global leadership, but instead anti-traditionalist.

that are being enforced and promoted within the EU. The democratic sentiment is a sentiment in which nobody can be seen as holding authority over anybody else, which is greedy in the said Platonic sense, but most essentially it is the perversion of the ideal of equality, where this has been taken with no logic to set any limits to it. It is as if the natural sources of authority in society were reversed: everywhere you can see parents silently and complacently letting their children behave without discipline, and similarly one can see politicians acting a role of a good guy instead of an informed and responsible authority. And this reflects a decline in *morale*; the easiest thing to do is to trust the image presented by a politician instead of demanding results, and similarly the easiest thing in parenting is to uphold an image of looking after one's children; a parent who doesn't have the courage to be an authority behaves this way because he is afraid of the judgement of neglect; he is playing it safe.

III-5. Information-Age Rhetorical Tactics

To look at modern rhetoric in terms of its underlying morals, it is worth acknowledging the history of Western dialectic and the role of public debate to resolve conflict. In a *democratic* setting, public debate has followed a Christian rhetoric where speakers are expected to speak on behalf of everybody as a family; as brothers and sisters. It has been this Christian *democratic spirit* that has underlain the practice whereby people, as separate parties, in a natural setting speak as representatives of their own parties and not for everybody. And now, today, we have a situation where the democratic spirit surely has disappeared and nobody would relate democracy to Christianity, as a result of atheist efforts to separate government from religion. But what we have left is the ritualized form of democracy where people are still expected to speak democratically instead of engaging in open conflict, and tabloid journalism has found a role in excoriating the public speakers that deviate from democratic standards, for example by using foul language or failing to hide their private life from stalking paparazzi. This sort of branding of democratic speakers is, of course, highly undemocratic, it causes makes the speakers vulnerable and therefore removes the level playing field when they try to carry out their public role. This is destructive to public democratic debate. For example, people report that a fear of having their actions misunderstood is the reason why they won't help a stranger who is lying in the street. It seems there is a general fear of getting involved; everyone has cameras in their mobile phones and whatever you do in a public setting can be presented as if your motive was insincere, so, it is easier not to get involved. We are very similar to the Chinese who would easily believe that the misfortune of accident would descend on you if you get involved by helping. And this situation creates an opportunity for those who are willing to behave in an undemocratic manner in the sense of blatantly advancing their personal interest or the interest of their financial benefactors, yet who can convincingly portray a democratic public image using the remnants of democratic norms that we have left.

PART III. SOCIO-POLITICAL ANALYSIS

The information age has provided an atmosphere of increased anonymity and therefore less restrictions for expressing opinions, and this has made people more short-sighted in terms of who they believe. The Finnish people, particularly, have a history of being suspicious and resistant to smooth words, and to gain trust, one is expected to show trustworthy actions instead of fine words. People of the information age, however, have a short attention span and the available time to form opinions has reduced. This has, among other things, brought in a wave of successful con artists, such as fake doctors—a new phenomenon in Finland—and at the same time has increased trust towards publicly known figures and suspicion towards unknown people, which is reflected in the job market. But the general development has been that people have become more reliant on impression and rhetoric, and there are many powerful people who get their salary from giant corporations and make their living from the art of demagoguery and illusion. Information age rhetoric has the distinct feature of always trying to sound like objective information, even when carrying powerful or even radical opinions underneath the surface. Two common features dominate the rhetorical scene. Firstly, there is a focus on the factual informational basis of arguments, which promotes arguments consisting of carefully constructed expressions that derive their credibility from *select factoids*, such as cherry-picked statistics, scientific sources or expert statements. These expert data or statements are professionally manufactured by information sources (such as news channels and newspapers that can collaborate with politicians) simply for the purpose of creating artificial credibility for an opinion presented to the public. A powerful tactic is to create a compact slogan that has some expert data backing it, then repeat the slogan *ad infinitum* in political rhetoric. A second tactic in argument is misusing terminology; that is, abusing the popularity of an existing concept by pushing it to a new meaning.

There is not enough scrutiny of the rhetoric of argument, so, I will try and briefly analyse some common rhetorical patterns; I'm not trying to make a comprehensive list and the use of these patterns might vary between countries in the Western world. All these patterns are fallacious

III-5. INFORMATION-AGE RHETORICAL TACTICS

in classical argumentative sense and are ways of drawing support in an anti-intellectual manner.

III-5-1. Personalization

A visible characteristic of information-age thought is the disappearance of our collective frameworks of shared values, such as religion, schools of thought, movements, new ideas and similar things that have traditionally united us. This development seems to reflect the information society and the increase in the number of technical means of social networking: groups are formed in a novel way and this happens out of sight. The overall situation could be described as utter confusion because we don't know our social groups, and there are no common values that we can use as references. On the level of rhetoric, this leads to the effectiveness of personalization, where one uses the individual characteristics of a person to appeal to his audience.

In *celebrity rhetoric*, which aims for idolization, or, to put it more mildly, to make the character appealing to follow. This includes publicizing the private life stories of important people, such as politicians or scientists, from the perspective of heroic personal struggle for important goals. The aim is to indirectly relate the success of reaching important status in society to their effort of reaching generous goals that traditionally are not at all related to status but the opposite. Think about it: "He was striving every day to help everybody and make the world better for everybody"... so, he achieved success by being a helper boy/bag carrier? Or do you mean he didn't wish for success but just to help... so, where did the success come from? A part of this rhetoric is trying to inspire awe and compassion by emphasizing how much work the individual has done or how much suffering he has had to endure. Such people can openly share select details of their personal lives to give an impression of having nothing to hide and that they are only humans, and this particular selection of such details gives the opportunity to select ones that can be expected to provoke a compassionate response.

PART III. SOCIO-POLITICAL ANALYSIS

And this method is successful because of a distinctive feature of the age of distrust: *people tend to trust concrete information as opposed to only vague words*. The modern public figure who shows his private life is like the kind customer who opens his bag at the supermarket counter to show he is not carrying any stolen items in his bag—he needs to do it because the standard is not trust but distrust. Shoplifting is a common crime, and so is a lying politician or any public figure, so, today people are instead fooled by the selection of pieces of information from that figure's private life and their compilation into a celebrity public image. Celebrity rhetoric has the downside that once you have publicly presented yourself in a particular image, any information that counters that image will harm it, and political competition generally involves snooping into the private lives of competitors in order to find pieces of information that can tarnish their public image. These pieces of information can be used to harm the figure by publishing them, or as negotiation leverage.

In *demonization rhetoric*, a person is associated with something publicly condemned, with the insinuation that they did so intentionality. This is different from defamation, which typically consists of false claims or false evidence, and where the individual is protected by national defamation laws. In the world of information and the printed word, important people are protected against false evidence and claims that cannot be shown to be true, but not against techniques where the relation to evil is implied and insinuated. I like to call it demonic due to the method of indirect harm; to bring forward a false claim about what somebody did is, at least in the common case, honest, and it is more likely that its presenter says it simply because he believes it himself, yet doesn't consider prudentially whether he has evidence to back up his accusation. But to *indirectly suggest* that somebody has done something harmful is the border area where a manipulating individual can test whether others share personal antipathies against somebody, without taking the risk of expressing his own sentiment aloud. Like Goethe's Mephistopheles, who manipulates Faust into murdering Valentin, the brother of his beloved Gretchen: when Valentin attacks Faust (and Mephistopheles) with a sword as an unidentified nightly intruder (unsure if there are one or two), Mephistopheles urges Faust not to retreat but to fight back together; he will only need to lunge and the devil will parry. The devil of this story (introducing himself as "The Spirit that Denies") manipulates by arousing anger and provoking action but acting himself in such a way as to avoid responsibility. Similarly, demonization is rhetoric where the credibility of an individual is attacked by provoking sentiments against him but in a way that accepts no responsibility by making direct suggestions, which implies that no supporting evidence exists to make such claims.

Defamation protection doesn't extend to international law, and completely fabricated claims about e.g. foreign heads of state are common in the Western media. This might add to the effect of international defamation, because the public are not subjected to direct accusations against their own countrymen, as they would need to be corroborated in court. When one makes outrageous claims about foreign heads of state, it might seem as if they must be true because the media dares to act so boldly. It just means that our concept of human rights doesn't extend to these countries, and we find it fair to beat anybody who is outside the protection of our legal system. Ironically, these accusations most typically concern human rights abuses by these foreign leaders.

III-5-2. Caricature

Kierkegaard wrote that every single action (except religious action) can be presented as a caricature. This would happen by taking a normal human feature and extending it to the human extreme. This is because all mental problems, and related stereotypes, are developments of people's normal human qualities but somehow developed unrestricted into an extreme. Caricature utilizes a *stereotype*: it presents the actions of a person as the actualization of a negative stereotype. In every successful demonization there must be a grain of truth, and this grain is that the actions of a person resemble a known negative stereotype. Incidentally, Kierkegaard himself was the target of numerous

PART III. SOCIO-POLITICAL ANALYSIS

caricatures both in picture and text by the local satirical periodicals, because he managed to enrage the local elite by his social critique. I will give some examples where a stereotypical behaviour is presented via caricature, and by this I am attempting to give a comprehensive 10-minute introductory lesson for a 20th-century media person with no previous history in journalism: *The ABC of evil remarks.*

- Being happy and satisfied in oneself can be presented as narcissism
- Being modest can be presented as having bad self-esteem
- Displaying one's credentials can be presented as boasting
- Generous behaviour can be presented as attempted bribery to win people over
- Good education can be presented as book-education
- Disapproving or reproachful behaviour can be presented as demonic restrictive behaviour; such as via association with Hitler
- Rhetorical skill and a convincing personality can be presented as populism and an attempt to please one's audience
- Having a sense of humour can be interpreted as being a clown of a person who needs to resort to jokes
- Being critical of a woman's behaviour can be presented as male chauvinism
- Being critical of immigration policies can be presented as racism
- Being critical of any phenomenon at all can be interpreted as 'something-phobia'
- Doing nothing at all can be presented as apathy

The 21st century professional politicians are aware of this and, first of all, will never publicly portray any action that would give an open chance for any of these caricatures, by being particularly calm and mild-mannered. Secondly, they will use their relationships to connect with the media to get them on their side, because they understand that only the media has the power to successfully employ these tactics to harm their reputation. Politicians can't successfully ridicule each other, except during presidential elections; it is the media who are in complete control of this activity, and there needs to be no apparent connection between the opinion of the media and the political parties; this connection takes place behind the scenes.

III-5-3. Facts

Our dominant theory of the mind is warped, and it is my understanding that this warped thought is widely taught in schools. There exists a popular rhetoric that abuses this weakness, in which something labelled 'facts', or something "based on evidence" (implying objectivity), is portrayed against something that implies subjectivity, such as opinions, beliefs, views or convictions. There is a latent presupposition that objectivity is good and the truth, and subjectivity is bad and false. Here lies also the fault of this rhetoric, as it doesn't recognize that reference to fact is a subjective choice, and a subjective belief in scientific objective results is nonetheless subjective belief. It is a very common error to confuse a *statement* and an *argument*: take the (rather silly) argument "Killing animals is wrong because 1+2=3"; it contains the elements "Killing animals is wrong", which is opinion, "1+2=3", which we can call a fact with reference to mathematical standard, and also the argument itself—the choice to justify the opinion with this fact—is an opinion. So, one could say that out of these three constituents of such a claim, only one part is fact and the rest is opinion. This sort of rhetoric can e.g. juxtapose religious faith against scientific results but doesn't do it correctly by juxtaposing religious faith against *belief* in scientific results. To unquestionably quote scientific results is no different from the standpoint of reason than to unquestionably quote Biblical truths, which is that there is no reason to it, as appeal to authority is simply a fallacy. The only difference is a change in our world in which today Christianity is not an authority; the scientific and Christian institutions simply act as standards of objectivity. The tactic in this rhetoric is to (subjectively) select the arguments that one wishes to use to justify one's opinion, such as scientific results, and *call them* (objective) fact.

PART III. SOCIO-POLITICAL ANALYSIS

The rhetoric can appear strong when used in live debate, if one has the ability to select one's facts beforehand when one's opposition hasn't done this, but to win such debate, one must point out *argumentum ad verecundiam*; one must show that the argument is not based on reason but authority. Another tactic is to base one's own argument on the same authority.

There is a great deal of warped pseudo-philosophical science, such as cognitivism and, say, economic psychology, etc., that pretends to study how our brain thinks, but that doesn't rest on a solid conceptual basis due to a lack of willingness to pay philosophical attention to the concepts used. I believe they tend to verify their concepts in the following manner:

- This is fact and that is opinion. *Facts are not opinions.*

- But what is a fact, really? What differentiates fact from opinion?

- Let science answer that. There are alternative theories, but while this process is reaching consensus, let's just work upon intuitive assumptions.

In this model, philosophical grounding work is *actively forgotten*, which implies regression, or, say, lobotomy. So, in this case, basically, when something is called *fact*, this is either a reference to the scientific institution or common sense, such as "rocks are hard". But this development can be described as an intellectual regression to a combination of institutional knowledge and common sense; similarly, to how earlier the Sun was seen to revolve around Earth based on both the Christian institution and common sense. This development represents the dismissal of both reason and philosophy, like a peasant in the old days who would believe two things: what his own eyes and hands could grasp, and what his wife and his priest (whom he trusts) said—all the rest he dismisses as unreliable, as he is prudentially smart enough to know he doesn't possess the intellect to tell truth from lie in such theoretical talk.

III-5. INFORMATION-AGE RHETORICAL TACTICS

III-5-4. Mystification

Classically, mystification is a rhetorical act of purposefully delivering one's topic in a grand manner, in reference to mystical and epic frames of reference such as universal laws, laws of nature, fate, destiny, harmony and so on. This has been the standard device for institutions such as the church and monarchy. It seems to me that this trick works particularly well today when presenting one's views as scientific facts, with a reference to the mystical institution of science. The efficiency is based on abusing the credulity of the listener, who will submit to the authority of the speaker in the absence of better knowledge. Commonly, the wielder of this rhetoric is not a scientific expert and the reference to scientific information may be weak, such as reference to a single article or opinion. To cover the weakness of one's actual knowledge, this rhetoric is commonly accompanied by a superior, arrogant and dismissive attitude towards questions or criticism, as if the opponent was too ignorant to be worthy of response. Try and pin such an 'expert' down to reveal the sources of his knowledge, and you'll soon find the topic of the conversation turning to your personal qualities as an *ad hominem* attack. But also, mixing information with illusion and entertainment can be used as a tool to retract one's argument when met with opposition that threatens one's credibility: "Ha, ha, ha! I was only kidding!"

Newspaper articles typically obscure their topics and justify this action by saying that the content is being made more 'accessible' or interesting (better hiding the actual lack of information quantity or quality). Information is woven into *a tale* of some sorts, such as the portrayed expert's personal tale, e.g. what he has been doing that day, or a tale about the particular topic itself in the light of history. A classical illusionist would use the same tactics when delivering his act, appearing from a cloud of mist in his exotic clothes and hypnotic gaze, delivering a tale about how he came into town and about the origin of the products he is selling.[256] Another line of rhetoric I've repeatedly noticed in

---

256 An illustration of this could be the private viewing scene at the beginning of the

PART III. SOCIO-POLITICAL ANALYSIS

Finnish newspaper headlines by experts is to claim that the topic is 'silenced' or a taboo (classical qualities of mystery). This tactic is used to portray oneself as a courageous messenger of justice, and, in effect, works to justify one's lack of knowledge via creating an atmosphere where speaking *only opinion* is expected. This kind of half-information-half-entertainment atmosphere naturally discourages people from paying attention to the source, consistency or the credibility of presented information.

III-5-5. Ignorance

In a functioning democracy we would see public discussion and argument in support of improvements to the system, which would then be delivered by like-minded MPs to parliament. In our current situation what we see is a very particular political rhetoric that consists of two elements. Firstly, the desired opinion is predetermined and assumed as *self-evident*, and can be accompanied by just a shrug and reference to common sense.[257] Secondly, the public rhetorical logic is directed to any *objections*: "Who opposes and why?" And this seems quite a powerful sleight of hand to capture people who don't pay very much attention to the logic of argument and who tend to sympathize with the speaker instead: the speaker omits supporting argumentation with an appeal to his own ignorance and the sympathetic listener will forgive this as something very human. This is comparable to buffoonery and the sort of activity we might expect from somebody who is not being responsible: "I think that's the case but that's just silly old me!" From the standpoint of rhetoric this means that the arguer is *actively ignoring* other options, and it is also worth noting that in democratic jurisprudence, objections are something that are presented against a

movie *Elephant Man*, where the owner of the circus freak delivers his act.
257 The US State Department refers to common sense regarding which party fired the rockets that downed an aeroplane, and there are some social media posts and Youtube video clips that support this view. This was said in a State Department press conference when a reporter pushed the Deputy Spokesperson to elaborate on evidence. A Youtube clip named "'Anything other than social media?' State Dept's MH17 evidence secret", Russia Today's Youtube channel, 22.7.2014. http://www.youtube.com/watch?v=oQRvINebeok [26.12.2019].

III-5. INFORMATION-AGE RHETORICAL TACTICS

decision or an action that is *already made*. The rhetoric can also take the form of denying intentionality; "I don't mean to"; I'm sure everybody has heard somebody say: "Now, I don't mean to be mean, but..." and then proceed to say the meanest possible things.[258]

The boom in ignorant rhetoric seems to be bound to the information society exactly because of the power of information as *evidence*. The popularity of natural science emphasizes the role of evidence, and e.g. Dawkins can say that there is no God because he is so ignorant as to have missed all the evidence, man-made climate change must be true because of amassing evidence, and we must change the concept of marriage to include gays because "Why not? (Ignorant as I am, I can't think of an opposing reason)." The wisdom behind the concept of *argumentum ad ignorantiam* as a fallacy is that the existence of evidence doesn't mean proof and it has nothing to do with justice, and the evidence can be used as a rhetorical device instead to reach falsity and injustice. Moreover, the relation between truth and evidence is not logical but methodical and authoritative. This implies the following: 1) the fact that no supporting evidence exists for a claim, or that no supporting evidence has been presented in argument, doesn't mean that the claim is false, and 2) the fact that supporting evidence exists, or supporting evidence has been presented, doesn't make a claim true. Whether truth is to be derived from evidence, this is in relation to, firstly, some strict and particular process, such as the one applied in natural science or the one applied in courts of law, and secondly, the existence of said institution where the process is applied, which produces truth via *authority*. This authority is shown in that the 'truths' of science can and do change from time to time, and similarly in legal justice, earlier verdicts can be repealed by another level of the legal system. The same applies to how it is said that in war the victor gets to write history: the last authority gets to write truth. Now, the said evidence rhetoric borrows strictly from the *methodology* of natural

---

[258] For example, President Obama was quite active in saying that the laws he just signed were not meant to be used. The American ambassador in Finland recently said that the economic sanctions the US imposed on Finland were not meant to hurt Finland. It seems like this might be standard political rhetoric in that part of the world.

science and extends it outside the institution of science. When, in science, students are taught to reason from evidence, they are taught to do their work within an institution that applies a methodology—one that is based on objective evidence—to serve a particular function in society. This system is what it is exactly because it serves this particular function, and because of this, it is crafted also to *produce* objective evidence, and has practices to protect the production of such evidence—if it wasn't so, the 'evidence' could just be something somebody made up. But if one now tries to extend this methodology outside such a system, one will notice that, firstly, there exists testimonial evidence that is subjective, and also there is evidence that cannot be produced, e.g. because it is known to be in the hands of somebody who will refuse to present it, and these facts will make it futile to claim objectivity as if one was a scientist whereas one is just being ignorant. And secondly, he doesn't have the support of the legal institution anymore, as if one was a judge, which will make his subjective judgments appear unjust and judgmental if they contradict people's sense of justice. So, all in all, common sense is what all people should possess, but to argue based on common sense—to say one's claim is true because of common sense—reveals that one is ignoring any rational evidence that might lie beyond common sense. And what does this phenomenon mean on the level of Western historical development? It means a reversion back to times when the ignorant were at the mercy of mumbo jumbo; where 'experts' in newspapers essentially are the charlatan fortune-tellers of old; delivering their money-motivated foresight via a powerful and colourful act. The media circus stays alive by rotating its actors. And wise people, those who are older and more experienced in this sort of trickery, will be more cautious before believing what is being presented.

III-5-6. Victimizing

Victimization—playing the victim—is a common psychological reaction and a rhetorical tactic that a subject may apply when they fail to get what they want. It is typically attributed to women and children rather than men, as this tactic employs the subject's known weaker sta-

III-5. INFORMATION-AGE RHETORICAL TACTICS

tus, but also stories of narcissistic domestic violence by men often involve victim playing to control a partner who is susceptible to guilting. It is noticeable that children of weak parents learn this at a young age: "I want it! No! I never get what I want! Always he gets it and I don't!" As a mother, if you fall for this tactic, then you'll be hearing a lot more of this in the future. Because victimization is a *primal* (infant-age) psychological tactic, it is very powerful, and thus useful as a society-level rhetoric and a propaganda tool. Victimization rhetoric was applied in the rise of fascism in the Second World War: workers and the masses were portrayed as victims of privileged Jews and foreigners who stole their jobs and pride. Similarly, Marxism applied victimization rhetoric to the relationship between the working class and the bourgeoisie—the Communist Manifesto is basically written in the form of "The bourgeoisie has done this and that." Victimization rhetoric takes the form of blaming experienced harm on a social group.

Feminism is one modern form of victimization, and in its common argumentative form it is an absolute contradiction: the goal of equality to be won via the method of sexism; that is, gender-based discrimination and discriminatory attitudes. Feminist argument typically applies the word 'equality' without a criterion, but as a value in itself: "Before such-and-such happens, there will be no real equality", and the meaning of the word itself can be traced to the fundamental democratic concept with its Christian/Stoic origin. The feminist argument is senseless or false, because Christian equality is *transcendent*. For example, UDHR reads:

> *All human beings are born free and equal in dignity and rights.*

The United States Declaration of Independence reads:

> *We hold these truths to be **self-evident**, that **all men are created equal**, that they are endowed by their **Creator** with certain unalienable **rights**.*

This divine transcendence means that this equality exists irrespective

PART III. SOCIO-POLITICAL ANALYSIS

of earthly matters, and therefore the definitive response to the feminist argument is: "We *are* equal, so why do you speak in conditional, as if we *were* equal *only after* some changes?" To put it another way, it is not possible to think how a transcendent quality would become true; rather its truth is attributed, and it would rather make sense to think about how such a quality would become *untrue*, which is, by having the group of people supporting this belief diminish in such a way that the word would disappear from active rhetoric or deviate from its original meaning. This change of original meaning is exactly what has happened; the wielder of the feminist argument doesn't seem to *believe* in equality in the sense of history and documents that constitute this equality. The feminist conception of equality is atheist, cynical and *material*, meaning that some determined material criteria will qualify equality, and then again, equality is never perfect but always proportionate. This makes it just to say that feminism is *socialist* in its conception of equality: the class difference is fundamental and the individual means nothing. If we acknowledge that capitalism is cynical because to a capitalist it makes no difference who loses as long as they themselves make a profit, and therefore the constituting emotion of capitalism is greed, we can certainly acknowledge that likewise the constituting emotion of socialism is *envy*, and once any socialist/feminist target is achieved, this envy will naturally jump to target the next group (disguised under the abstraction of class) that seems to be having a better time than one's own group. The feminist projects class struggle to men as a class and cynically disbelieves.

Winning women's suffrage is often attributed to feminist rhetoric, which is not true[259]... but even if it was true, what difference does it

---

259 Women's suffrage is historically an extension to women's rights, and its correct attribution needs to be made in the light of what made this extension possible. Finland was the first country in Europe to allow all women to vote, and this might best be attributed to Finland's unstable history with Sweden and Russia as an area with minimal natural resources and difficult to control. This has enforced local autonomy: increasing local rights diminishes external oppression. The second obvious cause is World War I and the need for the mobilization of women in support of the men in service. The international suffragette movement saw the increase in the civil importance of women as an opportunity and advanced with methodologies such as hunger strikes. The USA followed the UK's example. So, both historical causes for this extension of rights are related to war and dire

III-5. INFORMATION-AGE RHETORICAL TACTICS

make today when voter turnouts are ridiculous in general as politics is run via shadowy male lobbying? Feminist rhetoric involves a consistent contradiction between the feminist ideal and scientific truth; for example, a currently popular yet disgusting topic is the celebration of the female orgasm. Feminists consider this event the empowerment of women, and the goal is sensible as a part of the liberation of women, as women's equal needs are not traditionally considered in countries that feminists consider old-fashioned. But to look at the problem truthfully, it is exactly the feminist countries in which the safety of traditional sex roles has been stripped from the individual, and women in particular are confronted with external pressures (from women's magazines, among other sources) regarding the norms of sexual intercourse. As a result, the capability of women to enjoy intercourse has diminished, and now feminism once again steps in as if to help women by empowering them. I think a good parallel to this is when countries pose as military aids and partners to fight the problems they themselves have been instrumental in creating... this should be seen as a poor choice of method; if your method creates problems, you should switch method instead of trying to fix the problems using the same method. It is fundamentally irresponsible behaviour, and, morally, this sort of behaviour is meant to be tolerated and not condemned—when somebody plays victim, we need to take care of him, because we can't really know if he really is a victim or just playing victim—but it is not behaviour suitable for leadership, which is the actual goal of the feminists. Another form of modern victimization rhetoric is "sexual minority" propaganda: minorities aggressively regard themselves as victims, and demand changes in the legal system. I am using quotes round "sexual minority" because the concept is politicized and misleading, and, no doubt, crafted for this very purpose. The word 'minority' traditionally relates to unchangeable determining and thus classifying properties, such as age, gender, race, ethnicity, religion, or physical, economic or occupational status, but the use of the word has now been extended to include things that no longer relate to the original moral thought that *one can't be blamed for the things one can't change.* One's sexual

---

need under threat of annihilation, and the changes took place all over the Western world in a very short time scale.

PART III. SOCIO-POLITICAL ANALYSIS

preferences are correctly analysed under the concept of identity, and one's identity falls under the same category as taste in food or clothing, artistic taste, and such. Their whole rhetoric lies on the obviously false assumption that one's sexual identity is something that a person can't change, but despite a related strong devotion to one's identity group, and a dislike of its opposite, *identities change*. Now, considering the idea of whether one's identity can change, and therefore the question of whether the concept of "sexual minority" has a moral basis, the related 'unchangeable' experience is not physically or historically determined but the result of identification, and looking at identification as a phenomenon, one should rather make the contrary observation that identity, as a result of group identification, is something that changes much faster nowadays than in the past. Young people in particular change their identities all the time, and it's not uncommon for a liberal-minded person to e.g. inherit a relationship identity, then after a break-up inherit a homosexual identity, and after that lose interest e.g. get married and inherit a wife/husband identity.

What feminism has meant, in practice, is a *bar on the expression* of sex in a political setting, which in itself is completely contradictory as a human rights rhetoric, as the human right of freedom of speech is being attacked from a sexist basis, which itself is a breach of human rights. Similarly, the so-called 'rainbow' rhetoric is a bar on the expression of opinions that could be interpreted as anti-gay or anti-LGBT. Now, there are two kinds of bars: just and unjust ones; ones in which something considered wrong is being barred, and ones in which the thing that is being barred is considered right. A classic example of an unjust bar is alcohol prohibition, which is something that has been unsuccessfully tried all around the world. The underlying cause of the failure of prohibition is that the rhetoric with which it is driven is not fact but enforced propaganda, and that people comply with given directives doesn't mean that they will accept the underlying *morals*—if the directive is experienced as unjust, the problem will not disappear but find other forums of expression with likely illegal means. So now, regarding freedom of speech; this freedom is considered a moral right in the West and suppressing the freedom will not mean that opinions change, but on the contrary, they will be rampant and unrestricted. Regarding feminism; if men like to talk about women in a certain way, it is a very particular approach to condemn and restrict it instead of trying to understand what it is about men that makes them talk this way. Because if it so happens that they are not publicly allowed to be men any more, they will simply find other ways to be men... and today we live a time of shadow capitalism that is quite rampant from the perspective of public decision-making, but also a covert sexual subculture where people seek comfort from socially imposed inhibitions (expression is restricted) via more primitive dominant-submissive roles, and the related male-dominated pornography, where women are ritually demeaned and objectified, has shifted towards the mainstream from the status of being perverted and wrong. There is no doubt that while our public offices are being targeted with equality policies, sex quotas and such, said shadow capitalism is a completely patriarchal world of cowboys, bandits, partnerships and brotherhoods. Most people today are likely oblivious to the fact that the gender wealth disparity is increasing,[260] because modern public discourse works to hide facts that are inconvenient to these ideologies, which follows directly from said sexist bar on expression and free speech. Regarding rainbow rhetoric; at the same time as this rhetoric is trying to enforce LGBT rights, it is battling a rise in anti-gay (or homophobic) sentiments all around the world. And as these sentiments are barred on the level of public opinion, they take the form of violent attacks.

Another popular victimization rhetoric is used by modern atheists. First the atheist declares: "God is not true; I won't consider it; I won't talk about it either, and I'll attack if you try and force it. I do this *because I have the right to.*" And we empathize because we recognize this

---

[260] According to sociologist Mariko Chang, "gender wealth disparity has been on the rise since 1998 despite the recent decline in the income gap". In Australia, the gap is reported to have widened sharply. A. Perlberg, 'Women are Shortchanged by The Wealth Gap', Stanford Knowledgebase Research News, 7.4.2011, http://web.stanford.edu/group/knowledgebase/cgi-bin/2011/04/07/women-are-shortchanged-by-the-wealth-gap/ [26.12.2019]. M. Wade, 'Rich man, poor woman: the gender wealth gap widens', *The Sydney Morning Herald*, 9.11.2014, http://www.smh.com.au/national/rich-man-poor-woman-the-gender-wealth-gap-widens-20141108-11igay.html [26.12.2019].

freedom of religion and the right not to identify with one. But what the atheists do next is disrespecting and abusing this right and having the ideology evolve into radicalism: they start to see religion as an *evil*. They say religion

- causes wars (because wars are made in the name of religion),
- hurts children by scaring them about hell, or
- molests children (because paedophilia scandals are relatively common in institutions with clerical celibacy).

Here the atheists employ victimization rhetoric. They would consider themselves progressive and agitate people by saying that these are important truths that people or the government want to silence. What they fail to notice is that blaming issues on a group is not truth, but only a small grain of truth constitutes the efficacy of this rhetoric of hate. We have laws against this kind of agitation, for good reason. How difficult is it to abuse people's pain and fears; to say, when a child is run over by a car, that we should punish all drivers and car owners? This is rhetoric of hate that comes out of desperation and frustration; a wish for a different kind of justice and protection than one's system provides, as beautifully illustrated in the opening sequence of the movie *Godfather*. This wish for vengeance is the result of grief mixing with honour: one feels beaten but refuses to appear humiliated, stripped of one's pride. The victimizing radical personally needs an intellectual rational justification as his protection, and in this need he doesn't care if he is right or wrong; like Bonasera the undertaker, he succumbs to taking it because *it is available for him*.

III-5-7. Umbrage

Taking umbrage means taking offence at being slighted or wronged (shadowed; being unjustly put into somebody else's shadow). The person who takes umbrage at something is calling out that he, or somebody, is being slighted, and thus calling attention to this act to retain his honour or social status. The person using this rhetoric is being dramatic and calling attention to what is happening, as if responding to a perceived threat, and it should be noted that because this is actually an act of calling attention, the claims asserted by this rhetoric are often not factual, because they don't need to be. As an example, take the general-level feminist claim about the gender pay gap (that women earn less than men); this assertion is used as a rhetorical tool to take umbrage at the status of women. The assertion hides its basis, that it is calculated in a certain way; that is, simply by adding up overall earnings and not considering various things such as that men in general work more hours than women. But consider how outraged such a feminist orator would be if a man made a similar general level claim, such as "Men are stronger than women", while hiding the basis, which here is "in weight-lifting", which is a criterion that makes this claim true, while some other criteria might make the claim untrue. Such general-level claims should always be checked by asking for the criterion.

It is noteworthy that in, say, Asian countries, quarrels and acts of disrespect take place between individuals or groups, and there is no rhetoric to bring such an action into the public eye: on the contrary, pleading for mercy is rather a shameful action. I believe this culture was also the norm in pre-democratic Europe, apart from Western individualism and the coexisting tradition of chivalry, which had the effect of making honour disputes public displays of individual heroism or duels instead of traditional gang fights. In umbrage, public honour is insulted, and retaliation follows. Democratic rhetoric has brought the change that maintaining social harmony is considered the responsibility of all, which brings about a whole new rhetoric in which one makes public an action one considers disrespectful. First of all, it might be noted that the sympathy towards the plea for mercy is obviously of Christian origin; if someone is publicly showing "I am hurt!" the reaction could be the opposite of sympathizing, in other words thinking that being hurt is his own fault. It is the Christian sympathy and caring for one's brother that will make us care for those other than ourselves and our family, and it is quite ludicrous to see the current rhetoric of umbrage coexist with blatant disregard of the well-being of one's fellow man. This depicts profound confusion: people are torn between sympathizing strongly with, say, minority groups that they don't relate to at all (or even puppy dogs that are not humans), and coldly disregarding other groups such as Muslims or whomever the media happens to paint as the bad guys on any given day. Secondly, the security provided by joint responsibility derives from democratic equality, which is, apart from being a Christian value, based on the democratic society: it is the dividend the individual receives in return for following the rules of the democratic society, such as paying taxes, following politics, electing officials and participating in public opinion. But now newspapers have become political actors, and the way they are doing this is by taking umbrage at another country's actions, trying to convey the impression that the other country is slighting us. And this rhetoric is completely misleading, because the concept of being slighted is altogether a democratic principle that applies only within one's democratic society; why do you take offence at another culture slighting you, when you don't pay their taxes and are not in a position to elect their officials? Let it be said that in all sportsmanship it is customary to disrespect your opponent a bit before the match, which is considered an act of mutual respect: by publicly showing disrespect one brings one's honour into the match by making advance claims of victory, and by doing this, one also accepts the public loss of face as the result of one's defeat, which, in return, equals public respect for the victor. Disrespect before confrontation means betting on oneself. This is the very basis of healthy and *honour*able competition (where honour is at stake), in contrast with unhealthy competition which involves dishonourable acts.

III-5-8. Prudential

The concept of prudence dates from Aristotle and could be described as "practical wisdom", but it is very noticeable how public rhetoric has taken a turn towards prudence together with the development of increased authoritarianism. From the perspective of prudence, it is often wise not to say what you think or not to take the choice that is evident, and these come along with various forms of rhetoric of persuasion. Prudential rhetoric is something designed to make a choice appealing from the *personal* perspective, as opposed to a *moral* perspective in

III-5. INFORMATION-AGE RHETORICAL TACTICS

the sense of universality; it offers a deal between the speaker and the addressed: "Say yes to this and it will be better for you." When you are being approached with prudential rhetoric, somebody is interested in winning *you* (subjectively) over to *his* side, and the process can involve bribery, threat or both. The most visible one today is still the "manmade climate change" movement that applies a steady rhetoric of threatening with the obvious intent to gain financial control of global emissions, and thus production, for Western actors. At the same time, supporting scientific data is systematically exaggerated,[261] and critical scientific voices are branded 'denialists', placed on public lists, systematically bullied, smeared and laid off.[262] The increase in such rhetoric goes well with the modern movement of privatization, where public authority is being overrun by subjective business deals between, say, companies. Climate change argumentation also often takes the prudential form of *personal insurance*: "Although we are unsure whether climate change is happening or not, it is nevertheless reasonable to take all precautions to be on the safe side." I find this argument similar to: "We here at Ascendo© are ready to admit that we are somewhat unsure whether people in ugly coffins go to hell more often than people with an expensive and stylish coffin, but we urge you to buy our Ascendo Premium™ coffin for that maximal security a person of your quality will likely know to appreciate."

Another way to put it is to say that prudential rhetoric is working towards a subjective *agreement* contra *truth*. And what it contrasts with is our Western logic where the truth is the same for all, which, I believe, derives from two things: that our God (the objective authority) is the

---

[261] There are reports of climate data manipulation from around the world, where a decrease in temperature is reported as an increase. For example in this report official measurements from Switzerland, Australia and Paraguay are shown to be manipulated ('homogenized') by NASA to show an increasing temperature trend where such doesn't exist in raw data. M. Bastasch, 'More Countries Caught Manipulating their Climate Data', The Daily Caller, 19.5.2015, http://dailycaller.com/2015/05/19/more-countries-caught-manipulating-their-climate-data/ [26.12.2019].

[262] U.S. Senate Environment and Public Works Committee (Minority), U.S. Senate Minority Report: More Than 650 International Scientists Dissent Over Man-Made Global Warming Claims Scientists Continue to Debunk "Consensus" in 2008, 11.12.2008, https://www.hsdl.org/?abstract&did=233163 [26.12.2019].

same for all, and that our basic understanding of the meaning of concepts is based on science (with a Christian origin as the union of Christian monastery schools), which is also an objective organ. Therefore for a Westerner, it is *immoral* to agree something to be *true* that is shared only within a group, unless it is also believed to be universally true, and therefore a reason that is prudential in nature is not satisfactory, as it will not meet the requirement of objectivity. Outside the Western world, I believe, such a norm of objectivity doesn't exist. And people generally—I think, particularly today—are very poor at reaching for objective standards when something that is being said is subjectively appealing. Come to think of it, I think I could get almost anybody to agree on anything I wanted, if I just chose my words correctly,[263] and also the opposite: often you can meet a person in grumpy state (resembling a child that is woken up in the middle of sleep) in which he will refuse and deny without even considering. Here it would be key to undermine any ramifications of saying things that are not necessarily true; the best course would be to create a pressured situation in which telling a lie is a safe option without ramifications (the most extreme form of this would be torture alternated with sweet-talk). Also I find myself varying considerably in my, as it were, openness to what is being said; my willingness to agree or to disagree... my willingness to approach the matter from a perspective that will or will not contradict what is being said... and this applies to matters of subjective opinion. And this is to say that where there are no standards, there is no predictability. All in all, one could perhaps say that prudential rhetoric aims to abuse the human weakness to concur without setting any standards of the truth of what is being said.

III-5-9. Pathologizing

By pathologizing rhetoric, I mean the sort of *ad hominem* argument that attributes what is being said or done to the psychological or so-

---

[263] I saw an American video of a social experiment in which a reporter is trying to get a person on the street to tell a lie on camera. This seemed easy: usually all he had to do is just to tell him/her to repeat a line that is not true... and I think the pressure of being filmed will simply increase the person's compliance.

III-5. INFORMATION-AGE RHETORICAL TACTICS

cio-political qualities of the speaker. Such rhetorical attacks are targeted against any political people or groups; e.g. a group of demonstrators can be thoughtfully analysed from the socio-political perspective to thoroughly undermine their agenda as simply outrage born out of teenage angst. These attacks are effective because of the expert way they are carried out; a psychiatrist or a political analyst is trusted as a neutral expert, and such a text can be written in a highly civilized and expert manner. The concept of 'crazy' is very interesting, because it contains two elements: at the same time, it is a substantial claim about the mental health of another, but, more than anything, it is a prudential insinuation of *danger*. The target is considered abnormal; there is something wrong with him. It is not used in the sense of *worrying* about the mental health of another, which would be implied by somebody being in bad health, but rather it is very common to insinuate or to arouse suspicion about the mental qualities of a person, only with the intent to discredit. One who is called crazy is one who is not understood, but also one who is not worthy of being understood, because, it is implied, he cannot, or, he *will not*, be understood. Because the argument is anti-humane and unempathetic, it is almost never used in face-to-face communication but only in a communication context where one is sufficiently distanced from the target of the insinuation, for example in the position of a doctor or a football commentator. In face-to-face communication it will make the orator look inhumane and cruel. Also, psychological arguments have become common in *political commentary*, which is because of the reduced level of privacy of politicians. An interesting aspect to this rhetoric is to note how in movies or TV series that try to portray realism, the "crazy card" is often played as the *last resort* by somebody who is about to get caught in the light of evidence: when confronted with incriminating evidence and with no credible excuse available, the suspect calls his accusers crazy (and slowly moves towards the door to make a run for it). This is to say that if one was to tactically choose a rhetoric in one's defence (make up an excuse), this choice is quite weak.

Some examples of common psychological rhetorical tactics:

PART III. SOCIO-POLITICAL ANALYSIS

- "Check your medication" has become something of an Internet meme... implying that the speaker is under medication.

- Insinuating that *narcissism* has the same basis as "he thinks he is better than me". It essentially feeds on *class hatred* where inequalities brought about by difference in social class are subjectively blamed on another. I have seen many news headlines directly accusing notable politicians of narcissism.

- Scientific critics of man-made climate change, or parents who are suspicious about getting their children vaccinated (due to known cases of dreadful side-effects) are branded 'denialists'. The branding word is a smart choice, because it doesn't imply denying but being *in denial*, which is a psychological state.

- "Conspiracy theory" and "-theorist" are political branding words aimed at individuals who publicly suspect collusive action in their own government. The word works via its association to paranoia. Even public figures can be branded crackpots for making such public comments. Popular world-wide, it is public information that the term "conspiracy theory" *as a weapon* originates from a detailed CIA propaganda programme that was employed to discredit such theories and to rescue "the whole reputation of the American government" after the Warren Commission Report's findings on the murder of JFK.[264] There is a clear nationalistic logic in punishing the doubters of one's government *in wartime*, and even in this case the said propaganda recommendations included blaming conspiracy theories on the communists, thus implicating the foreign enemy. It's just that the USA is

---

264 L. deHaven-Smith, *Conspiracy Theory in America*, University of Texas Press 2014.

III-5. INFORMATION-AGE RHETORICAL TACTICS

always at war.[265,266]

- Religious people are associated with religious fundamentalism, and this association is used to imply that their thoughts are being manipulated from outside. In this rhetoric, religiousness is contrasted with *individuality*, which is a key Western attribute; it is implied that the person is not being an individual.

Scientific news has taken a psychological turn, commonly insinuating that people who don't believe experts are stupid and harmful, and this is not done with the intention of helping people but to explain that their *opinions* are wrong. The logic in this argument is that non-reliance on experts leads to political polarization, which is considered harmful—it is not the fault of politicized junk science, it is the fault of stupid people who don't believe what they are told to believe. Examples of such psychological political rhetoric that borrows from science: "Research shows the appeal of untestable beliefs, and how it leads to a polarized society" and "when facts are injected into the conversation, the symptoms of bias become less severe"[267] ('facts' here refers to whatever is produced by scientific experts). Another example:

---

[265] Between 2000 and 2015, the US armed forces were used in Bosnia, East Timor, Sierra Leone, Kosovo, Yemen, Iraq, Afghanistan, Ivory Coast, Liberia, Haiti, Horn of Africa, Lebanon, Libya, Central Africa (Uganda, South Sudan, Burundi, the Central African Republic and the Democratic Republic of Congo), Somalia, Niger, Jordan, South Korea, Ukraine, Poland, Senegal and Lithuania (omitting typhoon aid missions in the Philippines). These are the publicly admitted countries of military interest, but this doesn't yet include the use of special operations troops and mercenaries, training of foreign troops, arms sales etc. B. S. Torreon, *Instances of Use of United States Armed Forces Abroad*, 1798-2015, Congressional Research Service report, 15.1.2015. https://digital.library.unt.edu/ark:/67531/metadc501954/ [25.12.2019].

[266] In 2015 (10.3.2015) the USA declared Venezuela (its #4 crude oil supplier) a national security threat (Reuters). Since 2001, the military rhetoric systematically uses terrorism threat, and more recently, generally human rights, e.g. "cracking down on those who are violating human rights and, you know, abusers and those who are cracking down on civil society" (an excerpt from the US State Department Spokeswoman on the Venezuela issue). This 'crackdown' rhetoric extends into international conflicts from how a government would enforce justice on its own citizens—thus implying that the USA has the right to enforce justice on other countries.

[267] T. Campbell and J. Friesen, 'Why people "Fly from facts"', *Scientific American*, 3.3.2015, http://www.scientificamerican.com/article/why-people-fly-from-facts/ [26.12.2019].

PART III. SOCIO-POLITICAL ANALYSIS

> *[H]uman groups ... err much more in the direction of giving everybody a say than in the direction of deferring too much to experts. And that's quite obviously harmful on any number of issues, especially in science, where what experts know really matters and lives or the world depend on it — like vaccinations or climate change. ... [W]e need to recognize experts more, respect them, and listen to them.*[268]

So, here we see the political goals the article promotes with the rhetoric.

III-5-10. Propaganda Inserts

The prevailing model of 21st-century information warfare and psychological operations is very different from radio broadcasts, leaflets or the propaganda paintings of the last world war. And this is not only because we have many more information channels to influence people, such as online discussion forums and communities, but because the organizational structure of the involved parties is significantly different. We are no longer dealing with governments and the military, but a huge network consisting of various kinds of actors that are linked via, not nationality or, say, military pacts, but simply by money: the operators are subcontracting companies. A very interesting read for somebody who would like to understand how, in practice, a private political interest group can pay money to start a war, is the Hill & Knowlton PR campaign to help launch the US Persian Gulf invasion in 1990, which included something like a false testimony by a child actor in front of a panel disguised to look like a legal congressional committee in the widely televised video hearing.[269] This case serves as a good example because it has now been duly investigated and documented, unlike any potential contemporary cases. The underlying reason behind propa-

---

268 C. Mooney, 'The science of protecting people's feelings: why we pretend all opinions are equal', The Washington Post, 10.3.2015, http://www.washingtonpost.com/news/energy-environment/wp/2015/03/10/the-science-of-protecting-peoples-feelings-why-we-pretend-all-opinions-are-equal/ [26.12.2019].

269 J. R. MacArthur, *Second Front: Censorship and Propaganda in the Gulf War*, University of California Press, 2004.

III-5. INFORMATION-AGE RHETORICAL TACTICS

ganda is to influence public opinion to support political decisions, such as changes in the law, and, particularly, military operations. And the goal is not necessarily evil but may be simply to produce information that supports a political goal and is as credible as possible. Obviously there is a strong connection between governmental or globalist politics and commercial news channels, which makes our news biased. But there are also Internet articles, Internet sites, news articles, pictures or videos staged or taken out of context, false testimonies, people with false identities, etc. The art of deception is in manipulation: the information that is produced is most often targeted to frame the political opposition to be guilty of something bad, such as atrocities, which will portray you as the hero for bringing this to light and supporting action to counter their deeds. Another useful trick is that whenever one's own party is to be indicted, measures can be taken to alleviate incoming damages in publicity; say, if a minister knows of an incoming indictment, the prudential action is to find the least incriminating (human) excuse to leave office before the indictment becomes public, because the democratic press will pay most attention to the indictment of a minister and not the actual crime. Or, say, if incriminating material is known to surface, one can fabricate high-profile negative news against oneself in such a manner that the fabrication can easily be shown later, which has the impact of portraying him as falsely accused in the eyes of the public. Because the media only care about increasing readership by high-profile news, they won't care about the source of an article if they can avoid damage from suspicions that they are being too lenient in their publishing standards: fake news can mean money as long as one can insist that one didn't know it was fake. There is information that targets individuals, mainly political leaders of countries or otherwise important political actors, and information that targets groups. Ethnic or religious groups are particularly targeted: the propaganda is produced to carry symbols of ethnic or religious groups. Once information, incriminating the political opposition, has been brought to light, it is typically accompanied by political rhetoric—which pretends to be communicating a *political truth*—with the following features.

1) It is presented as if the implied accusations were self-evidently true without question and without further study. This tactic can also

be used directly to justify action.

2) It may be implied that further implicating proof exists, there is a sound reason why that information cannot be disclosed.

3) Any public questioning of the credibility of the information is regarded an insult; either an insult to one's public honour, or an insult against commonly shared values.

4) Any request to provide additional information is stonewalled.

5) Irrefutable evidence of misconduct is blamed on accident; responsibility over one's domain is never admitted.

One might think that if someone produces propaganda, they are likely to be found out, because crimes tend to come to light due to police investigations. But the position is different for governmental actors that possess the legal means to execute a part of the operations as intelligence operations that operate above the law, and that are justified because of the country's involvement in a military conflict. In this case the government can use subcontractors that work under a secret classification: say, there can be 1) active searches for trusted governmental subcontractors, and 2) a military propaganda programme that works under military secrecy and that uses designated subcontractors with such trusted status. It might be that, as with secret military missions, most of the people involved know only how to play their role and what to do, but don't know the final purpose or the big picture. I can easily imagine somebody producing, say, photographic or video evidence, working under a secret contract, not given any information about how the product is to be used, and having signed a contract to legally give away his intellectual rights and to honour the non-disclosure of any related information. In this mode, such work can be operated as a completely legitimate business. A viable model of collusion is one in which political actors are invited to cooperate with some governmental or corporate party, but with the precondition that no information is disclosed to outsiders. A viable model for such group meetings is the Chatham House Rule, which is a widely used methodology in various seminars that deal with delicate issues, and which dictates that any material produced is free to use with the condition that its accurate

III-5. INFORMATION-AGE RHETORICAL TACTICS

source is not revealed. For modern capitalist media, what is important in a piece of news is not its sources, and the verification of whether the news is true or a complete fabrication, but whether it can be used in a story that sells. For example, a one-man show by a Syrian defector, called the Syrian Observatory for Human Rights, is constantly cited as a source by many major news organizations, yet doesn't publicly disclose its sources.[270] Now, if sources are not published this doesn't by any means indicate that they are fraudulent, but it does relegate them to the status of anecdotal (undisclosed) evidence. As video evidence is particularly compelling in this era, video testimony can come from fabricated witnesses produced by e.g. PR offices, as in notorious Hill & Knowlton case previously mentioned. One should pay attention to what brings value to gossip news, which can be read from this comment from Amnesty International[271]: "Generally, the information on the killings of civilians is very good, definitely one of the best, including the details on the conditions in which people were supposedly killed." You can see that a 21st-century human rights organization takes the role of a journalistic media house or a PR office, because to them, one of the best *sources of information* is one that is *supposedly true*. Wartime news reporting, like all reporting in the modern world, has a yellow press attitude where checking the facts is not key (because they *cannot* be checked), but a great interest in detailed and colourful stories about individual people. And casualties and refugees—boy, are they colourful! You could perhaps try and find a generalization here that it would be difficult for organizations that make their biggest sales during wartime to be anti-war. If we think of human rights organizations as traditional companies operated by money and a responsibility to their benefactors, it is war, suffering, death and turmoil that justifies their existence in the first place. If we *really* care about human rights, as in standard modern global rhetoric, why is this advanced via grassroots organizations in the first place and not via governments conducting public policies of nonviolence as a sign of respecting the human rights of the people of foreign nations? This is why the concept of hu-

---

270 N. MacFarquhar, 'A Very Busy Man Behind the Syrian Civil War's Casualty Count', *The New York Times*, 9.4.2013, http://www.nytimes.com/2013/04/10/world/middleeast/the-man-behind-the-casualty-figures-in-syria.html [26.12.2019].
271 ibid.

man rights is completely meaningless today; those two words point to a utopia that has never been found, and its historical analysis is best performed by those after our generation who don't need to suffer the problematic of who was responsible of this development. There can be no system of Western nations built on the foundation of human rights—human rights is an idealist and secular derivative of Christianity but cannot establish social order because of the missing moral codes that would keep somebody from preaching the code of human rights while at the same time violating it and appearing credible to his followers. Many can do that for some time but there will be people who will not accept it but point out that it is contradictory and therefore (morally) wrong. Perhaps this moral issue could be momentarily tackled by writing songs in which people are made to say that it is right... to overcome the problem of morality by force.

III-5-11. Experts

In our information age we place increased emphasis on the credibility of the information, which elevates the status of picture and video material in particular (a picture paints a thousand words), eyewitness testimonials and various authorities with credentials, but at the same time news editors are in control of the news. I see two facets to consider in this; firstly, it's possible to note that most politically controversial topics are completely shunned by all commercial media, and high-profile newspapers have abandoned their editorial policies of giving equal opportunity voice to opposing opinion. This has given birth to forms of alternative media such as freelance investigative journalists and online blogging communities so that there is a class system of information in which commercial news channels inhabit the upper class. But secondly, one can easily find repetition in the news, which indicates that many news channels, particularly but not necessarily within the same media conglomerate, get their news readily scripted. The popular talk show host Conan O'Brien was able to publish news in a manner that got 27 TV channels to repeat the exact same phrasing and published the results in an amusing way in his show. A representative of WSBT

III-5. INFORMATION-AGE RHETORICAL TACTICS

news channel responded to the event, calling it a "dark secret" of the news business and explaining how such a thing is possible: "We take a wire copy and try to rewrite it."[272] A 2013 survey[273] brought out some figures from behind the scenes in US media:

- News content is routinely shared regionally or group-wide by stations owned by the same company.

- Three quarters of local TV stations share news content with other media stations.

- In 2013, 290 local TV stations were sold (compared to 95 in 2012); many of the stations ended up being separately owned but jointly operated. Almost half of US local TV markets operate with such joint service agreements.

- One fourth of local news stations don't originate *any* content.

- Both the number of people working in local TV news, and the amount of news aired, are at almost record highs.

The standard news method today is to quote information presented by 'experts'. The word 'expert' doesn't have any standards, like, say, the words 'doctor' or 'psychotherapist', so, the word is perfect for creating an appearance of expertise to serve the interest of the news publisher. In fact, because of the lack of a standard, the news source is technically able to use an impostor as an expert. When the news says "Experts say..." it translates to "This news channel recommends that you take the perspective of..." This is because of several distinguishable ways in which the news channel can manipulate the information being published:

- The news channel has the power to select the expert and to dictate the publication of the information. Even if they accidentally picked an expert that doesn't conform to their wanted opinion, they could

---

[272] M. Knox, 'How Did 27 Stations End Up With Identical Scripts For a Story About Conan O'Brien?', Adweek TVSpy, 4.11.2011, http://www.adweek.com/tvspy/how-did-28-stations-end-up-with-identical-scripts-for-a-story-about-conan-obrien/29043 [26.12.2019].

[273] D. Potter and K. E. Matsa, 'A Boom in Acquisitions and Content Sharing Shapes Local TV News in 2013', Pew Research Center, 26.3.2014, http://www.journalism.org/2014/03/26/a-boom-in-acquisitions-and-content-sharing-shapes-local-tv-news-in-2013/ [26.12.2019].

PART III. SOCIO-POLITICAL ANALYSIS

(and will) delete the parts they don't agree with in his comment or delete it altogether and switch expert. The wrong opinion will not be published, and even if it is published by accident, it can (and will) be withdrawn after its publication. It is also common in the case of major newspapers that the online news articles are edited after their publication, without annotating or even mentioning the edit anywhere.

• The expert can be a non-expert in the matters he/she is asked to comment about, yet still quoted as an expert.

• The expert can be opinionated and present his/her own recommendations instead of a scientific rigorously objective analysis, which is the framework of credibility under which his/her testimony is supposed to be operating. Those opinions can miraculously align with the opinions of the publisher.

• The expert can be completely anonymous. This can either mean that the expert is the rookie who writes the Sunday issue horoscopes, or it can mean that the expert is a national security intelligence agency. Sometimes news originating from an intelligence officer is thus quoted, sometimes not. Or keeping the expert anonymous may mean that what is published is the direct opinion of the publisher, and only when asked will they come up with the name of the source.

• In TV interviews the interviewers can employ very thoroughly scripted interview tactics to seek out the opinion of the publisher and to ensure that this opinion is published, and the interview is made to complement this opinion with additional fact. As an example, I'll describe a live interview about the murder of Boris Nemtsov, the news channels chasing for their own stories alongside the official murder investigation.[274] First the interviewer asks the interviewee to speculate about the murderer. After the speculation didn't turn out as she wanted, she asked if he had any evidence to support this claim and branded it a conspiracy theory (she initially asked him to speculate, but it turns out he speculated wrong). After he said he has evidence, too, the interviewer published a prepared excerpt from the deceased and asked the interviewee to speculate on that. When he didn't agree

---

274 Christiane Amanpour was interviewing a former United Russia parliament member Sergei Markov on CNN Live TV on 4.3.2015.

on that, the interviewer picked one expression ("fascist junta", in the context of the Ukrainian situation) from his comment and replied with a prepared opinion by the publisher to counter that with some individual fact. This means that even in live interview she must be employing a ready-made list of opinions to present against political keywords. This is something a politician would be expected to do when entering a live debate.

Then again, the credibility of real scientific experts is brutally politicized. In Europe, the job of the European Commission's scientific adviser was to make politicians accept the science behind set political goals first (obviously via lobbying). But refusal to do so on the part of any member countries would be interpreted as owing to social or cultural issues. A quote from the EU scientific adviser about genetically modified crops is given here.

> *I'm not an advocate for GM — all I'm saying is, let's look at the evidence. But if I look at how individual member states vote in the European Council, half of them vote no and the rest vote yes, even though the evidence is the same everywhere. So, it has to be a political opinion. What politicians should say is: 'I accept the evidence, but for social or cultural reasons my member state does not want this technology' — instead of saying that the evidence is incomplete, which makes citizens think that GM is dangerous.*[275]

Here we see that the EU works to make *politicians* "accept the evidence", which means that the EU considers politicians—not the scientific organ—to be the vessels of scientific truth. This model obviously has nothing at all to do with science *or* expertise, but the closest parallel that comes to mind is the medieval Church that enforced their political interpretation of true Christianity via arbitrary practices that originated from some secretive inner circles. The scientific adviser chair was recently abolished, after accusations of partiality and bias.

---

275 M. Peplow, 'EU science chief wants greater voice for experts', *Nature*, 23.6.2014, http://doi.org/10.1038/nature.2014.15445.

PART III. SOCIO-POLITICAL ANALYSIS

III-5-12. Dictatorship vs Democracy

There is a particular contemporary political rhetoric in which the word 'democracy' is consistently made to represent a set of contemporary Western political values. This set can variously include such values as equality, willingness to resist climate change, gay rights and resisting *dictatorships*, and the rhetoric uses the polarizing either-or fallacy that either you are pro these values or you are against them, implying that you are pro all those countries that are dictatorships. These values are simply taken as given in such political rhetoric and could be identified as a set of publicly accepted Western base values. But the interesting part is how these values are commonly referred to together—several of such values can be referred to in the same news article—and are used in juxtaposition with non-Western countries that are presented as dictatorships. So it seems to me that this rhetoric is *deliberately* juxtaposing Western values against whatever is seen as wrong in other countries, and thus is actively provocative, presenting 'us' as 'good' and the 'others' as 'bad'... so the implication is that what is wrong with those countries is that they are not Western; the mark of imperialism. This rhetoric carries a sense of the superiority of the Western world over other parts of the world; rhetoric in which nations that don't share these values are seen as inferior... which is quite silly considering that the values are not democratic but are just called such. Therefore, I suspect that the rhetoric is crafted, very much the same way as historically we have seen the crafting of a nationalistic sense of racial superiority. This rhetoric is meant to unify the Western countries under the same flag, and it obviously serves the interests of those who would prefer to see Europe as a federal state.

This rhetoric is a good reminder of what happens if one forgets one's *moral* basis in Christianity; if one forgets that what makes us Western is not just democracy, multiculturalism, liberalism, science and human rights, but that all of said values have their historical moral basis in us also being children of a Christian moral and social order. If any these words were to have any meaning, they have it in an ethical-ideological sense, which needs to be bound to a said basis. If one is to speak under the flag of any of these values, in order to be ethical, one is to first express the values in action. But this creates a paradox; how can one be democratic if one is to publicly argue with fallacies such as false dilemma? How can one promote multiculturalism against another culture? How can one promote liberalism—freedom of trade—by imposing economic sanctions on other nations? How can one promote science if one is to determine the truth about other cultures via the opinions of news commentators? And how can one promote human rights by provoking anger and war against other nations? This is possible only by taking said values as rituals, isolated from their spirit and ethical basis in which they at the same time obligate one. Such behaviour will be observed as arrogant and detached from reality from basically anywhere outside the West where moral values are based on tradition; it will look like the actions of a group of disorganized bandits. The ideological values, taken as slogans, will only further weaken Western unity, and will harm the Western image outside the West even more.

ACKNOWLEDGEMENTS

This book was written over a period of around ten years, during breaks from my day job. During this work, I have found myself unable to talk about it to anybody; ordinary people either expect a book to be a novel, or philosophy to be understandable by anybody, and academics are very busy.

I'd like to thank Allison McKechnie for her copy-editing work.

I am thankful to those few academics who have been able to give me encouraging comments. Particularly I am thankful to professor emeritus David Cockburn for our discussions.

I'd like to thank my mother who has always supported me in whatever silly things I wanted to do.

I have also been very grateful to my home country Finland and her social system that granted me education and leisure.

ABOUT THE AUTHOR

Jaakko Saaristo is a philosophy hobbyist. He got his MSc in computer science from University of Helsinki in 2008 while teaching part-time on programming and scientific writing courses and attending minor studies in theoretical philosophy. He has had a career as a freelance software expert for around 15 years at private business clients such as banks, government ministries and mobile technology. He finds philosophy of language a core fundament in computer science that on a practical level builds upon abstract languages and symbolism.

www.ingramcontent.com/pod-product-compliance
Lightning Source LLC
Chambersburg PA
CBHW031052080526
44587CB00011B/656